NBER Macroeconomics Annual 2024

NBER Macroeconomics Annual 2024

Edited by
Martin Eichenbaum, John Leahy, and Valerie Ramey

The University of Chicago Press
Chicago and London

NBER Macroeconomics Annual 2024, Number 39

Published annually by The University of Chicago Press.
www.journals.uchicago.edu/MA/

Subscriptions: For individual and institutional subscription rates, visit www.journals.uchicago.edu, email subscriptions@press.uchicago.edu, or call (877) 705-1878 (US) or (773) 753-3347 (international). Free or deeply discounted institutional access is available in most developing nations through the Chicago Emerging Nations Initiative (www.journals.uchicago.edu/inst/ceni).

Please direct subscription inquiries to Subscription Fulfillment, 1427 E. 60th Street, Chicago, IL 60637-2902. Telephone: (773) 753-3347 or toll free in the United States and Canada (877) 705-1878. Fax: (773) 753-0811 or toll-free (877) 705-1879. E-mail: subscriptions@press.uchicago.edu.

Standing orders: To place a standing order for this book series, please address your request to The University of Chicago Press, Chicago Distribution Center, Attn. Standing Orders/Customer Service, 11030 S. Langley Avenue, Chicago, IL 60628. Telephone toll free in the U.S. and Canada: 1-800-621-2736; or 1-773-702-7000. Fax toll free in the U.S. and Canada: 1-800-621-8476; or 1-773-702-7212.

Single-copy orders: In the U.S., Canada, and the rest of the world, order from your local bookseller or direct from The University of Chicago Press, Chicago Distribution Center, 11030 S. Langley Avenue, Chicago, IL 60628. Telephone toll free in the U.S. and Canada: 1-800-621-2736; or 1-773-702-7000. Fax toll free in the U.S. and Canada: 1-800-621-8476; or 1-773-702-7212. In the U.K. and Europe, order from your local bookseller or direct from The University of Chicago Press, c/o John Wiley Ltd. Distribution Center, 1 Oldlands Way, Bognor Regis, West Sussex PO22 9SA, UK. Telephone 01243 779777 or Fax 01243 820250. E-mail: cs-books@wiley.co.uk.

The University of Chicago Press offers bulk discounts on individual titles to Corporate, Premium and Gift accounts. For information, please write to Sales Department—Special Sales, The University of Chicago Press, 1427 E. 60th Street, Chicago, IL 60637 USA or telephone 1-773-702-7723.

This book was printed and bound in the United States of America.

ISSN: 0889-3365
E-ISSN: 1537-2642
ISBN: 978-0-226-84973-7 (pb.:alk.paper)
eISBN: 978-0-226-85002-3 (e-book)

University of Chicago Press's appointed EU Representative is Easy Access System Europe Oü, 16879218, Mustamäe tee 50, 10621 Tallinn, Estonia. Contact details: gpsr.requests@easproject.com, +358 40 500 3575.

Relation of the Directors to the Work and Publications of the NBER

1. The object of the NBER is to ascertain and present to the economics profession, and to the public more generally, important economic facts and their interpretation in a scientific manner without policy recommendations. The Board of Directors is charged with the responsibility of ensuring that the work of the NBER is carried on in strict conformity with this object.

2. The President shall establish an internal review process to ensure that book manuscripts proposed for publication DO NOT contain policy recommendations. This shall apply both to the proceedings of conferences and to manuscripts by a single author or by one or more co-authors but shall not apply to authors of comments at NBER conferences who are not NBER affiliates.

3. No book manuscript reporting research shall be published by the NBER until the President has sent to each member of the Board a notice that a manuscript is recommended for publication and that in the President's opinion it is suitable for publication in accordance with the above principles of the NBER. Such notification will include a table of contents and an abstract or summary of the manuscript's content, a list of contributors if applicable, and a response form for use by Directors who desire a copy of the manuscript for review. Each manuscript shall contain a summary drawing attention to the nature and treatment of the problem studied and the main conclusions reached.

4. No volume shall be published until forty-five days have elapsed from the above notification of intention to publish it. During this period a copy shall be sent to any Director requesting it, and if any Director objects to publication on the grounds that the manuscript contains policy recommendations, the objection will be presented to the author(s) or editor(s). In case of dispute, all members of the Board shall be notified, and the President shall appoint an ad hoc committee of the Board to decide the matter; thirty days additional shall be granted for this purpose.

5. The President shall present annually to the Board a report describing the internal manuscript review process, any objections made by Directors before publication or by anyone after publication, any disputes about such matters, and how they were handled.

6. Publications of the NBER issued for informational purposes concerning the work of the Bureau, or issued to inform the public of the activities at the Bureau, including but not limited to the NBER Digest and Reporter, shall be consistent with the object stated in paragraph 1. They shall contain a specific disclaimer noting that they have not passed through the review procedures required in this resolution. The Executive Committee of the Board is charged with the review of all such publications from time to time.

7. NBER working papers and manuscripts distributed on the Bureau's web site are not deemed to be publications for the purpose of this resolution, but they shall be consistent with the object stated in paragraph 1. Working papers shall contain a specific disclaimer noting that they have not passed through the review procedures required in this resolution. The NBER's web site shall contain a similar disclaimer. The President shall establish an internal review process to ensure that the working papers and the web site do not contain policy recommendations, and shall report annually to the Board on this process and any concerns raised in connection with it.

8. Unless otherwise determined by the Board or exempted by the terms of paragraphs 6 and 7, a copy of this resolution shall be printed in each NBER publication as described in paragraph 2 above.

Contents

Editorial

Martin Eichenbaum, *Northwestern University and NBER,* United States of America
John Leahy, *University of Michigan and NBER,* United States of America
Valerie Ramey, *Hoover Institution, NBER, and CEPR,* United States of America

The NBER's 39th Annual Conference on Macroeconomics brought together leading scholars to present, discuss, and debate five research papers on central issues in contemporary macroeconomics. In addition, it included a panel discussion on "Industrial Policy." Martin Eichenbaum moderated the panel, which included Laura Alfaro, Réka Juhász, Greg Mankiw, and Dani Rodrik.

This conference volume contains edited versions of the five papers presented at the conference, each followed by two written discussions by leading scholars and a summary of the debates that followed each paper.

Many economies experience credit cycles in which credit booms are followed by credit busts accompanied by recessions. The paper by Martin Kornejew, Chen Lian, Yueran Ma, Pablo Ottonello, and Diego Perez studies the role of bankruptcy institutions in softening the real effects of credit busts in the wake of credit booms. The authors use data on a panel of countries to study how the efficiency of bankruptcy institutions, measured using surveys of legal professionals across countries, affects gross domestic product (GDP) during a credit bust. The authors estimate a state-dependent local projection model that projects GDP growth on the interaction of credit growth during the previous 5 years with a measure of bankruptcy efficiency. The authors find large, statistically significant effects of bankruptcy efficiency—there is essentially no effect of a previous credit boom on GDP in countries with efficient bankruptcy institutions but large negative effects in countries with less efficient bankruptcy institutions. These results hold up across numerous robustness checks.

NBER Macroeconomics Annual, volume 39, 2025.
 https://doi.org/10.1086/735254

The authors also present a stylized model to interpret their empirical analysis. The model considers the situation of a distressed firm whose continuation value is greater than its liquidation value so that efficiency calls for reorganization rather than liquidation. In countries with more efficient bankruptcy institutions, reorganization is used more often than liquidation, which preserves more of the firm's value and therefore mitigates the negative macro effects of the credit bust.

Both discussants highlight the importance of the question and insights of the paper, as well as some limitations of the analysis. Dean Corbae points out that the authors assume only one type of error: liquidating firms that are going concerns. Corbae presents results from an alternative model where inefficiency can also arise from the converse case: allowing failing firms to continue to operate. His model reveals a host of fundamental issues, such as nonmonotonicities that may not be captured by the authors' empirical specification. He also notes how bankruptcy institutions also affect the nature of the preceding credit booms. Carola Frydman focuses on the challenges affecting the empirical analysis. First, she discusses some weaknesses of the authors' bankruptcy efficiency measure and recommends checking robustness against alternative measures. Second, she discusses an important issue that affects any cross-country analysis: omitted variable bias. In this context, it is likely that bankruptcy efficiency is correlated with many other aspects of a country's institutions, so we cannot be sure whether the effect measured is truly causal. Both discussants' comments suggest fruitful areas for further research into the interaction of credit cycles and bankruptcy institutions.

Monetary policy in the United States has important effects on the global economy. The precise mechanism that generates these effects matters for policy in the United States and abroad. The paper by Santiago Camara, Lawrence Christiano, and Hüsnü Dalgic uses time series methods and a sophisticated small open economy to understand how a US monetary policy shock propagates to the rest of the world. Their model embeds the type of frictions discussed in the literature: sticky-in-dollar export pricing, balance sheet effects associated with exchange rate depreciations, and distortions to uncovered interest parity because of factors such as risk appetite shifts.

Their time series results document that tighter US monetary policy leads to economic contractions in non-US countries, with emerging market economies exhibiting more pronounced contractions than advanced economies, as well as a decline in US imports and a price index of those imports. The price index response suggests that the decline in US imports reflects a decline in the US demand for imports rather than a decline in the supply of those imports by other countries.

Camara, Christiano, and Dalgic use their structural model to argue that the decline in US imports plays a critical role in the monetary propagation mechanism. Without the decline in US imports, the model cannot explain why exports fall substantially in the rest of the world in response to a US monetary policy contraction. Financial frictions do play an important role: absent financial frictions, the decline in imports after a contractionary US monetary policy shock would be small. In the presence of those frictions, the shock induces a contraction of investment and aggregate output in other countries that is quantitively consistent with their time series results.

Camara, Christiano, and Dalgic use their models to explore the efficacy of exchange rate interventions by other countries in response to a US monetary policy shock. They find that exchange rate interventions by other countries are ineffective in mitigating the effects of a contractionary US monetary policy shock when that shock induces a decline in US imports and inflation. However, exchange rate interventions are relatively effective in countering the contractionary effects of noise shocks in financial markets or a hypothetical US monetary policy shock that is not accompanied by a decline in US imports and inflation.

The first discussant, Jón Steinsson, reviewed the empirical results of Camara et al. and the associated methodology. He stressed that vector autoregressive (VAR) models may be associated with various biases and the potential advantages of local projections. He noted that the authors report results from local projections in the appendix. He compared the VAR-based and local projection–based results. Although the results are qualitatively the same, there are some interesting differences, especially in the response of exchange rates to a contractionary US monetary policy shock.

Steinsson also discussed the key result emerging from the structural model—namely, the importance of the trade channel. He highlighted features of the model that could be driving the result. He concluded that much more work on international financial frictions needs to be done before there can be a consensus on the nature of the international monetary transmission mechanism.

The second discussant, Şebnem Kalemli-Özcan, begins her discussion by noting that the Camara et al. is "an impressive paper that should be standard reading for graduate students in this area." However, she expresses skepticism about their conclusion that the trade channel is the critical element in the monetary transmission mechanism.

Kalemli-Özcan agrees that most episodes of US monetary policy contractions are associated with a decline in the US demand for imports and a retreat of US investors from foreign assets to US assets. In her view, the international transmission mechanism is primarily about the fall in US investors' demand for foreign assets and the resulting decline in foreign investment demand.

Kalemli-Özcan agrees that the authors' model incorporates a channel by which a contractionary US monetary policy shock leads to an increase in the demand of US investors for US assets and a decline in the demand for foreign assets. However, she disagrees with how the authors model the increase in the demand for US assets. In her opinion, incorporating her preferred way of modeling the increase in the demand for US assets would overturn the dominant role of the trade channel generated by the authors' model.

Like Steinsson, Kalemli-Özcan concludes that (1) more empirical work is necessary to establish whether the trade channel or financial frictions is the dominant factor in the international mechanism and (2) the resolution of this issue has very important policy implications.

The steep rise in inflation starting in 2021 reminded policymakers that the American public hates even moderate rates of inflation. However, standard macro models have trouble generating large costs of inflation to households. The paper by David Altig, Alan Auerbach, Erin Eidschun, Laurence Kotlikoff, and Victor Yifan Ye explores an overlooked channel—the interaction of inflation with the myriad government tax and benefit programs—and finds welfare costs of almost 7% from a permanent rise in inflation from 0% to 10%. The paper uses a proprietary software, designed to help households make financial decisions with respect to government programs, along with information on all households in the Survey of Consumer Finances to analyze the effects of inflation on a representative cross-section of US households. Imperfect inflation indexation in government tax and transfer programs leads to gains for some households but losses for many others. For example, taxation of nominal rather than real interest makes inflation costly for bondholders, and lagged cost-of-living adjustments make inflation costly for Social Security recipients.

Both discussants praise the authors' careful and comprehensive analysis of this understudied channel through which inflation affects households. Adrien Auclert puts the authors' estimates of the fiscal costs in context by summarizing and quantifying the other channels discussed in the literature, such as the opportunity cost of holding money, price dispersion, and nominal wealth redistribution. He finds that the authors' calculations of welfare losses are at the upper end of the calculated losses from the other channels, highlighting the potential importance of this channel. Deborah Lucas highlights the fact that the authors' model does not allow behavioral responses on the part of households, nor does it incorporate the important insurance aspects of government programs, two factors that could significantly change the welfare results. Both discussants also point out that the authors' exercise is partial equilibrium. Although general equilibrium effects could significantly change the welfare cost calculations, perhaps the most important omitted element is the government budget constraint. Inflation leads to an aggregate increase in government revenue and a decrease in spending. Considering the possibility of rebating the net revenue to households would significantly reduce the welfare costs. Future research can build on the authors' analysis.

Recent experience has renewed interest in the determinants of inflation. In their paper, "The Dominant Role of Expectations and Broad-Based Supply Shocks in Driving Inflation," Beaudry, Hou, and Portier argue that supply shocks operating through expectations of inflation are key to understanding what drives inflation.

The paper begins by demonstrating that expectation-augmented Phillips curves estimated to fit the prepandemic period work well in explaining the recent inflationary episode. As these Phillips curves are "flat," they leave very little room for the output gap to influence inflation. The authors argue that the rise and fall in inflation is instead largely explained by a rise and fall in inflation expectations. In the standard model with rational expectations, however, expected inflation reflects the impact of future costs. This raises the question, If costs do not affect inflation, how do future costs affect expected inflation?

The second part of the paper proposes a theory based on incomplete information and bounded rationality in which broad-based supply shocks affect inflation not through costs but through their impact on expectations. In their model, agents believe that sectoral inflation is a combination of a persistent common component and an idiosyncratic sector-specific component. Agents only see a subset of sectors, and when the idiosyncratic components on this subset of sectors align (a broad-based supply shock), agents misperceive sectoral inflation as aggregate inflation. Simulations of their model show that it can explain the recent experience.

Both discussants praised the paper as provocative and potentially important. Jonathan Hazell noted the parsimony of the authors' analysis of inflation. Frequently, the profession has found that popular models of inflation needed to be completely rethought when confronted with new data. In this case, the standard, expectations-augmented Phillips curve continues to fit the recent episode. What we need is a new model of expectations.

Both Hazell and Gabriel Chodorow-Reich pointed out that the authors' choice of household inflation expectations from the Michigan Survey of Consumers as their main measure of inflation expectations is critical to their success. Other measures of inflation expectations tend to leave a large portion of the recent run-up in inflation unexplained. Both authors also commented that whereas the authors show that their model fits the data, other models might do equally well. Chodorow-Reich argued that one cannot reject a model with a nonlinear Phillips curve, other measures of expectations, and a role for tight labor markets. Hazell speculated that inflation expectations might have responded to the large fiscal stimulus rather than supply shocks. Both thought that more work to identify and disentangle these various channels is warranted.

There has been a recent explosion of research investigating the implications of microeconomic heterogeneity for macroeconomic dynamics. As part of this movement, heterogeneous agent New Keynesian (HANK) models have become ubiquitous. These models allow for the incorporation of realistic financial frictions and for the income distribution and wealth distribution to affect monetary and fiscal policy in rich ways. The cost is added complexity, which often gives these models the feeling of a black box.

In "Heterogeneity and Aggregate Fluctuations: Insights from TANK Models," Debortoli and Galí show how to specify a two-agent New Keynesian (TANK) model so that it can mimic the aggregate implications of the more complex HANK model. They then use this simpler model to understand the many channels through which heterogeneity influences aggregate fluctuations. The main insight is to calibrate the TANK model to both the income share and the asset holdings of the constrained agents in the HANK model. In this way, the TANK model can capture not only the impact of labor income on the consumption of constrained agents but also the impact of asset prices and returns.

Both discussants value the contribution of the paper in highlighting the channels through which heterogeneity affects aggregate dynamics. Both wanted to better understand the limits of the authors' approximation. Johannes Wieland asked whether the authors' approach would extend to more complex environments such as the inclusion of durable consumption or large fiscal transfers that are saved.

Both commented that the main difference between HANK and TANK models is the intertemporal marginal propensity to consume of the constrained agents, that is, the marginal propensity to consume (MPC) in one period out of income in another. In TANK models, this MPC is 1 for current income and 0 for income in all other periods. In HANK models, this MPC often lies between 0 and 1. It peaks in the current period and decays as the gap between consumption and income widens. Matt Rognlie argued shocks with a more forward-looking component—persistent shocks or news shocks—would exacerbate the differences between HANK and TANK models by loading more on the propensity to consume in one period out of income in another. Both discussants commented that more research is needed to pin down the intertemporal MPCs in the data.

Endnote

Author email addresses: Ramey (vramey@stanford.edu), Eichenbaum (eich@northwestern.edu). The authors and the editors would like to take this opportunity to thank Jim Poterba and the National Bureau of Economic Research for their continued support for the NBER Macroeconomics Annual and the associated conference. We would also like to thank the NBER conference staff, particularly Rob Shannon, for his continued excellent organization and support. Financial assistance from the National Science Foundation is gratefully acknowledged. We also thank the rapporteurs, Andrea Ferrara and Erin Gibson, who provided invaluable help in preparing the summaries of the discussions. And last but far from least, we are grateful to Helena Fitz-Patrick for her invaluable assistance in editing and publishing the volume. For acknowledgments, sources of research support, and disclosure of the authors' material financial relationships, if any, please see https://www.nber.org/books-and-chapters/nber-macroeconomics-annual-2024-volume-39/editorial-nber-macroeconomics-annual-2024-volume-39.

Abstracts

1 Bankruptcy Resolution and Credit Cycles

Martin Kornejew, Chen Lian, Yueran Ma, Pablo Ottonello, and Diego J. Perez

We study how the macroeconomic dynamics following credit cycles vary with business bankruptcy institutions. Using data on bankruptcy efficiency and business credit around the world, we document that business credit booms are followed by severe declines in output, investment, and consumption in environments with poorly functioning business bankruptcy. On the contrary, in settings with well-functioning business bankruptcy, the aftermath of credit booms is characterized by moderate changes in economic activities. We use a simple model to lay out how and when efficient bankruptcy systems can mitigate the negative consequences of credit booms.

2 The International Monetary Transmission Mechanism

Santiago Camara, Lawrence Christiano, and Hüsnü Dalgıc

Time series analysis shows that a US monetary tightening leads to economic contractions in non-US countries. We develop small-economy models that capture these spillover effects onto advanced economies (AEs) and emerging market economies (EMEs). Using counterfactual experiments, we identify the decline in US imports as the primary mechanism by which a US monetary contraction affects other economies. We also document that EMEs exhibit more pronounced contractions compared with

NBER Macroeconomics Annual, volume 39, 2025.
 https://doi.org/10.1086/735255

AEs. Counterfactual experiments attribute this greater drop in EMEs to financial amplification associated with their greater exposure to dollar debt. We find that financial frictions are essential for understanding the propagation of US monetary shocks via the trade mechanism as well as via the classic interest rate mechanism.

3 Inflation's Fiscal Impact on American Households

David Altig, Alan J. Auerbach, Erin Eidschun, Laurence Kotlikoff, and Victor Yifan Ye

The post-COVID-19 price surge has reignited interest in inflation's impact on American households. Even if anticipated and with full market adjustments, inflation affects households through its interaction with the fiscal system, which is the focus of this paper. Inflation affects households through its interaction with the fiscal. We run the 2019 Survey of Consumer Finances (SCF), assuming different inflation rates, through the Fiscal Analyzer (TFA)—a life-cycle, consumption-smoothing tool incorporating all major federal and state fiscal programs. Before doing so, we adjust the SCF data to neutralize inflation's nonfiscal effects. A permanent increase in the inflation rate from 0% to 10% reduces median lifetime spending by 6.82%. This impact is smaller—4.74%—when fiscal cost of living adjustments (COLAs) are not lagged. But the big stories are the progressivity of inflation's increase in net taxation, its age pattern, and its heterogeneity. The 15.9% median lifetime spending loss of the top 1% from 10% inflation is roughly 2.5 times that of the bottom quintile. Middle-aged households are hit far harder because they have more asset income, which, with inflation, is taxed at a higher effective rate. The 25th percentile of spending changes is a reduction of 9.84%. The 75th percentile change is still a reduction of 4.83%. The maximum spending decline (increase) across all households is 64.9% (46.7%). Thus, the distribution of welfare is highly sensitive to significant, ongoing inflation.

4 The Dominant Role of Expectations and Broad-Based Supply Shocks in Driving Inflation

Paul Beaudry, Chenyu Hou, and Franck Portier

The object of this paper is to assess the role of supply shocks, labor market tightness, and expectation formation in explaining bouts of inflation. We begin by showing that a quasi-flat Phillips curve, which was popular prior to the pandemic, still fits the post-2020 US data well and that changes in short-term inflation expectations likely played an important role in propagating supply shocks in the recent inflation episode. We then document features of the joint dynamics of inflation and inflation expectations to form a baseline for what needs to be explained. Given the difficulty of reproducing these dynamics under rational expectations, we propose and evaluate a model with imperfect information and bounded rationality. In our model, agents see sectoral inflations as being driven by a component common to all the sectors of the economy and by sector-specific shocks. When supply shocks affect many sectors—what we refer to as a broad-based supply shock—agents infer that the common component of inflation has increased, which drives persistent inflation dynamics through their effect on expectations in a quasi-self-fulfilling way.

5 Heterogeneity and Aggregate Fluctuations: Insights from TANK Models

Davide Debortoli and Jordi Galí

We analyze the merits and limitations of simple tractable New Keynesian models (RANK [representative agent New Keynesian] and TANK [two-agent New Keynesian]) in accounting for the aggregate predictions of heterogeneous agent New Keynesian models (HANK). By means of comparison of a number of nested HANK models, we investigate the role played by (1) idiosyncratic income risk, (2) a binding borrowing constraint, and (3) a portfolio choice between liquid and illiquid assets. We argue that the effects of household heterogeneity can be largely understood by looking at the differential behavior of two types of households: hand-to-mouth and unconstrained. We find that a suitably specified and calibrated TANK model (which abstracts from idiosyncratic income risk) can capture reasonably well the aggregate implications of household heterogeneity and the main channels through which it operates. That ability increases in the presence of a policy rule that emphasizes inflation stability. In the limiting case of a strict inflation-targeting policy, heterogeneity becomes irrelevant for the determination of aggregate output.

1

Bankruptcy Resolution and Credit Cycles

Martin Kornejew, *Bocconi University,* Italy
Chen Lian, *University of California, Berkeley, and NBER,* United States of America
Yueran Ma, *University of Chicago, Booth School of Business, and NBER,* United States of America
Pablo Ottonello, *University of Maryland and NBER,* United States of America
Diego J. Perez, *New York University and NBER,* United States of America

I. Introduction

Credit cycles have been a leading topic in discussions about macroeconomic stability and macroprudential policies over the past decade. Following a growing body of evidence that credit booms often lead to economic turmoil (Schularick and Taylor 2012; Jordà, Schularick, and Taylor 2013; Mian, Sufi, and Verner 2017; Greenwood et al. 2022; Ivashina et al. 2024), researchers and policy makers have considered using macroprudential policies to restrain credit expansions and prevent crises. However, macroprudential policies also have costs (e.g., they can introduce regulatory burdens or lead to misallocations). Therefore, a critical task for guiding these policies is to identify the settings where credit booms are more or less likely to create real damage. In the aftermath of credit booms, real damage often arises from firms suffering through inefficient resolution of distress and default, which can disrupt economic activities and aggravate output losses. Accordingly, institutions for the resolution of distress and default can be important for the design of macroprudential policies.

In this paper, we study how institutions for business bankruptcy relate to the macroeconomic dynamics in credit cycles. Using data on bankruptcy efficiency and business credit across 39 countries, we document that business credit booms are followed by severe economic contractions in environments with poorly functioning business bankruptcy. On the contrary, in settings with well-functioning business bankruptcy, the aftermath of credit booms is characterized by moderate changes in output,

NBER Macroeconomics Annual, volume 39, 2025.
 https://doi.org/10.1086/735256

investment, and unemployment. We use a simple model to lay out how bankruptcy resolution affects macro outcomes and why more efficient bankruptcy systems can mitigate the negative consequences of credit booms.

At a high level, institutions for business bankruptcy resolve firms' distress and default through two main approaches. A traditional approach is to terminate firms' operations, liquidate their assets, and pay out the proceeds. This option is available in most countries. Another relatively more modern approach is to restructure viable firms where the continuation value from operations (i.e., "going-concern value") is greater than the liquidation value. For instance, in Chapter 11 restructuring in the United States, viable firms continue to operate, and creditors' payoffs are given by the going-concern (GC) value as verified and approved in court. Well-functioning restructuring systems are important because they reduce inefficiencies from liquidation, which can be substantial due to the loss of valuable organizational capital and the costs of redeploying specialized assets (Ramey and Shapiro 2001; Bernstein, Colonnelli, and Iverson 2019; Corbae and D'Erasmo 2021; Crouzet et al. 2022; Kermani and Ma 2023). However, these systems are challenging to build and relatively rare.

To measure the quality of a country's bankruptcy system, we follow the work of Djankov et al. (2008a) and the extension to 166 countries from 2003 to 2019 by World Bank (2020). This measure assesses the amount of value that can be preserved for a viable company in financial distress. Bankruptcy efficiency is higher if the viable company can continue to operate and the procedure does not take too long or incur too much cost. Default resolution for a viable company is economically important, given large deadweight loss from inefficient liquidation. It is also challenging to implement (well-functioning restructuring is difficult) and can reflect bankruptcy institutions' capacity to handle other issues more generally (e.g., their efficiency for liquidating nonviable companies), as we discuss in Subsection III.B, "Bankruptcy Efficiency." The data show that bankruptcy efficiency varies substantially around the world. For a standardized case where the company has continuation value 100 and liquidation value 70, the value that can be preserved after bankruptcy is 39 on average, with a standard deviation of 25.

Our empirical analysis proceeds by estimating state-dependent local projections, which trace out how economic activities evolve following changes in business credit to gross domestic product (GDP), in countries with high and low efficiency of business bankruptcy. We obtain data on business credit from the Bank of International Settlements (BIS), including both loans and bonds (Dembiermont, Drehmann, and Muksakunratana 2013). We use data on macroeconomic outcomes including GDP, investment, unemployment rate, and consumption from the World Economic Outlook and the World Bank World Development Indicator databases (International Monetary Fund 1999–2024; World Bank 2024). The combined sample has 39 countries due to the coverage of the BIS credit data.

We find that countries with better bankruptcy systems are less vulnerable to credit cycles. For instance, following a 10 percentage point increase in business credit to GDP over the past 5 years, output in the next 5 years declines by around 3 percentage points if bankruptcy efficiency is at the bottom quartile. In contrast, the decline is negligible when bankruptcy efficiency is at the top quartile. We also observe substantial declines of investment and consumption, as well as increases of unemployment in countries with low bankruptcy efficiency, but to a limited extent in countries with high bankruptcy efficiency. We perform a large set of robustness checks to verify that the differences in macroeconomic outcomes are not because of bankruptcy efficiency being correlated with other factors that affect macroeconomic stability, including development status, exchange rate pegging, countercyclicality of monetary and fiscal policies, or general rule of law. The results are similar when we instrument bankruptcy efficiency with legal origins following Djankov et al. (2008a). The results also hold when controlling for the size of the credit market (the level of business credit to GDP). Our exposition uses credit booms (i.e., positive changes in business credit to GDP) for simplicity, given the emphasis in the literature; the results are symmetric for negative changes in business credit to GDP after the first 2 years and stronger for credit booms before that.

To interpret our empirical findings, we develop a simple model that links credit cycles and bankruptcy efficiency. In the model, firms finance investments with defaultable debt. Following default, firms either liquidate or reorganize. Weaker bankruptcy institutions increase the likelihood of inefficient liquidation, which generates greater output losses. This setup resembles the baseline bankruptcy efficiency measure (Djankov et al. 2008a; World Bank 2020) and is supported by empirical evidence on substantial losses from liquidation (Ramey and Shapiro 2001; Bris, Welch, and Zhu 2006; Bernstein, Colonnelli, and Iverson 2019; Kermani and Ma 2023). We use the model to study both "fundamental" credit booms, driven by rational expectations of increases in firms' productivity, and "nonfundamental" credit booms, driven by increases in credit supply or credit demand because of changes in discount rates or biased beliefs.[1]

Our model analysis shows two main results. First, nonfundamental credit booms are followed by lower output and more defaults. Both our analyses and previous empirical studies of credit cycles (Schularick and Taylor 2012; Mian et al. 2017) observe such a pattern for credit booms overall. In this case, more efficient bankruptcy systems mitigate the negative consequences of these credit booms, by decreasing the likelihood of inefficient liquidation in default; this is also consistent with our main empirical evidence. Second, in our model, fundamental credit booms are followed by higher output and fewer defaults. In this case, a more efficient bankruptcy system dampens the positive impact of a credit boom because a more efficient bankruptcy system leaves less room for increases in firms' productivity when the amount of defaults and inefficient liquidations decrease. In the data, we draw on the findings by Müller and Verner (2024) and Ivashina et al. (2024) that credit booms in nontradable sectors appear nonfundamental (they are followed by worse macroeconomic outcomes), whereas credit booms in tradable sectors appear fundamental (they are followed by better macroeconomic outcomes). Interestingly, we also observe that bankruptcy efficiency dampens the negative effects of nontradable credit booms and also dampens the positive effects of tradable credit booms, exactly as our model predicts.[2]

Taken together, our analysis highlights the importance of incorporating default risk and bankruptcy institutions into models used for macroprudential policy design. Nonfundamental credit booms appear dominant both in our data and in previous research. In this setting, bankruptcy efficiency ameliorates the negative consequences of credit booms.

The importance of bankruptcy institutions for credit cycles is illustrated vividly by the experience of Japan in the last 2 decades of the twentieth century. Bankruptcy institutions in Japan were relatively underdeveloped until the late 1990s, with a tedious process and a focus on liquidation (Tan 2004; Anderson 2006). Business lending in Japan traditionally relied heavily on real estate, and a sharp business credit boom occurred when real estate prices surged in the late 1980s. The boom ended with the collapse of real estate prices, and Japan suffered substantially from negative macroeconomic consequences (Gan 2007; Caballero, Hoshi, and Kashyap 2008). With an inefficient bankruptcy system, bad debt problems were challenging to resolve. Correspondingly, firms were strained by debt overhang, whereas banks were burdened by nonperforming loans, and they often opted to evergreen such loans because default resolution was cumbersome. These issues exacerbated credit contractions, resource misallocations, and edconomic downturns. As bad debt problems proliferated,

Japanese policy makers recognized the importance of bankruptcy institutions and embarked on a major bankruptcy reform that lasted from 1996 to 2005.

In the United States, where business bankruptcy institutions are among the most developed in the world, business debt has not been a primary source of macroeconomic instability. Instead, households and financial institutions, where default resolution has been much more challenging, have played a central role in credit cycles that ended in economic turmoil (Gertler and Gilchrist 2018). However, business bankruptcy institutions perform poorly in many countries (Djankov et al. 2008a), and corporate credit booms appear to have been an important contributor to macroeconomic instability around the world in the twentieth century (Ivashina et al. 2024).

Our paper relates to several strands of literature. First, we extend the work on financial frictions and economic fluctuations. An influential line of research highlights that frictions in debt enforcement can exacerbate economic fluctuations (Kiyotaki and Moore 1997; Bernanke, Gertler, and Gilchrist 1999). A growing body of empirical work documents the negative consequences of credit booms in general (Schularick and Taylor 2012; Jordà et al. 2013; Greenwood et al. 2022) and corporate credit booms in particular (Müller and Verner 2024; Ivashina et al. 2024). The most closely related research is Jordà et al. (2022), who focus on recessions and show that greater frictions in corporate debt resolution are associated with slower recoveries. We do not restrict to recessions, and we study a variety of macroeconomic outcomes following changes in business credit to GDP in general (e.g., what happens after credit booms or contractions). Indeed, we observe that, in countries with lower bankruptcy efficiency, credit booms are followed by a higher likelihood of recessions in the first place. Moreover, in countries with lower bankruptcy efficiency, macro outcomes following credit booms are worse even without recessions. We also provide a model to delineate how bankruptcy efficiency matters for the macroeconomic impact of credit cycles.

Second, we connect law and macroeconomics. An important literature has examined how financial markets and firm outcomes are affected by legal systems in general (La Porta et al. 1998), as well as bankruptcy institutions in particular (Acharya and Subramanian 2009; Gilson 2012; Vig 2013; Becker and Josephson 2016; Ponticelli and Alencar 2016; Iverson 2018; Bernstein et al. 2019; Becker and Ivashina 2022). We focus on the macro consequences of credit cycles, which represent one of the most important challenges for economic stability. It is natural that the legal systems affect financial frictions, which in turn affect macroeconomic outcomes.

Third, we provide a new perspective on macroprudential policies. The traditional approach relies on regulatory tools to prevent credit booms, to avoid costly recessions in the aftermath of these booms (Hanson, Kashyap, and Stein 2011; Bianchi and Lorenzoni 2022). Our evidence suggests that the macroeconomic dynamics following credit booms depend on institutions for default resolution. Improving these institutions is another approach for enhancing macroeconomic stability. To the extent that existing macroprudential tools could be blunt or costly (Ottonello, Perez, and Varraso 2022; Andreasen et al. 2023; Dávila and Walther 2024), they may be less necessary in environments with high bankruptcy efficiency.

The rest of the paper is organized as follows. Section II outlines the economic functions of institutions for business bankruptcy. Section III describes the data. Section IV provides the empirical results on how bankruptcy efficiency relates to the macroeconomic consequences of credit booms. Section V uses a simple model to illustrate the mechanisms. Section VI concludes.

II. The Economics of Business Bankruptcy

Why are legal institutions for business bankruptcy important? We proceed in two steps in this section. In Subsection II.A, we discuss the relevance of default resolution for firm and macroeconomic outcomes. In Subsection II.B, we then discuss the relevance of legal institutions on business bankruptcy for default resolution. In Subsection II.C, we illustrate the importance of bankruptcy institutions for macroeconomic outcomes with the case of Japan.

A. Default Resolution and Economic Implications

Human civilizations have used debt contracts to support business activities for thousands of years. Since the earliest days, it has been well recognized that lenders are only willing to supply funding if they can expect to be paid back. There are several approaches to debt enforcement if borrowers default.

One approach is to impose severe punishment, such as debtors' prison (in ancient times) or autarky, analyzed in many studies of sovereign default (Eaton and Gersovitz 1981; Bulow and Rogoff 1989). This approach is perhaps rare for commercial credit in today's world. It can be rather inefficient, especially for "honest but unfortunate debtors" such as a viable company hit by adverse liquidity shocks (or firms during COVID-19).

Another approach is that firms pledge physical assets to borrow, which creditors can seize in the case of default. This approach exists in most countries and has influenced many macroeconomic models (Kiyotaki and Moore 1997; Bernanke et al. 1999). It is natural if property rights over assets can be enforced but cash flows are not verifiable. However, it can be inefficient, too, in the case of viable companies in financial distress (Diamond 2023).

A third approach is to implement financial restructuring and remunerate lenders with the continuation value of the company. This approach can be beneficial for viable companies in financial distress (Gilson 2010). It tends to rely more on cash flow verifiability. For instance, in Chapter 11 restructuring in the United States, viable firms continue to operate (instead of being liquidated), and creditors' payoffs are given by the "going-concern value" (i.e., the value of cash flows from ongoing operations) of the company postreorganization as verified and approved in court.

Default resolution affects ex post economic outcomes during distress. First, it has a direct impact on resource allocation. Ideally, viable companies in financial distress should be kept alive, and nonviable companies in economic distress should be liquidated. However, inefficient default resolution may liquidate viable companies or keep around nonviable firms whose assets have better use elsewhere. Second, poor business performance arising from inefficient default resolution can trigger real or financial amplifications (e.g., by reducing demand or asset prices) and exacerbate distress for other companies (Kiyotaki and Moore 1997; Bernanke et al. 1999; Benmelech and Bergman 2011; Bernstein et al. 2019). Third, inefficient default resolution can distort banks' lending decisions by creating stronger incentives for ailing banks to evergreen nonperforming loans instead of resolving them (Becker and Ivashina 2022). For these reasons, inefficient default resolution can exacerbate recessions.

Default resolution also affects ex ante credit availability and the determinants of firms' debt capacity. For example, with well-functioning restructuring systems, creditors' payoffs in default are tied to the going-concern value of the company, which facilitates borrowing against earnings (Lian and Ma 2021). Conversely, when liquidation dominates, pledging physical assets is especially important for borrowing, and companies' debt capacity can be more sensitive to real estate value.

What shapes the feasibility of each approach of default resolution? As mentioned above, the liquidation approach relies on property rights over assets, and the restructuring approach often relies on cash flow verifiability. In addition to these basic components, additional support from the legal system can be necessary, especially for restructuring, which tends to be a more complex process. We discuss the role of the legal institutions for business bankruptcy in the following.

B. *The Role of Bankruptcy Institutions for Default Resolution*

Bankruptcy is a legal process aimed to facilitate the resolution of financial and economic distress.[3] In the absence of legal institutions for business bankruptcy, private parties may encounter information frictions regarding the value of the debtors' assets and liabilities as well as coordination frictions among different claim holders. Both types of frictions can shrink the total size of the pie ex post and affect debt availability ex ante (Morris and Shin 2004; Smith and Strömberg 2005; Dou et al. 2021; Guntin 2024). Legal institutions, with a combination of statutes and court implementation, can improve the provision and verification of information and aid coordination.

In the case of liquidation, the key objective is to organize an orderly wind-down process. In this process, it is useful to verify the debtor's total assets and liabilities as well as the priority structure among different claim holders. It may also be useful to coordinate the liquidation process to maximize the receipts from asset sales (e.g., when assets pledged to different parties have complementarity).

In the case of restructuring, addressing information frictions and coordination frictions is even more important. In this process, it is crucial to verify the debtor's assets, liabilities, and cash flows. In addition, a significant amount of coordination among claim holders may be required to reach a restructuring plan. Unilateral actions taken by creditors to seize their collateral (out of concerns regarding the value of their assets, the priority they have with respect to other creditors, or actions taken by other creditors) can disrupt continuing operations and destroy viable businesses.

Finally, adjudicating whether a company is viable requires reliable information and considerable coordination. Coordination frictions are typically more severe for large companies with complex operations and liability structures. Information frictions can apply to both large and small companies.

The legal process for business bankruptcy addresses information frictions and coordination frictions in several ways. First, the court can provide a centralized forum for information gathering and disclosure. In the United States, debtors submit a variety of information to the court at the time of filing, including financial information, organizational structure, and lists of claim holders, among others. The court may also appoint trustees to collect additional information. In restructuring, the court approves the assessed value of the company, which is the basis of payments to claim holders. Second, the court may prohibit unilateral actions by claim holders that jeopardize orderly resolution or disrupt continuing operations of viable firms. In the United States, business bankruptcy features the automatic stay, which forbids asset seizure and debt collection upon bankruptcy filing.[4] Third, the court can design voting rules to help different claim holders reach an agreement. In the United States, claim holders with similar priority are grouped into one class, and each class needs to approve a restructuring plan with two-thirds in value and one-half in number. This voting rule aims to alleviate holdout problems and prevent powerful senior creditors from imposing their desires upon junior creditors (or vice versa).

The court may also help support the financing of firms' operations during restructuring. In the United States, the court can approve "debtor-in-possession" financing with super priority over prepetition claims (typically paid off when restructuring is completed), to provide liquidity and overcome debt overhang. In addition, the court can allow critical vendors to get paid for the goods and services they supply during the restructuring process (whereas other claim holders are not paid until restructuring is completed), to minimize production disruptions. Finally, bankruptcy laws often include provisions that allow the court to claw back payments made by the debtor during a certain time interval before the bankruptcy filing. Such provisions aim to prevent fraudulent behavior or unequal treatment of claim holders (e.g., the company tunneling funds toward certain parties in anticipation of the bankruptcy filing) and to correct such actions if they do occur.

Achieving these functions is a complicated endeavor that requires a combination of sophisticated statues and competent judges (Aghion, Hart, and Moore 1992; Smith and Strömberg 2005; Ponticelli and Alencar 2016; Antill 2022; Iverson et al. 2023). Often, bankruptcy laws are historically developed to liquidate failed businesses and are slow to serve the need of resolving financial distress for viable companies, because restructuring is a complex process that involves more information gathering,

Table 1
Summary Statistics

	(A) Full Sample						(B) Regression Sample					
	N	Mean	SD	Q25	Q50	Q75	*N*	Mean	SD	Q25	Q50	Q75
Bankruptcy efficiency (%)	1,759	39.3	24.6	21.3	32.4	51.0	560	63.1	23.5	42.9	68.6	83.0
Business debt-to-GDP ratio (%)	649	80.7	40.7	49.4	76.6	107.1	560	83.0	40.0	53.9	80.4	109.4
Business debt-to-GDP ratio, 5-year change (pp.)	621	6.5	15.0	−2.0	5.5	14.1	560	6.9	15.3	−2.0	6.1	14.6
Real GDP growth, annual (%)	1,964	4.1	8.8	1.4	4.0	7.3	560	2.8	3.8	1.0	2.7	4.6
Real investment growth, annual (%)	1,836	4.5	22.6	−1.8	4.8	11.5	560	2.8	9.6	−1.1	3.4	7.3
Unemployment rate (%)	1,915	6.9	4.8	3.6	5.4	9.1	560	7.4	4.3	4.6	6.8	8.7

Note: The table presents descriptive statistics for our main variables for years 2003–19. Panel A shows statistics for all countries covered by a given variable. Panel B shows statistics for our regression sample—that is, countries jointly covered by all five variables. The bankruptcy efficiency measure is from World Bank (2020). Business debt to gross domestic product (GDP) is from the Bank of International Settlements (BIS). Real GDP, real investment, and unemployment rate are from the World Economic Outlook and the World Development Indicator databases.

average bankruptcy efficiency is higher at 63%. Even in this case, the average loss of value is substantial. In the data, variations in bankruptcy efficiency are mainly across countries rather than within countries over time during the World Bank (2020) sample period (e.g., country fixed effects have R^2 around 0.9). Legal origins are important (Djankov et al. 2008a), with R^2 around 0.33.

There are two important reasons for low bankruptcy efficiency: (1) failure to preserve the viable firm and (2) long and costly bankruptcy process. In figure 1, we plot the total recovery rate on the *y*-axis for 2019, the latest year of data. The *x*-axis is the likely duration of the bankruptcy case across countries. The solid dots indicate countries where the viable company can continue to operate, and the hollow dots indicate places where it cannot. We see that the viable company is expected to survive in only about half of the countries. The recovery is naturally higher in these settings. In many countries, however, the company cannot survive, and the bankruptcy case is expected to take a long time. Accordingly, recovery is very low.

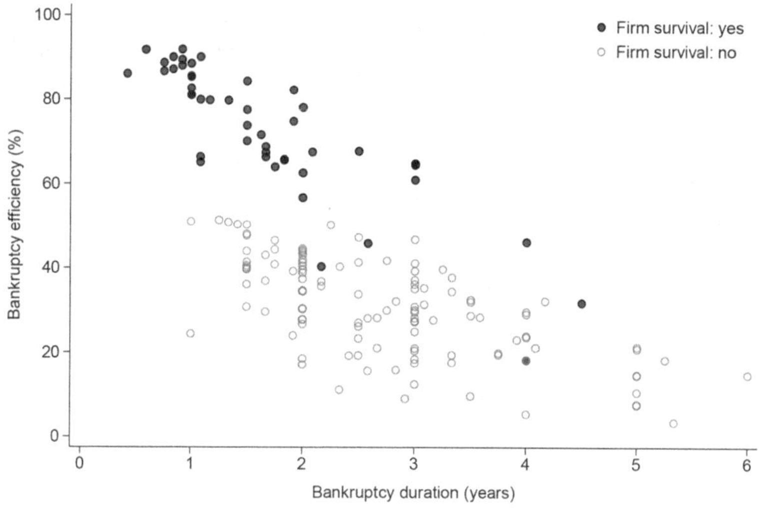

Fig. 1. Bankruptcy efficiency around the world. This figure shows a scatter plot for 166 countries in 2019, where each dot is a country. The data come from the World Bank Doing Business database (World Bank 2020) following the methodology of Djankov et al. (2008a). The solid dots represent countries where the business can continue to operate, and the hollow dots represent countries where the business is expected to be liquidated. Bankruptcy efficiency uses the fraction of economic value that can be preserved in bankruptcy. It measures total recovery less bankruptcy costs, discounted by resolution duration divided by the value from continuing operation (100).

In figure IA1, https://data.nber.org/data-appendix/c14994/appendix.pdf, we construct a proxy of realized default recovery rate and compare it with our bankruptcy efficiency measure. Specifically, we take the ratio of loan impairments relative to nonperforming loans in a given year from the BIS MiDAS Credit Loss database introduced by Ong, Schmieder, and Wei (2023), and use 1 minus this ratio as the imputed recovery rate. This imputation can be imprecise because we do not know the exact timing for nonperforming loans to translate into impairments. We observe a positive relationship between this imputed default recovery rate and the bankruptcy efficiency measure.

The baseline bankruptcy efficiency measure from World Bank (2020) focuses on default resolution for a viable company. Default resolution for a viable company is economically important because the deadweight loss from inefficient liquidation is substantial, due to high asset specificity (production assets are often specialized or immobile, so the liquidation value to second-best users can be limited) and valuable organizational capital. Ramey and Shapiro (2001) estimate that the average resale value of aerospace manufacturing equipment is 28 cents per dollar of replacement cost. Kermani and Ma (2023) find that the going-concern value from continuing operation is twice as much as the estimated total liquidation value (including cash, working capital, fixed assets, etc.) for nonfinancial firms in Chapter 11 bankruptcy, and about three times as much for US public nonfinancial firms in general.[6]

Efficiency of Resolving Nonviable Companies

Another aspect of bankruptcy efficiency is default resolution for a nonviable company. Our baseline measure does not capture this aspect, but the efficiency of default resolution for viable and nonviable companies is likely correlated.

First, if nonviable companies go through liquidation during the bankruptcy process, the efficiency is correlated with our baseline measure, as both are affected by the bankruptcy system's speed and expertise. The data set from the original Djankov et al. (2008b) work contains information for one question about the fraction of total liquidation value that can be obtained from liquidating a nonviable company.[7] In figure 2, we

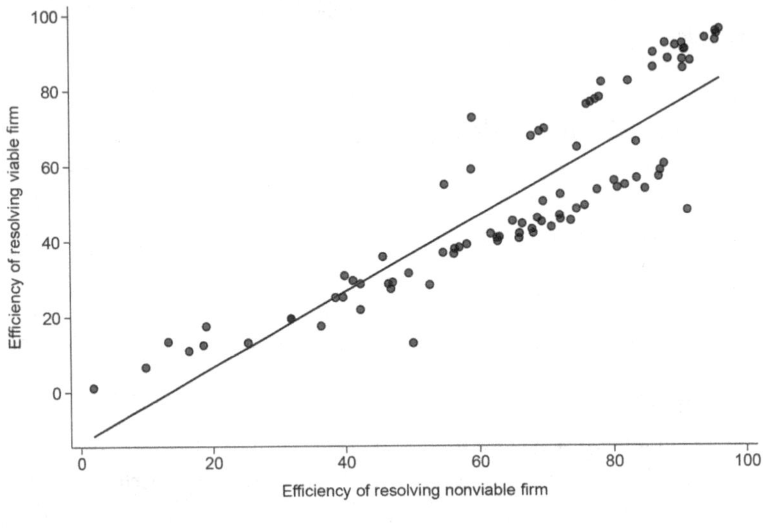

Fig. 2. Efficiency of resolving viable firm and nonviable firm. This figure shows a scatter plot for 88 countries in 2006, where each dot is a country. The data come from Djankov et al. (2008a). The *x*-axis shows the efficiency of liquidating a nonviable company—that is, the share of a nonviable company's liquidation value obtained in bankruptcy. The *y*-axis shows the efficiency of resolving a viable company—that is, the share of a viable firm's full value from continuing operation that can be preserved in bankruptcy.

observe a positive relationship between our baseline measure (y-axis) and the efficiency of liquidating a nonviable company (x-axis); both are for the year 2006 from the original Djankov et al. (2008a) data set. These two measures are 0.88 correlated.[8] Later, in Subsection IV.A, we show that among these two variables, the efficiency measure for a viable company is more important for differentiating macroeconomic outcomes following credit booms.

During the bankruptcy process, inefficient continuation of nonviable companies may not be common (Bernstein, Colonnelli, and Iverson 2019; Bernstein et al. 2019; Dou et al. 2021). Liquidating a company is more straightforward for courts to implement than keeping the firm alive. In addition, restructuring procedures often explicitly require that all creditors get paid no less than what they would obtain in liquidation.[9] Indeed, in the Djankov et al. (2008a) measure on the x-axis of figure 2, all countries report that the nonviable firm will be liquidated.

Second, inefficient continuation outside the bankruptcy process resulting from lenders evergreening their nonperforming loans may be more common (see, e.g., Caballero et al. 2008, and the literature on zombie lending reviewed by Acharya et al. 2022). Lenders are more likely to keep these firms continuing if bankruptcy processes are lengthy and costly, which are associated with lower bankruptcy efficiency in our baseline measure (as shown in fig. 1). Indeed, recent work finds that stronger bankruptcy institutions are associated with fewer zombie firms (Becker and Ivashina 2022; Altman, Dai, and Wang 2024).

In summary, default resolution for a viable company is economically important, given the high costs of inefficient liquidation. It is also a hard test, which can reflect bankruptcy institutions' capacity to handle other issues more generally (e.g., their efficiency in liquidating nonviable companies). Accordingly, previous data collection efforts have focused on this case. Our baseline measure follows them because of both data availability and economic relevance.

B. *Other Data*

We obtain data on business credit from the BIS. This data set contains both business credit issued by banks and credit extended by nonbanks (e.g., corporate bonds, see Dembiermont et al. 2013). Some work focuses on bank credit (Müller and Verner 2024; Ivashina et al. 2024). We focus on all business credit combined. We use data on GDP, investment, unemployment rate, and consumption from the World Economic

Outlook reports and the World Bank World Development Indicator database (International Monetary Fund 1999–2024; World Bank 2024). We drop countries with less than five million people, because small economies tend to be disproportionately exposed to international capital flows, and their economic performance can be more affected by external conditions.

Table 1 presents the summary statistics. Panel A shows the summary statistics for all country-years with respective data. Panel B shows the summary statistics for the regression sample that we use in Section IV, where we need data on bankruptcy efficiency, business credit, and economic outcomes. The size of the regression sample is limited by the coverage of the BIS business credit data. Figure IA2 shows the list of countries covered by the baseline regression sample.

IV. Bankruptcy Resolution and the Macroeconomic Impact of Credit Booms: Empirical Evidence

Credit cycles represent one of the most important challenges for macroeconomic stability. A growing volume of studies document that credit booms predict recessions and crises. We analyze how macroeconomic outcomes following credit booms vary with the efficiency of business bankruptcy institutions.

We follow the standard empirical specification in recent work on credit cycles, which performs a regression of subsequent economic outcomes on changes in credit as the key independent variable (Mian et al. 2017).[10] We include an interaction term between changes in credit and bankruptcy efficiency, to test how the relationship between changes in credit and subsequent economic outcomes varies with bankruptcy efficiency. Specifically, we estimate state-dependent local projections:

$$\Delta_h Y_{i,t+h} = \alpha_{i,h} + \beta_{1,h}\Delta_5 c_{i,t} + \beta_{2,h}(\Delta_5 c_{i,t} \times B_{i,t}) + \beta_{3,h}B_{i,t} + \gamma_h x_{i,t} + \epsilon_{i,t}, \qquad (3)$$

for annual horizons of $h = 1, \dots, 5$. The outcome variable $\Delta_h Y_{i,t+h}$ begins with the change in log real GDP; we also study log real investment, unemployment rate, and log real private consumption later on. The independent variable $\Delta_5 c_{i,t}$ is the change in business credit to GDP in the past 5 years in country i and year t using BIS data, and $B_{i,t}$ is the measure of bankruptcy efficiency.[11] We control for 5 lags of real GDP growth as well as the cumulative change in household credit relative to GDP since year $t-5$. We include horizon-specific country fixed effects $\alpha_{i,h}$. The sample covers annual data from an unbalanced panel of 39 countries over the period of 2003–19. We use Driscoll and Kraay (1998) standard errors with 5 lags.

A. *Basic Results*

Table 2 presents regression results for the path of GDP as the outcome variable. We interact the bankruptcy efficiency measure with the change in business credit to GDP over the past 5 years, as in equation (3). The regressions show that future output is significantly lower following increases in business credit when bankruptcy efficiency is low. Meanwhile, future output would stay roughly unchanged if bankruptcy efficiency were 100%.[12]

Figure 3 visualizes the GDP trajectory following a 10 percentage point increase in business credit to GDP over the past 5 years. The left (right) panel shows the result for low (high) bankruptcy efficiency, namely $B_{i,t}$

Table 2
Change in Log Real GDP

	(1)	(2)	(3)	(4)	(5)
	$h = 1$	$h = 2$	$h = 3$	$h = 4$	$h = 5$
Δ_5 Business credit/GDP × Bankruptcy efficiency	.143***	.319***	.546***	.633***	.669***
	(.048)	(.080)	(.114)	(.134)	(.172)
Δ_5 Business credit/GDP	−.146***	−.310***	−.490***	−.555***	−.576***
	(.046)	(.072)	(.103)	(.119)	(.145)
Bankruptcy efficiency	−.939	−1.385	−.700	−.260	−.082
	(.954)	(1.185)	(1.965)	(2.887)	(3.293)
Country FE	Yes	Yes	Yes	Yes	Yes
Controls	Yes	Yes	Yes	Yes	Yes
R^2 (within)	.14	.14	.18	.21	.25
Observations	560	522	484	446	408

Note: This table shows results from state-dependent local projections: $\Delta_h \log(\text{realGDP}_{i,t+h}) = \alpha_{i,h} + \beta_{1,h}\Delta_5 c_{i,t} + \beta_{2,h}(\Delta_5 c_{i,t} \times B_{i,t}) + \beta_{3,h}B_{i,t} + \gamma_h x_{i,t} + \epsilon_{i,t}$ for $h = 1, \ldots, 5$. The outcome variable is the change in log real GDP in country i from year t to year $t + h$. The independent variable $\Delta_5 c_{i,t}$ denotes the change of business credit to GDP in country i from year $t - 5$ to year t, and $B_{i,t}$ is the bankruptcy efficiency measure. The controls $x_{i,t}$ include contemporaneous and 5 lags of real GDP growth, as well as the cumulative change in household credit to GDP since year $t - 5$. Horizon-specific country fixed effects $\alpha_{i,h}$ are included. The sample contains annual data from an unbalanced panel of 39 countries. The sample period is 2003–19. Driscoll-Kraay standard errors are in parentheses. FE = fixed effects, GDP = gross domestic product.
$^{***}p < .01$.

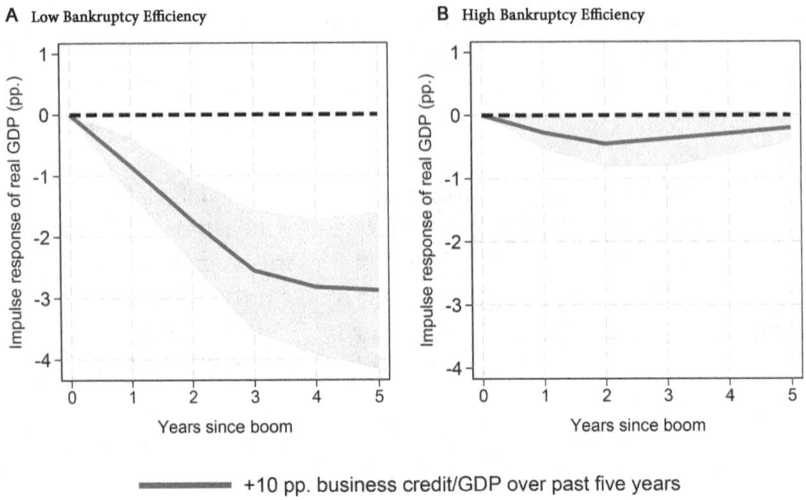

Fig. 3. Gross domestic product (GDP) following business credit booms. This figure shows the GDP trajectory following a 10 percentage point increase in the business credit to GDP ratio over the preceding 5 years. We estimate state-dependent local projections: $\Delta_h \log(\text{real GDP}_{i,t+h}) = \alpha_{i,h} + \beta_{1,h}\Delta_5 c_{i,t} + \beta_{2,h}(\Delta_5 c_{i,t} \times B_{i,t}) + \beta_{3,h}B_{i,t} + \gamma_h x_{i,t} + \epsilon_{i,t}$ for $h = 1, \ldots, 5$. The outcome variable is the change in log real GDP in country i from year t to year $t + h$. The independent variable $\Delta_5 c_{i,t}$ denotes the change of business credit to GDP in country i from year $t - 5$ to year t, and $B_{i,t}$ is the bankruptcy efficiency measure. The controls $\boldsymbol{x}_{i,t}$ include contemporaneous and 5 lags of real GDP growth, as well as the cumulative change in household credit to GDP since year $t - 5$. Horizon-specific country fixed effects $\alpha_{i,h}$ are included. The left (right) panel evaluates the impulse response using $B_{i,t}$ at the bottom (top) quartile, which is equal to 43% (83%). The sample contains annual data from an unbalanced panel of 39 countries. The sample period is 2003–19. Shaded areas mark 90% confidence intervals based on Driscoll-Kraay standard errors.

at the 25th (75th) percentile of the regression sample. Again, the economic magnitude is substantial. A business credit boom on the scale of a 10 percentage point increase in business credit to GDP occurs in roughly a third of our sample observations. Following a boom of this size, real GDP declines by about 3 percentage points in the next 5 years for a country at the bottom quartile of bankruptcy efficiency (left panel), whereas real GDP barely declines for a country at the top quartile of bankruptcy efficiency (right panel). The cumulative output loss over 5 years is about 9 percentage points larger under low bankruptcy efficiency than under high bankruptcy efficiency.[13] Interestingly, in low bankruptcy efficiency countries, real GDP does not yet recover by year 5. We verify in figure IA3 that the recovery gradually occurs between year 6 and year 10. However, since the bankruptcy efficiency data only began in 2003, the number of observations falls for longer-term local projections, so we use local projections for subsequent 5 years in the baseline results.

Jordà et al. (2022) find that recessions following business credit booms are more severe in countries with low bankruptcy efficiency. Their analysis conditions on the occurrence of recessions (i.e., negative GDP growth). Our previous analysis does not. Indeed, we observe that the results are not limited to recession severity. First, figure 4 shows that, in low bankruptcy efficiency countries, recessions are more likely to occur following credit booms. For example, 3 years after a 10 percentage point increase of business credit to GDP, countries at the bottom quartile of bankruptcy efficiency have higher cumulative recession probability by

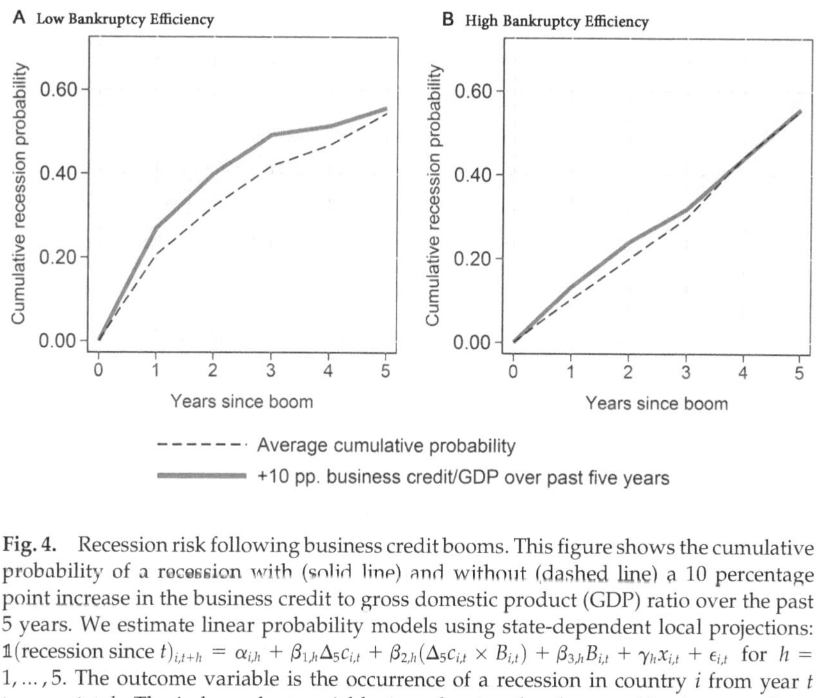

Fig. 4. Recession risk following business credit booms. This figure shows the cumulative probability of a recession with (solid line) and without (dashed line) a 10 percentage point increase in the business credit to gross domestic product (GDP) ratio over the past 5 years. We estimate linear probability models using state-dependent local projections: $\mathbb{1}(\text{recession since } t)_{i,t+h} = \alpha_{i,h} + \beta_{1,h}\Delta_5 c_{i,t} + \beta_{2,h}(\Delta_5 c_{i,t} \times B_{i,t}) + \beta_{3,h}B_{i,t} + \gamma_h x_{i,t} + \epsilon_{i,t}$ for $h = 1, \ldots, 5$. The outcome variable is the occurrence of a recession in country i from year t to year $t + h$. The independent variable $\Delta_5 c_{i,t}$ denotes the change of business credit to GDP in country i from year $t - 5$ to year t, and $B_{i,t}$ is the bankruptcy efficiency measure. The controls $x_{i,t}$ include contemporaneous and 5 lags of real GDP growth and recession indicators, as well as the cumulative change in household credit to GDP since year $t - 5$. Horizon-specific country fixed effects $\alpha_{i,h}$ are included. The left (right) panel evaluates the impulse response using $B_{i,t}$ at the bottom (top) quartile, which is equal to 43% (83%). The sample contains annual data from an unbalanced panel of 39 countries. The sample period is 2003–19. Shaded areas mark 90% confidence intervals based on Driscoll-Kraay standard errors.

about 7.4 percentage points, whereas there is no significant effect for countries at the top quartile of bankruptcy efficiency. Second, table IA1 (https://data.nber.org/data-appendix/c14994/appendix.pdf#page=14) shows that macro outcomes are also worse outside recessions. Relatedly, figure IA4 and table IA2 examine equation (3) with quantile regressions. We observe that both the 80th percentile and the 20th percentile outcomes are worse following credit booms in low bankruptcy efficiency countries. Taken together, the data suggest that low bankruptcy efficiency countries experience a systematic decline in output following credit booms: inefficient default resolution can generate more deadweight loss and reduce output in general. This makes economic outcomes worse both in and outside recessions, and a weaker economy also implies that recessions are more likely.

Robustness Checks

We perform a number of robustness checks in the rest of this section. First, we examine a large set of variables that can influence macroeconomic stability, and we verify that our main results are not driven by bankruptcy efficiency being correlated with these factors. Specifically, we add these variables and their interactions with the change in business credit ($\Delta_5 c_{i,t}$) to equation (3). Tables IA3 and IA4 start with country characteristics: table IA3 considers development status and log real GDP per capita; table IA4 controls for the general volatility of GDP growth. table IA1 and IA6 turn to macroeconomic policies: table IA5 considers exchange rate pegging; table IA6 controls for the countercyclicality of monetary policy (i.e., the country specific coefficient of regressing the changes in the policy rate on real output growth) and fiscal policy (i.e., the country specific coefficient of regressing changes in government spending to GDP on real output growth). Tables IA7, IA8, and IA9 turn to other aspects of legal institutions, including general rule of law, government effectiveness, regulatory quality, time to start a business, and time to enforce contracts.[14] In all cases, we find that macroeconomic outcomes following credit booms are substantially worse in countries with low bankruptcy efficiency. The results suggest that bankruptcy efficiency is a distinct factor from development status, standard macroeconomic stabilization policies, and general legal institutions.[15]

Second, a possible concern is reverse causality: Maybe bad economic conditions lead to low observed bankruptcy efficiency (e.g., courts get overcrowded when economic conditions are difficult). To address this concern, we also use bankruptcy efficiency fixed at the beginning of the sample in figure IA5 and table IA10 and examine macroeconomic outcomes thereafter. The results are similar to those in figure 3 and table 2.

Third, we follow previous work and instrument bankruptcy efficiency with legal origins. We use four indicator variables for legal origins: English, French, German, and Nordic, as in Djankov et al. (2008a). These legal origin variables explain about 30% of the variations in bankruptcy efficiency. The results instrumenting bankruptcy efficiency with legal origins are shown in figure IA6 and table IA11. The key patterns and magnitudes here are similar to those in the baseline results in figure 3 and table 2. Because legal origins may also affect general rule of law, in panel *B* of figure IA6 and table IA11, we additionally control for rule of law and its interaction with changes in business credit (as in table IA7) and obtain similar results. Indeed, bankruptcy efficiency is significantly related to legal origins, which often influence judicial philosophies, even when controlling for the general rule of law index. As Djankov et al. (2008a) document, French and German legal origins are especially unfriendly toward reorganization, automatic stay, and allowing existing management to remain, which tend to make it more challenging to preserve the continuing operation of the company as discussed in Subsection II.B.

Fourth, a possible question is whether countries with low bankruptcy efficiency happen to have high debt burden, so they are more vulnerable to negative shocks. We perform several checks. First, figure IA8 plots business credit to GDP against bankruptcy efficiency. If anything, we observe a positive correlation: Countries with high bankruptcy efficiency are those that bear more corporate debt relative to output. This is also consistent with the theoretical prediction in the model section below (Proposition 1) where a more efficient bankruptcy system leads to a larger credit market. Second, the baseline results are similar if we additionally control for the level of business credit to GDP at horizon 0 and its interaction with the change in business credit, as shown in figure IA9. In other words, for the same debt level, countries with low bankruptcy efficiency still experience worse macroeconomic outcomes subsequently.

Fifth, as mentioned in Subsection III.A, our baseline bankruptcy efficiency measure provides information about default resolution for a viable company. Figure 2 shows that our baseline measure is correlated with a secondary measure in Djankov et al. (2008a) on the value preserved in default resolution for a nonviable company. In table IA12, we compare the efficiency for resolving viable and nonviable companies. We take both variables measured for year 2006 from Djankov et al. (2008a) and use the fixed value for each country throughout the sample.[16] We observe that the efficiency of resolving a viable company appears more related to the path of output following credit booms. As discussed in Subsection III.A, there can be a lot more to lose from inefficient default resolution for a viable company.

Finally, figure IA7 shows that the main results are similar if we measure changes of business credit to GDP over alternative windows, such as the past 3 years or 8 years instead of the past 5 years above. Panel *A* (*B*) shows the path of output after a 6 (16) percentage point increase in business credit to GDP over the past 3 (8) years; in other words, we scale the change in business credit to GDP to 2 percentage points per year.

Nontradable and Tradable Booms

Work by Müller and Verner (2024) and Ivashina et al. (2024) finds that business credit booms driven by nontradable sectors are followed by worse macroeconomic outcomes, whereas business credit booms driven by nontradable sectors are followed by sustained output growth. Müller and Verner (2024) argue that nontradable sectors are more sensitive to nonfundamental shocks like "easy credit." In table IA13, we show that bankruptcy efficiency is associated with less economic damage following nontradable booms: the change in nontradable credit to GDP has a significantly negative coefficient on future output, but its interaction with bankruptcy efficiency has a significantly positive coefficient (i.e., the negative outcomes are milder in high bankruptcy efficiency countries). Later, in Section V, we analyze booms driven by nonfundamental shocks (e.g., lower discount rate of borrowers or lenders) and fundamental shocks (e.g., higher future productivity). In the former case, future output will be lower, but less so when bankruptcy efficiency is high; in the latter case, future output can be higher. The results in table IA13 are consistent with these predictions.

A common question is whether countries with high versus low bankruptcy efficiency experience different types of booms. We also examine this question for nontradable and tradable booms. In table IA14, column 1 shows that bankruptcy efficiency is positively associated with a higher share of nontradable credit (in total nontradable and tradable business credit), although the magnitude is economically small. Columns 2 and 3 show that how the share of nontradable credit changes in a credit boom is not significantly different for high versus low bankruptcy efficiency countries.[17] In other words, we do not observe that high bankruptcy efficiency countries have more or less nontradable credit booms in the first place. In sum, fundamental shocks that trigger good booms (e.g., positive news about total factor productivity [TFP]) and nonfundamental shocks that trigger bad booms (e.g., movements in discount rates or beliefs) can occur for other reasons, and bankruptcy efficiency does not have to be related to the relative prevalence of these shocks. Once nonfundamental shocks hit and trigger bad booms, bankruptcy efficiency is especially relevant for subsequent macroeconomic outcomes.

Symmetry of Credit Booms and Contractions

Our exposition illustrates the results using credit booms for simplicity given the emphasis on the adverse effects of credit booms in the literature. The underlying regressions in equation (3) use $\Delta_5 c_{i,t}$ directly, so the observations are not limited to credit expansions (i.e., $\Delta_5 c_{i,t} > 0$). For the case of credit expansions, the intuition is that *higher subsequent defaults* would contribute to larger (smaller) output decreases when bankruptcy efficiency is lower (higher). Analogously, for the case of credit contractions, the intuition is that *lower subsequent defaults* would contribute to larger (smaller) output increases when bankruptcy efficiency is lower (higher). We test whether the data show symmetric results for credit expansions and contractions (i.e., positive and negative changes in business credit to GDP). Figure IA10 panel *A* and panel *B* show the path of output following credit expansions and contractions, respectively. Table IA15 follows Ben Zeev, Ramey, and Zubairy (2023) to test against symmetric paths after credit booms and contractions. In particular, we use an indicator variable for credit booms (i.e., positive change in business credit to GDP over the past 5 years) and add a triple interaction of this indicator variable with credit booms and bankruptcy efficiency. In the first 2 years ($h = 1$ and $h = 2$), we observe stronger results for credit expansions. After that ($h = 3, 4$, and 5), the results are not significantly different for credit expansions and contractions.

B. *Other Outcomes*

We study a number of other outcomes in addition to aggregate output. In figures 5 and 6, we turn to the path of investment and employment following business credit booms. We observe that investment declines substantially and unemployment rises moderately in countries with low bankruptcy efficiency. These negative outcomes are less pronounced in countries with high bankruptcy efficiency. In figure IA11, we look at productivity using

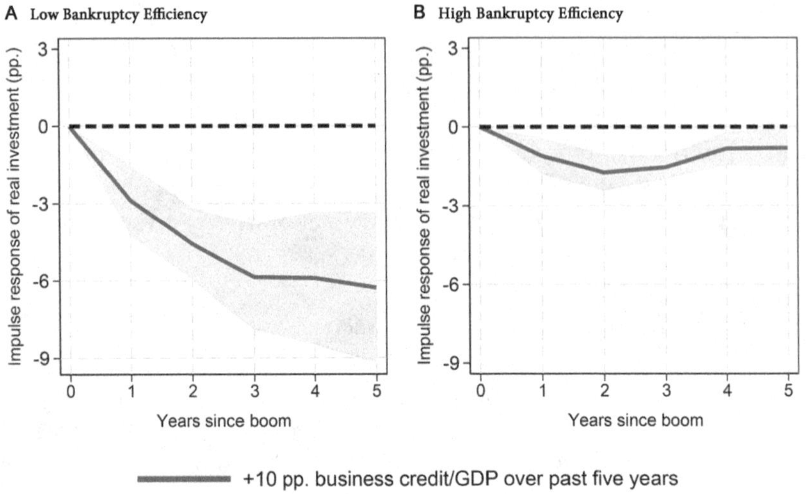

Fig. 5. Investment following business credit booms. This figure shows the investment trajectory following a 10 percentage point increase in the business credit to gross domestic product (GDP) ratio over the past 5 years. We estimate state-dependent local projections: $\Delta_h \log(\text{real investment}_{i,t+h}) = \alpha_{i,h} + \beta_{1,h}\Delta_5 c_{i,t} + \beta_{2,h}(\Delta_5 c_{i,t} \times B_{i,t}) + \beta_{3,h} B_{i,t} + \gamma_h x_{i,t} + \epsilon_{i,t}$ for $h = 1, \ldots, 5$. The outcome variable is the change in log real investment in country i from year t to year $t + h$. The independent variable $\Delta_5 c_{i,t}$ denotes the change of business credit to GDP in country i from year $t - 5$ to year t, and $B_{i,t}$ is the bankruptcy efficiency measure. The controls $x_{i,t}$ include contemporaneous and 5 lags of real GDP growth and real investment growth, as well as the cumulative change in household credit to GDP since year $t - 5$. Horizon-specific country fixed effects $\alpha_{i,h}$ are included. The left (right) panel evaluates the impulse response using $B_{i,t}$ at the bottom (top) quartile, which is equal to 43% (83%). The sample contains annual data from an unbalanced panel of 39 countries. The sample period is 2003–19. Shaded areas are 90% confidence intervals based on Driscoll-Kraay standard errors.

TFP from the Penn World Tables. We observe larger TFP declines following credit booms in low bankruptcy efficiency countries.

The negative consequences of firms' financial distress can be propagated across the economy in several ways. First, reductions in investment and employment can depress aggregate demand and in turn decrease consumption. In figure 7, we plot the path of consumption following business credit booms. We observe that consumption declines substantially in countries with low bankruptcy efficiency. In contrast, consumption remains largely stable in countries with high bankruptcy efficiency. Second, financial trouble among firms can depress capital markets and raise the cost of financing. In figure IA12, we look at the path of stock prices of nonfinancial corporations (using data from various sources compiled by Baron, Verner, and Xiong 2021 and Jordà et al. 2021 for 36 countries) and credit spreads (using data from Global Financial Data and other sources compiled by Mian et al.

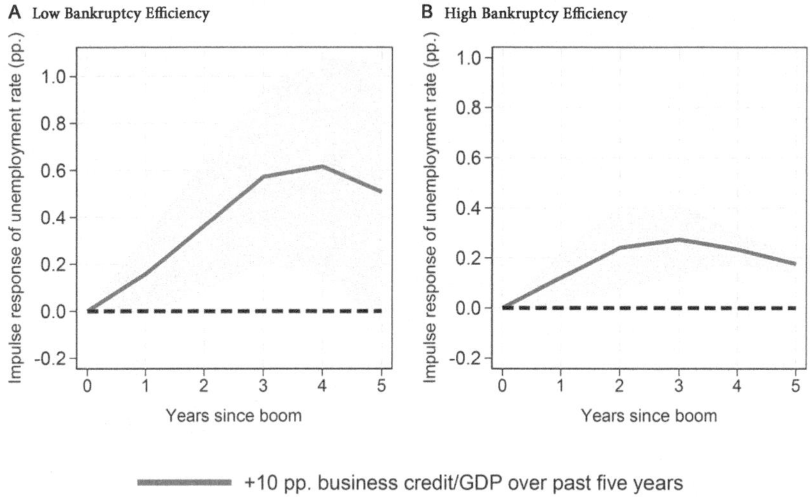

Fig. 6. Unemployment rate following business credit booms. This figure shows the unemployment rate trajectory following a 10 percentage point increase in the business credit to gross domestic product (GDP) ratio over the past 5 years. We estimate state-dependent local projections: $\Delta_h(\text{unemployment rate}_{i,t+h}) = \alpha_{i,h} + \beta_{1,h}\Delta_5 c_{i,t} + \beta_{2,h}(\Delta_5 c_{i,t} \times B_{i,t}) + \beta_{3,h}B_{i,t} + \gamma_h x_{i,t} + \epsilon_{i,t}$ for $h = 1, \ldots, 5$. The outcome variable is the change in unemployment rate in country i from year t to year $t + h$. The independent variable $\Delta_5 c_{i,t}$ denotes the change of business credit to GDP in country i from year $t - 5$ to year t, and $B_{i,t}$ is the bankruptcy efficiency measure. The controls $x_{i,t}$ include contemporaneous and 5 lags of real GDP growth and unemployment rate changes, as well as the cumulative change in household credit relative to GDP since year $t - 5$. Horizon-specific country fixed effects $\alpha_{i,h}$ are included. The left (right) panel evaluates the impulse response using $B_{i,t}$ at the bottom (top) quartile, which is equal to 43% (83%). The sample contains annual data from an unbalanced panel of 39 countries. The sample period is 2003–19. Shaded areas mark 90% confidence intervals based on Driscoll-Kraay standard errors.

2017 and Baron et al. 2021 for 20 countries, updated to 2019). We observe that stock prices decline and credit spreads rise in low bankruptcy efficiency countries but not in high bankruptcy efficiency countries; the standard errors are slightly larger in the smaller sample with asset price data. Deteriorating capital market conditions in countries with low bankruptcy efficiency could further exacerbate economic downturns.

Given the prominence of financial crises in recent research (Schularick and Taylor 2012; Chodorow-Reich 2014; Greenwood et al. 2022; Frydman and Xu 2023), we also examine the likelihood of financial crises following business credit booms in figure IA13. We use financial crisis coding by Baron et al. (2021). In our sample, business credit booms do not predict financial crises, regardless of bankruptcy efficiency. This is likely because our sample period is 2003–19 (because of the availability of bankruptcy

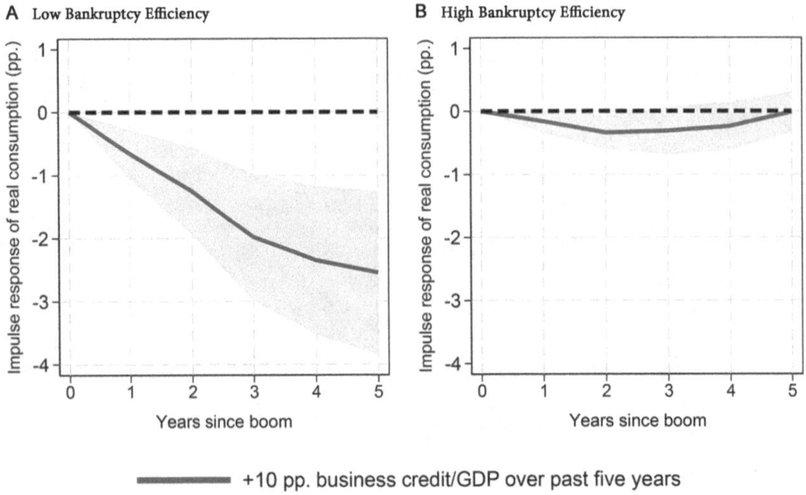

Fig. 7. Private consumption following business credit booms. This figure shows the trajectory of real private consumption following a 10 percentage point increase in the business credit to gross domestic product (GDP) ratio over the past 5 years. We estimate state-dependent local projections: $\Delta_h \log(\text{real consumption})_{i,t+h} = \alpha_{i,h} + \beta_{1,h}\Delta_5 c_{i,t} + \beta_{2,h}(\Delta_5 c_{i,t} \times B_{i,t}) + \beta_{3,h}B_{i,t} + \gamma_h x_{i,t} + \epsilon_{i,t}$ for $h = 1, \ldots, 5$. The outcome variable is the change in log real private consumption in country i from year t to year $t + h$. The independent variable $\Delta_5 c_{i,t}$ denotes the change of business credit to GDP in country i from year $t - 5$ to year t, and $B_{i,t}$ is the bankruptcy efficiency measure. The controls $x_{i,t}$ include contemporaneous and 5 lags of real GDP growth and real consumption growth, as well as the cumulative change in household credit to GDP since year $t - 5$. Horizon-specific country fixed effects $\alpha_{i,h}$ are included. The left (right) panel evaluates the impulse response using $B_{i,t}$ at the bottom (top) quartile, which is equal to 43% (83%). The sample contains annual data from an unbalanced panel of 39 countries. The sample period is 2003–19. Shaded areas mark 90% confidence intervals based on Driscoll-Kraay standard errors.

efficiency data), and the main financial crises during this time frame are related to the global financial crisis, which is more tied to household credit than business credit. Using a longer sample since 1940, Ivashina et al. (2024) find that corporate credit booms have substantial predictive power for financial crises. If bankruptcy efficiency measures can be extended further back in time, it is possible that financial crises are more likely to occur following business credit booms in countries with low bankruptcy efficiency.

V. Bankruptcy Resolution and the Macroeconomic Impact of Credit Booms: A Simple Theoretical Framework

Empirical evidence in the previous section shows that business credit booms are followed by severe economic downturns in countries with low bankruptcy efficiency but not in countries with high bankruptcy efficiency. In this section, we use a simple model to lay out how bankruptcy resolution affects macroeconomic outcomes and why more efficient bankruptcy systems can mitigate the negative consequences of credit booms. It also analyzes different sources of credit booms and their corresponding implications. The model is stylized and aims to provide a parsimonious illustration of the economic mechanisms.

A. *Environment*

Time is discrete, and there are two periods, $t \in \{1, 2\}$. The economy is populated by a representative unit mass of creditors and firms. Creditors are identical and have preferences described by $\mathbb{E}[c_1 + \beta c_2]$, where $\beta \in (0, 1)$ denotes the creditors' subjective discount factor and c_t denotes their consumption in period t. Firms' objective is to maximize $\mathbb{E}[\text{div}_{j1} + \beta_f \text{div}_{j2}]$, where $\beta_f \in (0, \beta)$ is their discount factor and div_{jt} are dividends transferred by firm j to its owners in period t.[18]

In the first period, each firm j has access to a risky investment opportunity, which requires an initial investment of $I > 0$ consumption goods and yields a stochastic cash flow of z_j consumption goods in the second period. To obtain analytical results, we assume that the cash flow of the risky project of firm j, z_j, is drawn from an i.i.d. (independently and identically distributed) uniform distribution with a measure 1 support, $[\underline{z}, \bar{z}]$, where $\underline{z} \geq 0$. That is, the probability density function is given by $\phi(z_j) = 1$ for $z_j \in [\underline{z}, \bar{z}]$, and the cumulative distribution function is given by $\Phi(z_j) = z_j - \underline{z}$ for $z_j \in [\underline{z}, \bar{z}]$.

Firms can borrow from creditors in competitive markets. In the second period, each firm j faces a nonnegative dividend constraint ($\text{div}_{j2} \geq 0$), which implies that debt is defaultable. Following a default, the firm obtains a dividend of 0. With probability $\xi \in (0, 1)$, the project can continue to operate (for simplicity, we assume that continuing operation is efficient) and maintain the cash flow z_j. With probability $1 - \xi$, the project gets liquidated inefficiently, obtaining a value $z^{\text{liq}} = \underline{z}$, which, for simplicity, is set to be the lowest realization of cash flow if the firm continues to operate. The parameter ξ, which governs the probability of continuing operation, captures bankruptcy efficiency in the economy and is the main focus of the comparative statics linked to our empirical evidence.[19] This setup aligns with the design of the bankruptcy efficiency measure. As discussed in Subsection III.A, empirical studies have found that the liquidation value of nonfinancial firms is fairly low (Ramey and Shapiro 2001; Kermani and

Ma 2023). In light of the evidence, $z^{\text{liq}} = \underline{z}$ is a reasonable assumption for the baseline model. In appendix IA2.6, https://data.nber.org/data-appendix/c14994/appendix.pdf, we relax this assumption and consider the case that $z^{\text{liq}} \in (\underline{z}, \bar{z})$, which allows the possibility of inefficient continuation. In that extension, we define bankruptcy efficiency as the probability of choosing the right outcome: continuation if $z > z^{\text{liq}}$ and liquidation if $z < z^{\text{liq}}$ (which nests the baseline model if $z^{\text{liq}} = \underline{z}$). We show that the main result Proposition 1 remains.

B. *Optimality*

The expected value for a firm j pursuing the investment opportunity is given by

$$V_f(\beta, \beta_f, \xi) = \max_{b \geq 0}(\text{div}_1 + \beta_f \mathbb{E}[\text{div}_2]) \tag{4}$$

$$\text{s.t. div}_1 + I = q(b, \beta, \xi)b, \tag{5}$$

$$\text{div}_2 = \begin{cases} z_j - b \text{ if } b \leq z_j \\ 0 \quad \text{ if } b > z_j \end{cases}, \tag{6}$$

where b is the face value of debt in period 2, and $q(b, \beta, \xi)$ is the debt price schedule faced by firms in period 1 (discussed further below). Equation (5) is the period-1 flow-of-funds constraint, which indicates that dividend payments and investment have to be financed with proceeds from borrowing. Equation (6) is the period-2 flow-of-funds constraint, which indicates that if the firm does not default, it transfers a dividend payment that is equal to the cash flow net of debt payment; otherwise, if the firm defaults, it does not transfer dividend payments. From equation (4), it follows that firms are willing to pursue the investment opportunity if and only if $V_f \geq 0$.

The debt price schedule is determined by the free entry of creditors to the lending market, and given by

$$q(b, \beta, \xi) = \beta \mathbb{E}\left[\mathbb{I}_{\{b \leq z_j\}} + \mathbb{I}_{\{b > z_j\}} \frac{(1 - \xi)z^{\text{liq}} + \xi z_j}{b}\right], \tag{7}$$

where $\mathbb{I}$ is the indicator function.

Finally, we make the following parametric assumption, which guarantees that the firm prefers investing to not investing in the first period:

Assumption 1. *The investment cost is such that* $I < \frac{\beta}{2}\left(\frac{1-\xi\frac{\beta_f}{\beta}}{2-\xi-\frac{\beta_f}{\beta}}\right) + \beta\underline{z}$.

C. *Macroeconomic Impact of Bankruptcy Resolution Efficiency*

The default resolution and bankruptcy procedure described above also lead to the expression for aggregate output, given the face value of debt b chosen in the first period (since all firms are ex ante identical, they choose the same face value of debt in the first period) and bankruptcy efficiency ξ. That is, for $b \in [\underline{z}, \bar{z}]$ (which holds for the optimally chosen face value of debt $b^*(\beta, \beta_f, \xi)$ in eq. [4]):

$$Y(b, \xi) = \mathbb{E}[z_j] - \underbrace{(1 - \xi)\int_{\underline{z}}^{b}(z_j - z^{\text{liq}})\phi(z_j)dz_j}_{\text{output loss from inefficient liquidation}}, \tag{8}$$

where the second term captures the output loss from inefficient liquidation, which depends on the probability of liquidation conditional on bankruptcy $(1 - \xi)$ and the output loss conditional on liquidation (liquidating a firm with cash flow z_j results in output loss of $z_j - z^{\text{liq}}$). From this expression, we can see that a more efficient bankruptcy system leads to higher aggregate output, conditional on the amount of borrowing. For $b \in (\underline{z}, \bar{z})$,

$$\frac{\partial Y(b, \xi)}{\partial \xi} = \int_{\underline{z}}^{b}(z_j - z^{\text{liq}})\phi(z_j)dz_j > 0. \tag{9}$$

That is, a higher ξ leads to more efficient allocations of resources: firms can continue to operate efficiently, instead of undergoing inefficient liquidation, which leads to higher aggregate output.

We now use the model to shed light on our empirical evidence. We consider both nonfundamental credit booms driven by increases in credit supply or demand because of changes in discount rates or biased beliefs and fundamental credit booms driven by rational expectations of increases in firms' productivity. We start with nonfundamental credit booms. We examine booms driven by credit supply, because of shocks to creditors' discount rates. In this case, a one unit increase in total business credit, $b^*(\beta, \beta_f, \xi)$, results from a $1/(\partial b^*(\beta, \beta_f, \xi)/\partial\beta)$ unit increase in the discount factor β. We also examine booms driven by credit demand, because of shocks to firms' discount rates. In this case, a one unit increase in total business credit, $b^*(\beta, \beta_f, \xi)$, results from a $1/(\partial b^*(\beta, \beta_f, \xi)/\partial \beta_f)$ unit increase in the discount factor β_f. In appendix IA2, https://data.nber.org/data-appendix/c14994/appendix.pdf, we additionally study the case where nonfundamental credit booms are driven by shocks to creditors' or firms' beliefs (rather than by shocks to their discount rates) as modeled in Dávila and Walther (2023), which does not affect our main results in Proposition 1.

Nonfundamental Credit Booms

Our empirical analysis examines macroeconomic outcomes following a one-unit change in total business credit (e.g., the response of output $Y^*(\beta, \beta_f, \xi) \equiv Y(b^*(\beta, \beta_f, \xi), \xi)$, which corresponds to

$$\varepsilon(\beta, \beta_f, \xi) = \frac{\frac{\partial Y^*(\beta,\beta_f,\xi)}{\partial \beta}}{\frac{\partial b^*(\beta,\beta_f,\xi)}{\partial \beta}} = \frac{\frac{\partial Y^*(\beta,\beta_f,\xi)}{\partial \beta_f}}{\frac{\partial b^*(\beta,\beta_f,\xi)}{\partial \beta_f}} = \frac{\partial Y(b^*(\beta, \beta_f, \xi), \xi)}{\partial b}, \tag{10}$$

in the model. Because credit booms only affect aggregate output $Y(b^*(\beta, \beta_f, \xi), \xi)$ through the impact on total business credit $b^*(\beta, \beta_f, \xi)$, the effect $\varepsilon(\beta, \beta_f, \xi)$ does not depend on whether the boom is driven by credit demand or credit supply.

We now examine the macroeconomic implications of a more efficient bankruptcy system.

Proposition 1. *Under assumption 1,*

1. *A more efficient bankruptcy system (a higher ξ) is associated with a larger credit market: $\partial b^*(\beta, \beta_f, \xi)/\partial \xi > 0$.*
2. *Nonfundamental credit booms have negative effects on macroeconomic outcomes: $\varepsilon(\beta, \beta_f, \xi) < 0$. Furthermore, a more efficient bankruptcy system (a higher ξ) dampens the negative impact of nonfundamental credit booms on macroeconomic outcomes: $\partial \varepsilon(\beta, \beta_f, \xi)/\partial \xi > 0$.*

Part 1 of the Proposition shows that a more efficient bankruptcy system leads to a larger credit market. An increase in bankruptcy efficiency, ξ, enhances the debt valuation given the face value of debt b, $q_b(b, \beta, \xi)$, because it increases creditors' payoffs in the event of bankruptcy. This higher debt valuation incentivizes firms to borrow more, which generates a larger credit market: $\partial b^*(\beta, \beta_f, \xi)/\partial \xi > 0$.

Part 2 of the Proposition shows that the impact of credit boom $\varepsilon(\beta, \beta_f, \xi) < 0$ is negative because it increases the promised debt payment $b^*(\beta, \beta_f, \xi)$ in the second period and leads to more defaults, which may be resolved inefficiently and negatively affect aggregate output $Y^*(\beta, \beta_f, \xi)$. Moreover, part 2 shows that a more efficient bankruptcy system mitigates the negative impact of a credit boom on macroeconomic outcomes and attenuates the credit cycle (even though the credit market is larger). To understand this, from equation (10) we recognize that the efficiency of the bankruptcy system, ξ, influences the impact of a credit boom, $\varepsilon(\beta, \beta_f, \xi)$, through two channels:

$$\underbrace{\frac{\partial \varepsilon(\beta, \beta_f, \xi)}{\partial \xi}}_{>0} = \underbrace{\frac{\partial^2 Y(b^*(\beta, \beta_f, \xi), \xi)}{\partial b \partial \xi}}_{>0} + \underbrace{\frac{\partial^2 Y(b^*(\beta, \beta_f, \xi), \xi)}{\partial b^2} \frac{\partial b^*(\beta, \beta_f, \xi)}{\partial \xi}}_{<0}. \quad (11)$$

First, holding the size of the credit market fixed at $b^*(\beta, \beta_f, \xi)$, a more efficient bankruptcy system mitigates the negative impact of a credit boom on aggregate output. That is, the first term in equation (11) is positive. Recall that the impact of a credit boom on aggregate output, $\partial Y(b^*(\beta, \beta_f, \xi), \xi)/\partial b < 0$ is negative because it leads to more defaults, which will generate inefficient liquidations with probability $1 - \xi$. A higher ξ lowers the probability of inefficient liquidations and dampens the negative impact of a credit boom on aggregate output: $\partial^2 Y(b^*(\beta, \beta_f, \xi), \xi)/\partial b \partial \xi > 0$. Second, by increasing the size of the credit market, $b^*(\beta, \beta_f, \xi)$, a more efficient bankruptcy system could exacerbate the negative impact of a credit boom. That is, the second term in equation (11) is negative because $\partial b^*(\beta, \beta_f, \xi)/\partial \xi > 0$ and $\partial^2 Y(b^*(\beta, \beta_f, \xi), \xi)/\partial b^2 < 0$. A larger promised debt payment, $b^*(\beta, \beta_f, \xi)$, means that the marginal firms that default have higher cash flows (firms with cash flows z_j up to $b^*(\beta, \beta_f, \xi)$ default) and suffer more output loss after inefficient liquidations. This exacerbates the negative impact of a credit boom on aggregate output. Part 2 of the Proposition shows that the first channel dominates the second channel, consistent with our empirical evidence.[20]

We note that the predictions in Proposition 1 are symmetric: the comparative statics apply to both credit booms and contractions. That is, the impact of credit contractions on macroeconomic outcomes is positive, because credit contractions lead to fewer subsequent defaults and inefficient liquidations. A more efficient bankruptcy system now dampens the positive impact of credit contractions: when default is less likely to end in inefficient liquidations, the efficiency gain from fewer subsequent defaults (after credit contractions) is smaller. In the data, we observe symmetry for horizons 3 years and above (fig. IA10 and table IA15).

Finally, appendix IA2 (https://data.nber.org/data-appendix/c14994/appendix.pdf) shows how Proposition 1 extends to alternative environments. First, we show that the results in the second part of Proposition 1 are robust to considering other sources of nonfundamental credit booms. We study booms driven by shocks to creditors' or firms' beliefs (rather than by shocks to their discount rates), following the long tradition of belief-driven credit cycles (Kindleberger 1972; Minsky 1986). We establish that higher bankruptcy efficiency still dampens the negative impact of credit booms in this setting. Second, we show that Proposition 1 extends to settings where the cash flow of the risky project z_j is drawn from a general class of distributions, not limited to the uniform distribution case examined in the main analysis. Third, we consider $z^{\text{liq}} \in (\underline{z}, \bar{z})$. In this extension, low bankruptcy efficiency can come from either liquidating a viable firm (inefficient liquidation) or keeping alive a nonviable firm (inefficient continuation). We show that Proposition 1 still holds.

Our model focuses on direct channels through which bankruptcy efficiency affects economic activity. In practice, some but not necessarily all firms experience distress following credit booms, and spillovers from firms in distress to other firms may also contribute to the empirical patterns we observe in Section IV. To account for such spillovers, our baseline framework could be extended to incorporate various amplification mechanisms, such as aggregate demand forces, financial amplification, or input-output linkages (Kiyotaki and Moore 1997; Bernanke et al. 1999; Christiano, Eichenbaum, and Evans 2005; Baqaee and Farhi 2019).

Overall, the predictions in Proposition 1 are consistent with the empirical evidence. First, credit booms are followed by worse macroeconomic outcomes, consistent with the growing literature on credit cycles (Schularick and Taylor 2012; Mian et al. 2017; Greenwood et al. 2022). Second, the negative outcomes are especially severe under inefficient bankruptcy systems, as shown in Subsection IV.A.

Fundamental Credit Booms

We then turn to credit booms driven by rational expectations of an increase in firms' future productivity. Formally, each firm j's risky cash flow z_j is now drawn i.i.d. from the uniform distribution $[\underline{z} + \Delta, \bar{z} + \Delta]$, where Δ captures shocks to firms' future productivity. Define aggregate output/

GDP $Y^*(\Delta, \xi) \equiv Y(\Delta, b^*(\Delta, \xi), \xi)$ based on the optimally chosen face value of debt $b^*(\Delta, \xi)$, where β and β_f are eliminated as arguments because they are fixed here.

Here, a one unit increase in total business credit, $b^*(\Delta, \xi)$, results from a $1/(\partial b^*(\Delta, \xi)/\partial\Delta)$ unit increase in Δ. The impact of a one unit increase in total business credit on subsequent macroeconomic outcomes is then given by:

$$\varepsilon(\Delta, \xi) = \frac{\frac{\partial Y^*(\Delta,\xi)}{\partial\Delta}}{\frac{\partial b^*(\Delta,\xi)}{\partial\Delta}}$$

$$= \underbrace{\frac{\partial Y(\Delta, b^*(\Delta, \xi), \xi)}{\partial\Delta} \cdot \left(\frac{\partial b^*(\Delta, \xi)}{\partial\Delta}\right)^{-1}}_{\text{direct productivity effect},>0} + \underbrace{\frac{\partial Y(\Delta, b^*(\Delta, \xi), \xi)}{\partial b}}_{\text{effect through credit changes},<0}.$$

Compared with equation (10), the impact of fundamental driven credit boom has an extra direct productivity effect. Indeed, this term dominates, and it overturns Proposition 1. As formalized in Proposition IA3 in appendix IA2.4 (https://data.nber.org/data-appendix/c14994/appendix.pdf), the impact of a fundamental driven credit boom on macroeconomic outcomes is now positive: $\varepsilon(\Delta, \xi) > 0$. The increase in firms' productivity means that credit booms driven by fundamentals are followed by fewer defaults and higher output because of fewer inefficient liquidations. Moreover, a more efficient bankruptcy system (a higher ξ) now dampens the positive impact of a credit boom on macroeconomic outcomes: $\partial\varepsilon(\Delta, \xi)/\partial\xi < 0$. This is because a more efficient bankruptcy system leaves less room for increases in firms' productivity to improve macroeconomic outcomes by decreasing the number of defaults and inefficient bankruptcies.[21]

For these predictions, we draw on findings by Müller and Verner (2024) and Ivashina et al. (2024) that credit booms in nontradable sectors appear nonfundamental (they are followed by worse macroeconomic outcomes), whereas credit booms in tradable sectors appear fundamental (they are followed by better macroeconomic outcomes). Interestingly, we see in table IA13 that bankruptcy efficiency dampens the negative effects of nontradable credit booms and dampens the positive effects of tradable credit booms, exactly as our model predicts. Overall, nontradable credit booms appear to dominate (Müller and Verner 2024), so business credit booms on average are followed by worse macroeconomic outcomes (Ivashina et al. 2024) and follow the predictions of nonfundamental credit booms in Proposition 1.

In summary, the model analysis in the section suggests that higher bankruptcy efficiency helps ameliorate the impact of nonfundamental credit cycles. Such credit cycles are well recognized to undermine macroeconomic stability. Accordingly, our results point to the importance of incorporating default risks and bankruptcy institutions in the theory and practice of macroprudential policy design.

VI. Conclusion

Legal institutions can influence the severity of financial frictions and, in turn, the contour of macroeconomic fluctuations. We explore these connections in the context of how business bankruptcy relates to the consequences of credit booms. The evidence supports the view that credit booms are especially detrimental when default resolution functions poorly. Indeed, this view has motivated reforms of bankruptcy institutions, as in the case of Japan.

In general, understanding default resolution in practice can be useful for macroeconomic analyses. In many macro models, default resolution is akin to liquidation. Models that feature restructuring are less common. In ongoing work, we aim to develop a quantitative model to analyze the macro implications of restructuring versus liquidation and evaluate how much different schemes of default resolution can affect economic fluctuations.

Endnotes

Author email addresses: Lian (chen_lian@berkeley.edu); Ma (Yueran.Ma@chicagobooth.edu); Ottonello (ottonell@umd.edu). We thank Dean Corbae, Carola Frydman, Simon Gilchrist, Jonathon Hazell, Diego Kanzig, Valerie Ramey, Jon Steinsson, Christian Wolf, Benjamin Schoefer, as well as seminar participants at the Bank of Portugal and Norges Bank for helpful comments and suggestions. We are grateful to Benjamin Castiglione and Chun Hei Hung for excellent research assistance. We acknowledge financial support from the NSF CAREER Award. For acknowledgments, sources of research support, and disclosure of the authors' material financial relationships, if any, please see https://www.nber.org/books-and-chapters/nber-macroeconomics-annual-2024-volume-39/bankruptcy-resolution-and-credit-cycles.

1. As in the empirical analyses, our exposition here uses credit booms (i.e., increases in business credit) for simplicity, but the model predictions are symmetric for decreases in business credit too.

2. We do not find that the prevalence of nontradable and tradable credit booms differs by the degree of bankruptcy efficiency.

3. Although the term "bankrupt" is often associated with business failure in popular culture, business bankruptcy is not the same as business failure. First, many businesses exit without bankruptcy proceedings. Formally, bankruptcy needs a petition to start, but business failures do not. Second, business bankruptcies in advanced economies may focus on restructuring financial obligations and streamline operations, and the company continues to operate instead of winding down.

4. Meanwhile, to ensure that creditors' rights are protected, payments will not be less than the liquidation value of their collateral.

5. The formula in Djankov et al. (2008a) is

$$\frac{100\mathrm{GC} + 70(1 - \mathrm{GC}) - 100c}{(1 + r)^t}, \tag{1}$$

where the variable GC takes value 1 if the company can continue to operate (0 if it shuts down), c captures the bankruptcy cost as a share of total value, r is the appropriate annual discount rate (the prevailing lending rate), and t denotes the bankruptcy duration in years. World Bank (2020) does not explicitly provide a formula but provides a similar verbal description about the calculation of the total recovery rate here: https://archive.doingbusiness.org/en/methodology/resolving-insolvency.

6. These estimates from collecting liquidation value data suggest an even larger gap between the liquidation value and the continuation value relative to the assumptions in the World Bank (2020) case (where the liquidation value is assumed to be 70% of the continuation value). This is in part because the firm in the World Bank (2020) design is a hotel (a type of firm that exists in every country), and correspondingly its assets can be more generic than those of manufacturers, for example.

7. The formula to compute the efficiency of resolving a nonviable firm is analogous to how Djankov et al. (2008a) compute the efficiency for resolving a viable firm:

$$\frac{100L + X(1 - L) - 100c}{(1 + r)^t}, \tag{2}$$

where L takes value 1 if the company is liquidated, X is the value of continuing operation (which is not reported in the paper and which cannot be backed out from the data since $L = 1$ for all countries), c captures the bankruptcy cost as a share of maximal value, r in the appropriate annual discount rate, and t denotes the bankruptcy duration in years.

8. For countries that liquidate the viable company, the y-axis and the x-axis are both directly affected by the liquidation efficiency. For countries where the viable company can continue to operate, the y-axis and the x-axis are both affected by the speed of the judicial system, and the y-axis gets shifted up since the liquidation deadweight loss is avoided.

9. Recent work finds that inefficient continuation seems rare in a country like the United States, even though the US bankruptcy institution has a strong emphasis on restructuring. Dou et al. (2021) estimate different sources of inefficiencies in US corporate bankruptcy and find that inefficiencies from excess continuation are quite small. Bernstein, Colonnelli, and Iverson (2019) and Bernstein et al. (2019) use the random assignment of bankruptcies to different judges and find that economic outcomes are better (worse) for those assigned to judges who are more prone to restructure (liquidate).

10. We provide detailed discussions about the sources of credit booms and whether they matter in Section V.

11. We follow the literature and measure credit cycles using changes in credit to GDP (Schularick and Taylor 2012; Mian et al. 2017; Müller and Verner 2024, among others). An alternative measure is the "Credit Gap" published by Bank for International Settlements (2024), which is the cyclical component in the credit to GDP ratio from a one-sided, backward-looking HP filter. Our results are very similar when using this measure.

12. Using data on bank debt of nonfinancial businesses collected by Müller and Verner (2024), we obtain similar results that are even stronger quantitatively. We also compare the average relationship between business credit growth and future output in our sample with results in Mian et al. (2017). We find that the negative relationship is approximately twice as large as that in Mian et al. (2017), but the 95% confidence interval includes their original point estimate.

13. The cumulative output loss is equal to the integral of the impulse responses in fig. 3 (cf. Ramey 2016). Under low bankruptcy efficiency, the annual losses over the first 5 years accumulate to around 10.8% of real GDP at $h = 0$. By contrast, they accumulate to only around 1.5% under high bankruptcy efficiency.

14. Bankruptcy efficiency is correlated with other aspects of the legal system, but this measure should be the most relevant statistic for the quality of default resolution.

15. We also consider Lasso regressions with all the control variables together and find that bankruptcy efficiency appears to be the most effective measure for differentiating output trajectory following credit booms.

16. As mentioned in Subsec. III.A, the efficiency of resolving a nonviable company is not covered in the World Bank (2020) extension of Djankov et al. (2008a). Accordingly, we can only use the value for 2006 (Djankov et al. 2008a). For the efficiency of resolving a viable company in table IA12, we can alternatively use the annual data from World Bank (2020) or the fixed value for 2006 from Djankov et al. (2008a), and the results are similar.

17. In table IA14, we measure the credit boom using 3-year changes in business credit to GDP instead of 5-year changes as in the baseline regressions. This is because the Müller and Verner (2024) data on nontradable versus tradable credit end in 2014, which further shrinks the sample period. Using 3-year change allows us to retain more years in the sample.

18. We assume that creditors are more patient than firms to ensure that firms borrow in equilibrium. For simplicity, we abstract from explicitly mentioning firms' owners, which can be thought of as an agent with preferences $\mathbb{E}[c_{f1} + \beta_f c_{f2}]$.

19. Note that in the limit case when $\xi = 1$, the model features no costs of default and the firm wants to borrow as much as possible. This extreme case is outside the range of the parameters considered. It is also simple to extend the model to feature deadweight losses from continuing operations in default.

20. As our discussant Dean Corbae points out, the impact of bankruptcy efficiency ξ on the level of aggregate output $Y(b^*(\beta, \beta_f, \xi), \xi)$ could be ambiguous. First, a higher ξ lowers the probability of inefficient liquidations given default, which increases aggregate output, similar to the first term in eq. (11), Second, a higher ξ increases the number of defaults (by increasing the size of the credit market), which potentially decreases aggregate output, similar to the second term in eq. (11). The net impact of the two channels can be either positive or negative for output (even though the first channel always dominates for the response of aggregate output to credit booms as in part 2 of Proposition 1).

21. The predictions in Proposition IA3 are again symmetric: the comparative statics apply to both fundamental driven credit booms and contractions.

References

Acharya, Viral V., Matteo Crosignani, Tim Eisert, and Sascha Steffen. 2022. "Zombie Lending: Theoretical, International, and Historical perspectives." *Annual Review of Financial Economics* 14:21–38.

Acharya, Viral V., and Krishnamurthy V. Subramanian. 2009. "Bankruptcy Codes and Innovation." *Review of Financial Studies* 22:4949–88.

Aghion, Philippe, Oliver Hart, and John Moore. 1992. "The Economics of Bankruptcy Reform." *Journal of Law, Economics, & Organization* 8 (3): 523–46.

Altman, Edward I., Rui Dai, and Wei Wang. 2024. "Global Zombie Companies: Measurements, Determinants, and Outcomes." *Journal of International Business Studies* 55:723–44.

Anderson, Kent. 2006. "Japanese Insolvency Law After a Decade of Reform." *Canadian Business Law Journal* 43:2–27.

Andreasen, Eugenia, Sofia Bauducco, Evangelina Dardati, and Enrique G. Mendoza. 2023. "Beware the Side Effects: Capital Controls, Trade, Misallocation and Welfare." Working Paper no. 30963, NBER, Cambridge, MA.

Antill, Samuel. 2022. "Do the Right Firms Survive Bankruptcy?" *Journal of Financial Economics* 144 (2): 523–46.

Bank for International Settlements. 2024. "Credit-to-GDP Gaps, BISWS_CREDIT_GAP 1.0" (data set). https://data.bis.org/topics/CREDIT_GAPS/data.

Baqaee, David Rezza, and Emmanuel Farhi. 2019. "The Macroeconomic Impact of Microeconomic Shocks: Beyond Hulten's Theorem." *Econometrica* 87 (4): 1155–203.

Baron, Matthew, Emil Verner, and Wei Xiong. 2021. "Banking Crises without Panics." *Quarterly Journal of Economics* 136 (1): 51–113.

Becker, Bo, and Victoria Ivashina. 2022. "Weak Corporate Insolvency Rules: The Missing Driver of Zombie Lending." *AEA Papers and Proceedings* 112:516–20.

———, and Jens Josephson. 2016. "Insolvency Resolution and the Missing High-Yield Bond Markets." *Review of Financial Studies* 29 (10): 2814–49.

Ben Zeev, Nadav, Valerie Ramey, and Sarah Zubairy. 2023. "Do Government Spending Multipliers Depend on the Sign of the Shock?" *AEA Papers and Proceedings* 113:382–87.

Benmelech, Efraim, and Nittai K. Bergman. 2011. "Bankruptcy and the Collateral Channel." *Journal of Finance* 66 (2): 337–78.

Bernanke, Ben S., Mark Gertler, and Simon Gilchrist. 1999. "The Financial Accelerator in a Quantitative Business Cycle Framework." *Handbook of Macroeconomics* 1:1341–93.

Bernstein, Shai, Emanuele Colonnelli, Xavier Giroud, and Benjamin Iverson. 2019. "Bankruptcy Spillovers." *Journal of Financial Economics* 133 (3): 608–33.

Bernstein, Shai, Emanuele Colonnelli, and Benjamin Iverson. 2019. "Asset Allocation in Bankruptcy." *Journal of Finance* 74 (1): 5–53.

Bianchi, Javier, and Guido Lorenzoni. 2022. "The Prudential Use of Capital Controls and Foreign Currency Reserves." In *Handbook of International Economics* 6, ed. Gita Gopinath, Elhanan Helpman, and Kenneth Rogoff, 237–89. Amsterdam: Elsevier.

Bris, Arturo, Ivo Welch, and Ning Zhu. 2006. "The Costs of Bankruptcy: Chapter 7 Liquidation versus Chapter 11 Reorganization." *Journal of Finance* 61 (3): 1253–1303.

Bulow, Jeremy, and Kenneth Rogoff. 1989. "Sovereign Debt: Is to Forgive to Forget?" *American Economic Review* 79 (1): 43–50.

Caballero, Ricardo J., Takeo Hoshi, and Anil K. Kashyap. 2008. "Zombie Lending and Depressed Restructuring in Japan." *American Economic Review* 98 (5): 1943–77.

Chodorow-Reich, Gabriel. 2014. "The Employment Effects of Credit Market Disruptions: Firm-Level Evidence from the 2008–9 Financial Crisis." *Quarterly Journal of Economics* 129 (1): 1–59.

Christiano, Lawrence J., Martin Eichenbaum, and Charles L. Evans. 2005. "Nominal Rigidities and the Dynamic Effects of a Shock to Monetary Policy." *Journal of Political Economy* 113 (1): 1–45.

Corbae, Dean, and Pablo D'Erasmo. 2021. "Reorganization or Liquidation: Bankruptcy Choice and Firm Dynamics." *Review of Economic Studies* 88 (5): 2239–74.

Crouzet, Nicolas, Janice C. Eberly, Andrea L. Eisfeldt, and Dimitris Papanikolaou. 2022. "The Economics of Intangible Capital." *Journal of Economic Perspectives* 36 (3): 29–52.

Dávila, Eduardo, and Ansgar Walther. 2023. "Prudential Policy with Distorted Beliefs." *American Economic Review* 113 (7): 1967–2006.

———. 2024. "Corrective Regulation with Imperfect Instruments." Working Paper no. 29160, NBER, Cambridge, MA.

Dembiermont, Christian, Mathias Drehmann, and Siripom Muksakunratana. 2013. "How Much Does the Private Sector Really Borrow—A New Database for Total Credit to the Private Non-Financial Sector." *BIS Quarterly Review* 2013 (March): 65–81. https://data.bis.org/topics/TOTAL_CREDIT/data.

Diamond, Douglas W. 2023. "Nobel Lecture: Financial Intermediaries and Financial Crises." *Journal of Political Economy* 131 (10): 2597–622.

Djankov, Simeon, Oliver Hart, Caralee McLiesh, and Andrei Shleifer. 2008a. "Debt Enforcement around the World." *Journal of Political Economy* 116 (6): 1105–49.

———. 2008b. "Replication Data for: Debt Enforcement around the World." *Journal of Political Economy* 116 (6): 1105–49. https://archive.doingbusiness.org/content/dam/doingBusiness/media/Methodology/Other/Debt-enforcement-database-NBER.xls.

Dou, Winston Wei, Lucian A. Taylor, Wei Wang, and Wenyu Wang. 2021. "Dissecting Bankruptcy Frictions." *Journal of Financial Economics* 142 (3): 975–1000.

Driscoll, John C., and Aart C. Kraay. 1998. "Consistent Covariance Matrix Estimation with Spatially Dependent Panel Data." *Review of Economics and Statistics* 80 (4): 549–60.

Eaton, Jonathan, and Mark Gersovitz. 1981. "Debt with Potential Repudiation: Theoretical and Empirical Analysis." *Review of Economic Studies* 48 (2): 289–309.

Frydman, Carola, and Chenzi Xu. 2023. "Banking Crises in Historical Perspective." *Annual Review of Financial Economics* 15:265–90.

Gan, Jie. 2007. "Collateral, Debt Capacity, and Corporate Investment: Evidence from a Natural Experiment." *Journal of Financial Economics* 85 (3): 709–34.

Gertler, Mark, and Simon Gilchrist. 2018. "What Happened: Financial Factors in the Great Recession." *Journal of Economic Perspectives* 32 (3): 3–30.

Gilson, Stuart C. 2010. *Creating Value through Corporate Restructuring: Case Studies in Bankruptcies, Buyouts, and Breakups*. 2nd ed. Hoboken, NJ: Wiley.

———. 2012. "Coming Through in a Crisis: How Chapter 11 and the Debt Restructuring Industry Are Helping to Revive the US Economy." *Journal of Applied Corporate Finance* 24 (3): 23–35.

Greenwood, Robin, Samuel G. Hanson, Andrei Shleifer, and Jakob Ahm Sørensen. 2022. "Predictable Financial Crises." *Journal of Finance* 77 (2): 863–921.

Guntin, Rafael. 2024. "Firms' Rollover Risk and Macroeconomic Dynamics." Working paper, University of Rochester.

Hanson, Samuel G., Anil K. Kashyap, and Jeremy C. Stein. 2011. "A Macroprudential Approach to Financial Regulation." *Journal of Economic Perspectives* 25 (1): 3–28.

International Monetary Fund. 1999–2024. "World Economic Outlook Database, version of Fall 2023." https://www.imf.org/en/Publications/WEO/weo-database/2023/October.

Ivashina, Victoria, Şebnem Kalemli-Özcan, Luc Laeven, and Karsten Müller. 2024. "Corporate Debt, Boom-Bust Cycles, and Financial Crises." Working Paper no. 32225, NBER, Cambridge, MA.

Iverson, Benjamin. 2018. "Get in Line: Chapter 11 Restructuring in Crowded Bankruptcy Courts." *Management Science* 64 (11): 5370–94.

———, Joshua Madsen, Wei Wang, and Qiping Xu. 2023. "Financial Costs of Judicial Inexperience: Evidence from Corporate Bankruptcies." *Journal of Financial and Quantitative Analysis* 58 (3): 1111–43.

Jordà, Òscar, Katharina Knoll, Dmitry Kuvshinov, Moritz Schularick, and Alan M. Taylor. 2021. "The Rate of Return on Everything, 1870–2015." *Quarterly Journal of Economics* 134 (3): 1225–98.

———, Martin Kornejew, Moritz Schularick, and Alan M. Taylor. 2022. "Zombies at Large? Corporate Debt Overhang and the Macroeconomy." *Review of Financial Studies* 35 (10): 4561–86.

———, Moritz Schularick, and Alan M. Taylor. 2013. "When Credit Bites Back." *Journal of Money, Credit and Banking* 45 (s2): 3–28.

Kermani, Amir, and Yueran Ma. 2023. "Asset Specificity of Nonfinancial Firms." *Quarterly Journal of Economics*. 138 (1): 205–64.
Kindleberger, Charles. 1972. *Manias, Panics, and Crashes: A History of Financial Crises*. Cham, Switzerland: Palgrave Macmillan.
Kiyotaki, Nobuhiro, and John Moore. 1997. "Credit Cycles." *Journal of Political Economy* 105 (2): 211–48.
La Porta, Rafael, Robert Vishny, Florencio Lopez de Silanes, and Andrei Shleifer. 1998. "Law and Finance." *Journal of Political Economy* 106 (6): 1113–55.
Lian, Chen, and Yueran Ma. 2021. "Anatomy of Corporate Borrowing Constraints." *Quarterly Journal of Economics* 136 (1): 229–91.
Mian, Atif, Amir Sufi, and Emil Verner. 2017. "Household Debt and Business Cycles Worldwide." *Quarterly Journal of Economics* 132 (4): 1755–817.
Minsky, Hyman. 1986. *Stabilizing an Unstable Economy*. New Haven, CT: Yale University Press.
Morris, Stephen, and Hyun Song Shin. 2004. "Coordination Risk and the Price of Debt." *European Economic Review* 48 (1): 133–53.
Müller, Karsten, and Emil Verner. 2024. "Credit Allocation and Macroeconomic Fluctuations." *Review of Economic Studies* 91 (6): 3645–76.
Ong, Li Lian, Christian Schmieder, and Min Wei. 2023. "Insights into Credit Loss Rates: A Global Database, 2023." BIS Working Paper no. 1101, https://www.bis.org/publ/work1101.htm.
Ottonello, Pablo, Diego J. Perez, and Paolo Varraso. 2022. "Are Collateral-Constraint Models Ready for Macroprudential Policy Design?" *Journal of International Economics* 139:103650.
Ponticelli, Jacopo, and Leonardo S. Alencar. 2016. "Court Enforcement, Bank Loans and Firm Investment: Evidence from a Bankruptcy Reform in Brazil." *Quarterly Journal of Economics* 131 (3): 1365–413.
Ramey, Valerie. 2016. "Macroeconomic Shocks and Their Propagation." In *Handbook of Macroeconomics*, ed. John B. Taylor and Harald Uhlig, 2:71–162. Amsterdam: Elsevier.
———, and Matthew D. Shapiro. 2001. "Displaced Capital: A Study of Aerospace Plant Closings." *Journal of Political Economy* 109 (5): 958–92.
Schularick, Moritz, and Alan M. Taylor. 2012. "Credit Booms Gone Bust: Monetary Policy, Leverage Cycles, and Financial Crises, 1870–2008." *American Economic Review*, 102 (2): 1029–61.
Smith, David C., and Per Strömberg. 2005. "Maximizing the Value of Distressed Assets: Bankruptcy Law and the Efficient Reorganization of Firms." In *Systemic Financial Crises*, ed. Patrick Honohan and Luc Laeven, 232–75. Cambridge: Cambridge University Press.
Tan, Charles. 2004. "Assessing the Corporate Insolvency Regime in Japan." Report by Moody's. Moody's Investor Service, Special Comment, Insolvency & Bankruptcy Committee, New York.
Vig, Vikrant. 2013. "Access to Collateral and Corporate Debt Structure: Evidence from a Natural Experiment." *Journal of Finance* 68 (3): 881–29.
World Bank. 2020. "Doing Business Reports: Historical Data." Doing Business Archive. https://archive.doingbusiness.org/en/data.
———. 2024. "World Development Indicators." World Bank DataBank. https://databank.worldbank.org/source/world-development-indicators.

Comment

Dean Corbae, *University of Wisconsin-Madison and NBER,* United States of America

I. Introduction

What may happen at the end of a firm's life influences all its prior decisions, even whether to enter in the first place. Thus, cross-country differences in firm resolution policies may have a quantitatively significant impact on the firm size distribution, misallocation, and output across countries. Kornejew et al. (2025, in this volume) tackle this important issue.

Specifically, they argue empirically that business credit booms are followed by severe economic downturns in countries with low bankruptcy efficiency but not in countries with high bankruptcy efficiency. Further they argue the results are symmetric implying more efficient bankruptcy systems are more stable. They then build a simple model to understand these data facts.

Perhaps one of the most important questions, both empirically and theoretically, is What is bankruptcy efficiency? I will focus on that in this discussion with particular emphasis on the applied theory part. The other discussant, Carola Frydman, is much more qualified to focus on the data than I am.

Hence, the discussion will be in two parts. Section II asks, What is bankruptcy efficiency in the data? The next set of sections asks, What is bankruptcy efficiency in the model? To answer that question, I summarize the model in Kornejew et al. (2025, in this volume) in Section III and draw out the implications of their benchmark equilibrium parameterization in Section IV. Specifically, under their benchmark parameterization, all liquidations are inefficient. Section V first documents that

NBER Macroeconomics Annual, volume 39, 2025.
 https://doi.org/10.1086/735257

there can be parameterizations consistent with US data that admit the possibility of efficient liquidation. I then draw out the equilibrium implications of that parameterization for aggregate output under different bankruptcy policies. In contrast to the authors' benchmark model, where all firms are ex ante homogeneous, I introduce a screening technology in Section VI that provides ex ante signals about a firm's ex post heterogeneous productivity, which nests the authors' benchmark. I use the technology to understand the interaction between ex ante screening and ex post bankruptcy resolution on the firm size distribution, and allocative efficiency and their implications for aggregate output. This opens up the question of how much of the greater stability across boom-bust cycles in the data is coming from ex post bankruptcy efficiency and how much comes from ex ante screening. Section VII concludes.

II. Data

What is bankruptcy efficiency in the data? Kornejew et al. (2025, in this volume) use measures of the quality of a country's bankruptcy system from Djankov et al. (2008) and World Bank (2020). Those papers ask bankruptcy lawyers across country i and time questions, such as

1. Would a bankrupt hotel with normalized value 100 if it continues in the face of a transient operating loss but worth only 70 units if sold piecemeal be kept as a going concern $GC_i = 1$ or liquidated $GC_i = 0$?
2. What is the likely duration τ_i and cost K_i to complete the bankruptcy?

The first item is the key hypothetical.

Then they compute country i's bankruptcy efficiency ξ_i as

$$\xi_i = \frac{100GC_i + 70(1 - GC_i) - 100 \cdot K_i}{(1 + r)^{\tau_i}}.$$

In their full sample, the mean ξ_i is 39.3 and its standard deviation is 24.6. In their sample that contains data on business credit from the Bank of International Settlements, which forms the basis of their regression analysis, the mean of ξ_i is 63.1 and its standard deviation is 23.5.

How should we interpret this bankruptcy efficiency measure? The hypothetical asked to lawyers bears an implicit assumption that reorganization is more efficient than liquidation with transitory losses because there is a 30% discount in liquidation.

A fundamental question, however, is whether liquidation is always inefficient and reorganization efficient. We know from Hopenhayn (1992) that in the presence of fixed operating costs, it may be efficient for persistently low productivity firms to exit.

To answer such a question, we should model the economic source of inefficiency. One such inefficiency arises from a commitment problem as modeled by Kornejew et al. (2025, in this volume). Here, there is a form of a debt overhang problem; it may be efficient to cancel the prior debt of a positive net present value firm experiencing a temporary loss instead of incurring liquidation costs associated with, say, a costly fire sale (at e.g., the 30% discount above). Such reorganization can, however, entail costs itself, and there can be inefficiencies in the renegotiation (e.g., bargaining) process. Another source of inefficiency, not explored here, is an information problem (more will be said about that in Sec. VI).

III. Model

What is bankruptcy efficiency in the model? Kornejew et al. (2025, in this volume) build an extremely simple model to help understand their regression results.

There are two periods $t \in \{1, 2\}$. There is a unit measure of ex ante identical risk neutral firms with discount rate β_f. There are also a large number of competitive risk neutral lenders with discount rate $\beta > \beta_f$. At $t = 1$ firms borrow b at price q to fund an investment project requiring an injection of goods of fixed size I. The project pays off $z \in \underline{z}, \bar{z}]$ drawn from a uniform distribution with density $\phi(z)$ at $t = 2$, where $\bar{z} - \underline{z} = 1$. All firms are ex ante ($t = 1$) homogeneous but ex post ($t = 2$) heterogeneous.

There is limited liability; if $b > z$, a firm declares bankruptcy. In that case, with probability ξ, the project is reorganized and continues to operate at cash flow $z^{\text{reorg}} = z$, whereas with probability $1 - \xi$, the project is liquidated, yielding $z^{\text{liq}} = \underline{z}$. Importantly, the parameter ξ captures bankruptcy efficiency; with a unit measure of firms, this also measures fraction of firms which are reorganized (i.e., Chap. 11 in the US bankruptcy code).

Because the paper is about bankruptcy on debt, the most important equilibrium conditions involve the pricing of that debt, which in turn depends on how much debt is chosen. Given there are no future repercussion to default at $t = 2$, there is a simple threshold default decision rule at $t = 2$, default if $b > z$ (i.e., default is more likely the higher amount you need to repay). Creditors recognize the borrowers' decision rule so that the competitive price of debt under the above bankruptcy policy is given by

$$q(b,\beta,\xi) = \beta\mathbb{E}_z\left[\mathbf{1}_{\{b\leq z\}} + \mathbf{1}_{\{b>z\}}\left(\frac{(1-\xi)z^{\text{liq}} + \xi z^{\text{reorg}}}{b}\right)\right], \tag{1}$$

where $\mathbb{E}_z[\cdot]$ integrates z using the density $\phi(z)$. Importantly, given $z^{\text{reorg}} = z \geq z^{\text{liq}} = \underline{z}$ creditors receive more in efficient bankruptcy systems, hence, interest rates are decreasing in ξ.

Taking prices as given, firms recognize that their debt choice affects the price they pay yielding the following borrowing decision rule:

$$\begin{aligned} b^*(\beta,\beta_f,\xi) &= \arg\max_{b\geq 0} q(b,\beta,\xi)\cdot b - I + \beta_f\int_b^{\bar{z}}(z-b)\phi(z)dz \\ &= \bar{z} - \frac{1-\xi}{2-\xi-\frac{\beta_f}{\beta}}. \end{aligned} \tag{2}$$

Kornejew et al. (2025, in this volume) establish in Proposition 1 that firms borrow more (i.e., $\partial b^*(\beta,\beta_f,\xi)/\partial\xi > 0$) because (ceteris paribus) creditors receive more (and hence charge lower interest rates) in more efficient bankruptcy systems.

IV. Benchmark Equilibrium: Inefficient Liquidation

The objective of the paper is to explore the macroeconomic implications, say, on aggregate output, of bankruptcy policy. Given a bankruptcy rule with $z^{\text{liq}} = \underline{z} \geq 0$, all liquidation is inefficient, because it destroys a non-negative value firm with a debt overhang problem. Aggregate output is given by

$$Y(b,\xi) = \mathbb{E}_z[z_j] - \underbrace{(1-\xi)\int_{\underline{z}}^{b}(z_j - \underline{z})\phi(z_j)dz_j}_{\text{output loss from inefficient liquidation}}, \tag{3}$$

with composition effect ξ and extensive margin effect $b = b^*$.

It is clear from equation (3) that to minimize output loss under the assumed exogenous bankruptcy system, the optimal policy is to set $\xi = 1$.[1] But then by equation (2), in the most efficient bankruptcy system

$$b^*(\beta,\beta_f,\xi = 1) = \bar{z}, \tag{4}$$

and hence 100% of firms default, because there's no cost to bankruptcy. This illustrates why modeling bankruptcy efficiency exogenously in a two-period model with $z^{\text{liq}} = \underline{z} \geq 0$, as in the paper, may be circumspect.

I think it is helpful to understand what is going on in the benchmark model through a set of figures. Specifically, figures 1–3 assume: $z^{\text{liq}} = \underline{z} = 0, \bar{z} = 1, \beta = 1, \beta_f = 0.9, I = 0.2$. This parameterization satisfies Assumption 1 of Kornejew et al. (2025, in this volume).[2]

Figure 1*A* graphs the set of equilibrium debt price menus (i.e., eq. [1]) for three different bankruptcy efficiency measures (i.e., the price charged $q(b, \beta = 1, \xi)$ for each level of debt b for $\xi \in \{0, 0, 5, 1\}$). The figure illustrates that (1) for any given ξ, interest rate offerings are increasing in debt b (standard result in equilibrium models of default), and (2) for any given debt level b, interest rate offerings (hard to observe unless you have great data) rise in less efficient bankruptcy systems ($\downarrow\xi$). Taking these menus as given, figure 1*B* illustrates the firm borrowing problem b^* which solves equation (2) off the given menu. Given the uniform distribution of z over a unit support, the figure also illustrates the probability of default. The figure illustrates that (1) equilibrium borrowing and default are increasing in bankruptcy efficiency (although the first prediction is consistent

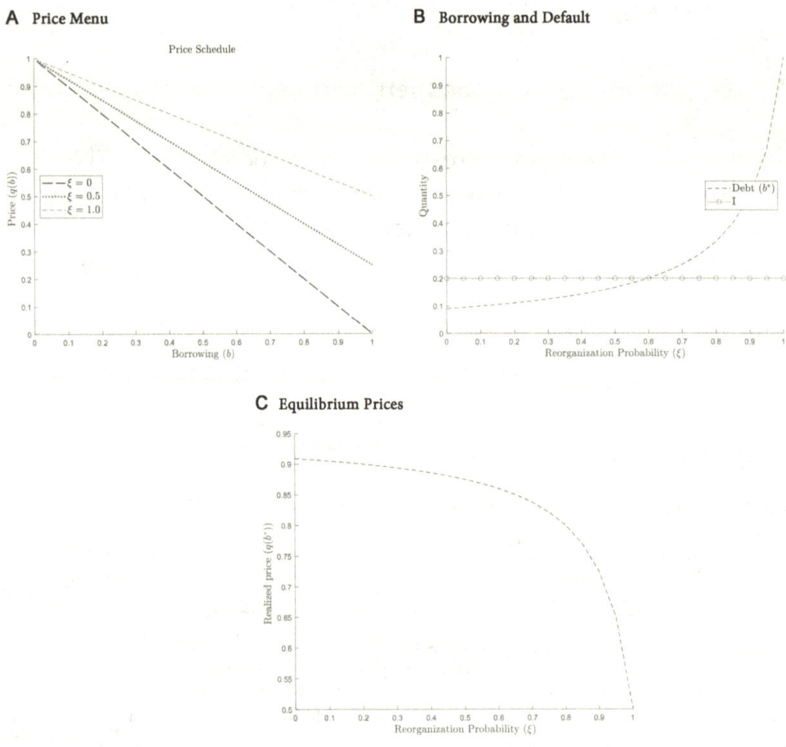

Fig. 1. Benchmark given reorganization probabilities (ξ).

with data, it is not clear the default prediction is consistent with data), and (2) low efficiency bankruptcy systems finance I with mix of debt and "equity" issuance $I - b^*$, which ensures some "skin in the game" for low bankruptcy efficient systems. This latter result questions how the regression results in Kornejew et al. (2025, in this volume) should account for other financing options (e.g., internal funds or via an informal sector). Given equilibrium borrowing choice b^*, figure 1C illustrates equilibrium prices $q(b^*, \beta = 1, \xi)$, which are easier to observe in the data than in the price menu. The figure illustrates that the model predicts that low bankruptcy efficient systems, which result in small amounts of borrowing, imply high observed prices $q(b^*, \beta = 1, \xi)$. In other words, the model predicts that observed interest spreads are bankruptcy efficient, a result which may not be consistent with data.

Dividends div_t accrue to the owners of the firm across the two periods. Specifically, the $t = 1$ dividend is given by $\text{div}_1 = q \cdot b - I$, whereas $\text{div}_2 = \max\{z - b, 0\}$. Figure 2 illustrates dividend issuance for different bankruptcy systems. It illustrates an important point; equity must be injected (i.e., $\text{div}_1 < 0$ in low bankruptcy efficient economies). This

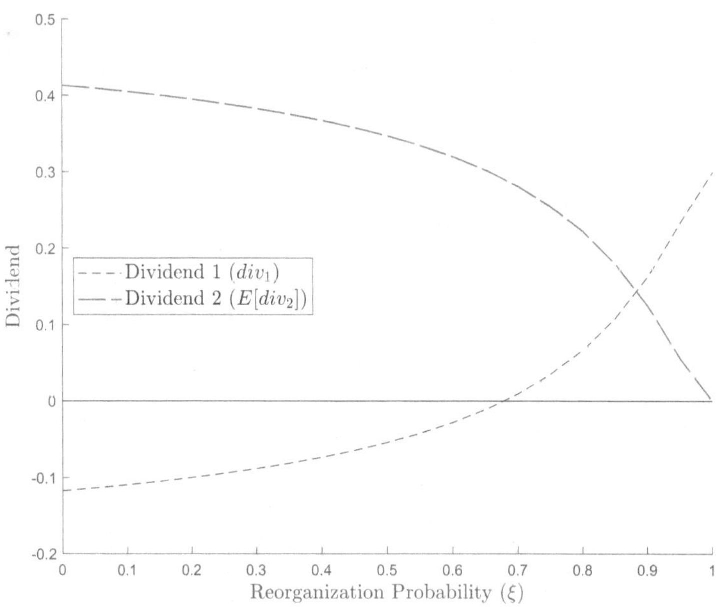

Fig. 2. Benchmark dividends given reorganization probabilities (ξ). Benchmark model ($\underline{z} = 0 = z^{liq}$).

provides evidence for an informal sector channel along the lines of D'Erasmo and Boedo (2012). The figure also illustrates that low bankruptcy efficient systems require high backloaded payoffs to induce investment (which yields another potentially testable prediction of the model).

Figure 3 illustrates the macroeconomic implications of bankruptcy systems on aggregate output. As is clear in the figure, with $z^{liq} = \underline{z} = 0$, it is efficient to reorganize all firms (i.e., the optimal $\xi = 1$, because they are all weakly positive value). But, importantly, the figure illustrates a nonmonotonicity arising from a trade-off:

1. For a given level of debt (and default), as ξ increases, the share of bankrupt firms resolved inefficiently decreases implying an increase in net output $Y - I$.
2. Because $\partial b^* / \partial \xi > 0$, default increases, implying a decrease in net output $Y - I$.

The composition effect (1) dominates for high ξ, whereas the extensive margin effect (2) dominates for low ξ. This nonmonotonicity may call into question local (linear) analysis of the data.

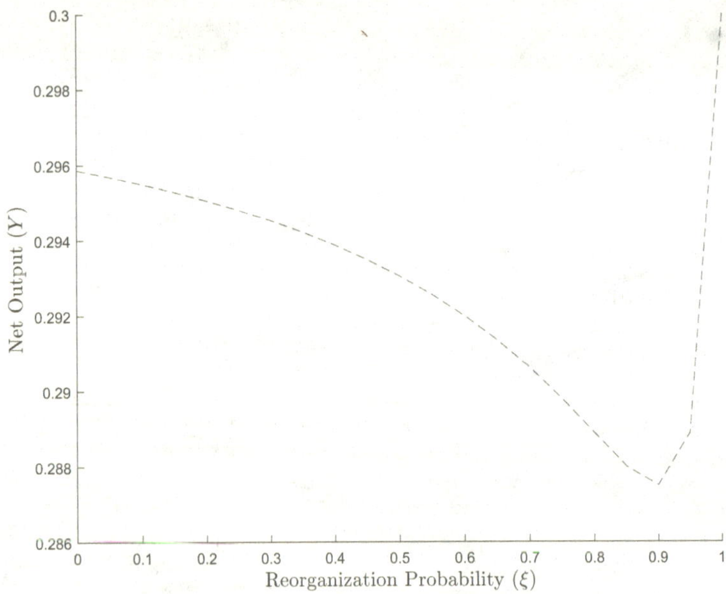

Fig. 3. Benchmark net output $(Y - I)$ given reorganization probabilities (ξ). Benchmark model $(\underline{z} = 0 = z^{liq})$.

V. Alternative Equilibria: Efficient Liquidation

Should all firms be reorganized? As shown above, in the benchmark model version of the model by Kornejew et al. (2025, in this volume), where $z^{liq} = \underline{z} = 0$, all firms with a debt overhang problem but with nonnegative value should be reorganized (i.e., $\xi = 1$) rather than liquidated. That is, liquidation of positive value firms is inefficient. But what if some firms in the economy are not positive value? In the context of this model, what if $\underline{z} < 0$? Such an assumption is similar to adding fixed operating costs along the lines of Hopenhayn (1992) shifting the entire support $[\underline{z}, \bar{z}]$ down. In that case, is it not efficient to liquidate firms with negative net revenue?

The point that liquidation in the presence of firms with negative operating revenue (i.e., those with $z \in [\underline{z}, 0]$ in the context of the model) is what we see in US Compustat data. Specifically, table 1 reproduces table 1 in Corbae and D'Erasmo (2021). To fix notation, in the United States, reorganization falls under Chapter 11 bankruptcy rules, whereas liquidation falls under Chapter 7. The table provides summary statistics on US Compustat firms from 1980 to 2014 and highlights two particularly important facts relevant for the Kornejew et al. (2025, in this volume) paper:

1. Bankrupt firms have negative operating income and interest coverage (EBITDA/interest) is declining across nonbankrupt (median 5) / Chapter 11 (−0.15) / Chapter 7 (−1.07) firms.

There is substantial heterogeneity involved in net debt to assets (i.e., Chap. 11 > Chap. 7 > Nonbankrupts) and size matters for bankruptcy choice: big bankrupt firms choose reorganization, whereas smaller firms choose liquidation.

Fact 1 documents that a relevant case for the model is $z \in [\underline{z}, 0]$. Fact 2 documents that there is substantial heterogeneity in debt and bankruptcy choices which is inconsistent with ex ante homogeneous borrowing choices and an exogenous probability ξ of reorganization. These two facts, negative value firms and heterogeneity, motivate my discussion in this section and in Section VI.

Importantly, the presence of negative value firms in Fact 1 has implications for the optimal bankruptcy resolution policy. In figure 4, we calculate net output comparing an economy where there are negative value firms ($\underline{z} = -0.1 < 0 = z^{liq}$) versus the benchmark parameterization, where ($\underline{z} = 0 = z^{liq}$). Unsurprisingly, the figure illustrates that

Table 1
Some US Compustat Facts from Corbae and D'Erasmo (2021): Balance Sheet and Corporate Bankruptcies 1980–2014

Moment						
Frequency of exit (%)			1.10			
Fraction of exit by Chapter 7 (%)			19.83			
Frequency of (all) bankruptcy (%)			.96			
Fraction of Chapter 11 bankruptcy (%)			79.15			
	Nonbankrupt		Chapter 11		Chapter 7	
	Avg.	Median	Avg.	Median	Avg.	Median
Capital (millions 1983$)	984.16	37.02	402.12*,***	68.42	76.95**	18.03
Cash (millions 1983$)	130.55	10.41	50.38*,***	5.84	13.39**	2.85
Assets (millions 1983$)	1415.11	100.49	485.28*,***	99.11	108.30**	33.45
Op. income (EBITDA)/assets (%)	5.29	10.86	−8.32*	−.52	−15.10**	−6.94
Net debt/assets (%)	9.00	11.19	30.71*,***	26.29	21.50**	20.11
Total debt/assets (%)	28.40	24.51	42.89*	37.48	43.30**	37.00
Frac. firms with negative net debt (%)	36.25	–	21.40*,***	–	32.26**	–
Secured debt/total debt (%)	43.66	40.61	49.07*	46.83	45.11	43.07
Interest coverage (EBITDA/interest)	14.10	4.95	−1.09*,***	−.15	−9.99**	−1.07
Equity issuance/asset (%)	4.79	.06	2.71*	.01	3.06**	.02
Fraction firms issuing equity (%)	22.12	–	12.88*	–	16.60**	–
Net investments/assets (%)	1.14	.33	−2.78*	−2.98	−2.24**	−2.17
Dividend/assets (%)	3.53	2.06	1.71*,***	.86	3.79**	2.56
Z-score	3.71	3.19	−1.16*	.12	−1.46**	.09
DD Prob. of default (%)	2.11	.01	3.47*	1.22	3.73**	1.27

Note: See Supplementary Appendix A.1 in Corbae and D'Erasmo (2021) for a detailed definition of variables and the construction of bankruptcy and exit indicators. Medians (average) reported in the table correspond to the time series average of the cross-sectional median (mean) obtained for every year in our sample. Nominal variables are deflated using the CPI index (US Bureau of Labor Statistics). Test for differences in means at 10% level of significance: *denotes Chapter 11 different from nonbankrupt, **denotes Chapter 7 different from nonbankrupt, ***denotes Chapter 11 different from Chapter 7. DD, distance to default, EBITDA, earning before interest tax, depreciation, and authorization. Reprinted from Corbae, Dean, and Pablo D'Erasmo. 2021. "Reorganization or Liquidation: Bankruptcy Choice and Firm Dynamics." *Review of Economic Studies* 88 (5): 2239–74, by permission of Oxford University Press.

the economy with lower mean productivity implies lower output. Surprisingly, however, maximum output is no longer achieved at $\xi = 1$ as in the benchmark but with $\xi = 0$. The maximum at $\xi = 0$ is because inefficient firms with $z < 0$ are liquidated, whereas at $\xi = 1$, they are not (but should be). This example simply illustrates that there are cases

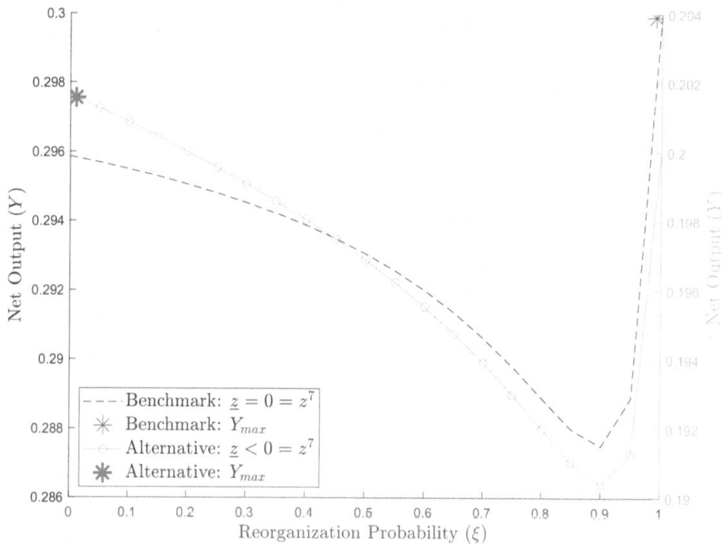

Fig. 4. Efficient liquidation ($\underline{z} < 0 = z^{\text{liq}}$) versus benchmark ($\underline{z} = 0 = z^{\text{liq}}$): net output. Left vertical axis corresponds to net output in benchmark (i.e., $[\underline{z}, \bar{z}] = [0, 1]$), whereas the right vertical axis corresponds to net output in efficient liquidation case (i.e., $[\underline{z}, \bar{z}] = [-0.1, 0.9]$).

where liquidation is not inefficient (as in the benchmark case) but potentially efficient with limited liability.[3]

VI. Ex Ante Firm Heterogeneity, Information, and Misallocation

As described above in Fact 2 of the Compustat data, there is substantial heterogeneity in debt holdings and bankruptcy choice; bigger bankrupt firms have more net debt and choose reorganization rather than liquidation. As in the Hopenhayn (1992) model, exit depends on persistence of revenue shocks (consistent with the "transient operating loss" question in Djankov et al. 2008). The more persistent a low revenue shock is, the lower the expected net present value of the firm and the more likely it should efficiently exit. In Corbae and D'Erasmo (2021), we estimate quarterly autocorrelation of operating income in Compustat is 0.9 which is similar to estimates in Cooper and Haltiwanger (2006). Importantly, besides its impact on the value of the firm, ex ante heterogeneity and persistence provides lenders with information to efficiently separate/screen unproductive firms, to which I now turn.

Suppose that instead of ex ante homogeneous firms as in the model of Kornejew et al. (2025, in this volume), we introduce signals $s(z)$ at the start of $t = 1$, before borrowing choices are made, about productivity $z \in [s - \Delta, s + \Delta]$ at $t = 2$. One can interpret these signals as an approximation to a Markov process over productivity as in Corbae and D'Erasmo (2021) or as firm credit ratings along the lines of credit scores in Chatterjee et al. (2023). This nests the previous benchmark ex ante homogeneous firm case when $\Delta = 0.5$ and a perfect signal case where $\Delta = 0$. Provided signals are observable to lenders, prices can also be conditioned on the signal (i.e., $\mathbb{E}_{z|s}$):

$$q(s, b, \beta, \xi) = \beta \mathbb{E}_{z|s}\left[\mathbf{1}_{\{b \leq z\}} + \mathbf{1}_{\{b > z\}}\left(\frac{(1 - \xi)z^{\text{liq}} + \xi z}{b}\right)\right]. \tag{5}$$

Figure 5 illustrates an important point that screening technologies (here modeled simply as informative signals) can aid in the "ex ante" efficient allocation of lending which can obviate the ex post need for more efficient bankruptcy systems. Specifically, in figure 5 we set $\xi = 0.7$, which is similar to the fraction of reorganization in the United States, keeping

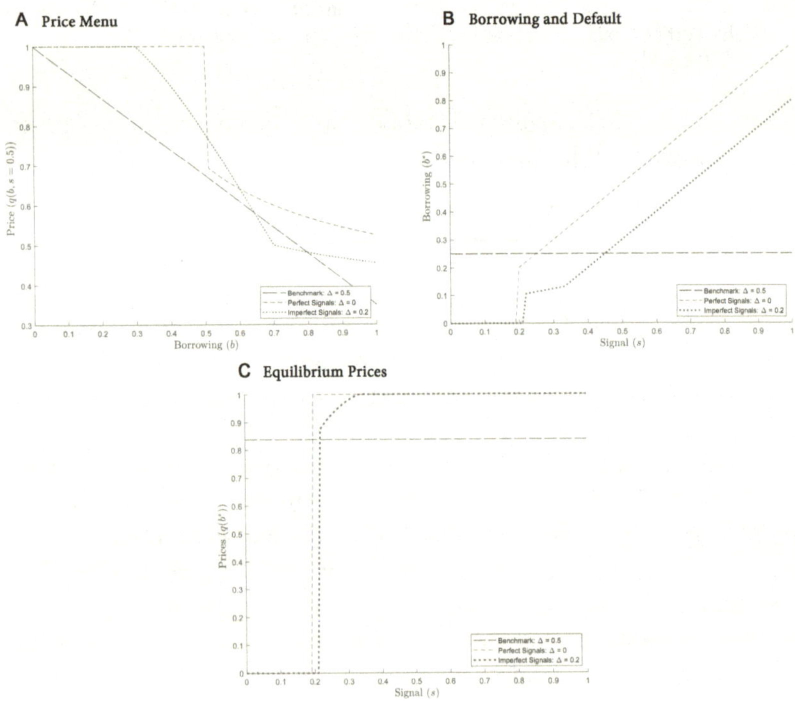

Fig. 5. Equilibrium prices across signal quality.

all other parameters as in the benchmark model (in particular, $z^{liq} = \underline{z} = 0$). Panel 5*A* plots price menus $q(s, b, \beta = 1, \xi = 0.7)$ in equation (5) for a particular signal $s = 0.5$. If the signal is completely uninformative (i.e., $\Delta = 0.5$), prices strictly decrease in the amount borrowed. On the other hand, if the signal is perfectly informative (i.e., $s = z$), given firms only default when $b > z$, lenders supply funds at the risk-free rate for $b \leq z$, whereas further borrowing leads to default, creditors still receive $((1 - \xi)z^{liq} + \xi z)/b = 0.35b^{-1}$, generating the remaining decreasing price menu. For partially informative signals with $\Delta = 0.2$, any $b < s - \Delta = 0.3$ leads to no default, so that a risk-free price is offered, whereas any borrowing beyond that level is risky and priced accordingly.

Facing price menus like panel 5*A* for each signal *s*, ex ante heterogeneous firms with signal $s \in [0, 1]$ choose how much they want to borrow (i.e., solve the *s* dependent analogue of equation (2) in panel 5*B*). With uninformative signals $\Delta = 0.5$, we are back in the benchmark case with a homogeneous borrowing level (i.e., independent of *s*). With perfectly informative signals $\Delta = 0$, sufficiently low productivity signals $s = z < I$ are rationed, whereas firms with higher productivity signals borrow increasing amounts. Again, with partially uninformative signals, creditors face more risk and require higher interest rates which generates lower equilibrium borrowing in panel 5*B*.

Given borrowing levels $b^*(s, \beta = 1, \beta_f = 0.9, \xi = 0.7)$ from panel 5*B*, panel 5*C* plots equilibrium prices $q(s, b^*, \beta = 1, \xi = 0.7)$ across signals *s* for each level of informativeness Δ. Uninformative signals $\Delta = 0.5$ correspond to the benchmark case which pools all firms with a spread of 16%. In that case, low risk (high *z*) firms at $t = 2$ are cross-subsidizing high risk (low *z*) firms in the credit market. At the other extreme where signals are perfect (i.e., $\Delta = 0$), lenders can efficiently separate and ration firms which are negative net present value (i.e., $z < I$) from those with positive net present value who receive funding at the risk-free rate equal to 0. With partially informative signals (i.e., $\Delta \in (0, 0.5)$, firms with $s > I + \Delta$ have guaranteed positive net present value projects and hence receive the risk-free rate. Those firms with $s < I - \Delta$ have negative net present value projects and face rationing. Those with $s \in [I - \Delta, I + \Delta])$ are risky so face a spread that is decreasing in s.

The implications of screening technologies for borrowing in figure 5 feeds into the determination of net output. Figure 6 illustrates the macro implications of bankruptcy resolution policies in the presence of screening technologies. Better screening technologies minimize the frequency of costly default. Output is lowest in the benchmark economy ($Y = 0.28$),

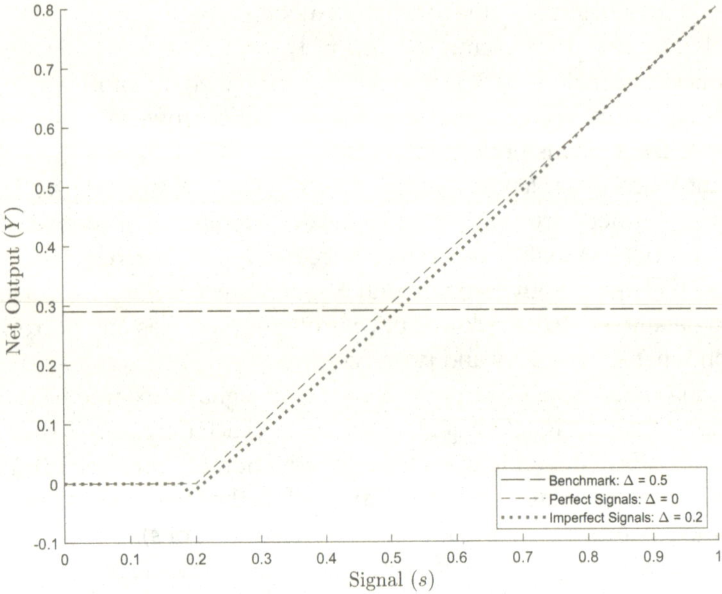

Fig. 6. Net output across signal quality.

increases by 11% with imperfect signals (some ex ante screening), and increases a further 3% with perfect signals (i.e., in a separating equilibrium).

In summary, the firm size distribution and misallocation depends critically on ex ante heterogeneity not modeled in Kornejew et al. (2025, in this volume). For instance, with perfect signals, ex ante screening means that no firms ever default so bankruptcy efficiency is not even relevant. Those negative net present value firms are rationed with implications for the firm size distribution and can lead to an efficient allocation of resources.

The impact of bankruptcy policies on the firm size distribution and misallocation in a quantitative model of firm dynamics is taken up in Corbae and D'Erasmo (2021). We parameterize our model to match current bankruptcy code and conduct a counterfactual change to bankruptcy policy like that in Aghion, Hart, and Moore (1992). We find that (1) better bankruptcy policy generates lower borrowing interest menu offerings and, despite higher equilibrium borrowing, lower (observed) equilibrium interest spreads, (2) an increase in measured productivity arising from selection and a change in the firm size distribution, and (3) measures of allocative efficiency rise closer to that of a frictionless economy.

VII. Conclusion

Kornejew et al. (2025, in this volume) have written a very thought-provoking and interesting cross-country paper on a fundamental question: How do policies aimed at financially distressed firms affect the boom-bust cycle? The answer to this question must address the sources of inefficiency: bankruptcy policy in light of commitment frictions and incomplete information. In this discussion, I have tried to extend the authors' analysis to understand how ex post liquidation of unprofitable firms may be efficient and how better ex ante screening technologies can achieve efficient rationing of unprofitable firms. This raises the question whether the authors' empirical findings of greater aggregate stability following a credit boom is coming from better ex post bankruptcy institutions or better ex ante credit screening. These extensions can have important implications for the firm size distribution, allocative efficiency, and financial stability. This seems like a fruitful avenue for future research.

Endnotes

Author email address: Corbae (corbae@ssc.wisc.edu). I wish to thank Charles Smith for excellent research assistance in preparing this discussion. For acknowledgments, sources of research support, and disclosure of the author's material financial relationships, if any, please see https://www.nber.org/books-and-chapters/nber-macroeconomics-annual-2024-volume-39/comment-bankruptcy-resolution-and-credit-cycles-corbae.

1. Although the authors restrict $\xi \in (0,1)$, I consider this limiting case to make the point clear.

2. That is, $0.2 = I < \frac{\beta}{2}\left(\frac{1-\xi\cdot\frac{\beta_f}{\beta}}{2-\xi-\frac{\beta_f}{\beta}}\right) + \beta\underline{z} = \frac{1}{2}\left(\frac{1-0.9\xi}{2-\xi-0.9}\right)$ for all values of $\xi \in [0,1]$.

3. In appendix IA2.6, Kornejew et al. (2025, in this volume) show that under a different assumption on investment costs, their main result in Proposition 1 on output dynamics following an exogenous increase in credit continues to hold.

References

Aghion, P., O. Hart, and J. Moore. 1992. "The Economics of Bankruptcy Reform." *Journal of Law, Economics, and Organization* 8 (3): 523–46.

Chatterjee, S., D. Corbae, K. Dempsey, and J.-V. Rios-Rull. 2023. "A Quantitative Theory of the Credit Score." *Econometrica* 91 (5): 1803–40.

Cooper, R., and J. Haltiwanger. 2006. "On the Nature of Capital Adjustment Costs." *Review of Economic Studies* 73 (3): 611–33.

Corbae, D., and P. D'Erasmo. 2021. "Reorganization or Liquidation: Bankruptcy Choice and Firm Dynamics." *Review of Economic Studies* 88 (5): 2239–74.

D'Erasmo, P. N., and H. J. M. Boedo. 2012. "Financial Structure, Informality and Development." *Journal of Monetary Economics* 59 (3): 286–302.

Djankov, S., O. Hart, C. McLiesh, and A. Shleifer. 2008. "Debt Enforcement around the World." *Journal of Political Economy* 116 (6): 1105–49.

Hopenhayn, H. A. 1992. "Entry, Exit, and Firm Dynamics in Long Run Equilibrium." *Econometrica: Journal of the Econometric Society* 60 (5): 1127–50.
Kornejew, M., C. Lian, Y. Ma, P. Ottonello, and D. J. Perez. 2025. "Bankruptcy Resolution and Credit Cycles." *NBER Macroeconomics Annual* 39:1–39.
World Bank. 2020. "Historical Data." *Doing Business* Archive. https://archive.doingbusiness.org/en/data.

Comment

Carola Frydman, *Northwestern University and NBER,* United States of America

The paper by Kornejew, Lian, Ma, Ottonello, and Perez provides an insightful analysis of the role that institutions for business bankruptcy resolution play on the impact of credit cycles on the real economy. The macroeconomic consequences of credit cycles for both households and firms have received much attention in recent decades. Perhaps surprisingly, the role of the process by which firm distress is dealt with has been largely ignored. This paper brings the institutional designs for debt resolution to the forefront, making a substantive contribution to our understanding of the consequences of credit cycles, macroeconomic dynamics, and macroprudential policies. In a nutshell, this is a big-picture paper that makes a really consequential point.

The paper bridges an important gap between two active and exciting areas of research. A substantive body of work in law and economics and, especially, in corporate finance has utilized microlevel data and empirical strategies such as differences-in-difference designs or instrumental variables to make a strong case for causal (and nuanced) effects of the design and enforcement of bankruptcy institutions on the outcomes of wide variety of firm outcomes (see, e.g., Ponticelli and Alencar, 2016; Iverson, 2018). But as convincing as these studies may be for establishing clean identification, their findings cannot be easily utilized to elicit robust aggregate effects. Separately, an extensive literature has used cross-country evidence to document the effects of credit cycles on the macroeconomy. Within this line of work, some recent papers have started to focus on corporate debt dynamics specifically (Mian, Sufi, and Verner 2017; Ivashina et al. 2024).

NBER Macroeconomics Annual, volume 39, 2025.
 https://doi.org/10.1086/735258

Still, there is much to learn about the underlying factors that may exacerbate the detrimental effects of corporate debt booms on the economy.

One important underlying factor may be the institutions that help resolve firm distress. If credit expansions lead to overleverage and higher corporate default rates, how the distressed assets are redeployed may have consequential implications for the aggregate economy. An important insight of this paper is that it is important to consider a country's bankruptcy system when designing macroprudential policies.

The paper tackles this question empirically and theoretically. Theoretically, it provides a simple framework to illustrate how the process for bankruptcy resolution can dampen the negative effects of credit cycles on the economy. I will not dwell on it here, but let me summarize the key intuition and predictions of the baseline model. The most interesting (and in practice the most common) case is nonfundamental credit booms that are not driven by increases in firm productivity. After a period of business credit growth, firms will be overleveraged. As they default, output will contract. Under the assumption that firms' continuation value is higher than liquidation value, a legal system that facilitates restructuring over inefficient liquidation will preserve more firms as a going concern and help minimize the decline in output. By contrast, an efficient bankruptcy system ameliorates the positive effects on output and defaults that follow fundamental booms. The theoretical framework helps convey the connection between bankruptcy efficiency and credit cycles that the authors have in mind, but this is at its core an empirical paper concerned with eliciting the effects of bankruptcy efficiency in the data.

The empirical evidence is based on 39 countries from 2003 to 2019. A bankruptcy system is deemed to be more inefficient when it fails to preserve as an ongoing concern a firm that should not be liquidated and when the legal process takes longer and is costlier. Using state-dependent local projections, the paper finds that following a 10 percentage point increase in business credit to gross domestic product (GDP) growth over a 5-year period, output declines by about three percentage points over the following 5 years when the efficiency of the country's bankruptcy system is in the bottom quartile. By contrast, the effects on output are essentially negligible for countries in the top quartile of the distribution of bankruptcy efficiency. An inefficient system also leads to more pronounced declines in investment and private consumption and to increases in unemployment following credit booms.

Importantly, this paper is not the first to make a connection between bankruptcy institutions and macroeconomic stability. Focusing solely on periods of output contractions, Jordà et al. (2022) show that when a recession starts after a 5-year business credit boom, the declines in GDP and investment that follow are deeper and longer in those countries with more inefficient bankruptcy systems. This paper follows essentially the same empirical design as Jordà et al. (2022), albeit with one very significant change: it does not condition the analysis on recessions. The main novel finding is, therefore, that the aggregate effects of legal institutions on the real economy following a credit boom are evidenced on average.

Although these average effects are the baseline specifications utilized throughout the paper, in light of the Jordà et al. (2022) findings, one obvious concern is that the negative effects of inefficient bankruptcy systems may still only operate during recessions. This is a point I raised in my discussion, and I am glad to see that the updated paper has incorporated it. Table IA1 in the paper shows clearly that bankruptcy efficiency helps undo the declines in real GDP that follow a 5-year credit expansion whether these declines are preceded by a recession year (panel *A*) or by a year in which GDP did not contract (panel *B*). Thus, this paper shows that legal regimes have a much broader impact on macroeconomic cycles than previously documented.

This finding naturally raises the question of what exactly the frictions are that create such losses of value even during good economic conditions. The paper is not too explicit on this, but it does point to the importance of asset specificity as a reason why liquidation may be inefficient, and it references empirical work based on US evidence that validates this empirically (Ramey and Shapiro 2001; Kermani and Ma 2023). But research using micro-level data to study the effects of bankruptcy on firm outcomes suggests that the mechanisms may be more complex. For example, Bernstein, Colonnelli, and Iverson (2019) show that the long-run use of real estate assets of liquidated firms is lower relative to reorganized firms only when markets are thin and access to finance is low. That means that financing frictions that limit the ability of liquidated assets to be redeployed quickly and efficiently may be significant for economic outcomes and may further exacerbate any distortions from asset specificity as well as reduce the likelihood of viable firms to be purchased whole. These financing frictions should be more severe during recessions and, especially, at times of financial distress. It is possible as well that they are more severe in countries that also happen to have weaker institutions and less efficient bankruptcy processes.

The fact that the legal system has such an impact on economic outcomes even during normal times raises some concerns about identification. In fact, the question the authors are tackling is one that is hard to answer convincingly, in no small part because the efficiency of the bankruptcy system is primarily explained by country fixed effects. The paper does a great job at controlling for a wide variety of potential confounding factors, by including one at a time controls for factors such as a country's income per capita level and volatility, exchange rate regime, general rule of law, and indicators for the quality of institutions. But the list cannot be exhaustive, and ultimately it is challenging to rule out the possibility that the measure of bankruptcy efficiency may be capturing other country characteristics that become salient at times of firm distress.

The omitted variable bias is obviously an easy comment to make, but I am worried in particular about one plausible omitted factor: the fact that the financial system may help some countries preempt or ameliorate firm distress more than others. Following the findings of Bernstein et al. (2019), one may be especially concerned about differences across countries in firms' access to finance, the existence of competitors with deep pockets that can absorb firms in distress, and especially, the ability of the government to rescue distressed firms or inject liquidity during difficult times. To address concerns of omitted bias beyond showing robustness to the inclusion of the controls mentioned above, the paper instruments bankruptcy efficiency with the country's legal origin. But this instrument is unlikely to satisfy the exclusion restriction. For example, a large body of work studies the importance of legal origins for financial development, in addition to many other outcomes (see La Porta, Lopez-de-Silanes, and Shleifer 2008, for a review of this literature). Thus, other financing frictions that may contribute to the efficiency in which assets are redeployed in the economy besides the bankruptcy process may be directly affected by the legal origin of the country. Ultimately, separating the effect of the legal system for bankruptcy resolution from other country-level factors that shape financial frictions—and therefore the likelihood of firm distress and its resolution—is simply extremely challenging. The paper does as much as possible given these constraints to put forth a convincing case for identification.

It is also challenging to obtain a comparable measure of how bankruptcy is resolved for a large set of countries, especially because the enforcement may vary across countries beyond differences in the letter of the law. To solve this, the authors rely on a strategy first introduced by Djankov et al. (2008), who present a made-up, stylized example of a viable firm in distress with multiple claimants to insolvency practitioners around the world. The key metric used in this paper—that is, bankruptcy efficiency—intends to capture claim holders' recovery relative to the continuation value. This measure has important advantages. Because it is not based on hard data but rather based on the narratives provided by legal professionals, it can be relatively easily obtained for most countries. In 2019, it is observed for 166 countries. In fact, it is more broadly available than data on business debt, which constrain the analysis to more efficient countries (see table 1 in the paper). Moreover, using the same hypothetical case allows for comparability across countries. It is also directly related to what one would like to measure (the efficiency of the system), which would be hard to do with real data.

But there are also important limitations of this hypothetical measure. The example considers a firm that should optimally continue as an ongoing concern and should not be liquidated. It also rules out by design the distortions that in practice may make reorganizations inefficient, such as the possibility for managers and shareholders to tunnel resources. In countries with weak institutions, a lengthy and unpredictable process of reorganization could conceptually lead to higher losses than the loss of value from liquidation, especially for complex bankruptcy cases. This measure also ignores out-of-court restructurings, which are an especially common method for addressing distress precisely in countries with weak institutions that may induce inefficient continuations (Franks and Lóránth 2004). It is also intended to be representative of insolvency for a midsize firm in many countries and therefore may not be representative of the process for larger firms, which are likely more systemically relevant.

Given these limitations, it seems critical to validate the findings with real data not based on the individual assessments of legal practitioners. I am pleased to see that the authors have taken a step in this direction in the revised paper. Specifically, figure IA1 shows a positive correlation between the bankruptcy efficiency measure and a proxy of the realized default recovery rate based on information on the values of loan impairments and nonperforming loans across countries. Although this is reassuring, there is much more variation in the realized recovery rate than in the efficiency measure. Given that the coverage of this alternative proxy is reasonably good, it would be helpful to show that the main results of the paper are also robust to this alternative measure. Further direct information linking the strength of the economic contraction following a credit boom to the prevalence and persistence of bankruptcies across countries could also be valuable.

Overall, the paper presents strong evidence that the legal institutions for the resolution of firm distress may play an important role for macroeconomic stability. What are the policy implications that emerge from this finding? The authors point to the value for macroprudential policies to take into account the design of the legal framework. This would allow policy makers to identify those settings in which intervention may not be that necessary (but equally costly) because credit booms are unlikely to hurt the economy. But this view does not take into account the endogeneity of credit growth to bankruptcy resolution. Djankov et al. (2008) find a 10-point increase in bankruptcy efficiency was associated with a 5–6 percentage point higher private credit-to-GDP ratio, suggesting that the effectiveness of the legal systems may contribute to financial development. If countries that are more effective at resolving bankruptcy are also those that experience large credit booms, then in practice one may see more of an impact on the economy in these cases. Large expansions in business debt during nonfundamental booms may still be costly even if the bankruptcy system can deal with firm defaults in an efficient manner.

An alternative strategy would be to reform legal systems to tilt them away from liquidations and toward reorganizations, as Japan did in the late 1990s and early 2000s. Although one may think that that is an unlikely path more generally, it is worth remarking that over time, the bankruptcy process has become more reorganization friendly, in part due to an understanding of the value of keeping firms as an ongoing concern. In the United States, the origins of court-mandated reorganization processes stem from the railroad equity receiverships of the late nineteenth century. At that time, the norm was for firms to be liquidated in default. But it became clear that railroad systems were worth more whole than the value that could be obtained by selling each of their lines separately (Skeel 2001), and the process for receivership—an ancestor to modern Chapter 11—was born. The World Bank Doing Business database utilized in the paper also points to broader changes in this direction. In addition to measuring bankruptcy efficiency, they have also collected information on bankruptcy reforms. The countries in the paper's main sample experienced 38 reforms over the sample period that made resolving insolvency easier (with an average increase in bankruptcy efficiency of about 6 percentage points) and only two reforms that made it harder (leading to a decline in efficiency of about 3 percentage points). As more countries make reorganizations during bankruptcy more likely, it becomes even more central to understand what these legal institutions imply for macroeconomic stability. In addition, in recent decades we have witnessed an increase in firms' intangible assets, and this trend will surely accelerate going forward. Because intangible assets are more difficult to collateralize and may be more specific to the firm, the frictions that underpin the findings of this paper may only become more salient. This paper makes a strong case for the importance of incorporating legal institutions for default resolution, and especially the distinction between reorganizations and liquidations, into macroeconomic analyses.

Endnote

Author email address: Frydman (c-frydman@kellogg.northwestern.edu). For acknowledgments, sources of research support, and disclosure of the author's material financial relationships, if any, please see https://www.nber.org/books-and-chapters/nber-macroeconomics-annual-2024-volume-39/comment-bankruptcy-resolution-and-credit-cycles-2-frydman.

References

Bernstein, Shai, Emanuele Colonnelli, and Benjamin Iverson. 2019. "Asset Allocation in Bankruptcy." *Journal of Finance* 74 (1): 5–53.

Djankov, Simeon, Oliver Hart, Caralee McLiesh, and Andrei Shleifer. 2008. "Debt Enforcement around the World." *Journal of Political Economy* 116 (6): 1105–49.

Franks, Julian, and Gyöngyi Lóránth. 2004. "A Study of Inefficient Going Concerns in Bankruptcy." https://ssrn.com/abstract=676356.

Ivashina, Victoria, Sebnem Kalemli-Özcan, Luc Laeven, and Karsten Müller. 2024. "Corporate Debt, Boom-Bust Cycles, and Financial Crises." NBER Working Paper 32225, NBER, Cambridge, MA.

Iverson, Benjamin. 2018. "Get in Line: Chapter 11 Restructuring in Crowded Bankruptcy Courts." *Management Science* 64 (11): 5370–94.

Jordà, Òscar, Martin Kornejew, Moritz Schularick, and Alan M. Taylor. 2022. "Zombies at Large? Corporate Debt Overhang and the Macroeconomy." *Review of Financial Studies* 35 (10): 4561–86.

Kermani, Amir, and Yueran Ma. 2023. "Asset Specificity of Nonfinancial Firms." *Quarterly Journal of Economics* 138 (1): 205–64.

La Porta, Rafael, Florencio Lopez-de-Silanes, and Andrei Shleifer. 2008. "The Economic Consequences of Legal Origins." *Journal of Economic Literature* 46:285–332.

Mian, Atif R., Amir Sufi, and Emil Verner. 2017. "Household Debt and Business Cycles Worldwide." *Quarterly Journal of Economics* 132 (4): 1755–817.

Ponticelli, Jacopo, and Leonardo S. Alencar. 2016. "Court Enforcement, Bank Loans, and Firm Investment: Evidence from a Bankruptcy Reform in Brazil." *Quarterly Journal of Economics* 131 (3): 1365–413.

Ramey, Valerie A., and Matthew D. Shapiro. 2001. "Displaced Capital: A Study of Aerospace Plant Closings." *Journal of Political Economy* 109 (5): 958–92.

Skeel, David A., Jr. 2001. *Debt's Dominion: A History of Bankruptcy Law in America*. Princeton, NJ: Princeton University Press.

Discussion

Valerie Ramey opened the discussion by pointing out that the appendix shows statistically and economically significant asymmetries between a credit boom and a credit bust, especially for the first 2 years after the shock. She suggested testing for asymmetries using the method developed by Ben Zeev, Ramey, and Zubairy and discussing the results in more detail in the paper's main text.

Yueran Ma thanked Valerie Ramey for the comment and agreed with her. However, she added that the literature has focused on credit booms generating damages, which is the paper's focus. For this reason, asymmetries are not a central discussion in the paper.

Then Frederic S. Mishkin pointed out that weaker institutions imply both lower growth for a country, as is well known, and larger effects regarding booms and busts, which is the paper's novelty. He added that bankruptcy data could better describe the quality of institutions than the rule of law measure used in the paper.

Ricardo Reis observed that the paper takes booms as given to see whether the consequences of a crash depend on bankruptcy law. However, from an ex ante perspective, bankruptcy law will likely affect why there was a credit boom in the first place and what its drivers were. This opens up exciting questions for future work: Does better bankruptcy law lead to fewer or more booms? Is the misallocation of capital during booms affected by bankruptcy law? Can bankruptcy law explain whether credit mostly goes to households or firms?

Yueran Ma replied, commenting that these are interesting questions. She added that, from an ex ante perspective, countries with more efficient

NBER Macroeconomics Annual, volume 39, 2025.
 https://doi.org/10.1086/735259

bankruptcy laws have more debt. She also pointed out that bankruptcy laws have heterogeneous effects across sectors. For example, preliminary evidence suggests that the nontradable goods sector, the main driver of credit booms, is the most affected by bankruptcy laws.

After that, Alan Auerbach pointed out that the paper measures the quality of bankruptcy law by how likely a firm with a positive going-concern value is to be restructured rather than liquidated. However, it is also important to determine how likely a firm with a negative going-concern value is to be liquidated. In this case, liquidation is the efficient outcome, and restructuring is inefficient. He further added that assessments of institutions should also consider this inefficient outcome.

Yueran Ma replied that, generally, the liquidation value of fixed assets is about 35% that of the replacement cost. Furthermore, a typical firm's continuation value is double the liquidation value even in Chapter 11 bankruptcy. She added that some data exist for the efficiency of liquidation and that empirically, the efficiency of restructuring plays a more important role for explaining macroeconomic outcomes following credit booms.

Gabriel Chodorow-Reich commented that the authors show that countries with more efficient bankruptcy laws have more cash flow–based lending rather than asset-based lending because creditors can recover their lending through the bankruptcy process. Hence, he pointed out that it is empirically challenging to disentangle whether the results in the paper should be thought of as keeping everything fixed except bankruptcy law or as varying the financial system and the credit contracts, given that these variables correlate with bankruptcy law.

Laurence J. Kotlikoff commented that understanding how long machinery is kept unutilized during the bankruptcy process is crucial to estimating the effects of bankruptcy on credit cycles.

Finally, Martin Eichenbaum pointed out that intangible capital is becoming more relevant. Furthermore, the consequences of bankruptcy law on intangibles are still an open and interesting question that should be considered in future works.

Yueran Ma agreed with Martin Eichenbaum. Returning to Alan Auerbach's comment, she added that this also points to why restructuring is usually better than liquidating for the typical firm. Finally, Yueran Ma thanked the discussants and participants for the useful comments.

2

The International Monetary Transmission Mechanism

Santiago Camara, *McGill University,* Canada
Lawrence Christiano, *Northwestern University and NBER,* United States of America
Hüsnü Dalgıc, *University of Mannheim,* Germany

I. Introduction

A. Background

Research over the past 2 decades has altered the consensus about international macroeconomics, summarized by the Mundell-Fleming model (M-F).[1] The new consensus, which remains in flux, reflects many developments. Recent advances in the measurement of exogenous US monetary policy shocks are particularly influential. Reliable measurement of these shocks makes it possible to trace out with some confidence the effects of a US monetary policy contraction.[2] As a result, much is known about how monetary shocks affect the US economy, and there has emerged a relatively settled consensus about the monetary transmission mechanism within the United States.[3] More recently, the literature has begun to explore the international effects of US monetary policy shocks, and this has produced evidence that is sharply at variance with M-F. A consensus is emerging that the key to the international transmission of US monetary shocks is financial and other frictions (see, e.g., Rey 2013; Degasperi, Hong, and Ricco 2020; Miranda-Agrippino and Rey 2020; Basu and Gopinath 2024). However, the new consensus assigns a relatively small role to trade in the transmission of monetary shocks.

NBER Macroeconomics Annual, volume 39, 2025.
 Published by The University of Chicago Press for the National Bureau of Economic Research. https://doi.org/10.1086/735260

B. *Our Main Finding*

We draw attention to the large decline in the US demand for imports that occurs after a US monetary contraction.[4] We argue that it is primarily via this decline that a US monetary contraction affects the rest of the world.[5] Informally, we reach this conclusion because we observe that the rest of the world experiences large export declines in response to a US monetary policy contraction. Absent a shift down in non-US countries' export demand, one would expect foreign exports to increase or at least stay the same when the dollar appreciates in the wake of a US monetary tightening.[6]

We begin by fitting a vector autoregression (VAR) to US data and estimating the impulse responses to a monetary shock. In our baseline analysis, we use the monetary shock produced by Bauer and Swanson (2023).[7] We also compute the response of a collection of advanced economies (AEs) and emerging market economies (EMEs), as well as Peru, because its central bank is known to engage actively in foreign exchange (FX) interventions. We use the impulse responses to characterize key facts about the international monetary transmission mechanism. Included among these facts are some (we believe) novel observations about the failure of uncovered interest rate parity (UIP). We then apply the impulse response matching procedure in Christiano, Eichenbaum, and Evans (2005) and Christiano, Trabandt, and Walentin (2011) to parameterize small open economy (SOE) models for Peru, as well the AEs and EMEs. Our models require as input the impulses to a US monetary tightening of three US variables: the US price level, the US interest rate, $R^*_{d,t}$, and US gross domestic product (GDP). These are the three US variables that matter for the residents of our AE, EME, and Peruvian models. They care about the US price level because it helps determine the terms of trade. They care about $R^*_{d,t}$ because they borrow and lend dollar assets. Finally, they care about US GDP indirectly because it shifts the demand for their exports. So, from the perspective of foreigners, a US monetary tightening represents three shocks: an $R^*_{d,t}$ shock, a terms of trade shock, and an export demand shock. We exploit the linearity of the VAR and of our linear approximation of the AE and EME models to represent the foreign impact of a US monetary tightening as the sum of the impact of these three shocks. We find that the US price shock has a negligible effect on the AEs and EMEs. The $R^*_{d,t}$ shock has a small impact. The overwhelming effect of a US monetary tightening on the AEs and EMEs appears to operate through export demand. The precise details about how a shock to US imports could have a nontrivial effect on the world economy are beyond the scope of our paper. The analysis in Di Giovanni and Hale (2022) suggests that the impact of a US trade shock may be substantial due to amplification effects associated with the global network of production.[8]

C. *The Role of Financial Frictions*

Our analysis differs from the conventional wisdom by giving trade a key role in the international transmission of a US monetary policy shock. At the same time, our analysis confirms the emerging conventional view that financial frictions play an important role in the international transmission mechanism.

Recent research on the transmission of monetary shocks considers a variety of factors such as the effects of balance sheet frictions,[9] sticky-in-dollar export prices,[10] deviations from interest rate parity and noise trading in FX markets,[11] FX interventions,[12] and other factors.[13] We require structural SOE models because understanding the role of trade and other frictions in the international monetary transmission mechanism requires contemplating counterfactuals: "What if US imports did not respond to a US monetary policy shock?" and "What if there were no balance sheet frictions?" and so forth.

To describe the role of financial frictions in our analysis, it is useful to first consider a stylized analysis of the foreign impact of a US interest rate rise in a Benchmark version of the M-F model. In this model, expenditure switching in response to a change in the exchange rate is a primary factor driving the US and foreign response to a US monetary policy shock.[14] Other factors, like financial frictions, are absent from the model. The M-F model implies that the US exchange rate appreciates following an increase in US interest rates and that the resulting expenditure switching effects drive US exports down and US imports up. With demand switching away from the United States, US GDP drops and GDP in the rest of the world expands. In contrast, the conventional view for at least a decade is that a US monetary contraction also has a contractionary impact on the rest of the world, a striking rejection of the M-F paradigm. A dramatic example of this shift in consensus is the so-called "Taper tantrum" in June 2013, when markets came to believe that the Fed intended to raise interest rates soon. In contrast to the rosy scenario implied by the simple M-F analysis, observers outside the United States (especially in the EMEs) came to expect financial instability, currency depreciation, and recession (Eichengreen and Gupta 2015). VAR evidence below provides support for the view that a rise in US interest rates leads to a reduction in rest-of-the-world output. The range of frictions listed above—balance sheet effects, interest parity frictions, and others—play an important role in the international monetary transmission mechanism.

Our VAR analysis suggests that when a US monetary policy shock perturbs the rest of the world, the latter effects do not rebound significantly back onto the United States. For this reason, and to facilitate the additive decomposition of a US monetary tightening described above, we model non-US economies as SOEs that take the United States as an exogenous source of US interest rate, US price, and export demand shocks. By not adopting a single general equilibrium model of the world economy, we avoid specifying the detailed path that a US monetary shock takes through the global trading network as it makes its way to the countries we study. This frees us to consider SOE models with a wide range of frictions.[15] We estimate our models to see which combination of frictions allows our models to reproduce our reduced-form representation of the international monetary transmission mechanism (i.e., our estimated impulse responses).

We now briefly summarize the financial frictions in the model and their role in the monetary transmission mechanism. We introduce balance sheet effects by adopting a version of the costly state verification (CSV) model in Bernanke, Gertler, and Gilchrist (1999). In this framework, there are entrepreneurs who wish to borrow to finance expenditures that drive investment. Entrepreneurs' ability to borrow is a function of their net worth. Their loans are funded in part by dollar borrowing. In this way, when a currency depreciation occurs in response to a US monetary tightening, entrepreneurs suffer capital losses, destruction of part of their net worth, and an increase in interest rate spreads. This limits their ability to borrow and drives investment down, contributing to a contraction. An outcome of our estimation exercise is that EME entrepreneurs fund a larger portion of their debt in dollars than do their counterparts in the AEs. This helps the models explain why EMEs contract more than AEs in response to the depreciation caused by a US monetary tightening.

Although the balance sheet considerations move the model in the right direction, they do not move it far enough. The literature reports extensive evidence against UIP (see, e.g., Gabaix and Maggiori 2015; Eichenbaum, Johannsen, and Rebelo 2021; Gourinchas, Ray, and Vayanos 2022; Itskhoki and Mukhin 2023; Dalgıc 2024). Our VARs suggest UIP violations may be even larger than is generally recognized. Not only do we report the well-known delayed overshooting observation (see,

finds results 1–3, as well as that EME GDP drops by more than US GDP. The Jarociński and Karadi (2020) results also take a VAR approach to identification. Still, their shock allows us to test the robustness of our results because their method of identifying a US monetary policy shock differs substantially from Bauer and Swanson's (2023). Section B in the appendix redoes the calculations in a way that makes no use of VARs at all, by doing local projections, as in Jordà (2005). The results of that analysis are consistent with 1–3 and, consistent with our baseline results, they suggest that EME GDP falls by more than US GDP.

We explore two variations on our baseline panel data VAR approach, and these imply that the fall in EME GDP, although greater than the fall in AE GDP, is about equal to the fall in US GDP. Both variations relax the restrictions in our panel VAR, without completely abandoning the VAR framework. One variation is reported in Section II.C and the other is reported in Subsection A.1 in the appendix.

All our robustness analyses support our central conclusions, 1, 2, and 3, listed above.

A. US Economy

Here, we do two things with the US data. First, in Subsection II.A, US Vector Autoregression, we estimate the response of US data to a shock in ε_t^m using a nine-variable US VAR with 12 monthly lags and treating ε_t^m as an exogenous variable, as in Paul (2020). The effects of monetary policy shocks on the US economy have been studied extensively. However, we include some variables, like imports, that do not usually appear in these studies. US imports play a key role in our analysis.

Second, in Subsection II.A, Three-Variable US VAR, we construct a three-variable, one-lag VAR that provides a near-perfect approximation to the first 3 years' responses in the three variables to a US monetary policy shock. That representation is incorporated into the SOE models estimated in Section IV. We require this representation in the models because the people in our SOEs must have a view about how three US variables—US inflation, the US interest rate, and US GDP—respond to ε_t^m.

US Vector Autoregression

Let Y_t denote the vector of endogenous US variables in the VAR. All variables are in levels, and prices and quantities are expressed in log form. The p-lag VAR is expressed as follows:

$$Y_t = A(L)Y_{t-1} + C\varepsilon_t^{mp} + u_t, \tag{1}$$

where $Eu_t u_t' = V$, and ε_t^{mp}, Y_{t-j}, $j > 0$ are orthogonal to the VAR disturbances, u_t. Also, L denotes the lag operator and

$$A(L) = A_1 + A_2 L + ... + A_p L^{p-1}.$$

We estimate V, C, and the A_i's using Bayesian methods with "Minnesota" priors. These priors suppose that all elements of Y_t are independent random walks. That is, the mean of the prior on A_1 is the identity matrix and the priors on A_i, $i > 1$ are zero matrices. In addition, under the priors the means of the elements C are zero. The prior density of $A_1, \dots, A_p$, C conditional on V is normal and the marginal density of V is inverse Wishart. So, the joint density of $V, A_1, \dots, A_p, C$ is normal inverse Wishart.[18]

The VAR is monthly and covers the period 2006–19. This sample is chosen primarily because many of the EMEs in our sample are characterized by different monetary and fiscal regimes before 2000. The nine variables in Y_t include GDP, the excess bond premium (EBP) first constructed in Gilchrist and Zakrajšek (2012), a default-free borrowing rate for firms, $R_{d,t}^*$, the personal consumption expenditures deflator (PCE), exports, imports, a trade-weighted measure of the nominal exchange rate, the S&P 500, and an index of import prices (see note to fig. 1 for additional details).[19]

Our measure of $R_{d,t}^*$ is the sum of the 2-year US Treasury bond rate plus the EBP.[20] The EBP is the excess of the interest rate paid by firms on loans over what the US Treasury pays, after adjusting for firm default risk. We assume that the EBP reflects various nonpecuniary liquidity services provided by Treasury securities, which are not provided by private debt.[21] In principle we could have computed $R_{d,t}^*$ by adding the 3-month US Treasury rate or the federal funds rate to EBP. This would have been more coherent with the SOE models we use to interpret the IRFs, in which the interest rate is a quarterly return. However, we found that with shorter-term rates, the rise in $R_{d,t}^*$ associated with a monetary tightening is much smaller. Indeed, in the case of 1-month Treasury yields, we found that $R_{d,t}^*$ actually drops. We attribute these results in part to the fact that Treasury rates with maturities shorter than 2 years are nearly constant and close to 0 for a substantial part of our sample. This is why, consistent with much of the literature, we decided to work with 2-year US Treasuries.

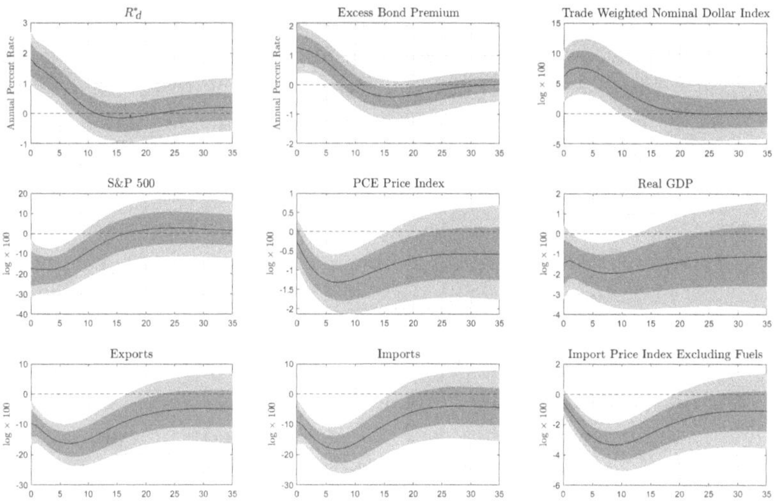

Fig. 1. Response to contractionary US monetary policy shock, United States. (1) Figure displays the response in US variables to a US monetary policy shock measured in Bauer and Swanson (2023). The dark lines are the median of the posterior distribution of the IRFs and the dark and light shaded areas correspond to 68% and 90% probability intervals. (2) The underlying 12-lag, 9-variable VAR is described in the text and is based on monthly data covering the period 2006–19. The Federal Reserve Bank of St. Louis's website, the Federal Reserve Economic Database (FRED), is the source for all variables except R^*_d, the excess bond premium, and the Standard & Poor's (S&P) 500. The mnemonic for the Import Price Index in FRED is IREXFUELS. R^*_d denotes an estimate of the interest rate paid on loans by private firms, after subtracting the component of their interest reflecting default risk (see the text for additional discussion). The excess bond premium is obtained from Favara et al. (2016). Monthly average data on the S&P 500 were obtained from Yahoo finance. (3) The S&P 500 is converted to real terms using the CPI, as are exports and imports. (4) US real gross domestic product (GDP) series are available on a quarterly basis. We use Stock and Watson's (2010) monthly GDP data obtained by multivariate interpolation of monthly real GDP series. PCE = personal consumption expenditure.

GDP, exports, imports, and the S&P 500 are converted into real terms by dividing by the consumer price index (CPI). We convert the data in this way because it facilitates matching the data results with our model where data are measured in units of the model CPI.[22] Finally, the quantity data are converted to logs when we estimate the VARs. All variables fed to the VARs are in levels or log levels.

The estimated IRFs to the ε_t^{mp} are displayed in figure 1. The dark lines are the mean of the posterior distribution of the IRFs to (not-normalized) ε_t^{mp} and the dark and light shaded areas correspond to 68% and 90% probability intervals. There are several things worth noting about this figure. First, for variables that overlap with other studies, the IRFs are qualitatively similar.[23] GDP, equity prices, and the price level drop. The exchange rate appreciates for a few periods before depreciating. We discuss this delayed overshooting feature of the exchange rate in Subsection V.E. Consistent with our interpretation of the EBP, that variable rises in the wake of a monetary tightening because a tightening is implemented by making liquidity scarce and thus increasing its marginal value. Second, note that the decline in imports is large by comparison with the percentage decline in GDP. Moreover, the probability interval around the mode is very tight and far from zero. Third, when we estimate the model with only one lag in the VAR, we get very similar results. In addition, when we further reduce the system to the three variables, $R^*_{d,t}$, GDP, and PCE, we also get similar results for those variables.

The final feature worth noting about the results in figure 1 is the decline in the price index for imports. As discussed in the introduction, the result for the price index suggests that the fall in imports is driven by US demand. It is not predominantly driven by a reduction in the supply of imported goods, caused by, say, an increase in financial frictions in non-US economies due to the US monetary tightening.

Three-Variable US VAR

In our model analysis, we require that people be able to forecast the impact of a US monetary tightening on three US variables, $R^*_{d,t}$, GDP, and PCE. Our computational strategy for analyzing the SOE models requires that we provide the IRFs in recursive form. In principle, we could simply insert our US VAR into the model. However, the empirical results reported above suggest that there exists a much simpler recursive representation for the IRFs.[24]

The variables that are of interest for people in foreign economies responding to a US monetary tightening are

$$\hat{Y}_t = \begin{pmatrix} 100\log\left(\frac{\pi^f_t}{\pi^f}\right) \\ 400\left(R^*_{d,t} - R^*_d\right) \\ 100\log\left(\frac{y^f_t}{y^f}\right) \end{pmatrix}. \tag{2}$$

Here, $\pi^f_t \equiv P^f_t/P^f_{t-1}$, where P^f_t denotes the US PCE price index. Also, y^f_t is a variable in our SOE model that corresponds to a transitory component of US GDP.[25] In each case, the variables are measured in log deviation from steady state. The middle term in $\hat{Y}_t$ is measured in annual percentage. We adopt the following recursive representation of $\hat{Y}_t$:

$$\hat{Y}_t = A\hat{Y}_{t-1} + D\varepsilon_t^{mp}, \tag{3}$$

where D is a 3×1 column vector and ε_t^p denotes the Bauer and Swanson (2023) monetary policy shock index.

Setting $\hat{Y}_0 = 0$, we compute n responses, $\hat{Y}_1, \ldots, \hat{Y}_n$ to $\varepsilon_1^{mp} = 1$ and $\varepsilon_t^{mp} = 0$ for $t > 1$ using equation (3). Then,

$$\hat{Y}_1 = D.$$

Also,

$$\hat{Y}_j = A^{j-1}\hat{Y}_1 = A^{j-1}D,$$

for $j = 2, \ldots, n$. In this way, we obtain the n IRFs, $[\hat{Y}_1, \ldots, \hat{Y}_n]$, are a function of D and A.

We convert the sequence, $[\hat{Y}_1, \ldots, \hat{Y}_n]$, into $[\hat{\mathcal{Y}}_1, \ldots, \hat{\mathcal{Y}}_n]$, where the second two terms in $\hat{\mathcal{Y}}_j$ coincide with the second two terms of $\hat{Y}_j$, and the first element of $\hat{\mathcal{Y}}_j$ is the cumulative sum of the first element of $\hat{Y}_j$, $j = 1, \ldots, n$. In this way, the first and third elements of $\hat{\mathcal{Y}}_j$ correspond to the response of $\log P_j^f$ and $\log \text{GDP}_j$ respectively. The way we handle GDP is determined by the assumption in our SOE model that GDP is the product of a temporary component, y_t^f, which is affected by ε_t^m and a permanent component, $\mathcal{Z}_t$, which is not affected by ε_t^m.

The empirical VARs that we estimate are based on monthly data, whereas the SOE models are quarterly. So, each of the n quarters is divided into 3 months. The first month of quarter t is $t - 2/3$, the second month is $t - 1/3$, and the third month is t, for $t = 1, \ldots, n$.

Let $\{\xi_t\}$ denote the $3n$ monthly IRFs from the VAR analysis (i.e., fig. 1). Here, the elements of ξ_t correspond to the monthly log price, monthly annualized interest rate, and monthly log GDP. Let ξ_t^Q, $t = 1, \ldots, n$ denote the corresponding quarterly data. We assume that quarterly price and GDP are well approximated by the geometric average over the months in the quarter. The interest rate is the arithmetic average. Thus,

$$\xi_t^Q = \frac{1}{3}[\xi_t + \xi_{t-1/3} + \xi_{t-2/3}],$$

for $t = 1, \ldots, n$.

Conditional on A and D we can compute the model's IRFs, $[\hat{\mathcal{Y}}_1, \ldots, \hat{\mathcal{Y}}_n]$, as described above. The empirical counterparts of $[\hat{\mathcal{Y}}_1, \ldots, \hat{\mathcal{Y}}_n]$ are $[\xi_1^Q,$

$\xi_2^Q, \ldots, \xi_n^Q]$. We set $D = \xi_1^Q$, where $t = 1$ denotes the period of the US monetary tightening shock. Now, we only need A to compute $[\hat{\mathcal{Y}}_1, \ldots, \hat{\mathcal{Y}}_n]$. We choose A to minimize a measure of distance between $[\xi_1^Q, \ldots, \xi_n^Q]$ and $[\hat{\mathcal{Y}}_1, \ldots, \hat{\mathcal{Y}}_n]$. Let σ_j denote the 3×1 column vector containing the standard deviations, under the posterior distribution, of each of the elements of $\xi_j^Q, j = 1, \ldots, n$. Then, A solves

$$\min_A \sum_{j=1}^{n} \left(\xi_j^Q - \hat{\mathcal{Y}}_j\right)' \Lambda_j^{-1} \left(\xi_j^Q - \hat{\mathcal{Y}}_j\right),$$

where Λ_j is a 3×3 diagonal matrix with the vector, σ_j, along its diagonal. In effect, in choosing the values of A we downplay the VAR IRFs, which are imprecisely measured.

The outcome of our algorithm for computing D, A with $n = 12$ based on the responses in figure 1 is

$$D = \begin{bmatrix} -0.58 \\ 0.41 \\ -1.42 \end{bmatrix}, A = \begin{bmatrix} 0 & -1.40 & -0.08 \\ 0.22 & 0.98 & 0.02 \\ 0.43 & -0.35 & 0.95 \end{bmatrix}, \quad (4)$$

where A has three eigenvalues, $0.5 \pm 0.31i$, 0.92. Consistent with the assumption in our SOE model, the three-variable VAR model we provide to it for the foreign variables is covariance stationary. Because all eigenvalues of A lie inside the unit circle, the impact of an ε_t^m shock eventually goes to 0.

The eigenvalues of the empirical VAR also lie, with one exception, inside the unit circle. The exception is an eigenvalue equal to 1.001. So, technically, the impact of shocks, including ε_t^m, eventually diverge in the estimated VAR underlying figure 1. Still, there are three reasons that we are comfortable providing the covariance stationary representation, equation (3), to our SOE models. First, Figure 2 shows that at the 3-year horizon, shocks appear to be converging. Second, though the impact of shocks diverge eventually, they remain centered at zero in the sense that probability intervals, although also diverging, include a zero response. Third, we also estimated a three-variable, one-period lag, VAR for ξ_t using monthly data. That estimated VAR produces IRFs for ξ_t very similar to the ones in figure 1, but they have all eigenvalues lying inside the unit circle. These three observations convince us that equation (3) provides a useful recursive representation of the response of US data over the 1- or 2-year horizon that our analysis focuses on.

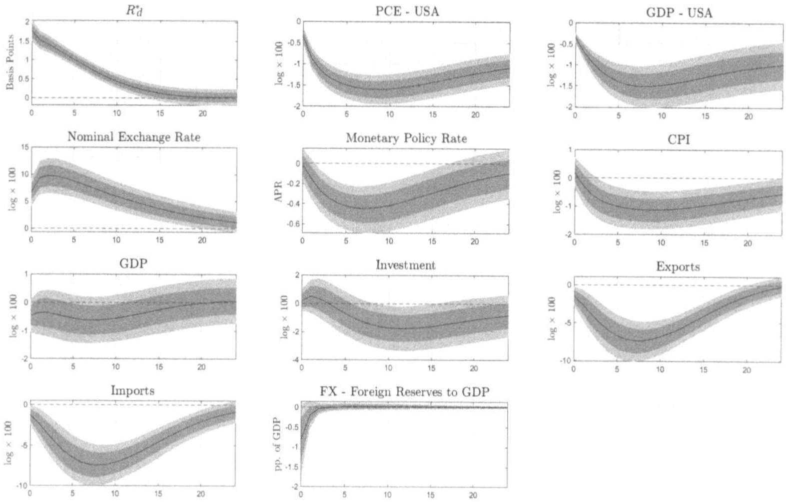

Fig. 2. Response to contractionary US monetary policy shock, AEs. Impulses from the panel VAR estimation for the AE countries: Australia, Canada, Germany, Israel, Japan, Norway, South Korea, Sweden, Switzerland, and United Kingdom. Solid lines correspond to the mode of the Bayesian posterior, dark shaded areas correspond to the 68% probability intervals, and the light shaded areas correspond to 90% probability intervals. The data sample is monthly, 2006–19. FX intervention, relative gross domestic product (GDP), obtained from Adler et al. (2024). The first row of graphs display the response of US variables to the monetary policy shock, when lagged values of the foreign variables are included in the VAR (see Subsec. II.B for discussion). Differences in the first-row responses from the corresponding impulse responses in figure 1 indicate feedback effects from the rest of the world to the United States, which we ignore in our modeling analysis. We interpret the graphs as indicating little (but not zero) feedback. PCE = personal consumption expenditure; CPI = consumer price index; FX = foreign exchange.

Figure 2 graphs the impulse response of the foreign interest rate, the log level of the PCE price index and the log level of GDP. The dots correspond to the simulations from the constructed model, equation (3). The solid lines are taken from figure 1, as are the dark (68%) and light (90%) shaded areas. The dots are "close" to the solid line in the sense that they are only barely distinguishable, visually, from the solid line.

Note that integer values of t in figure 3 correspond to months, which is inconsistent with the treatment elsewhere in this section, where integer values of t correspond to quarters. Throughout this paper we adopt the following convention: When VAR and SOE data are presented in the same graph, the time interval is monthly. When SOE data are displayed in a graph not including VAR data, then the time interval is quarterly.

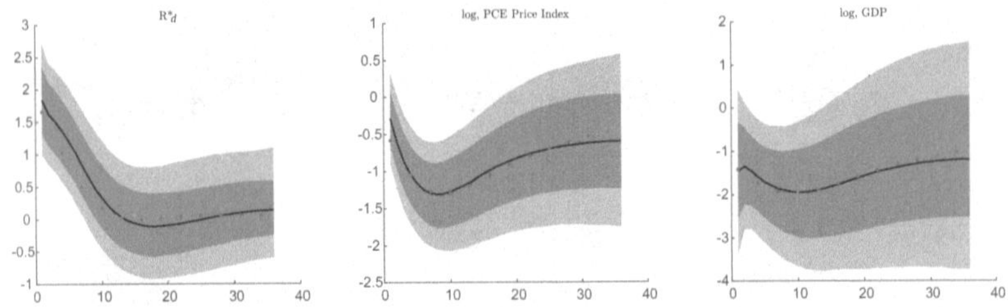

Fig. 3. Responses to US monetary shock implied by SOE model. Solid line: IRFs in figure 1 with the associated probability intervals in dark and light shade. Dots: IRFs to $\varepsilon_t^m = 1$ for $t = 1$ and $\varepsilon_t^m = 0$ for $t > 1$, with $\hat{Y}_0 = 0$. The dots correspond to the simulated $\hat{Y}_t$'s, after converting to $\hat{\mathcal{Y}}_t$ as discussed in the text. PCE = personal consumption expenditure; GDP = gross domestic product.

B. Non-US Economies

In this section we estimate the average impact of a contractionary US monetary policy shock on a set of AEs and EMEs. In addition, we report results for Peru.

In the case of each non-US VAR, we include data on the three US variables: the interest rate, inflation, and GDP. Including these US variables allows a monetary policy shock to have both a direct impact on non-US economies' data and an indirect impact via dynamic responses in the three US variables. In addition, we potentially allow non-US countries' variables to feed back onto the US economy. In our SOE model analysis, we abstract from the latter form of feedback. Comparing the IRFs with a US monetary policy shock in the three US variables—the interest rate, inflation, and GDP—with the corresponding IRFs in figure 1 sheds light on the appropriateness of our no-feedback assumption. We do see differences, but they appear to be quantitatively small.

In Subsection II.B, Panel VAR, we present our baseline VAR results. See the online appendix for robustness of our results to alternative measures of monetary policy shocks and alternative ways of estimating impulse responses.

Panel VAR

Our VAR for the *i*th non-US economy is

$$Y_{i,t} = A_1 Y_{i,t-1} + A_2 Y_{i,t-2} + C\varepsilon_t^{mp} + \varepsilon_{i,t}, \qquad (5)$$

where

$$Y_{i,t} = \begin{bmatrix} \tilde{Y}_t \\ Y_t^i \end{bmatrix}, \tag{6}$$

and $\tilde{Y}_t$ denotes the 3×1 vector of US variables composed of log GDP, R_d^*, and PCE. These are the US variables that affect foreign economies captured by our SOE models below. As noted above, we found that when the US analysis in Subsection II.A was redone with a US three-variable, one-lag VAR, the IRFs to the Bauer and Swanson (2023) shock are very similar to what we see in figure 1.

Also, Y_t^i denotes an 8×1 vector of variables for country i: GDP, nominal exchange rate (foreign currency per dollar), domestic monetary policy rate, CPI, gross private domestic investment, exports, imports, and a measure of central bank FX intervention, as a percentage of the 3-year moving average in GDP. The purpose of dividing by a backward-looking moving average of GDP is to reduce endogeneity of the denominator in the share, at least for the first few months after a shock. Apart from the FX intervention variable and the policy rate, all variables are measured in log levels and the sample mean is removed, thus setting the constant terms VARs to 0. We obtain the central bank FX intervention data from Adler et al. (2024).[26]

When we estimate the system in equation (5), we do not zero out the top right 3×8 blocks in A_1 and A_2 which govern feedback from movements in the foreign variables, Y_t^i, to the US variables, $\tilde{Y}_t$. This fact allows us to evaluate our assumption in the US VAR and in our model analysis that the rebound effect on the United States from the foreign impact of US monetary policy shocks is small.

The panel VAR is structured as follows:

$$\begin{bmatrix} Y_{1,t} \\ Y_{2,t} \\ \vdots \\ Y_{N,t} \end{bmatrix} = \begin{bmatrix} A_1 & 0 & \cdots & 0 \\ 0 & A_1 & & \vdots \\ \vdots & & \ddots & 0 \\ 0 & 0 & \cdots & A_1 \end{bmatrix} \begin{bmatrix} Y_{1,t-1} \\ Y_{2,t-1} \\ \vdots \\ Y_{N,t-1} \end{bmatrix} + \begin{bmatrix} A_2 & 0 & \cdots & 0 \\ 0 & A_2 & & \vdots \\ \vdots & & \ddots & 0 \\ 0 & 0 & \cdots & A_2 \end{bmatrix} \begin{bmatrix} Y_{1,t-2} \\ Y_{2,t-2} \\ \vdots \\ Y_{N,t-2} \end{bmatrix} + \begin{bmatrix} C \\ C \\ \vdots \\ C \end{bmatrix} \epsilon_t^{mp} + \begin{bmatrix} \epsilon_{1,t} \\ \epsilon_{2,t} \\ \vdots \\ \epsilon_{N,t} \end{bmatrix}, \tag{7}$$

where N denotes the number of countries and the dimension of C conforms with the dimension of $Y_{i,t}$. We apply a similar Bayesian method to estimate equation (7) as in the case of the US VAR in equation (1).

The difference here is the zero restrictions in equation (7) as well as the assumption that A_1, A_2, and C are the same across countries. In words, we impose that for each i, Y_t^i (*a*) responds only to the country's own lagged data and lagged data on the three US variables in $\tilde{Y}_t$, and (*b*) the responses are the same for all i's among the AEs and for all i's among the EMEs.

We impose (*a*) and (*b*) in part to minimize the number of parameters to be estimated. Our effective data sample is short. As noted above, this is due only in part to data limitations. We think that the monetary and regulatory regimes in place, especially in the EMEs, were very different before the 2000s, and we exclude these data, plus a few years to accommodate a transition, from the analysis. We interpret our IRFs for the AE and EME countries as an average over the individual country responses, which is perhaps more reliably estimated than the individual responses. Later, we show evidence that this interpretation is valid.

Impulse Responses of Estimated Panel VARs

The official International Monetary Fund (IMF) list of AEs is provided in IMF (2023). With one exception, we use data taken from the IMF's International Financial Statistics (IFS) to ensure cross-country comparability. The exception is that we take the FX intervention data from Adler et al. (2024) for the reasons explained above. In the case of AEs, we exclude some countries. In particular, we only include one country, Germany, from the euro area.[27] Similarly, we exclude Denmark because it pegs its exchange rate to the euro. Iceland, Taiwan, and Singapore are not included in our data analysis because their nominal GDP data do not appear in the IFS. Our AE panel consists of equation (7) with $N = 10$ countries: Australia, Canada, Germany, Israel, Japan, Norway, South Korea, Sweden, Switzerland, and United Kingdom.[28]

Turning to emerging markets, Duttagupta and Pazarbasioglu (2021) report that the IMF does not have an official definition of an EME. We work with the designation suggested in Duttagupta and Pazarbasioglu (2021), except that we also include Peru.[29] That country is of special interest to us because it is very transparent about its active intervention in the FX market. We exclude China because their nominal GDP is not included in the IFS. Our EME panel has $N = 14$ countries: Brazil, Chile, Colombia, Hungary, India, Indonesia, Mexico, Peru, the Philippines, Poland, Russia, South Africa, Thailand, Turkey. Our data set is monthly and covers the period 2006–19.

We begin by reporting the results for AEs displayed in figure 2. The top row of the figure displays the responses of the three US variables in $\tilde{Y}_t$. The model responses (the mode of the posterior distribution, the dark line) are similar to the corresponding responses in figure 1 in the sense that they lie inside the latter figure's 68% probability intervals. As noted above, the US IRFs in figure 2 are allowed to respond to lagged values of individual country variables. The similarity of the US responses across figures 1 and 2 is consistent with the idea that the rebound effect of US monetary shocks back onto the United States via their impact on non-US AEs is small.[30]

There are five other features of the results in figure 2 worth noting. First, the AE's exchange rate depreciates substantially after a US monetary tightening, as one would expect. In percentage terms, the magnitude is somewhat larger than the results for the trade-weighted US exchange rate reported in figure 1. This may reflect the absence from our data set of some countries that the United States trades with, especially China. Second, the mode of our results suggest that AE central banks sell dollars after a monetary tightening. But the probability intervals are sufficiently wide that they include the case of no response. Third, although the modal impulse response of GDP indicates that GDP falls, the percentage drop is substantially smaller than the nearly 2% drop in US GDP. Fourth, the drop in exports is substantially larger, in percentage terms, than the drop in GDP. Fifth, the relatively weak fall in GDP may reflect the estimated significant accommodative response by the AE monetary authorities (see the 2,2 panel of fig. 1).

Next, we turn to figure 4, which displays our results for the EMEs. First, note that as in the case of the AEs, there is a substantial currency depreciation. Second, the estimate of central bank FX interventions is fairly tightly centered on zero, with the 90% probability interval ranging from −0.5% to 0.5% of GDP. This is somewhat surprising in light of the evidence in Adler et al. (2024), which shows that EMEs conduct larger FX interventions than AEs. Third, the modal percentage drop in GDP is substantial, roughly three times the drop in the United States. Fourth, another difference between EMEs and the AEs is that the former actually raise the local currency units (LCU) policy rate whereas, as noted above, the latter reduce that rate. Fifth, by comparing figures 2 and 4, we can see that the LCU expected return on a round trip through the dollar exchange market rises by the same amount in the AEs and the EMEs. As a result, the rise in the EME interest rate premium relative to the rise in the AE interest rate premium can be inferred by the relative

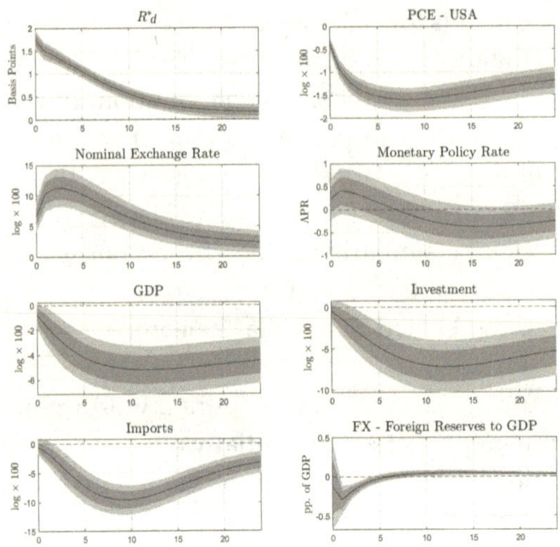

Fig. 4. Response to contractionary US monetary policy shock, emerging markets. Response to a unit shock in ε_t^m in panel VAR results for EMEs, Brazil, Chile, Colombia, Hungary, India, Indonesia, Mexico, Peru, the Philippines, Poland, Russia, South Africa, Thailand, and Turkey. For more information, see note to figure 2. PCE = personal consumption expenditure; GDP = gross domestic product; CPI = consumer price index; FX = foreign exchange.

movement of their policy rates. In particular, the relative rise in the EME premium is in the neighborhood of 20–40 basis points. Although interesting, this magnitude is small by comparison with the roughly 175 basis point rise in R_d^*.

We also report results for estimating equation (5) when *i* corresponds to Peru (see fig. 5). We do this in part because we are interested in analyzing the effects of FX intervention. According to data published by the Peruvian central bank, we can see that Peru frequently intervenes in FX markets (see fig. 27 in the appendix, http://www.nber.org/data-appendix/c14997/appendix.pdf). Note that the initial response of FX intervention to a US monetary tightening is to reduce FX reserves by about 4% of GDP. This mode for FX intervention is much larger than what we obtained based on all EMEs (see fig. 4), where the mode of the drop is small and the probability interval is also small. Also, the probability interval of the Peruvian data is tight enough to easily exclude zero. To have a sense of the size of this number, recall that we have not renormalized the US monetary tightening shock, and that R_d^* rises by about 170 basis points

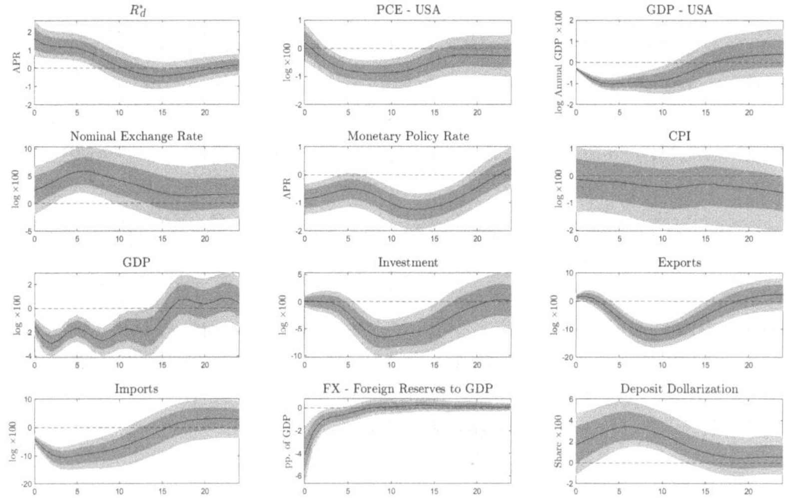

Fig. 5. Response to contractionary US monetary policy shock, Peru. For more information, see note to figure 2. Response to unit shock in ε_t^m in equation (5) for i corresponding to Peru. Parameters estimated on monthly data, 2006–19. Solid lines correspond to the mode of the Bayesian posterior, dark shaded areas correspond to the 68% probability intervals and the light shaded areas correspond to 90% probability intervals. PCE = personal consumption expenditure; GDP = gross domestic product; CPI = consumer price index; FX = foreign exchange.

at an annual rate. So, if we think of a 25 basis point US tightening then we must scale all the IRFs by approximately 7.

C. *Country-by-Country Impulse Responses*

The panel VARs studied in the previous section do not fully satisfy the assumptions underlying the derivation of the likelihood for the Bayesian VAR. In deriving the likelihood, Dieppe, Legrand, and Van Roye (2016) assume that $E\varepsilon_{i,t}\varepsilon_{j,t}^{'} = 0$ for $i \neq j$. At the same time, we include the US data in each $Y_{i,t}$ in equation (6) for each i, so that the covariance assumption on the disturbances cannot be satisfied. In addition, it seems implausible that shocks to different countries within the AEs and within the EMEs are uncorrelated. We avoid violating these covariance assumptions by estimating equation (5) separately for each country, i, in our sample. In addition, we delete the first three equations in equation (5), so that no covariance assumption is obviously violated in the VAR.

We compute IRFs for each country in our data set, except the United States. We then group the IRFs according to whether they come from an EME or an AE. The responses to a US monetary tightening are displayed in figure 6. The solid lines indicate the median, across countries in the AEs, of the median response at each horizon. The shaded area around the line presents the interquartile range of median responses at each horizon. Similarly, the starred line corresponds to EMEs and the shaded area around it indicates the associated interquartile range of responses. The figures convey roughly the same message as figures 2 and 4. GDP and investment falls by more in EMEs than in AEs, whereas the price level falls somewhat less in EMEs compared with what happens in AEs. There is one quantitative difference. The average fall in EME GDP after a US monetary contraction is smaller in figure 6 than is reported in figure 4. That fall is roughly equal to the fall in US GDP in the first year, and less so afterward.

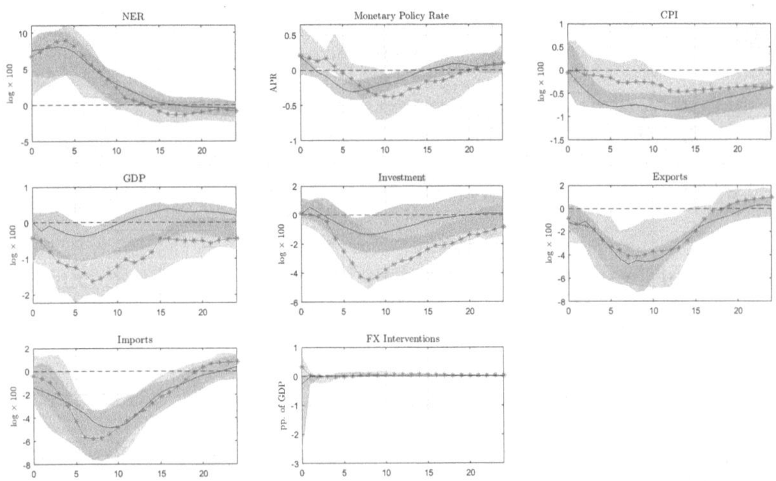

Fig. 6. Country-by-country impulse responses within EMEs and AEs. IRFs over 24 months to a US monetary tightening shock as measured in Bauer and Swanson (2023). We estimate a version of equation (5) separately for each country, *i*. The version of equation (5) that we use drops the first three equations but keeps the lagged US data as exogenous variables in the other equations. For each country we compute the median under the posterior distribution of the IRFs. The line in the above figure with stars (solid line) is the cross-country average of the median impulse response across the EME (AE) economies. At each lag, the shaded region around its respective line indicates the interquartile range across responses among EMEs (AEs). With one exception, the results convey a similar message as figures 2 and 4. An exception is that EME gross domestic product (GDP), although falling more than AE GDP, falls roughly the amount that US GDP falls in figure 1. All data are the same as the data underlying figure 1. Here, NER corresponds to "nominal exchange rate." CPI = consumer price index; FX = foreign exchange.

III. Model

The model we use is a fairly standard New Keynesian (NK) SOE model. It is closest to a streamed-down version of Christiano, Trabandt, and Walentin (2011), which in turn builds on Adolfson et al. (2007). The model is closely related to other models, including Gertler, Gilchrist, and Natalucci (2007) and Castillo and Medina (2021). The discussion below summarizes agents' problems and the market clearing conditions. For details about how a set of equilibrium conditions is derived and solved, see the appendix (http://www.nber.org/data-appendix/c14997/appendix.pdf).

One feature our model leaves out is the possibility of panic-based rollover crises, especially in response to capital losses resulting from exchange rate changes. This possibility has received a lot of attention, especially in the discussions of pre-2000s crises. In part, we leave this possibility out for tractability reasons. In part, the likelihood of such crises has been reduced in our sample period by regulations that move currency mismatch off the balance sheets of high-leverage banks and onto the balance sheets of lower-leveraged nonbank institutions (see Christiano, Dalgıc, and Nurbekyan 2021 for additional discussion). In addition, the greater dollar liquidity governments hold increases their ability to intervene in the case of trouble. Christiano, Dalgıc, and Li (2022) shows that in standard rollover crisis models, only a modest liquidity injection is sufficient to prevent a panic run from being an equilibrium.

A. Households

There is a representative household with preferences,

$$E_0 \sum_{t=0}^{\infty} \beta^t \left\{ u(C_t) - \frac{\ell_t^{1+\varphi}}{1+\varphi} - h_t(\Theta_t) \right\},$$

where ℓ_t denotes employment, C_t denotes consumption, and Θ_t denotes the household's share of financial wealth held in dollars. Also, $h_t(\Theta_t)$ denotes a nonpecuniary cost of deviating from a target portfolio, Y_t. In particular,

$$\Theta_t \equiv \frac{S_t D_t^*}{S_t D_t^* + D_t}, h_t(\Theta_t) = \frac{\gamma}{2}(\Theta_t - Y_t)^2, Y_t = Y + \gamma_{R^*}\left(R_{d,t}^* - R_d^*\right) + \gamma_\Theta(\Theta_t - \bar{\Theta}_{t-1}) + e_t^Y. \quad (8)$$

Here, Y_t denotes the time t target portfolio share of dollars, and Y denotes the value of that target in steady state. The term involving $\bar{\Theta}_t - \bar{\Theta}_{t-1}$ with portfolio inertia parameter $\gamma_\Theta < 0$, is a reduced-form representation of adjustment costs in adjusting portfolios' frictions. Such adjustment costs were proposed by Bacchetta, Davenport, and Van Wincoop (2022) to explain features of capital flows and asset prices. The object, e_t^γ, is a "noise" shock to the household's target, which has a first-order autoregressive representation. Also, the risk appetite parameter, $\gamma_{R_d^*} > 0$, captures the idea that when $R_{d,t}^*$ is high, people prefer dollar assets, perhaps because of a decrease in "risk appetite," or "flight to safety." The target portfolio cost parameter is given by $\gamma > 0$. The variable D_t^* denotes the household's end-of-period t holdings of dollar assets that pay $R_{d,t}^*$ gross interest in dollars in period $t + 1$. The variables S_t and D_t denote the number of LCU per dollar, and D_t denotes the end-of-period t holdings of LCU domestic assets that pay $R_{d,d}$ gross interest in LCU in period $t + 1$. The household's flow budget constraint is

$$S_t D_t^* + D_t + P_t^c C_t + E_t Q_{t,t+1} a_{t,t+1} = S_t R_{d,t-1}^* D_{t-1}^* + R_{d,t-1} D_{t-1} + W_t \ell_t + \Pi_t - T_t + a_{t-1,t}. \tag{9}$$

The terms on the left and right of the equality correspond to the household's period t purchases and receipts in LCU. In equation (9), W_t denotes a competitive wage. Also, Π_t and T_t denote lump-sum profits and taxes, respectively. In period t the household purchases $a_{t,t+1}$ units of LCU to be delivered conditional on the state of nature in period $t + 1$.[31] The price of one such unit of LCU, scaled by the period t conditional density of its state of nature, is denoted $Q_{t,t+1}$. The conditional expectation is a convenient way to express the total cost of all possible $t + 1$ Arrow securities in period t. The object, $a_{t-1,t}$ on the right of the above equality, represents the payoff on the Arrow security purchased in $t - 1$, given the realized state of nature in t. The Arrow security market is one in which households participate with domestic banks, and it is discussed further below. For later purposes, it is useful to note that household optimality requires that household consumption satisfy:

$$v_{t+1} \equiv \frac{\beta u'(C_{t+1})}{\pi_{t+1}^c u'(C_t)} = Q_{t,t+1}. \tag{10}$$

As is well known, one can derive the model's implications for interest parity from the optimality condition associated with the household's choice of Θ_t. After linearizing this expression about nonstochastic steady state,

$$E_t \log(S_{t+1}) - \log(S_t) + \log\left(R_{d,t}^*\right) + \Lambda_t = \log(R_{d,t}), \tag{11}$$

where the UIP deviation, Λ_t, has the following form:

$$\Lambda_t = \gamma(Y_t - \Theta_t). \tag{12}$$

The object on the left of the equality in (11) is the total return (i.e., the pecuniary and nonpecuniary parts) on holding dollar assets, in LCU. The first part, involving the prospective log change in the exchange rate, corresponds to the return on the round trip through the exchange market. The next term is the dollar return. Finally, the UIP deviation, Λ_t, is the nonpecuniary return on dollars. Note that when the share of dollars in the household's portfolio exceeds target then the nonpecuniary return is negative. UIP corresponds to $\gamma = 0$ and is violated in the IRFs presented above. For example, a period t US monetary tightening creates an anticipated depreciation from t to $t + 1$ and simultaneously raises the premium on the US interest rate, $R_{d,t}^* - R_{d,t}$, so that $\Lambda_t < 0$.

B. *Homogeneous Domestic Goods*

A homogeneous nontradable good, Y_t, is produced using domestic capital and labor using the Dixit-Stiglitz structure typical in closed economy NK models. In particular, Y_t is produced using a continuum of intermediate inputs, $Y_{i,t}$, $i \in [0, 1]$, as follows:

$$Y_t = \left[\int_0^1 Y_{i,t}^{\frac{\varepsilon-1}{\varepsilon}} di\right]^{\frac{\varepsilon}{\varepsilon-1}}, \varepsilon > 1. \tag{13}$$

The representative, competitive firm that produces Y_t takes the output price and input prices, P_t and $P_{i,t}$, $i \in [0, 1]$, as given. This firm maximizes profits and the first-order necessary condition associated with the choice of $Y_{i,t}$ constitutes the demand curve faced by a monopoly producer of $Y_{i,t}$.

The monopoly producer of $Y_{i,t}$ chooses a point, $Y_{i,t}$ and $P_{i,t}$, on the demand curve that maximizes profits subject to the production technology,

$$Y_{i,t} = \tilde{K}_{i,t}^{\alpha}(A_t \ell_{i,t})^{1-\alpha}, 0 < 1 < \alpha. \tag{14}$$

Here, $\tilde{K}_{i,t}$ and $\ell_{i,t}$ denote the quantity of capital labor services hired by the ith monopoly producer in period t. Also, A_t denotes the period t state of technology. In this paper we only consider foreign monetary policy shocks and we assume these have no impact on A_t, so A_t grows at its constant steady-state rate. That is, $\log(A_t/A_{t-1}) = \Delta a$, where $\Delta a > 0$ represents the steady-state growth rate of A_t. The assumptions about preferences and technology guarantee balanced growth, and we exploit that when solving the model.

In equilibrium, the aggregate capital services used by monopoly producers must be equal to supply, $\int_i \tilde{K}_{i,t}\, di = K_{t-1}$. The latter has time subscript $t-1$ because the time t supply of capital services is determined in period $t-1$ (see Sec. III.D).

Monopoly producers are subject to Calvo price frictions

$$P_{i,t} = \begin{cases} \tilde{P}_t & \text{with probability } 1-\theta \\ P_{i,t-1} & \text{with probability } \theta \end{cases}. \tag{15}$$

Monopoly producers are competitive in the input markets where they pay r_t and W_t for capital and labor services, respectively. They choose their price to maximize discounted profits subject to its demand curve, equations (14) and (15), and the given factor prices.

C. *Final Goods*

Three final goods are produced using constant elasticity of substitution production functions that combine domestic nontradable (the homogeneous good) and imports. Each production function is operated by a profit-maximizing representative, competitive producer taking the output and input prices as given. In equilibrium, these producers make zero profits. The first subsection discusses the consumption and investment goods. The second discusses the export good.

Consumption and Investment

The production functions are given by

$$I_t = \left[\gamma_I^{\frac{1}{\nu_I}} I_{d,t}^{\frac{\nu_I-1}{\nu_I}} + (1-\gamma_I)^{\frac{1}{\nu_I}} I_{m,t}^{\frac{\nu_I-1}{\nu_I}}\right]^{\frac{\nu_I}{\nu_I-1}},$$

$$C_t = \left[(1-\omega_c)^{\frac{1}{\eta_c}} (C_{d,t})^{\frac{\eta_c-1}{\eta_c}} + \omega_c^{\frac{1}{\eta_c}} (C_{m,t})^{\frac{\eta_c-1}{\eta_c}}\right]^{\frac{\eta_c}{\eta_c-1}},$$

where I_t and C_t denote investment and consumption goods, respectively. Also, ν_I and η_c denote the elasticities of substitution between the domestically produced homogeneous and imported goods. These are indicated by the subscripts, d and m, respectively. The prices of consumption and investment goods are P_t^c and P_t^I, respectively. The price of the domestic input is P_t in both cases, as discussed in Subsection III.B. The price of the imported good is $S_t P_t^f$, where P_t^f denotes the dollar price of foreign goods.

Exports and the Dominant Currency Paradigm

Foreign GDP, Y_t^f, is modeled as the product of a permanent component, $\mathcal{Z}_t$, and a transitory component, y_t^f, as follows:

$$Y_t^f = y_t^f \mathcal{Z}_t. \tag{16}$$

The monetary shock is assumed to affect Y_t^f exclusively via its transitory component, y_t^f (see Subsection II.A, Three-Variable US VAR), while leaving $\mathcal{Z}_t$ undisturbed. In a version of the model with more shocks, $\mathcal{Z}_t$ would be affected by technology shocks, which we assume are orthogonal to the monetary shock. Because our focus is on IRFs to monetary policy shocks, we can abstract from those other shocks.[32] We assume that $\mathcal{Z}_t$ grows at its steady-state rate, which we denote by Δa. The demand for exports, X_t, is given by

$$X_t = \left(\frac{P_t^X}{P_t^f}\right)^{-\eta_f} \left[\left(\frac{y_t^f}{y^f}\right)^{\gamma_f} \mathcal{Z}_t\right], \tag{17}$$

where P_t^X/P_t^f denotes the terms of trade; $\eta_f > 0$ denotes the elasticity of demand with respect to the terms of trade; and γ_f denotes the elasticity of the export demand shifter (the term in square brackets in eq. [17]) with respect to the transitory component of GDP.

The domestic production function for exports is

$$X_t = \left[\gamma_X^{\frac{1}{\eta_X}} (X_{d,t})^{\frac{\eta_X - 1}{\eta_X}} + (1 - \gamma_X)^{\frac{1}{\eta_X}} (X_{m,t})^{\frac{\eta_X - 1}{\eta_X}}\right]^{\frac{\eta_X}{\eta_X - 1}}, \tag{18}$$

where X_t denotes the quantity of exports. The quantities of the domestically produced good and imports are indicated by the subscripts d and m, respectively. The prices of the output good, P_t^X, and of the domestically produced good, $P_t^{d,X}$, and the imported good, P_t^f, are all denominated in dollars. Taking these as given, the representative exporter chooses inputs and output to maximize profits. In equilibrium, those profits are zero.

Gopinath et al. (2020) and others report that not only is much of world trade invoiced in dollars but the price of traded goods is actually sticky in dollars. To capture this observation, we adopt a version of the Calvo sticky-price mechanism in Subsection III.B, which implies that $P_t^{d,x}$ is sticky in dollars. We suppose that $X_{d,t}$ is produced by a representative competitive firm using a production function similar to equation (13):

$$X_{d,t} = \left[\int_0^1 X_{i,t}^{\frac{\varepsilon_X - 1}{\varepsilon_X}} di\right]^{\frac{\varepsilon_X}{\varepsilon_X - 1}}, \varepsilon_X > 1.$$

This production function is operated by a representative, competitive firm that takes the output price, $P_t^{d,X}$, and input prices, $P_{i,t}^{d,X}$, $i \in [0,1]$, as given. The ith input, $X_{i,t}$, is produced by a monopolist using $X_{i,t}$ units of the homogeneous good, taking its price, P_t, as given. This monopolist faces a version of the Calvo sticky-price mechanism, equation (15), with probability of not changing its price, θ^X.[33]

The total number of homogeneous goods, $X_{d,t}^*$, required to produce a given amount of $X_{d,t}$, depends in the usual Calvo way on the dispersion of $P_{i,t}^{d,X}$ for $i \in [0,1]$. In the special case of flexible prices, $\theta^X = 0$, then $P_{i,t}^{d,X} = [(1 - \tau_X)\varepsilon_X/(\varepsilon_X - 1)P_t]/S_t = P_t/S_t$ for all $i \in [0,1]$. Here, τ_X denotes a subsidy to the producer of $X_{i,t}$, financed by a lump-sum tax on households. Because $P_{i,t}^{d,X}$ is the same for all i when $\theta^X = 0$, it follows that all inputs for producing $X_{d,t}$ are used at the same scale, so that $X_{d,t} = X_{d,t}^* = \int_0^1 X_{i,t}\, di$. When $\theta^X > 0$ and there is some inflation in $P_t^{d,X}$, then $X_{d,t} < X_{d,t}^*$.

D. *Entrepreneurs and Banks*

To capture balance sheet effects of exchange rate changes and accelerator effects, we adopt an open economy version of the CSV adopted in Bernanke et al. (1999).[34] Entrepreneurs acquire capital and rent it to the intermediate good producers in the homogeneous good sector. Entrepreneurs find it desirable to leverage their own resources (net worth) by acquiring funds from a lender ("bank"). After the entrepreneur's capital is acquired and put to work, it experiences an idiosyncratic productivity shock, ω. Ex ante, there is no asymmetric information between bankers and entrepreneurs. Each knows the net worth of the entrepreneur and they know the common distribution, F, from which all entrepreneurs will independently draw ω. Ex post, the realized value of ω is observed by the entrepreneur, but it is only observable to the bank at a cost. Under these circumstances, a sharing contract between entrepreneur and bank does not work and the model assumes that entrepreneurs instead receive a standard debt contract: the entrepreneur receives a loan and must then pay a specified interest rate in the next period. If the entrepreneur cannot pay because its ω is too low, then it goes into default and, after being monitored by the bank, the entrepreneur must transfer all its assets to the bank. The interest rate in the standard debt contract is higher than the risk-free rate because loans to entrepreneurs are risky: entrepreneurs who draw a high value of ω must pay enough to cover the costs to the banks of defaulting entrepreneurs. Naturally, entrepreneurs with low net worth ("bad balance sheets") are restricted in the amount of debt they receive. This creates balance sheet effects, and these are potentially very large when there is a currency depreciation. To the extent that entrepreneurial loans are financed by dollar liabilities, entrepreneurial net worth falls when the exchange rate depreciates, and this reduces their capacity to borrow, forcing them to cut back on the purchase of capital, producing a fall in investment.

The CSV financial friction was first used in an open economy setting by Chang and Velasco (2001) and Céspedes, Chang, and Velasco (2004). The friction was later introduced into NK open economy models by Gertler et al. (2007) and Christiano, Trabandt, and Walentin (2011). The latter papers take extreme positions on the currency composition of entrepreneur loan liabilities, with either all entrepreneurial funding obtained in foreign currency or all in LCU. The data require something intermediate, and Dalgıc (2024) works out a model in which entrepreneurs choose endogenously the currency composition of their liabilities. Here, for simplicity, we adopt the approach developed in Castillo and Medina (2021) in which the currency composition of liabilities is exogenous (see also De Leo, Gopinath, and Kalmeli-Özcan 2022).

Entrepreneurs

We assume that entrepreneurs are members of the household and infinite-lived. Each entrepreneur has a history of idiosyncratic shocks, which determines its current net worth. To preserve our representative household assumption, we suppose that each household has a large number of entrepreneurs. The entrepreneurs in each household have the same distribution of net worth as in the economy as a whole.

Consider an entrepreneur with end-of-period t net worth, N_t. That entrepreneur goes to a bank and receives a loan contract, $(\bar{B}_t^e, \{Z_{t+1}\})$. Here,

$\bar{B}_t^e$ is a quantity of LCU money and Z_{t+1} is the LCU gross rate of interest the entrepreneur pays, which potentially depends on the period $t + 1$ realized aggregate state of nature. Combining its net worth and loan, the entrepreneur purchases K_t units of capital:

$$N_t + \bar{B}_t^e = P_t^k K_t, \tag{19}$$

where P_t^k is the period t market price of capital.

After purchasing a unit of capital, the entrepreneur's effective capital becomes ωK_t. The idiosyncratic shock is drawn from a log-normal distribution with $E\omega = 1$ and $var(\log \omega) = \sigma^2$. The entrepreneur rents out its effective capital in period $t + 1$ at the competitive rental rate, r_{t+1}. The entrepreneur sells the effective capital left over at the end of period $t + 1$ for $(1 - \delta)\omega K_t P_{t+1}^k$, where δ denotes the capital depreciation rate. So, the entrepreneur that buys K_t units of raw capital in t receives the following income in period $t + 1$:

$$K_t \omega r_{t+1} + (1 - \delta)\omega K_t P_{t+1}^k = K_t P_t^k \omega \left[\frac{r_{t+1} + (1 - \delta)P_{t+1}^k}{P_t^k}\right] = K_t P_t^k \omega R_{t+1}^k, \tag{20}$$

where R_{t+1}^k denotes the rate of return on a unit of effective capital, in LCUs. This rate of return is exogenous to the entrepreneur.

The standard debt contract specifies that the entrepreneur must pay the bank $Z_{t+1}\bar{B}_t^e$ in period $t + 1$. Let $\bar{\omega}_{t+1}$ denote the cutoff value of ω, which gives the entrepreneur just enough income to cover the interest and principal on its debt. That is,

$$\bar{\omega}_{t+1} = \frac{Z_{t+1}\bar{B}_t^e}{P_t^k K_t R_{t+1}^k}. \tag{21}$$

That the cutoff is indexed by $t + 1$ reflects that it is a function of the period $t + 1$ aggregate state of nature. Entrepreneurs with $\omega < \bar{\omega}_{t+1}$ go into default in $t + 1$ and must turn over all their resources to the bank, after those resources have been verified by the bank at a cost. The entrepreneur receives full consumption insurance from its household. In exchange, the household expects the entrepreneur to choose a debt contract that maximizes:

$$E_t \upsilon_{t+1} \int_{\bar{\omega}_{t+1}}^{\infty} \left[P_t^k K_t \omega R_{t+1}^k - Z_{t+1}\bar{B}_t^e\right] dF(\omega), \tag{22}$$

where υ_{t+1}, taken as exogenous by the entrepreneur, denotes the usual asset pricing kernel, defined in equation (10).

Banks

The entrepreneur chooses a standard debt contract from a menu that is determined in a competitive market equilibrium. To explain this, we need to examine the circumstances of the banks. For simplicity, consider a representative bank that specializes in making loans to entrepreneurs with net worth $N_t > 0$. Because the bank has no funds of its own, it must issue liabilities to finance $\bar{B}_t^e$ units of LCU loaned to entrepreneurs. Following Castillo and Medina (2021), we assume that the bank finances ϕ of its borrowing needs in an LCU credit market and $1 - \phi$ in dollars:

$$B_t^{LCU} = \phi \bar{B}_t^e,\ S_t B_t^{\$} = (1 - \phi)\bar{B}_t^e, \tag{23}$$

where B_t^{LCU} denotes the quantity of LCU borrowed at the gross interest rate, $R_{d,t}$. This interest rate must be paid in period $t + 1$ and is nonstate contingent. Also, $B_t^{\$}$ denotes dollars borrowed at the nonstate contingent dollar rate, $R_{d,t}^*$. The bank can borrow as much as it wants at the risk-free rates, $R_{d,t}$ and $R_{d,t}^*$, and there is no circumstance in which it cannot pay its liabilities. This is because the bank makes loans to a large population of entrepreneurs with net worth N_t. The population is large enough that the distribution of ω across the bank's borrowers matches the distribution, F.

Let $A_{t,t+1}$ denote bank receipts from entrepreneurs, net of monitoring costs and repayment of bank liabilities:

$$\begin{aligned} A_{t,t+1} = {} & [1 - F(\bar{\omega}_{t+1})]\bar{B}_t^e Z_{t+1} + (1 - \mu)G(\bar{\omega}_{t+1})P_t^k K_t R_{t+1}^k \\ & - R_{d,t}\phi \bar{B}_t^e - s_{t+1}(1 - \phi)\bar{B}_t^e R_{d,t}^*, \end{aligned} \tag{24}$$

where $s_{t+1} \equiv S_{t+1}/S_t$ denotes the rate of depreciation, $F(\bar{\omega}_{t+1})$ denotes the period $t + 1$ fraction of nonperforming entrepreneurs, and

$$G(\bar{\omega}_{t+1}) - \int_0^{\bar{\omega}_{t+1}} \omega dF(\omega_{t+1}). \tag{25}$$

The first term after the equality in equation (24) corresponds to payments by the $1 - F(\bar{\omega}_{t+1})$ nondefaulting entrepreneurs. The next term corresponds to the resources, net of monitoring costs, recovered from defaulting entrepreneurs. Total monitoring costs, in LCUs, are $\mu G(\bar{\omega}_{t+1})P_t^k K_t R_{t+1}^k$. Under the assumption of free entry, the ex ante value of banking must be zero:

$$E_t v_{t+1} A_{t,t+1} = 0. \tag{26}$$

In the presence of complete markets, this is the only restriction on profits. In particular, as of period t it is possible for the bank to have a "deficit,"

$A_{t,t+1} < 0$, in one period $t+1$ continuation state and a surplus, $A_{t,t+1} > 0$, in another period $t+1$ state. Household optimality in the Arrow securities market requires only that the prices, $Q_{t,t+1}$, equal v_{t+1} (see eq. [10]). With prices set in that way, households are willing to take a position opposite to the bank so that each period $t+1$ Arrow security market clears in period t, that is, $A_{t,t+1} + a_{t,t+1} = 0$ for each state of nature possible in $t+1$ conditional on t.

Equilibrium Contract

We assume that under competition, bankers offer a menu of contracts, $(\bar{B}^e_t, \{Z_{t+1}\})$, which satisfy equation (26). So, the equilibrium contract is the one that solves the problem in equation (22) subject to equation (26). In principle the entrepreneur could choose a contract in which Z_{t+1} is not contingent on the period $t+1$ state of nature. But this would come at a cost to the bank because it would force the bank to enter the Arrow security markets and potentially pay a high price for funds in a bad period $t+1$ state in exchange for funds in a good $t+1$ state, which have a lower relative price. This cost to the bank would be passed on to the entrepreneur in the form of a higher nonstate contingent interest rate, Z_{t+1}. In our computations we find that Z_{t+1} responds sharply to shocks, so that little use is made of Arrow securities in equilibrium (to save space, our discussion of this topic is brief and appears only in Sec. I in the appendix, http://www.nber.org/data-appendix/c14997/appendix.pdf).

As in Bernanke et al. (1999), the assumptions in the model allow us to determine aggregate capital, net worth, and borrowing without having to keep track of the distribution of these variables across individual entrepreneurs. An important property of the model is that the amount of loans an entrepreneur takes in a realized state of nature in period $t+1$ is, other things the same, an increasing function of its net worth in that state of nature. That is determined in part by the realization of its idiosyncratic shock in period $t+1$. In terms of aggregate variables, if R^k_{t+1} is realized to be high, because of a high realization of r_{t+1} or P^k_{t+1}, then the entrepreneur will be in a better position to borrow in that state of nature (see eq. [20]). A high r_{t+1} means capital purchased in period t brings in more income in period $t+1$, whereas a high P^k_{t+1} means that the entrepreneur earns a capital gain on capital purchased in t. In practice, capital gains and losses play an important role in the model because of the large coefficient, $1-\delta$, on P^k_{t+1} (see eq. [20]). When a shock causes P^k_{t+1} to go down, then the loss to entrepreneurs puts them in a bad position to borrow. There is a partially moderating factor to this capital gain effect. Because the price of capital is trend reverting, a fall in P^k_{t+1} triggers an expected capital gain from $t + 1$ to $t + 2$. Other things the same, this allows the entrepreneur to increase its leverage and borrow more. In practice, the dominant effect of a drop in P^k_{t+1} is the capital gains effect.

Now suppose that Z_{t+1} is high in $t + 1$, say because the exchange rate depreciates. Then, the entrepreneur will, other things the same, have less net worth in period $t + 1$ and will thus be driven to cut back borrowing. This is suggested by equation (24). Suppose that Arrow securities are used very little in equilibrium, so that $A_{t,t+1} \simeq 0$. Then, if s_{t+1} jumps, other things the same, Z_{t+1} must jump too. If, as is suggested by our numerical calculations, the equilibrium has the property that Arrow securities are not used, then effectively the entrepreneur borrows partially in dollars and partially in LCU if $0 < \phi < 1$ (recall eq. [23]). In LCUs, when s_{t+1} jumps, dollar debt is a drain on entrepreneurial net worth. This effect can be quite large in this model.

It is a property of the equilibrium that in period t the net aggregate earnings of all entrepreneurs can be expressed as a share, $1 - \Gamma(\bar{\omega}_t)$, of the aggregate gross earnings of all entrepreneurs, $P^k_{t-1}K_{t-1}R^k_t$. Here, $\Gamma: [0, \infty] \rightarrow [0, 1]$ and $\Gamma(\bar{\omega}_t)$ is increasing in $\bar{\omega}_t$. Note from equation (21) that, all other things being equal, $\bar{\omega}_t$ is increasing in Z_t. It is not surprising that with a higher Z_t, entrepreneurs receive a smaller share of their gross profits.

We assume that an exogenous fraction, γ^e, of an entrepreneur's period t earnings is transferred to its household and the entrepreneur keeps the rest. In addition, each entrepreneur receives a small LCU lump-sum transfer from households in the amount, W^e_t. The transfer ensures that even bankrupt entrepreneurs in period t, who receive income from their standard debt contract, nevertheless still have a small amount of net worth. It is a property of the model that if an entrepreneur has no net worth, then it cannot borrow at all. If $W^e_t = 0$, then, because all entrepreneurs experience bankruptcy at some point, all entrepreneurs would eventually be unable to borrow. It follows that the aggregate amount of net worth held by all entrepreneurs during period t after period t uncertainty is resolved and production has occurred is given by

$$N_t = \gamma^e[1 - \Gamma(\bar{\omega}_t)]P^k_{t-1}K_{t-1}R^k_t + W^e_t. \qquad (27)$$

where W^e_t denotes a transfer of net worth from households to entrepreneurs. The period t transfer to households from entrepreneurs is

$(1-\gamma^e)[1-\Gamma(\bar{\omega}_t)]P^k_{t-1}K_{t-1}R^k_t - W^e_t$, and this term is part of Π_t in the household's budget constraint, equation (9).

Additional technical details about the model are provided in the appendix (http://www.nber.org/data-appendix/c14997/appendix.pdf) to this paper.

E. *Government Policy*

Government Purchases of Goods and Services

We assume that the local government purchases domestic homogeneous goods:

$$G_t = g\mathcal{Z}_t, \tag{28}$$

where $\mathcal{Z}_t$ denotes the same trend term that appears in equation (16).

Interest Rate Policy

The central bank has two policy tools. The first is the traditional Taylor monetary policy rule:

$$\log\left(\frac{R_{d,t}}{R_d}\right) = \rho_R \log\left(\frac{R_{d,t-1}}{R_d}\right)$$
$$+ (1-\rho_R)\left[r_\pi \log\left(\frac{\pi_t}{\pi}\right) + r_y \log\left(\frac{y_t}{y}\right) + r_S \log(\tilde{S}_t)\right] + \epsilon_{R,t}.$$

Here, $\pi_t = P_t/P_{t-1}$ denotes homogeneous good inflation, y_t denotes Y_t/A_t, where Y_t denotes aggregate homogeneous good output.[35] We assume that the monetary authority targets local prices (rather than the CPI) in part because of our finding that the estimated rise in consumer price inflation is relatively strong after a US monetary tightening, whereas the response of local monetary authorities is relatively weak. Our decision to include π_t rather than π^c_t in the interest rate rule was also motivated by the argument in Egorov and Mukhin (2023), which suggests that this specification of the rule may be welfare improving. In addition, central banks tend to focus on "core inflation," a variable that is not sensitive to transitory shocks, and π_t may satisfy that condition because it is relatively insensitive to shocks in the exchange rate. We include y_t in the policy rule as a rough indicator of natural output. Also, $\tilde{S}_t$ corresponds to $S_t/(\psi^t\bar{S})$, where $\bar{S} > 0$ is a parameter. We indicate the nonstochastic steady state of a time-series variable by deleting its time subscript. We include $r_S > 0$ in the monetary policy rule because of our VAR evidence (see figs. 1, 2, and 4) that exchange rates appear to return to their unshocked levels after a US monetary policy shock.[36]

FX Interventions

In addition to the traditional monetary policy, we allow a central bank to conduct FX interventions. We assume that the central bank uses a Taylor-type intervention rule following Castillo and Medina (2021):

$$\frac{F_t^*}{\bar{F}_t^*} = \left(\frac{F_{t-1}^*}{\bar{F}_{t-1}^*}\right)^{\rho_{fx}} \left(\frac{R_{d,t}^* - 1}{R_d^* - 1}\right)^{-\theta_{R_d^*}}, \tag{29}$$

where F_t^* denotes the central bank holdings of dollar assets and $\bar{F}_t^*$ denotes a long-run target value for the central bank's target holdings of reserves. We construct $\bar{F}_t^*$ following the conventional wisdom about what the suitable foreign reserve target should be for a central bank (see, e.g., Greenspan 1999). According to this approach, the period t target for reserves is proportional to the gross dollar liabilities of the country at the start of period t. In our model, this is the term in the square brackets:

$$\bar{F}_t^* = \left(v^{cb}\right)^{1-\vartheta} \left[R_{d,t-1}^* B_{t-1}^\$ + \overbrace{P_t^m (I_{m,t} + C_{m,t})/S_t}^{\text{imports in units of dollars}} \right]^{1-\vartheta} \left(\bar{F}_{t-1}^*\right)^{\vartheta}. \tag{30}$$

In practice, we choose a value for v^{cb} so that the model's steady state is consistent with the average dollar reserves to GDP ratio of a country. We assume that FX interventions are sterilized in the following sense:

$$S_t\left(F_t^* - F_{t-1}^*\right) = B_t - B_{t-1}. \tag{31}$$

The central bank's FX strategy generates profits and losses on its balance sheet depending on movements in the exchange rate and interest rates. We assume these are rebated in lump-sum form to households. In our model, FX interventions have zero effect without the presence of UIP restrictions. For example, the frictions are turned off with $\gamma = 0$, then sterilized FX interventions are exactly undone by households, who willingly accept the dollar assets offered by the central bank in exchange for LCU bonds, without any change in market prices. The reason has to do with the fact that the households receive, in lump-sum form, any gains or losses that the central bank experiences on its portfolio. For example, if the central bank sells a lot of dollars to households, then household portfolios have a lot more exchange rate risk. They do not mind because their overall exposure to exchange rate risk, which takes into account the transfers from the government, has not changed. When $\gamma > 0$, then households have a particular interest in the composition of their own portfolio and sterilized interventions do have an effect. There is continuity, so that when $\gamma > 0$ but small, then the household buys nearly all of any amount of dollar assets the central bank sells, and they need only a very small market incentive to absorb those dollars. This could be some combination of a fall in $R_{d,t}$ or a rise in $R^*_{d,t} + E_t \log S_{t+1} - \log S_t$. Because $R^*_{d,t}$ is exogenous to the SOE, the latter would involve some combination of a fall in $\log S_t$ or rise in $E_t \log S_{t+1}$.

Finally, for measurement purposes we follow the approach of Adler et al. (2024). We measure FX interventions as a percentage of average annual GDP over the current and previous 11 quarters:

$$100 \frac{S_t\left(F_t^* - F_{t-1}^*\right)}{4/12 \sum_{i=0}^{11} P_{t-i}^c \mathrm{GDP}_{t-i}}, \tag{32}$$

where GDP_t denotes GDP in period t, measured in terms of consumption goods (see eq. [40]). We multiply by P_t^c to convert GDP into LCU. Division in the denominator by 12 gives the average and multiplication by 4 converts quarterly GDP into annual terms.

F. *Capital Production*

Capital is produced by competitive capital producers. These producers buy investment goods from investment good producers (see Subsec. III.C, Consumption and Investment) at a given price, $P_{I,t}$. Capital accumulation in the model is subject to Christiano et al. (2005) type investment adjustment costs. In period t the representative capital producer uses "old capital," x, and investment goods, I_t, to produce "new capital," k:

$$k = x + \left[1 - S\left(\frac{I_t}{I_{t-1}}\right)\right] I_t,$$

where $S(z) = S'(z) = 0$ and $S''(z) = \kappa > 0$, for $z = I_t/I_{t-1}$ along a steady-state growth path. Here, S' and S'' denote the first and second derivatives, respectively, and κ is a model parameter. The price of a unit of old capital, x, is the same as the price, P_t^k, of a unit of new capital, k. So, costs for the capital producer are $P_t^k x + P_t^I I_t$. The representative capital producer solves for sequences of x_{t+j}, I_{t+j} to optimize profits,

$$E_t \sum_{j=0}^{\infty} \beta^j \upsilon_{t+j} \left\{ P_{t+j}^k \left[x_{t+j} + \left(1 - S\left(\frac{I_{t+j}}{I_{t+j-1}}\right)\right) I_{t+j} \right] - P_{t+j}^k x_{t+j} - P_{t+j}^I I_{t+j} \right\},$$

where υ_{t+j} for $j \geq 0$ denotes the multiplier on the household's period $t + j$ flow budget constraint.

In equilibrium, $k = K_t$, the total quantity of capital purchased in period t. Also, $x = (1 - \delta)K_{t-1}$, the quantity of capital that was rented out in period t and depreciated by δ.

G. *Market Clearing, Balance of Payments, and GDP*

Financial Market Clearing

The supply of peso loans comes from households, D_t. The demand for pesos comes from banks, B_t^{LCU}, and government, B_t. We assume that foreigners do not participate in the market in local currency so that market clearing implies:

$$D_t = B_t^{LCU} + B_t. \tag{33}$$

The supply of dollars comes from households, D_t^*, and government, F_t^*, foreigners, F_t^o, and the demand, $B_t^\$$, comes from domestic banks. So, market clearing implies:

$$D_t^* + F_t^* + F_t^o = B_t^\$. \tag{34}$$

We also have clearing in the Arrow securities markets:

$$A_{t,t+1} = a_{t,t+1}, \tag{35}$$

where $a_{t,t+1}$ is pesos purchased by households (or sold if negative) in period t for a realized state in $t + 1$. Similarly, $A_{t,t+1}$ denotes LCU sold by banks in period t for delivery in a realized state of nature in $t + 1$.

Homogeneous Goods Market Clearing

For supply, Y_t, to equal demand in the homogeneous goods market requires:

$$Y_t = I_{d,t} + C_{d,t} + X_t^{d,*} + g\mathcal{Z}_t + \overbrace{\frac{\mu G(\bar{\omega}_t) P_{t-1}^k K_{t-1} R_t^k}{P_t}}^{\text{homog goods for monitoring by banks}}, \quad (36)$$

where $I_{d,t}$ and $C_{d,t}$ denote homogeneous goods used in the production of investment and consumption, respectively (see Subsec. III.C, Consumption and Investment). Also, $X_t^{d,*}$ denotes the quantity of homogeneous goods used to produce the domestic input into exports (see Subsec. III.C, Consumption and Investment), and the next term denotes government purchases (see eq. [28]). Finally, the last part of the equation corresponds to the total amount of homogeneous goods purchased by banks to monitor defaulting entrepreneurs (see Subsec. III.D, Banks). The object, $G(\bar{\omega}_t)$, is defined in equation (25).

Balance of Payments

The balance of payments is derived by starting with the household budget constraint and substituting out for profits and the government budget constraint. This leads to the following expression:

$$\begin{aligned} P_t^x X_t - P_t^m (C_{m,t} + I_{m,t} + X_{m,t}) &= F_t^* - R_{d,t-1}^* F_{t-1}^* \\ &+ D_t^* - R_{d,t-1}^* D_{t-1}^* - B_t^\$ + B_{t-1}^\$ R_{d,t-1}^*. \end{aligned} \quad (37)$$

Let $R_{d,t}^* = 1 + r_{d,t}^*$, so that the current account, CA_t, is net exports plus net interest earned from abroad:

$$CA_t = P_t^x X_t - P_t^m (C_{m,t} + I_{m,t} + X_{m,t}) + r_{d,t-1}^* \overbrace{\left(F_{t-1}^* + D_{t-1}^* - B_{t-1}^\$\right)}^{-F_{t-1}^o}. \quad (38)$$

Then, we have that equation (37) can be written as follows:

$$CA_t = F_t^* + D_t^* - B_t^\$ - \left(F_{t-1}^* + D_{t-1}^* - B_{t-1}^\$\right), \quad (39)$$

which states that the current account equals the change in net foreign assets. Because these assets have one maturity period, the change in net foreign assets is not affected by valuation effects. Given clearing in the dollar market, equation (34), the expression on the right of the equality in equation (39) can also be written as $-(F_t^o - F_{t-1}^o)$.

Gross Domestic Product

GDP is defined as domestic value added, or $C + I + G + X -$ imports. We have a real concept of GDP, which is expressed in units of the consumption goods. Adding these terms and taking into account the zero-profit conditions and first-order optimality conditions that hold in competitive markets with constant returns to scale, we find that:

$$\mathrm{GDP}_t = \frac{P_t Y_t - \mu G(\bar{\omega}_t) P^k_{t-1} K_{t-1} R^k_t}{P^c_t}. \tag{40}$$

The numerator is the LCU value of the homogeneous goods and division by P^c_t converts GDP to consumption units. The quantity, Y_t, includes monitoring costs (see eq. [36]), which are not part of GDP. That is why monitoring costs are subtracted in the numerator of equation (40).

H. Rest of the World

From the perspective of our SOE, the foreign variables, y_t, π^f_t, $R^*_{d,t}$, evolve exogenously, according to the specification in equation (3). People in an SOE are interested in US inflation because it helps to determine their country's terms of trade, and they use US GDP as a proxy for their country's export demand shifter. To people in the SOE, the US interest rate, $R^*_{d,t}$, is also of interest because they treat it as a risk-free rate in dollar terms, at which they can borrow and lend.

IV. Parameter Values

We use an approximate Bayesian approach to estimate the model parameters. The approach is a variant on the Bayesian impulse response matching estimator implemented in Christiano et al. (2005). The Bayesian procedure is described in Christiano, Trabandt, and Walentin (2010) and Christiano, Eichenbaum, and Trabandt (2016), and we apply the procedure using the code in version 6 of Dynare (see Adjemian et al. 2024).[37] Our IRFs are monthly, whereas the time period in our model is quarterly. We address this mismatch by applying a version of the impulse response procedure implemented in Jarociński and Karadi (2020). In particular, we associate the quarter j impulse response in the model with the estimated impulse response in the first month of quarter j. Our estimation in effect chooses values for the model parameters to optimize an objective subject to a penalty constraint. The estimation objective is the sum of squared deviations between estimated and model IRFs, weighted by the estimated sampling variance in the corresponding estimated IRF. The penalties correspond to Bayesian priors on the parameters.

A. *Parameter Values Not Estimated*

The rest-of-the-world variables, $\pi^f_t, y_t, R^*_{d,t}$ are assumed to evolve according to equation (3). The values of D and A are as given in equation (4).

Other parameters whose values are not estimated are listed in table 1. The values of these parameters are fairly standard in the macroeconomics literature. For example, they are similar to the ones reported in Christiano, Trabandt, and Walentin (2011) and Christiano, Motto, and Rostagno (2014). See those papers for discussion and for the related literature. One parameter that is somewhat nonstandard is r_s, the coefficient on the exchange rate in the Taylor rule. When $r_S > 0$, the exchange rate is stationary about the trend, ψ^t.[38] That is, the level of the exchange rate eventually returns to where it would have been in the absence of a shock. The exchange rate IRFs in figures 2, 4, and 5 suggest that at the 2-year horizon, the effect of a monetary policy shock on the level of the exchange rate is small in the data. Section J in the appendix (http://www.nber.org/data-appendix/c14997/appendix.pdf) looks at the longer-term impact of a monetary policy shock on the exchange rate, and the results are consistent with a zero long-term effect in the case of the EMEs, Peru, and the United States. We find some evidence of a nonzero, though small, long-horizon effect in the case of the AEs. For this reason, we set

Table 1
Common (Not Estimated) Model Parameters

Variable	Description	Value
β	Discount factor	.99
α	Capital share	.40
δ	Depreciation	.02
φ	Inverse Frisch	1.00
γ^e	Net worth retained by entrepreneur	.95
σ	Entrepreneur idiosyncratic productivity std	.22
μ	Monitoring cost rate	.25
$100\frac{W^e}{N}$	Steady-state transfers to entrepreneurs	.11
r_π	Taylor inflation coefficient	1.50
r_y	Taylor output coefficient	.05
r_S	Taylor exchange rate coefficient	.02
ϵ	Elasticity of substitution, intermediate goods	6.00
θ	Calvo parameter, intermediate goods	.75
ϵ^x	Elasticity of substitution, export goods	6.00

Note: Parameters are set a priori, as discussed in the text. In the case of $100W^e/N$, we in effect use the assumed value, 0.11, to determine the value of W^e conditional on the other model parameters. The idea was for W^e to be small but positive. We set $r_S = 0.00000002$ in the AE model.

$r_S = 0.02$ for the EMEs and Peru, and we set r_s to a much smaller, though positive, number for the AEs.[39]

B. *Estimated Parameters*

For ease of comparison, our point estimates for the three SOE models are reported in table 2. In the estimation, we adjusted our priors somewhat for two reasons. First, in the case of the EMEs, the model has difficulty reconciling the substantial depreciation with the relative absence of movement in consumer price inflation and the very substantial drop in GDP. Second, we adjusted home bias priors in the AEs and EMEs, $1 - \omega_c, \gamma_I, \gamma_x$, to help ensure empirically reasonable trade-to-GDP ratios for those economies. The latter objective could in principle have been accomplished by calibrating those parameters to ensure the trade targets are satisfied. Alternatively, the Bayesian "endogenous prior" methods

Table 2
Estimated Model Parameters

Parameter	Description	Peru	EME	AE
Γ	Target portfolio cost (UIP friction)	2.56	1.78	3.20
$\gamma_{R_d^*}$	Risk appetite (UIP friction)	22.46	29.46	44.78
γ_θ	Portfolio inertia (UIP friction)	−11.55	−19.47	−47.77
κ	Investment adjustment cost	3.16	5.85	1.78
$\theta_{R_d^*}$	FX intervention reaction coefficient	.42	.16	0
ρ^{FX}	FX intervention persistence	.78	.21	0
η_c	*C*, elasticity of substitution	.94	.41	1.53
η_x	*X*, elasticity of substitution	1.58	.70	1.18
ν_i	*I*, elasticity of substitution	1.17	.91	1.73
η_f	Elasticity of demand, exports	2.11	1.53	2.67
γ_f	Demand shifter, exports	4.02	5.67	3.86
θ^x	Export Calvo stickiness	.77	.80	.80
$1 - \omega_c$	Home bias, *C*	.83	.98	.90
γ_I	Home bias, *I*	.21	.71	.78
γ_X	Home bias, *X*	.51	.44	.77
ρ_R	Monetary policy persistence	.88	.82	.91
$1 - \phi$	Credit dollarization	.50	.45	.01
Υ	Steady-state deposit dollarization	.40	.47	.05
$\frac{F^*}{4\text{xGDP}}$	Steady-state reserves/GDP	.30	.15	.05

Note: (1) Steady-state reserves/GDP was estimated in the case of the EMEs, but it was simply taken from Castillo and Medina (2021) in the case of Peru and was set exogenously to 0.05 in the case of the AEs; (2) Υ is estimated in the case of the EMEs and Peru but simply set to 0.05 in the case of the AEs; in the case of ϕ, this parameter is not estimated for Peru or the AEs (see text for discussion). UIP = uncovered interest rate parity; AE = advanced economy; EME = emerging market economy; FX = foreign exchange; GDP = gross domestic product.

described in Christiano, Eichenbaum, and Rebelo (2011) that integrate moments of the data into the priors could have been used.[40] We did not use these approaches. This is why we call our approach an approximate Bayesian approach.

The first three rows of table 2 show that our models include a significant amount of UIP frictions. That such frictions are required is evident from the hump-shape response of AE, EME, and Peruvian exchange rates to a US monetary tightening (see figs. 2, 4, and 5). Those exchange rate responses differ significantly from the Dornbusch (1976) overshooting pattern one would expect in the absence of UIP frictions. We discuss the detailed role of the frictions below.

The value of the curvature parameter in investment, κ, is small, like the value estimated in Christiano et al. (2005), but much smaller than the values estimated in Christiano et al. (2014, 2016). The table indicates that the FX coefficients associated with the AEs are set to 0 because our IRFs suggests those economies do not engage in significant FX interventions after a US monetary tightening (see fig. 2).

Consider the elasticity of substitution between domestic and foreign inputs in the production of consumption, exports, and investment. In the case of the EMEs, these elasticities of substitution are relatively low, less than unity. As we explain below, these low elasticities help the SOE model explain the relatively large fall in economic activities in EMEs (see fig. 4). Consistent with this logic, elasticities of substitution are somewhat higher in Peru, where the drop in GDP after a US monetary tightening is not as great as it is in the EMEs more generally.[41] Empirical estimates of elasticities of substitution (see, e.g., Backus and Kehoe 1992; Eaton and Kortum 2002; Allen, Arkolakis, and Takahashi 2020) are generally higher than the values assigned in our estimation. That may reflect our relatively greater emphasis on the high-frequency component of the data. Auclert et al. (2021) and Bohr (2024) explain why elasticities of substitution may be much lower in the short run than they are over a longer horizon.

The parameters γ_f, η_f control the response of export demand to shifts in US GDP and the terms of trade, respectively (see eq. [17]). We expect the value of η_f to have little impact on the transmission of US monetary policy shocks. This is because, given the inertia in US prices and sticky-in-dollar export prices, we expect relatively little movement in the terms of trade. On the other hand, the substantial drop in US import demand that accompanies a US monetary tightening suggests that a large value of γ_f will be important for model fit. Indeed, table 2 reports a large value of γ_f, between approximately 4 and 6, for the different models. This means that when US GDP (i.e., Y_t^f in eq. [17]) falls by 1% due to its temporary component, the export demand shifter in the temporary component of Y_t^f, y_t^f in equation (16), falls 4%–5%. Section L in the appendix (http://www.nber.org/data-appendix/c14997/appendix.pdf) perturbs the values of γ_f, η_f in the EME model to verify the intuition just described about the relative unimportance for the model fit of variations in η_f and the importance of the value of γ_f.

Consistent with the dominant currency paradigm, we specify SOE export prices to be Calvo sticky in dollars (see Subsec. III.C, Exports and the Dominant Currency Paradigm). We include the relevant Calvo price stickiness parameter, θ^x, among the estimated parameters. The estimated values imply prices are sticky on average for about 5 quarters, only a bit higher than the 1 year or so found in studies of price stickiness in US data.

Next, we turn to the three home bias parameters. Notably, the home bias parameters take on relatively large values in the AEs. Not surprisingly, we show below that these large values imply counterfactually low trade shares in the AEs. A distinguishing feature of the VAR results is that GDP falls a relatively small amount in the AEs, compared with the United States, in the wake of a monetary tightening. Initially, we conjectured that the counterfactual implication that AE economies are relatively closed is the reason for our AE model's success at matching the relatively small drop in AE GDP. Section F in the appendix shows that this conjecture is incorrect. In the appendix, we reduce the value of the AE home bias parameters and find that this has essentially no impact on the drop in GDP and exports in the AEs. The reason the estimation chose high values for the home bias parameters was to avoid excessive passthrough of the exchange rate into inflation as well as an excessive drop in investment.

The large magnitude of the smoothing parameter in the monetary policy rule is consistent with estimates reported elsewhere.[42] Turning to credit dollarization, $1 - \phi$, we fixed this value at approximately zero for the AE model. In the case of Peru, we took the parameter value from Castillo and Medina (2021). For the EMEs, the parameter was included in the estimated parameters.

C. *Steady-State Properties of the Model*

Table 3 displays steady-state properties of the estimated models. The first column indicates the variable in each row. Here, *X*, *M*, *NX*, *NFA*

Table 3
Estimated Model Steady States

	AE (Data)	EME (Data)	Peru (Data)
C/GDP	.50 (.53)	.51 (.61)	.51 (.63)
I/GDP	.19 (.24)	.20 (.24)	.19 (.23)
X/GDP	.14 (.37)	.63 (.34)	.45 (.26)
M/GDP	.15 (.34)	.64 (.33)	.46 (.24)
NX/GDP	−.00 (.03)	−.01 (.01)	−.01 (.02)
G/GDP	.30 (.19)	.30 (.15)	.30 (.12)
NFA/GDP	.10 (.27)	.34 (−.28)	.30 (−.31)
K/GDP	2.01	2.03	2.01
L	2.58	2.56	2.58
100Bankruptcy	1.43	1.38	1.43
$400(Z-R)$	1.779	1.712	1.772
$400(Rk-R)$	7.738	7.509	7.715

Note: AE = advanced economy; EME = emerging market economy; GDP = gross domestic product.

denote exports, imports, net exports, and net foreign assets, respectively. The models' implications for the trade-to-GDP ratio, $(X + M)/\text{GDP}$, differ from the corresponding empirical estimates: the AEs understate that quantity and the EMEs and Peru overstate it. See Subsection IV.B above (and Sec. F in the appendix, http://www.nber.org/data-appendix/c14997/appendix.pdf) for a discussion of this result.

V. Fit of the Models and Counterfactual Experiments

Subsections V.A, V.B, and V.C evaluate the ability of our AE, EME, and Peru models to account for the empirical IRFs reported in Subection II.B. That the models account well for the empirical IRFs is important for the credibility of the counterfactual experiments that underly our conclusions.

One type of counterfactual experiment is reported in each of Subsections V.A, V.B, and V.C. As we noted earlier, a US monetary contraction moves the US interest rate, $R^*_{d,t}$, as well as the US price level and a US demand for imports shifter (in our model, the shifter is a function of US GDP).[43] By linearity of our VARs as well as of our model solution, the total effect of a US monetary tightening is the sum of the effects operating exclusively via the response of $R^*_{d,t}$ (the pure interest rate effect), the US price level (the pure price level effect), and US GDP (the pure GDP effect).[44] Because the price level effect is quantitatively very small and only operates through US import demand, we simply define the trade effect as the sum of the pure GDP and pure price level effects. In the first three subsections below, we document our main finding. The pure interest rate effect of a US monetary contraction is only a small part of the total effect of a US monetary policy contraction. The pure trade effect is the main channel by which a monetary policy contraction affects the rest of the world.

In Subsection V.C, we report additional counterfactual experiments for the Peruvian economy. Our results suggest that FX intervention is not particularly effective at insulating the Peruvian economy from a US monetary policy shock. However, it is effective at insulating the economy from noise trading in the FX market. By noise trading we mean FX trading that is not related to aggregate fundamentals and may reflect herd behavior or other exogenous factors that disturb FX markets. Recent research argues that a significant portion of exchange rate volatility is generated by non-fundamental noise trading shocks (Eichenbaum et al. 2021; Itskhoki and Mukhin 2021). That research tends to focus on AEs, but we know of no reason why noise would be less of a factor in EME FX markets.

The remaining subsections report results for a broader set of variables: consumption, the share of dollars in financial assets ("dollarization"), Θ_t, and the net worth of entrepreneurs. Subsection V.D documents again, looking at our wider set of variables, the central role played by the trade effect in transmitting a US monetary contraction to the rest of the world. We do counterfactual simulations to document the role of credit market frictions in the transmission of US monetary shocks. We find that credit market frictions only matter to the extent that there is credit dollarization. This is the case with the AEs, where our estimation assigns virtually no role to dollar borrowing ($\phi = 1$). Balance sheet effects do play an important role in the transmission of US monetary policy shocks in EMEs. Balance sheet effects play an important role regardless of whether we consider pure interest rate effects, pure price effects, or pure GDP effects. We then turn to sticky-in-dollar pricing, which shows that although this has some impact, it is not of the same order of magnitude as the trade effect or balance sheet effects.

Subsection V.E discusses the role in model fit of the UIP frictions characterized by γ, γ_Θ, $\gamma_{R_d^*}$. Here γ denotes the target portfolio parameter, γ_Θ denotes the portfolio inertia parameter, and $\gamma_{R_d^*}$ denotes the risk appetite parameter (see Subsec. III.A). Our first step uses the VAR-based IRFs to obtain a quantitative characterization of the failure of UIP (i.e., eqq. [11] and [12] with $\gamma = 0$). We display the well-known delayed overshooting puzzle. However, we argue that the problem with UIP is even worse than is suggested by delayed overshooting. We document a second puzzle, which we call the excess overshooting puzzle. We then explain the role of values assigned to γ, γ_{Θ}, $\gamma_{R_d^*}$ in resolving the two puzzles. We also discuss the general implications for the international monetary transmission mechanism of resolving the two UIP puzzles.

Finally, as a further check on the credibility of our SOE models, Subsection V.F examines the implications of the models for IRFs not used in model estimation. In particular, we evaluate the models' implications for the response of equity markets and interest rate spreads in the AEs and the EMEs.

A. *Advanced Economies*

Figure 7 reproduces the IRFs and probability intervals for AEs presented in figure 2. The corresponding IRFs from the estimated AE model are displayed in the dots (IRFs for other model variables are discussed later). The time unit on the horizontal axis is months, and the quarterly data from the model are displayed for the first month in each quarter. The stars present the model responses to a pure R_d^* shock.

Note that, overall, the model reproduces the solid black line reasonably well. The model does very well with GDP and investment. In the

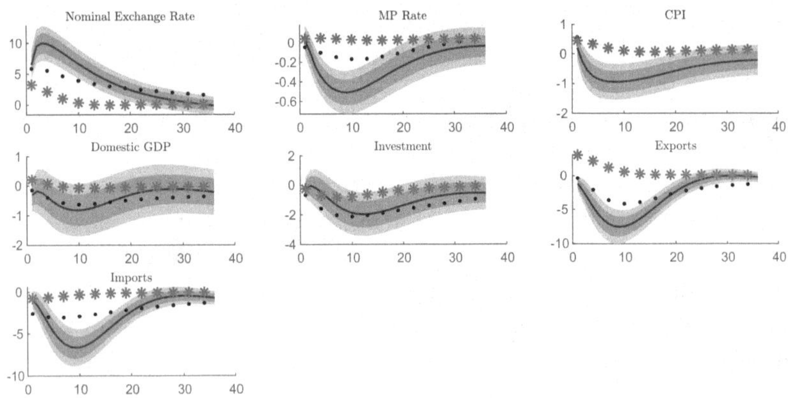

Fig. 7. AE: VAR IRFs, SOE IRFs, and SOE responses to pure R_d^* shock. (1) The time unit on the horizontal axis is months. Model data are quarterly and are reported in the third month of each quarter; (2) the dark solid line and shaded areas taken from figure 2; (3) dots correspond to IRFs implied by the estimated SOE model (for parameter values, see tables in Sec. IV); and (4) stars correspond to responses in estimated SOE model to a pure $R_{d,t}^*$ shock. Such a shock leaves the path of $R_{d,t}^*$ at its estimated value reported in figure 3, while zeroing out the response in the model's export demand shifter and foreign price. MP = Monetary policy; CPI = consumer price index; GDP = gross domestic product.

other cases, the model reproduces the rough pattern of the black line. The CPI is an exception because it rises for the first year rather than falling (the dots are partially obscured by the stars because they roughly coincide). The model is characterized by too much passthrough from the exchange rate depreciation to domestic prices.[45]

A key thing to note is how different the stars are from the dots in all cases with the exception of the CPI. With a pure R_d^* shock, the responses look more like what one expects from M-F expenditure switching in response to the exchange rate depreciation. Investment and imports fall a small amount, and there is a (small) rise in GDP. The difference between an $R_{d,t}^*$ shock and a pure $R_{d,t}^*$ shock is particularly stark in the case of exports. As in the data, exports fall sharply in the estimated SOE model in response to an $R_{d,t}^*$ shock. But, exports rise in response to a pure $R_{d,t}^*$ shock. Despite the sticky-in-dollars export pricing, exports increase. Notably, exports do not fall, as our estimates suggest. The difference between an R_d^* shock and a pure R_d^* shock is primarily due to zeroing out imports (zeroing out the US price level has very little effect). Thus, the decline in output and exports is mostly due to the decline in US imports. Also, much of the decline in AE investment and imports is due to the decline in US imports. AE imports are pulled down by the decline in AE GDP. According to our analysis, the decline in US imports is the key mechanism by which a US monetary tightening affects AEs.

Recall that the estimated portfolio friction parameters in table 2 are substantially higher for the AEs than for the EMEs and Peru. In addition, AEs have little credit dollarization ($\phi \simeq 1$). The stars in figure 8 show how the AEs would respond to a US monetary tightening if portfolio friction parameters (γ, γ_R, and γ_θ) were set to their estimated values in the EMEs and $\phi = 0.7$ (i.e., 30% credit dollarization). Note that the small drop in GDP in the estimated model (see the dots) is amplified substantially (the stars), by nearly 2 percentage points in the first year, before reverting to trend. The large drop in GDP is mainly due to a substantial acceleration in the drop in investment. The perturbation in the portfolio friction parameters plays a very small role in this. When ϕ is positive and there is significant credit dollarization, entrepreneurs make substantial losses when the exchange rate depreciates in response to a US monetary tightening. This leads entrepreneurs to cut back on the demand for capital, which in turn leads to the decline in investment demand that we see in figure 8. A review of the economic logic underlying these effects appears in Subsection III.D.

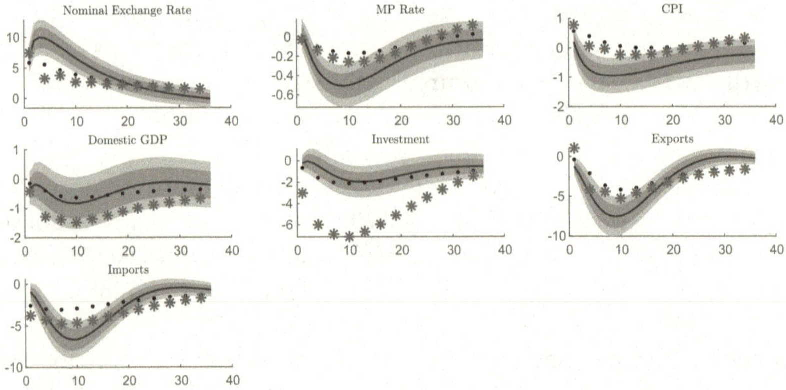

Fig. 8. Impact of high credit dollarization in AEs. See notes 1–3 in figure 7. Stars in the figure correspond to IRFs of the estimated AE SOE model in which the home bias parameters in consumption, investment, and exports are set to their values in the AE model (see table 2). MP = Monetary policy; CPI = consumer price index; GDP = gross domestic product.

Our estimated parameters imply that AEs trade much less than EMEs in the steady state even though the amount of AE and EME trade openness is similar according to the data. In Section F of the appendix (http://www.nber.org/data-appendix/c14997/appendix.pdf), we perturb the home bias parameter values in the estimated AE model so that they more closely resemble the home bias parameter values in the estimated EME model. When we do this, the perturbed AE model implies even more trade openness than we observe in the data. At the same time, the model's implication that GDP falls by a small amount after a monetary tightening is not changed. So, we conclude that the counterfactual implications of the AE model for trade openness are not the reason for the relatively modest decline in GDP after a US monetary policy shock. We show that the estimation procedure avoids the perturbed parameter values because smaller home bias increases passthrough from the exchange rate into inflation and magnifies the drop in investment. Overall, our results suggest that the main reason output falls more in EMEs than in AEs is that the former have more credit dollarization than the latter.

B. Emerging Market Economies

Our results for EMEs are displayed in figure 9. For baseline model parameter values, see Subsections IV.A and IV.B.

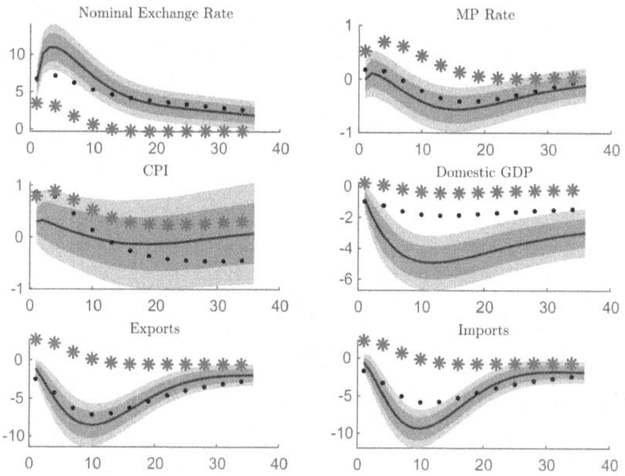

Fig. 9. EME: VAR IRFs, SOE IRFs, and SOE responses to pure R_d^* shock. See notes to figure 7. Also, "Reserves" follows Adler et al. (2024) in measuring FX intervention as a percentage of average annual gross domestic product (GDP) over the current and previous 11 quarters (see eq. [32]). MP = Monetary policy; CPI = consumer price index.

The estimated model reproduces the fact that EME GDP and investment fall substantially more than we observe in the AEs (recall fig. 7). The model understates our baseline VAR-based estimate of the drop in GDP (compare the solid line with the dotted line). This may not be a flaw. In the robustness tests for our VAR analysis, we did find some evidence that our estimates of the decline in GDP after a US monetary contraction may be overestimated in our baseline VAR analysis.[46] Investment in the model falls more, in percentage terms, than the decline in GDP. Model exports and imports closely follow the solid line. Bank reserves in the model and data match well too.

Consider the starred curves in figure 9, which display the response of the model to a pure $R_{d,t}^*$ shock. As in the case of the AEs, responses to a pure $R_{d,t}^*$ have an M F flavor. Exports increase in response to the exchange rate depreciation, despite sticky-in-dollar export pricing. Investment contracts, roughly canceling the positive effects of the rise in exports, so that the response of GDP is roughly flat, after a modest, temporary increase. The central bank sells reserves to support the exchange rate. Because the FX intervention rule is dominated by feedback onto $R_{d,t}^*$, reserves follow a similar path when there is an $R_{d,t}^*$ shock or a pure $R_{d,t}^*$ shock. There is substantial passthrough from the exchange rate and into local prices, though model inflation does not go substantially outside the probability interval. The difference between dots and stars is dominated by the impact of $R_{d,t}^*$ on the foreign demand for exports. As in the AE analysis, the model responses to the US monetary tightening (the dots) are dominated by the fall in the demand for AE exports.

C. *Peru*

Table 2 lists the estimated parameters for the Peru model. In figure 10, the dark solid line indicates the median estimated responses from the VAR analysis, and the shaded areas represent 68% and 90% probability intervals. The dots correspond to the IRFs in the estimated model. The match between model impulses and data impulses is reasonably good. The rise in $R^*_{d,t}$ is associated with a fall in the domestic interest rate and a short-run expected depreciation of the currency (compare the periods 0 and 1 values of the log exchange rate in panel 1,1). Households respond to the increase in $R^*_{d,t}$ by increasing the share of assets held in dollars, Θ_t (see panel 2,1).

The starred lines indicate the response of the estimated model to a pure $R^*_{d,t}$ shock, that is, one in which the import demand shifter and foreign inflation are held constant. Apart from the drop in FX reserves and the increased holdings of dollars, there is very little response in other variables.

The Role of FX Interventions after a US Monetary Tightening

The Central Bank of Peru is transparent about its active FX intervention policy (Castillo, Lama, and Medina 2019; Castillo and Medina 2021).[47]

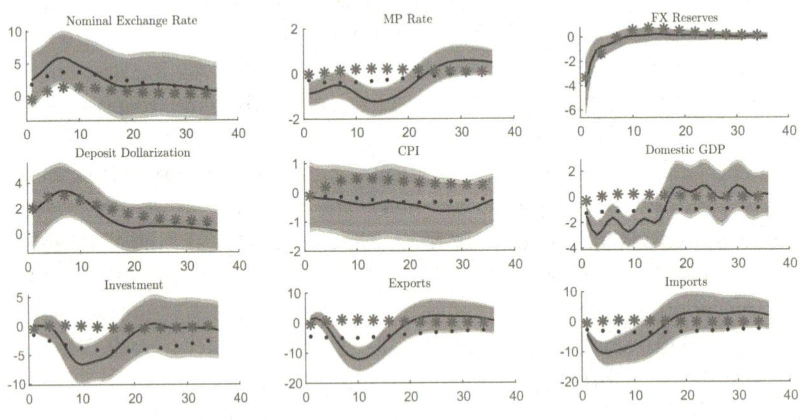

Fig. 10. Peru. See notes to figures 7 and 9. MP = Monetary policy; CPI = consumer price index; FX = foreign exchange; GDP = gross domestic product.

Using our model, we run several counterfactual experiments to quantitatively evaluate the effects of FX interventions. Figure 11 plots the IRFs of our estimated model, Benchmark, and a version of the model, No Intervention, in which the central bank does essentially no FX interventions ($\theta_{R_d^*} = 0$ in eq. [29]). We can see the effect of FX interventions in figure 11 by comparing the Benchmark curve with the No Intervention curve.

Central bank interventions are sterilized in that the sale of government dollar assets, F_t^*, are financed by the purchase of an equivalent amount of LCU government bonds, B_t (see eq. [31]). The 2,1 panel shows that, in the Benchmark version of the model, the central bank reduces its dollar reserves, F_t^*, by around 3% of GDP. The operation is reversed by the end of a year or so, when $R_{d,t}^*$ has returned to its preshock level.

Without UIP frictions, FX interventions have zero effect in our model. As explained in Subsection III.E, FX Interventions, $\gamma = 0$ implies that households are happy to take the opposite position of a sterilized intervention without the need for any change in market prices. In particular, $F_t^* + D_t^*$ remains unaffected and market clearing in LCU and dollar

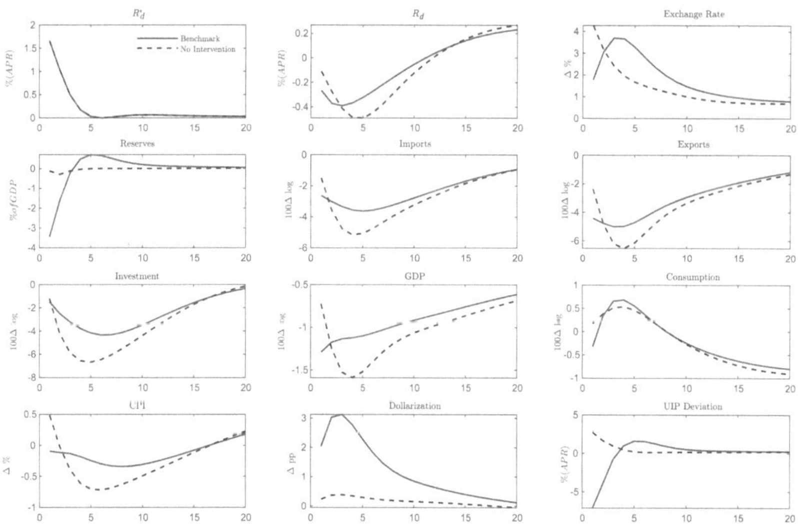

Fig. 11. Foreign exchange (FX) interventions in Peru: macro variables. The solid line reproduces the IRFs in response to a US monetary tightening from our estimated model (see the dotted lines in fig. 10). The dashed line shows what would have happened if $\theta_{R_d^*} = 0$ in the central bank's FX policy rule, equation (29). The "UIP Deviation" in panel 4,3 corresponds to Λ_t in equation (11). For the definition of "Reserves," see the note to figure 9. APR = annual percent rate; UIP = uncovered interest rate parity; CPI = consumer price index; GDP = gross domestic product.

bond markets is undisturbed.[48] With $\gamma > 0$ then FX interventions have real effects.

In the case with $\gamma > 0$, when the central bank reduces F_t^* in exchange for LCU government debt, households will not increase D_t^* without a decrease in Λ_t, that is, some combination of a decrease in $R_{d,t}$ and a rise in $R_{d,t}^* + E_t \log S_{t+1} - \log S_t$. The 4,3 panel in figure 11 shows that Λ_t falls substantially while F_t^* is low, and D_t^* rises (4,2 panel). Households do not fully raise D_t^* by the fall in F_t^* so that $F_t^* + D_t^*$ falls.[49] With the combination of the households and central bank selling dollars on net, it is intuitive that the domestic currency appreciates with the FX intervention (see the first month in panel 1,3). The appreciation helps reduce Λ_t. In addition, it has a negative effect on the price level, so that monetary policy drives $R_{d,d}$ down, also contributing to the fall in Λ_t.

A negative shock to $F_t^* + D_t^*$ has effects via the balance of payments. Abstracting from a change in $B_t^{\$}$, a fall in $F_t^* + D_t^*$ drives down the current account, according to equation (39). This, in turn, requires net exports to decrease, according to equation (38) (see panels 2,2 and 2,3). The market price that facilitates this move in net exports is the appreciation of the exchange rate.

The initial effect of the FX intervention on GDP is negative. This reflects in part that the FX intervention has a temporary negative impact on consumption, as households substitute toward holding more dollars in response to the increased LCU return on dollars, $R_{d,t}^* + E_t \log S_{t+1} - \log S_t$. It also reflects the fall in net exports. Finally, the impact on investment of the FX intervention is delayed. Over time, investment increases with the FX intervention so that the drop in investment that would occur absent FX intervention (the dashed line in panel 3,1) is muted (the solid line in panel 3,1). For the financial details about how FX interventions affect investment, including the response of leverage, interest rate spreads, nonperforming loans, net worth, bankruptcies, and monitoring costs, see Section I in the appendix (http://www.nber.org/data-appendix/c14997/appendix.pdf).

So, initially GDP is hurt by FX intervention and later it is boosted. To reduce the impact on GDP to a single number, we compute the cumulative GDP loss, $100 \times \Sigma_{t=0}^{\infty} \beta^t \Delta \log(\text{GDP}_t)$, where $\Delta \log(\text{GDP}_t)$ is the log deviation of GDP from its unshocked path. The cumulative loss is 19.75% in the absence of FX intervention and 17.04% with FX intervention. So, given the FX intervention rule that we study, FX interventions reduce 14% of the 19.75% GDP loss created by the US monetary tightening. FX intervention by the rule we use only provides modest insulation against a US monetary contraction. We leave it to future work to see how much insulation is desirable, by examining the Ramsey optimal equilibrium.

Noise Trading

Figure 12 plots IRFs for two versions of the Peruvian model in response to a shock, e_t^Y in equation (8), to the representative household's target share of dollars, Y_t, in its portfolio. Following Itskhoki and Mukhin (2021, 2023) and others, we refer to e_t^Y as a noise trading shock. The portfolio target is defined in equation (8), and we set $\gamma_{R_d^*} = \gamma_\Theta = 0$. The shock drives Y_1 from its steady-state value, 0.4, to 0.41, so the shock to e_1^Y is 0.01. The scalar first-order autoregressive process, e_t^Y, has autocorrelation, 0.95. We consider the following version of our FX intervention rule:

$$\frac{F_t^*}{\bar{F}_t^*} = \left(\frac{F_{t-1}^*}{\bar{F}_{t-1}^*}\right)^{\rho_{fx}} \left(\frac{Y_t}{\bar{Y}}\right)^{-\theta_Y}.$$

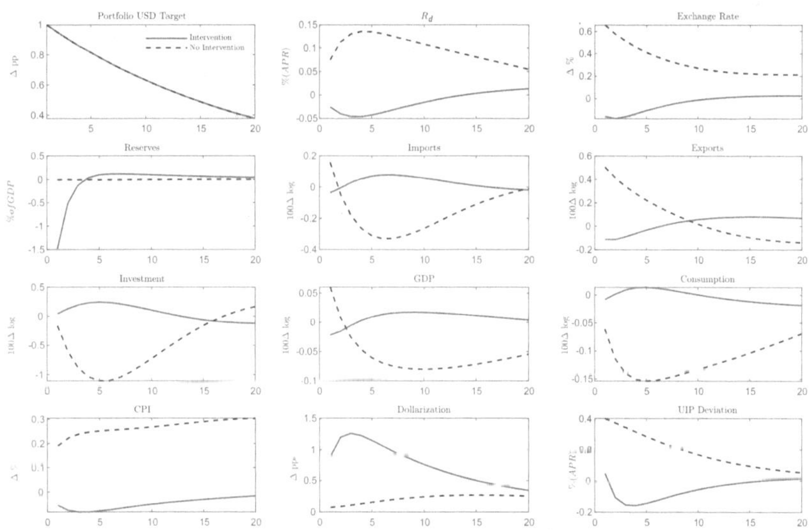

Fig. 12. The figure simulates the response of the estimated model (with $\gamma^*_{R_d} = \gamma_\Theta = 0$) to a (noise) shock, $e_1^v = 0.01$, in period $t = 1$ to the portfolio target, $v_1, v_2, \ldots$. The simulation is done under two scenarios: the central bank follows the estimated FX intervention rule described in the (unnumbered) equation in the text (solid line, θ_Θ) and a nonintervention rule (dashed line, $\theta_\Theta = 0$). With one exception, the intervention rule largely eliminates the impact of the noise shock on imports, exports, GDP, investment, consumption, and all but one of the other variables. The exception is central bank reserves, which fall by 1.5% of GDP. APR = annual percent rate; CPI = consumer price index; GDP = gross domestic product.

Here, $\theta_Y = 0$ corresponds to No Intervention (dashed line) and $\theta_Y = 3$ corresponds to the case where the monetary authority responds directly to the noise shock (admittedly, a heroic assumption). The IRFs in the case of $\theta_Y = 3$ are labeled Intervention and are depicted by the solid lines.

The 1,1 panel in figure 12 displays the impact of a noise shock on the dollar share target, $100(\Upsilon_t - \Upsilon)$, and the 4,2 panel in figure 12 reports the response of the actual dollar share, $100(\Theta_t - \Theta)$. Both variables are reported in percentage deviation from their (common) unshocked values, $\Upsilon = \Theta$. In the No Intervention case, the increase in the desire to hold dollars causes a depreciation (see panel 1,3). That in turn inflicts capital losses on entrepreneurs' balance sheets and, with a delay, leads them to cut back on investment. The maximal cut back on investment is a substantial 1%. The depreciation also drives up inflation (panel 4,1), so that the monetary authority raises the interest rate (panel 1,2). Households respond by substituting toward domestic assets by raising Θ_t by only a small amount, despite the rise in the target (panel 4,2). The small rise in Θ_t relative to Υ_t explains why Λ_t is positive (see panel 4,3). The rise in the interest rate, together with the fall in GDP, leads to a fall in consumption. Imports fall, because of both the depreciation and the fall in GDP. The depreciation stimulates a rise in exports, which is muted by the sticky-in-dollars export prices.

Now consider the effects of FX intervention, the Intervention case. With the intervention, reserves fall 1.5% of GDP (see panel 2,1). Roughly speaking, the FX intervention rule gives households the additional dollars that they want. Note that Λ_t remains close to 0 (see panel 4,2) and Θ_t roughly follows the path of Υ_t (panel 4,2). As a result, the FX intervention rule roughly insulates the economy from the noise shock. So, FX intervention can in principle be very effective at handling shocks for the demand for dollars.

The argument regarding FX interventions in the context of noise traders resembles a similar case made by Poole (1970) for dealing with money demand shocks. Suppose households experience a noise shock and they suddenly want to hold a larger fraction of their financial portfolio in the form of cash. It might be welfare improving for the monetary authority to give people the cash they want in exchange for assets and thereby prevent changes in financial market prices that might otherwise perturb the rest of the economy. Similarly, if a noise shock motivates people to change the fraction of their financial portfolio they want to hold in the form of dollars, then the central bank can enter the market and sell people the dollars they want in exchange for local currency assets, without the rest of the economy being disturbed by a significant jump in interest rates or the exchange rate. In effect, our simulations vindicate this view. For a version of this argument in a model with microfoundations, see Itskhoki and Mukhin (2023). In our simulations, a version of the FX intervention rule that we work with does insulate the economy against noise shocks in the exchange rate market. Undoubtedly a rule can be found that exactly insulates the economy from a noise shock. This observation gives rise to other questions: In practice, can a central bank distinguish a noise shock from other shocks, and if it cannot, does this affect the desirability of FX interventions? We suspect that in practice, noise shocks operate at a much higher frequency than other shocks so that a small amount of exchange rate smoothing may effectively target the noise shocks. We leave this conjecture for future research.

D. *The Importance of the Trade Channel, Sticky-in-Dollars Export Prices, the Elasticity of Substitution, and Balance Sheet Effects*

For each of the AE, EME, and Peru models, we display IRFs like in the previous graphs, except that we also include additional variables: consumption, the share of dollars in financial assets ("dollarization"), Θ_t, and the net worth of entrepreneurs. Figures 13, 14, and 15 correspond to the AE, EME, and Peru models, respectively. Each figure reproduces the IRFs of the estimated models ("Benchmark") as well as IRFs corresponding to single-parameter perturbations on the Benchmark.

We remove the balance sheet frictions by setting a high value for ϕ so that entrepreneurs have little exposure to dollar debt and the balance sheet effects associated with exchange rate movements are small ("Low Dollar Debt"). In the AE, the estimation results select a value of ϕ very close to 1, so we do not implement this perturbation in that case (see table 2). In the Peru model, we set $\phi = 1$, so entrepreneurs do not borrow in dollars at all. In the case of EMEs, for model solution reasons we set $\phi = 0.75$, so credit dollarization is substantially reduced but not eliminated.

We also consider the case in which the US monetary tightening does not change the foreign price level or the shifter in export demand ("No Import"). This is the case in which the trade channel is essentially shut down.[50] Finally, we consider the case "Flex Export," which corresponds to $\theta^X = 0$, that is, dollar prices in the export sector are set flexibly (see Subsec. III.C, Exports and the Dominant Currency Paradigm).

Consider the results for the AE model in figure 13. The Benchmark results are depicted by the solid lines, and we see the relatively modest 0.6% drop in GDP in the Benchmark model (panel 3,2). Note in the same

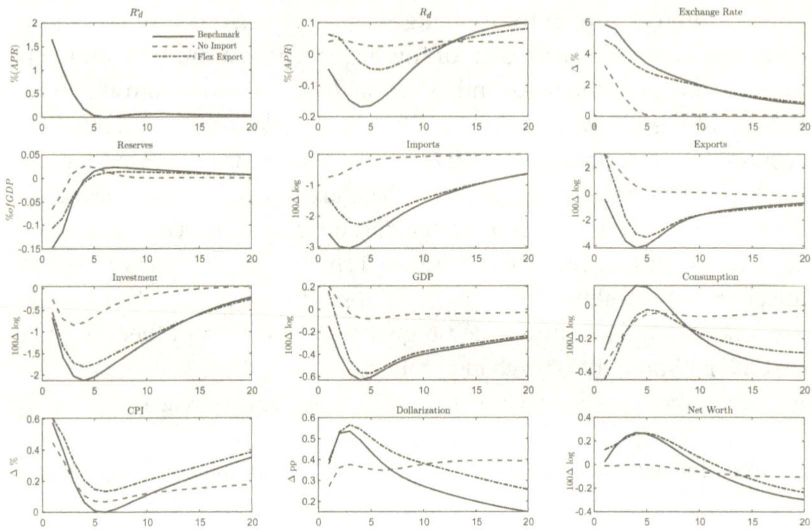

Fig. 13. AE: Baseline and baseline without two features. These graphs display the response of the AEs to a US monetary policy tightening. We include additional variables: consumption, the share of dollars in financial assets ("Dollarization"), Θ_t, and the net worth of entrepreneurs. The figure considers the effects of two perturbations on the Benchmark estimated model (solid line): zeroing out the impact of the monetary tightening on US import demand and the US price level ("No Import," dashed line), and eliminating the sticky-in-dollar assumption ("Flex Export," dot-dashed line) on intermediate good producers of the domestic component of exports (i.e., $\theta^X = 0$ in Subsec. III.C, Exports and the Dominant Currency Paradigm). Zeroing out US import demand has a very big impact. Flexible prices have only a small impact. See also the notes to figures 7 and 9. APR = annual percent rate; CPI = consumer price index; GDP = gross domestic product.

figure that allowing dollar export prices to be flexible does not have a big impact on dynamics; for example, the impact of flexible dollar prices on GDP is quantitatively small (panel 3,2). Qualitatively, the impact of flexible dollar prices on the response of exports is as expected (exports rise), but the effect is quantitatively small (see panel 2,3). By contrast, the impact of dropping the import channel is very large ("No Import"). In contrast to the previous result, when we drop the import channel, the effects of a US monetary contraction fall by an order of magnitude (dashed line). The key result in figure 13 is that dropping the trade channel eliminates most of the effects of a US monetary contraction. Indeed, GDP rises briefly before quickly returning to steady state. The role of variation in entrepreneurial net worth is small in the AE model because there is no exposure to dollar debt in that model. We include entrepreneurial net worth here for symmetry with the EME and Peru figures, where net worth plays an important role.

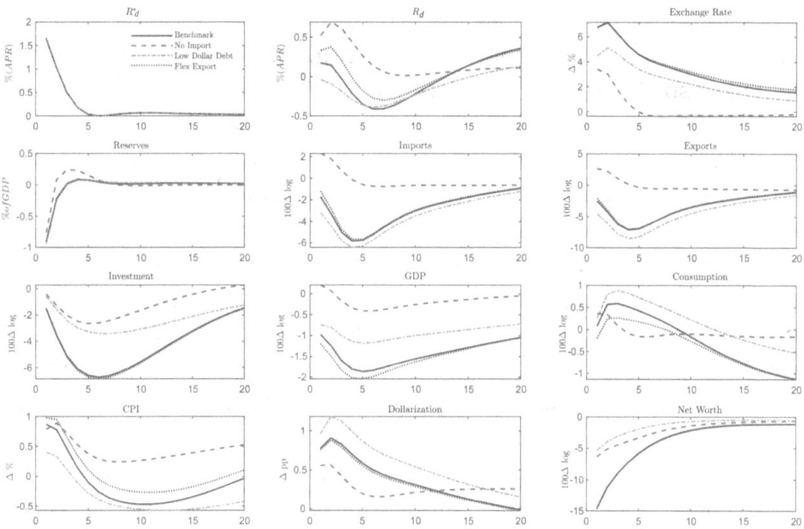

Fig. 14. EME: Baseline and baseline without three features. These graphs display the effects of three perturbations on the baseline, estimated model. These include the two perturbations in figure 13 (here, the "Flex Export" case corresponds to the dotted line) as well as a perturbation in which credit dollarization is reduced by raising the value of ϕ to 0.75 from its estimated value of roughly 0.5 ("Low Dollar Debt," dot-dashed line). As in the previous figure, zeroing out the response of US import demand of a monetary tightening has the consequence that a US monetary contraction has only a small impact on EME gross domestic product (GDP), consumption, and investment. Making export prices flexible in dollars has very little effect on the baseline IRFs. Reducing credit dollarization has a substantial impact by moderating the investment and GDP response to a US monetary tightening. See also the notes to figures 7 and 9. APR = annual percent rate; CPI = consumer price index.

Now consider the EMEs (fig. 14), in which ϕ is estimated to be in a neighborhood of 0.5. In this case, the depreciation triggered by a US monetary tightening inflicts capital losses on dollar-indebted entrepreneurs, causing a substantial, protracted fall in their net worth (see panel 4,3). The relatively small reduction in credit dollarization associated with an increase in ϕ from roughly 0.5 to 0.75 has a relatively large effect. The maximal drop in net worth falls by one-third, from 15% to 5% (see panel 4,3). The maximal drop in investment shrinks from roughly 7% to roughly 3% (panel 3,1). The maximal drop in GDP falls from roughly 1.75% to about 1.25% (panel 3,2). Consider the response of consumption, in panel 3,3. Note that it increases for a while before eventually falling. We do not include household consumption in our analysis, because consumption monthly data are either not available or they also include durables and so would not be a good match with our model. Still, the model could have produced an immediate fall in consumption if the elasticity of substitution between domestic and foreign inputs were lower. Our estimated elasticity of substitution is already quite low, at $\eta_c = 0.41$. In Section H of the appendix (http://www.nber.org/data-appendix/c14997/appendix.pdf), we display what happens when η_c is reduced further, to $\eta_c = 0.25$. In that case, consumption falls immediately. This makes the exchange rate depreciate even more (a good thing for model fit), but it makes the price of consumption goods rise too much, investment and GDP fall too much, and exports fall too little. (These observations are made relative to the VAR-based probability intervals reported in fig. 9.) We can see why the estimation does not "like" a lower value of η_c. Although that moves the exchange rate response in the direction of the data, at the same time it moves investment, GDP, the CPI, and exports away from the data.[51] Still, the results informally suggest that with low substitution between domestic and foreign inputs, one needs fewer balance sheet frictions to fit the EME IRFs.[52] This deserves further investigation, but we believe the outcome would not affect our basic result, that the foreign impact of a US dollar tightening operates primarily through the trade channel.

Finally, consider Peru (fig. 15). With two exceptions, the IRFs that zero out the shift in import demand are the ones closest to the zero line ("No Imports"). The first exception is reserves, which is no surprise because the FX intervention rule is still in operation and it is primarily a function of $R^*_{d,t}$ (see eq. [29]). The other exception is also no surprise. Net worth moves least when $\phi = 1$ so that there is zero credit dollarization and entrepreneurial net worth is not affected by movements in the exchange rate. It is interesting that eliminating credit dollarization by setting $\phi = 1$ (perhaps by regulation) does not insulate GDP from US monetary shocks. Although eliminating credit dollarization reduces the drop in investment, it increases the consumption response to a US monetary policy shock. This result is different from what we found for the EMEs, where a relatively small fall in credit dollarization cut the maximal drop in GDP in half (see fig. 14).

The key takeaway from these experiments is that the import channel plays a very important role in the transmission of US monetary policy shocks. Without the import effects, a monetary tightening is predicted to result in almost no change in GDP (panel 3,2 in the above three figures).

E. *UIP Deviations*

This section examines the role of the UIP frictions, parameterized by γ, $\gamma_{R^*_d}$, γ_Θ, in the international transmission of US monetary shocks. For

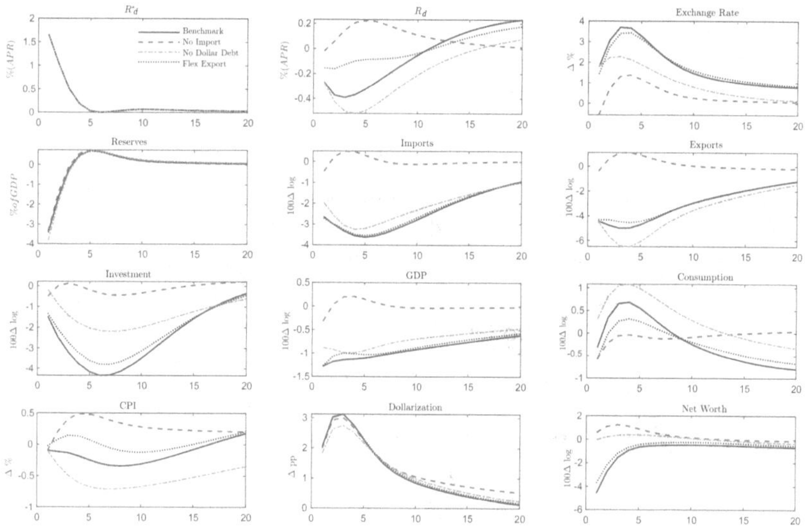

Fig. 15. Peru: Baseline and baseline without three features. See notes to figures 13 and 14. The results are similar to what we found for the AEs. The main takeaway is that zeroing out response of US import demand to a US monetary contraction greatly reduces the impact on Peru. APR = annual percent rate; CPI = consumer price index; GDP = gross domestic product.

convenience, we reproduce a variant on our expression for the UIP deviation, Λ_t, in equations (11) and (12):[53]

$$\begin{aligned} \Lambda_t &= R_{d,t} - \overbrace{\left[R^*_{d,t} + E_t \log\left(\frac{S_{t+1}}{S_t}\right)\right]}^{\text{expected return on dollar asset in LCUs}}, \\ \Lambda_t &= \gamma(Y_t - \Theta_t), \\ Y_t &= Y + \gamma_{R^*_d}\left(R^*_{d,t} - R^*_d\right) + \gamma_\Theta(\bar{\Theta}_t - \bar{\Theta}_{t-1}) + e^Y_t. \end{aligned} \tag{41}$$

Here, Θ_t denotes the portfolio share of dollars chosen by an individual household, and $\bar{\Theta}_t$ denotes the aggregate share of dollars in all households' portfolios.[54] The first expression in equation (41) defines, to a first-order approximation, the UIP deviation, Λ_t, in terms of the return on domestic assets and the return on dollar assets converted into LCU by the expected log change in the exchange rate. The second and third terms are our (reduced-form) model of the UIP deviation. A baseline in the SOE model literature is the seminal Dornbusch (1976) overshooting narrative, which assumes that UIP holds, that is, $\gamma = 0$.

In the first section below, we provide two quantitative characterizations of the failure of UIP. The first characterization corresponds to the standard, delayed overshooting puzzle. The second is (we believe) novel, and we call it the excessive overshooting puzzle. There are additional UIP puzzles, particularly in EMEs. Dalgıc (2024) documents the failure of UIP to hold even on average, and that the average deviation varies across EME countries depending on how much their currencies depreciate in a recession. Our model does not address this observation and implies that the deviation from UIP is approximately zero on average. Christiano et al. (2021) display a microfounded model in which hedging motives explain the observations that Dalgıc (2024) documents. In their model, the average deviation from UIP reflects an insurance mechanism under which some agents within a country insure others in the same country against business cycle income risk. Our VAR and SOE model analyses abstract from these considerations.

In the second subsection below, we do counterfactual simulations of our EME model to demonstrate the important role played by UIP frictions (i.e., the values of $\gamma, \gamma_{R_d^*}, \gamma_{\Theta}$) in accounting for the two UIP puzzles, as well as for the dynamics of aggregate measures of economic activity. We find that the primary role of $\gamma > 0$ is to activate the risk appetite parameter, $\gamma_{R_d^*}$, and the portfolio inertia parameter, γ_{Θ}. Both parameters help to account for the UIP puzzles documented in Subsection V.E, Characterization of the Failure of UIP, as well as the real effects of a US monetary tightening on investment and GDP. However, $\gamma_{R_d^*}$ has a relatively larger impact on aggregate economic activity and γ_{Θ} has a relatively larger impact on the UIP distortions.

Characterization of the Failure of UIP

This subsection examines our VAR evidence, and so the time unit, t, corresponds to months.[55] We consider the case in which $R_{d,t}^*$ and $R_{d,t}$ are 1-month, nominally risk-free assets. Recall that our empirical measure of $R_{d,t}^*$ pertains to an asset with 2-year maturity (see Subsec. II.A, US Vector Autoregression). At the end of this subsection, we explain that our empirical findings hold even more strongly when $R_{d,t}^*$ is measured by a shorter maturity interest rate.

In a slight abuse of notation, let $\Delta_j = R_{d,j}^* - R_{d,j}$ denote the period j response ($j = 1, 2, \ldots$) in the dollar premium, $R_{d,t}^* - R_{d,t}$, to a contractionary

US monetary policy shock in period $j = 1$. Similarly, let $\log S_j$ denote the period j response of the log exchange rate. We make the following assumption:

Assumption 1. Δ_j, $\log S_j \to 0$, as $j \to \infty$ and that convergence proceeds at a geometric rate.

By "proceeds at a geometric rate," we mean that the series eventually evolves like λ^j, for some $\lambda \in (-1, 1)$. Assumption 1 is satisfied in our linearly approximated SOE model solutions.[56] Our VAR analysis also appears to be consistent with assumption 1. For example, inspection of the figures for our baseline VARs suggest that $\log S_t$ converges to 0 after about 2 years (for the US, AE, EME, and Peruvian economies, see figs. 1, 2, 4, and 5, respectively). We study Δ_j, $\log S_j$ in Section J of the appendix (http://www.nber.org/data-appendix/c14997/appendix.pdf) up to period 600 (50 years), and assumption 1 seems plausible in that zero remains inside the 90% probability interval. To save space, the results in the rest of this section and the next are based on our analysis of the EME VARs.

Iterating on the first expression in equation (41) with $\Lambda_t = 0$ for all t, using assumption 1 and applying the law of iterated expectations, we obtain:

$$\log S_\ell^{\text{UIP}} = \sum_{j=0}^{\infty} \Delta_{\ell+j}. \tag{42}$$

Here, $\log S_\ell^{\text{UIP}}$ denotes the prediction of the UIP for the ℓth period response of the log exchange rate in an EME, to a US monetary policy shock, where $\ell = 1, 2, \ldots$ The object on the right of the equality in equation (42) is the sum of the IRFs of the dollar premium into the future. Also, $\ell = 1$ corresponds to the period in which the shock occurs.

Motivated by the above considerations, we use the EME IRFs and equation (42) to compute the IRFs in equation (12) for $\ell = 1, \ldots, 36$, under the truncation, $\Delta_t = 0$ for $t > 50$.[57] These IRFs appear as the dot dashed line in figure 16.[58] The dashed line reports the actual estimated exchange rate IRFs taken from panel 2,1 in figure 4. For reference, the solid line displays the IRFs of the dollar premium, $R_{d,\ell}^* - R_{d,\ell}$, for the EMEs, for $\ell = 1, \ldots, 36$.[59]

The UIP puzzle corresponds to the difference between the posterior median of the IRFs for $\log S_j^{\text{UIP}}$ (dot-dashed line) and $\log S_j$ (dashed line). The two sets of IRFs differ strikingly in two ways. First, the shape of the dot-dashed line is different from the hump shape displayed by the actual exchange rate IRF. The graph of $\log S_j^{\text{UIP}}$ displays the Dornbusch

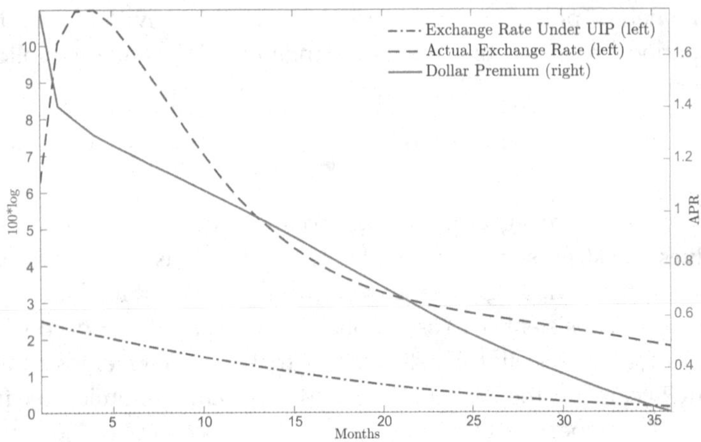

Fig. 16. Exchange rates and dollar premium in EMEs. The dashed line reproduces the estimated IRF for the EME's exchange rate from the 2,1 panel of figure (4). The solid line reports the IRFs for $R^*_{d,t} - R_{d,t}$, constructed by subtracting the IRF of $R_{d,t}$ in the 2,1 panel of figure 4 from the IRF of $R^*_{d,t}$ in the 1,1 panel of the same figure (the dollar monthly premium in the solid line is measured as an annual percentage rate). The dot-dashed line displays $100 \times \log S_j^{\text{UIP}}$ computed using equation (42) and the truncation, $\Delta_j = 0$ for $j > 50$. For the purposes of computing $100 \times \log S_j^{\text{UIP}}$, the dollar premium is measured at a monthly percentage rate. The dot-dashed line in period j is the sum of the values of the solid line (after division by 12) at horizons $j, j+1, \ldots, 50$. For additional discussion, see the text. UIP = uncovered interest rate parity; APR = annual percent rate.

(1976) overshooting effect, having the property that the maximal effect on the exchange rate occurs in the period of the shock. By contrast, the unrestricted estimate of the exchange rate response, $\log S_j$, displays the well-known delayed overshooting effect, in which the maximal effect occurs a few months later than the shock.[60] From the perspective of the UIP, the anticipated depreciation of the exchange rate on foreign currency after a US monetary tightening is puzzling because $\Lambda_1 < 0$. That is, because foreign currencies are expected to depreciate, anyone holding a foreign asset gets two boosts by selling that asset and buying a dollar asset: first, they get the higher nominal return on the dollar asset, and second, they get an additional bonus on the round trip through the FX rate market. The puzzle, from the perspective of the UIP, is:

'why do people hold any non–US assets right after a US monetary tightening?' (43)

The second puzzle follows from the obvious large difference in the overall level of the dashed line relative to the dot-dashed line predicted by the UIP. This is what we call the excessive exchange rate overshooting puzzle. The level of the exchange rate is much higher than is justified by the prospective move in the expected dollar premium.

Given that the currency eventually returns to its preshock level, the sharp ("excessive") depreciation of the currency must be followed by a bigger appreciation than the one implied by the dot-dashed line, which also converges to zero, but starting from a lower level. Because the appreciation of the currency under UIP (the dot-dashed line) exactly wipes out the advantage of holding dollar assets, the greater appreciation by the actual exchange rate must cause dollar assets to have a lower return than foreign assets, so that $\Lambda_\ell > 0$ after month 3. That is, the expected LCU return on the dollar, $R^*_{d,\ell} + \log S_{\ell+1} - \log S_\ell$, is less than $R_{d,\ell}$ after the first quarter, even though $R^*_{d,\ell} > R_{d,\ell}$. So, the second UIP puzzle is,

$$\text{why does any one hold dollar assets a few months after a US monetary tightening when dollar depreciation swamps the dollar premium?} \tag{44}$$

Finally, recall that in our empirical analysis, $R^*_{d,t}$ corresponds to the annualized percentage return on 2-year US Treasury securities. In the above analysis we interpreted $R^*_{d,t}$ as the annualized percentage return on a 1-month security. We redid our VARs using shorter-term US securities to measure $R^*_{d,t}$. In each case, we found that the premium, Δ_t, was even smaller although there was no impact on the other variables, including the response of the exchange rate to a Bauer and Swanson (2023) monetary tightening. In light of this result, we interpret the dot-dashed curve in figure 16 as an upper bound on what the UIP predicts for the exchange rate. Thus, the excessive exchange rate overshooting puzzle may be even bigger than what is suggested in figure 16. At the same time, the delayed overshooting result does not depend on how we measure $R^*_{d,t}$. We conclude that the two UIP puzzles discussed in this section are not an artifact of our measurement of $R^*_{d,t}$.

Interpreting Delayed and Excess Overshooting

In this section we ask: (1) How does our EME model explain the quantitatively large deviations from UIP? (2) Do the deviations from UIP matter for the international transmission of US monetary policy?

To save space, we make our points by focusing only on the EME case. The AE case is similar (for details, see appendix sec. K, http://www

.nber.org/data-appendix/c14997/appendix.pdf). For example, the 1,1 panels in figures 2 and 4 indicate that the exchange rate IRFs in the AEs and EMEs are very similar. Each follows a hump-shaped pattern with a high peak. The magnitude of the interest rate differentials, $R^*_{d,t} - R_{d,t}$, are not very different between AEs and EMEs, relative to the magnitude of the exchange rate depreciations and appreciations.

Because we work with our SOE model in this section, t now corresponds to quarters.

Our estimation procedure assigns values to the parameters, $\gamma, \gamma_{R^*_d}, \gamma_\Theta$, to enable the SOE to broadly match the IRFs described in Subsection V.E, Characterization of the Failure of UIP. Figure 17 displays the estimated EME model IRFs (solid line, Benchmark). Note from panel 1,3 that we obtain one period (quarter) delayed overshooting in that model. This matches the VAR evidence of a 3-month delay. The 3,3 panel of the figure shows that $\Lambda_1 < 0$ in the estimated model. In that model, people continue to hold at least some local assets, that is, $\Theta_1 < 1$, so $\Lambda_1 < 0$ contradicts household optimization under UIP. People do shift their portfolios somewhat toward dollars (panel 4,2) after a US monetary tightening, but with $\Lambda_1 < 0$ and $\Theta_1 < 1$ people walk away from a higher expected return by not increasing Θ_1 even more.[61] So, the model embeds an answer to the puzzle stated in equation (43).

According to panel 3,3, $\Lambda_1 < 0$ and $\Lambda_t > 0$ for $t = 2, \ldots$. This matches what we found in the analysis of the VAR above. That is, after one quarter has passed, the currency begins to appreciate so much that the LCU return on the dollar, $R^*_{d,t} + E_t[\log S_{t+1} - \log S_t]$, is less than the return on $R_{d,t}$ even though $R^*_{d,t} - R_{d,t} > 0$. Yet, according to the solid line, people continue to hold a relatively high share of dollars (panel 4,2). So, the model also embeds an answer to the puzzle stated in equation (44).

We now discuss the role of γ, γ_Θ, and $\gamma_{R^*_d}$ in answering our two questions.

The Role of γ. The version of the model with $\gamma > 0$ and $\gamma_{R^*_d} = \gamma_\Theta = 0$ in principle offers a reduced-form explanation for how $\Lambda_1 < 0$ can be part of an equilibrium. As people increase their holdings of dollar assets when $R^*_{d,t} - R_{d,t}$ jumps after a US monetary tightening, they exceed their target dollar share in assets, γ_1. On the margin they suffer nonpecuniary costs holding dollars, and this is why they are willing to forgo the additional pecuniary gains they can expect by raising Θ_t even more. Also, with $\gamma > 0$, the desire to back out of dollars after the first period puts people below target, eventually making $\Lambda_t > 0$. With a positive nonpecuniary return on dollars, they do not mind forfeiting the extra returns they could get if they reduced Θ_t faster.

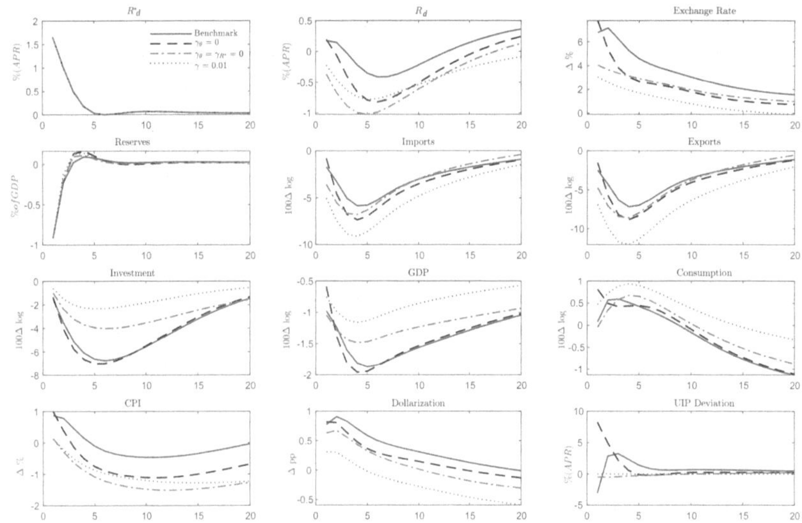

Fig. 17. The impact of portfolio friction parameters. Response to a US monetary tightening under different parameterizations of the model. The baseline parameterization corresponds to the version of the model with parameters set as in section IV. The horizontal axis is measured in quarters, consistent with the observations in Subsection II.A, Three-Variable US VAR. The monetary tightening shock occurs in period 1. APR = annual percent rate; UIP = uncovered interest rate parity; CPI = consumer price index; GDP = gross domestic product.

For the most part, the qualitative effects of $\gamma > 0$ move the model toward the data. One thing that the model misses with only γ is the delayed overshooting (see panel 1,3). But, at a quantitative level, it misses everything. It misses the excess overshooting in the level of the exchange rate. Investment and GDP fall relatively little.

When $\gamma = 0$, the model performs very badly (see the dotted line). Delayed overshooting is gone, and the level of the exchange rate rises only a little, similar to the dot dashed curve in figure 15. The model also performs poorly with real variables. The drop in investment and GDP are cut in half and are now quite modest.

The Role $\gamma_{R_d^*}$. The risk appetite parameter, $\gamma_{R_d^*} > 0$, has the consequence that a rise in R_d^* leads to an increase in the target share of dollars. We can see the effect of increasing the value of this parameter from $\gamma_{R_d^*} = 0$ (dot-dashed line) with $\gamma_{R_d^*} > 0$ (dashed line). The US monetary tightening only lasts for about a year, but it still has longer-term effects. The immediate effect is to increase share of dollars in people's portfolios, which in turn raises the exchange rate sharply, though only temporarily. So, $\gamma_{R_d^*}$

does not help with delayed overshooting. It also only helps a little to raise the overall level of the exchange rate as excessive overshooting calls for. Finally, $\gamma_{R_d^*}$ also does not help much with the pattern of UIP deviations in the 4,3 panel.

Where the parameter $\gamma_{R_d^*}$ appears to have a big impact is on economic activity. For example, note that the dashed line roughly coincides with the solid lines in the 3,1 and 3,2 panels. In particular, with a delay, investment falls in response to the sharp depreciation in the exchange rate (panel 1,3). The sharp depreciation that $\gamma_{R_d^*} > 0$ produces has the consequence that entrepreneurs experience substantial capital losses. Investment adjustment costs prevent an immediate response of investment, as entrepreneurs sustain spending for a while by substituting loans for their lost net worth. However, eventually investment falls as much as it does with all the UIP frictions, helping to drag down GDP. Investment stays low for a while because it takes time for net worth to recover. The delayed and dragged-out effects on investment of an exchange rate depreciation is discussed in detail in Section I in the appendix (http://www.nber.org/data-appendix/c14997/appendix.pdf). That discussion reviews the dynamics of interest rate premia on risky borrowers, the nonperforming loan rate, leverage, and issues relevant to the transmission of exchange rate shocks to investment via financial markets.

It is interesting to note that $\gamma_{R_d^*}$ only affects the pure interest rate effect and not the pure price level effect or the pure trade effect. In the previous section, we showed that the pure interest rate effect is small, and most of the impact of a US monetary contraction operates via the pure trade effect. So, how can $\gamma_{R_d^*}$ be "important" if it operates via a relatively unimportant channel? As it turns out, essentially the whole of the pure interest rate effect is due to $\gamma_{R_d^*} > 0$. For more details, see Section G in the appendix.

The Role of γ_Θ. As its name suggests, the portfolio inertia parameter, $\gamma_\Theta < 0$, acts like a portfolio adjustment cost. The impact of the value of that parameter can be assessed by comparing the dashed line in figure 16 with the solid line. The parameter γ_Θ has a significant impact on the UIP distortions. For example, panel 4,3 shows that that parameter allows the model to replicate the substantial switch between $\Lambda_1 < 0$ and $\Lambda_\ell > 0$ for $\ell > 1$. As people increase Θ_1, $\gamma_\Theta < 0$ reduces their incentive to raise Θ_1 by reducing the target share, Y_1. This helps to make Λ_1 more negative than otherwise (see panel 4,3). The parameter also allows the model to produce the delayed overshooting phenomenon (panel 1,3). The basic story about why people seem to leave money on the table by not acquiring more dollars in the quarter of a contractionary US monetary policy is that various factors sour them on dollars. Our model does not take a stand on the microfoundations of these factors, which could be a combination of habits in portfolio shares, regulatory rigidities, or something else.[62]

Eventually, people begin to reduce the share of their portfolios held in dollars (see panel 4,2). However, $\gamma_\Theta < 0$ works to slow the fall in the share of dollars as $\bar{\Theta}_t - \bar{\Theta}_{t-1} < 0$ because the parameter now has the effect of raising the target share of dollars. This suggests that $\gamma_\Theta < 0$ also helps with the puzzle in equation (44). The reason people do not get out of dollars faster is that there are portfolio adjustment costs. The fact that people continue holding dollars with $\gamma_\Theta < 0$ places upward pressure on the exchange rate at horizons $\ell > 1$. Thus, the parameter also helps the model to accommodate excess portfolio overshooting.

F. Out-of-Sample Model Evaluation

Our SOE model includes a rich array of financial frictions. For example, the credit market has implications for the interest rate spread for risky entrepreneurial borrowers (see Subsec. III.D). These implications were not used in the estimation of the model and provide us with a type of out-of-sample test for our model. The solid lines in figure 18 display estimates of the response of equity and lending spreads in AE and EME data. The dark and light shaded areas represent 68% and 90% confidence intervals, respectively. In each case, the empirical estimates are produced using the local projection method used elsewhere in our analysis. In particular, the left- and right-hand variables in these projections correspond to averages across the AE and EME countries for which we have data (for details, see app. B, http://www.nber.org/data-appendix/c14997/appendix.pdf).

We limited ourselves to the subset of our countries for which monthly data on equity and lending spreads are available from the IMF database, IFS. In the case of our measure of equity, for the AEs we have data on Canada, Japan, and the United Kingdom. In the case of spreads, we have data for Australia, Canada, Japan, Norway, Sweden, Switzerland, and the United Kingdom. Turning to the EMEs, we have data on equity from Brazil, Chile, Hungary, Mexico, the Philippines, Poland, Russia, South Africa, and Thailand. We have data on EME spreads for Brazil, Chile, Colombia, Dominican Republic, Hungary, Indonesia, Mexico, Peru, the Philippines, Russia, Serbia, South Africa, and Thailand.

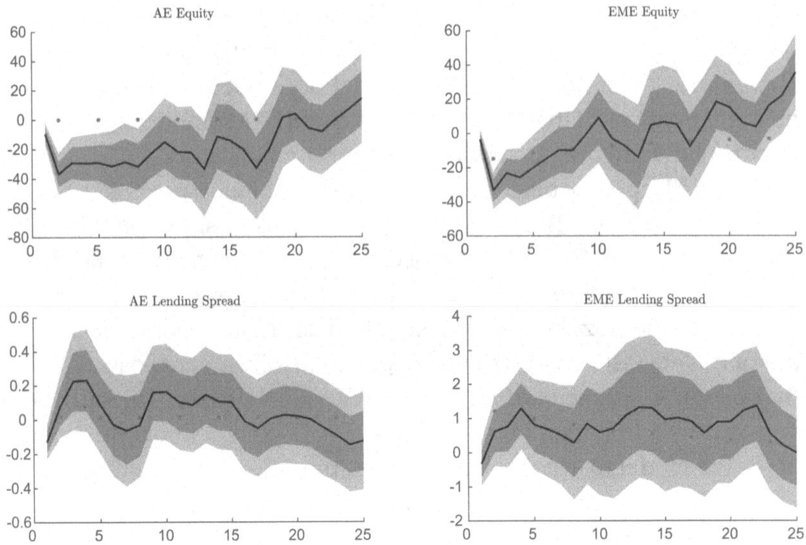

Fig. 18. Estimated model implications for equity and spreads. (1) The empirical equity data correspond to 100 times the log of an equity index reported in the IFS database. The empirical spread data are measured at an annual rate in decimal terms and are also obtained from the IFS. (2) Solid lines indicate point estimates by local projects discussed in the text. (3) Dark and light shaded areas correspond to 68% and 90% confidence intervals. (4) Equity data in the model are 100 times the log of entrepreneurial net worth, N_t (see eqq. [19] and [27]). (5) Dotted lines correspond to IRFs from our estimated models. (6) The date t spread variable in the model is measured by $E_t[Z_{t+1} - R_{t+1}]$, where Z_{t+1} denotes the LCU interest paid by risky entrepreneurs in period $t + 1$, for one unit of LCU borrowed in period t from a bank. Also, $R_{t+1} = R_{d,t}\phi + s_{t+1}(1 - \phi)R^*_{d,t}$ denotes the LCU interest rate paid by risk-free banks in period $t + 1$ on one unit of LCU borrowed in period t (as indicated in eq. [23], banks are assumed to be required to borrow a share, ϕ, in local currency and $1 - \phi$ in foreign currency). For additional discussion of entrepreneurs in the model, see Subsection III.D. AE = advanced economy; EME = emerging market economy.

Comparing the solid and dotted lines, we see that the model is roughly consistent with the empirical IRFs. The model misses somewhat in the case of AEs. The reason is that in that case ϕ is estimated to be close to unity. Even though the exchange rate response to an $R^*_{d,t}$ shock is substantial, it has little impact on entrepreneurs when they have no dollar debt. This is why our model implies that equity and the interest rate spread hardly respond to an $R^*_{d,t}$ shock in the AEs. Zero response in the interest rate spread is consistent with our empirical IRF for the AEs. However, zero response in equity lies outside the confidence intervals for the first three quarters in the AE IRF. Because we estimate ϕ to be substantially less than unity for the EMEs, exchange rate movements have a substantial impact on interest rate spreads and equity in the EMEs. The model responses closely mirror the corresponding empirical estimates.

Given that equity and interest rate spreads played no role in model estimation, we regard these results as providing support for our SOE models.

VI. Conclusion

We document that non-US countries contract after a US monetary tightening, with EMEs contracting more than AEs. In fact, the contraction in EME output is at least as big, maybe bigger, than the contraction in US output. In our analysis, bigger balance sheet frictions in the EMEs account for their greater sensitivity to US monetary shocks.

Our key novel finding concerns the role of US imports in the international transmission of US monetary shocks. We find that the primary channel by which non-US economies contract after a US monetary tightening operates through a fall in US demand for imports induced by the US monetary tightening. We reach this conclusion by doing counterfactual simulations using SOE models that we fit to the data.

Our analysis confirms much of the modern literature that focuses on a wide range of financial and other frictions. Violations of UIP are big (we believe they are bigger than previously reported), and these violations play an important role in the international propagation of US monetary policy shocks. Balance sheet effects appear to play an important role in EMEs.

We do not examine the details of how a fall in US imports propagates through the global trading network to have an impact on the non-US countries we study. The role of the global trading network is an exciting area of research.

We also ask whether a country can use FX interventions to shield itself from US monetary policy actions, while it pursues its own inflation and output objectives using, say, an interest rate targeting rule. We study a standard FX intervention rule and find that that rule only marginally insulates a representative EME economy from US monetary shocks. It has been argued that there are other shocks—sometimes they are called noise shocks or portfolio share shocks—that play an important role in exchange rate dynamics (see Eichenbaum et al. 2021; Itskhoki and Mukhin 2021). We find that FX interventions can be very useful at smoothing out the effects of these shocks.

Endnotes

Author email addresses: Camara (santiago.camara@mcgill.ca), Christiano (l-christiano@northwestern.edu), Dalgıc (cagri.dalgic@gmail.com). We are grateful for feedback from Paul Castillo and Mathias Trabandt, as well as for the research assistance and advice of Evan Majic. We also appreciate the thoughtful comments of our discussant, Dmitry Mukhin, at the Reykjavík Economic Conference, May 23–24, 2024. We owe a special debt for extensive interactions with Martin Eichenbaum and our discussants, Şebnem Kalemli-Özcan and Jón Steinsson, at the April 18–19, 2024, Macroeconomics Annual Conference. These also led to substantial improvements in the paper. Finally, we benefited from the extended audience feedback after the presentation at the Macroeconomics Annual Conference. This feedback, in particular from Adrien Auclert and Jordi Galí, prompted some revisions. Dalgıc gratefully acknowledges funding by the Deutsche Forschungsgemeinschaft (DFG, German Research Foundation) through CRC TR 224 (Project C02). For acknowledgments, sources of research support, and disclosure of the authors' material financial relationships, if any, please see https://www.nber.org/books-and-chapters/nber-macroeconomics-annual-2024-volume-39/international-monetary-transmission-mechanism.

1. See Fleming (1962) and Mundell (1963).

2. The literature on monetary policy shock identification stretches back over many decades. The recent literature on high-frequency identification (which actually starts around the turn of the century with Rudebusch [1998] and Kuttner [2001]) has injected new energy into shock identification. Ramey (2016) offers an excellent introduction and overview to the modern approach, and our work most closely follows Bauer and Swanson (2023).

3. This research is an important reason for the prominence of the New Keynesian macroeconomic model.

4. Others have documented a decline in US imports following a contractionary US monetary policy shock. For example, Miranda-Agrippino and Ricco (2021, fig. 7) and Degasperi et al. (2020, fig. 2) show that the peak percentage point decline in US imports is more than twice the peak decline in US industrial production after a US monetary contraction.

5. In principle, the fall in US imports could reflect tighter financial conditions for non-US exporters (see, e.g., Bruno and Shin 2021). To decide whether the drop in imports reflects a fall in demand or supply, we look at the impact on an export price index of a US monetary tightening. We conclude that US imports drop because of a decline in US demand because the price index falls (see fig. 1).

6. The point that a decline in US imports after a US monetary contraction could account for a fall in non-US country exports is also made in Cesa-Bianchi, Ferrero, and Li (2024). Although our two papers overlap in many ways, the modeling strategies and questions asked are different. We stress the central role played in the international monetary transmission mechanism by the decline in US imports.

7. See Camara (2021) for why the Bauer and Swanson (2023) is particularly useful in the international setting.

8. See also Di Giovanni and Rogers (2024) for related work.

9. See Di Giovanni et al. (2022) and Akinci and Queralto (2024).

10. See Goldberg and Tille (2008) and Gopinath et al. (2020).

11. See Eichenbaum et al. (2021), Kalemli-Özcan and Varela (2021), Kekre and Lenel (2021), Devereux, Engel, and Wu (2023), Fukui, Nakamura, and Steinsson (2023), Greenwood et al. (2023), Itskhoki and Mukhin (2023), and Jiang, Krishnamurthy, and Lustig (2024).

12. See Gabaix and Maggiori (2015), Cavallino (2019), and Itskhoki and Mukhin (2023).

13. See Adrian et al. (2021), Basu and Gopinath (2024), and Cesa-Bianchi et al. (2024) for other models that incorporate all these and other factors.

14. See, e.g., the baseline M-F model described in Krugman, Obstfeld, and Melitz (2023).

15. Cesa-Bianchi et al. (2024) work with a general equilibrium model of the world economy, but they only have two countries and thus avoid adopting an empirically founded model of the global trading network.

16. The underlying economics is similar to the analysis in Itskhoki and Mukhin (2023), and we also relate the logic to the classic paper by Poole (1970).

17. The monetary policy shock is computed in Bauer and Swanson (2023) in two steps. First, the first principle component of the four time series, $ED1, \ldots, ED4$, is computed. Here, EDi denotes the change, from 10 minutes before to 20 minutes after a Federal Open Market Committee (FOMC) announcement, in the 3-month Eurodollar futures rate on a loan starting $i - 1$ quarters in the future, $i = 1, \ldots, 4$. Second, the first principle component is orthogonalized with respect to information available at the time of the FOMC announcement. For extensive discussion, see Bauer and Swanson (2023).

18. After demeaning all variables, the VAR analysis is done using the code from Dieppe et al. (2016). This code and demeaning procedure is used for all VARs reported in this paper.

19. When the trade-weighted exchange rate rises, the nominal exchange rate corresponds to an appreciation in the dollar.

20. The 2-year Treasury bond rate is sampled on the last business day of the month and is obtained from the Federal Reserve Bank of St. Louis's online database, FRED.

21. See, e.g., Devereux et al. (2023).

22. In the US case, GDP data are only available on a quarterly basis. We use Stock and Watson (2010)'s monthly GDP data obtained by multivariate interpolation of the monthly real GDP series. So, our US GDP data are not measured in CPI units.

23. Note that the effect of the contemporaneous impact of the monetary shock on GDP is relatively large. This is puzzling because the Bauer and Swanson (2023) shocks are orthogonalized with respect to information available at the start of an FOMC meeting. This means that the drop in GDP in the month of a meeting must occur in the remaining time during the month of the meeting. This is implausible, especially for meetings that occur at the end of the month. We suspect that our results reflect that the Bauer and Swanson (2023) monetary policy shocks are correlated with subsequent revisions in the data. For example, suppose the statistical agencies apply the smoothing method suggested in Sargent (1989) to revise data over time. Seasonal adjustment also involves two-sided smoothing, which may inject a "look-ahead feature" into the data. Suppose that a contractionary monetary policy shock drives true GDP down in the months after the FOMC meeting. Two-sided smoothing then implies that later revisions of the data will adjust the reported GDP numbers down in the month of the monetary contraction.

24. Recall the third result reported for the US VAR in Subsec. II.A, US Vector Autoregression.

25. See eq. (16).

26. These data are intended to measure changes in reserves that reflect active purchases and sales by central banks in the FX market. They are not simply changes in central bank FX reserves. The latter changes can reflect changes in market valuation and changes in earnings on the underlying assets. There are other movements in central bank reserves that are stripped from the measure of FX intervention. For example, reserves can change because banks must deposit a portion of their dollar liabilities with the central bank, and these enter central bank reserves. Adler et al. (2024) also attempt to include central bank activity in futures markets in their measure of FX interventions.

27. We do not model the entire euro area as one economy because it is not an SOE.

28. We would include New Zealand, but the IFS does not provide monthly data for that country's price indices. Monthly data on the Australian consumption price index are not available, so we used their monthly data on the producer price index instead.

29. Duttagupta and Pazarbasioglu (2021) identify the following countries as emerging markets: Argentina, Brazil, Chile, China, Colombia, Egypt, Hungary, India, Indonesia, Iran, Malaysia, Mexico, the Philippines, Poland, Russia, Saudi Arabia, South Africa, Thailand, Turkey, and the United Arab Emirates.

30. The results do not prove the absence of rebound effects, because they could well be fully encoded in the parameters of the US VAR.

31. In this paper, the only states of nature we consider are different realized values of the foreign interest, $R^*_{d,t+1}$.

32. This argument relies on the accuracy of the linear approximation to the model, which is what we work with in practice.

33. An alternative model of sticky-in-dollar exports would assign the production function to the intermediate good producer with the Calvo price frictions. That would make P^x_t more sticky, by insulating P^x_t from shocks to P^f_t.

34. To our knowledge, the first paper to introduce CSV into a closed economy macroeconomics model is Williamson (1987a, 1987b). Another early influential contribution is Carlstrom and Fuerst (1997).
35. Homogeneous good output is essentially GDP in this model. The difference between Y_t and GDP is only that the former includes monitoring costs for banks, which does not appear in GDP. Bank monitoring costs are very small, as they presumably are in actual economies.
36. We simulated the VARs out 600 periods, and the upper and probability interval for the EME IRFs for the exchange rate blows up but includes zero in the interior. But, in the case of the AEs the lower bound of the probability interval blows up in a negative direction but appears bounded above by a negative number. So, the EMEs are more consistent than the AEs with the idea that the exchange rate returns to its unshocked level after a US monetary contraction. See Section J of the appendix (http://www.nber.org/data-appendix/c14997/appendix.pdf) for further discussion.
37. For another application of the impulse response procedure, see Cesa-Bianchi et al. (2024).
38. We set $\psi = 1$, though we believe our results are unaffected by this assumption.
39. Our model does not imply that the exchange rate is a random walk, as is suggested in much of the literature. Our results are not incompatible with that literature because we only look at the response of the exchange rate to one particular shock, a US monetary policy shock. Presumably, most movements in the exchange rate are due to other shocks.
40. Dynare offers the option in Christiano, Eichenbaum, and Rebelo (2011) as well as an alternative. Under the alternative, it offers the possibility of computing the posterior distribution of variables of interest, conditional on target variables (e.g., the share of trade in GDP) being in a region of particular interest.
41. According to fig. 5, Peruvian GDP falls by about 2% in the year after a US monetary tightening, whereas the drop is much larger in the EMEs (see fig. 4). This finding is robust to using the Jarociński and Karadi (2020) monetary policy shocks (see Sec. C in the appendix, http://www.nber.org/data-appendix/c14997/appendix.pdf).
42. See, e.g., Christiano, Trabandt, and Walentin (2011, p. 2025).
43. See Subsec. III.C, Exports and the Dominant Currency Paradigm.
44. Specifically, recall that the impulse responses of the US price level, interest rate, and output to a Bauer and Swanson (2023) shock are based on simulating the response of $\hat{Y}_t$, $t = 1, \ldots, n$ to $\varepsilon_1^{mp} = 1$ using eq. (3) (see Subsec. II.A, Three-Variable US VAR, for a full discussion). Denote the simulation results by the matrix, $\hat{Y} = [\hat{Y}_1, \ldots, \hat{Y}_n]$. The pure interest rate effect, $\hat{Y}_{R_d^*}$, is obtained by setting the elements of the first and last rows of $\hat{Y}$ to 0. The pure price level effect, $\hat{Y}_P$, is obtained by setting the elements of the second and third rows of $\hat{Y}$ to 0. The pure GDP effect, $\hat{Y}_{GDP}$, is obtained by setting the elements of the first and second row to 0. Let the responses of the SOE model to a US monetary contraction be denoted by $Y = L(\hat{Y})$, say. Under our linear approximation to the model solution, L is linear so that $Y = L(\hat{Y}) = L(\hat{Y}_{R_d^*} + \hat{Y}_P + \hat{Y}_{\text{GDP}}) = L(\hat{Y}_{R_d^*}) + L(\hat{Y}_P) + L(\hat{Y}_{\text{GDP}})$. The pure x effect of a US monetary contraction is $L(\hat{Y}_x)$, for $x = R_d^*, P$, GDP.
45. The dots and stars virtually coincide in the 1,3 panel of fig. 7.
46. The introduction to Sec. II provides a summary of our robustness analysis.
47. See Sec. E in the appendix (http://www.nber.org/data-appendix/c14997/appendix.pdf) for a graph of the Adler et al. (2024) measure of Peruvian FX intervention, based on data from the Central Bank of Peru's website. The interventions are frequent and large, as a fraction of (lagged) GDP.
48. The LCU and dollar market clearing conditions are given by equations (33) and (34), respectively.
49. This is qualitatively consistent with the empirical finding in Bayoumi, Gagnon, and Saborowski (2015). They argue that when a central bank sells 100 dollars of assets, that is, reduces F_t^* by 100, the sum of households and the central bank sell an amount of dollars in the range of 24–42, that is, D_t^* rises by 58–76 dollars.
50. Movements in domestic dollar export prices could still affect the terms of trade and, hence, exports. But, when the sticky-in-dollar export specification is adopted, the terms of trade are hardly affected in the "No Import" case.

51. The observation that a reduction in the elasticity of substitution between domestic and foreign inputs can help to trigger a contractionary depreciation has been emphasized recently in Auclert et al. (2021).

52. We were not able to establish the result more formally. In particular, when we examined the correlation between the elasticity of substitution and credit dollarization in the posterior distribution, we did not find a strong positive association.

53. We have expressed eq. (11) in a slightly different way, using the approximation $R_{d,t} \simeq 1 + \log(R_{d,t})$ for $R_{d,t}$ in a sufficiently small neighborhood of $R_{d,t} = 1$. The same approximation was applied in the case of $R^*_{d,t}$.

54. In equilibrium all households make the same choices.

55. Recall from Sec. II.A, Three-Variable US VAR, that the time unit in the empirical work is monthly and the time unit in the SOE model is quarterly. A detailed discussion of the mapping between quarterly and monthly is discussed in Sec. II.A, Three-Variable US VAR.

56. That assumption 1 holds for the interest rate differential in our SOE models is not surprising. That the log level of the exchange rate reverts to steady state after a US monetary tightening is a property of our SOE models because of our specification of the monetary policy rule, with $r_S > 0$. For discussion, see Subsecs. III.E and IV.A. That convergence proceeds at a geometric rate reflects that impulse responses are computed by iterating on a linear difference equation.

57. In the estimated IRFs for the dollar premium, $\Delta_t < 0$ for $50 < t < 100$. So, if we had adopted the different truncation, $\Delta_t = 0$ for $t > 99$, then the graph of $100 \times \log S_\ell^{\text{UIP}}$ would have shifted down by 0.65, in a roughly parallel way. Our conclusion regarding delayed overshooting would have been unaffected. Our conclusion regarding excess overshooting would have been even stronger. This is consistent with our overall conclusion, discussed below, that our estimate of $100 \times \log S_\ell^{\text{UIP}}$, which utilizes UIP, represents an upper bound for what the UIP implies for the exchange rate, given the estimated Δ_t's.

58. The dot-dashed line does not include posterior probability intervals. If we did incorporate them in a mechanical way, the probability intervals would be very wide because, according to equation (42), $\log S_\ell^{\text{UIP}}$ is a function of the IRFs of dollar premia into the indefinite future. At the same time, our VAR implies growing uncertainty into the future, and that uncertainty transmits without any discounting into $\log S_\ell^{\text{UIP}}$ for $\ell = 1, \ldots, 36$. But we do not have confidence in the VAR's implications for the long-term future, so we decided not to report probability intervals. We explored ways of formalizing our "distrust" of the long-run implications of the VAR but decided that developing these approaches is best left for future work.

59. The IRFs of the dollar premium for this purpose are measured in monthly percentage terms. That is the reason for the "100×" in front of $\log S_{\ell t}^{\text{UIP}}$.

60. For an early demonstration of the phenomenon of delayed overshooting in the wake of a monetary shock, see Eichenbaum and Evans (1995). The delayed overshooting result is somewhat, though not completely, robust. In appendix C, (http://www.nber.org/data-appendix/c14997/appendix.pdf) we show that our delayed overshooting is robust to the use of Jarociński and Karadi (2020) monetary policy shocks (see also Jarociński 2022). We examined whether delayed overshooting is robust to doing local projections. The results are reported in appendix B, but they are too noisy to say whether they support delayed overshooting or not. Müller, Wolf, and Hettig (2024) show that delayed overshooting is robust to the use of Romer and Romer (2004) shocks. Degasperi et al. (2020, fig. 2) and Miranda-Agrippino and Ricco (2021, fig. 6) show delayed overshooting in the US trade-weighted exchange rate. Degasperi et al. (2020, fig. 3) also look at the impact of three specific exchange rates, the euro, the British pound, and the yen. In each of these exchange rates, the peak value of the dollar occurs in the period of the US monetary tightening, so overshooting is not delayed in these cases. In our analysis of the country-by-country data underlying fig. 6, we also find, consistent with Degasperi et al. (2020, fig. 3), that there is no delay in the peak response of Japan's exchange rate. Our results for the euro area are statistically not significantly different from Degasperi et al.'s (2020, fig. 3) results. According to our point estimates, the peak effect of a US monetary tightening on the Eurodollar exchange rate is technically delayed, but the peak effect on the exchange rate is about the same as the immediate effect.

In the case of the United Kingdom, our point estimates indicate that the peak effect on the exchange rate is delayed, but determining whether our results are statistically significantly different from Degasperi et al.'s (2020, fig. 3) requires additional analysis. In our analysis of EMEs, we found that only two countries do not display delayed overshooting in their exchange rate after a US monetary tightening. We conclude that on average, across countries, there appears to be a delay in the response of the exchange rate to a US monetary tightening, but there are exceptions.

61. In principle, aversion to exchange rate uncertainty could prevent people from maximizing expected return on their portfolio. But it is well known that, with preferences of the kind we use, risk aversion plays very little role. Indeed, with our linearization method we abstract from risk aversion altogether.

62. In Gabaix and Maggiori (2015), people fear moving into dollars too much because they lack trust in the financial institutions they must deal with (see also Aoki, Benigno, and Kiyotaki 2016). In Itskhoki and Mukhin (2023), people are limited in how many dollars they can acquire because it is assumed that financial institutions must hold all the currency risk, and that the people who manage those institutions are much more risk averse to currency volatility than the representative household. We think of our reduced-form, modified UIP model as potentially encompassing the microfoundations in Gabaix and Maggiori (2015) or Itskhoki and Mukhin (2023). For other reduced-form approaches to UIP deviations analogous to the approach taken here, see Schmitt-Grohé and Uribe (2003), Christiano, Trabandt, and Walentin (2011), and Eichenbaum et al. (2021). A different approach to delayed overshooting is described in Ilut (2012) and considers alternatives to rational expectations. Ilut (2012) explains how ambiguity aversion makes people hesitant to acquire dollar assets in the immediate aftermath of a US monetary tightening because of a concern that the expected appreciation of the dollar may not occur.

References

Adjemian, Stéphane, Michel Juillard, Fréderic Karamé, Willi Mutschler, Johannes Pfeifer, Marco Ratto, Normann Rion, and Sébastien Villemot. 2024. "Dynare: Reference Manual, Version 6." Dynare Working Papers no. 80, Centre pour la Recherche Economique et ses Applications, Paris.

Adler, Gustavo, Kyun Suk Chang, Rui Mano, and Yuting Shao. 2024. "Foreign Exchange Intervention: A Dataset of Public Data and Proxies." *Journal of Money, Credit and Banking* 51 (6): 1455–90.

Adolfson, Malin, Stefan Laséen, Jesper Lindé, and Mattias Villani. 2007. "Bayesian Estimation of an Open Economy DSGE Model with Incomplete Pass-Through." *Journal of International Economics* 72 (2): 481–511.

Adrian, Tobias, Christopher J. Erceg, Marcin Kolasa, Jesper Lindé, and Pawel Zabczyk. 2021. *A Quantitative Microfounded Model for the Integrated Policy Framework*. Washington, DC: International Monetary Fund.

Akinci, Özge, and Albert Queralto. 2024. "Exchange Rate Dynamics and Monetary Spillovers with Imperfect Financial Markets." *Review of Financial Studies* 37 (2): 309–55.

Allen, Treb, Costas Arkolakis, and Yuta Takahashi. 2020. "Universal Gravity." *Journal of Political Economy* 128 (2): 393–433.

Aoki, Kosuke, Gianluca Benigno, and Nobuhiro Kiyotaki. 2016. "Monetary and Financial Policies in Emerging Markets." Unpublished paper, London School of Economics.

Auclert, Adrien, Matthew Rognlie, Martin Souchier, and Ludwig Straub. 2021. "Exchange Rates and Monetary Policy with Heterogeneous Agents: Sizing Up the Real Income Channel." Technical report, NBER, Cambridge, MA.

Bacchetta, Philippe, Margaret Davenport, and Eric Van Wincoop. 2022. "Can Sticky Portfolios Explain International Capital Flows and Asset Prices?" *Journal of International Economics* 136:1–27.
Backus, David K., and Patrick J. Kehoe. 1992. "Finn E. Kydland." *Journal of Political Economy* 100 (4): 745–75.
Basu, Suman, and Gita Gopinath. 2024. "An Integrated Policy Framework (IPF) Diagram for International Economics." Working Paper no. WP/24/38, International Monetary Fund, Washington, DC.
Bauer, Michael D., and Eric T. Swanson. 2023. "A Reassessment of Monetary Policy Surprises and High-Frequency Identification." *NBER Macroeconomics Annual* 37 (1): 87–155.
Bayoumi, Tamim, Joseph Gagnon, and Christian Saborowski. 2015. "Official Financial Flows, Capital Mobility, and Global Imbalances." *Journal of International Money and Finance* 52:146–74.
Bernanke, Ben S., Mark Gertler, and Simon Gilchrist. 1999. "The Financial Accelerator in a Quantitative Business Cycle Framework." *Handbook of Macroeconomics* 1:1341–93.
Bohr, Clement E. 2024. "Capacity Buffers: Explaining the Retreat and Return of the Phillips Curve." Manuscript, Northwestern University.
Bruno, Valentina G., and Hyun Song Shin. 2021. "Dollar and Exports." CEPR Discussion Paper no. 16311, Center for Economic and Policy Research, Washington, DC.
Camara, Santiago. 2021. "Spillovers of US Interest Rates: Monetary Policy & Information Effects." arXiv preprint arXiv:2111.08631.
Carlstrom, Charles T., and Timothy S. Fuerst. 1997. "Agency Costs, Net Worth, and Business Fluctuations: A Computable General Equilibrium Analysis." *American Economic Review* 87 (5): 893–910.
Castillo, Paul, Ruy Lama, and Juan Pablo Medina. 2019. "Foreign Exchange Intervention, Monetary Policy, and Liability Dollarization in Emerging Economies." Manuscript, Central Bank of Peru.
Castillo, Paul, and Juan Pablo Medina. 2021. "Foreign Exchange Intervention and the Global Financial Cycle in Emerging Economies." Manuscript, Central Bank of Peru.
Cavallino, Paolo. 2019. "Capital Flows and Foreign Exchange Intervention." *American Economic Journal: Macroeconomics* 11 (2): 127–70.
Cesa-Bianchi, Ambrogio, Andrea Ferrero, and Shangshang Li. 2024. "Capital Flows and Exchange Rates: A Quantitative Assessment of the Dilemma Hypothesis." CEPR Discussion Paper no. 18943, Center for Economic and Policy Research, Washington, DC.
Céspedes, Luis Felipe, Roberto Chang, and Andres Velasco. 2004. "Balance Sheets and Exchange Rate Policy." *American Economic Review* 94 (4): 1183–93.
Chang, Roberto, and Andres Velasco. 2001. "Monetary Policy in a Dollarized Economy Where Balance Sheets Matter." *Journal of Development Economics* 66 (2): 445–64.
Christiano, Lawrence, Hüsnü Dalgıc, and Xiaoming Li. 2022. "Modelling the Great Recession as a Bank Panic: Challenges." *Economica* 89 (S1): 200–38.
Christiano, Lawrence J., Hüsnü Dalgıc, and Armen Nurbekyan. 2021. "Financial Dollarization in Emerging Markets: Efficient Risk Sharing or Prescription for Disaster?" Working Paper no. 29034, NBER, Cambridge, MA.
Christiano, Lawrence J., Martin S. Eichenbaum, and Charles L. Evans. 2005. "Nominal Rigidities and the Dynamic Effects of a Shock to Monetary Policy." *Journal of Political Economy* 113 (1): 1–45.

Christiano, Lawrence J., Martin S. Eichenbaum, and Sergio Rebelo. 2011. "When Is the Government Spending Multiplier Large?" *Journal of Political Economy* 119 (1): 78–121.
Christiano, Lawrence J., Martin S. Eichenbaum, and Mathias Trabandt. 2016. "Unemployment and Business Cycles." *Econometrica* 84 (4): 1523–69.
Christiano, Lawrence J., Roberto Motto, and Massimo Rostagno. 2014. "Risk Shocks." *American Economic Review* 104 (1): 27–65.
Christiano, Lawrence J., Mathias Trabandt, and Karl Walentin. 2010. "DSGE Models for Monetary Policy Analysis." *Handbook of Monetary Economics* 3:285–367.
———. 2011. "Introducing Financial Frictions and Unemployment into a Small Open Economy Model." *Journal of Economic Dynamics and Control* 35 (12): 1999–2041.
Dalgıc, Hüsnü C. 2024. "Financial Dollarization in Emerging Markets: An Insurance Arrangement." *International Economic Review* 65 (3): 1189–219.
Degasperi, Riccardo, Seokki Hong, and Giovanni Ricco. 2020. "The Global Transmission of US Monetary Policy." Working Paper, Sciences Po. https://sciencespo.hal.science/hal-03373749/.
De Leo, Pierre, Gita Gopinath, and Şebnem Kalmeli-Özcan. 2022. "Monetary Policy Cyclicality in Emerging Economies." Working Paper no. 30458 (September), NBER, Cambridge, MA.
Devereux, Michael B., Charles Engel, and Steve Pak Yeung Wu. 2023. "Collateral Advantage: Exchange Rates, Capital Flows and Global Cycles." Technical report, NBER, Cambridge, MA.
Dieppe, Alistair, Romain Legrand, and Björn Van Roye. 2016. "The BEAR Toolbox." working paper, European Central Bank.
Di Giovanni, Julian, and Galina Hale. 2022. "Stock Market Spillovers via the Global Production Network: Transmission of US Monetary Policy." *Journal of Finance* 77 (6): 3373–421.
Di Giovanni, Julian, Şebnem Kalemli-Özcan, Mehmet Fatih Ulu, and Yusuf Soner Baskaya. 2022. "International Spillovers and Local Credit Cycles." *Review of Economic Studies* 89 (2): 733–73.
Di Giovanni, Julian, and John Rogers. 2024. "The Impact of US Monetary Policy on Foreign Firms." *IMF Economic Review* 72 (1): 58–115.
Dornbusch, Rudiger. 1976. "Expectations and Exchange Rate Dynamics." *Journal of Political Economy* 84 (6): 1161–76.
Duttagupta, Rupa, and Ceyla Pazarbasioglu. 2021. "Miles to Go: Emerging Markets Must Balance Overcoming the Pandemic, Returning to More Normal Policies, and Rebuilding Their Economies." *Finance and Development*, June. https://www.imf.org/external/pubs/ft/fandd/2021/06/pdf/the-future-of-emerging-markets-duttagupta-and-pazarbasioglu.pdf.
Eaton, Jonathan, and Samuel Kortum. 2002. "Technology, Geography, and Trade." *Econometrica* 70 (5): 1741–79.
Egorov, Konstantin, and Dmitry Mukhin. 2023. "Optimal Policy under Dollar Pricing." *American Economic Review* 113 (7): 1783–824.
Eichenbaum, Martin, and Charles L. Evans. 1995. "Some Empirical Evidence on the Effects of Shocks to Monetary Policy on Exchange Rates." *Quarterly Journal of Economics* 110 (4): 975–1009.
Eichenbaum, Martin S., Benjamin K. Johannsen, and Sergio T. Rebelo. 2021. "Monetary Policy and the Predictability of Nominal Exchange Rates." *Review of Economic Studies* 88 (1): 192–228.

Eichengreen, Barry, and Poonam Gupta. 2015. "Tapering Talk: The Impact of Expectations of Reduced Federal Reserve Security Purchases on Emerging Markets." *Emerging Markets Review* 25:1–15.

Favara, Giovanni, Simon Gilchrist, Kurt F. Lewis, and Egon Zakrajšek. 2016. "Updating the Recession Risk and the Excess Bond Premium." FEDS Notes, Board of Governors of the Federal Reserve System, Washington, DC.

Fleming, J. Marcus. 1962. "Domestic Financial Policies under Fixed and under Floating Exchange Rates." *Staff Papers, International Monetary Fund* 9 (3): 369–80.

Fukui, Masao, Emi Nakamura, and Jón Steinsson. 2023. "The Macroeconomic Consequences of Exchange Rate Depreciations." Technical report, NBER, Cambridge, MA.

Gabaix, Xavier, and Matteo Maggiori. 2015. "International Liquidity and Exchange Rate Dynamics." *Quarterly Journal of Economics* 130 (3): 1369–420.

Gertler, Mark, Simon Gilchrist, and Fabio M. Natalucci. 2007. "External Constraints on Monetary Policy and the Financial Accelerator." *Journal of Money, Credit and Banking* 39:295–330.

Gilchrist, Simon, and Egon Zakrajšek. 2012. "Credit Spreads and Business Cycle Fluctuations." *American Economic Review* 102 (4): 1692–720.

Goldberg, Linda S., and Cédric Tille. 2008. "Vehicle Currency Use in International Trade." *Journal of International Economics* 76 (2): 177–92.

Gopinath, Gita, Emine Boz, Camila Casas, Federico J. Díez, Pierre-Olivier Gourinchas, and Mikkel Plagborg-Moller. 2020. "Dominant Currency Paradigm." *American Economic Review* 110 (3): 677–719.

Gourinchas, Pierre-Olivier, Walker D. Ray, and Dimitri Vayanos. 2022. "A Preferred-Habitat Model of Term Premia, Exchange Rates, and Monetary Policy Spillovers." Technical report, NBER, Cambridge, MA.

Greenspan, Alan. 1999. "Currency Reserves and Debt." Speech before the World Bank Conference on Recent Trends in Reserves Management, Washington, DC, April.

Greenwood, Robin, Samuel Hanson, Jeremy C. Stein, and Adi Sunderam. 2023. "A Quantity-Driven Theory of Term Premia and Exchange Rates." *Quarterly Journal of Economics* 138 (4): 2327–89.

Ilut, Cosmin. 2012. "Ambiguity Aversion: Implications for the Uncovered Interest Rate Parity Puzzle." *American Economic Journal: Macroeconomics* 4 (3): 33–65.

IMF (International Monetary Fund). 2023. *World Economic Outlook*. Washington, DC: IMF.

Itskhoki, Oleg, and Dmitry Mukhin. 2021. "Exchange Rate Disconnect in General Equilibrium." *Journal of Political Economy* 129 (8): 2183–232.

———. 2023. "Optimal Exchange Rate Policy." Technical report, NBER, Cambridge, MA.

Jarociński, Marek. 2022. "Central Bank Information Effects and Transatlantic Spillovers." *Journal of International Economics* 139:103683.

Jarociński, Marek, and Peter Karadi. 2020. "Deconstructing Monetary Policy Surprises—the Role of Information Shocks." *American Economic Journal: Macroeconomics* 12 (2): 1–43.

Jiang, Zhengyang, Arvind Krishnamurthy, and Hanno Lustig. 2024. "Dollar Safety and the Global Financial Cycle." *Review of Economic Studies* 91 (5): 2878–915.

Jordà, Òscar. 2005. "Estimation and Inference of Impulse Responses by Local Projections." *American Economic Review* 95 (1): 161–82.

Kalemli-Özcan, Şebnem. 2019. "U.S. Monetary Policy and International Risk Spillovers." Working Paper no. 26297 (September), NBER, Cambridge, MA.

Kalemli-Özcan, Şebnem, and Liliana Varela. 2021. "Five Facts about the UIP Premium." Technical report, NBER, Cambridge, MA.

Kekre, Rohan, and Moritz Lenel. 2021. "The Flight to Safety and International Risk Sharing." Working Paper no. 29238 (September), NBER, Cambridge, MA.

Krugman, Paul, Maurice Obstfeld, and Marc Melitz. 2023. *International Economics: Theory and Policy*. 12th ed. Essex: Pearson.

Kuttner, Kenneth. 2001. "Monetary Policy Surprises and Interest Rates: Evidence from the Fed Funds Futures Market." *Journal of Monetary Economics* 47 (3): 523–44.

Miranda-Agrippino, Silvia, and Hélène Rey. 2020. "US Monetary Policy and the Global Financial Cycle." *Review of Economic Studies* 87 (6): 2754–76.

Miranda-Agrippino, Silvia, and Giovanni Ricco. 2021. "The Transmission of Monetary Policy Shocks." *American Economic Journal: Macroeconomics* 13 (3): 74–107.

Müller, Gernot, Martin Wolf, and Thomas Hettig. 2024. "Delayed Overshooting: The Case for Information Rigidities." *American Economic Journal: Macroeconomics* 16 (3): 310–42.

Mundell, Robert A. 1963. "Capital Mobility and Stabilization Policy under Fixed and Flexible Exchange Rates." *Canadian Journal of Economics and Political Science* 29 (4): 475–85.

Paul, Pascal. 2020. "The Time-Varying Effect of Monetary Policy on Asset Prices." *Review of Economics and Statistics* 102 (4): 690–704.

Poole, William. 1970. "Optimal Choice of Monetary Policy Instruments in a Simple Stochastic Macro Model." *Quarterly Journal of Economics* 84 (2): 197–216.

Ramey, Valerie A. 2016. "Macroeconomic Shocks and Their Propagation." *Handbook of Macroeconomics* 2:71–162.

Rey, Hélène. 2013. "Dilemma Not Trilemma: The Global Financial Cycle and Monetary Policy Independence." Technical report, Proceedings—Economic Policy Symposium, Jackson Hole, WY.

Romer, Christina D., and David H. Romer. 2004. "A New Measure of Monetary Shocks: Derivation and Implications." *American Economic Review* 94 (4): 1055–84.

Rudebusch, Glenn D. 1998. "Do Measures of Monetary Policy in a VAR Make Sense?" *International Economic Review* 39 (4): 907–31.

Sargent, Thomas J. 1989. "Two Models of Measurements and the Investment Accelerator." *Journal of Political Economy* 97 (2): 251–87.

Schmitt-Grohé, Stephanie, and Martın Uribe. 2003. "Closing Small Open Economy Models." *Journal of International Economics* 61 (1): 163–85.

Stock, James, and Mark Watson. 2010. "Monthly GDP and GNI—Research Memorandum." Manuscript, Princeton University.

Williamson, Stephen D. 1987a. "Costly Monitoring, Loan Contracts, and Equilibrium Credit Rationing." *Quarterly Journal of Economics* 102 (February): 135–45.

———. 1987b. "Financial Intermediation, Business Failures, and Real Business Cycles." *Journal of Political Economy* 95 (6): 1196–216.

Comment

Jón Steinsson, *University of California, Berkeley and NBER,* United States of America

Camara, Christiano, and Dalgic have written an interesting and important paper on an important topic in international macroeconomics. The paper has both a substantial empirical component and a substantial theoretical component. The main empirical results of the paper are that a US monetary tightening leads output in other countries to fall and that it leads output in emerging market (EM) countries to fall more than in advanced economies (AEs). The main theoretical result in the paper is that the trade channel explains the bulk of this negative international transmission.

I. Empirical Results

I will start by considering how the authors reach their empirical conclusions. They use monthly data from 2006 to 2019. This is a rather modest amount of data: only a little more than one business cycle in the United States. This choice therefore limits the strength of the statistical inference and may make it sensitive to special features of this 14-year period. The authors make this choice because "many of the EMEs [emerging market economies] in our sample are characterized by different monetary and fiscal regimes before 2000."

The authors use monetary shocks constructed by Bauer and Swanson (2023) from high-frequency data around Federal Reserve Board (Fed) announcements. They run Bayesian vector autoregression (VAR) with "Minnesota" priors, that is, priors that shrink coefficients of their (vector) autoregressive system toward a random walk. They first run a VAR with

NBER Macroeconomics Annual, volume 39, 2025.
 https://doi.org/10.1086/735261

9 variables and 12 lags for the United States and then a panel VAR with 11 variables (3 US and 8 local) but only 2 lags separately for 10 AEs and 14 EMEs.

Figure 1 of the paper presents the results of the US VAR. The results are—for the most part—relatively standard. The main ways in which the results are unusual are (1) gross domestic product (GDP) drops on impact rather than falling gradually, which is more common in this type of analysis; and (2) the response of imports and exports is very large. The peak response of imports and exports is almost a 20% fall (about 10 times larger than the proportional response of GDP).

Figure 3 of the paper reports the responses of AEs to a US monetary tightening. Output and prices fall. Imports and exports fall by very large amounts. These foreign AEs ease monetary policy in response to the Fed tightening. Initially, the exchange rate depreciates, but after a few months, it begins appreciating and appreciates rapidly for over 2 years.

Figure 4 reports responses for EMEs. Overall, these responses are similar to those for AEs. One notable difference is that the fall in output is larger than for AEs. The fall in imports and exports is estimated to be very large. In contrast to AEs, the EMEs are estimated to tighten monetary policy even though output and prices are falling. These estimates, thus, indicate that the EMEs do not typically adopt countercyclical monetary policy in response to economic softening caused by Fed tightening. As with AEs, the exchange rate first depreciates and then appreciates rapidly.

The authors are not the first researchers to estimate the international transmission of US monetary policy shocks. In fact, there is a robust recent literature on this topic using similar methods to the ones the authors use. A notable recent paper in this literature is Degasperi, Hong, and Ricco (2023). Figure 2 of that paper presents results that are broadly similar to those of the present paper. In response to a US monetary tightening, output and prices fall in AEs and EMEs. The fall in output in EMEs is smaller than the headline estimates in the present paper (more similar to some of the robustness analysis in the appendix of the present paper). Trade volumes respond strongly (but not as strongly as in the present paper). Monetary policy eases for both AEs and EMEs. This is more in line with Leo, Gopinath, and Kalemli-Özcan (2024) than with the results of this paper. Another notable difference is that the estimated response of the exchange rate is quite a bit smaller.

Although there are some differences, the strong overall similarity of the results of Degasperi et al. (2023) to the results of the present paper is reassuring. Degasperi et al. (2023) make different choices regarding a number of important aspects of the analysis. For example, they use about twice as much data in the time series (their sample period is 1990–2018). They also use data from more AEs (15 rather than 10). They make the more standard assumption for a monthly VAR to have 12 lags as opposed to 2 lags. And they use a different monetary shock series—the one from Miranda-Agrippino and Ricco (2021) rather than the one from Bauer and Swanson (2023). These differences in methodological choices suggest that the core empirical findings of this paper are relatively robust to changes in various choices made by the authors.

II. Empirical Methods: VAR versus LP

The empirical exercise performed in the paper is an exercise in dynamic causal inference. The authors are interested in estimating the dynamic effects of US monetary policy on various macroeconomic outcomes in other countries. They have a series of monetary shocks, which they take from an earlier paper (Bauer and Swanson 2023). Their goal is to estimate how these shocks affect the various macroeconomic outcomes at different horizons.

As I mentioned above, the method the authors use to perform this exercise is a Bayesian VAR with Minnesota priors. An alternative method would be to use LPs, or "local projections." An LP is simply fancy macro jargon for directly regressing the variable of interest on the exogenous shock at the researchers' disposal. The researcher is interested in the effect of ϵ_t on Y_{t+h}. Why not simply regress Y_{t+h} on ϵ_t? In other words: Why not use an LP?

This question is closely related to another question: Why use a VAR? Conceptually, there are two quite distinct reasons why a researcher may choose to use a VAR, and it is important to keep the distinction between these two reasons clear. One reason for using a VAR is to identify exogenous shocks. A number of different strategies for identifying exogenous shocks in macro rely on VAR methods. This includes Cholesky decompositions, long-run restrictions, sign restrictions, and so on. This is not what the present paper is doing. The present paper has an exogenous shock series constructed by other researchers, which was identified using high-frequency methods. The rationale for using a VAR in the present paper must therefore be something else.

The other rationale for employing a VAR (rather than an LP) is to enhance statistical power when constructing impulse responses. This is what the authors are using the VAR for in this paper. The authors have a relatively modest data set—14 years, a little more than one business cycle—yet their empirical procedure yields a considerable amount of statistical power (modestly sized confidence intervals). They are leaning on the VAR and Minnesota priors to shrink their standard errors and smooth out the impulse responses.

The variance reduction of a VAR comes at a potential cost in terms of bias. LPs make minimal assumptions and are therefore unbiased. But they can be very noisy if the data are not very informative. VARs, on the other hand, make stronger assumptions. This reduces variance, but if the assumptions embedded in the VAR are not valid, it introduces bias. This raises a question: Are the empirical conclusions in the paper driven by the data or by the assumptions in the VAR?

VARs are a bit of an odd tool to reduce variance because they are extremely highly parameterized. The US VAR estimated by the authors has 108 parameters and 168 data points. Estimating so many parameters raises the issue of overfitting. Recent advances in econometrics have focused very strongly on this overfitting problem. In particular, controlling overfitting is a core goal of machine learning methods. For example, Lasso and Ridge regressions shrink parameters for the purpose of limiting overfitting. The authors' approach to limiting overfitting is to use Minnesota priors. These shrink the impulse responses toward unit roots. This will work well if the true data-generating process is close to a unit root but less well if it is not.

A second issue is that VARs contain lagged dependent variables. Regressions with lagged dependent variables are biased. In particular, the coefficient on the lagged dependent variable is biased downward. (The direction of bias of other coefficients is more complex.) With only 14 years of data, this type of bias may be substantial. The Minnesota prior pushes against this bias. But it is not clear which way the net bias will go in the authors' setting.

It is useful to consider a few specific impulse response estimates in the paper with the issues discussed above in mind. First, consider the response of GDP in the US VAR. As I mentioned before, GDP jumps down on impact. This is an unusual result. The whole impulse response looks like a unit root response. Are the authors estimating this because the data call for it or because of their prior? Because this VAR has 108 parameters and only 168 data points, the overfitting concern is very severe. My guess is that the Minnesota priors are rather tight. Or in other words, the empirical results are likely being shrunk toward a unit root pretty aggressively.

Contrast this with the response of the nominal exchange rate in the EM VAR. Exchange rates are usually considered to be very close to a unit root. But in this case, the authors estimate an impulse response that is quite far from a unit root. The exchange rate is estimated to appreciate very rapidly after it stops depreciating. One worries that this might be due to downward bias in the largest root of the estimated autoregressive system.

The authors do present results from an LP in the appendix (fig. 23). These results are useful in helping to assess what is really coming from the data and what is coming from the VAR assumptions. A notable difference in results is that the nominal exchange rate response in the LP looks much more like a unit root. In their LPs, the authors take averages of the variables that they are interested in across countries within AEs and EMs. They include 24 lagged controls in these regressions. With only 168 data points, even this raises some potential concerns about overfitting. One noticeable aspect of the LP impulse responses is that the confidence bands are quite jagged, implying that one can reject a smooth response. This suggests that these confidence intervals are narrower than they should be. Nevertheless, it is valuable to have these LP estimates as they come closer to showing the reader what is coming purely from the data before stronger assumptions are layered on.

III. The Trade Channel and Financial Channels

Let me now turn to the theoretical part of the paper. The recent literature has emphasized the financial channel of the transmission of US monetary policy to other countries. Most prominently, Hélène Rey and coauthors have emphasized the notion of a Global Financial Cycle (Rey 2013; Miranda-Agrippino and Rey 2022). This theme is prominent in a large body of recent work, including the papers by Şebnem Kalemli-Özcan and Riccardo Degasperi and coauthors cited above. The present paper uses a structural model to assess the mechanisms through which US monetary policy affects other countries. The authors conclude that it is the trade channel that explains most of the transmission.

In a vanilla open economy model, a US monetary tightening has two effects: First, the US dollar appreciates, which implies that the currencies of other countries depreciate. This results in expenditure switching away from US goods and toward foreign goods. This should result in positive transmission toward other countries, that is, an expansion of output in other countries. The other basic channel in a vanilla model is that a US monetary tightening causes demand in the United States to fall. Because the United States is a big country, this lowers demand in other countries as well. This causes negative transmission toward other countries, that is, a slowdown of output in other countries.

If the second of these channels is stronger than the first, then a US monetary tightening will result in foreign output falling. It seems to me that this is basically what is going on in the present paper. The authors assume dollar pricing (as opposed to producer currency pricing), which helps mute the expenditure switching effect. There is strong evidence for this assumption in the literature. But then there is the question of the strength of the demand channel. In the present paper, it is estimated to be quite strong. Might it be too strong?

One of the points that I made in my discussion of the paper at the conference was that I worried about this issue. The authors have since revised their paper addressing this issue. The estimation of the model in the draft of the paper presented at the conference implied that the small open economy was very exposed to US demand. In the model, the "foreign" region is equated with the United States and the estimation in the earlier draft implied that the weight of US goods in the home consumption basket was 46% for EMs and the weight of US goods in the home investment basket was 71%. I remarked that these seemed much too large, and I worried that this made the trade channel too strong in the model. The revised draft of the paper adjusts the priors in the Bayesian estimation exercise to reduce the weight of US goods in the home consumption and investment baskets. For EMs these are now 2% and 31%, respectively. Because this large change has not materially affected the results, my worries about this are mitigated.

The authors' model incorporates a wide range of different financial frictions. But the authors demonstrate convincingly that to the extent that these frictions affect the response of AEs and EMEs to a US monetary shock in their model, it is mostly through the trade channel. This is clearly demonstrated in figures 7 and 9, which present the fit of the model to the estimated impulse responses for AEs and EMEs, respectively. These figures show that the authors' model is able to generate a substantial fall in output, investment, and exports in response to a US monetary policy tightening. However, the ability of the model to match the response of the nominal exchange rate, the response of domestic monetary policy, and the response of the price level are rather poor for AEs (better for EMEs). In particular, the model generates a substantially smaller response of the nominal exchange rate than the data do (and no delayed overshooting).

Figures 7 and 9 also present a counterfactual where the authors only hit the AEs and EMEs with the change in US interest rates, not the response of US GDP and prices to the US monetary shock. The response of output and investment is much smaller in this counterfactual, and the response of exports has the opposite sign relative to the data. This shows that the model is not generating much action in foreign countries from pure changes in US interest rates independent of their effect on US demand.

Why does the model come to this conclusion? One potential reason is that there may be no other mechanism in the model to generate a substantial fall in foreign output. But the model does incorporate a large range of financial frictions. After all, the idea is to give financial frictions a fair shot at generating the foreign bust.

One potential difficulty is that the response of the nominal exchange rate implies large excess returns on the foreign country currencies after a few months. Initially, the US dollar keeps appreciating (delayed overshooting). This generates excess returns on US dollars. But after a few months, the US dollar begins to depreciate and does so quite rapidly for several years. This generates high returns on the currencies of the foreign countries.

High returns on the foreign currencies should generate capital inflows into the foreign countries and therefore should push in the direction of a boom in the foreign countries. This is, of course, exactly the opposite of what the authors "need" to match the fall in foreign output they estimate in the data. I worry that this issue is part of why the financial channels are not playing a bigger role in the authors' model. But I have to admit that I do not think I fully understand how all the different features of the authors' model interact to generate their results. This implies that I do not feel that I have a great grasp on why they come to the conclusion they come to in the theoretical part of the paper.

Let me conclude by saying that I enjoyed reading this thought-provoking paper. I learned a lot thinking about it over the past few months. It is really striking how large the effects of US monetary policy seem to be on other countries. The authors' conclusions are provocative in terms of the breakdown of these effects into a trade channel and a financial channel. But I think we need a lot more work on international financial frictions before we can generate a consensus on these issues.

Endnote

Author email address: Jón Steinsson (jsteinsson@berkeley.edu). For acknowledgments, sources of research support, and disclosure of the author's material financial relationships, if any, please see https://www.nber.org/books-and-chapters/nber-macroeconomics-annual-2024-volume-39/comment-international-monetary-transmission-mechanism-2-steinsson.

References

Bauer, M. D., and E. T. Swanson. 2023. "A Reassessment of Monetary Policy Surprises and High-Frequency Identification." *NBER Macroeconomics Annual* 37:87–155.

Degasperi, R., S. S. Hong, and G. Ricco. 2023. "The Global Transmission of U.S. Monetary Policy." Working paper, Sciences Po OFCE no. 09/2021.

Leo, P. D., G. Gopinath, and Ş. Kalemli-Özcan. 2024. "Monetary Policy and the Short-Rate Disconnect in Emerging Economies." Working Paper, University of Maryland.

Miranda-Agrippino, S., and H. Rey. 2022. "The Global Financial Cycle." In *Handbook of International Economics, Volume 6*, ed. G. Gopinath, E. Helpman, and K. Rogoff, 1–43. Amsterdam: Elsevier.

Miranda-Agrippino, S., and G. Ricco. 2021. "The Transmission of Monetary Policy Shocks." *American Economic Journal: Macroeconomics* 13:74.

Rey, H. 2013. "Dilemma not Trilemma: The Global Cycle and Monetary Policy Independence." Proceedings—Economic Policy Symposium—Jackson Hole, Federal Reserve of Kansas City, 285–333.

Comment

Şebnem Kalemli-Özcan, *Brown University and NBER,* United States of America

The paper by Santiago Camara, Lawrence Christiano, and Hüsnü Dalgıc is on an important and extensively researched question, and yet it provides us with new insights. It is rich in its analysis, both theory and empirics, covering a lot of ground. The authors develop a quantitative small open economy (SOE) model with several frictions and other interesting bells and whistles to study the international transmission of the US monetary policy. They have written an impressive paper that should be standard reading for graduate students in this area.

The authors start from two well-established facts. First, emerging markets (EMs) experience sharper contractions when US monetary policy tightens vis-à-vis the advanced economies (AEs) (Kalemli-Özcan 2019), and second, SOEs contract almost as much as the United States itself when the United States tightens the monetary policy (Dedola, Rivolta, and Stracca 2017; Akinci and Queralto 2018; Gourinchas 2018). The current literature explains these findings either with financial frictions (Cesa-Bianchi, Ferrero, and Li 2024; Shaghil, Akinci, and Queralto 2024) or with changing risk sentiments/risk shocks (Miranda-Agrippino and Rey 2020; Di Giovanni et al. 2022; Degasperi, Hong, and Ricco 2023) or both (Akinci, Kalemli-Özcan, and Queralto 2021). The authors provide a different explanation: declining US import demand. The authors show that, in model counterfactuals, once the decline in US demand is shut down, there is no international transmission. That is, if US consumers do not reduce their import demand when the Federal Reserve tightens the monetary policy, there will be no effect on Mexico. The overarching

NBER Macroeconomics Annual, volume 39, 2025.
 https://doi.org/10.1086/735262

implication of this result is that the global financial cycle (Rey 2013) is not playing an important role in the international transmission of US monetary policy.

I will argue that this sole dominance of trade channel in international monetary transmission is theoretically possible but empirically not relevant. Let me start with the well-known episode of Taper Tantrum in May 2013. This episode was triggered with an exogenous and unanticipated US monetary policy shock. In fact, a key requirement to understanding monetary policy transmission mechanism (in the United States or globally) is to have an exogenous measure of US monetary policy as shown by a large literature, starting with the seminal work of Gertler and Karadi (2015).[1]

During this—widely accepted as an exogenous US tightening—episode of Taper Tantrum, US import demand did not decline at all; however, a very strong international transmission to EMs was observed with lower growth, capital outflows, exchange rate depreciations, and output declines, as extensively documented (e.g., Sahay et al. 2014; Bems et al. 2020; De Leo, Gopinath, and Kalemli-Özcan 2022). This episode clearly shows that the international transmission of US monetary policy does not need a fall in US import demand, at least for EMs that account for the half of world gross domestic product (GDP) and 60% of its growth (Obstfeld and Zhou 2023).

Of course, the Taper Tantrum episode does not deny the importance of declining US demand in international monetary transmission. In reality, most episodes of US monetary policy tightenings are associated with two types of declines: US consumers' import demand and US investors' retrieval to US assets with low demand for foreign assets (e.g., Kalemli-Özcan and Unsal 2023). In fact, it is extremely valuable that the authors are focusing on the declining US import demand channel, because most of the traditional literature on SOEs ignores this channel when the foreign (US) interest rate shock is exogenous and has no effect in the foreign (US) country. There is a parallel recent literature that also studies the same channel as that of the authors, that is, declining US imports, in global general equilibrium, where imports go down both in SOE and in the United States (e.g., Cesa-Bianchi et al. 2024; Shaghil et al. 2024). This new literature poses a challenge for the authors' model because, in spite of the fact that they incorporate the exact reduction in US import demand, these papers still show that the financial channel dominates the trade channel and that international transmission is not about fall in US import demand for Mexican exports but rather about a fall in

US investors' demand for Mexican and global assets that feeds back to lower global investment demand, leading to contractions in rest of the world.

Why does the authors' model miss this channel, in spite of the fact that they include several financial frictions? In the authors' model, a pure US interest rate shock (R^*) will have no effect (figures 7 and 9 of the paper for AEs and Ems, respectively). In the aforementioned papers, a pure R^* shock will depreciate the non-US country currency—depressing net worth, increased spreads, and uncovered interest parity (UIP) premium—and lower domestic absorption through investment. Then this lower investment feeds back to asset prices and spreads. This feedback mechanism is not allowed in this paper, although the authors allow for financial frictions (balance sheet, dollar pricing, and UIP deviations). Hence, the middle loop of interactions in figure 1 is missed in the authors' framework, making the trade channel dominant. If the middle loop is allowed, then the financial channel becomes the dominant channel of international transmission due to the higher cost of credit, as shown by the aforementioned papers.

How can the feedback effect be this powerful? In the authors' model, with higher US interest rates, there is more demand for dollars, and this dollar demand depreciates the other currencies and hurts balance sheets with dollar debt and local currency assets. Such weak balance sheets will hurt investment. However, these effects are not quantitatively powerful in the authors' model compared with other quantitative models. When authors do a pure R^* shock, as the rest of the literature does, without

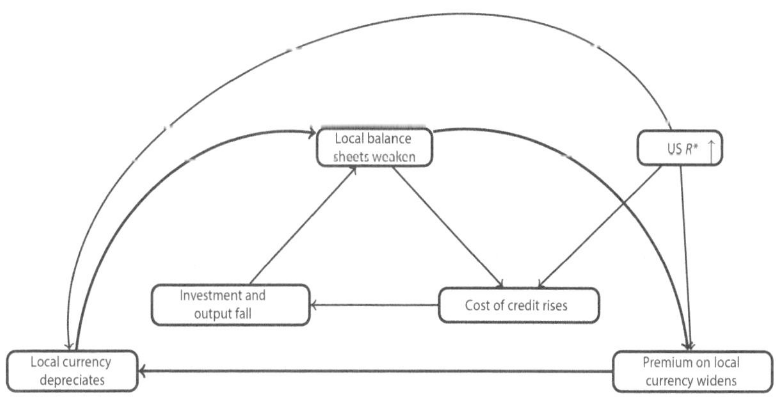

Fig. 1. Impact of a pure R^* shock in alternative frameworks.

a decline in US imports, even they observe a decline in SOE investment due to the above balance-sheet mechanism; this is not big and can easily be fixed with foreign exchange (FX) interventions that stop the depreciations. The key reason why the authors' model cannot generate large output declines through this financial channel is that their UIP wedge is small and does not feed back to firms' borrowing costs (hence a small decline in investment). The small UIP wedge can be offset with throwing more dollars to firms, and hence it plays a small role in the authors' setup.

I made this point in my discussion at the conference as I was worried that the way the authors treat UIP deviations (exogenous noise trader shocks) prevents their model from giving the finance channel a chance to dominate the trade channel. The authors have since revised their paper addressing this issue. They add UIP deviations and show that they not only can fit the model now to widely observed UIP puzzle of delayed overshooting but also shown excess overshooting, that is, high volatility in the exchange rate that also shows up in the UIP, especially of EMs. Since now their model can match these patterns; they argue that the model fits empirically observed UIP deviations and also fits even better to EM data, because the large depreciation of the EM exchange rate makes it easier for the model to match EM facts of large drops in GDP and investment in the wake of a US monetary tightening. Their main conclusion stays even after these changes, though the main channel of international transmission of US monetary policy is declining US imports. This is because UIP deviations quickly revert with mean reversion in exchange rates.

The data tell a different story on endogenous UIP deviations. The mean reversion is there in AEs, so UIP holds on average in AEs even though there is significant month-to-month variation. However, in EMs, it has never held with volatile and persistent time-varying movements, as documented in Kalemli-Özcan and Varela (2021), from the late 1990s to the present. These authors also show delayed and excessive overshooting, however; even though exchange rates go back to the original level after several months following a monetary policy shock, UIP stays elevated a long time, given the persistent interest rate differentials. The authors' linear approach will miss such persistence—hence the feedback from UIP to firms' borrowing costs. Their additional analysis confirms this. The linearization omits the fact that aversion to exchange rate uncertainty could prevent people from maximizing the expected return on their portfolio, that is, under UIP deviations, investors will hold less EM assets and more dollar assets even when EM assets offer more including the risk premium. The nonlinear models mentioned before include this channel, leading to a strong feedback effect. The authors defend their linear approach by showing that the risk appetite only affects the pure interest rate effect. Hence, they conclude the risk appetite effect cannot be important, as it operates via a relatively unimportant channel. They detail this in appendix G, which shows that even risk appetite can have huge impact; in a linear model, its effect is minimized, hence leading to small effect of pure R^* shock. As a result, the feedback from UIP deviations to borrowing costs will be missed; hence, the decline in investment and output cannot be driven by the financial channel, and decline in output is attributed to drop in exports by construction.

Let me conclude by saying that I really enjoyed and learned a lot from this paper. It provides a lot of food for thought. The jury is still out on which channel dominates the international transmission of US monetary policy. The answer depends on the modeling approach: two different class of models, linear versus nonlinear deliver different channels dominating, trade versus finance, because different approaches give different weights to the role played by UIP deviations affecting firms' borrowing costs. In reality, both trade and finance channels are operative, but to be sure which one is dominant, we need a lot more work on the empirical front. This is a key research priority, as policy implications depending on which channel dominates the international transmission will starkly differ. If the UIP wedge has a small role and does not feed back into borrowing costs, then the optimal policy is an FX intervention. However, if there is a feedback to borrowing costs, then FX intervention is not optimal: It will partially absorb the shock and earn a carry profit, but this comes at the cost of output destabilization (e.g., Basu et al. 2020).

I started my discussion with the episode of Taper Tantrum in 2013, where even though US imports did not fall, we experienced international transmission of US monetary policy because there was a financial shock as picked up by UIP premia increasing, capital flowing out, and exchange rates depreciating. During 2022–2023, we also experienced a period of US monetary policy tightening with no fall in US imports and no observable international transmission (Kalemli-Özcan and Unsal 2023). The authors argue that this recent episode is further evidence for the trade channel dominance. I would argue, instead, that the recent episode showing the dominance of the financial channel as the key difference in 2023 from 2013 is the fact that the financial shock was missing in 2023. The 2022–2023 US tightening was not associated with an increasing UIP, capital outflows, and exchange rate depreciations for EMs, as was observed in 2013.

Endnotes

Author email address: Şebnem Kalemli-Özcan (sebnem_kalemli-ozcan@brown.edu).
For acknowledgments, sources of research support, and disclosure of the author's material financial relationships, if any, please see https://www.nber.org/books-and-chapters/nber-macroeconomics-annual-2024-volume-39/comment-international-monetary-transmission-mechanism-kalemli-ozcan.

1. Simply looking at the effect of US interest rates on other countries' macro outcomes does not yield a readily interpretable empirical magnitude, because US interest rates are responding endogenously to the US economy. This literature is constantly advancing in terms of measuring exogenous US monetary policy shocks (e.g., Nakamura and Steinsson 2018; Stock and Watson 2018; Cieslak and Schrimpf 2019; Jarociński and Karadi 2020; Bauer, Bernanke, and Milstein 2023; Bauer and Swanson 2023; Miranda-Agrippino and Ricco 2023).

References

Akinci, Ozge, Şebnem Kalemli-Özcan, and Albert Queralto. 2021. "Uncertainty Shocks, Capital Flows, and International Risk Spillovers." Technical report, National Bureau of Economic Research, Cambridge, MA.

Akinci, Ozge, and Albert Queralto. 2018. "Exchange Rate Dynamics and Monetary Spillovers with Imperfect Financial Markets." Staff report, Federal Reserve Bank, New York.

Basu, Suman S., Emine Boz, Gita Gopinath, Francisco Roch, and Filiz D. Unsal. 2020. *A Conceptual Model for the Integrated Policy Framework*. Washington, DC: International Monetary Fund.

Bauer, Michael D., Ben S. Bernanke, and Eric Milstein. 2023. "Risk Appetite and the Risk-Taking Channel of Monetary Policy." *Journal of Economic Perspectives* 37 (1): 77–100.

Bauer, Michael D., and Eric T. Swanson. 2023. "A Reassessment of Monetary Policy Surprises and High-Frequency Identification." *NBER Macroeconomics Annual 2022* 37 (1): 87–155.

Bems, Rudolfs, Francesca Caselli, Francesco Grigoli, and Bertrand Gruss. 2020. "Gains from Anchoring Inflation Expectations: Evidence from the Taper Tantrum Shock." *Economic Letters* 188 (March): Article 108820.

Cesa-Bianchi, Ambrogio, Andrea Ferrero, and Shangshang Li. 2024. "Capital Flows and Exchange Rates: A Quantitative Assessment of the Dilemma Hypothesis." Working paper, Bank of England. https://drive.google.com/file/d/1mpj1bS1FkoE5s9xLvHEtQIv_BFrWe1kv/view.

Cieslak, Anna, and Andreas Schrimpf. 2019. "Non-Monetary News in Central Bank Communication." *Journal of International Economics* 118:293–315.

De Leo, Pierre, Gita Gopinath, and Şebnem Kalemli-Özcan. 2022. "Monetary Policy Cyclicality in Emerging Economies." Working paper, National Bureau of Economic Research, Cambridge, MA.

Dedola, Luca, Giulia Rivolta, and Livio Stracca. 2017. "If the Fed Sneezes, Who Catches a Cold?" *Journal of International Economics* 108:S23–S41.

Degasperi, Riccardo, Seokki Hong, and Giovanni Ricco. 2023. "The Global Transmission of US Monetary Policy." Working paper 2023-02, Center for Research in Economics and Statistics (CREST), Palaiseau, France.

Di Giovanni, Julian, Şebnem Kalemli-Özcan, Mehmet Fatih Ulu, and Yusuf Soner Baskaya. 2022. "International Spillovers and Local Credit Cycles." *Review of Economic Studies* 89 (2): 733–73.

Gertler, Mark, and Peter Karadi. 2015. "Monetary Policy Surprises, Credit Costs, and Economic Activity." *American Economic Journal: Macroeconomics* 7 (1): 44–76.

Gourinchas, Pierre-Oliver. 2018. "Monetary Policy Transmission in Emerging Markets: An Application to Chile." In *Monetary Policy and Global Spillovers: Mechanisms, Effects and Policy Measures*, ed. Enrique G. Mendoza, Ernesto Pastén, and Diego Saravia, 25:279–324. Santiago: Central Bank of Chile.

Jarociński, Marek, and Peter Karadi. 2020. "Deconstructing Monetary Policy Surprises—The Role of Information Shocks." *American Economic Journal: Macroeconomics* 12 (2): 1–43.

Kalemli-Özcan, Şebnem. 2019. "US Monetary Policy and International Risk Spillovers." Proceedings—Economic Policy Symposium—Jackson Hole, Federal Reserve of Kansas City Economic Symposium. https://www.kansascityfed.org/Jackson%20Hole/documents/6951/Ozcan_JH2019.pdf.

Kalemli-Özcan, Şebnem, and Filiz D. Unsal. 2023. "Global Transmission of Fed Hikes The Role of Policy Credibility and Balance Sheets." Technical report, Brookings Papers on Economic Activity, Washington, DC.

Kalemli-Özcan, Şebnem, and Liliana Varela. 2021. "Five Facts about the UIP Premium." Technical report, National Bureau of Economic Research, Cambridge, MA.

Miranda-Agrippino, Silvia, and Hélène Rey. 2020. "US Monetary Policy and the Global Financial Cycle." *Review of Economic Studies* 87 (6): 2754–76.

Miranda-Agrippino, Silvia, and Giovanni Ricco. 2023. "Identification with External Instruments in Structural VARs." *Journal of Monetary Economics* 135:1–19.

Nakamura, Emi, and Jón Steinsson. 2018. "High-Frequency Identification of Monetary Non-Neutrality: The Information Effect." *Quarterly Journal of Economics* 133 (3): 1283–1330.

Obstfeld, Maurice, and Haonan Zhou. 2023. "The Global Dollar Cycle." Technical report, National Bureau of Economic Research, Cambridge, MA.

Rey, Hélène. 2013. "Dilemma not Trilemma: The Global Financial Cycle and Monetary Policy Independence." Proceedings—Economic Policy Symposium—Jackson Hole, Federal Reserve of Kansas City Economic Symposium. https://www.kansascityfed.org/Jackson%20Hole/documents/4575/2013Rey.pdf.

Sahay, Ratna, Vivek Arora, Thanos Arvanitis, Hamid Faruqee, Papa N'Diaye, Tommaso Mancini-Griffoli, and an IMF Team. 2014. "Emerging Market Volatility: Lessons from Taper Tantrum." Technical report, International Monetary Fund, Washington, DC.

Shaghil, Ahmed, Ozge Akinci, and Albert Queralto. 2024. "U.S. Monetary Policy Spillovers to Emerging Markets: Both Shocks and Vulnerabilities Matter." Staff report, Federal Reserve Bank, New York.

Stock, James H., and Mark W. Watson. 2018. "Identification and Estimation of Dynamic Causal Effects in Macroeconomics Using External Instruments." *Economic Journal* 128 (610): 917–48.

Discussion

Gabriel Chodorow-Reich opened the discussion. He noted that some illustration of raw variation would be helpful to see before the vector autoregression (VAR) analysis on the international impact of a US monetary policy shock. Furthermore, he highlighted two significant contractionary outliers in the Bauer–Swanson monetary policy shock data: one at the peak of the US business cycle before the Great Recession (2007Q4) and one coinciding with the Lehman Brothers collapse (2008Q3). He remarked that these outliers helped him understand the quick reaction of gross domestic product to monetary policy shocks in the VAR results. He suggested that the authors try excluding these outliers given the nature of the shocks, noting that, among other things, there was a considerable trade collapse around these events that was not just caused by US monetary policy.

Şebnem Kalemli-Özcan responded to concerns over the sample period highlighted in Chodorow-Reich's comments and Jón Steinsson's discussion. She noted that although the main sample for the VAR covers 2006–2019, the authors repeat the analysis with data from the 1990s and the only result that changes is the policy rate response. She added that her recent Brookings Papers on Economic Activity (BPEA) paper contains further robustness checks, and the policy rate response remains the only change throughout.

Supplementing Kalemli-Özcan's response, Lawrence Christiano confirmed they achieved the same results when starting the sample period in 1990.

Jordi Galí expressed concerns over the use of exogenous monetary policy shocks. Although he emphasized that there was nothing technically

NBER Macroeconomics Annual, volume 39, 2025.
 https://doi.org/10.1086/735263

wrong with the paper's approach, he cautioned against interpreting certain episodes with changing interest rates as being the result of exogenous monetary policy shocks. In particular, the recent rise in interest rates in the United States cannot be interpreted as an exogenous monetary policy shock because interest rates clearly responded to developments in the economy (a Federal Reserve response to higher inflation). Endogenous variations in US policy rates may have very different implications for other countries' exports from exogenous monetary policy shocks. He concluded by noting that some of the model's results could possibly be captured by the most basic small open economy model with a low elasticity of substitution between domestic and foreign goods.

Laura Alfaro followed up with a comment regarding the elasticity of substitution between domestic and foreign goods. She noted that the paper's sample period coincides with the development of global value chains, meaning that countries need to import to export. She noted that this connection eliminates the expenditure switching effect seen in small open economy toy models of the 1960s and 1970s and explains the observed collapse of trade. She furthered her point with the example of Mexico, noting that it is fully integrated with the United States, with all trade being intermediated through multinational enterprises. She also offered Mexico as an example to explain the limited evidence for foreign exchange intervention by emerging market economies: In Mexico, 60% of exchange rate transactions involve foreign agents or occur on derivatives markets, so it is unsurprising that these transactions are absent from capital flows.

Lawrence Christiano responded, noting that needing imports to produce exports is already built into their model. Following up on comments about the elasticity of substitution, he agreed that it is an interesting parameter. However, he noted that they gave the model complete freedom for this parameter and likely cannot get much more out of it.

Adrien Auclert continued the discussion with three points. First, he commented that the paper's exchange rate results provide direct evidence for an uncovered interest rate parity (UIP) mechanism. He remarked that this was his first time seeing the Dornbusch overshooting mechanism in action. Next, he noted that the paper finds that the trade channel dominates the dollar debt channel in transmitting a US tightening to the rest of the world. He suggested that the authors should also consider a real income channel, which could be incorporated into their model with a low elasticity of substitution and two agents. Finally, he suggested that the interaction between dollar debt and UIP frictions might explain why dollar debt does not matter in the model. He recommended that the authors remove the UIP friction and rerun the model to see if the trade channel still dominates.

Finally, Lawrence Christiano closed the discussion by thanking the discussants for their insightful comments. In response to Kalemli-Özcan's discussion, he noted that they plan to extend the paper to consider other implications of financial market frictions, including, for example, bankruptcy rates, equity markets, and spreads for risky borrowers. He clarified that the paper's results support the existence of a global financial cycle but suggest that it is merely a symptom rather than a cause of global co-movement: The co-movement of asset prices worldwide is caused by the contraction of imports, not by supply effects.

3

Inflation's Fiscal Impact on American Households

David Altig, *Federal Reserve Bank of Atlanta,* United States of America

Alan J. Auerbach, *University of California, Berkeley, and NBER,* United States of America

Erin Eidschun, *Boston University,* United States of America

Laurence Kotlikoff, *Boston University, NBER, and Fiscal Analysis Center,* United States of America

Victor Yifan Ye, *Boston University, Opendoor Technologies, and Stanford DEL,* United States of America

I. Introduction

Understanding inflation's welfare costs is a long-standing question, interest in which is surely enhanced by the post-COVID-19 surge in prices. This paper measures welfare in terms of households' levels of expected (over different survival paths) remaining lifetime spending. Inflation's impacts are, of course, financial as well as fiscal, where *financial* refers to transactions between private-sector entities and *fiscal* entails transactions between the private and government sectors. All else equal, inflation is zero-sum.[1] In this case, gains to net winners, present and future, are offset by losses to net losers, present and future. This zero-sum property, enforced by intertemporal budget constraints, holds whether the economy is static or dynamic or open or closed.[2]

Yet, even when inflation has no overall impact, tracing winners and losers from its financial impacts—for example, changes in real wages or the real values of financial assets and liabilities—is a major challenge given available data.[3] In this paper, we look over the longer term, when financial impacts may be less important, and limit our focus to inflation's fiscal impacts, which are more readily measured using household data and detailed information on government programs.[4] The US fiscal system is far from inflation-neutral. Federal and state income taxation of nominal, not real asset, income is a most important example. Another is the failure to index modified adjusted gross income thresholds beyond

NBER Macroeconomics Annual, volume 39, 2025.
 Published by The University of Chicago Press for the National Bureau of Economic Research. https://doi.org/10.1086/735264

which Social Security benefits are subject to federal income taxation and, in ten states, state income taxation. A third is the choice not to index Medicare's Part B top premium (IRMAA)[5] bracket. A fourth is the inability of corporations to deduct depreciation and inventory acquisition costs on an inflation-adjusted basis rather than at historic cost. Yet another is permitting corporations to deduct nominal rather than real interest.

There are also delays in the timing of the government's inflation adjustments. For instance, Social Security's annual cost of living adjustment (COLA), which occurs on January 1, is calculated based on inflation that arose as far back as 15 months. With ongoing inflation, Social Security recipients receive permanently lower real benefits as a result of this lag. For example, with only a 1-year adjustment lag, a permanent increase in inflation from 0% to 10% would reduce real benefits by the middle of the first year by 5%, and they would remain 5% lower, on average, forever. Inflation indexation of federal and state income tax brackets is also lagged, albeit less severely. The same holds for federal and state benefit programs.

This paper uses the Fiscal Analyzer (TFA) to study inflation's fiscal impacts on the total expected (over potential survivor paths) remaining lifetime spending of respondents to the 2019 Survey of Consumer Finances (SCF). Each year's spending includes discretionary spending, bequests (when the household reaches a terminal state), housing expenses, and annual in-kind consumption of Medicare and Medicaid benefits. Total expected lifetime spending is the sum of the present values of these survivor-path-specific annual outlays multiplied by the path's probability and the value of home equity.[6]

TFA is a life-cycle, consumption-smoothing research tool that incorporates all major federal and state tax and transfer programs, including cash and in-kind programs.[7] It has been used to study inequality and fiscal progressivity (Auerbach, Kotlikoff, and Koehler 2023), marginal lifetime net taxation (Altig et al. 2023), Social Security collection decisions (Altig, Kotlikoff, and Ye 2022), marriage taxation (Ilin, Kotlikoff, and Pitts 2022), and the distribution, across states, of gains from the 2017 Tax Cuts and Jobs Act (Altig et al. 2020). We benchmark the SCF data to national aggregates and augment the survey with imputations of state residency, benefit-program participation, expected retirement age, survival probabilities, and real earnings growth. Our description of TFA, including our imputations, draws heavily and often verbatim from these studies.

TFA smooths consumption subject to borrowing constraints. To be precise, TFA smooths households' living standards, where *living standard* is defined as a household's discretionary spending divided by the number of household members with adjustments for economies of shared living and the relative cost of children. *Smoothing*, for purposes of this paper, refers to keeping the household's annual living standard constant without violating the household's annual cash-flow constraints.[8] The expected present value of remaining lifetime spending on housing plus spending arising from in-kind medical transfers is treated as nondiscretionary.

Inflation's fiscal effects on the expected present value of spending—discretionary and nondiscretionary—arise via two channels. The first is changes in real taxes and benefits given the tax and benefit programs the household faces. The second is changes in program eligibility. Our results capture both channels. To isolate inflation's fiscal-based effects that are not caused by financial factors, we modified all SCF observations to ensure that, absent fiscal policy, TFA's results were independent of inflation. Specifically, we fully inflation-indexed each household's future labor earnings, pensions, mortgage and other loan repayments, property taxes and other housing costs, real estate and other income, and retirement account benefits. This assumes that inflation is fully anticipated going forward and was fully anticipated at the time each household's financial contracts, such as their mortgages, were established. Hence, one may view our analysis as considering the long-term effects of inflation operating through the fiscal system once financial adjustments have occurred. We confirm TFA's inflation financial neutrality by running TFA with all fiscal policies turned off and then verifying that, regardless of TFA's specified inflation rate, each sample household enjoys precisely the same lifetime as well as annual real spending, including real primary and vacation housing expenses[9] and in-kind real transfers of health-care benefits.

Our study considers 0%, 5%, and 10% rates of inflation. We find, using our inflation-neutral data, that an immediate and permanent increase in inflation from 0% to 5% reduces median household spending by 3.62%. The corresponding median reduction in moving from 0% to 10% permanent inflation is 6.82%. Absent lags in inflation adjustments, median expected household lifetime spending declines by 2.65% and 4.74% for 5% and 10% inflation, respectively. Inflation, as we show, is a highly progressive form of net taxation. The average percentage lifetime-spending decline when we switch to 10% inflation is roughly twice that for the top 1% as for those in the bottom quintile. Inflation also hits those in their middle ages particularly hard. This reflects the relative importance of assets in the remaining lifetime resources of this age group coupled with inflation's taxation of nominal, not real asset, income.

The median losses from inflation are economically meaningful. But they mask enormous heterogeneity, with some households benefiting dramatically and others losing dramatically from inflation's fiscal effects. Indeed, with 10% inflation, the 75th percentile spending change is −4.83%. The 25th percentile change is −9.84%. The maximum spending decline across all households is 64.9%, and the maximum spending increase is 46.7%. As documented below, the 64.9% spending decline reflects the dramatic rise in the effective tax rate on real asset income imposed on a household with very sizable financial wealth, none of which is sheltered in municipal bonds. The huge, 46.7% gain from moving to 10% inflation reflects the household in question becoming eligible for Medicaid. Specifically, the decline in their real Social Security benefits due to the lag in Social Security's COLA lowers the household's income by enough to satisfy Medicaid's income test. In sum, even ignoring financial impacts, inflation is far from neutral. It represents a nontrivial and seemingly capricious net tax on American households. Moreover, inflation's net taxation is highly progressive. The top 1% median declines are roughly twice as big for both inflation experiments as those for the bottom quintile.

Our paper proceeds as follows. Section II examines previous research on inflation's fiscal nonneutralities. Section III presents our life-cycle framework. Section IV describes TFA's computation method and our means of verifying its accuracy. Section V describes our 2019 SCF data, imputations, and inflation adjustments to achieve financial neutrality. Section VI presents results, including household-specific case studies that clarify the sources and magnitudes of inflation's fiscal impacts. Section VII summarizes and concludes.

II. Inflation's Fiscal Impacts—Prior Studies

A limited number of prior studies seek to assess inflation's fiscal impacts. Most date to the 1970s, when inflation was last a serious US concern. None evaluated inflation's fiscal impacts on a comprehensive basis. Kelley et al. (1977) identified two key ways in which inflation raised real rates of taxation during this period. The first was nominal bracket creep combined with a decline in the real values of exemptions and credits. The second was the taxation of nominal, not real, asset income. Federal personal income tax brackets are now inflation-indexed, albeit with a lag. This is not the case for the two Social Security tax brackets beyond which first 50% and then 85% of benefits are subject to income taxation. These two brackets are fixed at their 1983 nominal values. The top IRMAA (Medicare Part B premium) bracket is not adjusted for inflation either. And households and businesses are still taxed on nominal, not real, interest income and nominal, not real, capital gains. In addition, inflation continues to raise businesses' real tax bills by reducing the real values of historic cost depreciation allowances and FIFO-based inventory deductions. On the other hand, businesses are able to deduct nominal rather than real interest payments. Feldstein, Green, and Sheshinski (1978), Feldstein and Summers (1979), and Auerbach (1981) are prominent studies exploring inflation-induced mismeasurement of real corporate capital income and its impact on real corporate net tax liabilities. Fischer and Modigliani (1978) consider a different issue: inflation's taxation of real money balances.

Our research goes well beyond previous studies in many respects, some previously mentioned. First, TFA incorporates, in close detail, the entire federal and state fiscal systems. Second, TFA considers inflation's fiscal impact on lifetime spending, not just its impact on current-year net taxes. Third, we control for purely financial inflation-based changes in lifetime spending. Fourth, our welfare measure is the expected present value of remaining lifetime spending, where the expectation is over all household potential survival paths. In the case of married or partnered households, TFA calculates all relevant taxes and benefits for all survival paths—that is, not just the path under which each spouse/partner lives to their maximum age of life. Fifth, expected lifetime spending incorporates bequests net of estate taxes due on those bequests.

Table 1 provides a compressed list of TFA's fiscal programs. The full list is far longer. The reason is that most benefit programs are state-specific. For example, there is not one but 51 different Medicaid programs because each state, including the District of Columbia, has its own Medicaid provisions. The same is true of Temporary Assistance to Needy Families (TANF), food stamps, and other benefit programs. Indeed, TFA incorporates the precise details of close to 1,000 fiscal policies—some strictly federal, some strictly state, but most federal with state-specific provisions.

III. Our Remaining Lifetime Framework

Denote a potential survival path as i. Along path i, the intertemporal budget constraint is satisfied:

$$S_i = R_i - T_i, \tag{1}$$

where S_i is the realized present value of total remaining lifetime spending—the sum of discretionary and nondiscretionary spending—along

Table 1
List of Tax and Transfer Programs Included in TFA

Taxes	Personal income tax (federal and state)
	Corporate income tax (federal and state)
	Federal Insurance Contributions Act (FICA) Tax (federal)
	Sales taxes (state)
	Medicare Part B premiums (federal)
	Estate and gift tax (federal)
Transfer programs	Earned income tax credit (federal and state)
	Child tax credit (federal)
	Social Security benefits (federal)
	Supplemental security income (SSI) (federal)
	Supplemental Nutritional Assistance Program (SNAP) (federal and state)
	Temporary Assistance for Needy Families (TANF) (federal and state)
	Medicaid (federal and state)
	Medicare (federal)
	The Affordable Care Act (ACA) (federal and state)
	Section 8 Housing Vouchers (state and county)
	Energy assistance (state)
	Childcare assistance (state and county)

Note: Section 8 housing benefits and childcare assistance are also county-specific. Affordable Care Act subsidies are also ZIP code specific. The Fiscal Analyzer lacks data on county or ZIP codes needed to calculate benefits based on county or ZIP code.

survival path i. Nondiscretionary spending includes housing costs, net taxes, repayment of loans, and other off-the-top expenses. It also includes government benefits provided on an in-kind basis, particularly Medicare and Medicaid benefits. And it includes involuntary bequests, net of estate taxes, arising when a household's last survivor dies prior to or upon reaching their maximum age of life. On the right-hand side is the realized present value of lifetime net resources. The value of lifetime net resources is calculated as $R_i - T_i$, where R_i is path i's realized present value of remaining lifetime resources, and T_i is path i's realized present value of net taxes, including estate taxes.

Note the following relationship:

$$R_i = W + H_i. \tag{2}$$

R_i consists of the household's current net wealth W (and so lacks subscript i) and survival path i's realized present value of future labor earnings, H_i. The expected lifetime present values of these variables are calculated for each household using survival probabilities:

$$S = \sum_i p_i S_i, \tag{3}$$

$$H = \sum_i p_i H_i, \tag{4}$$

$$T = \sum_i p_i T_i, \tag{5}$$

$$R = \sum_i p_i R_i, \tag{6}$$

where p_i is the probability the household experiences survival path i. The above equations imply

$$R = W + H, \tag{7}$$

$$S = R - T. \tag{8}$$

IV. The Fiscal Analyzer

TFA incorporates the tax and benefit programs listed in table 1 in smoothing households' living standards.[10] The relationship between a household's discretionary spending in year t, C_t, and its underlying living standard per effective adult, c_t, is given by

$$C_t = c_t(N + \lambda K)^{\gamma}, \tag{9}$$

where N is the number of adults in the household and K is the number of children. λ reflects how "expensive" children are relative to adults, whereas γ parameterizes economies of joint living. We set λ to 0.7, that is, we assume that children are 70% as expensive as adults. We set γ to 0.642, which implies that 2 can live as cheaply as 1.6. TFA's default assumption is that households desire to perfectly smooth their living standards across time and survival states, and they do so subject to cash-flow nonnegative life insurance holdings (no annuitization) constraints. However, the program can run with any desired age–living standard profile, any age-specific child–adult equivalency factors, any degree of economies of shared living, and chosen maximum ages of life of household heads and spouses/partners. Household heads who are not single need not have the same maximum lifespan as their spouse/partner. Here, we set maximum longevity at 100 for heads, spouses, and partners.

Our 2019 SCF data provide the TFA with values for marital status; birth dates of spouses, partners, and children; current-year labor earnings; regular and retirement account holdings (both tax-deductible and Roth accounts); regular asset holdings; contributions to retirement accounts; defined benefit pensions; housing expenses; real estate holdings; and household debts. We supplement these data with an assumed pre–all-tax nominal rate of return, an assumed inflation rate, imputed state residency, imputed future labor earnings, imputed participation in benefit programs, imputed retirement dates, imputed Social Security retirement-benefit collection dates, and imputed retirement account withdrawal start dates. Our imputations are detailed below.

A. *TFA's Solution Method*

TFA uses dynamic programming to smooth each household's living standard per equivalent adult (c_t), subject to borrowing constraints. The program simultaneously calculates not only the household's smoothest living standard path if both the household head and spouse/partner live to their maximum ages of life but also the household's year-specific demands for life insurance (and, thus, the life insurance premiums it will pay each year) to ensure that survivors have at least the same living standard as would otherwise have been the case.[11] The program also determines each of the household's above-referenced taxes and transfer payments along each of its potential survivor paths.

The problem TFA solves is computationally challenging for four reasons. First, there are tens of thousands of survivor-path-specific state variables. These are the levels of regular as well as spouse/partner-specific tax-deferred and Roth retirement accounts. Take, for example, a 40-year-old couple who could live to age 100. They have more than 200,000 survivor-contingent regular and retirement account state variables. Second, taxes, transfer payments, discretionary spending, and life insurance holdings must be determined for all years of all survivor paths. Third, spending, insurance amounts, and net taxes on any survivor path are interdependent. Indeed, they are also interdependent across paths. Hence, one needs a simultaneous equations solution. Fourth, the program needs to run in finite time.

TFA forms its calculations using three dynamic programs. One program does consumption smoothing subject to borrowing constraints. A second dynamic program calculates annual household taxes and benefits for all programs listed in table 1. The third dynamic program calculates the life insurance, subject to a nonnegativity constraint, needed to maintain the household's living standard if survivors live to their maximum ages of life. A key by-product of TFA's life insurance algorithm is determining the lifetime spending and net taxes of households along each survivor path. The programs run sequentially, with each transmitting its results to the other two. Processing continues until the three programs precisely converge to mutually consistent solutions. Dynamic programming of intertemporal consumption choice based on kinked functions that arise from borrowing constraints introduces interpolation error that compounds as one programs backward in time. To ensure precision to many decimal places, TFA utilizes a sparse grid method between iterations.[12]

B. *Confirming TFA's Results*

The accuracy of TFA's algorithm is easy to check. There are eight ways to confirm that TFA's calculations are correct. First, the present value of lifetime discretionary spending (including terminal bequests) equals, to the dollar, human plus nonhuman wealth less the present value of fixed spending less the present value of net taxes (including estate taxes). Second, the household's living standard, measured in today's dollars, is constant through time unless the household faces cash-flow constraints or TFA is told to adjust discretionary spending through time to match a specified age–living standard profile. For example, we could specify a 1% annual decline starting at age 75.

Third, the household's difference in regular assets between years t and $t + 1$ equals its saving in year t—that is, flows and stocks are mutually consistent. Fourth, terminal regular assets are zero apart from specified desired bequests, equity bequests, reserve funds, and funeral expenses. Fifth, regular assets are zero in the year before the household's borrowing constraint is relieved. Sixth, nonnegative life insurance amounts are, to the dollar, what survivors need to maintain their living standard through their maximum ages of life. Seventh, lifetime budget balance holds to the dollar for all survivor outcomes. Eighth, all tax and benefit amounts are correctly calculated.[13]

Testing for Financial Neutrality Absent the Fiscal System

As stated, we adjust SCF inputs to ensure financial inflation neutrality. This entails inflation-indexing all receipts, including wages, self-employment earnings, and asset income, as well as all off-the-top outlays, including mortgage payments, alimony, property taxes, loan repayments, and so forth. We test financial system inflation neutrality by (1) setting all TFA-generated taxes and benefits to zero whether they are calculated for the base trajectory (household heads and spouses live to their maximum ages of life) or survivor trajectories, (2) running TFA assuming alternative paths of inflation, and (3) verifying that the present value of lifetime discretionary spending as well as all survivor-contingent discretionary spending paths remain unchanged.

V. Benchmarking, Imputations, and Adjustments

The SCF is a cross-section survey conducted every 3 years. The survey oversamples wealthy households in the process of collecting data from, in the case of the 2019 Survey, 5,777 households.[14] These data include detailed information on household labor and asset income, assets and liabilities, and demographic characteristics.[15]

Running TFA requires additional information not provided by the SCF. First, it needs state identifiers to calculate state-specific taxes and transfer payments. The public-use SCF release does not provide state identifiers, so we allocate SCF households to different states based on the 2016 American Community Survey (ACS).[16] Second, TFA requires future earnings to calculate resources along survival paths and past and future covered earnings to calculate Social Security benefits. Here, we use Current Population Survey (CPS) data to backcast and forecast each SCF respondent's past and future earnings through retirement.

Third, not all SCF respondents answer questions about retirement, and those who do appear to be too optimistic. Therefore, following Altig et al. (2023), we use the 2019 ACS to impute age- and demographic-specific retirement hazards. Fourth, the SCF provides limited information about welfare program take-up. We use the TFA to directly calculate eligibility and combine SCF data with data from the Annual Social and Economic Supplement (ASEC) to the CPS to infer household- and program-specific take-up. Finally, TFA requires a measure of the pretax rate of return on national wealth for our savings and lifetime wealth calculations. The following subsections detail our benchmarking process and methods for these four imputations.

A. Benchmarking the 2019 SCF to National Aggregates

SCF household-weighted totals of various economic and fiscal aggregates differ from their direct counterparts in the National Income and

Product Account (NIPA) and Federal Reserve Financial Accounts (FA). To assure concordance, we follow the approach outlined in appendices A and B in Dettling et al. (2015), which benchmarks the 2016 SCF based on "conceptually equivalent" values. Specifically, we set SCF benchmark factors to ensure that SCF-weighted aggregates coincide with conceptually comparable NIPA and FA aggregates. We use FA2018 Q4 aggregates for wages, self-employment income, and assets. Benchmarking assets and net worth reported in the SCF requires several adjustments to the FA values. Using the approach outlined in Dettling et al. (2015), our first asset adjustment is to reduce SCF-reported home market value by 7.3% to match the 2018 Q4 FA measure. Second, we increase the SCF-reported equity in noncorporate businesses by 33.3% to match the 2019 Q3 FA estimate. Third, we increase reported retirement account assets by 11.3% to match the total reported in the FA for 2018 Q4. Table 2 details aggregate values, their sources, and our benchmark adjustments. We inflate all SCF-reported wage income by 22.3% to match the NIPA 2018 measure of employee compensation and deflate all SCF-reported self-employment income by 28.4% to match the NIPA 2018 proprietorship and partnership income total.[17]

B. *Imputing State Residency*

We impute state residency based on a statistical match to the ACS. Having done so, we calculate the distribution across states of ACS households with specific cell characteristics used in the match. Next, we assign each SCF household to each of the 50 states and Washington, DC—51 "units"—in appropriate proportion such that the sum of each household's unit-specific weights equals its original SCF weight. To be precise,

Table 2
SCF Benchmarking Adjustments and Targets

	SCF Unadjusted	Benchmarking Coefficient	SCF Adjusted	Target	% Diff.
Wages	7,382	1.22	9,027	9,027	0
Self-employment income	2,237	.72	1,601	1,601	0
Market value of homes	28,048	.93	25,992	25,877	.4
Noncorp. business equity	9,795	1.33	13,055	13,055	0
Regular assets	50,904	.69	35,373	35,374	0
Retirement accounts	14,307	1.11	15,923	15,824	.6

Note: All values are presented in billions of 2018 US dollars. SCF = Survey of Consumer Finances.

we partition households into distinct cells based on the household head's age, race/ethnicity, marital status, and educational attainment, as well as home ownership status, total household income in 2018, and the number of children in the household under 17 years of age.[18] For households in a given cell, we create the household's weight for each unit by multiplying their SCF sample weight by the weighted fraction of the cell's households in the 2019 ACS that reside in that unit. Thus, the sum of all unit weights for each unit will equal the population of that unit. We then run TFA 51 times, once for each state plus DC, incorporating, in the process, each unit's specific tax and transfer policies.

Note that the categorization of rich and poor by resources is done at the national level. For example, California has a higher weighted fraction of its households (17.1%) in the top 10% of lifetime resources than does Mississippi (4.5%) and has significantly more residents. Thus, resource-rich households in the United States are much more likely to be located in California than in Mississippi (18.2% of the top decile of households are in California versus 0.4% in Mississippi).

C. *Earnings Imputations*

To impute annual labor earnings, we first group CPS observations by age, sex, and education. Next, we estimate annual earnings growth rates by age and year for individuals in each sex and education cell. These cell growth rates are used to backcast and forecast each individual's earnings history. Past and future cell growth rates ignore earnings heterogeneity within cells. To deal with such heterogeneity, we assume that observed individual deviations in earnings from cell means are partially permanent and partially transitory, based on an underlying earnings process in which the permanent component (relative to group-trend growth) evolves as a random walk and the transitory component is serially uncorrelated. We also assume that such within-cell heterogeneity begins in the first year of labor force participation.

In particular, suppose that, at each age, for group i, earnings for each individual j evolve (relative to the change in the average for the group) according to a shock that includes a permanent component, p, and an i.i.d. (independent and identically distributed) temporary component, e. Then, at age a (normalized so that age 0 is the first year of labor force participation), the within-group variance will be $\alpha\sigma_p^2 + \sigma_e^2$. Hence, our estimate of the fraction of the observed deviation of individual earnings from group earnings, $(y_{i,j}^a - \bar{y}_i^a)$, that is permanent is $a\sigma_p^2/(a\sigma_p^2 + \sigma_e^2)$. This share grows with age, as permanent shocks accumulate. Using this estimate, we form the permanent component of current earnings for individual j, $\hat{y}^a_{i,j}$,

$$\hat{y}^a_{i,j} = \bar{y}^a_i + \left(\frac{a\sigma_p^2}{a\sigma_p^2 + \sigma_e^2}\right)(y^a_{i,j} - \bar{y}^a_i) = \left(\frac{a\sigma_p^2}{a\sigma_p^2 + \sigma_e^2}\right)y^a_{i,j} + \left(\frac{\sigma_e^2}{a\sigma_p^2 + \sigma_e^2}\right)\bar{y}^a_i, \quad (10)$$

and assume that future earnings grow at the group average growth rate. Further, we make the simplifying assumption that permanent and temporary earnings shocks have the same variance. In so doing, we follow Meghir and Pistaferri (2011) and Moffitt and Gottschalk (2011). Then (11) reduces to

$$\hat{y}^a_{i,j} = \left(\frac{a}{a+1}\right)y^a_{i,j} + \left(\frac{1}{a+1}\right)\bar{y}^a_i. \quad (11)$$

For backcasting, we assume that earnings for individual j were at the group mean at age 0 (i.e., the year of labor force entry) and diverged smoothly from this group mean over time so that the individual's estimated earnings t years prior to the current age a are

$$\bar{y}_i^{(a-t)} + \left(\frac{a-t}{a}\right)(\hat{y}^a_{i,j} - \bar{y}^a_i)\left(\frac{\bar{y}_i^{(a-t)}}{\bar{y}^a_i}\right) = \left(\frac{t}{a}\right)\bar{y}_i^{(a-t)} + \left(\frac{a-t}{a}\right)\hat{y}^a_{i,j}\left(\frac{\bar{y}_i^{(a-t)}}{\bar{y}^a_i}\right). \quad (12)$$

That is, for each age, we use a weighted average of the estimate of current permanent earnings, deflated by general wage growth for group i, and the estimated age a, group i mean also deflated by general wage growth for group i, with the weights converging linearly so that, as we go back, we weight the group mean more and more heavily, with a weight of 1 at the initial age, which we assume is age 20.

D Imputing Retirement Hazards with ACS Data

As discussed in Altig et al. (2022), SCF respondents are asked about their expected ages of retirement. Not all respond, and those who do appear to be overly optimistic.[19] This squares with the tendency of workers in general to overestimate how long they will work (Center for a Secure Retirement 2019). As an alternative, we use the 2000 through 2020 waves of the ACS to impute retirement age based on two questions in the survey. The ACS asks respondents the number of weeks that they worked last year and the number of hours they are currently working in a typical week. We define a person as having "retired" when that person worked more than 26 weeks in the previous year and works less than 21 hours a week this year.[20] We segregate ACS working respondents by year of birth, age, gender, marital status, and education, assuming no retirement prior to age 50. This lets us calculate, for each cohort and combination of cell attributes, sample retirement probabilities in more than 20 ACS surveys.

We smooth these values and use the resultant smoothed function to determine retirement probabilities. For cohorts retiring after 2020, we linearly project retirement hazards at each age based on 2000–2020 trends through 2040 and assume constant hazards thereafter. These cohort- and characteristics-specific retirement hazards are used to randomly assign retirement ages for each SCF respondent under age 80. We assume that all households retire at 80 if they have not yet been probabilistically retired.[21] We also assume that collection of Social Security retirement benefits begins immediately upon retirement.

The predicted age-specific fraction of ACS respondents working after 55 increases over time. The drivers here include higher educational achievement among successive cohorts and a rise in the fraction of working women. Consequently, within each cohort we project some, but rather limited, increases in retirement ages through 2040, with married 50-year-old men with 4-year college degrees or more retiring at an average age of 65.9, approximately 0.6 years later than their 2020 counterparts. Figure 1 plots our cohort-specific smoothed retirement hazard functions—the likelihood of working "full time" (more than half time) at different

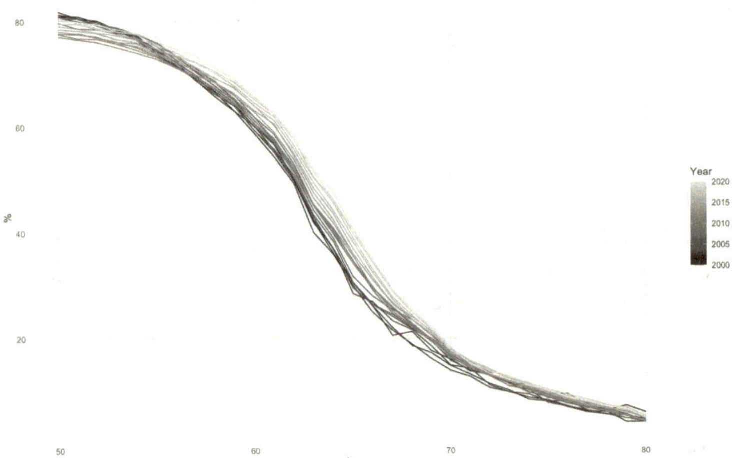

Fig. 1. Fraction of respondents working more than 20 hours per week, ACS 2000–2020.

Table 3
Projected Average Retirement Age

		Age-50 Workers in 2020		Age-50 Workers in 2040	
Marital status	Education	Male	Female	Male	Female
	High school or less	63.0	59.4	63.1	59.0
Single	Some college	62.9	61.0	62.7	60.8
	4 Yr. college or more	63.2	61.5	63.3	61.7
	High school or less	64.9	58.1	65.4	58.4
Married	Some college	64.9	58.5	65.1	58.9
	4 Yr. college or more	65.3	58.3	65.9	58.5

ages—for alternative birth cohorts. Two things are immediately clear: First, regardless of year of birth, the probability of working "full time" declines dramatically starting at age 50. Second, recent cohorts are more likely to work after age 60, but the differences are small and decrease with age.

Table 3 shows projected average retirement ages for workers aged 50 in 2020 and 2040. Results are broken down by marital status and education. First, predicted average retirement ages are only slightly higher for future than for current age-50 workers. Second, single females with college educations are projected to "retire" roughly 2 years later, on average, than those with a high school diploma or less. Third, for males, education makes little difference in average "retirement" ages holding fixed marital status. Fourth, married males "retire," on average, roughly 2 years later than single males across all levels of education. Fifth, males "retire" later than females, with the difference in average ages declining from roughly 4 years to roughly 2 years as one moves from lower to higher levels of education.

Table 4 reports the probability of working "full time" at ages 65 and 70 for 50-year-old workers in 2020. The table is quite revealing. First,

Table 4
Probability of Working More than 20 Hours, Age-50 Workers in 2020

		Prob. of Working More than 20 Hours at Age 65		Prob. of Working More than 20 Hours at Age 70	
Marital status	Education	Male	Female	Male	Female
Single	High school or less	44.2	24.5	20.0	6.9
	Some college	43.2	34.0	17.3	11.0
	4 Yr. college or more	45.3	35.9	18.4	10.5
Married	High school or less	56.5	17.9	26.6	3.9
	Some college	56.0	20.3	25.1	4.7
	4 Yr. college or more	58.6	18.9	26.5	3.9

holding education and marital status fixed, the chances of working "full time" are substantially higher at age 65 than at age 70. Take, for example, married males with some college education. Their chances of being "fully employed" are 56% at age 65 and 25.1% at age 70. Second, females are substantially less likely than males to work "full time." Third, married males are more likely to keep working "full time" than single males. And fourth, education significantly raises the likelihood of single, but not of married, females working "full time."

E. *Adjusting for Take-Up Rates of Benefit Programs*

As is well known, not all households file for all or, indeed, any of the welfare benefits for which they are eligible (Moffitt 1983; Chien 2015; Giannarelli 2019). We make a variety of adjustments, imputations, and assumptions to assign take-up of each benefit to eligible SCF respondents. The adjustments include benchmarking each program's take-up rate to accord with the program's national take-up rate as reported by relevant government agencies. These are summarized in table 5. Our analysis relies, in part, on benefit-participation data reported in the ASEC to the CPS. The ASEC includes participation data for the following programs whose participation is not fully recorded by the SCF: Supplemental Nutritional Assistance Program (SNAP), Section 8 housing, the Affordable Care Act, the earned income tax credit (EITC), Adult and Child Medicaid, and the Child Tax Credit (CTC).

As for the SCF, it records household Medicaid participation, but it does not report whether participants are children, adults, or both. The SCF also indicates if the household is receiving benefits from one or more of TANF, food stamps, Supplemental Security Income (SSI), or other programs. However, it does not report the exact program, and the total amount is often unreported. The ASEC is also problematic for inferring take-up. It generally underreports participation rates relative to official figures. For example, in the ASEC, 40% of eligible households participate in SNAP, whereas the official take-up rate is 67.6%. Hence, using the ASEC to predict SNAP take-up among SCF respondents requires first benchmarking SNAP participation in the ASEC to the official figure.

We do so by assigning participation to a set of ASEC respondents who did not report participating in SNAP. The set of reassigned respondents was determined based on a logit regression relating reported SNAP participation in the ASEC against respondent characteristics. The reassigned respondents are those non-SNAP participants with highest predicted SNAP

Table 5
Estimated Participation and Take-Up of Public Assistance Programs

	Number of Participating Individuals ('000)	Number of Eligible Individuals ('000)	Take-Up Rate (%)
SNAP	40,776	60,334	67.6
Housing choice voucher	5,249	46,559	11.3
Medicaid for adults[a]	18,040	24,096	79.9
Medicaid for children/CHIP[b]	35,953	38,370	93.7
ACA subsidy	9,593	112,942	8.5
EITC	N/A	N/A	78.1
CTC	48,962	58,081	84.3
TANF	1,213	4,869	24.9
CCDF childcare subsidy	2,099	8,417	24.9

Source: Number of eligible individuals for each program are computed using the Policy Rules Database (Ilin and Terry 2022) applied to the 2019 Annual Social and Economic Supplement. Supplemental Nutritional Assistance Program (SNAP) enrollment numbers are from SNAP Data Tables, Food and Nutrition Service, US Department of Agriculture (https://www.fns.usda.gov/pd/supplemental-nutrition-assistance-program-snap). Section 8 housing voucher enrollment data are from 2019 Picture of Subsidized Households, US Department of Housing and Urban Development (https://www.huduser.gov/portal/datasets/assthsg.html#2009-2021_data). Enrollment in Medicaid and CHIP is from Open Data, Center for Medicare and Medicaid Services (https://data.medicaid.gov/dataset/6165f45b-ca93-5bb5-9d06-db29c692a360); Affordable Care Act (ACA) Premium Subsidy enrollment is from 2019 Marketplace Open Enrollment Period Public Use Files, Center for Medicare and Medicaid Services (https://www.cms.gov/Research-Statistics-Data-and-Systems/Statistics-Trends-and-Reports/Marketplace-Products/2019_Open_Enrollment). Estimates of the earned income tax credit (EITC) take-up are taken directly from the Internal Revenue Service (https://www.eitc.irs.gov/eitc-central/participation-rate/eitc-participation-rate-by-states). Number of tax returns with Child Tax Credit (CTC) are from Estimates of Federal Tax Expenditures for Fiscal Year 2019–2023, Joint Committee on Taxation (https://www.jct.gov/publications/2019/jcx-55-19/). Data on the number of participating and eligible units for Temporary Assistance for Needy Families (TANF) are taken from Giannarelli (2019). Data on the number of participating and eligible units for Childcare Defense Fund (CCDF) are taken from Chien (2019).

[a]Excluding dual Medicaid-Medicare enrollees and nonelderly adults with disabilities.

[b]Excluding children with special needs care.

participation probabilities. Thus, if we need X more ASEC respondents to participate in SNAP to equate the ASEC SNAP participation rate with the national rate, we reassign the top X ASEC nonparticipants, where "top" references participation probability ranking.

Next, we estimate a second ASEC logit model using covariates that are common to the ASEC and SCF, specifically marital status, household size, income, education, and the amount they would receive if participating. Then, we assign SNAP program participation to SCF households based on their regression-based ranking of predicted program participation. The cutoff for SCF SNAP participation is set to achieve the national rate. We follow this procedure for benchmarking each of the other benefits whose participation is solicited in the ASEC.

We also impute take-up in the SCF for several programs not included in the ASEC. In the case of SSI and Energy Assistance, we assume full take-up by eligible SCF households. As for the Childcare Defense Fund (CCDF), we randomly assign participation to eligible SCF households. For the remaining programs, we take the following approach. We know if a household is receiving benefits from either SNAP, TANF, or SSI, but we do not have information on the specific program(s) from which the benefits are received. If an SCF household (1) reports receiving benefits from any of the three programs, (2) is not eligible for SSI, and (3) is eligible for SNAP, we assume that they are receiving SNAP benefits only, as very few households receive TANF. This produces close to 30% participation. We impute the remainder using the logit regression approach outlined above. Child Medicaid has a very high participation rate—93.7%. If an SCF household that reports receiving Medicaid is eligible for Child Medicaid and has children younger than 18, we assume they participate in Child Medicaid. If they report receiving Medicaid, are childless, and are eligible for Adult Medicaid, we assume they participate in Adult Medicaid. As for adults otherwise unassigned to Adult Medicaid but who are eligible, we use our logit-based assignment method. Finally, we randomly assign TANF to those who are eligible to reach our benchmark for the program. Table 6 summarizes the results of our imputation for the programs for which we have aggregate participation rates. As shown, the procedure matches weighted participation rates for SCF respondents to within 0.2% age points of estimated national take-up rates.

F. *Survival-Path Probabilities*

As discussed in Auerbach et al. (2023), our survival-path probabilities are constructed from underlying mortality rates estimated by the Committee on the Long-Run Macroeconomic Effects of the Aging US Population (2015). This study sorts Health and Retirement Study (HRS) respondents between 1992 and 2010 by average wage-indexed earnings between ages 40 and 50. For married or partnered couples, average indexed earnings are divided by the square root of 2 prior to sorting. This is a rough adjustment for economies in shared living. It then estimates post–age-50 mortality rates as functions of age and sex. We follow the

Table 6
Summary Statistics for Welfare Program Participation Imputation

	Total Eligible	Total Assigned	Unweighted Participation Rate (%)	Weighted Participation Rate (%)	Take-Up Rate Target	Difference
SNAP	905	631	69.7	67.7	67.6	.1
Section 8	646	72	11.1	11.3	11.3	0
Medicaid adult	706	579	82.0	80.1	79.9	.2
Medicaid child	420	392	93.3	93.8	93.7	.1
ACA	1,657	126	15.4	8.6	8.5	.1
EITC	572	459	80.2	78.1	78.1	.1
CTC	1,351	1,062	78.6	84.3	84.3	0
TANF	74	19	25.7	24.9	24.9	0
CCDF	338	85	25.1	25.1	24.9	.2

Note: ACA = Affordable Care Act, SNAP = Supplemental Nutritional Assistance Program, EITC = earned income tax credit, CTC = Child Tax Credit, TANF = Temporary Assistance for Needy Families, and CCDF = Childcare Defense Fund.

same procedure, except we sort SCF respondents based on average wage-indexed earnings from age 25 through age 60.

G. *Real Rate of Return*

A key component of our calculations involving saving and wealth is the before-tax rate of return on household saving. Following the method detailed in Auerbach et al. (2023), we use the average return on national wealth for the period 1948–2015 based on data from the NIPA accounts and the Federal Reserve's Flow of Funds data. The real return rate in a given year is a fraction whose numerator is national income less labor income, defined as the sum of wages and salaries and the income earned by proprietors and partnerships attributable to labor.[22] The denominator is aggregate wealth of the household sector plus financial wealth (negative if a net liability) of federal, state, and local government sectors. The resulting average real before-tax rate of return of 6.371% is used in all our TFA runs.

H. *Inflation Indexation*

Not all elements of the US fiscal system are indexed for inflation and those that are adjusted experience different delays and are based on different inflation measures. Where available, 2018 values of fiscal-system components are taken as published. There are nuances to each part of the fiscal system for indexing beyond 2018, however. In describing the indexation in detail, the specified inflation rate (0%, 5%, or 10%) in simulated years is referred to as *X*%.

Federal income tax brackets in 2018 equal the official values in that year. Federal income tax brackets for 2019 are calculated by growing the 2018 brackets by one-third times the inflation rate in 2019 (*X*%) plus two-thirds times the Chained Consumer Price Index for All Urban Consumers (C-CPI-U) from the data in 2018.[23] Brackets for 2020 cannot be calculated using *X*% and the 2019 C-CPI-U from the data, however. This is because, given that the TFA takes the most recent year of data to be 2018, any values of the C-CPI-U from 2019 onward do not exist, from the point of view of the TFA. Instead, 2020 brackets are calculated as the 2019 brackets grown by one-third times the inflation rate in 2020 (*X*%) plus two-thirds times an imputed C-CPI-Uate for 2019. The imputed C-CPI-U rate for 2019 is calculated by extending the C-CPI-U from 2018 (from the data) by *X*%, subtracting off a factor, and converting this number to a rate. The factor is constructed such that it maintains the historical difference that has been present between the C-CPI-U and the Consumer Price Index for All Urban Consumers (CPI-U).[24] Tax brackets for $t \geq 2021$ are calculated in the same way: by extending $t - 1$ tax brackets by one-third times *X*% plus two-thirds times the imputed C-CPI-U rate for $t - 1$. These mechanisms capture indexing lags.

State income tax brackets for 2018 are also taken as published. Starting in 2019, these brackets are adjusted in the same manner as the federal tax brackets—based on *X*% inflation and the same composition of lags. The only difference is that the CPI-U is used in all calculations instead of the C-CPI-U, and the subtraction of the factor mentioned in the previous paragraph is unnecessary. The Federal Insurance Contributions Act (FICA) cap and property taxes grow by the specified inflation rate of *X*% starting in 2019 with no lag applied.

Indexing Social Security benefits is more complex. These benefits are adjusted using COLAs calculated based on changes to the Consumer Price Index for Urban Wage Earners and Clerical Workers (CPI-W). Published COLAs from the Social Security administration are used prior to 2018 to determine benefits. Benefits in subsequent years are based on a sequence of imputed CPI-W numbers. To determine this sequence, the following procedure is followed. Calculate the 2018 imputed CPI-W as the 2017 CPI-W from the data, extended by three-quarters times the inflation rate in 2017 (the CPI-U in 2017 from the data) plus one-quarter times the inflation rate in 2016 (the CPI-U in 2016 from the data). The 2019 imputed CPI-W is calculated by extending the 2018 imputed CPI-W by three-quarters times the inflation rate in 2018 (*X*% plus one-quarter times the inflation rate in 2017 (the CPI-U in 2017 from the data). Iterating this formula forward, the 2020 imputed CPI-W is equal to the 2019 imputed CPI-W, grown by this lagged sum of inflation rates from 2019 and 2018, which are both *X*%. Thus, from 2020 onward, the imputed CPI-W is equal to the prior year's imputed CPI-W, extended by *X*%. Now, given this sequence of imputed CPI-W's, the differences between each of these numbers form the annual COLA adjustment used to determine Social Security benefits.

Medicare Part B brackets are taken as published from 2018 data. Because the top bracket (which determines whether the household must pay IRMAA) does not adjust with inflation, the associated income threshold is fixed at $500,000 and $750,000 for single and joint married filers, respectively. The lower brackets are equal to the 2018 brackets, extended each year by the corresponding year value in the imputed CPI-W series described above. Therefore, all Medicare Part B brackets except the top one grow by *X*% each year starting in 2020.

Finally, Medicare and Medicaid benefits are indexed. Because these amounts are typically only available for 1 year, which may not be 2018, the 2018 value is imputed where applicable. This indexing is done using CPI-U data. From 2019 onward, *X*% is used to index benefits. Thus, these benefits are indexed in perfect synchronization with inflation. All other federal and state benefits are also imputed to the 2018 value where applicable by the CPI-U. Starting in 2019, they are extended by *X*%.

Timely Adjustment

We also consider timely adjustment of those tax and benefit provisions that are subject to inflation indexation. The difference between our timely indexing and baseline results indicates how much of inflation's fiscal impacts reflect lagged adjustments. The TFA is a discrete-time model. Time-*t* labor earnings, spending (discretionary and nondiscretionary, including in-kind government transfers from Medicare and Medicaid), taxes, benefits, and receipt of asset and other income all occur at the end of period *t* concomitant with the time *t* increase in prices. Hence, timely indexing simply entails adjusting, at the end of time *t*, all time-*t* fiscal values, such as tax bracket thresholds, that are inflation-indexed.

I. *Incorporating Inflation's Fiscal Effects on Asset Income*

In addition to imperfect or lagged indexation of brackets, thresholds, and ceilings in tax and benefit programs, the other major channel through which inflation changes the real values of net tax burdens is via its various impacts on capital income tax bases, at both the individual and business levels. The key components at the individual level are the taxation of nominal interest income and capital gains. At the business level, firms' taxable income is overstated by the use of historical cost deductions for depreciation and inventories and understated by the deductibility of nominal interest payments. We incorporate each of these effects in the manner described by the following subsections.

Nominal Interest Income

We assume that the nominal interest rate obeys Fisher's Law. Because our inflation experiments hold the real return fixed, the nominal interest rate adjusts according to the standard formula.[25] Because all TFA tax calculations are done in nominal returns before being deflated into current end-of-year dollars, the TFA automatically taxes inflation-induced higher nominal asset income. This, of course, raises the effective taxation of real asset income.

Nominal Capital Gains

We assume that inflation has no impact on firm dividend yields, consistent with our assumption that there are no purely financial effects of inflation. Thus, the inflation-induced increase in nominal equity income that individuals receive takes the form of capital gains. We assume that these additional gains are taxed at the same effective rate as real gains, that is, that individuals realize inflation-induced gains following the same pattern as underlying real gains over time. The TFA is designed to defer the realization of capital gains until they are needed to limit or fully mitigate cash-flow constraints. The program includes settings for the share of regular assets invested in municipal bonds, the share of nonmuni regular asset income received in the form of dividends and realized capital gains, the share of nonmuni regular asset income received in the form of realizations of unrealized long-term capital gains, and the share of nonmuni regular asset income received in the form of interest and other ordinary asset income. The TFA also inputs amounts of unrealized capital gains or losses.

Business-Level Inflation Effects

For both corporate and noncorporate businesses, the effects of inflation on tax liabilities translate into changes in net taxes at the individual level, whether through the ownership of corporate equity (directly, through mutual funds, or through retirement accounts) or direct business ownership (in the case of pass-through entities, including partnerships, sole proprietorships, and S corporations). There are two main channels through which inflation alters taxable business income. First, depreciation deductions and, for firms using FIFO inventory accounting, the costs of goods sold are measured based on historical cost, which generally understates costs and overstates income when there is inflation. Second, as the taxes on interest received and tax deductions for interest paid are based on nominal interest, that is, including the inflation premium, increases in the inflation premium reduce the tax base of a business to the extent that it is a net debtor.

In appendix A, we detail our calculation of inflation-induced adjustments to income for the corporate and noncorporate sectors as well as how these adjustments are integrated into our analysis. For the corporate sector, we find that, relative to a 0% rate of inflation, a 5% rate of inflation increases the tax base by 0.16% of equity. For the noncorporate sector, we find a drop of 0.66% of equity for the same experiment. The effects of a 10% rate of inflation are simply twice as large. The difference in sign is attributable to both the capital consumption adjustment (CCA) and inventory valuation adjustment (IVA) being higher (as a share of equity) in the corporate sector and the net interest-bearing debt as a share of corporate equity being lower.[26]

VI. Results

Section A presents results from TFA using our inflation-neutral data. Section B shows alternate results, assuming the fiscal system is adjusted in a timely manner for inflation, and compares results with those based on actual lagged adjustments. Section C presents case studies that decompose extreme changes to lifetime spending resulting from inflation's fiscal impact.

A. Baseline Results

Figure 2 plots, for given levels of lifetime resources, the percentage change in lifetime spending from 5% and 10% permanent inflation. The 5% and

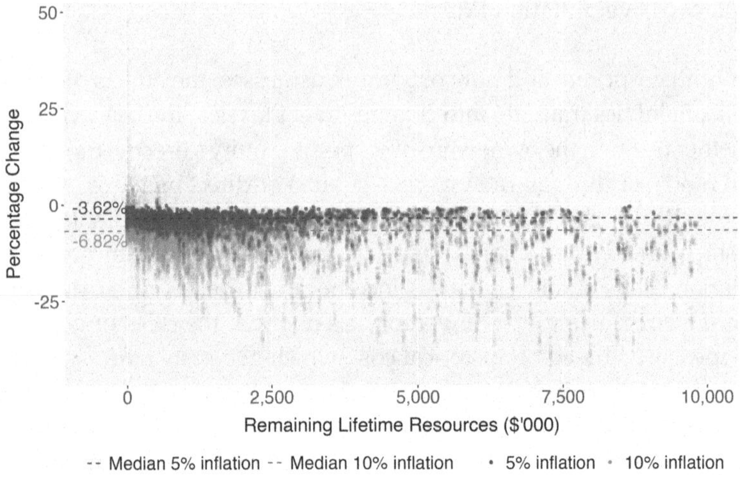

Fig. 2. Percentage change in remaining lifetime spending, ages 20–79.

10% weighted-median changes are −3.62% and −6.82%, respectively. Hence, typical households are almost twice as worse off when inflation is 10% rather than 5%.

Virtually all households are hurt by inflation. But richer households typically face larger percentage losses, thanks to their higher share of asset income relative to labor income. Figures 3 and 4 show median and mean percentage changes in lifetime spending. The top 1% median values are nearly 2.5 times as big, for both inflation experiments, as those

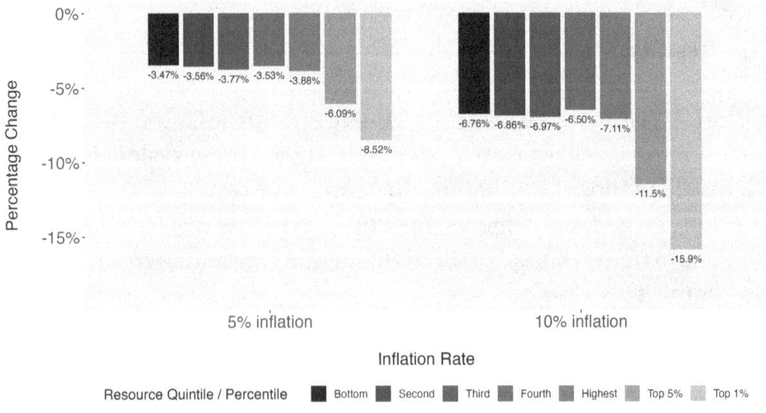

Fig. 3. Median percentage change in remaining lifetime spending by resource quintile, ages 20–79.

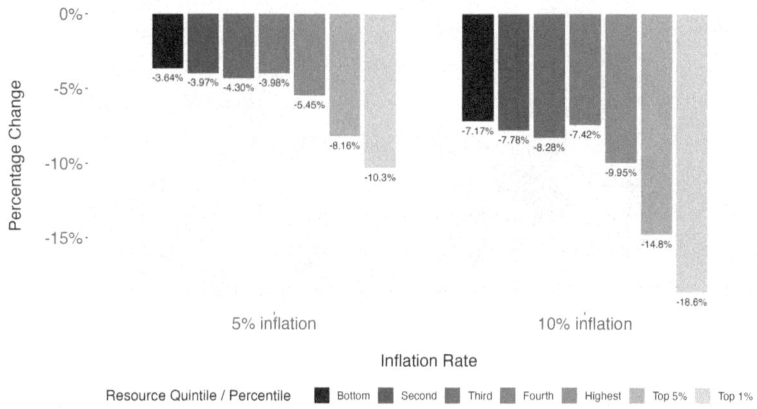

Fig. 4. Average percentage change in remaining lifetime spending by resource quintile, ages 20–79.

for the bottom quintile. The top 1%'s 5% and 10% inflation spending losses are 8.5% and 15.9%, respectively. Under 5% inflation, the other quintiles face losses between 3% and 6%. Under 10% inflation, their losses are between 6% and 12%. As for mean impact, in the 10% inflation case, the mean loss for the richest 1% of households is remarkably large—more than 18%. This is over 2.5 times the corresponding mean lifetime spending decline among those in the lowest quintile. The fact that the ratio of means to medians rises with resources indicates that inflation's fiscal impacts are greater for the rich.

Figure 2's most remarkable feature may be the dispersion of impacts. As detailed in figure 5, coefficients of variation are substantial for all resource groups. For the second, third, and fourth quintiles, they exceed 1.75. For the 10% inflation case, the impact on certain households exceeds 30%. On the other hand, a small fraction of low-resource households experience higher lifetime spending when inflation is either 5% or 10%. Section C explores the underlying dynamics of such cases in detail.

Figures 6 and 7 decompose figure 2 at the age-cohort level, revealing significant cross-cohort variation. The age 50–59 cohort is hurt most by inflation. This is expected, because a larger share of the resources of this cohort comprises financial assets. The reverse is true for young workers in the 20–29 cohort, with their lower savings limiting the impact of inflation.

Appendix B shows the average decomposition of lifetime spending by resource quintile. Several common patterns arise. Federal and state income taxes go up, and benefits decline.[27] Consequently, average net

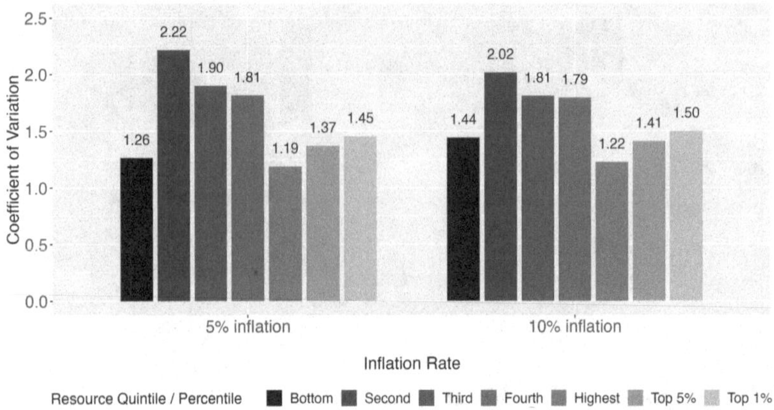

Fig. 5. Coefficients of variation, lifetime spending by resource quintile, ages 20–79.

taxes increase with inflation. For households in the third quintile, average net taxes increase to the extent that households in this group change from being owed money by the government to owing money to the government on net. Households, particularly those in the top quintile, also experience a decline in sales taxes as a result of reductions to cash expenditures.

Figure 8 shows inflation's impact on lifetime net taxes. There is considerable heterogeneity in the net tax response of bottom-quintile households. Households below the 45-degree line correspond to households that have lower net taxes in the face of inflation. The number of households below the line decreases with lifetime resource: For those in the

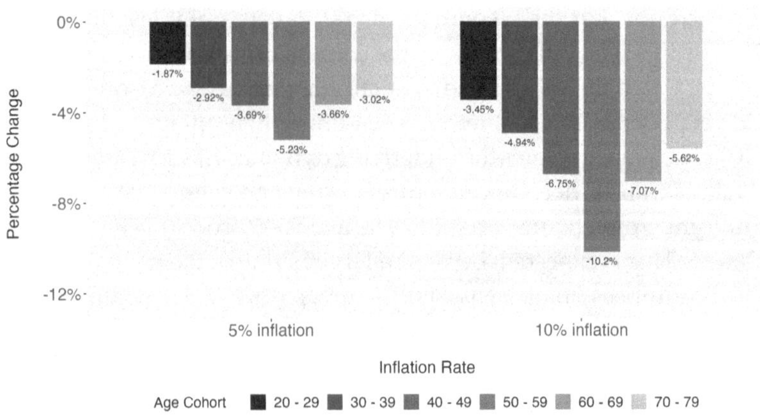

Fig. 6. Median percentage change in remaining lifetime spending by age cohort.

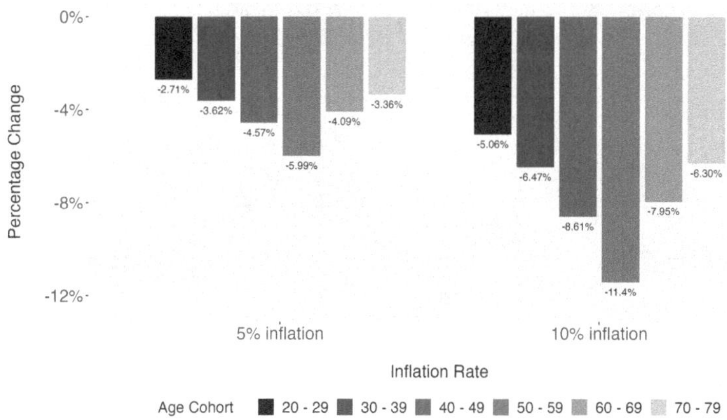

Fig. 7. Average percentage change in remaining lifetime spending by age cohort.

highest quintile, almost all households are subject to higher net taxes. What is driving this heterogeneity? Inflation increases lifetime federal and state income taxes for nearly every household. Yet it does so to a larger degree for rich households. This is the message of figures 14a and 15a.

Finally, although not a component of net taxes, in-kind benefits (Medicare and Medicaid) adjust very differently across resource quintiles in the face of inflation. This is a key driver of total spending. From figure 9, it is clear that lower resource quintiles see the most variation in changes to Medicare and Medicaid benefits. Higher resource quintiles see relatively little change being mostly located along the 45-degree line.[28] Detailed explanations of why these benefits change, for select households, are presented in Section C.

B. *Timely Indexing*

Figure 10 is otherwise identical to figure 2 but with timely indexing. As expected, inflation is more benign, yet the difference is moderate. The median change in lifetime spending is −2.65% under 5% inflation and is −4.74% under 10% inflation. These values are not dramatically different from the −3.62% and −6.82% baseline results. Patterns across resource groups are also very similar. As with the results in Section A, there is considerable variation in lifetime spending response by age cohort, shown in figures 11 and 12. Age cohort 50–59 is, similarly, the most affected, as measured by both weighted-median changes and weighted-average changes.

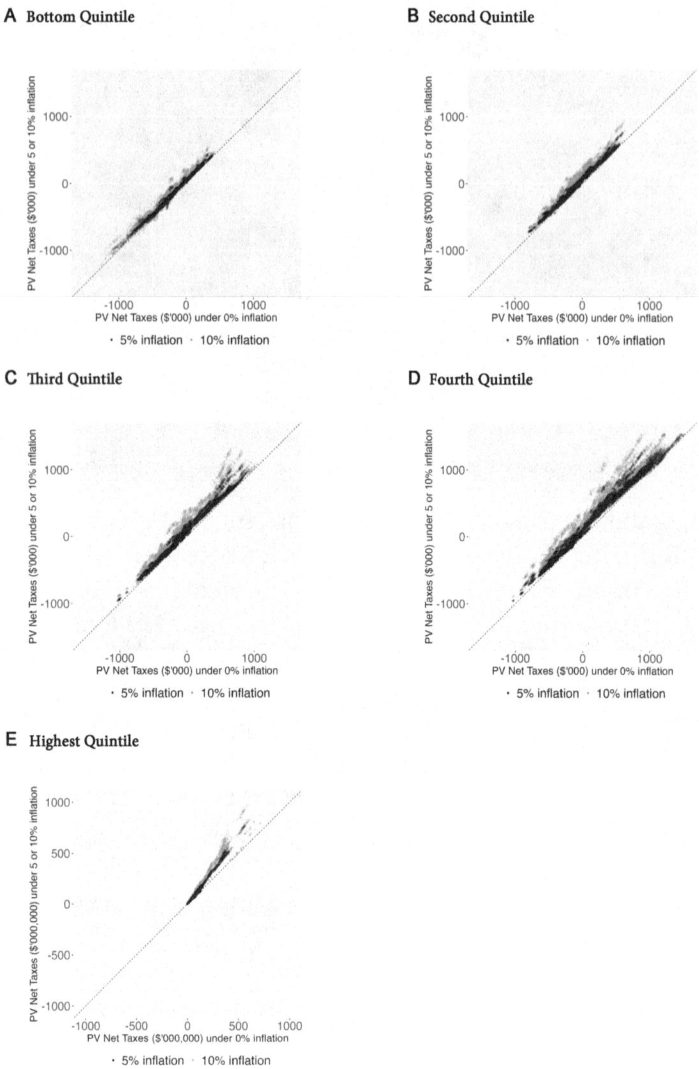

Fig. 8. Net taxes by resource quintile, ages 20–79.

Figure 13 decomposes figure 10 by household positions in the lifetime-resource distribution. Clearly, as measured by median percentage decline, households in the highest quintile of the resource distribution suffer the most. The results for mean changes and for coefficients of variation in appendix C also show patterns similar to those in our baseline analysis.

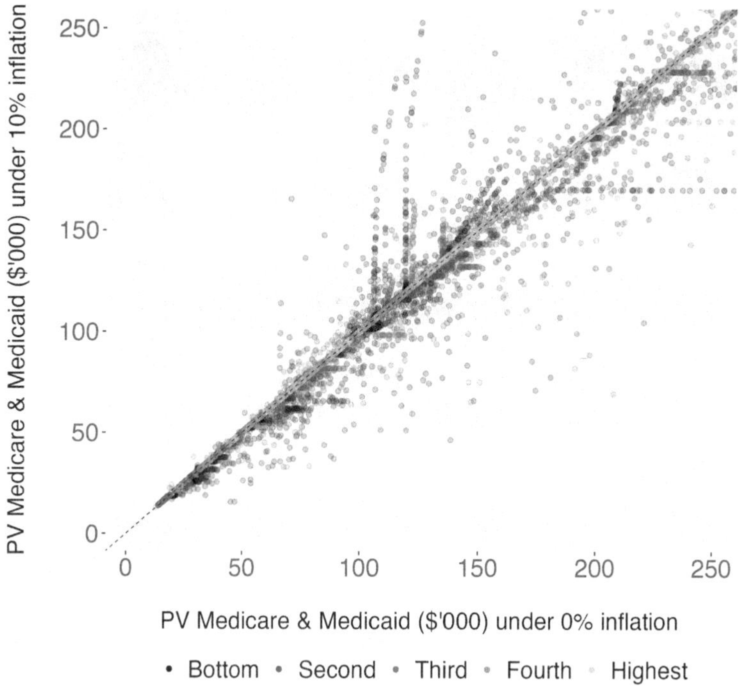

Fig. 9. In-kind benefits by resource quintile, ages 20–79.

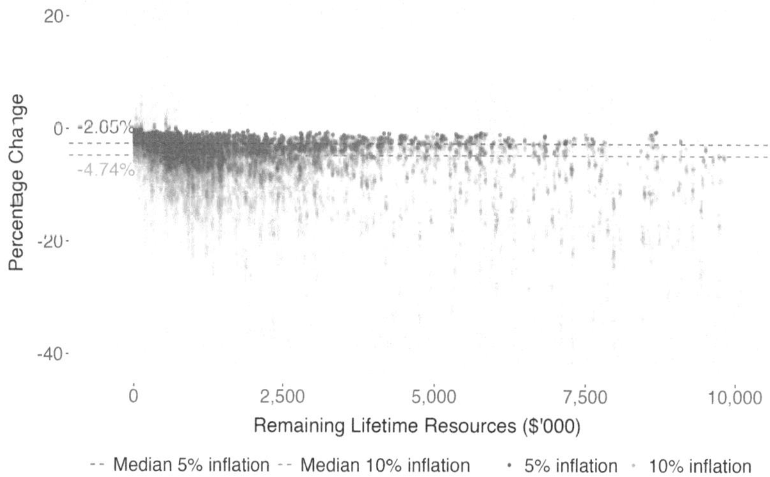

Fig. 10. Percentage change in remaining lifetime spending with timely adjustment by lifetime resources, ages 20–79.

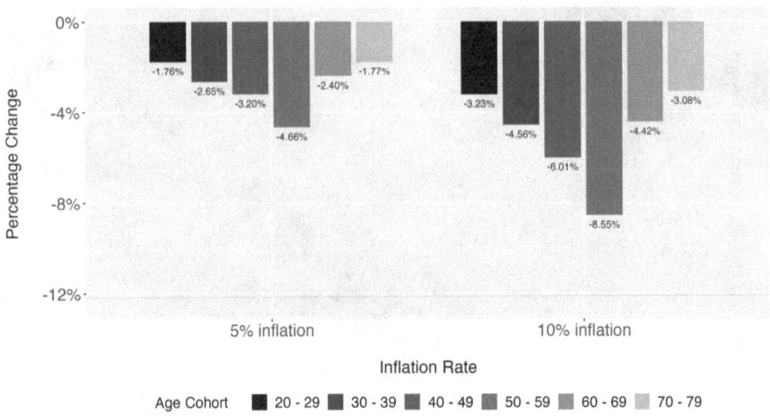

Fig. 11. Median percentage change in remaining lifetime spending with timely adjustment by age cohort.

Figure C3 in appendix C shows changes to lifetime net taxes by resource quintile. The patterns are similar to those in figure 8. As expected, the removal of lags dampens the effects of inflation. Compared with the baseline case, however, the absence of lags in indexing the fiscal system makes little difference to the distribution of spending impact across age cohorts and resource quintiles.

Inflation's fiscal effect on spending can be seen by comparing key components of the fiscal system with and without timely indexing. Figure 14 compares the distribution of federal income taxes across baseline

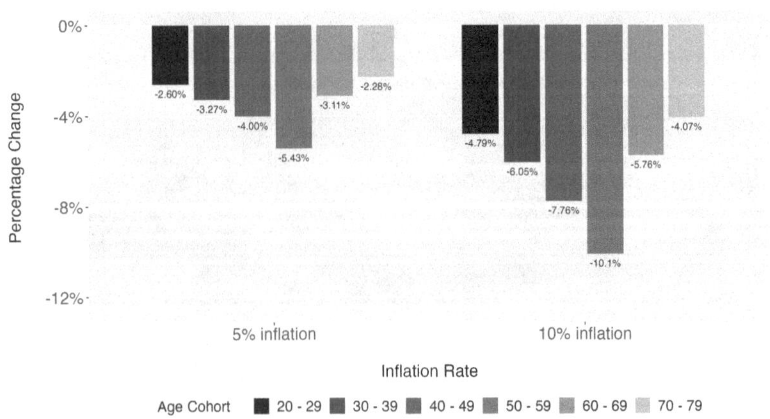

Fig. 12. Average percentage change in remaining lifetime spending with timely adjustment by age cohort.

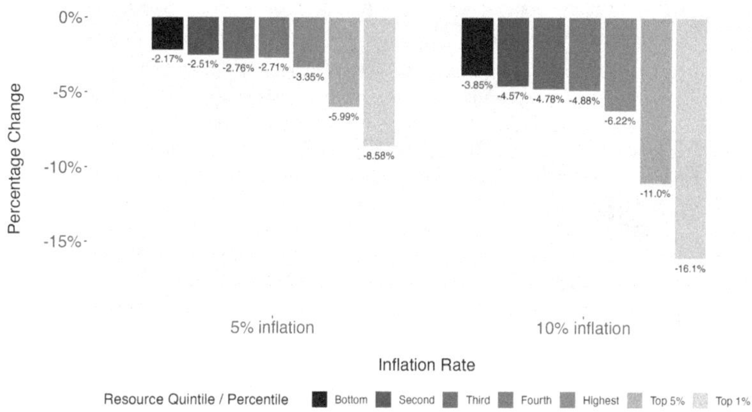

Fig. 13. Median percentage change in remaining lifetime spending with timely adjustment by resource quintile, ages 20–79.

and timely indexing cases in the presence of 10% inflation. The 45-degree line is plotted to emphasize that federal income taxes almost uniformly increase when households face inflation. Figure 15 repeats the exercise for state income taxes.[29] From these two figures, there are no pronounced differences in the distribution of the inflation shock. Finally, figure 16 compares Social Security benefits. Again, there are no major differences in the distribution of benefit changes across quintiles; however, the effects of the COLA lags on Social Security benefits are visible. Social Security benefits for nearly all households decline in the presence of inflation but more so in the baseline case.

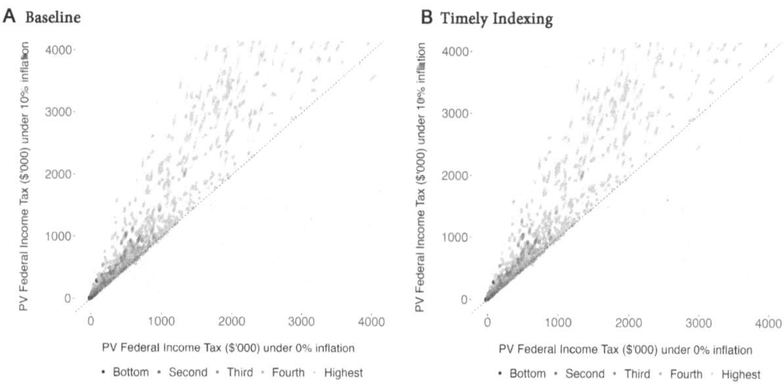

Fig. 14. Federal income tax by resource quintile, ages 20–79.

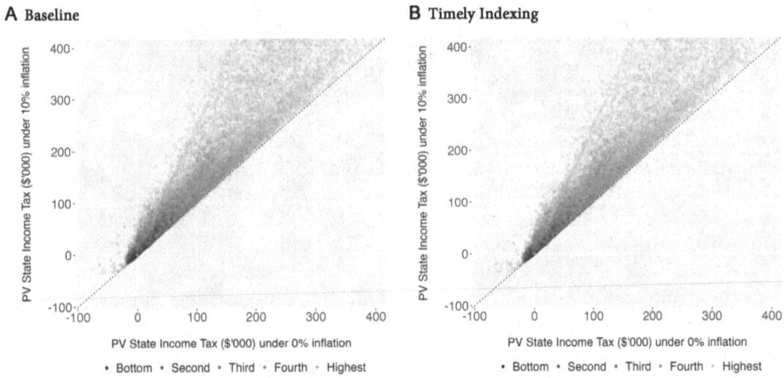

Fig. 15. State income tax by resource quintile, ages 20–79.

C. *Case Studies*

This section examines the impact of 10% inflation on two households each that (1) experience approximately the median increase in remaining lifetime spending among households that experience increases; (2) experience the greatest increase in remaining lifetime spending; (3) same as (1), but for households experiencing decreases; and (4) experience the greatest reduction. The decomposition of spending of each household characterized by (1) and (2) is shown in table 7. Those for (3) and (4) are shown in table 8.

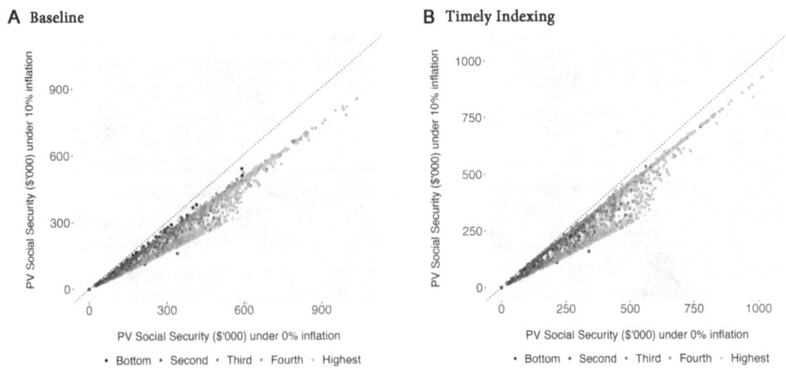

Fig. 16. Social Security benefits by resource quintile, ages 20–79.

Table 7
Decomposition of Level Changes in Total Spending for Select Better-Off Households

Household/State	5,289, MA	4,047, DC	4,314, ND	2,290, DE
Federal income tax	0	0	0	0
State income tax	−4	0	0	0
Other taxes	−2,382	−5,314	−3,248	−1,278
Total taxes	−2,386	−5,314	−3,248	−1,278
Social Security	−38,864	−57,772	−41,541	−28,584
ACA	0	0	0	0
Medicaid	29,848	49,458	136,121	110,055
Medicare	0	0	0	0
Section 8	0	0	10,827	8,364
SSI	120	0	2,247	3,479
Other transfers	786	−9,100	−11,235	1,607
Transfer payments	−8,110	−17,414	96,419	94,921
Net taxes and in-kind benefits	−24,124	−37,358	−235,789	−206,252
Total spending	24,124	37,358	235,789	206,252

Note: All numbers shown are calculated as the present value in the inflation run minus the present value in the base run. "Total Spending" refers to the sum of discretionary spending, nondiscretionary spending, and in-kind benefits. ACA = Affordable Care Act, SSI = Supplemental Security Income, MA = Massachusetts, DC = District of Columbia, ND = North Dakota, and DE = Delaware.

Table 8
Decomposition of Level Changes in Total Spending for Select Worse-Off Households

Household/State	5,751, IL	4,449, TN	1,458, CA	2,045, CA
Federal income tax	85,580	1,446,763	12,407,995	56,823,448
State income tax	20,259	17,766	4,249,723	18,659,611
Other taxes	8,785	−27,164	−1,279,710	−6,607,645
Total taxes	114,624	1,437,365	15,378,008	68,875,414
Social Security	−117,429	−80,445	−88,221	−77,280
ACA	0	0	0	0
Medicaid	0	0	0	0
Medicare	0	0	0	0
Section 8	0	0	0	0
SSI	0	0	0	0
Other transfers	−21	0	0	0
Transfer payments	−117,450	−80,445	−88,221	−77,280
Net taxes and in-kind benefits	232,075	1,517,811	15,466,230	68,952,693
Total spending	−232,075	−1,517,811	−15,466,229	−68,952,693

Note: All numbers shown are calculated as the present value in the inflation run minus the present value in the base run. "Total Spending" refers to the sum of discretionary spending, nondiscretionary spending, and in-kind benefits. ACA = Affordable Care Act, SSI = Supplemental Security Income, IL = Illinois, TN = Tennessee, and CA = California.

Household 5,289, in Massachusetts

This single-person household's lifetime total spending increases by 3.18%. They receive only pension income and Social Security. Inflation lowers the real value of Social Security benefits through the system's lagged COLA. Consequently, the household becomes eligible, on an ongoing basis, for 18 more years of Medicaid, food stamps, and SSI. The additional Medicaid amounts to approximately $30,000. The household also owes more than $2,000 less in taxes, comprised primarily declines in Medicare Part B premiums and sales taxes. Medicare Part B premiums are tied to household overall income, including the household's reduced Social Security benefits. Sales taxes fall with lower cash expenditures. The aggregate change entails an increase in lifetime spending of $24,000.

Household 4,047, in District of Columbia

This age-78 household experiences a 3.19% increase in lifetime spending. Their only income is Social Security benefits, which erode. This makes them eligible for energy assistance and 10 more years of Medicaid. The additional $49,000 of Medicaid offsets the $58,000 Social Security income decline. Whereas the household has approximately $140,000 in assets, they are poor enough to owe zero income taxes. They do owe sales tax, federal excise taxes, and Medicare Part B premiums, however, which decline in aggregate by more than $5,000. The result is a nearly $40,000 increase in lifetime spending.

Household 4,314, in North Dakota

This North Dakota household experiences a dramatic, seemingly implausible 40.7% increase in lifetime spending. Yet the explanation is straightforward. All expenditures of this age-68 individual, apart from housing, are covered by Social Security benefits. The same mechanism from case 4,047 applies: Social Security benefits drop, making the household eligible for 17 additional years of Medicaid and other income-tested benefits. Increased Medicaid participation leads to almost $140,000 more in lifetime benefits. This is more than 13 times the amount that was received in the 0% case. Medicaid also covers the respondent's Medicare Part B premium. Over the household's remaining lifetime, the respondent receives, in present expected value, approximately $135,000 more in Medicaid benefits. The household also becomes eligible for 10 more years of food stamps, receives more in Section 8 benefits, and becomes eligible for SSI. Paying lower sales taxes and federal excise taxes follows as a consequence of having lower cash expenditures. In total, these changes more than compensate for the decline in Social Security payments.

Household 2,290, in Delaware

This household experiences the largest increase: 46.7%. This is a 69-year-old divorced female with no children in the bottom resource quintile. Her only income after 2018 comes from Social Security benefits and a small pension. She owes no federal or state income tax. However, other taxes decrease by roughly $1,300, mostly driven by declines in Medicare Part B premiums. On the benefits side, Social Security benefits decline. This makes her eligible for SSI, food stamps, and 15 more years of Medicaid eligibility. The change in Medicaid eligibility generates $110,055 more in lifetime benefits. Given that the household is in the bottom resource quintile (its total lifetime spending equals only $441,247 in the 0% inflation case), its percentage increase in lifetime spending is very large.

Household 5,751, in Illinois

This household, comprised a married couple with no children, experiences a 6.83% reduction—approximately the median among worse-off households. They have $609,000 in remaining lifetime wages and $2.9 million in nonstock assets. Because the nominal rate of return on these assets is nearly 17% each year, the amount of taxable income, none of which is derived from munis, increases substantially year after year. Consequently, they face much higher real taxation due to income taxation of the inflation component of nominal asset income. As a result, federal income taxes increase by more than $85,000. Holding stock dampens the tax increase. Recall the section called "Business-Level Inflation Effects"—for the noncorporate sector, 10% inflation decreases the tax base by 1.32% of equity. If the couple did not hold their money in stock, federal taxes would have increased even further.[30] In addition, they face a $9,000 net increase in other taxes. Sales and federal excise taxes decrease due to reduced cash expenditures, but this is insufficient to counter increases in Medicare Part B premiums and higher corporate taxation. Social Security benefits also decline. In total, they lose more than $230,000 in lifetime spending.

Household 4,449, in Tennessee

This household also experiences a 6.83% reduction in lifetime spending, the bulk from owing $1.4 million more in taxes. The household is exceptionally asset heavy, with more than 100 times more assets than lifetime wages ($20 million vs. $180,000). Bracket creep more than doubles their federal and state income taxes. Other taxes go down, in net, by $27,000. Of these, corporate taxes increase by over $75,000 due to the household's huge stock holdings. This burden is partially reduced by a reduction in Medicare Part B premiums, federal excise taxes, and sales taxes. The decline in Social Security benefits deepens the blow. In total, they lose over $1.5 million in remaining lifetime spending.

Household 1,458, in California

This household experiences the second largest reduction: 60.7%. Similar to household 4,449, they are in the top quintile, holding $45 million in assets and $1.5 million in lifetime wages. They hold no stock. Bracket creep results in their federal and state income taxes increasing by over $12 million and $4 million, respectively. Declines in other taxes are relatively minor. Social Security benefits also decline. The losses total over $15 million in lifetime spending. The large discrepancy between households 4,449 and 1,458 in how income taxes behave can be attributed to asset composition. Household 4,449 holds 70% of their assets in stock, whereas 1,458 holds none. Had household 4,449 held zero assets in stock, then their federal and state income taxes would have increased by $3.7 million and $47,000, respectively.

Household 2,045, in California

This household sees the largest decline—64.9%—in lifetime spending. They are extremely wealthy, with almost $195 million in assets, which is substantial relative to their $976,000 in lifetime wages. Virtually all of their taxable income is asset income, and they hold no municipal bonds or stock. As a result, they face much higher taxation. Under zero inflation, their current-year taxable income is $12.2 million. With 10% inflation, this nearly triples to $32.6 million. Reductions in other taxes are small in comparison. As usual, Social Security benefits decline.

VII. Conclusion

This paper uses TFA, a life-cycle consumption-smoothing tool, in conjunction with the 2019 Survey of Consumer Finances to study inflation's impact through the fiscal system on the level and distribution of expected remaining lifetime spending. We focus on the fiscal system's interaction with inflation for two reasons. First, tracing the financial impacts of inflation on the course of wages and the valuations of particular stock holdings would necessarily be highly speculative, given data limitations, or highly episode dependent were we to consider a specific historical inflation occurrence. Second, inflation's interaction with the fiscal system can be readily examined using the TFA's detailed coding of all major federal and state fiscal policies.

To isolate inflation's fiscal impacts, we adjust our SCF data to make it inflation-neutral. That is, absent fiscal policy, our 2019 SCF households experience no impact whatsoever on their annual path of annual or lifetime spending from inflation. Using these adjusted data ensures that our results tell us just about inflation's interaction with elements of the fiscal system—some of which are indexed, albeit with longer or shorter lags, and some of which, such as the taxation of Social Security benefits and asset income, are not.

As we show, depending on the household's age, resource level, resource composition, and participation in welfare programs, inflation can substantially decrease or, indeed, increase lifetime living standards. A permanent increase in the rate of inflation from 0% to either 5% or 10% reduces median lifetime spending by 3.62% and 6.82%, respectively. Whereas a share of these effects is due to the lagged adjustment of tax and benefit programs to inflation, most impacts reflect other channels, including changes in benefit-program eligibility. Inflation-induced decline in real Social Security benefits arising from the lagged nature of its COLA is, paradoxically, a key trigger for household eligibility for Medicaid and other income-tested benefits. For households experiencing the largest reduction in lifetime spending, the main factor is their large net wealth relative to human wealth coupled with their failure to invest in municipal bonds or inability to fully defer capital gains taxation.

Inflation's net taxation is highly progressive, with the richest 1% experiencing nearly 2.6 times the average percentage decline in lifetime spending as those in the bottom quintile. And those in their middle ages are particularly hard hit. Both findings reflect the fact that the rich and middle-aged are disproportionate asset holders and, therefore, suffer disproportionately from inflation's increase in the effective rate of taxation of real asset income. Our study's other major finding regards heterogeneous impacts. For an increase in the rate of inflation from 0% to 10%, the 25th percentile spending change is −9.84%, whereas the 75th percentile change is −4.83%. A small fraction of households experience extreme changes in lifetime spending, with the maximum reduction equaling 64.9%. The maximum increase equals 46.7%.

In summary, even were inflation fully anticipated and, thus, financially neutral, it would have a major and quite progressive impact, via the fiscal system, on the average level and distribution of Americans' lifetime spending.

Appendix A

Calculating the Effects of Inflation on Business Income

Here, we provide details regarding the calculation of the changes in business income due to inflation and how these estimated changes are used to calculate the impact of inflation on tax burdens. There are two main components to changes in measured business income. The first is the sum of the IVA, which accounts for input costs not being valued at current prices, and the CCA, which accounts for depreciation deductions not being based on current capital costs.[31] The second is the change in net interest due to the inflation premium on debt. Generally, the first component will increase taxes, and the second will reduce taxes (because the business sector in the aggregate is a net debtor). We calculate these two adjustments for both the noncorporate and the corporate sectors.

To compute the inflation component of the CCA, we start with figures for both corporate and noncorporate sectors from the NIPA, table 7.6.[32] For the IVA, we use NIPA table 6.14D.[33] The corporate and noncorporate values are in rows 2 and 14, respectively.

Because S corporations are taxed as noncorporate (i.e., pass-through) businesses but are treated as corporations in the NIPA data, we need to shift their share of the CCA and IVA corrections to the noncorporate sector. We can do this using the Federal Reserve's Release Z.1, the Flow of Funds (FOF) data, which also groups S corporations with other corporations.[34] In FOF table L.224 (Corporate Equities), total corporate equity in the domestic sector at market value is in line 2. S corporation equity at market value is in line 31, so we divide the latter by the former to get the S corporation share and then multiply this fraction by the CCA and IVA corrections to form adjusted corporate and noncorporate IVA and CCA corrections.[35]

To compute the adjusted corporate CCA and IVA corrections as a share of equity values, we divide by the market value of domestic corporations adjusted to remove S corporations (line 2 minus line 31 in table L.224 of the FOF data). To replicate this step for noncorporate business, we need a market value of noncorporate equity, adjusted to include S corporate equity. To compute this, we add line 31 (S corporation equity) in FOF table L.224, line 27 (Equity in Noncorporate Business) in table L.104 (Nonfinancial Noncorporate Business), and line 32 (Equity in Noncorporate Business) in table L.130 (Brokers and Dealers).[36]

To calculate the increase in the corporate and noncorporate tax bases due to the CCA and IVA from inflation, as a fraction of equity values, we multiply the adjusted CCA and IVA ratios for the corporate and noncorporate sectors derived above by the ratio of the inflation rate assumed in our simulations (either 5% or 10%) to the actual inflation rate during the period when the CCA and IVA are measured. Given that the CCA and the IVA fluctuate from year to year (even with little change in the inflation rate), we use the average of 2017, 2018, and 2019 for adjusted CCA and IVA values and inflation factors in computing the numerators of these ratios to equity values.

Turning now to the effect of inflation on net deductible interest payments, we begin by calculating the net interest-bearing debt for the corporate and noncorporate sectors, starting with FOF tables L.103 (Nonfinancial Corporate Business) and L.104 (Nonfinancial Noncorporate Business). For corporations, we define net interest-bearing debt as gross taxable interest-bearing debt [line 28 (Debt securities) – line 30 (Municipal securities)[37] + line 32 (Loans) + line 36 (Intercompany debt)] – gross taxable interest-bearing assets [line 4 (Time and savings deposits) + line 5 (Money market fund shares) + line 7 (Debt securities) – line 11 (Municipal securities) + line 13 (Loans) + line 16 (Intercompany debt)]. For noncorporate business, the corresponding calculation from table L.104 is line 18 (Loans) + line 22 (Intercompany debt) – line 3 (Time and savings deposits) – line 4 (Money market fund shares) – line 5 (Debt securities) + line 7 (Municipal securities) – line 8 (Loans). Note that these calculations are for the nonfinancial sector. Comparable calculations for the financial sector would be much more difficult because of the many special tax regimes that apply and the complexity of determining the impact of inflation on net income for different classes of assets and liabilities beyond simple debt obligations. Therefore, we do not attempt to include a measure of the impact of inflation on the taxable financial income of financial companies.[38] With these calculations of net debt for the corporate and noncorporate sectors in hand, we again make an adjustment for S corporations, to move the net debt of the S corporate sector to the noncorporate sector. To do this, we assume that S corporations' share of total corporate net debt is the same as their share of total corporate equity.

Next, we divide this adjusted net debt into the corporate and noncorporate sectors by the respective adjusted values of corporate and noncorporate equity derived above. This gives us net debt as a share of equity value in both the corporate and noncorporate sectors. To calculate the decrease in the corporate and noncorporate tax bases as a fraction of equity values due to the deduction of the inflation premium on net interest-bearing debt, we multiply the corporate and noncorporate ratios just computed by the inflation rate assumed in our calculations.

Adding the results for the CCA and IVA and net debt together for both corporate and noncorporate sectors, we now have inflation-induced net changes in the tax base as a share of corporate and noncorporate equity values. For corporations, one final adjustment is required. Because some equity held by households is in foreign corporations, whose taxable earnings we do not expect to be directly affected by the US inflation rate, we wish to apply the corporate ratio only for domestic US equities. We do this by multiplying the corporate ratio just computed by 0.72, based on a recent estimate by Rosenthal and Mucciolo (2024) of the share of US-held equity that is foreign-issued.[39]

Finally, we integrate our estimates of the impact of inflation on business income (as a share of business equity) into our TFA simulations. For the corporate sector, we multiply the combined federal and state marginal corporate tax rate for 2018 taken from the OECD tax database [.2584] by the inflation-induced change in income as a share of equity, +0.16% for 5% inflation and +0.32% for 10% inflation, to get the increased corporate taxes as a share of corporate equity. The TFA then automatically calculates the reduced level of individual consumption that results, based on individual holdings of corporate equity directly, through mutual funds and through retirement savings accounts. For the noncorporate sector, the change in business income due to inflation for each household is −0.66% of equity for 5% inflation and −1.32% of equity for 10% inflation, so we multiply these percentages by the value of the household's noncorporate business assets and add this (negative) adjustment to taxable income.[40]

Appendix B

Decomposition of Spending by Resource Quintile

Table B1
Breakdown of Spending, Lowest Resource Quintile

	0%	5% Inflation	10% Inflation
Federal income tax	38,982	43,701	50,795
State income tax	5,713	6,922	8,629
Other taxes	52,324	52,116	53,966
Total taxes	97,019	102,739	113,390
Social Security	187,796	165,094	147,399
ACA	9,416	9,510	9,214
Medicaid	10,475	10,007	9,928
Medicare	113,798	113,798	113,798
Section 8	5,034	5,883	6,223
SSI	7,804	7,642	7,499
Other transfers	3,847	3,197	3,011
Transfer payments	338,170	315,131	297,072
Net taxes and in-kind benefits	−365,424	−336,197	−307,406
Total spending	894,212	864,601	835,794

Note: All numbers are in present value terms. Weighted mean values are presented. In appendix tables B1–B5, "Total Spending" refers to the sum of discretionary spending, nondiscretionary spending, and in-kind benefits. Changes in net taxes and in-kind benefits need not equal changes in total spending due to employer-paid FICA and employer-paid health insurance. These may change due to Social Security rules and lagged indexing. ACA = Affordable Care Act and SSI = Supplemental Security Income.

Table B2
Breakdown of Spending, Second Resource Quintile

	0%	5% Inflation	10% Inflation
Federal income tax	79,312	88,735	100,848
State income tax	12,197	14,630	17,729
Other taxes	78,592	79,142	82,253
Total taxes	170,101	182,507	200,830
Social Security	213,546	184,212	162,087
ACA	4,037	3,623	3,043
Medicaid	1,415	1,274	1,292
Medicare	112,368	112,368	112,368
Section 8	929	948	1,012
SSI	802	822	828
Other transfers	1,198	677	572
Transfer payments	334,295	303,924	281,202
Net taxes and in-kind benefits	−277,977	−235,059	−194,032
Total spending	1,156,800	1,113,835	1,072,773

Note: All numbers are in present value terms. Weighted mean values are presented. ACA = Affordable Care Act and SSI = Supplemental Security Income.

Table B3
Breakdown of Spending, Third Resource Quintile

	0%	5% Inflation	10% Inflation
Federal income tax	150,205	170,035	190,215
State income tax	23,593	28,346	33,653
Other taxes	119,346	120,511	123,906
Total taxes	293,144	318,892	347,774
Social Security	274,754	235,065	204,856
ACA	1,513	1,007	797
Medicaid	216	208	208
Medicare	130,756	130,756	130,756
Section 8	238	238	244
SSI	116	144	165
Other transfers	297	153	120
Transfer payments	407,890	367,571	337,146
Net taxes and in-kind benefits	−245,719	−179,643	−120,336
Total spending	1,627,953	1,561,389	1,500,469

Note: All numbers are in present value terms. Weighted mean values are presented. ACA = Affordable Care Act and SSI = Supplemental Security Income.

Table B4
Breakdown of Spending, Fourth Resource Quintile

	0%	5% Inflation	10% Inflation
Federal income tax	293,725	319,070	343,344
State income tax	46,307	54,153	61,748
Other taxes	192,664	193,534	194,087
Total taxes	532,696	566,757	599,179
Social Security	334,484	285,499	248,241
ACA	1,510	918	768
Medicaid	231	35	32
Medicare	144,241	144,241	144,241
Section 8	2	2	3
SSI	19	18	16
Other transfers	117	54	37
Transfer payments	480,604	430,767	393,338
Net taxes and in-kind benefits	−92,381	−8,287	61,568
Total spending	2,338,169	2,250,440	2,176,245

Note: All numbers are in present value terms. Weighted mean values are presented. ACA = Affordable Care Act and SSI = Supplemental Security Income.

Table B5
Breakdown of Spending, Fifth Resource Quintile

	0%	5% Inflation	10% Inflation
Federal income tax	1,628,769	2,029,170	2,357,605
State income tax	244,135	309,408	363,911
Other taxes	664,191	641,302	618,604
Total taxes	2,537,095	2,979,880	3,340,119
Social Security	398,689	340,813	296,442
ACA	146	18	15
Medicaid	16	11	12
Medicare	149,162	149,162	149,162
Section 8	0	0	5
SSI	1	1	1
Other transfers	38	23	23
Transfer payments	548,052	490,028	445,660
Net taxes and in-kind benefits	1,839,867	2,340,680	2,745,285
Total spending	7,205,076	6,697,324	6,286,326

Note: All numbers are in present value terms. Weighted mean values are presented. ACA = Affordable Care Act and SSI = Supplemental Security Income.

Appendix C

Timely Indexing Results

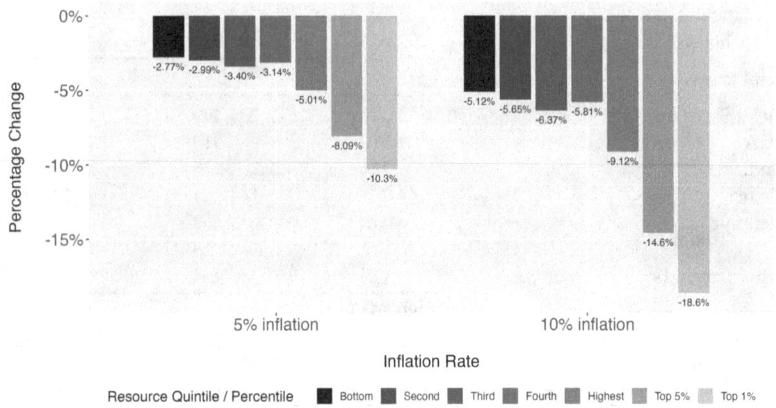

Fig. C1. Average percentage change in remaining lifetime spending with timely adjustment by resource quintile, ages 20–79.

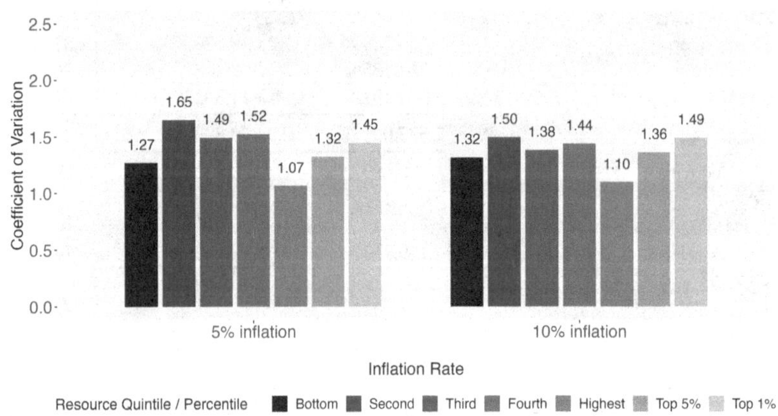

Fig. C2. Coefficients of variation with timely adjustment by resource quintile, ages 20–79.

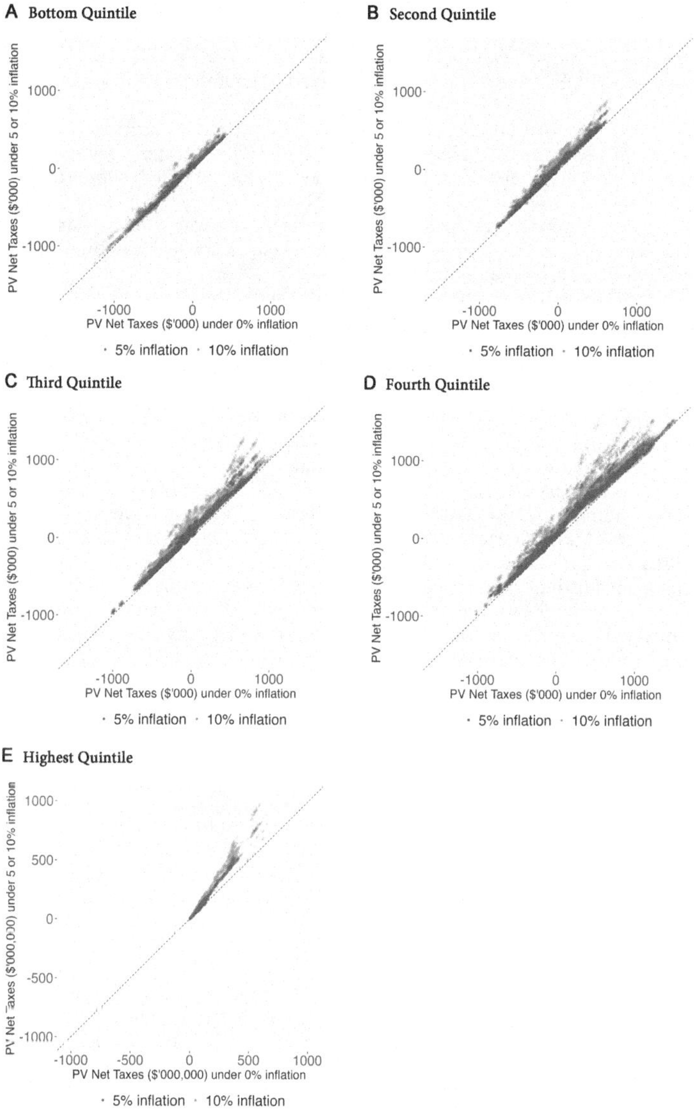

Fig. C3. Net taxes with with timely adjustment by resource quintile, ages 20–79.

Endnotes

Author email address: David Altig (Dave.Altig@atl.frb.org), Alan J. Auerbach (auerbach@econ.berkeley.edu), Erin Eidschun (eidschun@bu.edu), Laurence Kotlikoff (kotlikoff@gmail.com), Victor Vifan Ye (victor@yifanye.com). We thank Adrien Auclert, Deborah Lucas, Valerie Ramey, and other NBER 2024 Macro Annual Conference participants for their valuable comments. We thank the Federal Reserve Bank of Atlanta, Boston University, the Goodman Institute, and Economic Security Planning Inc. for their research support. The authors are solely responsible for the paper's contents. For acknowledgments, sources of research support, and disclosure of the authors' material financial relationships, if any, please see https://www.nber.org/books-and-chapters/nber-macroeconomics-annual-2024-volume-39/inflations-fiscal-impact-american-households.

1. This includes, critically, the assumption that there is no change in the course of government consumption and no change in economic incentives.

2. See Kotlikoff (2002).

3. For a recent analysis of the financial effects of recent inflation in Europe, see Pallotti et al. (2023).

4. Note that we treat losses to government bondholders as financial impacts and hence exclude them from our definition of fiscal effects.

5. Income-related monthly adjustment amount.

6. Home equity captures the present expected value of annual imputed rent on owned homes plus the present expected value of the terminal housing bequest less the current outstanding mortgage. The term *expected* is used for consistency because the present value of inputted rent plus the present value of the household's realized equity bequest are equal, for each survivor path, to the current value of home equity.

7. TFA uses MaxiFi Planner's computation engine. MaxiFi Planner is an economics-based financial planning tool developed by Economic Security Planning Inc., Laurence Kotlikoff's software company.

8. TFA can smooth a household's living standard in accordance with any prespecified age–living standard profile.

9. Housing expenses include mortgage payments, property taxes, insurance, maintenance, condo fees, rent, equity bequests, and holding costs—that is, imputed rent.

10. Detailed TFA documentation is available at https://kotlikoff.net.

11. TFA generates positive life insurance holdings only for years when the insured's death would leave survivors with a lower living standard than were the household head and, if not single, their spouse/partner to live to their maximum ages.

12. TFA is not open source due to its reliance on Economic Security Planning's (ESP's) MaxiFi Planner computation engine. However, the tool is available for use by academics upon request. To date, more than a dozen economists (two foreign) in academe and the Federal Reserve have used TFA for research, including modifying its source code as needed.

13. TFA's Social Security benefit calculations are checked against the agency's benefit calculators when such comparisons are feasible. TFA's federal and state income taxes, FICA taxes, and IRMAA values are determined by strictly following federal tax forms. MaxiFi Planner's thousands of users continually check these calculations. As for non–Social Security benefits, TFA's calculations are cross-checked with independently coded measurements produced by the Federal Reserve Bank of Atlanta in its Cliff career-choice tool.

14. The SCF combines an area-probability sample of households with a "list" sample of generally wealthier households from administrative tax records gleaned from the Internal Revenue Service (IRS). The SCF includes sampling weights to account for oversampling of wealthier households from inclusion of the "list" sample and for differential response rates among wealthier groups. Wealthier households have lower response rates, particularly at the highest levels. See Bricker et al. (2016). The oversampling of wealthy households allows for inference about households in the top 1% of the resource distribution. For the 2004 SCF, Kennickell (2007) shows that 15.8% of sampled households were in the top 1% of the net worth distribution for the United States with 96.4% of these coming from the list sample. Another 38.5% of the 2004 SCF-sampled households were in the

bottom 50% of the net worth distribution with only 5.7% of these households coming from the list sample.

15. Using a multiple imputation algorithm, the Fed includes each household's record in the public-use SCF data set in five so-called replicates to account for estimation of nonreported values (item nonresponse) or for disclosure limitations. We use the first replicate for our analysis. Auerbach et al. (2017, 2023) report no significant differences in results across replicates.

16. Although the nonpublic-use SCF data set includes state identifiers, its household weights are national—that is, not state-specific. This data set is, therefore, of no value for our purposes of appropriately allocating SCF households by state.

17. The fact that we need to inflate wage income and significantly deflate self-employment income to match national aggregates may reflect, in part, a tendency of SCF respondents to report wage earnings as self-employment income.

18. We generate age groups in 10-year intervals. The 10–19 age group is combined with the 20–29 group, and the 90–99 group with the 80–89 group. We bin race/ethnicity groups to white or nonwhite, and education to three bins: high school diploma or less, some college, and college diploma. Income groups are designated using total income quintiles. The number of under-17 children is top-coded at 3.

19. Among 45- to 62-year-old 2019 SCF male respondents, the average age of expected full retirement is 70.3 years old, calculated using sample weights. For females, the weighted self-reported full retirement age is 68.9 years old. In 2018, the Social Security Administration (2019) reported an average retirement benefit claiming the age of 64.8 among men and 64.7 among women.

20. We include 20 hours as retired because many ACS respondents report exactly 20 hours. These respondents are likely earning less than the Social Security earnings test threshold and hence are likely taking Social Security retirement benefits.

21. Summaries of average retirement ages and conditional probabilities of working at ages 65 and 70 for 50-year-old workers in 2020 are provided in tables 3 and 4.

22. We assume that labor's share of proprietorship and partnership income equals the economy's overall labor share.

23. The IRS began indexing federal income tax brackets by the C-CPI-U starting in 2018 with the implementation of the Tax Cuts and Jobs Act (TCJA).

24. The factor is the average difference of geometric means of the C-CPI-U and CPI-U in years of data they have in common. Subtracting this factor in calculating the imputed C-CPI-U maintains the historical difference between the C-CPI-U and the CPI-U; the C-CPI-U moves in a lower trajectory than the CPI-U does.

25. That is, one plus the nominal rate equals one plus the inflation rate times one plus the real rate.

26. The impact of inflation on the taxation of business income lowers median lifetime spending by an additional 0.73% for an increase from 0% to 5% inflation and an additional 1.13% when inflation rises from 0% to 10%.

27. The decline in Social Security benefits, which constitute a nontrivial component of households' spending budget, is especially important.

28. This figure excludes households above the top 95th percentile of in-kind benefits, for ease of viewing.

29. Both of these figures exclude households above the top 75th percentile in respective income taxes, for ease of viewing.

30. Simulating this counterfactual leads to an increase in federal taxes of $100,290.

31. A second component of the capital consumption adjustment relates to the fact that depreciation deductions are accelerated relative to economic depreciation. We ignore this component in our calculations.

32. Note that the inflation component of the noncorporate CCA is available only for nonfarm sole proprietorships and partnerships. To cover all noncorporate firms, we calculate the ratio of the inflation component to the full CCA for noncorporate nonfarm sole proprietorships and partnerships (line 18 divided by line 16) and multiply this by the overall noncorporate CCA (line 13).

33. This is for nonfarm incomes, as the method of calculating the cost of goods sold for farm businesses does not give rise to an IVA.

34. All of the FOF tables we use are in levels, rather than flows.

35. This assumes that the CCA and IVA as a share of equity are the same for S corporations as for the corporate sector as a whole.

36. According to FOF table L.225b, noncorporate business equity equals the sum of these last two items. Following this, we will assume that the financial sector except for brokers and dealers is corporate (C + S).

37. We exclude municipal securities here and in the following calculations because they are wholly tax exempt for federal purposes and substantially tax exempt for state purposes.

38. To the extent that the taxable financial sector as a whole is a net creditor, and assuming similar effects of inflation on income and deductions, this omission may cause us to understate the increase in taxes due to inflation.

39. This adjustment implicitly assumes that US corporations have income solely in the United States and foreign corporations have income solely abroad. In reality, there are cross-holdings that would have offsetting effects on our calculations.

40. For the noncorporate sector, the change is negative, as the increase in interest deductions exceeds in magnitude the increase in the tax base associated with the CCA and IVA.

References

Altig, D., A. J. Auerbach, P. C. Higgins, D. R. Koehler, L. J. Kotlikoff, M. Leiseca, E. Terry, and Y. Ye. 2020. "Did the 2017 Tax Reform Discriminate against Blue State Voters?" *National Tax Journal* 73 (4): 1087–1108.

Altig, D., A. J. Auerbach, L. J. Kotlikoff, E. Ilin, and V. Ye. 2023. "The Marginal Net Taxation of Americans' Labor Supply." Working paper, National Bureau of Economic Research, Cambridge, MA.

Altig, D., L. J. Kotlikoff, and V. Y. Ye. 2022. "How Much Lifetime Social Security Benefits are Americans Leaving on the Table?" Technical report, National Bureau of Economic Research, Cambridge, MA.

Auerbach, A. J. 1981. "Inflation and the Tax Treatment of Firm Behavior." *American Economic Review* 71 (2): 419–23.

Auerbach, A. J., L. J. Kotlikoff, D. Koehler, and M. Yu. 2017. "Is Uncle Sam Inducing the Elderly to Retire?" *Tax Policy and the Economy* 31:1–42.

Auerbach, A. J., L. J. Kotlikoff, and D. R. Koehler. 2023. "U.S. Inequality, Fiscal Progressivity, and Work Disincentives: An Intragenerational Accounting." *Journal of Political Economy* 131 (5): 1249–93.

Bricker, J., A. Henriques, J. Krimmel, and J. Sabelhaus. 2016. "Measuring Income and Wealth at the Top using Administrative and Survey Data." *Brookings Papers on Economic Activity* 2016 (1): 261–331.

Center for a Secure Retirement. 2019. "A Growing Urgency: Retirement Care Realities for Middle-Income Boomers." https://www.centerforasecureretirement.com/posts/retirement-care-realities-for-middle-income-boomers.

Chien, N. 2015. "Estimate of Child Care Eligibility and Receipt for Fiscal Year of 2012." ASPE Issue Brief. Office of the Assistant Secretary for Planning and Evaluation, Washington, DC. https://aspe.hhs.gov/system/files/pdf/153591/ChildEligibility.pdf.

Chien, N. 2019. *Factsheet: Estimates of Child Care Eligibility & Receipt for Fiscal Year 2015*. Washington, DC: US Department of Health and Human Services, Office of the Assistant Secretary for Planning and Evaluation.

Committee on the Long-Run Macroeconomic Effects of the Aging US Population. 2015. *The Growing Gap in Life Expectancy by Income: Implications for Federal Programs and Policy Responses*. Washington, DC: National Academies Press.

Dettling, L., S. Devlin-Foltz, J. Krimmel, S. Pack, and J. Thompson. 2015. "Comparing Micro and Macro Sources for Household Accounts in the United States: Evidence from the Survey of Consumer Finances." FEDS Working Paper no. 2015-086, *SSRN*, https://papers.ssrn.com/sol3/papers.cfm?abstract_id=2669590.

Feldstein, M., J. Green, and E. Sheshinski. 1978. "Inflation and Taxes in a Growing Economy with Debt and Equity Finance." *Journal of Political Economy* 86 (2, part 2): S53–S70.

Feldstein, M., and L. Summers. 1979. "Inflation and the Taxation of Capital Income in the Corporate Sector." *National Tax Journal* 32 (4): 445–70.

Fischer, S., and F. Modigliani. 1978. "Towards an Understanding of the Real Effects and Costs of Inflation." *Review of World Economics* 114 (4): 810–33.

Giannarelli, L. 2019. "What Was the TANF Participation Rate in 2016?" Urban Institute. https://www.urban.org/sites/default/files/publication/100521/what_was_the_tanf_participation_rate_in_2016_0.pdf.

Ilin, E., L. J. Kotlikoff, and M. Pitts. 2022. "Is Our Fiscal System Discouraging Marriage? A New Look at the Marriage Tax." Technical report, National Bureau of Economic Research, Cambridge, MA.

Ilin, Elias, and Ellyn Terry. 2022. "Estimating Occupation and Location Specific Wages over the Life Cycle." *Business and Economic Research* 12 (2): 46–60.

Kelley, W. A., J. H. Hall, A. J. B. Aronsohn, F. W. Hickman, H. Sweeney, and L. Carroll. 1977. "Indexing for Inflation." *Tax Lawyer* 31 (1): 17–35.

Kennickell, A. B. 2007. "Look and Listen, But Don't Stop: Interviewers and Data Quality in the 2007 SCF." Proceedings of the Survey Research Methods Section. American Statistical Association. http://www.asasrms.org/Proceedings/y2007/Files/JSM2007-000648.pdf.

Kotlikoff, L. J. 2002. "Generational Policy." In *Handbook of Public Economics*, ed. Alan J. Auerbach and Martin Feldstein, 4:1873–1932. New York: Elsevier.

Meghir, C., and L. Pistaferri. 2011. "Earnings, Consumption and Life Cycle Choices." In *Handbook of Labor Economics*, ed. Orley Ashenfelter and David Card, 4:773–854. New York: Elsevier.

Moffitt, R. 1983. "An Economic Model of Welfare Stigma." *American Economic Review* 73 (5): 1023–35.

Moffitt, R. A., and P. Gottschalk. 2011. "Trends in the Covariance Structure of Earnings in the US: 1969–1987." *Journal of Economic Inequality* 9:439–59.

Pallotti, F., G. Paz-Pardo, J. Slacalek, O. Tristani, and G. L. Violante. 2023. "Who Bears the Costs of Inflation? Euro Area Households and the 2021–2022 Shock." Working paper, European Central Bank.

Rosenthal, S. M., and Mucciolo, L. 2024. "Who's Left to Tax? Grappling with a Dwindling Shareholder Tax Base." *Tax Notes Federal* 183:91–107.

Social Security Administration. 2019. "Annual Statistical Supplement to the Social Security Bulletin, 2019." https://www.ssa.gov/policy/docs/statcomps/supplement/2019/index.html#:~:text=Download%20entire%20publication.

Comment

Adrien Auclert, Stanford University, CEPR, and NBER, United States of America

What are the costs of inflation? In a classic article, Fischer and Modigliani (1978) observed that "there is no convincing account of the economic costs of inflation that justifies the typical belief—of the economist and the layman—that inflation poses a serious economic problem, relative to unemployment." Their paper presented "a systematic account of the real effects of inflation that [the authors hoped] will contribute to understanding of and continuing research on the costs of inflation." Almost 50 years later, a large body of research has, in fact, formalized and quantified the various costs of inflation that Fischer and Modigliani identified in their seminal paper. This paper by Altig et al. (2025, in this volume) is an important part of this continuing research effort.

The paper focuses on one component of the total cost of inflation, which the authors call its "fiscal impact." The fiscal impact of inflation arises from the fact that the US tax system—like all tax systems I know of—is not robust to the presence of inflation. The best-known example of fiscal impact is the "bracket creep" phenomenon. In the late 1970s and early 1980s, inflation was running over 10% a year, but the US federal income tax brackets were fixed in nominal terms. This pushed many taxpayers into higher tax brackets, meaningfully increasing marginal tax rates (e.g., Saez 2003). Today, partly as a result of this episode, most of the tax system is indexed, with tax brackets revised each year. But indexation is still incomplete—it only occurs once a year—and it is also imperfect: To give an example that has been in the news lately, it does not apply to brackets determining the taxation of Social Security benefits. Official projections from the

NBER Macroeconomics Annual, volume 39, 2025.
 Published by The University of Chicago Press for the National Bureau of Economic Research. https://doi.org/10.1086/735265

Congressional Budget Office (CBO) show that "real bracket creep" amounts to a meaningful source of projected tax revenue, growing to 1.5% of gross domestic product by 2049 (Congressional Budget Office 2019). So fiscal impacts can be large in the aggregate, and it is clearly relevant to study them.

A lesser-known fiscal impact occurs because federal and state income taxes apply to nominal, rather than real, interest paid on assets and liabilities. When inflation is higher, nominal interest rates are higher, in part to compensate investors for higher expected inflation. However, because nominal interest is taxed, the compensation for inflation is taxed as well. This affects asset holders with lots of nominal interest income the most and, on the other hand, benefits liability holders who make large nominal interest payments that they can deduct from their taxes. Because the distribution of assets and liabilities is very unequal, the fiscal impacts are very unequally distributed. This paper reports the distribution of household-level fiscal impacts.

The paper quantifies these household-level fiscal impacts by asking the following question: What fraction of lifetime consumption would each household in the Survey of Consumer Finances be forced to give up if inflation were to increase permanently by π%, holding everything else fixed, and assuming that the only costs of inflation are fiscal costs?

As I have argued, this question is clearly interesting and relevant, and I believe the paper is the first of its kind to provide a comprehensive quantitative answer. This discussion makes two main points: one on scope and one on method.

Regarding scope, there are clearly nonfiscal costs of inflation in addition to fiscal costs. The answer provided by this paper, however comprehensive on the fiscal costs, is therefore only a part of what we ultimately want to know, which is the total cost, at the household level, of increasing inflation. A related point is about general equilibrium. Imperfect indexation of the tax system means that when inflation rises, the household sector loses and the government benefits. The paper is silent on what the government does with these extra resources, but this would clearly matter in a comprehensive assessment. The first part of my discussion will try to provide the relevant context for the magnitudes found in the paper.

Regarding method, the paper does its calculations using proprietary software. This makes it quite difficult to understand where its quantitative answers are coming from. The second part of my discussion will argue that these magnitudes appear reasonable, based on simple back-of-the envelope calculations, and provide an alternative route to the use of proprietary software to do these calculations.

Before diving in, let me also mention that the thought experiment that the paper is after fundamentally relies on the idea that "government institutions are sticky." Just like a simple Calvo model of price stickiness is inconsistent with evidence that the frequency of price change increases with the rate of inflation, a simple model of government institution stickiness is inconsistent with the fact that US tax brackets started getting indexed after the bracket creep of the 1970s. We can still use these models to get a baseline quantitative answer, but it is important to recognize that it will likely be an upper bound as institutions adapt to rising inflation.

I. The Costs of Inflation in Context

Because the Altig et al. paper focuses on a component of the cost of inflation, it is useful to go back to Fischer and Modigliani's taxonomy to understand how it fits in the literature and to provide context for its answers. The headline number from Altig et al. (2025, in this volume) is that a permanent increase in the inflation rate from 0% to 10% reduces median lifetime spending by 6.82%. How does this compare with the other, consumption-equivalent (CE) welfare costs of inflation that the literature has calculated?

I will focus on three other well-known calculations of the costs of inflation that were also laid out in the Fischer and Modigliani (1978) measurement agenda: two from the aggregate costs of inflation and one that focuses on the heterogeneity and has many parallels to those of the Altig et al. (2025, in this volume) paper. Table 1 summarizes the results from my discussion below. We will see that a 6.8% number is quite large, but not unheard of, and that the heterogeneity in welfare effects that they

Table 1
Fischer and Modigliani (1978)'s Costs of Inflation and Their Modern Quantification

Cost	Relevant Literature	CE Welfare Loss from $\pi = 10\%$
Opportunity cost of holding money	Friedman rule—Lucas (2000)	1%
Price dispersion	New Keynesian—Nakamura et al. (2018)	>5% (Calvo), ~0.5% (Menu costs)
Redistribution of nominal wealth	Fisher effect—Doepke and Schneider (2006)	0.8% average (−14%–66% across cohorts)
Nominal government institutions	Fiscal impact—Altig et al. (2025, in this volume)	6.8% average (3%–9% across cohorts)

document is actually comparable to, or a little smaller than, the heterogeneity from the impact of nominal wealth redistribution.

Fischer and Modigliani (1978) proposed to understand the costs of inflation using a series of thought experiments. First, they thought, imagine that we are living in a fully indexed economy: Wage and price contracts are indexed, debt instruments are indexed (except for currency, which pays no nominal interest), tax brackets and other payments fixed by law are indexed, real rather than nominal returns on assets are taxed, there are no nominal interest rate ceilings, and so on. In this economy, they reasoned, there would only be one main effect from an increase in inflation: The opportunity cost of holding currency would increase.[1]

A. *Cost from Higher Nominal Interest Rates*

This effect has since been quantified as the welfare cost of departing from the Friedman rule, for instance, in settings where money enters the utility function or there is a cash-in-advance constraint (see, among many others, Lucas and Stokey 1983, Woodford 1990, and Chari and Kehoe 1999). The basic idea for quantifying the welfare effect goes back to Bailey (1956) and has since been revisited by Lucas (2000). Suppose, as in the Sidrauski (1967) model, that the utility function is $U(c, M/P)$ where c is consumption and M/P is real money balance. Suppose that we are in a steady state where c is constant and M and P grow at the same rate π. Then, across steady states with different inflation rates π, the real interest rate is the constant $r = \rho$, the time discount rate, and the nominal interest rate is $i = \rho + \pi$. The demand for money is determined by the first-order condition $U_m/U_c = i$.

Let $w(i)$ be the percentage increase in steady-state consumption needed to leave a household indifferent between a steady-state interest rate of i and one of 0. Let $m(i)$ be the steady-state money demand to consumption ratio M/Pc when the interest rate is i. Then, by definition, we have

$$U((1 + w(i))c, m(i)c) = U(c, m(0)c),$$

for any i. It follows that, around any steady state where the interest rate is i, we have

$$w'(i) = -\frac{U_m}{U_c} m'(i) \simeq -im'(i) = m \times \left(-\frac{dm/m}{di/i}\right) = m \times \eta,$$

where $\eta \equiv -(dm/m)/(di/i)$ is the interest elasticity of money demand. This equation is helpful because it allows us to relate the welfare effect of inflation to measurable quantities m and η. Since across steady states with different inflation rates π, we always have $i = \rho + \pi$, in particular we have $di = d\pi$. This leads to the famous Bailey (1956)–Lucas (2000) formula for the welfare cost of inflation:

$$dw = w'(i)di = m \times \eta \times d\pi. \tag{1}$$

Equation (1) says that the CE welfare loss from an increase in inflation of $d\pi$% is the product of the money balance-consumption ratio m and the interest elasticity of money demand η times $d\pi$. Using Lucas (2000)'s estimates of $\eta = 0.5$ and $m = 0.2$, this implies a welfare cost of reducing the annual rate of inflation from 10% to 0% at $0.2 \times 0.5 \times 10 = 1\%$ of real consumption. This provides us with a useful benchmark against which to compare the 6.8% average number in the Altig et al. paper. We see that the fiscal impact is substantially larger than the effect of departure from the Friedman rule, at least under conventional estimates of the money demand elasticity.

B. *Cost from Price Dispersion under Nominal Rigidities*

Fischer and Modigliani (1978) next proposed to consider the effects of adding price stickiness to their fully indexed economy, causing "distortions of relative prices [that are fixed] at different times." The New Keynesian literature has since developed a framework that allows us to quantify these effects of price dispersion. Suppose that flow utility is $u(c) - v(n)$, and that we consider the steady state of a standard New Keynesian model where inflation is π and price dispersion is Δ. In this framework, price dispersion acts as a productivity loss, with the production possibility frontier being $c = n/\Delta$. The first-order condition for consumption versus labor is $v'(n)/u'(c) = 1/\Delta$. Moreover, the CE welfare loss from an inflation rate of π is now defined by the equation

$$u\left((1 + w(\pi))\frac{n}{\Delta}\right) - v(n) = u(n) - v(n).$$

These equations lead us to an expression for the welfare loss from inflation in terms of the sensitivity of price dispersion to inflation around a zero-inflation steady state with $w = 0$ and $\Delta = 1$:

$$dw = w'(\pi)d\pi = \Delta'(\pi)d\pi. \tag{2}$$

Hence, price dispersion is also a measure of the CE welfare loss from inflation. Now we can use the expression for price dispersion in the canonical New Keynesian model with constant returns to scale in production to derive:

$$\begin{aligned} w(\pi) &= \Delta(\pi) - 1 \\ &= (1-\theta)^{\frac{-1}{(\epsilon-1)}}\left(1-\theta(1+\pi)^{\epsilon-1}\right)^{\frac{\epsilon}{(\epsilon-1)}}\left(1-\theta(1+\pi)^{\epsilon}\right)^{-1} - 1 \qquad (3) \\ &\simeq \frac{\epsilon}{2}\frac{\theta}{(1-\theta)^2}\pi^2, \end{aligned}$$

where θ is one minus the frequency of price change and ϵ is the elasticity of substitution between goods, and the last equation provides a quadratic approximation around $\pi = 0$.

Nakamura et al. (2018) quantify these kinds of effects using $\theta = 0.899$ (a frequency of price change of 0.101 per month) and an ϵ of 7, which is a typical value for the New Keynesian literature. Then the percentage annual consumption loss from going from 0% to 10% inflation because of price dispersion is $w \simeq 5.5\%$, which is much larger than the quadratic approximation of $7/2 \times 88 \times (0.1/12)^2 = 2\%$ because the model becomes highly nonlinear as inflation rises. Here we actually see that the welfare cost of inflation under a Calvo model is quite comparable to Altig et al.'s (2025, in this volume) estimate of the average fiscal impact.

However, this is probably an overstatement of the true cost of price dispersion. The baseline effect from the Calvo model is generally thought to be implausibly large. As Nakamura et al. (2018) argue, it is also dramatically mitigated when price setting occurs under menu costs rather than under a Calvo model. In their calibration, the welfare loss from price dispersion under menu costs stays bounded at around 0.5% without being much affected by the aggregate inflation rate (see their fig. 2).

C. *Cost from Nominal Redistribution*

Fischer and Modigliani (1978) then proposed to add in the effects of unanticipated inflation through existing assets and liabilities fixed in nominal terms, which, they pointed out, generate "redistribution from the private to the public sector and between private debtors and creditors." An important paper by Doepke and Schneider (2006) proposed a systematic quantification of these "Fisher" effects (a reference to Irving Fisher's debt-deflation theory of recessions—Fisher (1933)—not to be confused with Stanley Fischer!), using micro data on household nominal asset and liability holdings. They found these effects to be very large.

Quantifying these effects is somewhat less straightforward than the two I just discussed. In part, this is because they are conceptually different because they are transitional effects: They arise on the impact of a transition from one steady-state inflation rate to another, as a result of the redenomination of the value of assets and liabilities. To first order, the formula for the real present value effect of a permanent increase in inflation by $d\pi$ for a household h with a net nominal position NNP_h is

$$dPV_h = -NNP_h \cdot \text{Duration}_h \cdot d\pi,$$

where Duration_h is the duration of the net nominal position (see Doepke and Schneider 2006; Auclert 2019). A household with a positive net nominal position—say, holding long-term nominal government bonds—stands to lose from higher inflation in proportion of the product of his nominal position and its duration: Not only does a higher price level today erode the nominal value of these bonds today but the anticipation of higher inflation in the future raises nominal interest rates and therefore results in a capital loss that is larger when the duration is larger. On the flip side, a household with a negative net nominal position—say, holding a fixed rate nominal mortgage—stands to gain from higher inflation.

To convert a present value effect into a steady-state CE welfare effect dw_h, we need to divide dPV_h by the present value of consumption of household h, that is, lifetime spending $PV(c_h)$. So we have that the CE welfare loss from inflation for household h is

$$dw_h = \frac{NNP_h \cdot \text{Duration}_h}{PV(c_h)} d\pi. \tag{4}$$

Doepke and Schneider (2006)'s table 2 gives the headline result, reporting $NNP \cdot \text{Duration}/y\ d\pi = 7.3\%$ for the household sector as a whole when $d\pi = 5\%$ (this is what they call the "full surprise" scenario). We have to double this number to get the effect for increasing inflation by 10% and then divide by the annuitization factor $PV(c)/y$ to obtain an expression for the average CE welfare loss in (4). In the simplest possible life-cycle model, the lifetime spending/income ratio is given by $PV(c_h)/y_h = (1+r)/r(1-(1/(1+r))^{T_h})$ where r is the real interest rate and T_h is the number of years of life remaining; assuming an average of 40 years remaining, this gives us an annuitization factor of 18. Hence, the average welfare loss from inflation for the household sector as a whole from the Fisher effect is $7.3 \times 2/18 = 0.8\%$. This seems substantially smaller than the average fiscal effect.

However, the very striking finding from Doepke and Schneider (2006) was not the average effect but the heterogeneity. Their table 5 reports the amount of wealth redistribution for each group relative to income y_h, that is, $NNP_h \cdot \text{Duration}_h / y_h \, d\pi$ for $d\pi = 5\%$. Converting these numbers for each cohort, assuming an average lifetime of 85 years, provides us with a cohort-level estimate of the welfare loss or gain from inflation, presented in table 2.

The table shows that the heterogeneity in effects is substantial. Some, especially older agents, hold a very substantial amount of nominal wealth, causing 75-year-olds to potentially lose 65% in CE welfare from a 10% increase in inflation. On the other side some, especially younger, agents have very substantial nominal liabilities, causing 35-year-olds to potentially gain 14% in CE welfare from that same 10% increase in inflation. The heterogeneity in the fiscal cost reported by Altig et al. (2025, in this volume) is of the same order of magnitude, and across cohorts it is actually less. In both cases, this is because there is substantial heterogeneity in wealth across the population, and these effects tend to affect households in proportion to their wealth.

There is an important conceptual difference between this calculation and those from the earlier two. Whereas the welfare cost of departing from the Friedman rule and that of price dispersion are fundamentally general equilibrium calculations, those from Doepke and Schneider (2006) are a fundamentally partial equilibrium exercise. This is clear from the fact that net nominal positions always net out to zero in the economy as a whole: Any nominal debtor has a nominal creditor in some part of the economy and vice versa; there is no net supply of nominal assets. This is clear from Doepke and Schneider (2006)'s table 2: their 7.3% loss for the household sector, combined with a 5.2% loss from the rest of the world, which also holds nominal assets in the aggregate, is

Table 2
Doepke and Schneider (2006)'s Costs of Inflation in Consumption Equivalent Units

Age Cohort	Lifetime Spending/ Income	Losers (% of Cohort)	Mean CE Loss (%)	Mean CE Gain (%)
≤35	19.5	25	−2.1	13.8
36–45	18.7	29	−4.9	9.7
46–55	17.2	40	−6.1	4.9
56–65	14.8	58	−11.7	2.4
66–75	10.9	73	−18.2	2.1
>75	4.55	84	−65.6	3.1

counterbalanced by a 13% gain for the government. But in general equilibrium, a gain from government must accrue back to the household sector somehow. Hence, the costs are probably overestimated, but the exact way in which to rebate gains and losses will matter for the final calculation.[2]

D. *Fiscal Impact*

Finally, Fischer and Modigliani (1978) suggested adding the "effects of nominal government institutions: imperfect indexation of tax brackets, taxation of nominal interest income and capital gains, and so on." This is what Altig et al. (2025, in this volume) call the fiscal impact, and they quantify this piece under current tax law, using individual household data and a model of the household response to changes in their environment. In many ways, their paper is therefore parallel to the Doepke and Schneider (2006) paper but focusing on the fiscal impact rather than the Fisher effect. Just like Doepke and Schneider (2006), they find large and heterogeneous effects, which are unexpected and will likely shift priors. I report the headline number of 6.8% loss, together with the minimum and the maximum across cohorts from their figure 7b in my table 1, to complete the comparison to the literature.

Just like Doepke and Schneider (2006), the calculation done in Altig et al. (2025, in this volume) is a partial equilibrium one in nature. The losses to the household sector are gains to government, which by the logic of the intertemporal budget constraint will eventually rebate those gains back to household and mitigate the losses. Here again, the exact nature and timing of rebates would matter for the final calculation, which is why it is outside of the scope of this paper to do so. However, it is important to bear this in mind when thinking about the overall magnitude.

E. *Combining the Effects*

Obviously, in the real world, the effects that Fischer and Modigliani (1978) discussed are all present to some extent. I have provided context for each effect in isolation, but it is noteworthy that the formulas presented in (1), (2), and (4)—as well as formula (7), which I will derive for the fiscal impact in the next section—are all linear. Therefore, a reasonable estimate of the total costs, including at the household level, is just to add them all up. Obviously, each particular model is nonlinear (as we saw with Δ in the Calvo model), and Altig et al. (2025, in this volume) themselves find some evidence of nonlinearity: Their estimates from 10% inflation are a little less than double the effects at 5% inflation, that is, they find some modest concavity in size (although the Calvo model is highly convex in size.) To truly assess the magnitude of these nonlinearities as well as the potential interactions between the different effects of inflation, one would need a model in which all the effects are present at once. This would be an interesting avenue for future research.

II. The Fiscal Effects of Inflation: A Simple Calculation

Having provided context for the magnitudes found by Altig et al. (2025, in this volume), I now would like to move on to the core of their calculation of the fiscal impact. The paper does an impressive amount of work, but it is difficult to follow the details of the calculation, because the quantitative answers are all obtained from a proprietary software (MaxiFi) that is fed information from the Survey of Consumer Finances. Moreover, there are scant details about how the algorithm itself actually works, though we may be comforted by the fact that "the program runs in finite time." Obviously, this is not ideal for transparency.

In this section, I will proceed along similar lines as for the other three effects I discussed, by deriving a formula for the CE welfare costs from first principles and then seeing whether the magnitudes obtained by the authors seem reasonable in that light. I will find that they do. Hopefully, this also provides a useful set of intuitions for what may be going on inside the MaxiFi software.

Just as in Altig et al. (2025, in this volume)'s calculation, my objective is to provide a partial equilibrium estimate of the CE welfare gain or loss from the fiscal impact.

The model I will solve is a simplified model of that used in Auclert et al. (2021), augmented with a nominal tax system that is imperfectly indexed to inflation. Households in the model solve the following maximization problem:

$$\max \sum_{j=0}^{T} \beta^j \Phi_j u(c_{jt}), \tag{5}$$

where j represents age, β is the discount factor, u is instantaneous utility, and Φ_j is the probability of surviving until age j.

Income taxation is progressive; for simplicity I assume a two-bracket system with B_t giving the threshold at which the marginal tax rate jumps from τ_1 to $\tau_2 > \tau_1$. Hence, the retention function from pretax income $W_t y_j$ (the product of current wage per efficiency unit of W_t and age-specific efficient labor supply e_j) is

$$\mathcal{R}_t(W_t y_j) = \begin{cases} (1-\tau_1)W_t y_j & W_t y_t \leq B_t \\ (1-\tau_1)B_t + (1-\tau_2)(W_t y_j - B_t) & W_t y_t \geq B_t \end{cases}.$$

Agents invest in nominal assets. The nominal budget constraint reads

$$P_t c_{jt} + \phi_j A_{jt} = (1 + i_t(1-\tau_a))A_{j-1,t-1} + \mathcal{R}_t(W_t e_j) + T_t,$$

where τ_a is the tax rate on asset income, and T_t represents government-provided benefits, which we assume to be lump sum.

There are two "sticky government institution" frictions. First, the adjustment of tax brackets and benefits is lagged by one period, so we have that $B_t = bP_{t-1}$ and $T_t = tP_{t-1}$ for some constant b and t. And second, it is nominal, rather than real, interest that is taxed. To see how much these matter for real income at different levels of inflation π, we rewrite these constraints in real terms. Using $a_j \equiv A_{jt}/P_t$, and focusing on someone who makes more than B_t for simplicity, the real budget constraint is

$$c_j + a_j = +(1-\tau_2)we_j + \frac{(\tau_2 - \tau_1)b + t}{1+\pi},$$

where the term in $\tau_2 - \tau_1$ on the right disappears if income falls inside the first bracket. Now, enforcing the Fisher equation $(1+i)/(1+\pi) = 1 + r$, we have the following budget constraint:

$$c_j + a_j = (1 + r(1-\tau_a))a_{j-1} + (1-\tau_2)we_j \underbrace{- \tau_a \frac{\pi}{1+\pi} a_{j-1}}_{\text{taxation of nominal interest}} + \underbrace{\frac{(\tau_2 - \tau_1)b + t}{1+\pi}}_{\text{imperfect indexation of benefits}}. \quad (6)$$

Equation (6) shows clearly the two fiscal effects from higher inflation in this model. First, because of imperfect indexation, inflation erodes the real value of tax brackets and transfers, and affects households with higher transfers and those in higher tax brackets the most. And second, because of taxation of nominal interest, inflation creates a real income loss for households with asset holdings, which is larger the more asset holdings one has and is negative if one has liabilities whose interest payments are tax deductible.

A household optimizes (5) subject to (6), and this is in essence what the MaxiFi planner does, though it has the particularity of assuming an elasticity of intertemporal substitution in consumption of 0. Altig et al. (2025, in this volume) proceed by simulating trajectories for each household under different assumptions about π and reporting the effect on the present value of consumption. Here, I follow a simpler route: I note that, taking the present value on both sides of (6), we have

$$PV(c_j) = (1 - \tau_2)PV(we_j) - \tau_a \frac{\pi}{1+\pi} PV(a_{j-1}) + \frac{(\tau_2 - \tau_1)PV(b) + PV(t)}{1+\pi}.$$

Now, the first-order effect on $PV(c_j)$ from increasing π starting from $\pi = 0$, which is the CE welfare effect, is

$$dw_j = \frac{dPV(c_j)}{PV(c_j)} = -\left(\tau_a \frac{PV(a_j)}{PV(c_j)} + (\tau_2 - \tau_1)\frac{PV(b_j)}{PV(c_j)} + \frac{PV(t_j)}{PV(c_j)}\right) d\pi, \quad (7)$$

where again, the second term only applies to households who have a marginal tax rate of τ_2.

Equation (7) is useful because it gives another linear expression for the CE welfare costs of inflation—this time for the fiscal impact. It also shows the determinants of both the overall level as well as the heterogeneity: we need to know the terms $(PV(a_j))/(PV(c_j))$, $(PV(b_j))/(PV(c_j))$ (for all the brackets below the applicable marginal tax rate), and $(PV(t_j))/(PV(c_j))$. The first will be larger for middle-aged households who have high assets relative to remaining consumption, the second for high marginal tax rate households, and the third for households with large benefits.

To quantify, a simulation of a simple version of the Auclert et al. (2021) model shows that $PV(a_j)/PV(c_j)$ starts around 5 at age 20, peaks around 8 at age 50 and then slowly declines toward 0, averaging around 4. Moreover, we have that $PV(b_j)/PV(c_j)$ is likely around 0.5 for rich households and 0 for poor households, and $PV(t_j)/PV(c_j)$ is likely around 0.5 for poor households and 0 for rich households. Putting this together with $\tau_a = 20\%$ and $\tau_2 - \tau_1 = 20\%$, we find that an average household has a CE welfare loss from $d\pi = 10\%$ of $0.2 \times 4 + 0.2 \times 0.25 + 0.25 = 0.8 \times 10\% = 8\%$, which is quite close to the headline number. Moreover, the number rises to $0.2 \times 8 + 0.2 \times 0.25 + 0.25 = 1.6 \times 10\% = 16\%$ for 50-year-olds, in line with their higher $PV(a_j)/PV(c_j)$, and is smaller for younger and older households, consistent with figure 7 in the paper.

The general patterns of heterogeneity by income are also broadly consistent with this back-of-the envelope calculation.

III. Conclusion

Just as Doepke and Schneider (2006) shifted my priors on the empirical magnitude of the Fisher effect of inflation, this paper by Altig et al. (2025, in this volume) shifts my prior on the likely magnitude of the fiscal impact of inflation. In both papers, the large CE welfare losses from some segments of the population are to be taken with a grain of salt given the pure partial equilibrium nature of the exercise; however, the heterogeneity is large and fascinating and would likely survive a general equilibrium calculation. Moreover, the calculations are subject to the caveat that government institutions are likely not to be that sticky in practice, as evidenced by the indexing of tax brackets that followed the bracket creep episode of the 1970s. Nevertheless, these costs are likely substantial and heterogeneous in practice, and I hope that the paper reignites interest in this relatively unexplored intersection of macroeconomics and public finance.

Endnotes

Author email address: Adrien Auclert (aauclert@stanford.edu). I thank the authors for helpful discussions and Gianluca Violante for suggesting the term "sticky government institutions." For acknowledgments, sources of research support, and disclosure of the author's material financial relationships, if any, please see https://www.nber.org/books-and-chapters/nber-macroeconomics-annual-2024-volume-39/comment-inflations-impact-american-households-auclert.

1. They also discuss the fact that firms would incur larger menu costs from changing their prices more frequently. I will treat this effect in a moment as one that comes from price stickiness.

2. I explore this issue in some more detail in Auclert (2019), Section IID.

References

Altig, David, Alan J. Auerbach, Erin Eidschun, Laurence Kotlikoff, and Victor Yifan Ye. 2025. "Inflation's Fiscal Impact on American Households." *NBER Macroeconomics Annual* 39:159–207.

Auclert, Adrien. 2019. "Monetary Policy and the Redistribution Channel." *American Economic Review* 109 (6): 2333–67.

———, Hannes Malmberg, Frederic Martenet, and Matthew Rognlie. 2021. "Demographics, Wealth, and Global Imbalances in the Twenty-First Century." NBER Working Paper 29161, National Bureau of Economic Research, Cambridge, MA.

Bailey, Martin J. 1956. "The Welfare Cost of Inflationary Finance." *Journal of Political Economy* 64 (2): 93–110.

Chari, V. V., and Patrick J. Kehoe. 1999. "Chapter 26: Optimal Fiscal and Monetary Policy." In *Handbook of Macroeconomics*, ed. John B. Taylor and Michael Woodford, 1: 1671–745. Amsterdam: Elsevier.
Congressional Budget Office. 2019. "How Income Growth Affects Tax Revenues in CBO's Long-Term Budget Projections." https://www.cbo.gov/publication/55368.
Doepke, Matthias, and Martin Schneider. 2006. "Inflation and the Redistribution of Nominal Wealth." *Journal of Political Economy* 114 (6): 1069–97.
Fischer, Stanley, and Franco Modigliani. 1978. "Towards an Understanding of the Real Effects and Costs of Inflation." *Review of World Economics* 114 (4): 810–33.
Fisher, Irving. 1933. "The Debt-Deflation Theory of Great Depressions." *Econometrica* 1 (4): 337–57.
Lucas, Robert E. 2000. "Inflation and Welfare." *Econometrica* 68 (2): 247–74.
———, and Nancy L. Stokey. 1983. "Optimal Fiscal and Monetary Policy in an Economy without Capital." *Journal of Monetary Economics* 12 (1): 55–93.
Nakamura, Emi, Jón Steinsson, Patrick Sun, and Daniel Villar. 2018. "The Elusive Costs of Inflation: Price Dispersion during the U.S. Great Inflation." *Quarterly Journal of Economics* 133 (4): 1933–80.
Saez, Emmanuel. 2003. "The Effect of Marginal Tax Rates on Income: A Panel Study of 'Bracket Creep.'" *Journal of Public Economics* 87 (5): 1231–58.
Sidrauski, Miguel. 1967. "Rational Choice and Patterns of Growth in a Monetary Economy." *American Economic Review Papers and Proceedings* 57 (2): 534–44.
Woodford, Michael. 1990. "Chapter 20: The Optimum Quantity of Money." In *Handbook of Monetary Economics*, ed. Benjamin M. Friedman and Frank Hahn, 2: 1067–152. Amsterdam: Elsevier.

Comment

Deborah Lucas, *Massachusetts Institute of Technology and NBER,* United States of America

A surge of high and now lingering postpandemic inflation has rekindled concerns about its costs and distributional impacts. In this timely and ambitious analysis, Altig et al. explore imperfectly indexed fiscal policy as a potentially important channel for inflation to have real effects. Although economists have long recognized the potential for distortions to arise from the interaction of inflation with fiscal rules, this analysis represents a significant advance over past studies along several dimensions: (1) The analysis incorporates most major tax and benefit policies at both the federal and state levels; (2) costs are measured in terms of the percentage consumption change over a household's remaining lifetime rather than at a point in time; and (3) the results are broken out by age and wealth quintile, illuminating distributional effects.

The main hypothetical that the authors examine is, What would happen to discretionary expenditures if inflation were to permanently rise to 10% annually, all else equal? That is, what happens if the paths of real wages, real asset returns, current law policy, and so forth are held constant. The answer is that on average, taxes net of benefits would rise, leaving households in aggregate with lower lifetime consumption expenditures. Notably, the effects are heterogeneous across wealth and age groups, with a few big winners as well as some big losers. The effects are progressive, with the biggest losses borne by very wealthy households and with significant gains for some poorer households. An important takeaway is that the current fiscal system is far from inflation-neutral

NBER Macroeconomics Annual, volume 39, 2025.
 https://doi .org/10.1086/735266

and that modifying policies to make it more neutral could avoid unintended consequences arising from future inflationary episodes.

In the discussion that follows, I briefly recap the modeling approach to highlight some of its unconventional features that may cause the magnitude of estimated expenditure reductions to be larger than what would be predicted by a more standard optimizing model. I then focus on the question whether the finding of progressivity is robust, and I suggest several factors that could reverse or significantly weaken that conclusion. Turning to aggregate and policy implications, I consider whether average lifetime spending would still be predicted to fall if an explicit government budget constraint had been incorporated. I conclude with a short discussion of why limited indexation of taxes, although redistributive, might be a second-best policy.

I. Modeling Approach

The major advance of this analysis over previous efforts to quantify the effects of inflation via fiscal channels was made possible by use of the Fiscal Analyzer (TFA), an existing tool for retirement planning that several of the authors developed and commercialized and that has been used in previous academic papers. Most critically for this analysis, the model's code incorporates the rules determining taxes and benefits for hundreds of tax and benefit programs, which in turn affect each individual households' path of earnings and asset holdings over its lifetime. The TFA is a partial equilibrium model that assumes households will smooth deterministic expenditure paths over their remaining lifetime to the maximum extent possible, subject to borrowing and wealth constraints and using actuarially fair life insurance to stabilize the consumption paths of surviving spouses. Any bequests are accidental. The cross-section of households represented and imputations about their characteristics and program participation are based on demographic and economic data from the 2019 Survey of Consumer Finances and other government data sources.

The authors emphasize several mechanisms that are important for the results. The interactions of inflation and fiscal policies that drive changes in real household expenditures are primarily due to lags in, or the absence of, indexation related to the computation of taxes and benefits and from the incomplete indexing of thresholds and ceilings that alter benefit program eligibility. The lower-wealth households that benefit from higher inflation do so primarily because of expanded eligibility for valuable Medicare and other social insurance benefits. The wealthier households that bear the largest costs are hit with much higher effective tax rates on nominal interest receipts and capital gains.

Although the qualitative effects of these driving mechanisms seem intuitively robust, the predicted magnitudes are likely to be quite sensitive to specific modeling choices. The framework used in this paper differs fundamentally from those of standard life-cycle models. The pattern of expenditures and asset allocations are not the solution to a constrained intertemporal optimization problem. There is no choice about when to retire, how many hours to work, or the size of bequests. There is no possibility for firms to change the structure of their liabilities to avoid the additional taxation of nominal interest or capital gains (e.g., by replacing bonds with dividend-paying stocks). Household portfolio allocations do not respond to rebalancing incentives—for instance, taking more care to hold bonds only in tax-protected retirement accounts.

Although the simplifying assumptions in the TFA may be necessary to accommodate the complexity introduced by incorporating realistic fiscal rules, those assumptions tend to all go in the direction of precluding likely behavioral changes that would mitigate reductions in expenditures. For example, people might reduce intentional bequests, work more hours or retire later, or rebalance their portfolios toward assets that are less heavily taxed. This suggests that the reported magnitudes of expenditure reductions, both for different groups of households and in aggregate, are upper bounds rather than expected values. For the households that potentially benefit from inflation's interaction with fiscal policies, behavioral changes would tend to increase those benefits.

It also remains an open question whether the behavior implied by the TFA model, which was designed to be prescriptive rather than descriptive, is realistic overall and for different wealth and age cohorts. It would be useful to compare the implied expenditure paths in the model with observed patterns for different groups to verify that the assumed behavior is plausible. More ambitious but also very worthwhile, the fiscal apparatus could be incorporated into a more traditional optimizing model and the results compared.

The focus on inflation permanently moving to a rate of 10% (or 5%) demonstrates that large distortions via fiscal effects are theoretically possible. However, because those scenarios seem unlikely to occur, it would be interesting to also consider the effects of a permanent 3% inflation rate. Extrapolating from the reported results for 5% inflation, I would expect those effects to be quite small. Nevertheless, that exercise would be interesting because it is germane to the current conversation about the pros and cons of moving to a 3% inflation target.

II. Are the Findings of Progressivity Robust?

The authors provocatively claim that inflation is a highly progressive form of net taxation, albeit only in the context of its interactions with the fiscal system. For instance, they note that the 15% median lifetime spending loss for the top 1% is roughly twice that for the bottom quintile (in the 10% inflation scenario). I argue here that there are important omitted considerations that, if taken into account, would weaken or even reverse the conclusion that the effects of inflation via the fiscal system are progressive.

An important omission from the model is the insurance value of benefit programs, particularly for low-income households. Such programs provide valuable protection against catastrophically low consumption realizations. In interpreting their findings, the authors implicitly take average expenditure changes as an adequate proxy for welfare changes. However, for programs with an important insurance component, using average expenditures as a measure of welfare effects can be misleading.

A simple model illustrates the potential magnitude of the omitted costs associated with reductions in social insurance protection caused by higher inflation—for instance, because higher nominal income causes a household to lose program eligibility. Consider a low-income household that earns relatively low wages most of the time. Unemployment or health shocks cause it to periodically qualify for government benefit programs. Consumption is hand to mouth. Period utility exhibits constant relative risk aversion with curvature parameter γ:

$$U(c) = \frac{c^{(1-\gamma)}}{(1-\gamma)}.$$

Income when employed is $35,000 annually, the top of the bottom quartile of income. Own income when unemployed is $5,000. Government benefits when unemployed are $10,000. Hence, total income when unemployed is $15,000 annually.

Expected utility in any period, either (1) with social insurance or (2) without social insurance is given by

$$p\,U(35{,}000) + (1-p)U(15{,}000) \tag{1}$$

$$p\,U(35{,}000) + (1-p)U(5{,}000). \tag{2}$$

It is straightforward to calculate how much income the household would willingly give up whenever it is in an employed state for benefit program eligibility when unemployed. The willingness to pay, X, solves

$$p\,U(35{,}000 - X) + (1 - p)U(15{,}000) = p\,U(35{,}000) + (1 - p)U(5{,}000). \quad (3)$$

Table 1 shows the willingness to pay for a range of assumptions about risk aversion and the probability of unemployment, and it compares the expected premium payment based on willingness to pay with the actuarially fair premium for the social insurance. Willingness to pay far exceeds actuarial cost even with moderate risk aversion. For example, for risk aversion of 1.5 and a 10% chance of being unemployed, the actuarially fair value of the premium is 0.1 × \$10,000 = \$1,000. The willingness to pay is found to be \$7,300. It is only paid in the employed state, making its expected value 0.9 × \$7,300 = \$6,576. The value of the insurance to the household therefore is more than 6.5 times its actuarially fair value. That large multiple underscores that the value of social insurance, particularly for low-wealth recipients facing the risk of very low income, can be many times greater than the expected value of benefits received.

As the above example illustrates, the economic value of government insurance benefits is likely to greatly exceed the expected payments received for low-income households exposed to catastrophic income risk. The economic value of government insurance programs for young and middle-income households of working age is also likely to exceed the value of expected payouts, even though take-up is rarer than for poor households. By contrast, benefit programs aimed at older households generally have less of an insurance element, and estimates of value based on average benefit receipts is more appropriate. For example, Social Security payments and Medicare health insurance subsidies provide a level stream of resources rather than episodic cash infusions. For wealthier households, consumption floors provided by government programs are too low and too unlikely to bind to provide significant insurance value.

Insurance benefits are hard to directly quantify using the TFA. The model abstracts from the cost of risk, and the assumption of maximal expenditure smoothing would be likely to cause the estimated benefit of government insurance to be lower than if the limited smoothing by many low-income households were taken into account. A partial remedy could be via discount rate adjustments. Specifically, value flows could be discounted at exogenously determined discount rates that are risk adjusted. Notably, risk adjustment could imply negative discount rates for benefits from programs with high insurance value. The authors

Table 1
Social Insurance: Willingness to Pay Versus Actuarial Value

90% chance employed; $\gamma = 0, .5,$ or 1.5					
Probability employed	.9	Probability employed	.9	Probability employed	.9
Employed income	35,000	Employed income	35,000	Employed income	35,000
Unemployed income	5,000	Unemployed income	5,000	Unemployed income	5,000
Unemployed income + benefits	15,000	Unemployed income + benefits	15,000	Unemployed income + benefits	15,000
CRRA[a]	0	CRRA	.5	CRRA	1.5
Expected benefit	1,000	Expected benefit	1,000	Expected benefit	1,000
Voluntary employed premium	1,111	Voluntary employed premium	2,119	Voluntary employed premium	7,306
Voluntary expected premium	1,000	Voluntary expected premium	1,907	Voluntary expected premium	6,576
50% chance employed; $\gamma = 0, .5$ or 1.5					
Probability employed	.5	Probability employed	.5	Probability employed	.5
Employed income	35,000	Employed income	35,000	Employed income	35,000
Unemployed income	5,000	Unemployed income	5,000	Unemployed income	5,000
Unemployed income + benefits	15,000	Unemployed income + benefits	15,000	Unemployed income + benefits	15,000
CRRA	0	CRRA	.5	CRRA	1.5
Expected benefit	5,000	Expected benefit	5,000	Expected benefit	5,000
Voluntary employed premium	10,000	Voluntary employed premium	16,689	Voluntary employed premium	27,200
Voluntary expected premium	5,000	Voluntary expected premium	8,344	Voluntary expected premium	13,600

[a]Constant relative risk aversion.

currently discount all value streams at a single rate based on average real investment returns in the US economy. A move to risk-adjusted discounting would also be helpful for more accurately capturing the costs of tax distortions on different categories of investment income.

Another source of omitted regressivity is that the asset limits in many anti-poverty programs are not indexed for inflation. In fact, eligibility for low-income benefits is subject to severe asset limits for programs like Supplementary Security Income (SSI) (elderly and disabled poor), Medicaid (low-income health), Temporary Assistance for Needy Families (welfare), and Supplemental Nutrition Assistance Program (SNAP) (food stamps). Typical limits are only $2,000 to $3,000 for individuals. Limits vary by state and can be complicated.[1] For example, in North Dakota, a one-person household receives $3,000, two people receive $6,000, and another $25 is allowed for each additional person thereafter. Unlike the 1- or 2-year inflation adjustment lags in most major programs, the asset limit for SSI was last raised in 1989. The price level has increased by factor of 2.5 since that time. What counts as an asset varies by state, but often cash, bank accounts, cars, and retirement accounts are included. The affected population is large. In 2021, there were 41 million SNAP participants, and in 2022, there were 7.6 million SSI participants, including a million children with disabilities. Many economists have emphasized the high economic costs of the limits, which tend to lock people into poverty. For example, without assets, workers cannot afford to spend time searching for better jobs. The effect is to reduce lifetime expenditures and welfare, although it is uncertain by how much.

Turning to the upper end of the income distribution, an omitted effect that makes higher inflation less progressive because it favors the wealthy is the lag in updates to the property values that feed into property tax assessments. Property taxes represent a significant share of total tax revenues, and they are the largest source of state and local revenues. Property taxes collected in 2023 totaled $778 billion. By comparison, total state income tax revenues were $546 billion, and total federal tax revenues were $4,439 billion in the same year. Property value typically is reassessed every 1–5 years. A back-of-the-envelope calculation shows that with a 3-year lag in valuation updates, and an increase from 0% to 10% inflation, the present value of property taxes over 20 years is 8.3% lower at the 10% inflation rate.

Another effect that is likely to mute the expenditure reductions of wealthier households relative to the predictions of the model is reductions in planned bequests. Recall that the model assumes all bequests are involuntary, but the data suggest otherwise. Presumably, part of the response to higher tax bills would be to cut back on the size of planned inheritances.

A. *Aggregate and Policy Implications*

The aggregate result that the authors emphasize is that a permanent shift in the rate of inflation from 0% to 10% reduces median lifetime spending by 6.09%. That finding seemed at odds with my intuition that in this type of "all else equal" experiment with no changes in real output or real investment returns, the average effect on expenditures should be close to 0. A natural question, then, is, Why does the model predict a drop in average or median expenditures?

I think the explanation lies in what the government is implicitly assumed to do outside of the tax and benefit programs explicitly modeled. Inside the model, aggregate tax collections increase relative to aggregate benefit expenditures, leaving people with less money to spend. If other government revenues and expenditures are also held constant, and if there are no changes to the real economy, then the government will run larger surpluses than it did prior to the inflation increase. If the larger surpluses are saved rather than spent, then government debt will decrease over time. In a Ricardian world, households would expect cuts to future tax rates or some other form of rebate, and expenditures would be higher than predicted in anticipation of lower future taxes. Therefore, if the analysis were to take into account the government's budget constraint and if the usual transversality condition were imposed, as a first approximation, no change in aggregate expenditures would be predicted. Presumably, the predictions about the cross-sectional distribution of expenditure effects would be similar to those reported but with a higher mean and median.

Although the authors do not make policy recommendations, some might cite their findings to argue for fully indexing the fiscal system to inflation, thereby avoiding unintentional taxes and transfers. There is a strong case for avoiding unnecessary distortions. However, it may be that in a second-best world, full indexation would not be optimal. Budget analysts have long warned of ballooning debt and deficits and the need for some combination of increased taxes and reduced benefits to move to a sustainable path. However, such policy changes are politically unpopular, particularly for entitlement programs like Social Security and

Medicare, which enjoy broad public support. The "failure" to index adjusted gross income thresholds for Social Security or to index Medicare's Part B top premium may be one of few politically feasible channels to limiting spending growth and increasing revenues. Congress can then reverse unwanted distortionary effects with much less resistance by lowering taxes and increasing benefits. It is notable that full indexing in the private sector is also unusual, and a better understanding of why that is so would help inform the question of optimal indexation in the public sector.

Endnotes

Author email address: Lucas (dlucas@mit.edu). For acknowledgments, sources of research support, and disclosure of the author's material financial relationships, if any, please see https://www.nber.org/books-and-chapters/nber-macroeconomics-annual-2024-volume-39/comment-inflations-impact-american-households-2-lucas.

1. Thanks are due to Monroe Gamble, who provided me with data on program rules.

Discussion

Jonathan Parker opened the discussion by raising concerns about the nature of the paper's counterfactuals. He noted that inflation is zero sum; thus, from an accounting perspective, the government must still find a way to raise the money it would have raised anyway. As such, he suggested that the counterfactual costs for households should be measured relative to some other realistic way that the government could raise the same amount of revenue. He proposed that this might be conducted using the progressivity of the current tax system (i.e., if everyone's taxes were just increased by whatever percent necessary to raise the same revenue). This counterfactual, he explained, might lead to the conclusion that inflation is regressive—a very different message from that of the paper.

Laurence J. Kotlikoff thanked Parker for the comment and agreed with the importance of accounting for countervailing fiscal policy in the counterfactual. However, he stated there is no way to know how these adjustments would be made. He added that whereas the current counterfactual—namely, implicitly assuming an offsetting increase in government discretionary spending in response to inflation-based net taxation—may be imperfect, they find it useful for characterizing some features of the fiscal system that sometimes escape scrutiny due to the system's complicated and state-specific nature.

Alan Auerbach reinforced Kotlikoff's response. He added that even taking the progressivity of the countervailing fiscal policy as given, it would be challenging to incorporate, because it would require accounting for future generations who are not currently in the calculations.

NBER Macroeconomics Annual, volume 39, 2025.
 Published by The University of Chicago Press for the National Bureau of Economic Research. https://doi.org/10.1086/735267

Ricardo Reis commented on the assumption of perfect foresight: In the paper, inflation is a permanent shock that everyone immediately realizes and agrees on. However, in the last couple of years, the data show much disagreement on expected inflation. In particular, at the start of 2021, young people thought the inflation shock would be transitory, whereas older people thought it would be persistent. This should make a significant impact in terms of how people across different cohorts adjust to inflation. Furthermore, commenting on the paper's thought experiment about a change in the inflation target, he noted that evidence suggests that rich households seem to incorporate news about a rising inflation target faster than poor households do. He concluded that heterogeneity in how expectations change with bouts of inflation or changes in the inflation target could be just as important as the heterogeneity across asset positions.

Building on Reis's comments, Valerie Ramey noted that noneconomists often think that transitory inflation means transitory increases in the price level. Thus, even if a person's expectations are correct about the transitory nature of inflation, they might not realize the impact on the price level.

Responding to comments by the discussants, Laurence J. Kotlikoff clarified that the paper's purpose was strictly to illuminate inflation nonneutralities in the fiscal system. For this, considering a permanent, fully anticipated increase in inflation seems most appropriate.

As for the model's inner workings, he conceded that the model might seem like a black box. But he laid out during the meeting and in a subsequent exchange seven different ways to check that the Fiscal Analyzer's (TFA) calculations are precisely correct. First and foremost, each household respondent's lifetime present value budget constraint is exactly satisfied along each survival path. Second, along each survivor path, the annual flow of saving equals that year's change in net wealth. Third, households' living standard per person (calculated in light of the household's demographic composition and economies in shared living) is perfectly smooth during years when the household is not cash constrained. Fourth, when a cash-flow constraint stops binding, the household's living standard jumps onto a higher smooth path. Fifth, household net wealth is zero at the end of each cash-constrained interval. And, sixth, life insurance, when positive, provides survivors with precisely enough resources to maintain their living standard.

He explained that the TFA solves a problem involving hundreds of state variables, specifically, year and survivor-state-specific values of regular and retirement account assets. TFA's algorithm overcomes the curse of dimensionality via iterative dynamic programming. Specifically, the algorithm features three dynamic programs that iterate with one another to convergence, which typically takes less than one second. Convergence is defined by mutually consistent survivor-path-specific paths of annual discretionary spending—smooth consumption over the path subject to annual cash-flow constraints, survivor-path-specific paths of annual net taxes, and survivor-specific, annual, nonnegative life insurance holdings—that ensure no reduction in survivors' living standards. Mutual/internal consistency is essential because, for each survival path, the spending path depends on the path of net tax paths and life insurance premium paths, and each of the latter two paths depends on the other two paths. The algorithm also uses a proprietary method of sparse grids to overcome another major hurdle: doing backward induction over nondifferentiable policy functions.

In 1999, Kotlikoff's company, Economic Security Planning Inc. (ESP), received a method's patent—US 6611807B1—for its MaxiFi Planner algorithm, which is the company's principle financial planning tool. TFA was developed starting roughly a decade ago as a research version of MaxiFi Planner. Because MaxiFi Planner has run flawlessly for tens of thousands of ESP-client households, TFA's algorithm has been thoroughly tested. In particular, there have been no convergence problems, which would suggest multiple solutions. He expressed gratitude to the Federal Reserve, the Sloan Foundation, the National Institute of Aging, Boston University, and ESP for their support in building TFA. He also pointed out that this old but still breakthrough technology can be tested by any economist by simply requesting a free license to MaxiFi Planner.

Kotlikoff then addressed the desire for a unified framework of fiscal and financial costs of inflation expressed by the discussants. He explained that this was their initial goal, but they realized the interaction between the fiscal and financial costs was very episode-specific, depending on factors such as the extent to which inflation was anticipated and how quickly wages responded.

Finally, Kotlikoff pointed out that TFA has been and is being used to address other fundamental economic issues, such as inequality in remaining lifetime spending, the level and distribution of lifetime marginal net taxes on labor supply and saving, the size and distribution of cash-flow constraints, the taxation of marriage, the gains from lifetime Social Security benefit optimization, and the study of fundamental tax reform. TFA includes roughly 100 federal and state fiscal policies. As such it represents, in Kotlikoff's view, a veritable Webb telescope for assessing the fiscal system.

Alan Auerbach further addressed calls for a unified framework of fiscal and financial costs. He noted that Adrien Auclert's discussion provided a very helpful example that resulted in an expression where, after taking a derivative, the fiscal and financial effects are additive. He explained that, unfortunately, this does not work for discrete changes and that there is a complicated interaction between fiscal and financial effects.

Auerbach additionally responded to comments from Deborah Lucas's discussion regarding the impact of risk adjustment on progressivity. Assuming constant relative risk aversion and the same risk profile versus average effect for people of different income groups, the ratio of utility loss to the mean loss should be the same for the two groups. In the paper, they find a higher coefficient of variation for the highest income group than for the lowest income group. Thus, Auerbach thought incorporating the missing risk adjustment would support their progressivity finding rather than work against it. He acknowledged, however, that they need to worry about extreme values that might result in near-zero consumption at the bottom of the income distribution.

4

The Dominant Role of Expectations and Broad-Based Supply Shocks in Driving Inflation

Paul Beaudry, *University of British Columbia and NBER,* Canada
Chenyu Hou, *Simon Fraser University,* Canada
Franck Portier, *University College London and CEPR,* United Kingdom

I. Introduction

Although inflation in many countries has been coming down quickly from the heights of 2022, core inflation has been coming down at a slower pace, and this can be challenging for central banks that aim for a timely return to a prepandemic level of near 2%. For the United States, this pattern for core inflation can be seen in figure 1.

One of the main tools used by central bankers to understand inflation is the expectations-augmented Phillips curve, which links inflation to expectations of future inflation and overall market tightness, either measured by an output gap, an unemployment gap, or a vacancy-to-unemployment ratio.[1] When viewed through the lens of the Phillips curve, the persistent period of high inflation that is not explained by supply shocks can be attributed to either an overly hot labor market or by elevated expectations of inflation. A third possibility is that the Phillips curve is a rather unstable object and should be considered of limited value for thinking about current inflation. The latter, more unorthodox view is sometimes motivated by perceived repeated failures of the Phillips curve. For example, in the decade between the "Great Financial Crisis" and the pandemic, instead of underpredicting inflation as has recently been common, the Phillips curve often led to a "missing deflation puzzle."

This paper begins by examining what a pre-2020 view of the Phillips curve tells us about the recent determinants of inflation and whether such

NBER Macroeconomics Annual, volume 39, 2025.
 https://doi.org/10.1086/735268

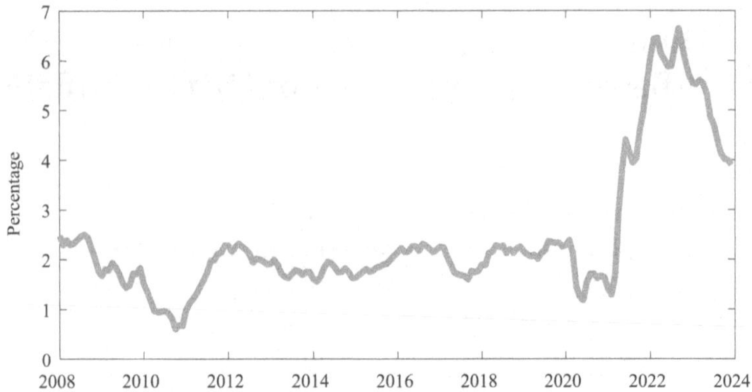

Fig. 1. US core CPI inflation, 2008m1–2023m12. The observed series is Consumer Price Index for All Urban Consumers: All Items Less Food and Energy in U.S. City Average. We plot monthly observations of the percent change from one year ago to obtain a slightly smoother picture. In the rest of the paper, we will use quarter-to-quarter changes.

a Phillips curve actually remains a good tool for understanding inflation. We complement our Phillips curve analysis with a vector-autoregression (VAR) analysis of the joint dynamics of inflation, inflation expectations, and labor market tightness, where inflation expectations used in both cases are taken from the Michigan Survey of Consumers. The VAR analysis is especially relevant as it will become the target for our later structural analysis of how inflation and inflation expectations interact to create a rich joint dynamics following different supply shocks. Both our Phillips curve exploration and our VAR analysis come to similar conclusions. First, the recent episode does not suggest any important break from past behavior. Second, both analyses suggest that inflation is mainly driven by expectations and quasi-i.i.d. (independently and identically distributed) supply shocks, with labor market tightness playing a very secondary role. In other words, the data maintain support for a close-to-flat Phillips curve view, with short-term inflation expectations being an important driver of inflation. In particular, the VAR analysis highlights how inflation expectations formed at t almost perfectly match realized inflation at $t + 1$, whereas inflation and inflation expectations are almost unrelated to labor market outcomes. We finish this section by showing why a Phillips curve model with rational expectations does poorly in accounting for the joint dynamics of inflation and inflation expectations.

We then turn to examining some of the empirical determinants of household inflation expectations. In particular, we show that these inflation expectations react to sectoral inflation measures in a way that deviates markedly from their importance in the overall consumer price index (CPI) basket. Instead, inflation expectations seem to be influenced by the common component of sectoral data, where the main common component places very different weights than the CPI across items/sectors. So agents appear to update their expectations very differently if inflation is driven by a broad-based increase in prices (as measured by the common component) than if the same level of inflation is driven by only one or two items. This observation will be a key element in our model of inflation expectations.

In the fourth section of the paper, we propose a model of the joint determination of inflation and inflation expectations that builds on the previously mentioned empirical patterns with the aim of explaining the VAR patterns. For the determinants of inflation, our model simply imports the New Keynesian Phillips curve specification we discuss and evaluate in Section II. For the determinant of inflation expectations, we make two departures relative to a full information rational expectations (FIRE) benchmark. First, we endow agents with two inflation realizations: a realization of headline inflation and a realization of an inflation signal that can be interpreted as reflecting broad-based shocks. Second, we model the agents as quite sophisticated but not fully informed of the data generating process. They extract a common component from their sectoral inflation signals using a Kalman filter and use this common component to predict future inflation. In this filtering process, agents treat the realization of the common component in inflation as uncorrelated with the noise in their signal, even though the two may not be independent in equilibrium due to the role of expectations themselves driving inflation. In doing so, agents depart from a fully rational benchmark. We show that such a model of inflation expectations can capture very well the joint dynamics of inflation and inflation expectations, as described by the VAR presented in Section III, while simultaneously being consistent with easily observable moments of the inflation process, so that agent's beliefs are almost self-confirming.

Although the narrative behind our model is most easily expressed with reference to the role of broad-based inflation shocks in driving inflation expectations, we do not actually use the disaggregated data in the estimation of our model. Instead, the "broad-based" inflation signal is treated as a latent variable, and we complete our analysis by showing that our estimate of this latent variable correlates closely with the common component directly estimated from the disaggregated data.

The narrative that arises from our model of inflation and inflation expectations can be expressed as follows. Inflation can be seen as mainly driven by two different types of shocks:[2] first, by narrow supply shocks that create very few dynamics because such shocks are not readily transmitted to expectations as they do not create a perceived generalized increase in prices; second, by a broad-based supply shock that transmits to inflation expectations and thereby creates something close to a self-fulling inflation episode, albeit ignited by exogenous forces. In our setup, the persistent movements of inflation expectations do not come from perceived current and future marginal costs as implied by the standard New Keynesian Phillips curve with Full Information Rational Expectation, as the slope of the Phillips curve is estimated to be quite small. Instead, positive, temporary, broad-base supply shocks trigger large initial responses of inflation expectations, which affect the prices the agents observe in the future. As the agents fail to recognize that inflation expectations are driving the inflation they observe, these future price changes make them believe that there is generalizable inflation. Their inflation expectations will remain high for a long time. As a result, temporary broad-base shocks trigger persistent responses of inflation and inflation expectations. In this setup, the presence of even a very weak persistent fundamental factor—such as labor market tightness—is enough for the inflation expectation formation process to be fooled by temporary supply shocks in creating persistent inflation.[3] Such a model explains why inflation can remain stable during long periods in the presence of narrow and unsynchronized supply shocks. But, in contrast, inflation tends to be amplified and made persistent when the economy is hit simultaneously by supply shocks across different sectors, even if the shocks are temporary in nature.

Related literature. Our paper contributes to the recent literature on the persistence of high inflation after the global supply chain disruptions caused by the COVID-19 pandemic. Ball, Leigh, and Mishra (2022) and Benigno and Eggertsson (2023) explain the recent episode through an overly heated labor market and argue for a nonlinear Phillips curve. Blanchard and Bernanke (2023) find instead that most of the inflation surge that began in 2021 was driven by shocks to prices given wages. Our paper finds that inflation expectations play a crucial role in explaining the persistent responses of inflation to these price shocks. Similar to us, Acharya et al. (2023) document high and persistent inflation expectations of European households and show how high inflation expectations can lead to broad-based inflation. Our paper provides a theoretical explanation for why households' inflation expectations respond to supply shocks and, more specifically, why transitory supply shocks can have a persistent effect on inflation expectations and inflation. Our results are also related to the empirical findings in Carrière-Swallow et al. (2023), where the authors show that supply chain shocks have smaller pass-through in countries with inflation targeting or better-anchored inflation expectations.

Our empirical analysis is a small contribution to the vast literature on the estimation of expectation augmented Phillips curve. Our baseline estimates builds on Hazell et al. (2022) and Beaudry, Hou, and Portier (2024). Our findings suggest that the use of real-time survey data on expectations helps identify a stable slope of the Phillips curve, as proposed in Coibion, Gorodnichenko, and Kamdar (2018). Our finding that households' inflation expectations are particularly important to explain inflation dynamics are in the same spirit as Coibion and Gorodnichenko (2015b), although the key mechanism we propose focuses more on the role of broad-based supply shocks rather than narrowed ones like energy price shocks.

Finally, our model setting on a household's expectation is motivated by both the theoretical and empirical literature on the formation of inflation expectation. Our agents solve a signal-extraction problem as in Sims (2003), Woodford (2001), Coibion and Gorodnichenko (2015a), and Carvalho et al. (2023). However, similar to D'Acunto et al. (2020), the signals our agents use to form expectations are sectoral price changes rather than noisy observations of the realized aggregate inflation. As a result, agents treat idiosyncratic sectoral shocks mainly as noise in our framework, with boundedly rational expectation formation. Bounded rationality and learning have been introduced in New Keynesian models by (among others) Hommes and Zhu (2014), Gelain et al. (2019), and Hommes et al. (2023). Our modeling is close in spirit to Lansing (2009), but we focus on the short run and not on the low frequency properties of inflation.

II. Should We Maintain or Throw Out the Flat Phillips Curve View?

Prior to the COVID-19 pandemic, many studies of the Phillips curve suggested that its slope was quite flat. Although the identification of the slope of the Phillips curve can be difficult, the work by Hazell et al. (2022) advanced on this point by exploiting cross-state variation. Their finding was that the slope of the Phillips curve was significantly positive but nevertheless quite small. Furthermore, they found that this flatness property did not arise post-1990s but appeared to be a feature of the data going back into the 1960s. They concluded that inflation expectations likely played a dominant role in the inflation episode on the 1970s and early 1980s. In related work (Beaudry et al. 2024), we found similar results, with the inflation expectations drawn from the Michigan Survey of Consumers helping to explain much of the variation in inflation since late 1960.

In this section, we aim to examine whether the recent inflation episode should lead one to revise/reject/update the flat Phillips curve view. To this end, we start with the following very parsimonious view of the (quarterly) Phillips curve:[4]

$$\pi_t = \beta \pi^e_{t+1} + \gamma_g \text{ gap}_t + e_t. \quad (1)$$

π_t is quarter-to-quarter headline CPI inflation and π^e_{t+1} is the mean of the 1-year-ahead expectation of CPI inflation drawn from the Michigan Survey of Consumers.[5] The gap represents labor market tightness and is initially measured by the minus unemployment gap.[6] Later we discuss the implications of using the vacancy-to-unemployment rate instead.

One important issue in our analysis relates to the most appropriate measure to use for inflation expectations. In figure 2, we plot a different measure for 1-year-ahead expectation of CPI inflation. As prices are set by

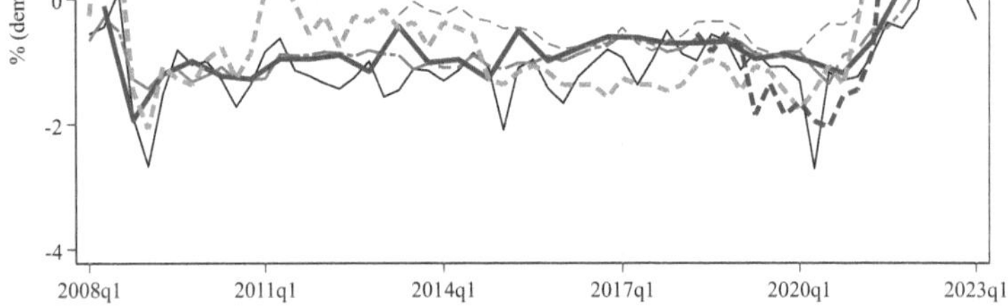

Fig. 2. Different measures of 1-year inflation expectations. "Cleveland Fed" is the inflation expectations series published by the Federal Reserve Bank of Cleveland, "SPF" is the Survey of Professional Forecasters published by the Federal Reserve Bank of Philadelphia, "Livingston" is the Livingston Survey series published by the Federal Reserve Bank of Philadelphia, "MSC" is the Michigan Survey of Consumers published by the University of Michigan, "SCE" is the Survey of Consumer Expectations series published by the Federal Reserve Bank of New York, "SoFIE" is the Survey of Firms' Inflation Expectations series published by the Federal Reserve Bank of Cleveland. All series have been demeaned.

firms, using a measure of business expectations would be our preferred approach. However, such measures are not readily available over a long time span. For example, the Cleveland Fed Survey of Firms' Inflation Expectations (SoFIE) has been available only since 2018Q2. Over the sample 2018Q2–2023Q1, it is interesting to note that the correlation between the Michigan Survey of Consumers' inflation expectations and those of the Cleveland Fed Survey of Firms is 0.9330. For this reason, we choose to exploit the Michigan Survey of Consumers measure for CPI inflation expectations as our main measure of inflation expectations as it both goes back all the way to the 1960s and is highly correlated with firm measures of inflation expectations.[7] This contrasts with professional forecasts or market-based forecasts, which are much less correlated with the SoFIE firms' inflation expectations than those obtained from consumers.

We initially do not estimate this Phillips curve but choose commonly accepted parameters values. In particular, γ_g is set to 0.0138 according to what is estimated in Hazell et al. (2022),[8] and β is set to 0.99, which is a common value in the literature. We refer to this as our baseline Phillips curve. Note that given the low value of γ_g, that Phillips curve is pretty flat.

From this baseline Phillips curve, we construct residuals $\hat{e}_t = \pi_t - 0.99\pi^e_{t+1} - 0.0138\ \text{gap}_t$ over the period 2008q1–2023q1 and plot them against our measure of the gap. This is the plot in panel *A* of figure 3.[9] The dark dots are Phillips curve residuals for the post-2020 period, whereas the gray dots cover the period from 2008q1 to 2019q4. We overlayed on these figures two estimated relations between the Phillips curve residuals and labor market tightness over 2008q1–2019q4: one in linear form and one in cubic form. The coefficients for this regression are presented in columns 1 and 2 of table 1. We also calculate the standard deviation σ_ϵ of the Phillips curve residuals for this sample as well as that from the prior sample running from 1968q1 to 2007q4. The first thing to note is that the standard deviation of the Phillips curve residuals is only slightly higher over the period 2008q1–2023q1 than over the period 1968q1–2007q4, although we are considering headline inflation and not controlling for supply shocks. More interestingly, we detect no significant link between these residuals and the unemployment gap.[10] If the residuals were strongly and positively associated with the labor market tightness measure, including possibly in a nonlinear fashion, this would put in question the validity of a flat Phillips curve view in the more recent data. However, these forecast errors do not suggest that a steeper Phillips curve would better explain the more recent data episode. The same exercise is repeated using core CPI inflation as a measure of inflation. As it

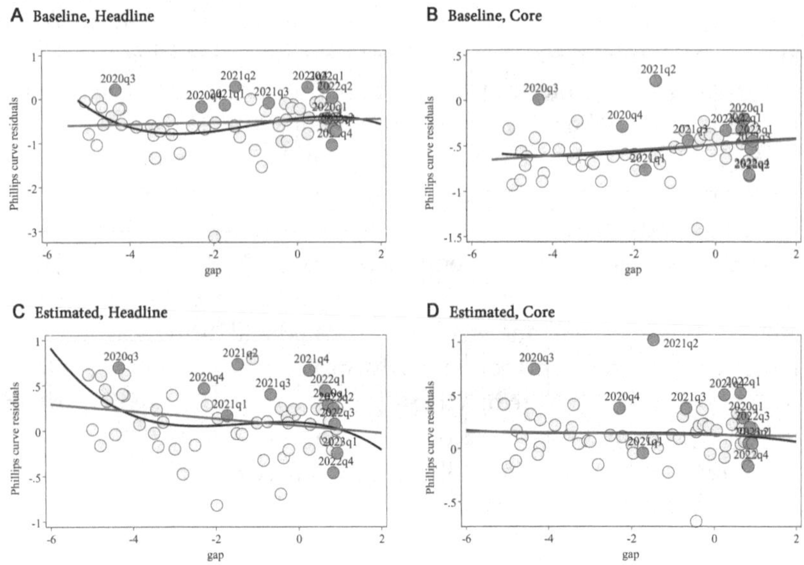

Fig. 3. Out-of-sample residuals from Phillips curves. Panels *A* and *B* of this figure plot the out-of-sample residuals of the baseline Phillips curve (1) against a measure of labor market tightness (minus) the US Congressional Budget Office unemployment gap, for two measures of inflation (headline and core consumer price index). The gray lines show the estimated linear or cubic relation between residuals and labor market tightness (see table 1 for the estimated coefficients). Light dots correspond to pre-2020 observations and dark ones to post-2020. We exclude 2020q2 from this graph. Panels *C* and *D* of this figure repeat the analysis with the augmented estimated Phillips curve (2).

can be seen in columns 3 and 4 of table 1 and on panel *B* of figure 3, there is again no sign of a steepening of the Phillips curve. Furthermore, the standard deviation of the Phillips curve residuals is now smaller post-2008 as compared with previously. If anything, this flat Phillips curve fits better post-2008 data than over the period 1968–2007.

In addition to this baseline Phillips curve, we also directly estimate a Phillips curve over the sample 1969q1–2007q4 and look at the implied out-of-sample forecast errors for the period 2008q1–2023q1. Details of this estimation are provided in the appendix (http://www.nber.org/data-appendix/c14985/appendix.pdf) and follow Beaudry et al. (2024). Because the determinants of inflation in Phillips curve are endogenous, we follow Barnichon and Mesters (2020) and estimate our Phillips curve by instrumental variables using estimated monetary shocks as instruments.[11] To reduce the risk of biases, we estimated the Phillips curve using core inflation and, as argued in Beaudry et al. (2024), we include the real interest

Table 1
Projection of the Phillips Curve Residuals $\hat{e}$ on the Gap, 2008–2023

	Headline		Core		Headline		Core	
	Baseline		Baseline		Estimated		Estimated	
	Linear	Nonlinear	Linear	Nonlinear	Linear	Nonlinear	Linear	Nonlinear
	(1)	(2)	(3)	(4)	(5)	(6)	(7)	(8)
gap	.02	.11	.03	.04	−.04	−.03	−.01	−.02
	(.035)	(.113)	(.016)	(.056)	(.022)	(.072)	(.016)	(.055)
gap^2		−.05		.00		−.04		−.01
		(.087)		(.043)		(.056)		(.042)
gap^3		−.02		.00		−.01		.00
		(.015)		(.007)		(.009)		(.007)
N	60	60	60	60	60	60	60	60
$\sigma_{\hat{e},60-07}$	.324		.315		.276		.291	
$\sigma_{\hat{e},08-23}$	.528		.256		.338		.245	

Note: In columns 1–4, the Phillips curve residuals are obtained from the baseline Phillips curve (1). In columns 5–8, they are obtained from the augmented Phillips curve (2) estimated over the sample 1969Q1–2007Q4. $\sigma_{\hat{e}}$ is the standard deviation of the Phillips curve residuals. The standard errors of estimated coefficients are between parentheses.

rate as an additional explanatory variable to capture a potential cost channel of monetary policy.[12] The estimated Phillips curve is therefore

$$\pi_t = \beta\pi^e_{t+1} + \gamma_g \text{ gap}_t + \gamma_r(i_t - \pi^e_{t+1}) + e_t. \tag{2}$$

Table 2 displays the results from estimation. The coefficients we obtain for γ_g are quite close to that of our baseline Phillips curve, with the exception that we obtain a slightly steeper Phillips curve than that reported in Hazell et al. (2022). Our estimate of γ_g is 0.04 and significant at standard levels, which is more than twice that of 0.0138 from Hazell et al. (2022) but not significantly different from it. Our estimate for β is also 0.99.

In panel *D* of figure 3, we report the out-of-sample Phillips curve residuals from our estimated model for the period 2008q1–2023q1 plotted against our measure of labor market tightness, with again a linear and cubic fit superimposed. We see a very similar pattern to that observed in panels *A* and *B*, with very little link between the forecast errors and labor market tightness, even though these are out-of-sample forecast. The estimated coefficients for these linear and cubic fits are displayed in columns 7 and 8 of table 1. So again, these observations do not suggest that a steeper Phillips curve is helpful/needed to explain the 2008q1–2023q1 period. Note that the fit of this estimated Phillips curve, as measured by

Table 2
Estimated Phillips Curves, 1969–2007

	Headline	Core
β	1.15[a]	.99[a]
	(.031)	(.048)
γ_g	.07[a]	.04[a]
	(.020)	(.015)
γ_r	.13[a]	.25[a]
	(.031)	(.042)
Observations	144	144
J test	15.201	10.684
(jp)	(.887)	(.986)
Weak ID test	7.825	12.245

Note: All results are using IV-GMM procedure; Newey-West HAC standard errors with six lags are reported in parentheses. The constant term is omitted from the table. Real oil price and its lag are also omitted for the regression with headline CPI. All regressors are instrumented using six lags of Romer and Romer (2004) shocks (as extended by Wieland and Yang 2020) and their squares as instruments. [a]indicates significance at 5%. Sample is 1969Q1–2007Q4.

the standard deviation of the residuals $\sigma_{\hat{e}}$, is better out of sample than in sample. In appendix A (http://www.nber.org/data-appendix/c14985/appendix.pdf), we confirm similar finding using the vacancy-to-unemployment rate as an alternative measure of labor market tightness, as well as exploring the effect of the use market base measures of expectations. For completeness, panel C of figure 3 and columns 5 and 6 of table 1 repeat the analysis when using the headline CPI to estimate the Phillips curve. Results are similar.

The overall out-of-sample fit of the baseline Phillips curve can also be seen in panels *A* and *B* (for headline) and *C* and *D* (for core) of figure 4. As can be seen, the forecasted inflation tracks actual inflation reasonably well, with exceptions such as 2021q2, where actual inflation was well above predicted, as is consistent with a strong supply shock in that quarter associated with transport bottlenecks. In panels *A* and *C*, we also plot a counterfactual path of inflation over the period, assuming that the unemployment gap had been equal to its sample mean over the forecast horizon. Here we see that this counterfactual inflation series is very similar to the predicted inflation path using the full model. This reflects the very weak direct role that labor market tightness is playing in our estimated Phillips curve given that the slope is quite small. The second counterfactual we examine imposes that inflation expectations are constant over the

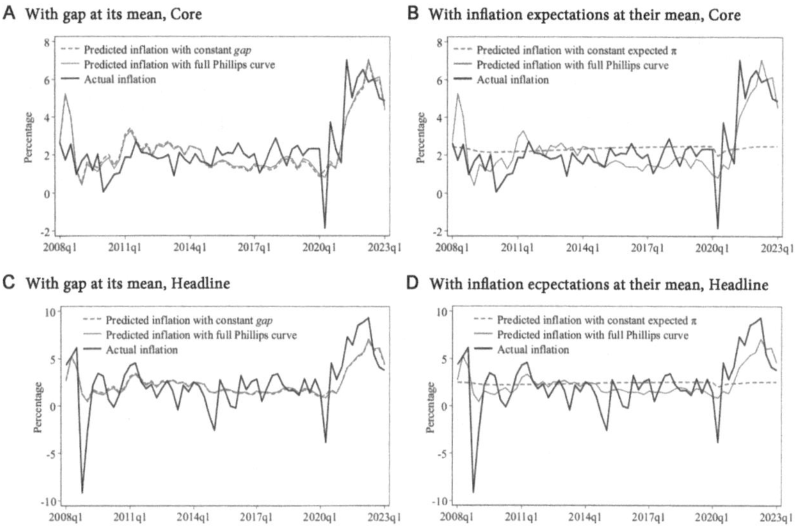

Fig. 4. Counterfactual simulations from the baseline Phillips curve. These counterfactual simulations are done using the baseline Phillips curve (1), using either headline or core consumer price index.

forecast period and set at their average. This counterfactual path is reported together with our forecasted rates of inflation in panels *B* and *D*. Here we see clearly that it is expected inflation that mainly drives the fit of the predicted inflation, because when we omit the role of inflation expectations, the fit greatly deteriorates.

In summary, figures 3 and 4 illustrate how a very simple, three-variable Phillips curve, either estimated prior to the recent periods of missing deflation and high inflation or based on the work of Hazell et al. (2022), fits the post-2007 data and post-2020 quite well. The lack of a relationship between forecast errors and labor market tightness indicates that the Phillips curve is likely still quite flat. The forecast error is also close to i.i.d., which is consistent with them being interpreted as supply shocks. The ongoing flatness of the Phillips curve implies that persistently high levels of core inflation in 2022 and early 2023 are unlikely explained by labor market tightness. Instead, it appears primarily driven by elevated levels of inflation expectations. Such observations can be both reassuring and uncomfortable. On the one hand, they support the view that the Phillips curve framework likely remains a relevant framework for thinking about inflation developments. However, they also suggest that the main driver of inflation is expected inflation itself. The latter observations can be uncomfortable, as they question/downplay the traditional role of pure demand management as key to controlling inflation and instead push forward the central importance of expectations management—and the more amorphous role of inflation psychology—in controlling inflation.

III. The Joint Dynamics of Inflation, Inflation Expectations, and Labor Market Tightness

In this section, we first provide VAR-based evidence to give further support to the view that inflation dynamics appear to be largely explained by inflation expectations, with labor market tightness playing a very secondary role. We then show that our baseline Phillips curve model with rational expectations and full or incomplete information is unlikely to account for the observed joint dynamics.

A. VAR Evidence

To this end, figure 5 plots impulse response generated from a bivariate VAR using inflation and the inflation expectations estimated over the period 1969q1–2023q2. The data for inflation remain headline inflation, and that for expectations are again drawn from the Michigan Survey of Expectations. The figure corresponds to impulse response associated with a Choleski orthogonalization of the VAR residuals, where the shock ϵ_2 does not have impact effect on inflation expectations and the shock ϵ_1 is orthogonal to ϵ_2. We do not claim that these impulses responses capture the effects of structural shocks. Instead, we simply view them as a means of summarizing properties of the data. In particular, these two shocks will eventually be interpreted as combinations of the structural shock in our modeling of Section V. In figure 5, together with the response of inflation to the two shocks $\{\pi_t\}_{t=1}^{20}$, we also represent (dashed line) the expected inflation response $\{\pi^e_{t+1}\}_{t=1}^{19}$ shifted by one period.

Two properties of this joint dynamics can be observed. First, inflation expectations formed at time t match very closely realized inflation at $t + 1$. This is true for both shocks, and therefore for any linear combination of these shocks. Accordingly, it suggests that either agents are very good at predicting inflation or instead that expected inflation may be an important driver of inflation. Second, these impulse responses suggest that there is some combination of shocks (that forms ϵ_2) that do not transmit to expected inflation, and this leads to a very temporary rise in inflation.

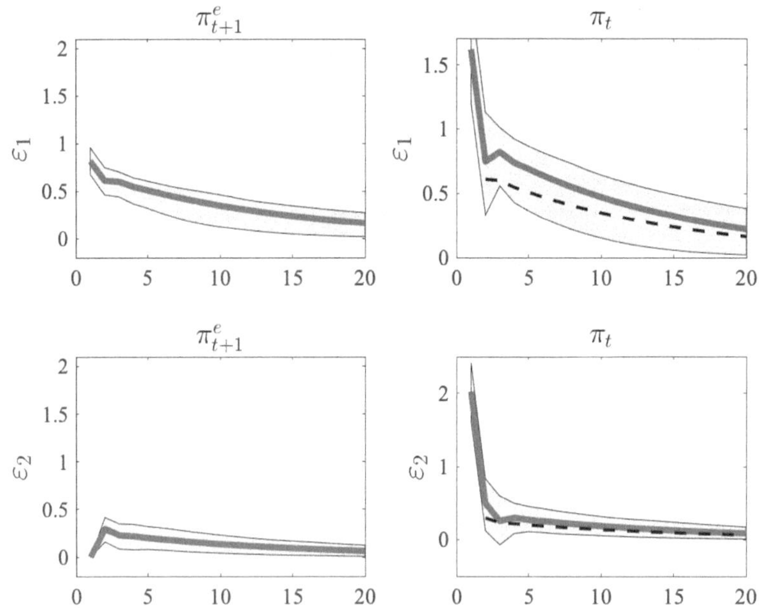

Fig. 5. Impulse responses in the 2-VAR (π_t, π^e_{t+1}). This figure plots the impulse responses to a 1 standard deviation shocks ε_1 and ε_2. These shocks are obtained from a Choleski orthogonalization. The estimated VAR features two lags of headline consumer price index inflation and of the Michigan Survey of Consumers inflation expectations. The dashed line is the expected inflation response $\{\pi^e_{t+1}\}_{t=1}^{19}$ shifted by one period. Sample is 1969Q1–2023Q1. Shaded area represents the 95% confidence band. VAR = vector autoregression.

Meanwhile, on the other hand, there is some combination of shocks (that forms ε_2) that have a large effect of inflation and transmit to expected inflation, and this is associated with persistent inflation. Indeed, in the response to ε_1, the first and second serial correlations of inflation response are 0.45 and 0.44, whereas for ε_2, they are 0.19 and 0.06. It should also be noted that the short-run variance of inflation accounted for ε_2 is close to 50%, implying that a substantial fraction of the variance of inflation does not transmit to expectations. So one needs at least two quite distinctive types of shocks to explain the joint behavior of inflation and inflation expectations.

In appendix C (http://www.nber.org/data-appendix/c14985/appendix.pdf#page=12), we show that these impulse responses are essentially unchanged if we change the number of lags or if we drop post-2008 data from the estimation. It also holds if the VAR is estimated on 2008–23.[13] This suggests that the recent inflation dynamics continue to obey the dynamics that were observed earlier, suggesting no substantial break in the process.

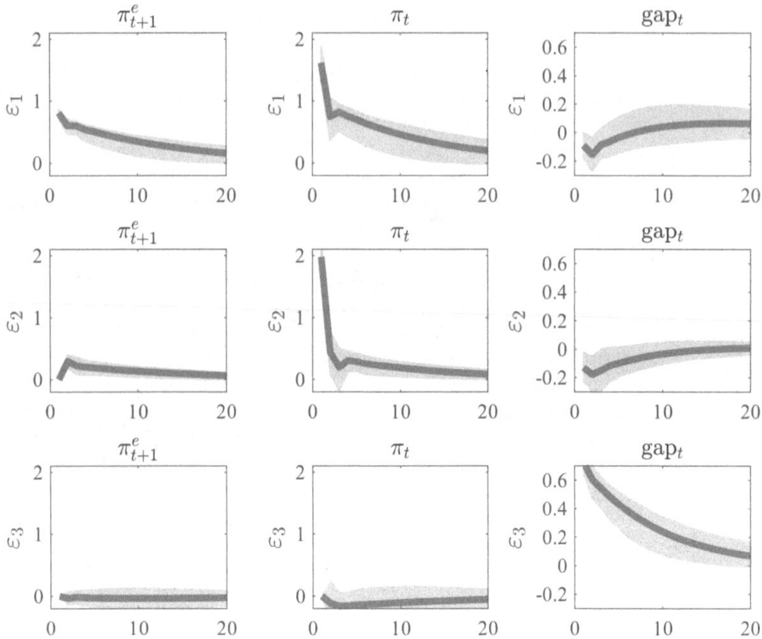

Fig. 6. Impulse responses in the 3-VAR (π_t, π^e_{t+1}, gap$_t$). This figure plots the impulse responses to a 1 standard deviation shocks ε_1, ε_2, and ε_3. These shocks are obtained from a Choleski orthogonalization. The estimated VAR features two lags of headline consumer price index inflation, the Michigan Survey of Consumers inflation expectations and of (minus) the employment gap. Sample is 1969Q1–2023Q1. Shaded area represents the 95% confidence band.

In figure 6, we present the impulse responses from a trivariate VAR that builds on our bivariate VAR by including (minus) the unemployment gap as the third variable. We use a Choleski indentification: ε_3 affects only the gap on impact, ε_2 affects only the gap and inflation on impact, and ε_1 is unrestricted but to be orthogonal to the two other shocks.

The main feature we want to highlight from this figure is the quasi-complete separation between inflation and inflation expectations, on the one hand, and labor market tightness, on the other hand. This can be seen by examining how the subblock of impulse response to ε_1 and ε_2 for inflation and inflation expectations generated by this three-variable VAR is almost identical to that generated by our two-variable VAR. Furthermore, we can see that the shock to unemployment ε_3 has essentially no impact on inflation or inflation expectations, whereas the two other shocks that drive almost all the variance of inflation and expected inflation have very little effect on unemployment. In summary, these two (nonstructural) VARs appear consistent with the view that the Phillips curve is likely very flat and that the persistent component of inflation may well be driven by expected inflation.

B. *The Challenge in Explaining the Joint Dynamics of Inflation and Inflation Expectations under Rational Expectations*

As we have argued above, inflation expectations appear to potentially be an important driver of inflation. However, this may only be a proximate cause. It may well be the case that both inflation and inflation expectations are driven by a third variable, and expectations are simply good at capturing this force. Accordingly, we ask in this subsection whether the joint dynamics of inflation and inflation expectations reflected in our bivariate VAR could be produced by our baseline Phillips curve model under rational expectations, where the dynamics of the labor market tightness and supply shocks would be the more fundamental factor. To that end, first assume that inflation is generated from the baseline Phillips curve

$$\pi_t = \beta\pi^e_{t+1} + \gamma_g \text{ gap}_t + e_t, \tag{3}$$

with $e_t \sim N(0, \sigma_e^2)$, $\beta = 0.99$, $\gamma_g = 4 \times 0.0138$[14] and where we use quarterly (annualized) headline inflation, the Michigan Survey of Expectations and (minus) the unemployment gap. As discussed in the previous section, the fit of the baseline Phillips curve has not worsened in the recent period, as illustrated on figure 7.

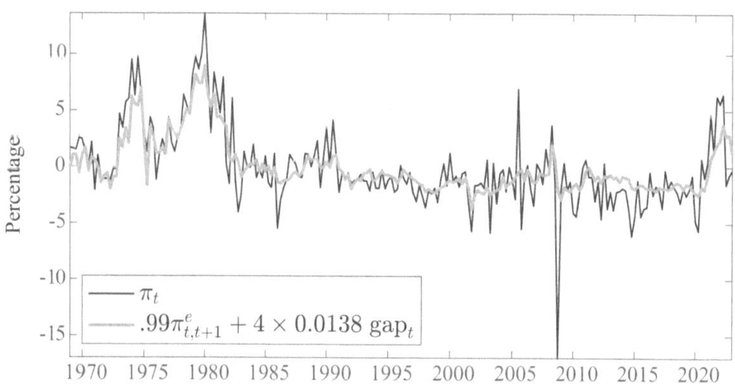

Fig. 7. The fit of the baseline Phillips curve, 1969–2023. This figure plots headline consumer price index inflation together with inflation predicted by the baseline Phillips curve (1).

We also assume that the gap follows an exogenous autoregressive process

$$\text{gap}_t = \rho\,\text{gap}_{t-1} + v_t, \tag{4}$$

with $v_t \sim N(0, \sigma_v^2)$. We estimate this autoregressive process for gap_t.[15] The estimated parameters are $\rho = 0.89$ (SE = 0.03) and $\sigma_v^2 = 9.05$ (SE = 0.33). We obtain an estimate of $\sigma_e^2 = 5.00$ from the residual of equation (3).

Now let us solve that Phillips curve and gap process model under rational expectations and with or without full information and show that data generated by such models cannot replicate our VAR findings.

FIRE. When economic agents form rational expectations, they use the correct model (eqq. [3]–[4]) and form expectations $\pi_{t+1}^e = E_t^{\text{FIRE}}[\pi_{t+1}]$. Under full information, gap_{t-1}, v_t, and e_t are observed. The solution to the model is given by

$$\pi_t = \frac{\gamma_g}{1-\beta\rho}\,\text{gap}_t + e_t, \tag{5}$$

$$E_t^{\text{FIRE}}[\pi_{t+1}] = \frac{\gamma_g \rho}{1-\beta\rho}\,\text{gap}_t. \tag{6}$$

FIRE with persistent supply shock. Looking at the properties of the Phillips curve residual $\hat{e}$, it is significantly autocorrelated, although the autocorrelation coefficient is small. When we estimate an AR(1) process, we find low autocorrelation, with an estimated $\rho_e = 0.165$ (SD = 0.05). Could this admittedly low persistence reverse the results we obtain with the i.i.d. supply shocks FIRE model? To answer that question, we also consider an extension of the FIRE model where we allow e_t to be persistent. The solution to such a FIRE model with persistent e_t is given by

$$\pi_t = \frac{\gamma_g}{1-\beta\rho}\,\text{gap}_t + \frac{1}{1-\beta\rho_e}\,e_t, \tag{7}$$

$$E_t^{\text{FIRE}}[\pi_{t+1}] = \frac{\gamma_g \rho}{1-\beta\rho}\,\text{gap}_t + \frac{\rho_e}{1-\beta\rho_e}\,e_t. \tag{8}$$

Incomplete information rational expectations (IIRE). Here we look at a counterpart of our Section IV main model but with rational expectations. We assume that agents correctly understand the model (eqq. [3]–[4]) but that they do not observe the gap and the aggregate supply shock e_t. Instead, we assume that the economy is composed of N sectors with sector-specific supply shocks. In sector j, sectoral inflation is generated by

$$\pi_{j,t} = \beta\pi^e_{t+1} + \gamma_g \text{ gap}_t + e_{j,t}, \tag{9}$$

where $e_{j,t} \sim N(0, \sigma_j^2)$. We assume that agents observe a signal that adds-up demand inflationary pressures γ_g gap$_t$ and a subset S of the sector-specific supply shocks e_{jt}:

$$s_t = \gamma_g \text{ gap}_t + \sum_{j\in S} e_{j,t} \tag{10}$$

and we will use the notation

$$\epsilon_t = \sum_{j\in S} e_{j,t}, \tag{11}$$

with $\epsilon_t \sim N(0, \sigma_\epsilon^2)$. Economic agents have rational expectations and know that inflation is generated by

$$\pi_t = \beta\pi^e_{t+1} + \gamma_g \text{ gap}_t + \epsilon_t + w_t, \tag{12}$$

where $w_t = e_t - \epsilon_t$ is the residual supply shock. The agents use Bayes Rule and the knowledge of the model to form beliefs of e_t and gap$_t$ and to compute $\pi^e_{t+1} = E_t^{\text{IIRE}}[\pi_{t+1}]$. Denoting K the Kalman gain in this computation, the solution to the model is[16]

$$E_t^{\text{IIRE}}[\pi_{t+1}] = (1 - K\gamma_g)\rho E_{t-1}^{\text{IIRE}}[\pi_t] + \frac{\gamma_g\rho K}{1 - \beta\rho}(\gamma_g \text{ gap}_t + \epsilon_t), \tag{13}$$

$$\pi_t = \beta(1 - K\gamma_g)\rho E_{t-1}^{\text{IIRE}}[\pi_t] + \frac{\gamma_g^2 K\rho\beta + (1 - \beta\rho)\gamma_g}{1 - \beta\rho} \text{ gap}_t$$
$$+ \frac{K\rho\beta\gamma_g + (1 - \beta\rho)\gamma}{1 - \beta\rho}\epsilon_t + w_t. \tag{14}$$

We estimate σ_ϵ by simulated method of moments. The model is simulated 200 times, the (π_t, π^e_{t+1}) VAR is estimated in each simulation, and σ_ϵ is set to minimize the distance between the average impulse response functions obtained from the model with their empirical couterpart, when the same Choleski decomposition is used for model and data. The resulting estimate is $\sigma_\epsilon = 1.08$, and this implies $\sigma_w = 1.96$.

Results. For each of the three models considered, using the estimated parameters, we simulate 200 random samples with the same length as the data. With these generated data, we estimate the bivariate VAR and

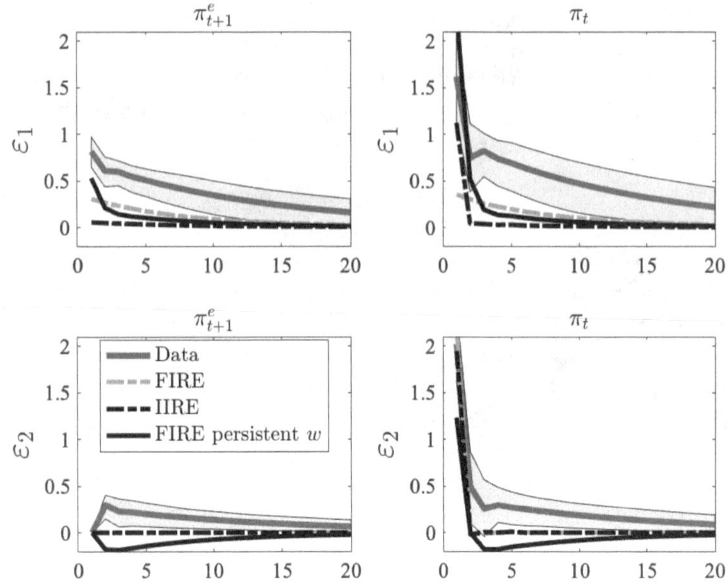

Fig. 8. The joint process of π and π^e_{t+1} in the data and in models with rational expectations. On this figure, the solid gray line plots the impulse responses to a 1 standard deviation shocks ε_1 and ε_2 estimated with data from Michigan Survey of Consumers inflation expectations and headline consumer price index. Sample is 1969Q1–2023Q1. Shaded area represents the 95% confidence band. The other lines plot the average impulse responses (over 200 simulations of length 216) obtained from the same vector autoregression estimated on simulated data, when the data generating process is either the FIRE model (eqq. [5]–[6]) assuming w_t is i.i.d., the IIRE model (eqq. [13]–[14]), or the FIRE model assuming w_t is persistent. FIRE = full information rational expectations, i.i.d. = independently and identically distributed, IIRE = incomplete information rational expectations.

see how well it can match the impulse responses derived from our empirical bivariate VAR. The result can be seen in figure 8. The impulse responses from the generated data do not match that derived from actual data either in shape or in level, even if in the case of IIRE model we estimate σ_ϵ to deliberately match these impulse response functions (IRFs).

We can also illustrate the performances of these models in matching the joint dynamics of inflation and inflation expectations by looking at the set of moments presented in table 3. We see that none of the rational expectations models can create inflation as volatile as the data. The simulated data have much lower persistence and variances in both realized and expected inflations, as compared with the actual data.

In part, this should not be too surprising. Given the rather small slope of the Phillips curve implied by the work of Hazell et al. (2022) and the

Table 3
Moments of π and π^e_{t+1} in the Data and in Models with Rational Expectations

	$\text{var}(\pi_t)$	$\text{cov}(\pi_t, \pi_{t-1})$	$\text{cov}(\pi_t, \pi_{t-2})$	$\text{var}(\pi^e_{t+1})$	$\text{corr}(\pi^e_{t+1}, \pi^e_t)$
Data	12.52	7.70	6.99	3.92	.90
FIRE	5.49	.45	.39	.42	.87
IIRE	5.10	.05	.04	.00	.87
FIRE, persistent w_t	7.59	1.61	.57	.61	.64

Note: For the three models, the moments are computed as the average across 200 random samples of same length as the data. FIRE = full information rational expectations, IIRE = incomplete information rational expectations.

low persistence of the supply shocks, it is hard to see how shocks to labor market tightness or supply shocks could generate important volatility in inflation expectations. In particular, the difficulty for the rational expectations models to match the VAR observations reflects the difficulty to generate both large and persistent responses of inflation expectations. Rational agents understand that the underlying persistent factor moving inflation plays only a limited role. As a result, they should not expect future inflation to have persistent movement as well. Moreover, limited information does not help with the situation. In fact, the IIRE case has the most muted response among all three models and generates the least volatile as well as the least persistent inflation. This is not only because the rational agents understand the persistent labor market condition plays little role. They also realize that their signals are not informative because of the large noise-to-signal ratio due to low γ_g. As a result, their expectations do not respond much to the movements in labor market conditions.

Our takeaway from this section is that the VAR dynamics for inflation and inflation expectations are unlikely to be explained by a Rational Expectations New Keynesian Phillips curve model.[17] In the next section, we explore what may drive inflation expectations.

IV. The Information Encoded in Inflation Expectations

In this section, we provide some preliminary evidence for our conjecture that inflation expectations may be driven by a perceived common component across sector-specific inflations. Our narrative is quite simple. Inflation is defined as a generalized increase in prices. So when agents (both firms and households) see prices increase in many sectors (although not necessarily in all sectors), they take this to be sign that inflation is taking hold. This affects their expectations, and this incite firms to increase prices.

To provide support to this conjecture, we take the set of sectoral inflation data for the 24 expenditure categories used by the US Bureau of Labor Statistics (BLS) to construct the CPI (see table D.1, http://www.nber.org/data-appendix/c14985/appendix.pdf#page=15, for a description) and extract the common component of these sectoral inflations. To do so, we estimate a dynamic factor model[18] in which sectoral inflations are driven by one common persistent factor C_t, which follows an AR(1) process. The model takes the following form:[19]

$$\pi_{j,t} = \alpha_j C_t + e_{j,t}, \tag{15}$$

$$C_t = \rho_C C_{t-1} + v_t, \tag{16}$$

where j stands for the sector/category and $\pi_{j,t}$ is the month-to-month inflation of each sector/category j. How the common component C_t affects different $\pi_{j,t}$ may be different, and that is captured by α_j. Data are monthly over the sample 1978m1–2023m5 for 17 sectoral inflations and shorter for the remaining seven (see table D.1). We estimate that model with Kalman filter smoothing using a Maximum Likelihood Estimator that accounts for the missing observations. Estimated parameters are ρ_C and $\{\alpha_j, \sigma_j^2\}_{j=1}^{24}$. Note that σ_v^2 is not separately identifiable from α_j's, so we normalize it to 1. The parameters estimates we obtained are presented in table D.2 (http://www.nber.org/data-appendix/c14985/appendix.pdf#page=15). The important element to note is that all the α_j's are positive, so C_t is indeed capturing a common component in inflation. In figure 9, we plot expected inflation and the common component C_t. As can be seen, the common component of sectoral inflations tracks the expected inflation quite well.

It is interesting to compare the (normalized) weights of each category in the common components to the expenditure share of that category, as used by the BLS to compute CPI. The weights in the common component are computed as the relative Kalman gain associated to each sectoral inflation in updating the common component. Those two sets of weights are represented in figure 10. It is evident that they are very different. The correlation between these two sets of weight is 0.15, with a 95% confidence set [−0.01, 0.32]. This shows that the common component encodes some information about broad-based shock, as the weights significantly differ from the CPI ones.

It is also interesting to note which sectors are most disproportionately affecting the common component. One sector that is particular important

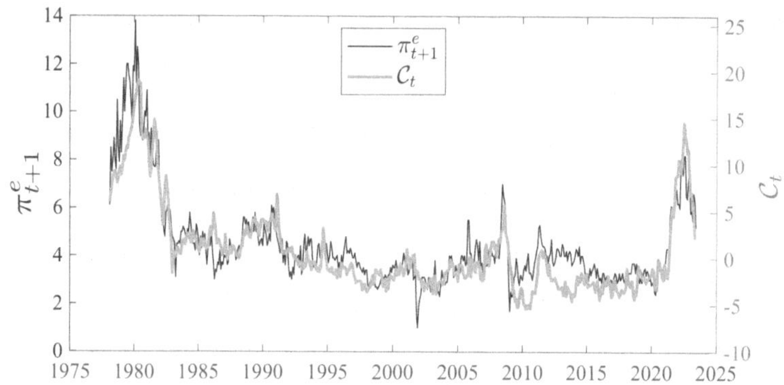

Fig. 9. Michigan Survey of Consumers inflation expectations π^e_{t+1} and the common component C_t. This figure plots inflation expectations (as measured by the Michigan Survey of Consumers) together with the common component C_t. C_t is obtained from the estimation of equations (15) and (16) on the 24 expenditure categories used by the Bureau of Labor Statistics to construct the consumer price index.

is full-service meals. This is a sector that combines aspects of both food and services inflations, and in that sense it is quite broad based by construction. Similarly, limited-service meals and other foods away from home are also important components. Shelter, in contrast, has an important weight in the common component, but its weight is significantly below its weights in the CPI. Cereals and bakery products are also disproportionately important contributors. Overall, this common component appears to be especially affected by components that combine food and service costs, in addition to more traditional categories like energy and shelter.

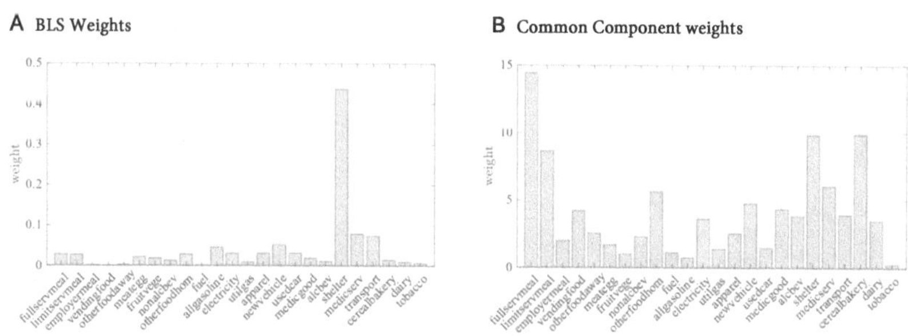

Fig. 10. Comparing the weights in the common component and in the consumer price index (CPI) basket. Panel *A* plots the weight of each category in the CPI basket, whereas panel *B* plots the (normalized) weights in the common component C_t. BLS = Bureau of Labor Statistics.

We then regress our measure of expected inflation (from the Michigan Survey of Consumers) on the common component of the disaggregated inflation data and annualized month-to-month CPI (headline) inflation. The resulting regression is (with standard errors between parenthesis)

$$\underset{}{\pi^e_{t+1}} = \underset{(0.09)}{0.66} + \underset{(0.02)}{0.78}\ C_t + \underset{(0.01)}{0.09}\ \pi^{\text{HL}}_t + u_t, \tag{17}$$

where the data are at a monthly frequency with 545 observations and an adjusted R^2 of 0.82. The common component enters significantly in the regression on top of headline CPI, which indicates that economic agents (here the households) may be using it to forecast inflation. The adjusted R^2 of regressing inflation expectations from the Michigan Survey of Consumers on only common component is 0.80, and the adjusted R^2 of regressing inflation expectations on only headline CPI is merely 0.45.

It is also interesting to compare the behavior of the common component extracted from disaggregated data to the behavior of oil prices. To this end, on figure 11 we superimpose the behavior of the year-to-year oil price changes[20] to that of expected inflation to parallel figure 9. As can be seen, over the recent bout of inflation (post-2020), expectations moved closely with oil price inflation. If one only focused on this type of period, it could suggest that the price of oil is the dominant force behind inflation expectations. However, as can also be seen in the figure, there have been many extended periods where oil price inflation and inflation expectations have diverged considerably. Over the whole sample from 1978 to 2023, the correlation between expected inflation and oil price inflation

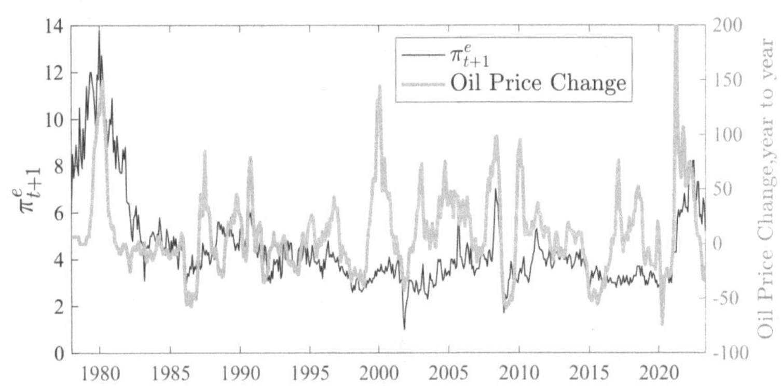

Fig. 11. Michigan Survey of Consumers inflation expectations π^e_{t+1} and the change of oil prices. This figure plots inflation expectations (as measured by the Michigan Survey of Consumers) together with the year-to-year change of oil prices.

is only 0.35. In contrast, the extracted common component closely follows inflation expectations over the entire sample with a correlation of 0.90, thereby offering a better basis to build a theory of inflation expectations. In particular, figures 11 and 9 suggest that agents are likely downplaying the role of oil prices in forming inflation expectations when only oil prices are moving, but when oil prices and many other goods are increasing in tandem, then inflation expectations react strongly.

V. A Bounded Rational Model of Inflation and Inflation Expectations Dynamics with Broad-Based Supply Shocks

In this section, our aim is to take up the following challenge: we want to combine our baseline Phillips curve with a particular bounded rationality theory of inflation expectations to see whether it can match the bivariate VAR for inflation and expected inflation. Our theory of expectations will build on the idea that agents may form expectations by extracting a common component from disaggregated data. However, agents' perception of the data generating process will be slightly simpler than the actual data generating process. In particular, we will assume that they do not conceptualize the data generating in its structural form. Instead, they view persistent inflation as driven by a common component that they need to infer from the data.

A. *The Model*

The model has two main departures from the FIRE case. First, agents observe only a subset of the sectoral inflations when forming their inflation expectations. This is the source of imperfect information. Second, they believe that sectoral inflations depend on a common persistent component and a transitory sector-specific component but fail to fully understand the relations between these two components. The latter is the source of bounded rationality.

Sectors. The model directly adopts the baseline aggregate Phillips curve discussed in the previous sections as part of the data generating process:

$$\pi_t = \beta \pi^e_{t+1} + \gamma_g \, \text{gap}_t + e_t. \tag{18}$$

The headline aggregate inflation π_t is a weighted average of sector-specific inflations. Consider that each sectoral inflation obeys a sectoral Phillips curve similar to the aggregate one:[21]

$$\pi_{j,t} = \beta \pi^e_{t+1} + \gamma_g \text{ gap}_t + e_{j,t}, \tag{19}$$

where j stands for a specific sector and $e_{j,t}$ is the i.i.d. sector-specific shock with distribution $N(0, \sigma_j^2)$. We will describe the expectations formation process after we have introduced the agents perceived laws of motion. As in Subsection III.B, the gap follows an AR(1) process:[22]

$$\text{gap}_t = \rho \text{ gap}_{t-1} + v_t. \tag{20}$$

Assuming there are N categories in the CPI, headline inflation is the weighted average of the sectoral series:

$$\pi_t = \sum_{j=1}^{N} \omega_j \pi_{j,t}, \tag{21}$$

where the ω_js are the sectoral weights, and $\Sigma_j \omega_j = 1$. We can therefore rewrite the Phillips curve as

$$\pi_t = \beta \pi^e_{t+1} + \gamma_g \text{ gap}_t + \sum_{j=1}^{N} \omega_j e_{j,t}. \tag{22}$$

Imperfect information. We assume that economic agents observe only a subset or the sectoral inflations.[23] This subset of sector indexes j is denoted $\mathcal{S} \subseteq \{1, 2, \ldots, N\}$, and its cardinality is $m \leq N$. Agents will use these sectoral inflations as signals $s_{j,t} = \pi_{j,t}$ to form expectations. In our framework, it is mathematically equivalent to replace the set of signals $\{s_{j,t}\}_{j \in S}$ by one aggregate signal s_t. Indeed, for independent signals $j = 1, \ldots, m$ with different precisions $1/\sigma_j^2$, observing m different signals is equivalent to observing a signal with precision: $\Sigma_{j=1}^{m} 1/\sigma_j^2$.[24]

Perceived law of motion and bounded rationality. We have shown in Section III that neither the FIRE nor the IIRE models could easily match the joint dynamics of inflation and inflation expectations, as obtained from a simple VAR. Accordingly, in this section, we build on our analysis in Section IV by assuming that agents form their inflation expectations by extracting a common component from their observations of sectoral inflations. In particular, the agents are assumed to observe $\{\pi_{j,t}\}_{j \in S}$ and to form expectations using this information.[25] The element of bounded rationality is that they perceive the law of motion for sectoral inflations as being composed of a common persistent component $\tilde{z}_t$ and sector-specific transitory components $\tilde{e}_{j,t}$, instead of the sectoral Phillips curves (eq. [22]). Their estimate of the persistent component will be used to form expectations about future aggregate inflation.[26]

Formally, agents have the following perceived law of motion of the economy:

$$\pi_{j,t} = \tilde{z}_t + \tilde{e}_{j,t} = s_{j,t}, \tag{23}$$

$$\pi_t = \tilde{z}_t + \sum_{j \in S} \omega_j \tilde{e}_{j,t} + \sum_{j \notin S} \omega_j \tilde{e}_{j,t}, \tag{24}$$

$$\tilde{z}_t = \tilde{\rho}_z \tilde{z}_{t-1} + \tilde{\epsilon}_{z,t}, \tag{25}$$

with $\tilde{e}_{j,t} \sim N(0, \tilde{\sigma}_j^2)\ \forall\ j$ and $\tilde{\epsilon}_{z,t} \sim N(0, \tilde{\sigma}_z^2)$. The parameters $\tilde{\rho}_z$, $\tilde{\sigma}_j^2$, and $\tilde{\sigma}_z^2$ denote the perceived persistence and variances for the law of motion. Here also, the perceived independent $\tilde{e}_{j,t}$ with different precisions $1/\tilde{\sigma}_j^2$ can be collapsed into a single $\tilde{\epsilon}_t$ with precision: $1/\tilde{\sigma}_\epsilon^2 = \Sigma_{j=1}^m 1/\tilde{\sigma}_j^2$.

The agents endowed with this perceived law of motion will be quite sophisticated. They will use the observed sectoral inflation series to infer the state $\tilde{z}_t$—the perceived common component affecting inflation—and take these beliefs about $\tilde{z}_t$ to form expectations of aggregate inflation. However, they are bounded rational in the sense that they treat the state-space system (eqq. [23]–[25]) as a standard signal-extraction problem in which the noise generated by not observing all the sectors is treated as uncorrelated with the state $\tilde{z}_t$. Because the sectoral inflations are common to all the agents, when the aggregate expectation responds to the signals, these signals will affect the state variable, which will feed back to the signals via the Phillips curve (eq. [22]). As agents fail to recognize that the hidden state may be correlated with the noise in their signals, this has the potential to create a positive feedback loop from noise to inflation.[27] This misinterpretation of the data is the key to creating an amplification mechanism in our expectations formation model.[28]

Solving the model. Using equation (23) together with the aggregate inflation (eq. [24]), we obtain the observational equations from the agent's perspective:

$$\begin{cases} s_t = \tilde{z}_t + \tilde{\epsilon}_t \\ \pi_t = \tilde{z}_t + \tilde{\eta}_t \end{cases}, \tag{26}$$

whereas the actual signal and aggregate inflation are generated by

$$\begin{cases} s_t &= \beta\pi^e_{t+1} + \gamma_g \text{ gap}_t + \epsilon_t \\ \pi_t &= \beta\pi^e_{t+1} + \gamma_g \text{ gap}_t + \eta_t \end{cases}. \tag{27}$$

In these equations, s_t is an average signal from the m independent sectoral signals, with precision $1/\tilde{\sigma}^2_\epsilon$. Using equations (22) and (24), we denote $\eta_t = \Sigma^N_{j=1}\omega_j e_{j,t}$ and $\tilde{\eta}_t = \Sigma^N_{j=1}\omega_j\tilde{e}_{j,t}$, with $\eta_t \sim N(0, \sigma^2_\eta)$ and $\tilde{\eta}_t \sim N(0, \tilde{\sigma}^2_\eta)$. ϵ_t stands for the broad-based shock. The information encoded in s_t is also reflected in π_t so that ϵ_t and η_t are correlated with correlation ρ. For the same reason, $\tilde{\epsilon}_t$ and $\tilde{\eta}_t$ are correlated with correlation $\tilde{\varrho}$. It is possible that $\varrho \neq \tilde{\varrho}$ and both are nonzero.[29]

The agents face the state-space model described by equations (25) and (26). They solve a signal-extraction problem to form belief about the perceived common component, $\tilde{z}_t$, and use it to form expectations about inflation. Because expectations formed in the current period will also affect current inflation and signals that the agents see, we need to be specific about the timing of expectations formation and when expectations affect inflation. In the baseline version of the model, we will allow information extracted from the disaggregated data to be simultaneously determined with inflation, whereas we will assume that aggregate inflation (CPI) is released to households with a lag. This implies that any residual information in aggregate inflation does not feed back contemporaneously to itself.[30] Accordingly, we solve the model adopting the following steps, which is easiest to present as having each period t being composed of two subperiods:[31]

Step 1: In the first subperiod of t, the gap_t realizes. Economic agents form expectations using the signal s_t. We denote the expected inflation formed in this subperiod as $\pi_{t+1|t,0}$. This is the expectation π^e_{t+1} that enters in the Phillips curves (eqq. [18] and [19]). Consistent with the treatment in Sections II and III, we take these expectations as those observed in the Michigan Survey of Consumers.

Step 2: In the second subperiod of t, agents also observe aggregate inflation π_t. They use this extra information to update their belief about future inflation, denoted as $\pi_{t+1|t,1}$. This will be the prior on inflation that will be carried over to the next period $t + 1$.

Step 3: Both expectations $\pi_{t+1|t,0}$ and $\pi_{t+1|t,1}$ are formed from beliefs on the common component $\tilde{z}_t$. We denote these beliefs as $\tilde{z}_{t|t,0}$ and $\tilde{z}_{t|t,1}$. From equations (25) and (26), we see that the links between expected inflation and the common component are

$$\pi_{t+1|t,k} = \tilde{z}_{t+1|t,k} = \tilde{\rho}_z \tilde{z}_{t|t,k} \;\; \forall\, k = 1, 2. \tag{28}$$

Step 4: Denote the innovations in agents' perceived information (signal and aggregate inflation)-generating process (eq. [26]) as

$$\begin{pmatrix} \tilde{\epsilon}_t \\ \tilde{\eta}_t \end{pmatrix} \sim N(\mathbf{0}, \tilde{R}), \;\; \tilde{R} \equiv \begin{pmatrix} \tilde{\sigma}_\epsilon^2 & \tilde{\varrho}\tilde{\sigma}_\epsilon\tilde{\sigma}_\eta \\ \tilde{\varrho}\tilde{\sigma}_\epsilon\tilde{\sigma}_\eta & \tilde{\sigma}_\eta^2 \end{pmatrix}. \tag{29}$$

The agents form weights on $\tilde{\epsilon}_t$ and $\tilde{\eta}_t$, according to the Kalman filter, using their beliefs that s_t and π_t are correlated. Denoting ι_n a $n \times 1$ vector of ones, the stationary Kalman filter is given by

$$\widehat{K} = \tilde{\sigma}^2 \iota_2{}' (\iota_2 \tilde{\sigma}^2 \iota_2{}' + \tilde{R})^{-1}, \tag{30}$$

$$\tilde{\sigma}^2 = \tilde{\rho}_z^2 \left(\tilde{\sigma}^2 - \widehat{K}\iota_2 \tilde{\sigma}^2 \right) + \tilde{\sigma}_z^2, \tag{31}$$

where $\tilde{\sigma}^2$ is the stationary posterior variance of belief on $\tilde{z}_t$. Now note the $\widehat{K}$ is a 1×2 vector, with the first element being the weight on the signal coming from the observed sectoral inflations and the second being the weight on aggregate inflation π_t: $\widehat{K} \equiv (K \quad k)$.

Step 5: In the first subperiod of t, agents observe s_t and form a nowcast of $\tilde{z}_t$:

$$\tilde{z}_{t|t,0} = (1 - K)\tilde{z}_{t|t-1,1} + K s_t. \tag{32}$$

Step 6: In the second subperiod of t, agents observe π_t and update belief on $\tilde{z}_t$:

$$\tilde{z}_{t|t,1} = ((1 - K - k)\tilde{z}_{t|t-1,1} + K s_t + k\pi_t). \tag{33}$$

Following these six steps, the solution of the model will be given by

$$\pi^e_{t+1} = \pi_{t+1|t,0} = \frac{\tilde{\rho}_z(1 - K)}{1 - K\beta\tilde{\rho}_z}\tilde{z}_{t|t-1,1} + \frac{\tilde{\rho}_z K \gamma_g}{1 - K\beta\tilde{\rho}_z}\,\text{gap}_t + \frac{\tilde{\rho}_z K}{1 - K\beta\tilde{\rho}_z}\epsilon_t, \tag{34}$$

$$\pi_t = \beta\pi_{t+1|t,0} + \gamma_g\,\text{gap}_t + \eta_t, \tag{35}$$

$$\begin{aligned} \tilde{z}_{t+1|t,1} &= \tilde{\rho}_z \left(1 - (K + k)\frac{1 - \beta\tilde{\rho}_z}{1 - K\beta\tilde{\rho}_z} \right) \tilde{z}_{t|t-1,1} \\ &+ \tilde{\rho}_z \frac{(K + k)\gamma_g}{1 - K\beta\tilde{\rho}_z}\,\text{gap}_t + \tilde{\rho}_z \left(\frac{K + \tilde{\rho}_z K k \beta}{1 - K\beta\tilde{\rho}_z} \right) \epsilon_t + k\tilde{\rho}_z\eta_t, \end{aligned} \tag{36}$$

$$\text{gap}_t = \rho\, \text{gap}_{t-1} + v_t. \quad (37)$$

Note that signal s_t and aggregate inflation π_t are realized according to equation (27), so expectations $\pi^e_{t+1} = \pi_{t+1|t,0}$ and signal s_t will be simultaneously determined.

The above expectations formation process has the potential to create persistent bouts of inflation in a quasi-self-confirming way. When an adverse (positive) broad-base supply shock ϵ_t hits the economy, economic agents observe an inflation hike in many disaggregate inflation series. This causes them to update their view of the common component $\tilde{z}_t$. If agents believe that their signal is quite informative, this will increase their expected inflation. Because the disaggregated inflations are public signals, the average expectation will increase, which drives up the disaggregate prices they observe. This feedback channel can thereby amplify the response of expected inflation to broad-base shocks on impact.[32] Moreover, in the second subperiod, agents observe π_t, which is also pushed up by expectations. This further supports their belief of positive realization in the common component. As a result, economic agents enter next period with a prior of high inflation. This then creates very persistent responses of both actual and expected inflations to broad-base price shocks. Furthermore, after the initial period of the shock, actual inflation will react almost one to one with expectations, which corresponds to the observation we made in the empirical VAR.

B. *Illustrating the Respective Roles of Imperfect Information and Bounded Rationality Using a Static Version of the Model*

It may be useful to first consider a static model that conveys most of the intuitions for the mechanism at play in the dynamic one. In that static model, equilibrium inflation π depends on expected inflation (within the period) π^e and a shock that is i.i.d. normal $e \sim N(0, \sigma_e^2)$:

$$\pi = \beta \pi^e + e, \quad (38)$$

with $\beta \in [0, 1]$. Economic agents do not observe inflation, but a noisy signal S:

$$S = \pi + \epsilon, \quad (39)$$

with $\epsilon \sim N(0, \sigma_\epsilon^2)$.

Consider first the rational expectation solution in which $\pi^e = E[\pi|s]$. Agents filter the signal S to infer a conditional expectation of e, understanding that their conditional expectation of π influences inflation via equation (38). The equilibrium inflation is then given by

$$\pi^{RE} = \frac{1-(1-\kappa)\beta}{1-\beta}e + \frac{\kappa\beta}{1-\beta}\epsilon, \text{ with } \kappa = \frac{\sigma_e^2}{\sigma_e^2+\sigma_\epsilon^2}. \tag{40}$$

Both the noise ϵ and the shock e contribute the variability of π.

It is convenient to look at the case where the variance of fundamental shock e goes to 0 ($\sigma_e^2 \to 0$). In that case, $\kappa = 0$ so that equilibrium inflation $\pi^{RE} = 0$, even if the signal S is noisy ($\sigma_\epsilon^2 \neq 0$). It is the same solution with full information ($\sigma_\epsilon^2 = 0$) or with imperfect information ($\sigma_\epsilon^2 \neq 0$).

Consider now a model with bounded rationality in which, instead of knowing equation (38), agents believe that inflation is i.i.d.:

$$\pi = \tilde{e}, \tag{41}$$

where $\tilde{e} \sim N(0, \tilde{\sigma}_e^2)$. Observing the signal S, agents read it as $S = \tilde{e} + \varepsilon$ and believe that $\tilde{e}$ and ε are orthogonal. Doing that signal extraction, one can obtain expected inflation and replace it in equation (38) to obtain equilibrium inflation:

$$\pi^{BR} = \frac{1}{1-\tilde{\kappa}\beta}e + \frac{\tilde{\kappa}\beta}{1-\tilde{\kappa}\beta}\epsilon, \tag{42}$$

with $\tilde{\kappa} = \tilde{\sigma}_e^2/\tilde{\sigma}_e^2 + \sigma_\epsilon^2$. It is useful to look again at the limit case $\sigma_e^2 \to 0$. We obtain in that case

$$\pi^{BR} = \frac{\tilde{\kappa}\beta}{1-\tilde{\kappa}\beta}\epsilon. \tag{43}$$

Here the noise accounts for *all* the variability of inflation, whereas it was totally eliminated with rational expectations. The reason is that because of their beliefs (eq. [41]), the agents fail to see that inflation is orthogonal to the noise. Because $\tilde{e}$ is a latent variable, there is no way they can detect that this correlation is not 0. Therefore, noise shocks ϵ affect expectations, therefore inflation, therefore expectations, and so on . . . , which explains the "multiplier" term $1/(1-\tilde{\kappa}\beta)$ in the equilibrium inflation equation.

One should nevertheless note that generically the variance of the signal S will not be equal to the agents' belief $\tilde{\sigma}_e^2 + \sigma_\epsilon^2$. It is reasonable to believe that agents would eventually notice that discrepancy and will change their belief to reach a "self-confirming" situation in which $\tilde{\sigma}_e^2 + \sigma_\epsilon^2$ equals to the variance of the signal S. Would that kill the current "noise multiplier" we have previously highlighted? There are potentially multiple self-confirming equilibrium in this setup.[33] If $\beta > 1/2$, the self-confirming equilibrium most likely to arise under learning is $\tilde{\sigma}_e^2 = (2\beta - 1/(1-\beta)^2)\sigma_\epsilon^2$. In that case, noise shocks are magnified in a quasi-self-fulfilling way, all the volatility of inflation comes from the noise ϵ, and the model equilibrium is qualitatively different from the case of rational expectations. Futhermore, the agents' belief that inflation is volatile cannot be contradicted by the observation given (eq. [41]), that is, under their model of the economy. As we will see, a similar mechanism is at play in our dynamic model.

C. *Quantitative Analysis*

Our aim is not to estimate the model's parameters by matching the impulse responses of the (π_{t+1}^e, π_t) VAR while simultaneously imposing that the parameters governing the agents' perceived law of motion be supported by the data. In particular, we want the parameters of the perceived law of motion to be consistent with that implied by the observed variance as well as the first and second autocovariances of aggregate inflation. In that sense, the model is disciplined in two ways: first, it aims at reproducing the VAR impulse responses; and second, it ensures that there are no large discrepancies between what agents believe and what they observe.

We fix the values of β, ρ, γ_g, σ_η, and σ_v at the values discussed in Section A, when we use the baseline Phillips curve. We estimate the other parameters $\tilde{\rho}_z$, $\tilde{\sigma}_\epsilon$, $\tilde{\varrho}$, ϱ, $\tilde{\sigma}_z$, $\tilde{\sigma}_\eta$, and σ_ϵ by minimum distance as in Gourieroux, Monfort, and Renault (1993). Denote the vector of parameters to be estimated as Θ, the estimates are given by

$$\hat{\Theta} = \text{argmin}_\Theta \begin{pmatrix} \hat{\mathcal{M}} - \frac{1}{N}\sum_n^N \hat{\mathcal{M}}_T^n(\Theta) \\ \\ \mathcal{M}_{\text{beliefs}}(\Theta) - \mathcal{M}_{\text{model}}(\Theta) \end{pmatrix}' W \begin{pmatrix} \hat{\mathcal{M}} - \frac{1}{N}\sum_n^N \hat{\mathcal{M}}_T^n(\Theta) \\ \\ \mathcal{M}_{\text{beliefs}}(\Theta) - \mathcal{M}_{\text{model}}(\Theta) \end{pmatrix}. \quad (44)$$

In this minimization problem, we minimize the weighted norm of a vector composed of two sets of elements. The first set corresponds to fitting the data. $\hat{\mathcal{M}}$ is the vector of moments to match—that is, the 20 periods impulse response functions estimated from the bivariate VAR in Subsection III.A. $\hat{\mathcal{M}}_T^n(\Theta)$ is computed as the average estimated IRF from N simulated random sample of the model with parameter Θ. T is the length for the simulated random sample, which is set to be the same as our actual sample 1969–2023. The second set corresponds to the requirement for consistency of beliefs. $\mathcal{M}_{\text{beliefs}}(\Theta)$ gathers the variance, first- and second-order auto-covariances of inflation as computed from the perceived law of motion, whereas $\mathcal{M}_{\text{model}}(\Theta)$ gathers the same moments as generated by the model. In our baseline estimation, we use the identity matrix as the weighting matrix W. The parameters obtained from the New Keynesian Phillips curve and the minimum distance estimation are reported in table 4.

Figure 12 shows how well the estimated model matches the empirical impulse responses we obtained in Section III.[34] In the signal-extraction problem, economic agents form expectations using the perceived law of motion and their subjective parameters. The large $\tilde{\sigma}_z$ and $\tilde{\rho}_z$ make the agents believe the disaggregated inflation series are very informative about the common component, $\tilde{z}_t$. However, in reality, most of the variations in the disaggregate signals they observe are actually coming from the broad-base supply shock ϵ_t, as σ_ε point estimate is relatively large. As a result, they respond to the broad-base supply shock more aggressively. For this reason, this model with imperfect information and bounded rationality can trigger larger movements of expectations than those with rational expectations, and full or imperfect information. Meanwhile, their beliefs of such high $\tilde{\sigma}_z$ and $\tilde{\rho}_z$ are supported by the realized aggregate inflation that they observe, as we have imposed that consistency of beliefs restriction in our estimation.

Table 4
Parameters

Phillips Curve Parameters			
β	.99	ρ	.89
σ_ν	3.02	γ_g	.0138
σ_η	2.24		
Estimated Parameters (Minimum Distance)			
$\tilde{\sigma}_z$	.73	σ_ϵ	5.88
$\tilde{\rho}_z$	.96	$\tilde{\sigma}_\eta$	2.22
ϱ	.43	$\tilde{\sigma}_\epsilon$	2.24
$\tilde{\varrho}$	.96		

Note: The Phillips curve estimates use the baseline estimation with Hazell et al. (2022) estimate of γ_g. σ_η implied by the variance of the residual e from the Phillips curve.

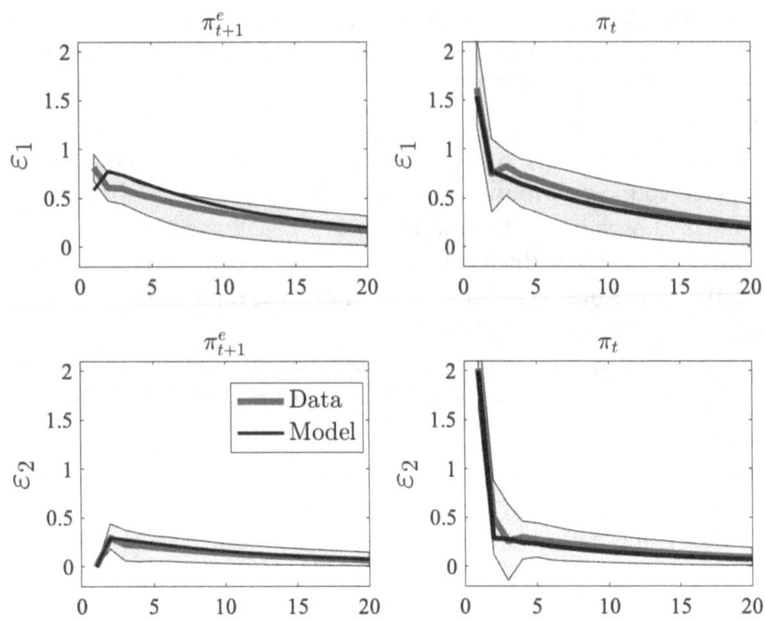

Fig. 12. Impulse responses from data and estimated model. The thick gray line is the IRF from the 2-VAR with actual data, and the black line is the average IRF from simulated data across 200 random samples. The estimated VAR is a VAR(2) with Cholesky decomposition, ordering π^e_{t+1} first. The shaded area represents 95% confidence interval. VAR = vector autoregression, IRF = impulse response function.

From the perspective of the model, the VAR shock ε_1 corresponds to combinations of demand (v) and broad-base (ϵ) shocks. Because the actual variation in v_t is quite small, the shape of the IRF mainly reflects the impact of the broad-based shock. The other VAR shock, ε_2, corresponds to the residual supply shocks η, which is orthogonal to the broad-based shock ϵ. To better illustrate this point, we can construct an orthogonalized normal random variable w_t:

$$w_t = \eta_t - \frac{\operatorname{cov}(\epsilon_t, \eta_t)}{\sigma^2_\epsilon}\epsilon_t = \eta_t - \frac{\varrho\sigma_\eta}{\sigma_\epsilon}\epsilon_t. \tag{45}$$

By construction, w_t is uncorrelated to ϵ_t. This constructed "shock" represents the supply shock that is not used to form the within-period expectations. Because agents observe aggregate inflation only after having formed the expectations that they report, this shock affects measured inflation on impact but reported inflation expectations only with a lag. The VAR shock ε_2 then corresponds to the residual supply shock w_t.

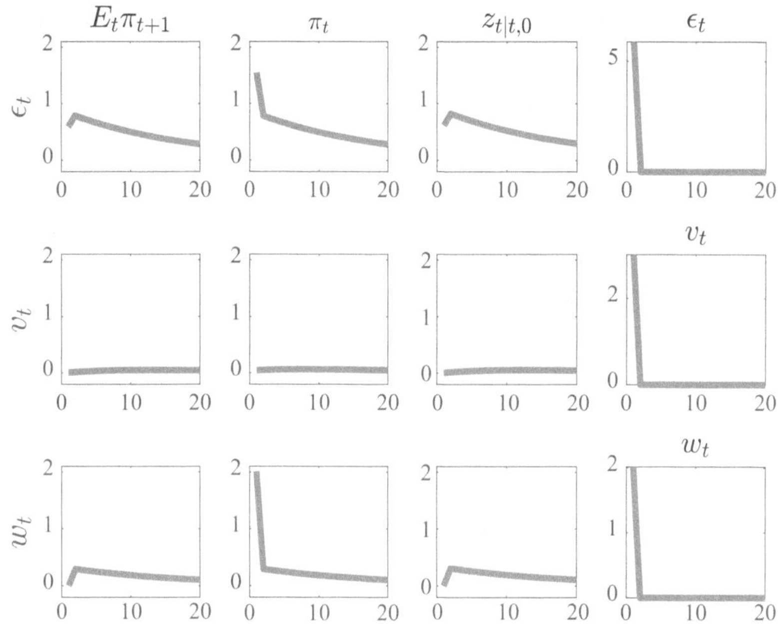

Fig. 13. Impulse responses to structural shocks in the estimated model. These impulse responses to structural shocks are computed from the model solution (eq. [34]) to (eq. [37]) with estimated parameters.

In light of this, figure 13 shows the implied model impulse responses to the three structural shocks: the broad-based supply shock ϵ_t, the demand shock v_t, and the residual supply shock w_t. We see why the broad-based supply shock ϵ_t plays a dominant role in shaping the response to ε_1 in figure 12. This is because the variation in inflation created by v_t is minimal due to the flatness of the Phillips curve. Meanwhile, the response to ε_2 corresponds to a residual supply shock w_t. Moreover, the broad-based shock ϵ_t itself only increases inflation on impact by a factor ϱ. But the broad-based shock triggers a large increase of inflation expectations, which push up aggregate inflation. In comparison, the residual supply shock w_t increases aggregate inflation substantially on impact but does not affect expectations right away. As a result, the response of aggregate inflation is more transitory.

It is worth noting that the three main parameters of the perceived law of motion, $\tilde{\rho}_z$, $\tilde{\sigma}_v$, and $\tilde{\sigma}_\varepsilon$, will be directly reflected in the process for inflation. For example, given the perceived law of motion, $\text{cov}(\pi_t, \pi_{t-2})/\text{cov}(\pi_t, \pi_{t-1})$ gives an estimate of $\tilde{\rho}_z$. Similarly, $\tilde{\sigma}_v$ could then be inferred using $\tilde{\rho}_z$ and $\text{cov}(\pi_t, \pi_{t-1})$. Accordingly, if these moments for actual inflation

Table 5
Variance and Auto-Covariance of Inflation

	Data	PLM	Model
$\text{var}(\pi_t)$	12.52	11.34	11.34
$\text{cov}(\pi_t, \pi_{t-1})$	7.70	6.18	6.28
$\text{cov}(\pi_t, \pi_{t-2})$	6.99	5.92	5.82

Note: PLM stands for "perceived law of motion." The "PLM" and "model" moments are the average moment across 200 random samples. In the estimations, we penalize distance between data and model 2-VAR responses as well as distance between these three moments in the perceived law of motion and in the model. VAR = vector autoregression.

were far from those implied by the agent's subjective model and if agents were learning, they would realize the discrepancy between their subjective model and reality and will adjust their beliefs accordingly. Table 5 therefore reports the first three moments of the inflation auto-covariance function generated by the model and those implied by the beliefs of agents. As we can see, they are very close to implying that agents would have little reason to change their beliefs had we allowed them to learn.

Finally, in our estimation procedure, we did not directly use the gap as one observable and did not try to match the empirical trivariate VAR (π_t, π^e_{t+1}, gap_t) that we estimated in Section III. In figure 14, we compare these estimated impulse responses with those obtained from the same trivariate VAR estimated with 200 random samples of our estimated model. The match is indeed very good. Note that the model responses of gap_t to the first two shocks ε_1 and ε_2 are 0 by construction, as gap_t is modeled as an exogenous shock.

D. *Filtered Shocks and Counterfactuals*

Using the state-space representation of our estimated model, we can use Kalman filter smoothing to form projections of the latent states and the shocks implied by the model. The latent variable $\tilde{z}_{t+1|t,1}$ corresponds to the common component C_t the agents perceived using the disaggregate signals. The three shocks to the economy are the demand shock v_t, the broad-based supply shock ϵ_t, and the residual supply shock w_t. Shocks are displayed in figure 15. Because the Phillips curve is quite flat, the data on inflation and expected inflation do not depend much on the gap and therefore contain little information on it. As a result, the recovered series on v_t is imprecise but mainly irrelevant. This can be partly seen from the fact that the variance of recovered v_t is merely 0.04, whereas the true variance of v_t should be 3.01.

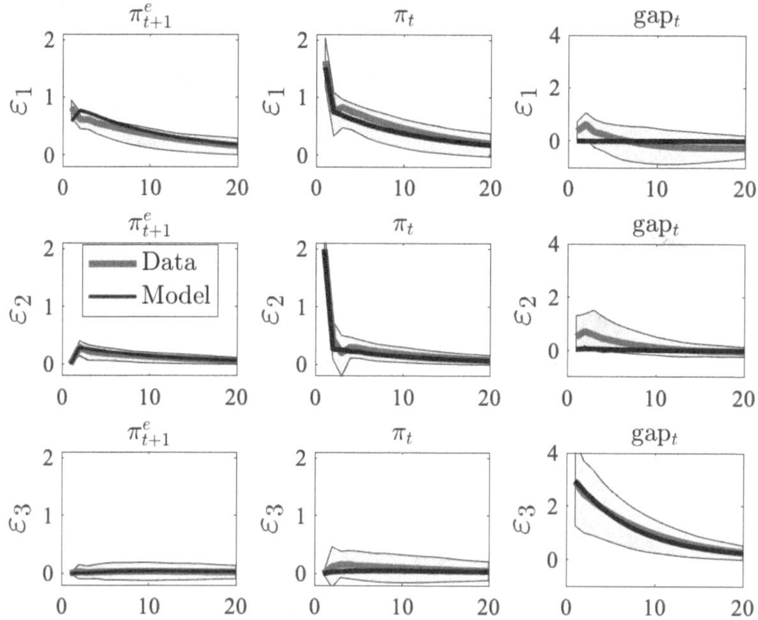

Fig. 14. Trivariate VAR IRF from data and model simulation. Thick gray line is IRF from 3-VAR with actual data, and black line is average IRF from simulated data across 200 random samples. The shaded area represents the 95% confidence interval. IRF = impulse response function, VAR = vector autoregression.

On the contrary, the recovered series for ϵ_t and w_t are quite trustworthy, because the observables contain lots of information on these two shocks. We illustrate these points using simulated data in appendix H (http://www.nber.org/data-appendix/c14985/appendix.pdf#page=25).

In our model, the system of inflation and expected inflation is driven by a latent variable $\tilde{z}_{t+1|t,1}$, which is the common component the agents perceived using the disaggregate signals. This variable can be obtained using the Kalman filter smoothing approach mentioned above. In figure 16, we scatter the backed-out $\tilde{z}_{t+1|t,1}$ against the common component C_t we extracted using the actual CPI disaggregated inflation series in Section C. The correlation between these two series is 0.91, suggesting that the perceived common component in our model contains similar information to the common component directly extracted from disaggregated data, although only aggregate data are used in the model.

We then perform a counterfactual simulation starting in 2020. We simulate the economy with the broad-based shock ϵ_t. The resulting paths for headline inflation and inflation expectations give the contribution of

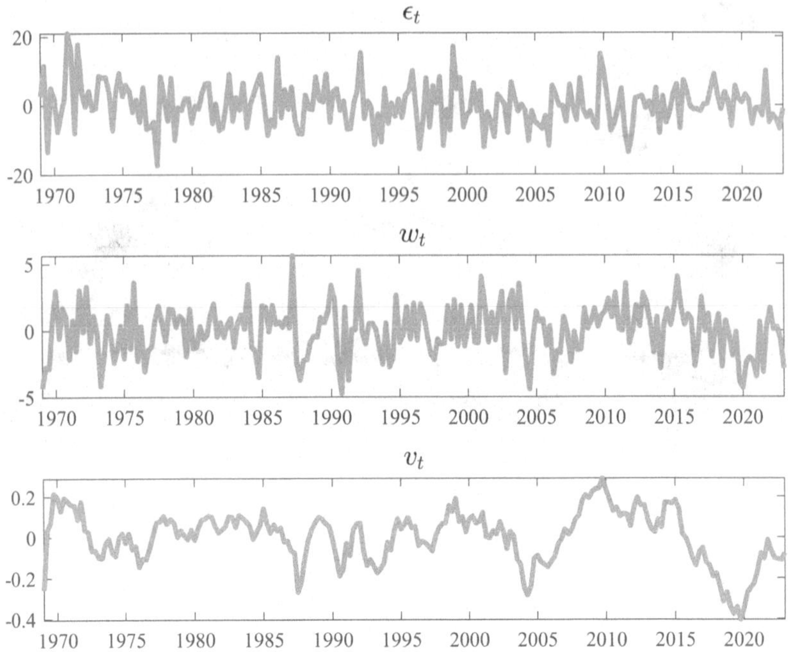

Fig. 15. Filtered shocks from the estimated model. The demand shock v_t, the broad-based supply shock ϵ_t, and the residual supply shock w_t are recovered by Kalman filter smoothing using the estimated model.

that shock to realized headline inflation and inflation expectations. Figure 17 shows these counterfactual paths. Inflation is much more volatile than expectations, because in the model, it is a filtered version of the broad-based shock that determines expectations. For example, in 2022Q1, the broad-based shock puts headline inflation at 8.2%, whereas it would have been 4.1% absent of shocks and was actually 10.6%. More than half of the deviation of headline inflation from its unconditional mean is therefore attributable to the broad-based shock. In the same quarter, inflation expectations are 7.5% with the broad-based shock, instead of 4.7% unconditionally and 7.9% in the data. Virtually all the deviation of expectations from their unconditional mean is explained by the broad-based supply shock.

VI. Conclusion

This paper began by presenting evidence in support of the prepandemic view that the Phillips curve is quasiflat and that supply shocks are mainly

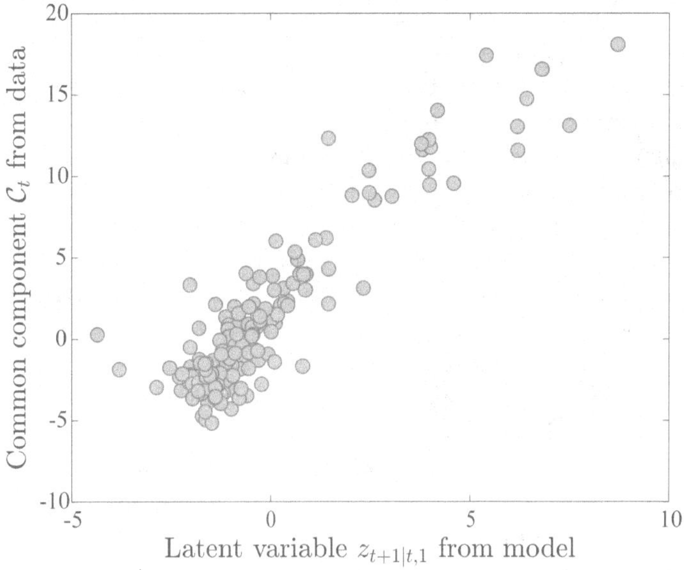

Fig. 16. Filtered shocks from the estimated model. On this figure, the latent variable $\tilde{z}_{t+1|t,1}$ is the "common component" the agents perceived using the disaggregate signals, as obtained from Kalman filter smoothing using the estimated model. It is plotted against the common component C_t extracted from the consumer price index components in Section IV.

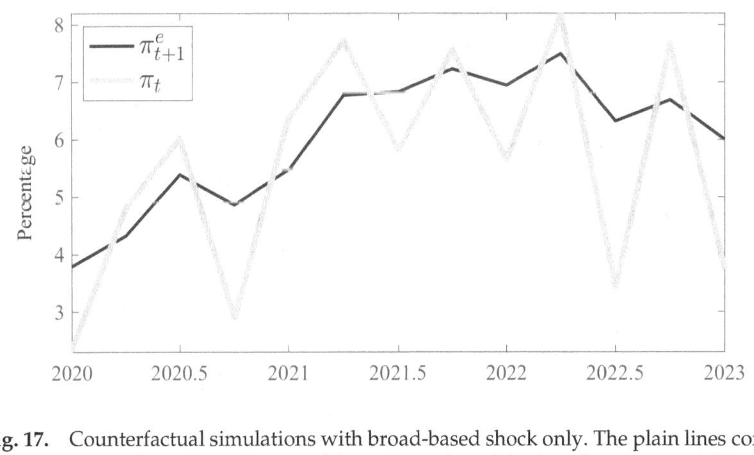

Fig. 17. Counterfactual simulations with broad-based shock only. The plain lines correspond to counterfactual simulations of the estimated model, when the economy is hit only by the broad-based shock ϵ_t for both expected inflation and actual inflation. Note that in the model the unconditional mean of inflation is 4.1%.

temporary. We also presented VAR evidence indicating that inflation expectations and one-step-ahead inflation move very closely together, suggesting that either agents are very good at predicting inflation or that inflation expectations are potentially an important driver of inflation. After failing to explain the VAR patterns under rational expectations, we proposed an explanation to the observed inflation dynamics based on bounded rationality whereby agents have an incomplete understanding of the data generating process driving inflation.

In our bounded rational framework, persistent inflation arises when the economy is simultaneously hit by supply shocks across many sectors, even if the shocks themselves are not persistent. When agents see prices rise in many sectors, they revise their view about the common force that drives inflation. This revision leads to higher-than-expected inflation, which makes the initially temporary disturbances propagate through time in a quasi-self-fulfilling way. In contrast, when agents see prices rise in only a small set of sectors, they recognize that this is not an aggregate phenomenon and therefore do not revise their expectations much. This results in sector-specific shocks causing only minor movements in inflation. Both these features are needed to match the joint dynamics of inflation and inflation expectations as captured by a bivariate VAR. In support of our model's main assumption, we showed that the common component extracted from a large set of disaggregate data correlates closely with measured inflation expectations. We also showed that this common component extracted from disaggregated data correlates closely with the model counterpart inferred only from aggregate data. Together, we believe these elements support a theory of persistent bouts of inflation driven primarily by temporary but broad-based supply shocks that get transmitted to expectations. The sectors that seem to disproportionately affect the common component of inflation, and therefore drive potential bouts of inflation, are full-service meals, limited-service meals, and other foods away from home. Keeping watch of inflation in these sectors, in addition to shelter and energy, may help identify mounting inflation pressure early on.

Endnotes

Author email addresses: Beaudry (Paul.Beaudry@ubc.ca), Hou (sevhou1989@gmail.com). We thank our discussants Gabriel Chodorow-Reich and Jonathon Hazell; editors John Leahy, Martin Eichenbaum, and Valerie Ramey; as well as the participants in the NBER Macroeconomics Annual 2024 conference and the various seminars in which that work was presented. For acknowledgments, sources of research support, and disclosure of the author's material financial relationships, if any, please see https://www.nber.org

/books-and-chapters/nber-macroeconomics-annual-2024-volume-39/dominant-role-expectations-and-broad-based-supply-shocks-driving-inflation.

1. The latter has been advocated as a better proxy for labor market tightness by, among others, Ball et al. (2022), Michaillat and Saez (2022), and Benigno and Eggertsson (2023).

2. Demand shocks also affect inflation in our setup, but this effect is very weak because of the flat Phillips curve.

3. Moreover, as the agents are not fully informed about the actual data generating process, they will use some perceived law of motion to help them form expectations. We will restrict this perceived law of motion to generate inflation moments that are close to the actual ones.

4. To derive such a Phillips curve, one generally needs to assume that agents' expectations satisfy the law of iterative expectations (see Galí 2015). In a later part of the paper, we will propose a model for the formation of inflation expectations where agents do not have a full understanding of the data generating process. However, these agents will nonetheless be statistically sophisticated, and their expectations will satisfy the law of iterative expectations.

5. Our preference would be to use quarter-to-quarter expected inflation. However, the Michigan Survey of Consumers reports expectations for CPI inflation for the next year. To extract a quarter estimate from these data, we rescale the 1-year-ahead expected inflation assuming survey respondents believe that quarter-to-quarter inflation follows a first order autoregressive process with persistence $\tilde{\rho}$, which needs not be equal to the actual persistence of inflation. The estimated $\tilde{\rho} = 0.89$. This adjustment only affects the point estimate of β. For more details, we refer to Beaudryet al. (2024).

6. The unemployment gap is computed as the unemployment rate minus the noncyclical rate of unemployment from the Federal Reserve Bank of St. Louis database FRED (code NROU).

7. Reis (2021) analyzes the business-cycle dynamics of the discrepancy between market and survey measures but focuses on long-run inflation expectations.

8. In Hazell et al. (2022), the authors provide an implied aggregate slope of the Phillips curve, with R-CPI as the measure of inflation and negative unemployment gap as the measure of market slackness. From footnote 24 in Hazell et al. (2022), this aggregate slope of the Phillips curve $= 0.58 \times 0.0062 + 0.42 \times 0.0243 = 0.0138$.

9. In our analysis for post-2008 data, we exclude the 2020q2 observation given that measuring labor market tightness at a time of massive lockdowns is very controversial.

10. Endogeneity issues can complicate inference from this figure. Under the null hypothesis that our Phillips curve is well specified, forecast errors should reflect supply or markup shocks. In contrast, if the slope is misspecified, then the forecast errors would also include a term directly related to labor market tightness. In this latter case, such misspecification should show up as a systematic relationship between forecast errors and labor market tightness. However, a strong endogenous relation between supply shocks and labor market tightness could hide this effect. Although we see this as a possibility, we believe it is likely of second-order importance over this sample. We have explored the potential relevance of this issue by using high frequency identified monetary shocks to instrument labor market tightness when regressing forecast errors on labor market tightness. We have not found evidence of endogeneity bias.

11. To be specific, we use 12 lags of the Romer and Romer (2004) shocks (extended by Wieland and Yang 2020) and their square as instruments.

12. Also note that the presence of direct cost channel matters in the context of asking which expectations are more relevant when estimating Phillips curve. See a comprehensive discussion in Reis (2023).

13. In that case, we keep only one lag in the VAR, as the sample is small.

14. We multiply the Hazell et al. (2022) estimate by four because we use here annualized quarterly inflation and expected inflation.

15. When we estimate an AR process with more lags, only the estimate on the first lag is significant.

16. The detailed derivations are left to appendix F (http://www.nber.org/data-appendix/c14985/appendix.pdf#page=21).

17. We show in appendix F that the VAR dynamics cannot be matched by a hybrid Phillips curve in a model where a fraction of agents uses adaptive expectations or where agents adopt k-level thinking as in Beaudry, Carter, and Lahiri (2023).

18. See Stock and Watson (2011) for a thorough review.

19. There are no constants in the model because we use standardized sectoral inflations $\pi_{j,t}$.

20. We use Spot Crude Oil Price: West Texas Intermediate (WTI) as our proxy for oil prices.

21. Note that we could allow for different responses of disaggregate inflations to expectations (β_j) and labor market conditions ($\gamma_{g,j}$). This would give some extra degrees of freedom to the model in our quantitative analysis later. At this stage, we abstract for this extra layer of heterogeneity between sectors and assume $\beta_j = \beta$ and $\gamma_{g,j} = \gamma_g$ for all j. We could also introduce both aggregate expected inflation expectations and sector j-specific expected inflation. Again, we keep minimal the deviations from the standard model and only introduce aggregate expected inflation.

22. In our model specification, we are not explicitly discussing monetary policy. However, our framework is implicitly assuming that monetary policy is such that (1) it ensures that the gap is centered at 0 and (2) inflation in the long run is well anchored.

23. We do not take a stand on what the causes are for the agents not being fully attentive to all the sectoral inflations. Many frameworks such as rational inattention (Sims 2003) or sparsity (Gabaix 2014) can create such a partial information environment.

24. See appendix E (http://www.nber.org/data-appendix/c14985/appendix.pdf#page=18) for the derivation.

25. For example, D'Acunto et al. (2020) document prevalent evidence that consumers use prices they are exposed to in their daily shopping experience to form inflation expectations.

26. Such a signal-extraction formulation is widely used in the literature about inflation expectations. Examples are among others Coibion and Gorodnichenko (2015a) and Bordalo et al. (2020).

27. In the perceived law of motion, the information relevant for forming expectation is the common component. As a result, the agent will treat the transitory sectoral supply shock $\tilde{e}_{j,t}$ as a noise. However, $\tilde{e}_{j,t}$ is different from a pure "noise shock," as in Lorenzoni (2009), which is typically interpreted as a demand shock. The crucial difference is that $\tilde{e}_{j,t}$ will have direct impact on actual inflation even if it does not pass into expectation.

28. Another feature of the above observational equation is that the signals are weighted by their precisions that do not depend on their actual weights ω_j in the aggregate price index. In other words, a category that has a very low weight in the aggregate price index can be more informative as a category that has significant weight but with a lower signal-to-noise ratio. This feature is in line with our finding in Section IV that the weights of disaggregate price indices in the CPI basket are not highly correlated with the estimated weights from Kalman filter smoothing.

29. See appendix E (http://www.nber.org/data-appendix/c14985/appendix.pdf#page=18) for complete derivations of equations (27) and (26).

30. In appendix I (http://www.nber.org/data-appendix/c14985/appendix.pdf#page=30), we reestimate the model under the assumption that inflation expectations are reported *after* observing current inflation. Differences in the results are minor.

31. An alternative formulation would be thinking of the belief on z_t as formed conditional on information set $\mathcal{I}_t = \{\pi_{t-1}, s_t\}$ in each period t. The two will give equivalent representation of the model.

32. Note that this amplification comes from the fact that the agents fail to understand expectations $\pi_{t+1|t,0}$ as part of the perceived common component $\tilde{z}_t$. More precisely, they fail to understand the hidden state is correlated with the noise of their signal. This arises because the signals the agents observe are endogenous.

33. An obvious self-confirming equilibrium is one in which $\tilde{\sigma}_\varepsilon^2 = 0$. If the agents believe that inflation is a constant, they will attribute all the variations in the signal to the noise ($\tilde{\kappa} = 0$), and we will have indeed $\sigma^2_{\pi^{BR}} = 0$. We are back to rational expectations and inflation is not reacting to the noise. But under simple learning schemes, it can be shown that the agents will not converge to this equilibrium.

34. In appendix G (http://www.nber.org/data-appendix/c14985/appendix.pdf#page=24), we also include the IRFs using actual and simulated data from our baseline model with an alternative order of variables for the Choleski decomposition. Because the Choleski VAR is here used as a way to summarize the joint dynamics of inflation and inflation expectations, we would expect the data generated by a correct model to give similar results as the actual data when summarized with a different ordering of the variables. Appendix G shows that this is indeed the case.

References

Acharya, V. V., M. Crosignani, T. Eisert, and C. Eufinger. 2023. "How Do Supply Shocks to Inflation Generalize? Evidence from the Pandemic Era in Europe." Working Paper no. 31790, NBER, Cambridge, MA.

Ball, L. M., D. Leigh, and P. Mishra. 2022. "Understanding U.S. Inflation during the COVID Era." Working Paper no. 30613, NBER, Cambridge, MA.

Barnichon, R., and G. Mesters. 2020. "Identifying Modern Macro Equations with Old Shocks." *Quarterly Journal of Economics* 135 (4): 2255–98.

Beaudry, P., T. J. Carter, and A. Lahiri. 2023. "The Central Bank's Dilemma: Look through Supply Shocks or Control Inflation Expectations?" Working Paper no. 31741, NBER, Cambridge, MA.

———, C. Hou, and F. Portier. 2024. "Monetary Policy when the Phillips Curve Is Quite Flat." *American Economic Journal: Macroeconomics* 16 (1): 1–28.

Benigno, P., and G. B. Eggertsson. 2023. "It's Baaack: The Surge in Inflation in the 2020s and the Return of the Non-Linear Phillips Curve." Working Paper no. 31197, NBER, Cambridge, MA.

Blanchard, O. J., and B. S. Bernanke. 2023. "What Caused the US Pandemic-Era Inflation?" Working Paper no. 31417, NBER, Cambridge, MA.

Bordalo, P., N. Gennaioli, Y. Ma, and A. Shleifer. 2020. "Overreaction in Macroeconomic Expectations." *American Economic Review* 110 (9): 2748–82.

Carrière-Swallow, Y., P. Deb, D. Furceri, D. Jiménez, and J. D. Ostry. 2023. "Shipping Costs and Inflation." *Journal of International Money and Finance* 130:102771.

Carvalho, C., S. Eusepi, E. Moench, and B. Preston. 2023. "Anchored Inflation Expectations." *American Economic Journal: Macroeconomics* 15 (1): 1–47.

Coibion, O., and Y. Gorodnichenko. 2015a. "Information Rigidity and the Expectations Formation Process. A Simple Framework and New Facts." *American Economic Review* 105 (8): 2644–78.

———. 2015b. "Is the Phillips Curve Alive and Well after All? Inflation Expectations and the Missing Disinflation." *American Economic Journal: Macroeconomics* 7 (1): 197–232.

Coibion, O., Y. Gorodnichenko, and R. Kamdar. 2018. "The Formation of Expectations, Inflation, and the Phillips Curve." *Journal of Economic Literature* 56 (4): 1447–91.

D'Acunto, F., U. Malmendier, J. Ospina, and M. Weber. 2020. "Exposure to Grocery Prices and Inflation Expectations." *Journal of Political Economy* 129 (5): 1615–39.

Gabaix, X. 2014. "A Sparsity-Based Model of Bounded Rationality." *Quarterly Journal of Economics* 129 (4): 1661–1710.

Galí, J. 2015. *Monetary Policy, Inflation, and the Business Cycle: An Introduction to the New Keynesian Framework and Its Applications*. 2nd ed. Princeton, NJ: Princeton University Press.

Gelain, P., N. Iskrev, K. J. Lansing, and C. Mendicino. 2019. "Inflation Dynamics and Adaptive Expectations in an Estimated DSGE Model." *Journal of Macroeconomics* 59:258–77.

Gourieroux, C., A. Monfort, and E. Renault. 1993. "Indirect Inference." *Journal of Applied Econometrics* 8:S85–S118.

Hazell, J., J. Herreño, E. Nakamura, and J. Steinsson. 2022. "The Slope of the Phillips Curve: Evidence from U.S. States." *Quarterly Journal of Economics* 137 (3): 1299–1344.

Hommes, C., K. Mavromatis, T. Özden, and M. Zhu. 2023. "Behavioral Learning Equilibria in New Keynesian Models." *Quantitative Economics* 14 (4): 1401–45.

———, and M. Zhu. 2014. "Behavioral Learning Equilibria." *Journal of Economic Theory* 150:778–814.

Lansing, K. 2009. "Time Varying U.S. Inflation Dynamics and the New Keynesian Phillips Curve." *Review of Economic Dynamics* 12 (2): 304–26.

Lorenzoni, G. 2009. "A Theory of Demand Shocks." *American Economic Review* 99(5): 2050–84.

Michaillat, P., and E. Saez. 2022. "$u^* = \sqrt{uv}$." Working Paper no. 30211, NBER, Cambridge, MA.

Reis, R. 2021. "The People versus the Markets: A Parsimonious Model of Inflation Expectations." Discussion Paper no. 15624, CEPR, Washington, DC.

———. 2023. "Four Mistakes in the Use of Measures of Expected Inflation." *AEA Papers and Proceedings* 113:47–51.

Romer, C. D., and D. H. Romer. 2004. "A New Measure of Monetary Shocks: Derivation and Implications." *American Economic Review* 94 (4): 1055–1084.

Sims, C. A. 2003. "Implications of Rational Inattention." *Journal of Monetary Economics* 50 (3): 665–90, Swiss National Bank/Study Center Gerzensee Conference on Monetary Policy under Incomplete Information.

Stock, J. H., and M. W. Watson. 2011. "35 Dynamic Factor Models." In *The Oxford Handbook of Economic Forecasting*, ed. Michael P. Clements and David F. Hendry. Oxford: Oxford University Press.

Wieland, J., and M.-J. Yang. 2020. "Financial Dampening." *Journal of Money, Credit and Banking* 52 (1): 79–113.

Woodford, M. 2001. "Imperfect Common Knowledge and the Effects of Monetary Policy." Working Paper no. 8673, NBER, Cambridge, MA.

Comment

Jonathon Hazell, *London School of Economics,* United Kingdom

I. Overview

This paper tackles one of the most—if not *the* most—important business cycle questions of the postpandemic period in the United States: Why did inflation rise so much? Beaudry, Hou, and Portier offer an important and convincing answer in two steps. First, they show that the flat and linear Phillips curve, which accurately characterized the relationship between inflation and real activity before 2020, continues to fit the data well after 2020. According to the Phillips curve, the proximate cause of rising inflation was a rise in inflation expectations. Second, the authors advance a theory of why inflation expectations rose. They consider a model with incomplete information and bounded rationality. When supply shocks hit many sectors at the same time—a "broad-based supply shock"—then inflation expectations rise. Inflation itself rises, too, via the Phillips curve.

This comment has two parts. First, I summarize the context of the paper and its main findings while replicating the main results of the paper. Second, I discuss the scope of the contributions. I argue that the choice of inflation expectations is critical, and the results hint at an important role for fiscal policy. I expect that Beaudry et al.'s paper will become central to the fast-growing literature on the postpandemic inflation.

NBER Macroeconomics Annual, volume 39, 2025.
 https://doi.org/10.1086/735269

II. Inflation Dynamics before and after 2020

A. Background: Inflation Dynamics before 2020

This paper studies the New Keynesian Phillips curve, the relationship

$$\pi_t = \beta\pi^e_{t,t+1} - \kappa\tilde{u}_t + \varepsilon_t, \tag{1}$$

between inflation π_t, inflation expectations $\pi^e_{t,t+1}$, the current gap between unemployment and its "natural rate" under flexible prices $\tilde{u}_t$, and supply shocks ε_t.

Before 2020, a consensus formed that the Phillips curve was positively sloped but flat. That is, the comovement between real activity and inflation was weak. Equivalently, the "slope" coefficient κ in equation (1) was positive but near 0. A variety of methods arrived at this result. For instance, Hazell et al. (2022) found a flat Phillips curve using state level inflation data. Various limited- and full-information time series methods applied to aggregate data arrived at the same conclusion—for instance, Blanchard (2016), Ball and Mazumder (2019), Stock and Watson (2020), and Del Negro et al. (2020), among others.

The flat Phillips curve is appealing because it makes sense of the major inflation episodes between 1978 and 2020 in a unified framework. Consider the "Missing Disinflation" during the Great Recession. Inflation failed to fall by much even as unemployment rose dramatically (Coibion and Gorodnichenko 2015). The flat Phillips curve rationalizes the data, given a weak relationship between unemployment and inflation. Or consider the "Missing Reinflation" of the late 1990s and late 2010s. Robust expansions led to low unemployment, yet inflation failed to increase much. The flat Phillips curve makes sense of the data via the decoupling of inflation and real activity. The flat Phillips curve can also explain the "Volcker Disinflation," the large fall in inflation in the early 1980s. Through the lens of equation (1), disinflations happen via large falls in inflation expectations, which indeed happened in the early 1980s.

B. The Flat Phillips Curve: Post Hoc Theorizing?

The flat Phillips curve can successfully explain past data. But this success may not be reassuring. History is full of examples in which some version of the Phillips curve successfully explains past data but then fails to explain the latest inflation episode. One apt term is "post hoc theorizing."

A theory may well be able to rationalize the data it was designed to explain, without making sense of newer data. Ball and Mazumder (2019) discuss this danger in a wonderful quote that summarizes the troubled history of Phillips curve estimation: "Unfortunately, researchers have repeatedly needed to modify the Phillips curve to fit new data. Friedman added expected inflation to the specification in Samuelson and Solow (1960). Subsequent authors have added supply shocks, time variation in the Phillips-curve slope, and time variation in the natural rate of unemployment. Each modification helped explain past data, but, as Stock and Watson (2010) observe, the history of the Phillips curve 'is one of apparently stable relationships falling apart upon publication.'"

This quote explains the stakes of Beaudry et al.'s paper. As figure 1 shows, the 2020s were another major inflation episode in which inflation rose from around 2% to almost 7%. Beaudry et al. ask whether the flat Phillips curve can rationalize the new data. Alternatively, the flat Phillips curve might be post hoc theorizing, which "falls apart" with new data. If so, then the Phillips curve is of questionable value. A relationship that makes sense of past episodes but must be modified with each successive episode is surely of limited use.

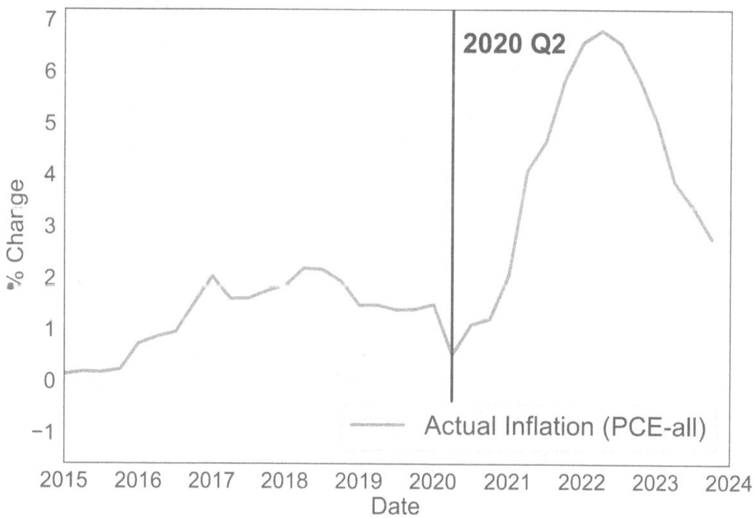

Fig. 1. Inflation before and after 2020. This figure plots headline personal consumption expenditures (PCE) inflation from 2015Q1 to 2023Q3, where inflation is the percent difference in the price level over the previous four quarters.

C. *The Flat Phillips Curve: An Illustration*

I now illustrate the success of the flat Phillips curve before 2020. In doing so, I develop an empirical framework to be used throughout the comment, which parallels Beaudry et al.'s paper. I estimate the regression

$$\pi_t = \beta\pi^e_{t,t+4} - \kappa\tilde{u}_t + \gamma e_t + \varepsilon_t, \tag{2}$$

where π_t is annualized quarterly personal consumption expenditures (PCE) headline inflation, $\pi^e_{t,t+4}$ is households' median 1-year-ahead inflation expectations from the Michigan Consumer Survey, $\tilde{u}_t$ is the difference between quarterly unemployment and its natural rate as measured by the Congressional Budget Office, e_t is annualized quarterly PCE energy inflation, and ε_t is a regression residual that may be interpreted as a supply shock. In the regression, κ is the parameter of interest, the "slope" of the Phillips curve. I estimate this regression by ordinary least squares (OLS) from 1984Q1 to 2020Q2. In using OLS, I ignore the important issue of omitted variable bias (e.g., McLeay and Tenreyro 2020).[1]

Figure 2 shows that the flat Phillips curve can rationalize inflation dynamics before 2020. In the figure, I plot annualized quarterly inflation in the thick black line and inflation predicted by regression equation (2) in the thick, light gray line for 1995–2020. The model is successful: actual and predicted inflation align closely. In the dark-dashed line, the light-dashed line, and the thick, dark gray line, I plot the contribution due to inflation expectations, energy, and the unemployment gap. The contribution of unemployment to inflation is small, because the line associated with unemployment varies little—even though changes in unemployment were often large. As such, the Phillips curve is flat.

D. *Contribution 1: The Flat Phillips Curve Fits after 2020*

Beaudry et al.'s first contribution shows that the flat Phillips curve fits the data well after 2020. To replicate this analysis, I extend the previous empirical exercise. I take the coefficients of the Phillips curve estimated using data from before 2020Q2; combine them with unemployment, inflation expectations, and energy growth after 2020; and predict inflation after 2020. If the flat pre-2020 Phillips curve fits the post-2020 data, then predicted and actual inflation will align. If the flat Phillips curve cannot explain the postpandemic inflation, then predicted inflation will fall below actual inflation.

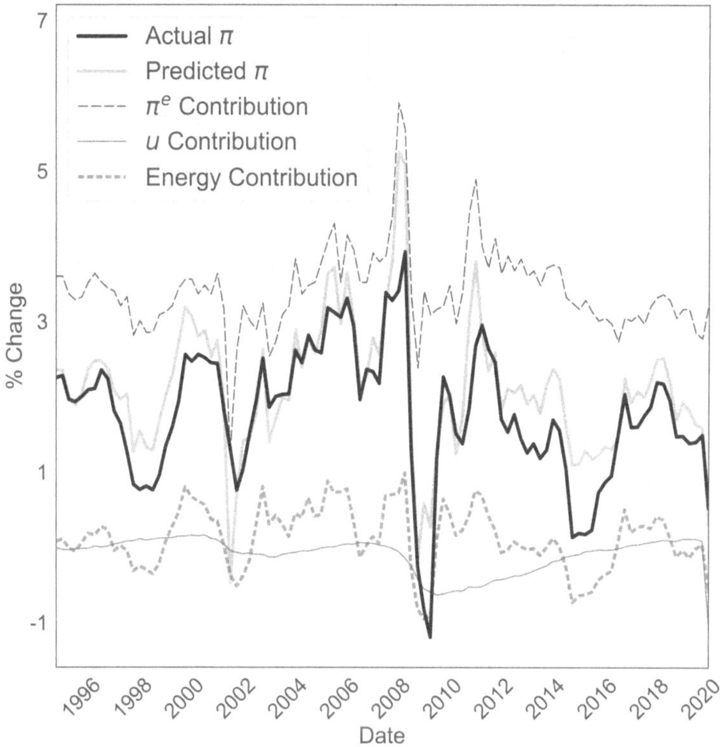

Fig. 2. Inflation dynamics: a historical decomposition. This graph estimates the Phillips curve, equation (2), relating personal consumption expenditures (PCE) inflation to median 1-year-ahead household inflation expectations from the Michigan survey, the unemployment gap, and PCE energy price growth, using 1984Q1–2020Q1 data. The figure plots actual inflation and inflation predicted by the model. The figure also plots the contribution of each individual regressor toward explaining overall inflation.

Figure 3 shows that the flat pre-2020 Phillips curve characterizes the postpandemic inflation well. In the figure, the black line plots the evolution of annualized quarterly inflation before and after 2020. There is the sharp increase in inflation from 2021 onward, with inflation peaking at around 7%. The thick, light gray line shows the key finding of the paper. Predicted inflation, using the pre-2020 Phillips curve coefficients and the subsequent path of $\pi^e_{t,t+4}$, $\tilde{u}_t$ and e_t, closely matches actual inflation.

Beaudry et al.'s finding is remarkable and invites several comments. First, the model is successful out of sample. The coefficients are estimated only using data up to 2020Q2, and yet, the post-2020 fit is good. Second, the Phillips curve can explain the data well, despite its flatness. The dashed dark line shows that the contribution of unemployment to

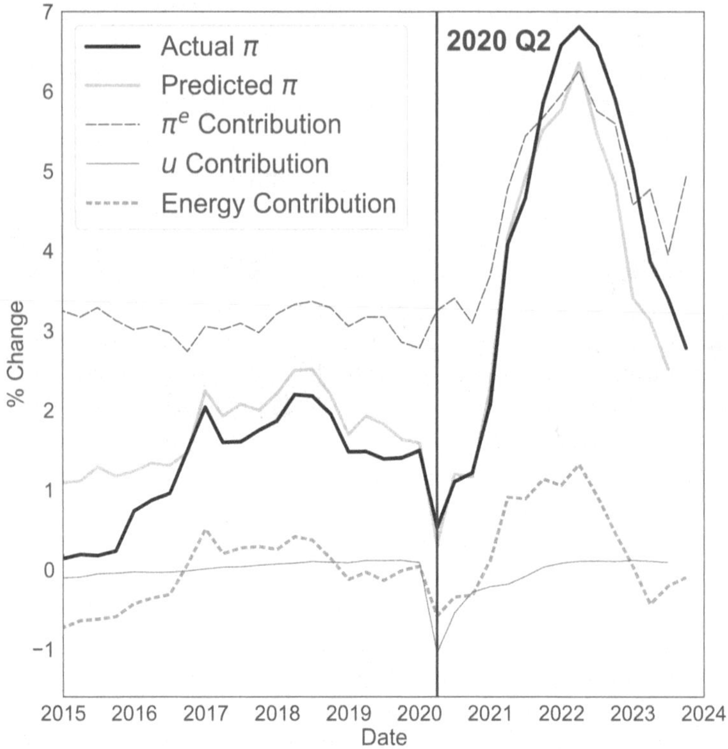

Fig. 3. Predicting post-2020 inflation using pre-2020 Phillips curve. The figure uses estimated regression coefficients from estimating equation (2)—the relationship between inflation, inflation expectations, the unemployment gap, and energy price growth—using data up to 2020Q2. The figure then uses the realized path of inflation expectations, the unemployment gap, and energy price growth after 2020, combined with the pre-2020 regression coefficients, to predict inflation after 2020. The figure also plots the contribution associated with each regressor to predicting overall inflation.

explaining inflation is small, as before 2020. Third, the proximate cause of higher inflation is higher inflation expectations. The thick, dark gray line is the contribution of inflation expectations to actual inflation, which is by far the largest contributor. The reason for this large contribution is that household inflation expectations increased rapidly, as figure 4 shows.

E. *Contribution 2: Inflation Expectations and "Broad-Based Supply Shocks"*

The first contribution, then, is that the flat Phillips curve characterizes the postpandemic inflation, and that the proximate cause was rising

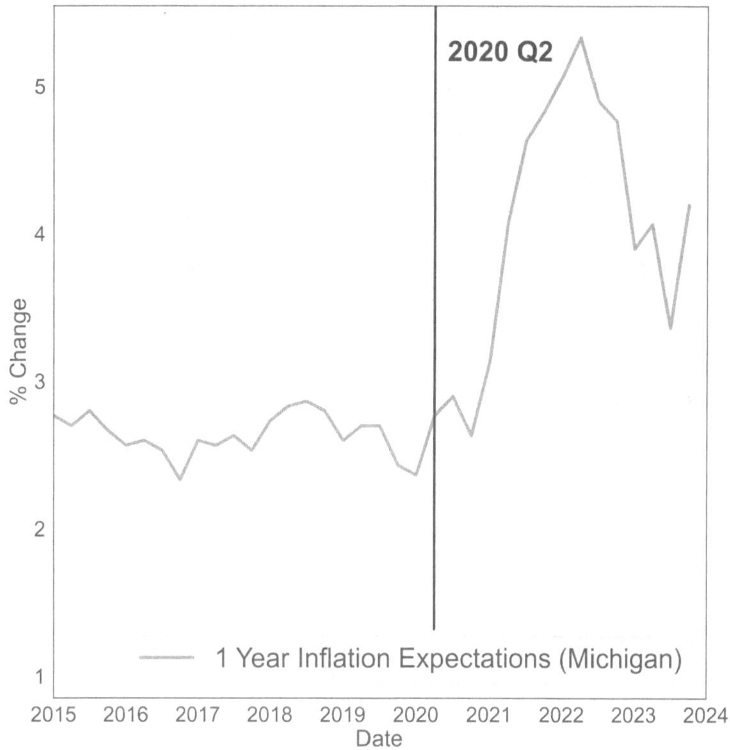

Fig. 4. Michigan consumer survey inflation expectations. This figure plots median household inflation expectations over the next year, at quarterly frequency, from the Michigan Consumer Survey. The sample period is 2015Q1–2023Q3.

inflation expectations. The second contribution is a model of why inflation expectations rose by so much.

The authors propose a theory with incomplete information and bounded rationality. In the model, inflation obeys the New Keynesian Phillips curve, as in equation (1). There are a number of sectors that together form an aggregate Phillips curve. The novelty is how the authors model expectation formation. Agents in the model perceive inflation as a common component $\tilde{z}_t$ as well as sectoral supply shocks $\tilde{e}_{jt}$ to inflation in sector j. Agents believe that the common component $\tilde{z}_t$ follows an AR(1) process. Agents infer the common component based on observing inflation in a subset of sectors J, following a standard signal extraction problem. There is incomplete information in that agents do not observe inflation in all sectors to infer the aggregate component. There is also bounded rationality in that agents' beliefs about the common component of inflation $\tilde{z}_t$ do not respect the Phillips curve.

One example of the mechanism is people who extrapolate overall inflation expectations from observing inflation in only a few goods. For instance, people might form inflation expectations based on observing rent, food, and gas prices. There is a burgeoning literature documenting precisely this behavior (e.g., D'Acunto et al. 2021).

In the authors' model, "broad-based supply shocks" increase inflation expectations. For instance, supply shocks specific to only rent, food, and gas may increase the aggregate component of inflation expectations. Intuitively, agents solve a signal extraction problem to estimate the aggregate component $\tilde{z}_t$. When sufficiently many sectoral supply shocks raise inflation, agents infer that $\tilde{z}_t$ has increased. Then inflation expectations increase.

Therefore, the authors' model can rationalize the increase in inflation expectations that they have documented. Because their model obeys a Phillips curve, higher inflation expectations also raise inflation itself. The rise in inflation expectations is "quasi-self-confirming." Actual inflation does end up rising, precisely as agents believed would happen via their inference over the common component $\tilde{z}_t$. The authors then parameterize and estimate a version of the model. The model successfully accounts for inflation dynamics, both during the postpandemic inflation and earlier.

The role of supply shocks is different from the standard New Keynesian model. In the standard model, supply shocks increase inflation through a direct effect on marginal costs—that is, the ε_t term in equation (1). In Beaudry et al.'s calibration, these effects are relatively small. Rather, supply shocks indirectly raise inflation to the extent that they increase inflation expectations via the "broad-based supply shock" mechanism.

III. Recap and Comments

Beaudry et al. have produced a remarkable paper, which is essential for understanding the postpandemic inflation. Their finding that a flat pre-2020 Phillips curve fits the postpandemic inflation will be influential.

Their finding is an out of sample explanation using a standard model. As such, the paper contrasts with a fast-growing literature proposing a range of 2020s specific modifications to the Phillips curve. For instance, Ball, Leigh, and Mishra (2022) and Benigno and Eggertsson (2023) argue that the slope of the Phillips curve increases when the labor market is tight, as in the early 2020s. Both papers advocate different measures of labor market slack—other than unemployment—which were particularly tight during the early 2020s. Blanco et al. (2024) suggest that the slope of the Phillips curve increases after large shocks, such as the rapid increase in real activity after the pandemic. Di Giovanni et al. (2022) and Bai et al. (2024) suggest that new kinds of supply shocks, arising from "bottlenecks," are important. Papers such as Barro and Bianchi (2023) and Bianchi, Faccini, and Melosi (2023) are motivated by the large rise in deficits in the early 2020s and argue for the "Fiscal Theory of the Price Level."

Beaudry et al. suggest a simple explanation: the flat and linear New Keynesian Phillips curve can explain the data. In this view, there is no need to modify the conventional wisdom about inflation dynamics from before 2020. Rather, the same process characterizes inflation both before and after 2020. Their explanation has at least three virtues. First, Beaudry et al. use a model that was conceived and estimated prior to 2020. As such, they avoid post hoc theorizing—the traditional pitfall of Phillips curve estimation. The 2020s specific alternative explanations may be more vulnerable to this critique. Second, the model is parsimonious, containing three simple and off-the-shelf explanatory variables for inflation. Nevertheless, figure 3 shows that the model is remarkably successful at explaining inflation dynamics, despite their unusual size and speed. Third, the result suggests a tantalizing possibility. There is a unified equation that can make sense of all of the major inflation episodes after the 1960s. The flat and linear Phillips curve seems broadly applicable.

To round off this excellent paper, Beaudry et al. then explain why inflation expectations rose by so much. They advance a novel, plausible, and quantitatively successful theory of rising inflation expectations. I expect future work will develop the ideas they have advanced. In the rest of this discussion, I make two comments that provide context to the paper.

A. The Importance of Household Inflation Expectations

Beaudry et al.'s Phillips curve uses household inflation expectations from the Michigan Consumer Survey. This choice is ex ante reasonable but turns out to be crucial for their results. To make this point, I carry out the exercise from figure 3 but use alternative measures of inflation expectations. That is, I estimate the Phillips curve equation (2) using data from 1978 to 2020 but with different measures of inflation expectations. I use not only household expectations from Michigan but also adaptive expectations (the fourth lag of inflation), expectations from the Survey of Professional Forecasters, 1-year-ahead inflation expectations from swaps, and the 2-year-ahead inflation expectation measure provided by the Cleveland Federal Reserve. This last measure is a weighted average of expectations from profession forecasters and swaps. Then, for each inflation expectations measure, I calculate the predicted value of inflation after 2020, using the pre-2020Q2 regression coefficients and the post-2020 data.

Figure 5 reports the results and shows that the success of the Phillips curve depends on using household inflation expectations. In the figure, the solid black line is actual inflation. The other lines show predicted

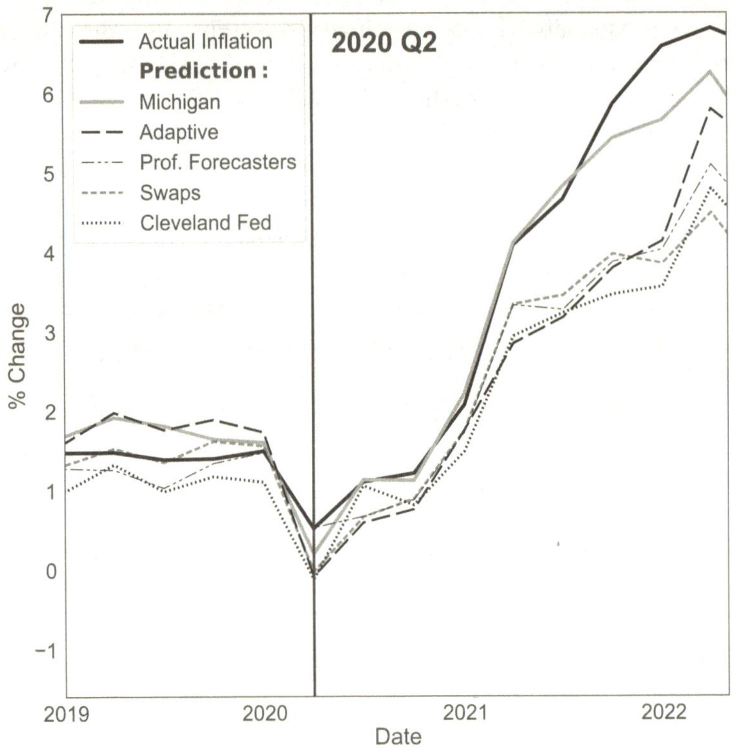

Fig. 5. Prediction of inflation with different expectations measures. The figure uses estimated regression coefficients from estimating equation (2)—the relationship between inflation, inflation expectations, the unemployment gap, and energy price growth—using pre-2020Q2 data. The regression is estimated for five different measures of inflation expectations, from Michigan households, swaps, professional professional forecasts, the Cleveland Fed, and adaptive expectations (the fourth lag of inflation). The figure then uses the realized path of inflation expectations, separately for each measure, as well as the unemployment gap and energy price growth after 2020, combined with the pre 2020Q2 regression coefficients, to predict inflation after 2020.

inflation using Michigan household expectations (solid gray), adaptive expectations (dashed black), professional forecasters (dashed light gray), swaps (dashed medium gray), and Cleveland Fed expectations (dotted black). Evidently, the other inflation expectations measures perform worse—there is a two percentage point difference between actual and predicted inflation according to the other measures, throughout 2021.

This figure clarifies a source of disagreement in the literature. Influential papers such as Benigno and Eggertsson (2023) argue that the Phillips curve slope became steeper during the postpandemic inflation. This paper uses the Cleveland Fed and professional forecaster measures, not household expectations as in Beaudry et al.

Michigan household expectations are ex ante a reasonable measure for at least two reasons. First, household expectations perform better for Phillips curve estimation prior to the postpandemic inflation. For instance, Coibion and Gorodnichenko (2015) show that household expectations are critical for understanding the "Missing Disinflation" during the Great Recession. Coibion, Gorodnichenko, and Kamdar (2018) show that household expectations perform better for Phillips curve estimation over the whole US time series. Second, from a conceptual standpoint, what matters for the Phillips curve is firms' inflation expectations. Arguably, household expectations are a better proxy for firms' expectations than are professionals' expectations. After all, most firms do not hire professional forecasters and are run by households. In support of this view, Beaudry et al. show that during the 2020s, household expectations closely correlate with firm expectations from the Cleveland Federal Reserve's SoFIE measure.

B. *Fiscal Stimulus May Matter Even with a Flat Phillips Curve*

To remind the reader, the narrative of this paper is that supply shocks caused higher inflation by raising inflation expectations. An alternative narrative through which inflation expectations and inflation rose is fiscal stimulus. The United States experienced enormous fiscal stimulus during the postpandemic inflation. Thirteen percent of annual 2020 gross domestic product (GDP) was disbursed in two rounds of fiscal stimulus of late 2020 and early 2021, via the Consolidated Appropriations Act and the American Rescue Plan Act. Shortly after this stimulus, inflation rose significantly. Furthermore, the United States experienced a third large stimulus of 10% of annual 2020 GDP in early 2020, via the CARES (Coronavirus Aid, Relief, and Economic Security) Act.

The fiscal stimulus suggests a possible alternative cause of inflation. A demand shock from fiscal stimulus could have caused inflation and inflation expectations to rise. If the shock were sufficiently large and persistent, inflation could rise even with a flat albeit positively sloped Phillips curve. Higher inflation then arises without limited information or bounded rationality.

A back of the envelope exercise suggests that this alternative narrative is plausible. To carry out this exercise, one can write the Phillips curve equation (1) in terms of output and then solve forward for the inflation expectations term. One arrives at an equation

$$d\pi_t = \kappa_y \mathcal{M} E_t \sum_{j=0}^{\infty} \beta^j \frac{dG_{t+j}}{\bar{Y}}, \tag{3}$$

where $d\pi_t$ is the response of inflation at time t to a sequence of shocks to government spending $\{dG_{t+j}\}$ relative to steady state output $\bar{Y}$. κ_y is the slope of the Phillips curve in terms of output, and $\mathcal{M}$ is the "cumulative multiplier" (e.g., Ramey and Zubairy 2018), defined as $\mathcal{M} \equiv E_t\Sigma_{j=0}^{\infty}\beta^j dY_{t+j}/E_t\Sigma_{j=0}^{\infty}\beta^j dG_{t+j}$.

One can plug some rough numbers into equation (3) to gauge the approximate effect of the 2020s fiscal stimulus on inflation. An annual calibration with a flat Phillips curve suggests $\kappa_y = 0.08$, using the numbers of Hazell et al. (2022) and Beaudry et al.[2] There was a fiscal shock of 13% of GDP in 2021, excluding the 2020 CARES Act and including the two later stimulus bills. The cumulative multiplier $\mathcal{M}$ could potentially be as high as 2. This high multiplier is possible if monetary policy was loose and the Federal Reserve was "behind the curve." Moreover, the stimulus was deficit financed, which may lead to large multipliers (e.g., Auclert, Rognlie, and Straub 2024).

The back of the envelope number suggests that fiscal stimulus raised inflation in 2021–22 by 2.2 percentage points. This contribution is sizable, given that PCE inflation in 2022 was 6.4%. Therefore, fiscal stimulus is potentially important for inflation expectations and for inflation. The core reason is that fiscal stimulus was large. Therefore, stimulus could raise inflation despite a flat Phillips curve, as several observers noted in 2021 (e.g., Blanchard 2021).

More detailed analysis again suggests that fiscal stimulus was important for the postpandemic inflation, even with a flat Phillips curve. For instance, in Hazell and Hobler (2024), we provide "high frequency narrative evidence" that the 2021 fiscal stimulus raised inflation by around two percentage points in 2021 and 2022. We use the release of deficit news around the 2021 Georgia Senate election runoffs to show that markets expected inflation to rise by several percentage points due to the anticipated stimulus. We also find that a standard heterogeneous agent New Keynesian model, combined with a flat Phillips curve, can rationalize the inflation response.

IV. Conclusion

Beaudry et al. have produced one of the most important papers to date on the postpandemic inflation. A range of papers have tackled the question of why inflation rose in the United States and around the world in the 2020s. What sets Beaudry et al. apart is the parsimony of their explanation. Without 2020s specific ingredients, and only using the conventional flat Phillips curve from before 2020, they are able to make sense of the dramatic post-2020 inflation episode. In tracing the proximate cause of the inflation to inflation expectations, they ask exciting questions about why inflation expectations rose so much. Their model offers a thought-provoking answer that will be influential for future work.

Endnotes

Author email address: Jonathon Hazell (jadhazell@gmail.com). For acknowledgments, sources of research support, and disclosure of the author's material financial relationships, if any, please see https://www.nber.org/books-and-chapters/nber-macroeconomics-annual-2024-volume-39/comment-dominant-role-expectations-and-broad-based-supply-shocks-driving-inflation-hazell.

1. This framework was originally estimated in unpublished slides circulated by James Stock.

2. To convert between a Phillips curve in output versus employment, I assume a production function $Y = N^{\alpha}$ with $\alpha = 2/3$.

References

Auclert, A., M. Rognlie, and L. Straub. 2024. "The Intertemporal Keynesian Cross." *Journal of Political Economy* 132 (12): 4068–121.

Bai, X., J. Fernández-Villaverde, Y. Li, and F. Zanetti. 2024. "The Causal Effects of Global Supply Chain Disruptions on Macroeconomic Outcomes: Evidence and Theory." Working Paper no. 32098, NBER, Cambridge, MA.

Ball, L., D. Leigh, and P. Mishra. 2022. "Understanding US Inflation during the COVID-19 Era." *Brookings Papers on Economic Activity* 1:54.

Ball, L., and S. Mazumder. 2019. "A Phillips Curve with Anchored Expectations and Short-Term Unemployment." *Journal of Money, Credit and Banking* 51 (1): 111–37.

Barro, R. J., and F. Bianchi. 2023. "Fiscal Influences on Inflation in OECD Countries, 2020–2022." Discussion paper, NBER, Cambridge, MA.

Benigno, P., and G. B. Eggertsson. 2023. "It's Baaack: The Surge in Inflation in the 2020s and the Return of the Non-Linear Phillips Curve." Discussion paper, NBER, Cambridge, MA.

Bianchi, F., R. Faccini, and L. Melosi. 2023. "A Fiscal Theory of Persistent Inflation." *Quarterly Journal of Economics* 138 (4): 2127–79.
Blanchard, O. 2016. "The Phillips Curve: Back to the '60s?" *American Economic Review* 106 (5): 31–34.
———. 2021. "In Defense of Concerns over the 1.9 Trillion Dollar Relief Plan." Peterson Institute for International Economics, February 18.
Blanco, A., C. Boar, C. J. Jones, and V. Midrigan. 2024. "Non-Linear Inflation Dynamics in Menu Cost Economies." Discussion paper, NBER, Cambridge, MA.
Coibion, O., and Y. Gorodnichenko. 2015. "Is the Phillips Curve Alive and Well after All? Inflation Expectations and the Missing Disinflation." *American Economic Journal: Macroeconomics* 7 (1): 197–232.
Coibion, O., Y. Gorodnichenko, and R. Kamdar. 2018. "The Formation of Expectations, Inflation, and the Phillips Curve." *Journal of Economic Literature* 56 (4): 1447–91.
D'Acunto, F., U. Malmendier, J. Ospina, and M. Weber. 2021. "Exposure to Grocery Prices and Inflation Expectations." *Journal of Political Economy* 129 (5): 1615–39.
Del Negro, M., M. Lenza, G. E. Primiceri, and A. Tambalotti. 2020. "What's Up with the Phillips Curve?" *Brookings Papers on Economic Activity* 1 (Spring): 301–73.
Di Giovanni, J., Ş. Kalemli-Özcan, A. Silva, and M. A. Yildirim. 2022. "Global Supply Chain Pressures, International Trade, and Inflation." Discussion paper, NBER, Cambridge, MA.
Hazell, J., J. Herreño, E. Nakamura, and J. Steinsson. 2022. "The Slope of the Phillips Curve: Evidence from US States." *Quarterly Journal of Economics* 137 (3): 1299–344.
Hazell, J., and S. Hobler. 2024. "Do Deficits Cause Inflation? A High Frequency Narrative Approach." CFM-DP2024-39, London School of Economics and Political Science, London, UK.
McLeay, M., and S. Tenreyro. 2020. "Optimal Inflation and the Identification of the Phillips Curve." *NBER Macroeconomics Annual 2019* 34 (1): 199–255.
Ramey, V. A., and S. Zubairy. 2018. "Government Spending Multipliers in Good Times and in Bad: Evidence from US Historical Data." *Journal of Political Economy* 126 (2): 850–901.
Samuelson, P. A., and R. M. Solow. 1960. "Analytical Aspects of Anti-inflation Policy." *American Economic Review* 50 (2): 177–94.
Stock, J. H., and M. W. Watson. 2010. "Modeling inflation after the Crisis." Working Paper no. 16488, NBER, Cambridge, MA.
———. 2020. "Slack and Cyclically Sensitive Inflation." *Journal of Money, Credit and Banking* 52 (S2): 393–428.

Comment

Gabriel Chodorow-Reich, *Harvard University and NBER,* United States of America

Beaudry, Hou, and Portier (hereafter BHP) have written an excellent and provocative paper. Rather than attempt to comment on each element of the analysis, I will focus my discussion on two main claims. First, the paper makes an empirical case that a linear and flat Phillips curve can explain inflation during 2021–23. Second, it provides a theory through which broad-based supply shocks change inflation expectations and hence inflation itself and fits this theory to the US experience.

I can state my bottom line succinctly up front: the paper makes a strong case that supply shocks can drive inflation expectations. I remain less convinced of the claim in the paper's title that these forces are dominant in driving inflation and, by implication, that tight labor markets play a subordinate role.

I structure my comment in the order of the paper. Section I reviews the New Keynesian Phillips curve (NKPC). The theory motivates a few changes to the empirical exercise assessing nonlinearity in the Phillips curve slope, which I implement in Section II. Although my perspective shares ingredients with existing work (Benigno and Eggertsson 2023; Gagliardone and Gertler 2023), this part of the comment contains some novel theoretical and empirical arguments. I conclude that the US time series are perfectly consistent with a nonlinear Phillips curve in which only very tight labor markets cause inflation, although I acknowledge that the time series lack the variation to make a stronger claim. Section III illustrates the main mechanics of the BHP model using a simplified version and offers some comments.

NBER Macroeconomics Annual, volume 39, 2025.
 https://doi.org/10.1086/735270

I. Review of NKPC

I start with a review of the textbook NKPC. The key decision concerns the reset price of a firm changing its price at date t and that expects to change its price with probability $1 - \alpha$ each period thereafter. This firm sets its price to minimize deviations from the expected desired markup over marginal cost over the course of the price spell. Letting $p_{t|t}$ denote the reset price, μ^*_{t+h} the desired markup at date $t + h$, p_{t+h} the nominal price level, and $c_{t+h|t}$ the firm's marginal cost all in log deviation from their steady state values, and letting β denote the firm's discount factor, this equation takes the form:

$$0 = \mathbb{E}_t \sum_{h=0}^{\infty} (\alpha\beta)^h \left[\underbrace{p_{t|t}}_{\text{Reset price}} - \left(\underbrace{\mu^*_{t+h}}_{\text{Desired markup}} + \underbrace{p_{t+h} + c_{t+h|t}}_{\text{Nominal marginal cost}} \right) \right]. \quad (1)$$

Equation (1) can be solved and written to express the period t optimal reset price as a weighted average of the price set in period t under fully flexible prices and the expected optimal reset price in $t + 1$:

$$p_{t|t} = (1 - \omega)(\mu^*_t + p_t + c_{t|t}) + \omega \mathbb{E}_t p_{t+1|t+1}, \quad (2)$$

where $\omega \equiv (\alpha\beta + \alpha\beta\chi)/(1 + \alpha\beta\chi)$ and $\chi > 0$ denotes the (opposite of the) elasticity of a firm's relative marginal cost to its relative price. Using the definition of inflation and its decomposition into the extensive and intensive margin $\pi_t = p_t - p_{t-1} = (1 - \alpha)(p_{t|t} - p_{t-1})$, one can manipulate the reset price equation to arrive at the marginal cost Phillips curve:

$$\pi_t = \lambda(\mu^*_t + c_t) + \beta \mathbb{E}_t \pi_{t+1}, \quad (3)$$

where $\lambda \equiv (1 - \alpha/\alpha)(1 - \alpha\beta/1 + \chi)$.

These steps illustrate three key points for measurement. First, expectations enter directly through price setters considering what price they would like in the future. Higher expected inflation implies a higher future desired price, which implies a higher price today and hence more inflation today. Importantly, price setters' expectations of their future costs and desired markups matter.[1] Second, a theory of price setters implies the appropriate measure of inflation is the gross domestic product (GDP) price index, not the consumer price index (CPI). Third, the theory predicts a linear relationship between inflation and log marginal cost. Estimations of the Phillips curve instead typically relate inflation to the output gap. This switch results from an unheralded divine coincidence between the central bank's dual mandate of inflation and output and what researchers can more easily measure in the data, because marginal cost typically is not directly observed.[2] Of course, this switch requires determining the relationship between aggregate output and marginal cost, which may introduce nonlinearity.

II. Evidence of Nonlinearity

I now make a simple case in the spirit of the BHP exercise for a steepening Phillips curve during 2021–23. My analysis incorporates three theory-motivated changes to the data. First, I use the GDP price index to measure inflation. Second, I use professional forecasters' inflation expectations in place of the Michigan survey. Third, I use either the vacancy-unemployment ratio or the expected vacancy duration as the measure of labor market tightness rather than the unemployment gap. I have already discussed the rationale for using the GDP price index, and this change matters relatively little to the results. I now motivate the alternative measures of expectations and the output gap before presenting the results.

A. Inflation Expectations

According to equation (2), the NKPC wants firms' expectations of their desired price growth. Coibion and Gorodnichenko (2015) argue that household expectations from the Michigan survey best fit a (linear) Phillips curve and suggest that in the absence of direct measurement of firm expectations, there is no reason not to think they coincide with expectations of households. BHP follow this line. Figure 1 (short-dashed line) shows the Michigan expectations.

Following publication of Coibion and Gorodnichenko (2015), new measures of firm expectations have come into being. Figure 1 (solid line) plots the Federal Reserve Bank of Atlanta firm expectations of their own cost growth, referred to as business inflation expectations (BIE). The BIE arguably comes closest among existing survey measures to the proper theoretical construct, because what enters into the firm's pricing decision is its expectation of its own desired future price.[3] Meyer and Sheng (2021) offer an extensive empirical exploration of the BIE.

The main drawback of the BIE is that it starts only in 2011. However, figure 1 (long-dashed line) shows that the median forecast of GDP price index inflation from the Survey of Professional Forecasters (SPF) closely

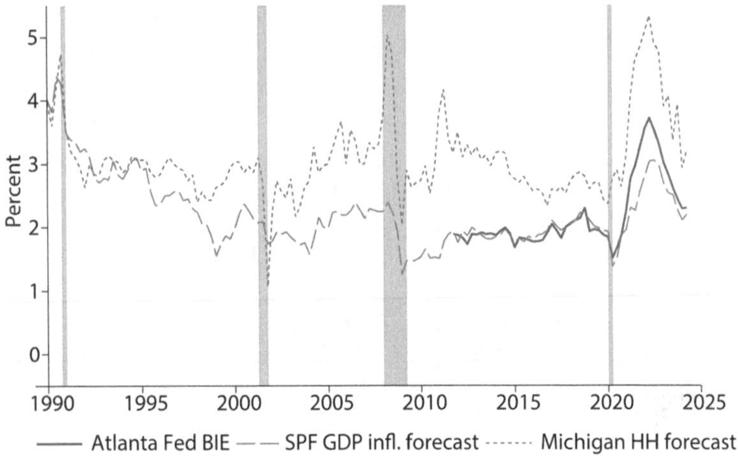

Fig. 1. Measures of expected inflation. BIE = business inflation expectations, GDP = gross domestic product, SPF = Survey of Professional Forecasters, HH = household.

tracks the BIE. Importantly, both measures differ notably from the Michigan survey; during the 20teens, both the BIE and SPF have roughly rational forecasts of inflation of 2%, whereas the Michigan survey expectations are always too high and excessively volatile. In what follows, I equate expected inflation in the Phillips curve with the SPF forecast to obtain a longer sample. Given the short time series of the BIE, I understand that reasonable people may disagree with this choice, although I do not think that reasonable people can disagree that it is a plausible measure of price setters' expectations.

B. *Relation of Marginal Cost to Labor Market Tightness*

Figure 2 shows why the choice of the measure of the output gap might matter. The figure shows three series: the gap between the unemployment rate u and the Congressional Budget Office (CBO) estimate of the nonaccelerating inflation rate of unemployment (NAIRU) u^*; the vacancy-unemployment ratio $\theta = V/U$ (setting V equal to JOLTS [Job Openings and Labor Turnover Survey] job openings and extended backward by Barnichon 2010); and the Davis, Faberman, and Haltiwanger (2013) measure of expected vacancy duration (extended forward by me). The gap u^*/u, here shown in logs, is the paper's preferred measure. Because u is typically above u^*, $\log(u^*/u)$ is typically negative. One can immediately see why this measure does not generate nonlinearity in the Phillips

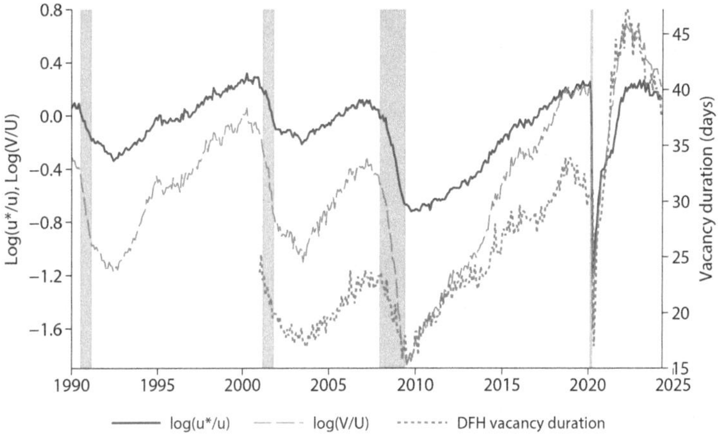

Fig. 2. Measures of the business cycle. DFH = Davis, Faberman, and Haltiwanger (2013).

curve; given the downward trend in the NAIRU, it shows a tighter labor market in 2000 than in 2019 and about the same tightness in 2019 and 2022. Furthermore, because purely frictional unemployment appears to bound u from below at around 3.5%, the unemployment gap becomes less informative in very tight labor markets.

In contrast, both θ and vacancy duration are historically high in 2021–22. The high sensitivity of θ and vacancy duration in tight labor markets reflects their unboundedness from above. I next argue that this feature also may capture an important economic force—a high level of vacancies signals that firms face capacity constraints.

In the remainder of this subsection, I provide a simple theory that puts θ into the Phillips curve and shows why nonlinearity might arise. Broadly, there are two (non–mutually exclusive) ways to link θ to inflation, either through wages (Benigno and Eggertsson 2023; Blanchard and Bernanke 2023; Moscarini and Postel-Vinay 2023) or through recruiting costs (Gagliardone and Gertler 2023). I adopt the latter formulation. Relative to Gagliardone and Gertler (2023), by adopting a more general matching function and not linearizing, I illustrate two sources of nonlinearity in the relationship between θ and marginal cost. This contribution is new.

The model consists of workers, wholesale firms, and retail firms. Competitive wholesalers transform labor into output with a linear technology:

$$Y_{i,t} = L_{i,t}, \tag{4}$$

where $Y_{i,t}$ and $L_{i,t}$ are output and labor input of wholesaler i at date t. Wholesalers take the price of their output C_t as given. They must hire each period, so that

$$L_{i,t} = \bar{L}_i + H_{i,t}, \tag{5}$$

where $\bar{L}_i$ is the firm's fixed stock of labor, $H_{i,t}$ is the number of new hires, and I assume that $\bar{L}_i$ is small enough that firms always hire.[4] The number of hires equals the product of the equilibrium job-filling rate, $q(\theta_t)$, and the number of vacancies posted by the firm, $V_{i,t}$:

$$H_{i,t} = q(\theta_t)V_{i,t}, \tag{6}$$

where $\theta_t = V_t/U_t$, V_t is the aggregate quantity of vacancies, U_t the aggregate quantity of unemployed job-seekers, and $q(\theta_t)$ follows from the Haan, Ramey, and Watson (2000) matching function:

$$q(\theta_t) = \frac{1}{(\eta + (1-\eta)\theta_t^{\rho})^{\frac{1}{\rho}}}, \tag{7}$$

where $\eta \subseteq [0, 1]$ and $\rho \geq 0$ are parameters of the matching function.[5] Firms pay a flow cost k per vacancy and pay all workers a wage W_t.

The wholesaler's marginal cost, denoted $C_{i,t}$, equals the sum of the recruiting cost and the wage:

$$C_{i,t} = \frac{k}{q(\theta_t)} + W_t. \tag{8}$$

In the competitive equilibrium, the wholesaler's marginal cost equals the output price of the wholesaler sector, $C_{i,t} = C_t$. That is, taking the output price C_t as given, wholesalers hire until marginal cost equals C_t. In log deviation form, the wholesale price then satisfies:

$$c_t \equiv \ln\left(\frac{C_t}{C^*}\right) = -R(\theta_t)\ln\left(\frac{q(\theta_t)}{q(\theta^*)}\right) = R(\theta_t)h(\theta_t)\ln\left(\frac{\theta_t}{\theta^*}\right), \tag{9}$$

$$\text{where } R(\theta_t) = \frac{k}{q(\theta_t)C_t}, \tag{10}$$

$$h(\theta_t) = \left(\frac{(1-\eta)\theta_t^{\rho}}{\eta + (1-\eta)\theta_t^{\rho}}\right), \tag{11}$$

and, importantly, the share of recruiting costs in total marginal cost $R(\theta_t)$ satisfies $R'(\theta_t) > 0$ and the inverse elasticity of the job-filling rate to tightness $h(\theta_t)$ satisfies $h'(\theta_t) > 0$ as long as $\rho > 0$.[6]

Retailers transform one unit of the wholesale good into one unit of a differentiated final good and reset their price with Calvo probability $1 - \alpha$. Thus, the retail price Phillips curve is given by equation (3) with a constant markup and marginal cost given by equation (9). One can close the model by positing a process for nominal demand.

To summarize, in this model the correct output gap measure in the Phillips curve is $\ln \theta_t$ because marginal cost depends on the hiring cost. Because the Beveridge curve is nonlinear (unemployment is bounded from below), in general equilibrium $\ln \theta_t$ is a nonlinear function of u, and a Phillips curve in unemployment gap space inherits this nonlinearity. Furthermore, the slope of the Phillips curve in θ space is nonlinear because as tightness increases, recruiting costs become a larger share of marginal cost and the elasticity of the hiring rate to θ_t diminishes.

C. *Evidence of Nonlinearity*

I now undergo an exercise in the spirit of BHP figure 3 but with the three changes just discussed: (1) I use the GDP price index to measure inflation; (2) I use the SPF to measure inflation expectations; and (3) I use log θ or log vacancy duration instead of the unemployment rate gap. I make one final change required by changing the output gap measure: instead of calibrating the slope of the Phillips curve, I impose a coefficient of 0.99 on expected inflation and plot $\pi_t - 0.99\mathbb{E}_t\pi_{t+1}$ against the output gap measure.

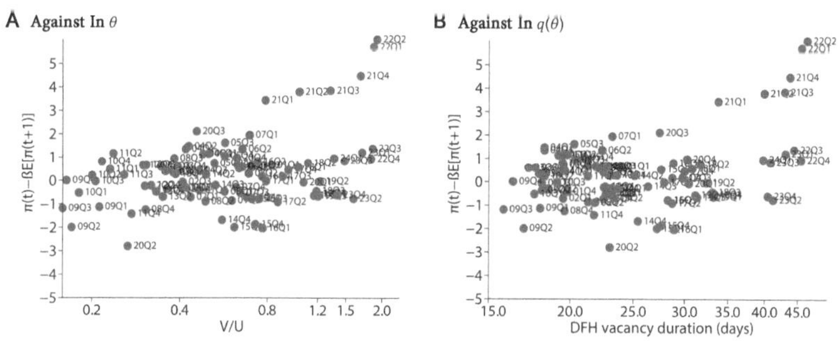

Fig. 3. Phillips curve nonlinearity. DFH = Davis, Faberman, and Haltiwanger (2013).

Panel A of figure 3 shows the results with $\ln \theta$ as the output gap measure. Panel B shows the results using the Davis et al. (2013) vacancy duration, which is the inverse of the job-filling rate and hence in logs equal to $-\ln q(\theta)$. The period from 2021 to 2022 stands out in both panels as having very high tightness and high excess inflation. The main difference in the tightness measures occurs in 2021Q1–2021Q3, which register as even tighter using vacancy duration than θ. I suspect these measures may even understate labor market tightness during this period, as some establishments remained closed because of the difficulty of finding workers.

In the context of this theory and calibration, the confluence of very high labor market tightness in 2021–22 and high excess inflation has two possible interpretations, because $\pi_t - 0.99\mathbb{E}_t\pi_{t+1} = R(\theta_t)h(\theta_t)\ln(\theta_t/\theta^*) + \epsilon_t$. Either the Phillips curve slope $R(\theta_t)h(\theta_t)$ has a strong nonlinearity, or large positive supply shocks ϵ_t happened to coincide with the period of maximum tightness in the sample.

The aggregate JOLTS-era post-2000 data cannot on their own distinguish these two explanations. Benigno and Eggertsson (2023) point to a similar episode of high inflation during the last period of high θ in the late 1960s, doubling the effective sample size to two. Clearly, the aggregate time series data leave room for disagreement. Hence my statement at the outset that the US time series are perfectly consistent with a nonlinear Phillips curve in which only very tight labor markets cause inflation, without rejecting the possibility of the alternative view.

III. The BHP Model

I now turn to the BHP model of expectations formation. Subsection III.A provides a simplified version of the model. Subsection III.B offers some comments.

A. A Simplified Version

My simple version has two ingredients, a flat Phillips curve and an equation for expectations formation:

$$\pi_t = \beta\mathbb{E}_t[\pi_{t+1}] + \epsilon_t, \tag{12}$$

$$\mathbb{E}_t[\pi_{t+1}] = a\pi_{t-1} + b\pi_t. \tag{13}$$

Solving this system:

$$\pi_t = \frac{\beta a \pi_{t-1} + \epsilon_t}{1 - \beta b}, \tag{14}$$

$$\mathbb{E}_t[\pi_{t+1}] = \frac{a}{1 - \beta b}\pi_{t-1} + \frac{b}{1 - \beta b}\epsilon_t. \tag{15}$$

The impulse response of inflation to a transitory supply shock is

$$\frac{d\pi_{t+h}}{d\epsilon_t} = \frac{1}{1 - \beta b}\left(\frac{\beta a}{1 - \beta b}\right)^h. \tag{16}$$

Equations (14)–(16) contain the key amplification and persistence present in the full BHP model. The dependence of expected inflation on current inflation generates amplification of supply shocks ϵ_t through higher expected inflation. The backward-looking component of the expectations process, $a > 0$, generates persistent inflation in response to a transitory supply shock.

B. Comments

My "1960s version" of the BHP model yields the key result that transitory supply shocks can have amplified and persistent effects on overall inflation by raising inflation expectations. In fact, setting $b = \tilde{\rho}K$, the impact effect of inflation coincides with the impact in the BHP model. In this sense, the information frictions and bounded rationality in BHP serve the purpose of microfounding the contemporaneous and backward-looking components of expectations formation.

Information frictions in price setting have a distinguished history that includes Lucas (1972) and Mankiw and Reis (2002). In the BHP microfoundation, the main friction concerns price setters' belief formation, taking account of an imprecise signal of contemporaneous inflation and neglecting that the error in their signal is correlated with actual inflation. Broadly, this seems plausible.[7] The details have interesting implications, including that inflation expectations exhibit less sensitivity to movements in oil prices than to other items because agents understand that oil is a volatile sector subject to large supply shocks. This implication runs counter to much conventional wisdom, but BHP provide some evidence in favor of it.

Endnotes

Author email address: Gabriel Chodorow-Reich (chodorowreich@fas.harvard.edu). For acknowledgments, sources of research support, and disclosure of the author's material financial relationships, if any, please see https://www.nber.org/books-and-chapters/nber-macroeconomics-annual-2024-volume-39/comment-dominant-role-expectations-and-broad-based-supply-shocks-driving-inflation-2-chodorow-reich.

1. This statement holds true even if expectations of other agents influence future costs, as discussed in Reis (2023). For example, consumer demand may depend on consumers' inflation expectations through the Euler equation. However, consumer demand affects prices through either changing marginal costs or desired markups. Likewise, workers' inflation expectations may affect wage demands, but these influence prices through firms' costs.

2. See Gagliardone et al. (2023) for a recent attempt at estimation of a marginal cost Phillips curve. Of course, potential output and hence the output gap also is not directly observed.

3. Of course, linking the desired future price to expected cost growth imposes a constant markup. Surprisingly, I am not aware of any survey that circumvents this assumption by directly asking firms about what price they would like to have at future dates. The Federal Reserve Bank of Cleveland reports an expectation of CPI inflation from a panel of CEOs, but this variable contains many differences from the firm's own desired price growth.

4. This formulation simplifies the exposition by making the wholesaler's marginal cost a static function of its hiring. More complicated laws of motion are possible.

5. If $\rho = 0$, the matching function is Cobb-Douglas and the vacancy-filling rate is $q(\theta_t) = \theta^{\eta-1}$.

6. The condition $\rho > 0$ corresponds to gross complementarity between vacancies and searchers in the matching function. This property seems intuitively appealing. For example, consider adding either 1% more vacancies or 1% more searchers. With $\rho > 0$, the relative change in matches from 1% more vacancies diminishes as θ increases. Empirical evidence of ρ remains scarce. Haan et al. (2000) internally calibrate a value of 1.27, whereas Lange and Papageorgiou (2020) find evidence consistent with $\rho < 0$.

7. A minor quibble with the details. Price setters in the BHP model incorporate into their expectations the current inflation rate, which itself depends on the actions of those same price setters. On the one hand, such criticism runs a little cheap: we are all guilty of writing down simultaneous systems of equations to determine equilibrium without fully specifying the adjustment process (Dogra 2024). On the other hand, in a model of expectations formation, such details have greater bite. In his exploration of the pass-through of expected to current inflation, Werning (2022) goes so far as to date the expectation in the Phillips curve as based on only $t - 1$ information.

References

Barnichon, Regis. 2010. "Building a Composite Help-Wanted Index." *Economics Letters* 109 (3): 175–78.

Benigno, Pierpaolo, and Gauti B. Eggertsson. 2023. "It's Baaack: The Surge in Inflation in the 2020s and the Return of the Non-Linear Phillips Curve." Working Paper no. 31197, NBER, Cambridge, MA.

Blanchard, Olivier J., and Ben S. Bernanke. 2023. "What Caused the US Pandemic-Era Inflation?" Working Paper no. 31417, NBER, Cambridge, MA.

Coibion, Olivier, and Yuriy Gorodnichenko. 2015. "Is the Phillips Curve Alive and Well after All? Inflation Expectations and the Missing Disinflation." *American Economic Journal: Macroeconomics* 7 (1): 197–232.

Davis, Steven J., R. Jason Faberman, and John C. Haltiwanger. 2013. "The Establishment-Level Behavior of Vacancies and Hiring." *Quarterly Journal of Economics* 128 (2): 581–622.

Dogra, Keshav. 2024. "Paradoxes and Problems in the Causal Interpretation of Equilibrium Economics." Staff Report no. 1093, Federal Reserve Bank of New York.

Gagliardone, Luca, and Mark Gertler. 2023. "Oil Prices, Monetary Policy and Inflation Surges." Working Paper no. 31263, NBER, Cambridge, MA.

Gagliardone, Luca, Mark Gertler, Simone Lenzu, and Joris Tielens. 2023. "Anatomy of the Phillips Curve: Micro Evidence and Macro Implications." Working Paper no. 31382, NBER, Cambridge, MA.

Haan, Wouter J. den, Garey Ramey, and Joel Watson. 2000. "Job Destruction and Propagation of Shocks." *American Economic Review* 90 (3): 482–98.

Lange, Fabian, and Theodore Papageorgiou. 2020. "Beyond Cobb-Douglas: Flexibly Estimating Matching Functions with Unobserved Matching Efficiency." Working Paper no. 26972, NBER, Cambridge, MA.

Lucas, Robert E. 1972. "Expectations and the Neutrality of Money." *Journal of Economic Theory* 4 (2): 103–24.

Mankiw, N. Gregory, and Ricardo Reis. 2002. "Sticky Information versus Sticky Prices: A Proposal to Replace the New Keynesian Phillips Curve." *Quarterly Journal of Economics* 117 (4): 1295–328.

Meyer, Brent H., and Xuguang Simon Sheng. 2021. "Unit Cost Expectations and Uncertainty: Firms' Perspectives on Inflation." Working Paper no. 2021-12b, Federal Reserve Bank of Atlanta.

Moscarini, Giuseppe, and Fabien Postel-Vinay. 2023. "The Job Ladder: Inflation vs. Reallocation." Working Paper no. 31466, NBER, Cambridge, MA.

Reis, Ricardo. 2023. "Four Mistakes in the Use of Measures of Expected Inflation." *AEA Papers and Proceedings* 113:47–51.

Werning, Iván. 2022. "Expectations and the Rate of Inflation." Working Paper no. 30260, NBER, Cambridge, MA.

Discussion

Jón Steinsson opened the discussion by observing that, so far, there had been no real mention of monetary policy in a discussion about inflation in this session. He asked whether we can think about inflation without considering monetary policy. The initial Phillips curve system presented in the paper assumes AR(1) processes for both the employment gap and the supply shock. This system fails to account for the joint dynamics of inflation and inflation expectations, thereby motivating the rest of the paper. Steinsson noted that the employment gap equation governs demand in this economy and, thus, must also implicitly contain monetary policy. Consequently, he expressed concerns that this system fails to accurately capture monetary policy. To illustrate the point, he considered a slight adjustment to the system with β set equal to 1, yielding a vertical long-run Phillips curve. Under this system, if the central bank were to change the inflation target—a long-run change in monetary policy—it would never affect the employment gap or enter the system. He continued that, with β less than one, a change to the inflation target would mean a permanent change to the employment gap, but this cannot be captured by the system's AR(1) specification. Overall, he concluded that although he was sympathetic to the overall story of the paper, he felt that the system was not doing justice to the impact of monetary policy, especially with respect to persistent changes in monetary policy.

Following up on the previous comment, Ricardo Reis noted that a search of the paper produced only four results for the word *monetary*–all in titles in references or in one footnote. This was odd in a paper about

NBER Macroeconomics Annual, volume 39, 2025.
 https://doi.org/10.1086/735271

inflation. Further, the paper proposed a reduced-form model that linked expected inflation to existing variability in sectoral prices. Changes in monetary policy should affect how agents interpret the signals of sectoral price changes to form their inflation expectations and therefore change this reduced-form map. Finally, Reis responded to the discussion on the correct measure of inflation expectations in empirical Phillips curves, stating that the Survey of Professional Forecasters (SPF) was not right for the recent period. He explained that the SPF mimics the central bank's forecast, so whenever the central bank gets things wrong—as it did in 2021—the SPF also gets it wrong. Households are more skeptical and their expectations (say, measured in the Michigan Survey of Consumers) are more useful to study large movements in inflation, not the SPF. The recent experience confirms this.

Johannes Wieland further endorsed Steinsson's concerns over the lack of monetary policy. He explained that the Phillips curve shifted out in the 1970s and 1980s, and inflation resulted because the monetary authority decided to accommodate that shift. He continued that, similarly, in the current episode, one can think about what would have happened if the Fed had raised interest rates to 10% in April 2021. Had this been the case, he stated, there probably would not have been 8% inflation. He clarified that he is not necessarily saying that the Fed made a poor choice in this instance but that it is hard not to talk about what monetary policy did or did not do when considering the path of inflation.

Paul Beaudry thanked everyone for the discussion and responded to the recurring comments on the lack of monetary policy in the paper's framework. He agreed that monetary policy is certainly relevant to a discussion of inflation. However, he explained that they had adopted the simplifying assumption that the economy remained in a stable regime for most of the studied period, assuming long-run inflationary expectations remained relatively flat. He noted that they initially had set up the model to be relative to long-run expectations, allowing for a clearer consideration of monetary policy. However, they found this was not making much of a difference and made the setup less tractable. He reinforced that he thinks monetary policy matters and that the way they wrote the model was just a simplification, adding that they should perhaps be clearer about the simplifying assumptions. Addressing comments on the different measures of inflation expectations, he noted that when inflation spikes, it seems like the consumers—rather than the professionals—get it right. He explained that this is not because consumers are better at predicting inflation but because they cause high inflation when they expect it.

Frederic Mishkin commenced by noting that he took issue with how much of the literature treats estimated Phillips curves as structural. He explained that a key issue is the endogeneity of monetary policy: If monetary policy achieves its stated objectives, then estimates of the Phillips curve will be biased toward supporting a flat Phillips curve. Furthering the point, he added that, under the theorem of optimal control, if monetary policy is optimal, there will be zero correlation with the policy. Thus, well-designed policies lead directly to a flat Phillips curve. Overall, he stated that he found the story of supply shocks leading to an increase in expected inflation very interesting but found the exclusion of monetary policy troubling. He noted that the Federal Reserve probably waited longer than they otherwise would have to raise rates in the recent inflationary episode because they believed in a flat Phillips curve. He warned that assuming a flat Phillips curve in setting policy, rather than understanding that good monetary policy itself creates a flat Phillips curve, can lead to policy mistakes.

James Stock opened his comments by noting his appreciation for the paper and the discussion. He stated that there are a few interesting regularities surrounding the current inflationary episode. For one, a Phillips curve estimated through 2020 using all straightforward variables—including the unemployment gap and expected inflation from the household survey—fits well through the entire episode. He noted that he liked the authors' explanation of this fact but added that prior research has established that inflation expectations from the Michigan survey seem to track the level of gasoline prices. Consequently, he suggested that the current inflationary episode was heavily driven by energy shocks rather than broad-based supply shocks. He added that the second regularity around this episode is that a Phillips curve estimated using SPF expectations, the unemployment gap, and personal consumption expenditures (PCE) energy inflation from 1968 to 1983 also fits well over the current period. He noted concern over this fact.

Martin Eichenbaum continued the discussion by expressing the need for future research on the correct theory of expectations. He suggested regressing inflation expectations on some measure of the cross-sectional dispersion of price increases might provide some insight into whether salience or some other theory prevails. He explained that, in the paper's theory of expectation formation, there are two things an agent learns: The first is about an exogenous process, but the other is about endogenous variables. He added that, typically, rational expectations serve as the benchmark for monetary policy, so learning about endogenous variables raises the question of the rate of convergence. He assumed that there would be a very slow rate of convergence in the paper's model, meaning that a Bayesian agent would not change their mind very quickly. He stated that this might mean rational expectations policy design is terrible as an approximation for real world policy analysis—a possibility that has only recently started to be explored.

Lawrence Christiano commented that a student of his wrote a paper about a nonlinear Phillips curve. That paper, he noted, was finished in 2021 and written to explain the flattening of the Phillips curve. However, the same model predicted that inflation would take off precisely the way it did in the most recent episode because of an intersectoral shift in demand. The basic ingredient in that paper's model is that capital is ex post difficult to adjust, leading agents to hold a bit extra. Thus, the Phillips curve got flatter because people held larger capital buffers due to markups growing over time. He explained that the intersectoral shift in demand—a result of demand shifting from services to goods during COVID-19—led to a shortage of physical capital, which provides an alternative story. Furthermore, he expressed discomfort with the idea in Beaudry et al.'s paper that expected inflation moves current inflation. He explained that although this is true in some sense, it ignores the effect of the output gap. He stated that, per the work of Clarida, Galí, and Gertler, the reason for high inflation in the 1970s was that inflation expectations fed immediately into inflation, and the Federal Reserve did nothing to slow things down. The subsequent low inflation era resulted from anchored inflation expectations. He added that this means that when inflation expectations go up, inflation starts to rise, but when the central bank comes in and tightens policy, it forces the economy—and the output gap—down so that inflation is somewhat anchored. He concluded that it is worrying for policy that this channel is found to be very weak in the paper.

Jordi Galí offered a comment on the micro foundations of the paper. He noted that inflation results from some firms adjusting prices and that, in New Keynesian models, these pricing decisions are based on firms' expectations for discrepancies between markups and desired markups. He continued that, under auxiliary assumptions, the markup gap can be related to the output gap, and, more importantly, inflation is related to the sequence of discounted expectations of future output gaps. If the law of iterated expectations is satisfied, this discounted sum can be collapsed into the simple recursive formulation, but there is no separate channel for expected inflation aside from long-run inflation. As a result, he explained that the reason why expected inflation enters here, when considering the micro foundations, is that it is a sufficient statistic for the expected future output gap. He suggested it would be interesting to look at proxies for the expected future output gap to see if they have a separate influence on inflation and whether that influence is correlated with measures of expected inflation. He added that, if measures of subjective expectations are used because inflation is thought not to be rational, then that specification should be questioned because it is derived under the assumption of rational expectations. In addition, he noted that the authors use the unemployment rate as a proxy for the output gap. As such, he recommended that they try looking at a Phillips curve specification with wage inflation because there are micro foundations that relate wage inflation to unemployment but not that relate price inflation to the unemployment rate. He concluded that it would be interesting to see if inflation expectations are just proxying lagged inflation.

Paul Beaudry closed the discussion by thanking everyone and acknowledging that he lacked sufficient time to respond to all the comments. He added that Chodorow-Reich's discussion covered the question whether there is still evidence for a nonlinear Phillips curve well and added that if expectations do not move much, there is a lot of room for nonlinearities.

5

Heterogeneity and Aggregate Fluctuations: Insights from TANK Models

Davide Debortoli, *ICREA-Universitat Pompeu Fabra, Centre de Recerca en Economia Internacional (CREI), and Barcelona School of Economics (BSE), Spain*

Jordi Galí, *Centre de Recerca en Economia Internacional (CREI), Universitat Pompeu Fabra, Barcelona School of Economics (BSE), and NBER, Spain*

I. Introduction

Differences in income, wealth, education, and, more generally, economic fortune are a pervasive feature of modern economies. Yet macroeconomists have largely ignored such heterogeneity for decades, under the widespread belief that it is largely irrelevant for understanding aggregate outcomes and their interaction with macro policies. Consistently with that view, and given its analytical convenience, the assumption of an infinitely lived representative household became a staple of macro models, without raising any eyebrows. The representative agent New Keynesian (henceforth, RANK) model is a prominent example of that approach.

An emerging class of models, often referred to as HANK (for heterogeneous agent New Keynesian), has challenged the dominance of the representative household paradigm. Heterogeneity in those models is usually introduced by assuming that households experience idiosyncratic income shocks that cannot be insured against because of incomplete financial markets. The presence of some assets allows households to partly smooth their consumption while giving rise to a nondegenerate wealth distribution. The latter thus becomes one of the model's state variables, which evolves over time in response to aggregate shocks, also influencing how the economy responds to those shocks. The previous features are then combined with a supply block that is similar (if not fully identical) to that characterizing the standard New Keynesian (NK) model. In particular,

NBER Macroeconomics Annual, volume 39, 2025.
 https://doi.org/10.1086/735272

the supply block assumes monopolistically competitive firms as well as nominal rigidities, thus allowing monetary policy to have real effects.[1]

In the present paper, we seek to advance our understanding of the implications of heterogeneity for aggregate fluctuations in the NK model. Our ultimate goal is twofold. First, we want to understand the mechanisms through which heterogeneity, in the form of idiosyncratic income risk, affects aggregate fluctuations and the transmission of shocks in HANK models. As discussed below, we do so by comparing the properties of a number of nested HANK models, a strategy that allows us to isolate the role played by different elements found in conventional versions of those models. Second, we want to investigate whether there are simple tractable models that can capture reasonably well the mechanisms that we identify as most relevant in richer models.[2]

Throughout, our analysis relies heavily on the distinction between hand-to-mouth and unconstrained households. That distinction arises endogenously in conventional HANK models. It is also central to two-agent New Keynesian (TANK) models, though in the latter it is introduced in a rather stark way.[3] Although the tractability and transparency of TANK models are generally viewed as advantages relative to conventional HANK models, it is not clear that the former can capture well the aggregate implications of the latter. This motivates a key objective of our analysis, namely, the evaluation of the ability of TANK models to approximate the aggregate equilibrium dynamics generated by HANK models.

To be clear, we are not the first to compare the properties of a baseline HANK model to those of simpler, more tractable frameworks.[4] The key difference lies in the particular approach we adopt, which stresses the differential behavior of hand-to-mouth versus unconstrained households. It is in that sense that we analyze the properties of HANK models through the lens of their TANK counterparts, thus motivating our title. We believe this provides an interesting and useful perspective to understanding the mechanisms at work in HANK models.

Our analysis starts by laying out a HANK model that we use as a baseline throughout the paper. Our baseline HANK model describes an economy with a continuum of households subject to idiosyncratic income shocks. All households have access to two assets: bonds and stocks. Bonds are fully liquid, whereas stocks are fully or partly illiquid. Holdings of the two assets are subject to constraints: a borrowing constraint in the case of bonds, a nonnegativity constraint in the case of stocks.

We view the presence of idiosyncratic income shocks (in the absence of complete markets) as a defining feature of HANK models, relative to tractable models like RANK or TANK. It is also a main factor behind its nontrivial equilibrium dynamics, because it gives rise to a time-varying wealth distribution that becomes an infinite-dimensional state variable. By way of contrast, we define a tractable model as one that abstracts from the presence of idiosyncratic income risk, assuming instead a small number of household types. For each type, a time-invariant set of households that are identical, both ex ante and ex post, is assumed. The equilibrium conditions of such tractable models, linearized around a steady state, can be solved analytically, arguably rendering them more suitable for use in the classroom or for communication with policy makers.

Our approach in the present paper consists of (1) analyzing the equilibrium properties of three versions of the HANK model,[5] (2) proposing a tractable counterpart for each of them, and (3) assessing the extent to which the equilibrium properties of the tractable model provide a reasonable approximation to those of the corresponding HANK economy.[6]

We proceed sequentially by considering models with increasing complexity. Thus, we start by analyzing a version of the HANK model (which we refer to as HANK-I) in which borrowing constraints are not binding in equilibrium and stocks are fully illiquid, a framework we took as a benchmark in earlier work (Debortoli and Galí 2024). We show that the NK model with a representative agent (RANK), which also displays no binding borrowing constraints, provides a good approximation to the aggregate behavior of HANK-I.

Next, we consider a version of the HANK model (HANK-II) similar to HANK-I except for the fact that the borrowing constraint on bonds is binding in equilibrium for a (time-varying) fraction of households. In the equilibrium of HANK-II, we can identify two types of households at any point in time: those which are unconstrained and those for which the borrowing constraint is binding. We refer to the latter as hand to mouth because their marginal propensity to consume (MPC) is one. We compare the equilibrium properties of the previous model to those of simple TANK models, in which a time-invariant subset of households behaves in a hand-to-mouth fashion. First, we show that the standard version of the TANK model, which we refer to as TANK-I, fails to capture two key channels determining the response of aggregate consumption to aggregate shocks in HANK-II: (1) the *interest rate exposure channel*, whereby changes in interest rates have a direct effect on the net cash-on-hand and, hence, consumption of hand-to-mouth households and (2) *the income distribution channel*, which captures the impact of changes in the average price markup on the distribution of income between unconstrained and hand-to-mouth households, given that the average labor productivity and, hence, the relative importance of labor versus capital income differs across those two household types. Those missing channels prevent the TANK-I model from approximating well some of the aggregate properties of HANK-II. We then propose a straightforward modification of TANK-I, which we label TANK-II, where the hand-to-mouth (1) own a fraction of the existing (illiquid) stocks; (2) have a lower labor productivity than the unconstrained; and (3) are permanently against an implicit borrowing constraint, thus servicing the interest on a constant level of debt. We show that a suitably calibrated version of the TANK-II model approximates well the aggregate properties and key underlying mechanisms of the HANK-II model.

Finally, we analyze a version of the HANK model (labeled as HANK-III) which is arguably closer to the baseline HANK models found in the recent literature. The main difference with respect to HANK-II is that HANK-III relaxes the assumption of fully illiquid stocks by allowing adjustments in the holdings of the illiquid asset, subject to a transaction cost and a no short-sale constraint. The resulting model is similar to versions of the HANK model found in the literature, generally referred to as *two-asset* HANK models. A property of the equilibrium of HANK-III is that at any point in time, three different types of households coexist: (1) the unconstrained, (2) those for whom the borrowing constraint on the liquid asset is binding, but not the short-sale constraint on the illiquid asset, and (3) those for which both constraints are binding. Following the literature, we refer to (2) and (3) as the *wealthy hand to mouth* and the *poor hand to mouth*, respectively. We show that the introduction of portfolio adjustment costs and the emergence of wealthy hand-to-mouth agents alter significantly some key properties of the model: in particular, the response to technology shocks. The main reason for this is that in HANK-III, changes in dividends are not immediately converted into cash on hand, because that conversion requires liquidation of part of the illiquid asset.

We propose a tractable counterpart to HANK-III, which we refer to as TANK-III. In the latter, and relative to TANK-II, we introduce in a parsimonious way the distinction between poor and wealthy hand-to-mouth households found in HANK-III while abstracting from the presence of idiosyncratic income risk. The resulting model matches reasonably well the predictions of HANK-III.

The bulk of our analysis below is carried out under the assumption of an exogenous real interest rate. We choose that approach so that the response of aggregate variables to different shocks is not affected by any particular assumption regarding the monetary policy rule, which would generally lead to different paths of the real rate across environments that differ in terms of the behavior of variables that the central bank responds to. When we relax that assumption and assume instead a more realistic Taylor-type rule as a description of monetary policy, we find that the similarity in the aggregate properties of the different models considered (RANK, TANK, and HANK) increases dramatically. The intuition for that result is straightforward: all the previous models share a common supply block, which features a NK Phillips curve displaying the "divine coincidence" property. Policies that tend to stabilize inflation (like the assumed Taylor rule) also close the gap between output and its natural counterpart, which is invariant to heterogeneity. As a result, equilibrium output tends to converge across models. Furthermore, we show that in the limiting case of a strict inflation targeting, policy heterogeneity becomes completely irrelevant for the determination of aggregate output.

Our paper is related to two main strands of the literature. On the one hand, the HANK literature explores the implications of introducing household idiosyncratic income risk and incomplete markets into an otherwise standard NK framework with nominal rigidities. Some examples are the works of Guerrieri and Lorenzoni (2018), McKay, Nakamura, and Steinsson (2016), Farhi and Werning (2019), Gornemann, Kuester, and Nakajima (2016), Kaplan, Moll, and Violante (2018), McKay and Reis (2016), Werning (2015), Auclert (2019), Auclert, Rognlie, and Straub (2024), Luetticke (2020), and Ravn and Sterk (2021), among others.

On the other hand, the paper builds on a literature that develops simple, tractable models that assume some stylized form of ex ante household heterogeneity with regard to access to financial markets. That literature was pioneered by Campbell and Mankiw (1989), who proposed a simple, two-agent framework with unconstrained and hand-to-mouth households, thus departing from the representative household formalism dominant at that time. Galí, López-Salido, and Vallés (2007) and Bilbiie (2008) are early examples, embedding that structure into the NK model, giving rise to the so-called TANK models. More recent contributions include Bilbiie (2020), Broer et al. (2020), and Cantore and Freund (2021), among others.[7]

Our paper connects the two literatures in two respects. First, we rely on the distinction between hand-to-mouth versus unconstrained households—the hallmark of TANK models—to better understand the mechanisms at work in HANK models. Second, we assess the ability of tractable models in the spirit of TANK to approximate the aggregate properties of richer HANK models.

The remainder of the paper is organized as follows: Section II introduces the baseline elements that are common across all the HANK models considered. Section III analyzes a HANK model without binding borrowing constraints (HANK-I) and its tractable RANK counterpart. Section IV introduces an occasionally binding borrowing constraint (HANK-II) and compares its properties with a standard TANK model as well as a modified version of the latter (TANK-II). Section V considers a HANK model with liquid bonds and partially illiquid stocks (HANK-III) in comparison to a suitably modified TANK model (TANK-III). Section VI analyzes the consequences of endogenizing monetary policy. Section VII relates some of our findings to the existing literature. Section VIII concludes.

II. A Baseline HANK Model

In this section, we describe the elements of a baseline HANK framework that are shared across the different models considered below.

A. Households

We assume a continuum of infinitely lived households, indexed by $j \in [0,1]$. Each household seeks to maximize utility $\mathbb{E}_0 \Sigma_{t=0}^{\infty} \beta^t U(C_t(j), \mathcal{N}_t(j))$, where $C_t(j) \equiv (\int_0^1 C_t(i,j)^{1-\frac{1}{\epsilon}} di)^{\epsilon/(\epsilon-1)}$ is an index of the quantities consumed of the different available goods $i \in [0,1]$, with ϵ denoting the elasticity of substitution among goods. $\mathcal{N}_t(j)$ denotes hours worked. We assume $U(C,\mathcal{N}) \equiv (C^{1-\sigma} - 1)/(1-\sigma) - \mathcal{N}^{1+\varphi}/(1+\varphi)$, where σ is the coefficient of relative risk aversion and φ is the inverse of the Frisch labor supply elasticity.

Household j's labor income in period t is given by $\Xi_t(j) W_t \mathcal{N}_t(j)$, where W_t is the (real) wage per efficiency unit of labor and $\Xi_t(j) \equiv \exp\{\zeta_t(j)\}$ is an exogenous idiosyncratic shock to the household's supply of efficiency units per hour worked, with $\int_0^1 \Xi_t(j) dj = 1$. For brevity, we refer to $\Xi_t(j)$ as the idiosyncratic income shock.

There are two assets in the economy. The first asset is a one-period, riskless real bond, with holdings by household j denoted by $B_t(j)$.[8] Bonds are assumed to be fully liquid, that is, they can be bought and sold in a competitive market with no transaction costs, yielding a safe gross real return R_t. Bond holdings are subject to the borrowing constraint:

$$R_t B_t(j) \geq \underline{B}, \tag{1}$$

where $\underline{B}$ indicates the borrowing limit.

The second type of asset ("stocks") are shares in firms' equity, which generate an aggregate dividend D_t every period. In two of the models considered (HANK-I and II), stocks are illiquid, with each household being allocated a fraction of firms' profits according to a rule specified below.

By contrast, in HANK-III stocks are held directly by a competitive financial intermediary. Households can borrow or lend from the financial intermediary at a competitive interest rate R_t and subject to a borrowing constraint. In addition, they can maintain in the latter an equity account to which they can add or withdraw funds subject to a portfolio adjustment cost, following the formalism in Kaplan et al. (2018) and Auclert et al. (2024).

The resulting period budget constraint for household j can thus be written as

$$C_t(j) + B_t(j) = R_{t-1}B_{t-1}(j) + \Xi_t(j)W_t\mathcal{N}_t(j) + F_t(j),$$

where $F_t(j)$ denotes the net additions to the household's cash on hand associated with equity holdings (dividends and/or sales/purchases of equity positions).

We assume a wage schedule given by

$$W_t = \mathcal{M}_w C_t^{\sigma} N_t^{\varphi}, \tag{2}$$

where $C_t \equiv \int_0^1 C_t(j)dj$ and $N_t \equiv \int_0^1 \mathcal{N}_t(j)dj$ denote aggregate consumption and hours, respectively. Note that $C_t^{\sigma} N_t^{\varphi}$ can be interpreted as an "average" marginal rate of substitution (MRS), with $\mathcal{M}_w > 1$ thus playing the role of an average wage markup, determined by workers' market power.[9] Given the wage, firms determine the quantity of hours hired, which are assumed to be distributed uniformly across all households, that is, $\mathcal{N}_t(j) = N_t$ for all $j \in [0, 1]$.[10] Accordingly, household j takes its labor income $\Xi_t(j)W_tN_t$ as exogenous.

B. *Firms*

The supply side, common to all the models analyzed below, is kept as simple as possible. In particular, we make assumptions that guarantee that it is not affected by the presence of heterogeneity. This allows us to focus on the impact of the latter on aggregate demand (which coincides with aggregate consumption in our simple model).

On the production side, we assume a continuum of firms, indexed by $i \in [0, 1]$. Each firm produces a differentiated good with the linear technology:

$$Y_t(i) = A_t N_t(i), \tag{3}$$

where $N_t(i)$ is the quantity of labor (expressed in efficiency units) hired by firm i, and $A_t \equiv \exp\{a_t\}$ is an exogenous technology parameter common to all firms, which follows the AR(1) process $a_t = \rho_a a_{t-1} + \varepsilon_t^a$.

Each firm sets the price of its good optimally each period, subject to a quadratic adjustment cost $(\xi/2)(P_t Y_t)(P_t(i)/P_{t-1}(i) - 1)^2$, where $\xi > 0$, and a sequence of demand constraints $Y_t(i) = (P_t(i)/P_t)^{-\epsilon} Y_t$, where Y_t denotes aggregate output. Profit maximization, combined with the symmetric equilibrium conditions $P_t(i) = P_t$ and $Y_t(i) = Y_t$ for all $i \in [0, 1]$, implies

$$\Pi_t(\Pi_t - 1) = \mathbb{E}_t\left\{\Lambda_{t,t+1}\left(\frac{Y_{t+1}}{Y_t}\right)\Pi_{t+1}(\Pi_{t+1} - 1)\right\} + \frac{\epsilon - 1}{\xi}\left(\frac{\mathcal{M}}{\mathcal{M}_t} - 1\right), \tag{4}$$

where $\Pi_t \equiv P_t/P_{t-1}$ is (gross) price inflation rate, $\mathcal{M}_t$ is the gross price markup, with $\mathcal{M} \equiv \epsilon/(\epsilon - 1) > 1$ being its desired (or flexible price) counterpart, τ is a constant employment subsidy and $\Lambda_{t,t+1}$ is the firm's stochastic discount factor. Aggregate profits are given by $D_t = Y_t\Delta(\Pi_t) - (1 - \tau)W_t N_t - T_t$, where $\Delta(\Pi_t) \equiv 1 - (\xi/2)(\Pi_t - 1)^2$ and T_t are lump-sum taxes on firms that finance the employment subsidy. We set τ so that $\mathcal{M}(1 - \tau) = 1$, which implies that the zero-inflation steady state is efficient and involves zero profits. The latter property guarantees that the distribution of wealth and consumption in the stochastic steady state is not affected by assumptions on the allocation of profits across households and instead depends exclusively on the presence of idiosyncratic income shocks.

A first-order approximation of equation (4) around the zero-inflation steady state yields the inflation equation:

$$\pi_t = \beta\mathbb{E}_t\{\pi_{t+1}\} - \lambda\hat{\mu}_t, \tag{5}$$

where $\hat{\mu}_t \equiv \log(\mathcal{M}_t/\mathcal{M})$ and $\lambda \equiv (\epsilon - 1)/\xi$. Noting that $\mathcal{M}_t = A_t/(1 - \tau)W_t$ and using the wage schedule above we obtain

$$\hat{\mu}_t = -(\sigma + \varphi)\hat{y}_t + (1 + \varphi)a_t, \tag{6}$$

where $y_t \equiv \log(Y_t/Y)$. Moreover, we can determine the (log) natural output (i.e., the equilibrium level of output under flexible prices), denoted by y_t^n, by setting $\hat{\mu}_t = 0$ in equation (6). This yields $y_t^n \equiv ((1 + \varphi)/(\sigma + \varphi))a_t$. Thus, under our assumptions, natural output is not affected by the presence of idiosyncratic income risk, the set of assets available, or the existence of binding borrowing constraints.

Combining equations (5) and (6) yields a version of the familiar NK Phillips curve:

$$\pi_t = \beta \mathbb{E}_t\{\pi_{t+1}\} + \kappa(y_t - y_t^n), \tag{7}$$

where $y_t - y_t^n$ is the output gap and $\kappa \equiv \lambda(\sigma + \varphi)$. Note that equation (7) is invariant to the presence of household heterogeneity and the nature of the latter.

C. *Monetary Policy*

Regarding monetary policy, we assume that the central bank controls the real interest rate R_t. In our baseline specification, we assume that the central bank keeps the real interest rate constant in the face of aggregate shocks (other than monetary policy shocks). Under that approach, the response of aggregate variables to different (nonmonetary) shocks is not affected by any particular assumption regarding the monetary policy rule, which would generally lead to different paths of the real rate across environments associated with different responses of aggregate variables.[11] On the other hand, when we analyze the effects of monetary policy shocks, we assume an exogenous process for the real rate, given by

$$R_t = R \exp\{v_t\},$$

where $v_t = \rho_v v_{t-1} + \varepsilon_t^v$.

The assumptions of a real bond and an exogenous process for its real return jointly imply that we can solve for equilibrium output without any reference to the supply side of the model and, hence, independently of the specific form of the Phillips curve. In Section VI, we bring back (eq. [7]) into the analysis when studying the consequences of endogenizing monetary policy, for which purpose we assume a simple Taylor-type rule for the nominal rate while allowing also for nominal bonds.

D. *Baseline Calibration and Solution Method*

The baseline calibration of our economy is summarized in table 1. Each period is assumed to correspond to a quarter. We set the coefficient of risk aversion $\sigma = 1$, which corresponds to log utility, and the (inverse) Frisch elasticity of substitution $\varphi = 1$. In addition, we set the average wage markup $\mathcal{M}_w = 1.10$, the elasticity of substitution among good varieties $\epsilon = 11$, which implies an average price markup of $\mathcal{M} = 1.10$, and

Table 1
Calibration

Model Parameters		
Σ	Coefficient of risk aversion	1
Φ	(Inverse) Frisch elasticity	1
$\mathcal{M}$	Average price markup	1.10
$\mathcal{M}_w$	Average wage markup	1.10
K	Slope of Phillips curve	.10
Θ	Fraction of profits distributed as lump-sum	.5
R	Steady-state (gross) interest rate	1.005
	→ Discount factor β:	
	RANK, TANK (I, II, III)	.995
	HANK (I, II, III)	.9937, .9838, .9905
Shocks Processes		
ρ_r	Persistence monetary policy shocks	.5
ρ_a	Persistence technology shocks	.9
ρ_z	Autocorr. of idiosyn. earnings	.966
σ_z	Std. dev. of idiosyn. earnings	.5
Solution Method		
n_z	Gridpoints for idiosyn. earnings	11
n_a	Gridpoints for liquid asset	500
$(\underline{B}, \bar{B})$	Bounds on grid for liquid asset:	
	HANK-I	$(-36.33Y, 300Y)$
	HANK-II and III	$(-2Y, 50Y)$

the price adjustment cost parameter ξ so that the resulting slope of the Phillips Curve is $\kappa = 0.10$, in line with available estimates.

Following Auclert et al. (2021), we calibrate the parameters of the K-state Markov process for idiosyncratic income using the Rouwenhorst method to match the volatility and persistence of an AR(1) process $\zeta_t(j) = \rho_\zeta \zeta_{t-1}(j) + \varepsilon_t^\zeta(j)$, where $\varepsilon_t^\zeta(j) \sim N(0, \sigma_\zeta\sqrt{1-\rho_\zeta^2})$, with $\rho_\zeta = 0.966$ and $\sigma_\zeta = 0.5$.

For each model considered below, we calibrate the discount factor β so that the real risk-free rate is 2% (in annual terms) in the steady state. This results in a discount factor $\beta = 1/R = 0.995$ in the RANK and TANK models, and to $\beta = (0.9937, 0.9838, 0.9905)$ for HANK-I, HANK-II, and HANK-III, respectively.

For the economy without a binding borrowing constraint of Section III, we set the borrowing limit at $\underline{B} = -Y\exp\{\min_j \zeta(j)\}/r$, which constitutes the "natural debt limit," given aggregate output and interest rate at their steady-state values (Y, r).[12] For the remaining economies, we set $\underline{B} = -2Y$, which implies a steady-state share of hand-to-mouth households of 30%, as suggested by the evidence in Kaplan, Violante, and Weidner (2014).

The calibration of parameters pertaining to the determination of $F_t(j)$ is discussed below in the respective sections.

Regarding the numerical solution method, we build a grid for individual assets of 500 points, equally distanced (in logs) between the lower bound described above, and an upper bound set to 300 times quarterly income for the model of Section III and to 50 times income for the other models.

For given values of the real interest rate, we solve for the households' policy functions—using the endogenous gridpoints method described in Carroll (2006)—which are then used to calculate the implied equilibrium asset distribution. We solve for the steady state iterating on the value of the discount factor β so that the stationary asset distribution implied by the households' choices satisfies the market clearing condition $\int B_t(j)dj = 0$ at an (annualized) steady-state real rate of 2%.

For the transition dynamics, we adopt the sequence-space Jacobian approach described in Auclert et al. (2021). This amounts to finding the first-order approximation of the equilibrium responses to arbitrary sequences of anticipated monetary policy and technology shocks, that is, under perfect foresight over a finite horizon (set to $T = 300$ quarters). Unless otherwise noted, we set the persistence parameters $\rho_r = 0.5$ for monetary policy shocks and $\rho_a = 0.9$ for technology shocks. Due to certainty equivalence, the resulting dynamics are equivalent to the ones that would be obtained solving the linearized rational expectations model—for example, as in Reiter (2009) and Ahn et al. (2018).[13] Also, by construction, the approximate responses to positive and negative aggregate shocks are fully symmetric, and proportional to the size of the shocks. Most importantly, the assumption of perfect foresight (or certainty equivalence) with respect to aggregate shocks implies that idiosyncratic income shocks are the only source of individual uncertainty.

III. A HANK Economy without Binding Borrowing Constraints

In this section, we consider a version of the HANK model with a natural debt limit, fully illiquid stocks, and a profit allocation rule. This framework, which builds on our earlier work (Debortoli and Galí 2024), helps us identify the specific role of idiosyncratic income shocks as a factor underlying aggregate fluctuations. For brevity, we refer to this version of the HANK model as HANK-I.

We assume aggregate operating profits D_t are distributed among households according to the rule

$$F_t(j) = [\vartheta + (1 - \vartheta)\Xi_t(j)]D_t$$
$$\equiv \Theta_t(j)D_t,$$

where parameter ϑ defines the fraction of profits that are distributed uniformly across households in the form of dividends, whereas $1 - \vartheta$ is the corresponding fraction which is distributed as "bonuses" in proportion to each household's productivity $\Xi_t(j)$.[14] As discussed below, the setting of ϑ is potentially important in determining how a given change in income is allocated across households in response to a shock, with the consequent implications for aggregate consumption.

The previous assumption on the allocation of profits allows us to write the period budget constraint of a typical household as

$$C_t(j) + B_t(j) = R_{t-1}B_{t-1}(j) + \Xi_t(j)W_tN_t + \Theta_t(j)D_t.$$

The assumption of a natural debt limit, together with $\lim_{C\to 0}U_{c,t} = +\infty$, implies that the borrowing constraint is never binding in equilibrium for any household. In turn, the latter fact implies that the following Euler equation holds for all t and $j \in [0, 1]$:

$$1 = \beta R_t \mathbb{E}_t\left\{\left(\frac{C_{t+1}(j)}{C_t(j)}\right)^{-\sigma}\right\}. \tag{8}$$

To understand how the dynamics of aggregate consumption in the HANK-I model differ from those of RANK, it is useful to derive the log-linear approximation to equation (8). As shown in the appendix, equation (8) can be approximated and then aggregated across households to yield the log-linear Euler equation for aggregate consumption:

$$c_t = \mathbb{E}_t\{c_{t+1}\} - \frac{1}{\sigma}\hat{r}_t - \frac{\sigma + 1}{2}\hat{v}_t, \tag{9}$$

where $c_t \equiv \log C_t$ with $C_t \equiv \int_0^1 C_t(j)dj$ denoting aggregate consumption, $\hat{r}_t \equiv 1/\beta R((R_t - R)/R)$, and $v_t \equiv \int(C_t(j)/C_t)v_t(j)dj$, where $v_t(j) \equiv \text{var}_t\{c_{t+1}(j)\}$ is a measure of "individual consumption risk," and $\hat{v}_t \equiv v_t - \mathbb{E}\{v_t\}$.

The impact of idiosyncratic income risk is captured by the *risk-shifter* term v_t in the Euler equation for aggregate consumption. We assume that due to the presence of idiosyncratic income risk, variations in v_t are of the same order of magnitude as variations in aggregate variables resulting from aggregate shocks. This is in contrast with a model with a representative household, in which by construction, $\text{var}_t\{c_{t+1}\}$ is of second order relative to aggregate consumption and other aggregate variables and is thus generally ignored when approximating the Euler equation for aggregate consumption.

Iterating forward we obtain

$$\begin{aligned}\hat{c}_t &= -\frac{1}{\sigma}\sum_{k=0}^{\infty}\mathbb{E}_t\{\hat{r}_{t+k}\} - \frac{\sigma+1}{2}\sum_{k=0}^{\infty}\mathbb{E}_t\{\hat{v}_{t+k}\} \\ &= -\frac{1}{\sigma(1-\rho_r)}\hat{r}_t - \frac{\sigma+1}{2}\sum\nolimits_{k=0}^{\infty}\mathbb{E}_t\{\hat{v}_{t+k}\},\end{aligned} \tag{10}$$

where $\hat{c}_t \equiv \log C_t/C$ and where we have used the fact that $\lim_{T\to\infty}\mathbb{E}_t\{c_{t+T}\} = c$, where c is the mean of the ergodic distribution for $c_t(j)$. Note that, in addition to the real interest rate, aggregate consumption depends inversely on current and anticipated values of the risk shifter which capture the extent of precautionary savings. Our simulations of a calibrated version of HANK-I discussed below allow us to assess the importance of that factor in accounting for fluctuations in aggregate consumption.

As a tractable counterpart to the HANK-I economy analyzed above, we propose the standard RANK model. The latter corresponds to a special case of the HANK-I model above with $\Xi_t(j) = 1$ for all t and $j \in [0,1]$. The representative household's optimality condition is given by

$$1 = \beta R_t \mathbb{E}_t\left\{\left(\frac{C_{t+1}}{C_t}\right)^{-\sigma}\right\},$$

or, in log-linearized form,

$$c_t = \mathbb{E}_t\{c_{t+1}\} - \left(\frac{1}{\sigma}\right)\hat{r}_t.$$

Iterating forward and imposing $\lim_{T\to\infty}\mathbb{E}_t\{c_{t+T}\} = c$ yields:

$$\hat{c}_t = -\left(\frac{1}{\sigma(1-\rho_r)}\right)\hat{r}_t.$$

Thus, under our assumptions, equilibrium output in the RANK economy is a function of the exogenous state variable, $\hat{r}_t$, and is invariant to the specification of the supply side. Output does not display any endogenous persistence.

The gap between aggregate consumption in the HANK-I and RANK models is thus given by

$$\hat{c}_t^{\mathrm{HA}} - \hat{c}_t^{\mathrm{RA}} = -\frac{\sigma + 1}{2} \sum_{k=0}^{\infty} \mathbb{E}_t\{\hat{v}_{t+k}\}, \tag{11}$$

that is, it depends exclusively on current and expected future values of the risk shifter. Accordingly, the presence of idiosyncratic risk will affect the aggregate response of consumption and output to a given aggregate shock only if the latter has an impact on the risk-shifter $\hat{v}_t$. The latter is an endogenous variable that cannot be solved in closed form, so we need to (numerically) solve for the equilibrium of the HANK-I model to evaluate quantitatively the size of that gap. In doing so, and in addition to the calibrated values introduced above, we assume $\vartheta = 0.5$, implying that half of aggregate profits are distributed to households in proportion to their idiosyncratic labor productivity.

Panel *A* of figure 1 shows the impulse response of equilibrium output to monetary policy and technology shocks in HANK-I (line with circles) and RANK (line with crosses). In the case of a monetary policy shock, we consider a 25 basis point reduction in the real rate on impact (which corresponds to a 1 percentage point in annualized terms). The presence of idiosyncratic risk in HANK-I leads to an amplification of the output effects of the shock: the effects are stronger on impact and more persistent. The difference is, however, quantitatively very small.

The previous assessment is confirmed by panel *B* of figure 1, which displays the simulated time series for (log) output generated by HANK-I and RANK in response to a sequence of monetary policy surprises drawn from a normal distribution. In a way consistent with the impulse responses, we see that the volatility of output under HANK-I is slightly larger (by a 1.22 factor), but the correlation between the two is very high (0.97), pointing to a limited impact of the additional dynamics resulting from changes in the wealth distribution, an endogenous state variable present in HANK-I but not in RANK.

In Debortoli and Galí (2024), we sought to understand the reasons behind the small gap between the output responses in the two models. Given equation (11), that finding must ultimately be associated with a small response of the risk shifter to a shock. The basic intuition for that small response can be obtained from the following approximation derived in that paper:

$$v_t(j) \simeq \psi_t(j)^2 \sigma_\xi^2,$$

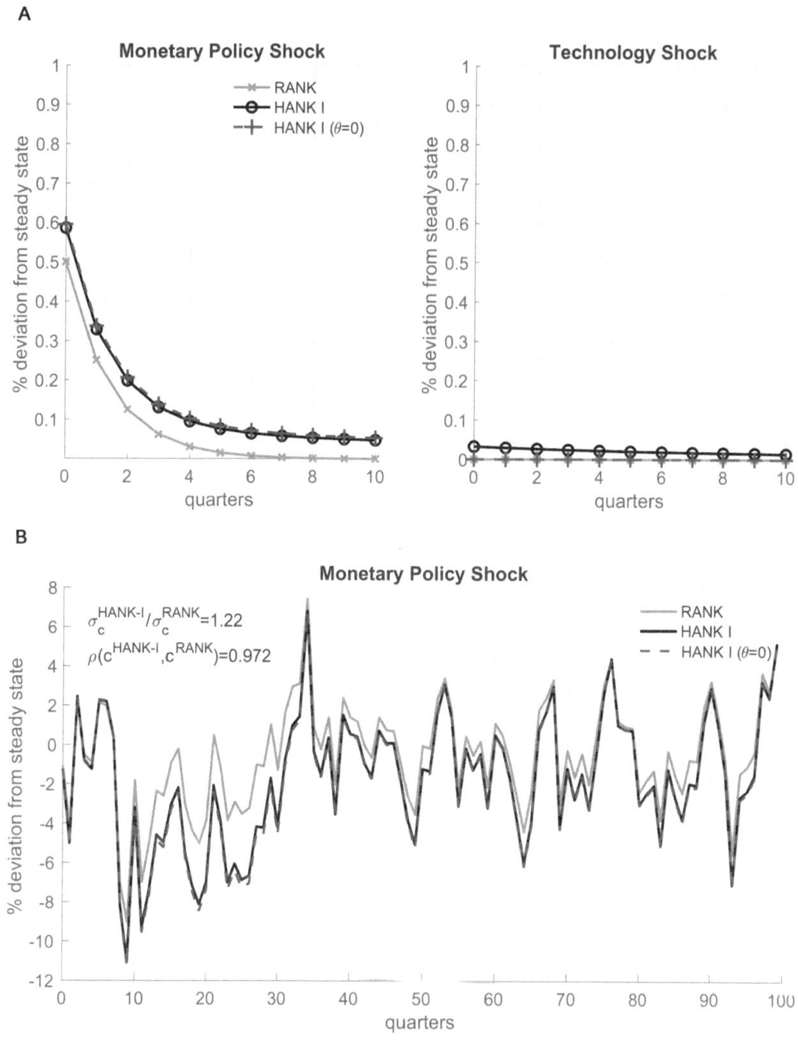

Fig. 1. RANK versus HANK-I. Panel *A* shows the response of output to a 1% decrease in the (annualized) real interest rate (left), and to a 1% positive technology shock (right) in a representative agent model (line with crosses) and in the heterogeneous agent model with no binding borrowing constraint, with or without an income distribution channel (line with circles and dashed line with "pluses," respectively). Panel *B* shows a simulated path of consumptions in response to monetary policy shocks.

where $\psi_t(j)$ is the elasticity of individual consumption with respect to the idiosyncratic shock. Hence

$$v_t \simeq \sigma_\xi^2 \int \frac{C_t(j)}{C_t} \psi_t(j)^2 dj, \tag{12}$$

where $\psi_t(j)$ is household j's elasticity of consumption with respect to the innovation in the idiosyncratic income process, and σ_ξ^2 is the variance of the latter. In response to an aggregate shock the following approximation holds:

$$\frac{dv_{t+k}}{d\varepsilon_t} \simeq \sigma_\xi^2 \int \frac{C_t(j)}{C_t} \frac{d\psi_{t+k}(j)^2}{d\varepsilon_t} dj.$$

As shown in figure 2, drawn from Debortoli and Galí (2024), $\psi_t(j)^2$ is *decreasing and (strongly) convex in the level of consumption*, capturing the fact that the consumption of households with less liquid wealth and closer to the natural debt limit is more responsive to shocks that change that wealth (i.e., their MPC is higher). Accordingly, and in response to

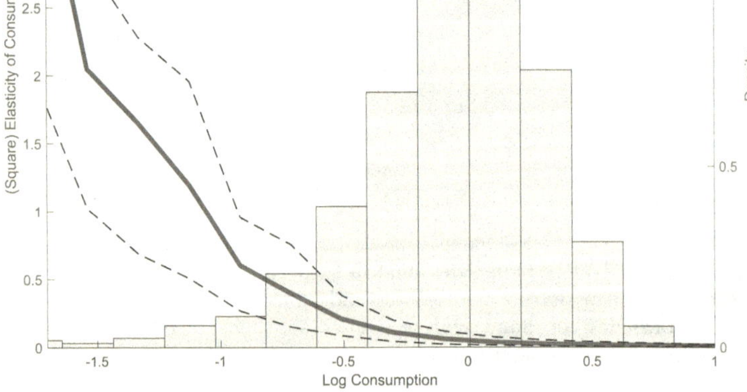

Fig. 2. Elasticity of consumption in steady state. The figure shows the relationship between log consumption (horizontal axis) and the elasticity of consumption (left vertical axis) in steady state. For each value of consumption, the figure reports the average elasticity (solid line) and the 5%–95% interval of the distribution (dashed lines), whereas the histogram indicates the steady-state distribution (right vertical axis).

shocks that shift the wealth distribution in either direction, $d\psi_{t+k}(j)^2/d\varepsilon_t$ is quantitatively significant only for poor households. Because the weight of those households in aggregate consumption is small, the dynamic response of the aggregate risk shifter becomes muted, thus accounting for the small gap between $\hat{c}_t^{HA}$ and $\hat{c}_t^{RA}$.

We can apply the previous reasoning to understand the impact of idiosyncratic risk on the responses to a monetary policy shock. In particular, note that an expansionary monetary policy shock has two effects that tend to offset each other, above and beyond the intertemporal substitution in response to a change in the real interest rate that is already captured by the RANK model. First, the interest rate reduction implies a redistribution from (rich) lenders to (poor) borrowers, which reduces wealth dispersion. We refer to this as the *interest rate exposure* channel. On the other hand, the monetary expansion raises average labor income but lowers aggregate dividends. For households with productivity above a certain threshold, total (noninterest) income increases, but this is not the case for low-productivity households, which experience a decline in that income. To see this formally, define a household's income (excluding interest) as

$$Y_t(j) \equiv \Xi_t(j)W_tN_t + \Theta_t(j)D_t,$$

which we can rewrite in terms of aggregate output and the markup as follows:

$$Y_t(j) = \left[\Xi_t(j)\frac{\mathcal{M}}{\mathcal{M}_t} + \Theta_t(j)\left(1 - \frac{\mathcal{M}}{\mathcal{M}_t}\right)\right]Y_t .$$

Differentiating the previous expression and using equation (6), we obtain

$$\frac{dY_t(j)}{Y} = [\Xi_t(j) - \vartheta(1 - \Xi_t(j))(\sigma + \varphi)]dy_t + \vartheta(1 - \Xi_t(j))(1 + \varphi)da_t. \quad (13)$$

Accordingly, in response to an expansionary monetary policy shock, which raises aggregate output, $dY_t(j) > 0$ if and only if $\Xi_t(j) > \vartheta(\sigma + \varphi)/(1 + \vartheta(\sigma + \varphi))$. Thus, through this mechanism and to the extent that $\theta > 0$, income is redistributed from poor/low-productivity households to rich/high-productivity households. This is what we call the *income distribution* channel.[15]

Thus, and as long as $\vartheta > 0$, the interest rate exposure and income distribution channels work in opposite directions and thus tend to neutralize the impact of the shock on the wealth distribution and, as a result, on the difference in the response of aggregate consumption and output between RANK and HANK-I. In addition, whatever net redistribution there is, it affects mostly the consumption risk of poor households, so the impact on the aggregate risk shifter and aggregate consumption are small. This is consistent with the small difference uncovered in the impulses responses shown in figure 1.[16]

To assess the importance of each channel, the dashed line in the figure shows the response of aggregate output when setting $\vartheta = 0$—that is, when we turn off the income distribution channel. The tiny gap between that response and the one implied by our baseline calibration suggests a very small role for that channel in shaping the aggregate response to the shock. In that case, the interest rate exposure channel redistributes resources from the rich to the poor, thus reducing the overall consumption risk and amplifying the response of output relative to RANK, albeit in a small amount, given the low weight of poor households' consumption in the aggregate.

Let us now turn to the effects of technology shocks. The second panel in figure 1 shows that a 1% positive technology shock has no effect on output in the RANK model because the central bank keeps the real rate constant, thus preventing aggregate demand from increasing. By contrast, the output effect of the same shock in HANK-I is positive, albeit very small. The intuition for the increase in output in HANK-I is as follows: at any given initial level of output, the shock raises dividends while reducing labor income by the same amount. As equation (13) makes clear, that adjustment does not affect everyone equally: it raises the income of households with productivity below the mean ($\Xi_t(j) < 1$), for which dividends account for a larger share of their income, while lowering it for the remaining households. Thus, the shock implies a redistribution of income from rich to poor households. The reduction in consumption risk for the poor more than offsets the small increase in that risk experienced by the rich, implying an overall decline in precautionary savings, with the consequent expansion in aggregate demand and output captured in figure 1. Again, the effect is quantitatively small because the reduction in precautionary savings affects mostly households with a low consumption share to begin with. The response in the counterfactual case with $\vartheta = 0$ is represented by the dashed line, which overlaps perfectly with the zero response associated with RANK, for in that case, there is no income redistribution and hence no change in consumption.

Next, we assess the role of idiosyncratic income risk as a source of endogenous persistence. As is well known, in the basic RANK model, there are no state variables beyond the exogenous variables themselves. This is not the case in HANK models generally, in which, as discussed above, the distribution of wealth is itself a state variable. To assess to what extent the dynamic response of that distribution is capable of generating endogenous persistence (i.e., persistence beyond that of the exogenous driving forces), we report in figure 3 the dynamic response of output to purely transitory monetary policy and technology shocks in the HANK-I model, next to the corresponding responses in RANK. The figure makes clear that although the presence of idiosyncratic risk generates persistence in the output response, the effect beyond the initial period is quantitatively small. In other words, the endogenous response of the wealth distribution to an aggregate shock has quantitatively small implications for aggregate output.[17]

We conclude from the previous exercises that RANK provides a good approximation to the response of aggregate output to both monetary and technology shocks implied by the HANK-I model, that is, a version of the HANK model without binding borrowing constraints. Next we study whether the introduction of occasionally binding borrowing constraints in the HANK model leads to a different conclusion.

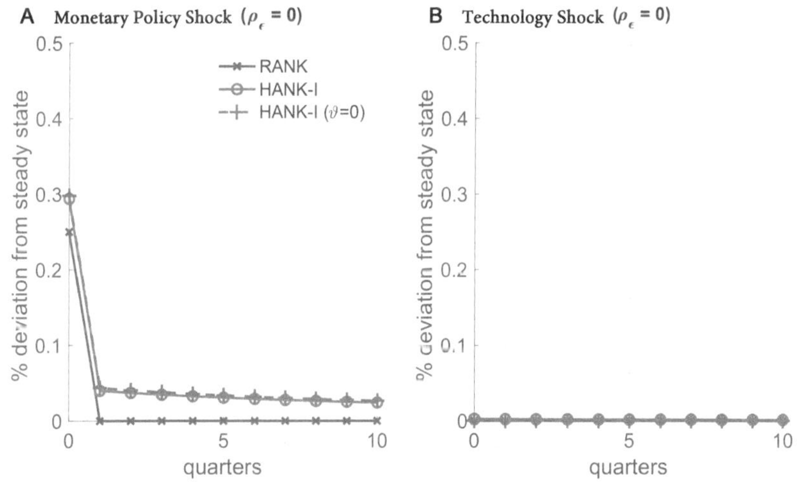

Fig. 3. Impulse responses, RANK versus HANK-I (purely transitory shock). The figure shows the response of output to a purely transitory 1% decrease in the (annualized) real interest rate (panel *A*) and to a purely transitory 1% positive technology shock (panel *B*) in a representative agent model (line with crosses) and in the heterogeneous agent model with no binding borrowing constraint with or without an income distribution channel (line with circles and dashed line with "pluses," respectively).

IV. A HANK Economy with Binding Borrowing Constraints

In the previous section, we analyzed a version of the HANK model without binding borrowing constraints, in which the consumption Euler equation held for all households at all times. This allowed us to derive an approximate aggregate consumption Euler equation and to insulate the role of idiosyncratic income risk. By contrast, in the present section, and following much of the HANK literature, we assume a borrowing limit tighter than the natural debt limit. As a result, the borrowing constraint is binding in equilibrium for a nonnegligible fraction of households, which we label as hand to mouth. That fraction evolves endogenously, with its value in period t denoted by λ_t^H.

More specifically, the borrowing limit is now assumed to be given by

$$\underline{B} = -\psi Y .$$

The remaining assumptions are the same as in HANK-I. We refer to the resulting model as HANK-II.

Households who are unconstrained in period t, satisfy the Euler equation:

$$1 = \beta R_t \mathbb{E}_t \left\{ \left(\frac{C_{t+1}(j)}{C_t(j)} \right)^{-\sigma} \right\}, \tag{14}$$

which thus holds for all $j \in \mathcal{U}_t \equiv \{j \in [0, 1] : R_t B_t(j) > -\psi Y\}$.

As shown in the appendix, one can approximate and then average the resulting equation across unconstrained households to yield the log-linearized Euler equation:

$$\hat{c}_t^U = \mathbb{E}_t\{\hat{c}_{t+1}^U\} - \frac{1}{\sigma}\hat{r}_t - \frac{\sigma + 1}{2}\hat{v}_t^U - \hat{h}_t^U, \tag{15}$$

where $\hat{c}_t^U \equiv \log C_t^U / C^U$ with $C_t^U = 1/(1 - \lambda_t^H) \int_{j \in \mathcal{U}_t} C_t(j) dj$ and $v_t^U \equiv 1/(1 - \lambda_t^H) \int_{j \in \mathcal{U}_t} C_t(j)/C_t^U v_t(j) dj$, measuring, respectively, average consumption and average consumption risk (the latter weighed by relative consumption) of households who are unconstrained in period t. In addition, we have $h_t^U \equiv \mathbb{E}_t\{(C_{t+1}^U - C_{t+1|t}^U)/C_t^U\}$ where $C_{t+1|t}^U \equiv 1/(1 - \lambda_t^H) \int_{j \in \mathcal{U}_t} C_{t+1}(j) dj$ is the average consumption in $t + 1$ of households who were unconstrained in period t. Note that h_t^U emerges as a result of changes in the composition of subset $\mathcal{U}_t$, associated with the fact that some households that are unconstrained at t become constrained at $t + 1$, and vice versa, so that in general we have $C_{t+1}^U \neq C_{t+1|t}^U$. We refer to this additional term in the Euler equation as the *composition shifter*. The presence of both the risk-shifter $\hat{v}_t^U$ and the composition shifter $\hat{h}_t^U$ is tied to the existence of idiosyncratic income risk. In the absence of the latter, $\hat{v}_t^U$ would be of second order, and $\hat{h}_t^U$ would be zero.

Iterating equation (15) forward, we can write the gap between average consumption of the unconstrained in HANK-II and that in the RANK model as

$$\hat{c}_t^U - \hat{c}_t^{RA} = -\frac{\sigma+1}{2}\sum_{k=0}^{\infty}\mathbb{E}_t\{\hat{v}_{t+k}^U\} - \sum_{k=0}^{\infty}\mathbb{E}_t\{\hat{h}_{t+k}^U\}, \tag{16}$$

whose quantitative significance we seek to evaluate below.

For the remaining households, for which the borrowing constraint is binding, consumption is given by

$$C_t(j) = \Xi_t(j)W_tN_t + \Theta_t(j)D_t + R_{t-1}B_{t-1}(j) + \frac{\psi Y}{R_t}, \tag{17}$$

which holds for all $j \in \mathcal{H}_t \equiv \{j \in [0,1] : R_tB_t(j) = -\psi Y\}$. Note that, at the margin, any change in household j's current income $\Xi_t(j)W_tN_t + \Theta_t(j)D_t$ while constrained leads to a one-for-one change in consumption (i.e., the MPC is one). Thus, and following the literature, we refer to that subset of households as *hand to mouth*.

Averaging equation (17) over $j \in \mathcal{H}_t$ yields

$$\begin{aligned} C_t^H &= \frac{1}{\lambda_t^H}\int_{j\in\mathcal{H}_t} C_t(j)dj \\ &= \Xi_t^H W_tN_t + \Theta_t^H D_t - \psi Y\left(\Omega_{t-1}^H - \frac{1}{R_t}\right) \\ &= \left[\Xi_t^H\frac{\mathcal{M}}{\mathcal{M}_t} + \Theta_t^H\left(1-\frac{\mathcal{M}}{\mathcal{M}_t}\right)\right]Y_t - \psi Y(\hat{R}_t + \Omega_{t-1}^H - 1), \end{aligned} \tag{18}$$

where $\hat{R}_t \equiv (R_t-1)/R_t$, $\Xi_t^H \equiv 1/\lambda_t^H\int_{j\in\mathcal{H}_t}\Xi_t(j)dj$ and $\Theta_t^H \equiv 1/\lambda_t^H\int_{j\in\mathcal{H}_t}\Theta_t(j)dj$ are, respectively, the average productivity of and the average fraction of aggregate profits accruing to hand-to-mouth households in period t, whereas $\Omega_{t-1}^H \equiv -1/\lambda_t^H\int_{j\in\mathcal{H}_t}(R_{t-1}B_{t-1})(j)/\psi Y dj$ denotes the average debt maintained in period $t-1$ by period t hand-to-mouth households, expressed as a ratio to the debt limit ψY.

Equation (18) reveals explicitly the role of the interest rate exposure channel and the income distribution channel in determining the consumption of constrained households. First, note that to the extent that most currently constrained households were either already constrained or close to being constrained in the previous period, we would expect Ω_{t-1}^{H} to be positive and close to 1. As a result, $\partial C_t^H/\partial R_t < 0$, revealing the presence of the interest rate exposure channel. Moreover, and given that average productivity among hand-to-mouth households will (naturally) be below the mean (i.e., $\Xi_t^H < 1$), we will have $\Theta_t^H > \Xi_t^H$ (as long as $\vartheta > 0$). Accordingly, an increase in the average markup will, ceteris paribus, raise hand-to-mouth consumption, that is, $\partial C_t^H/\partial \mathcal{M}_t > 0$. The reason is that it implies an increase in dividends, and a reduction in labor income, and thus a redistribution of income toward low-productivity, constrained households (for whom dividend income is relatively more important).

Aggregate consumption can thus be written as

$$\begin{aligned} C_t &= \lambda_t^H C_t^H + (1-\lambda_t^H)C_t^U \\ &= \Phi_t Y_t - \lambda_t^H \psi Y(\hat{R}_t + \Omega_{t-1}^H - 1) + (1-\lambda_t^H)C_t^U, \end{aligned} \tag{19}$$

where C_t^U satisfies equation (15) and $\Phi_t \equiv \lambda_t^H[\Xi_t^H(\mathcal{M}/\mathcal{M}_t) + \Theta_t^H(1-(\mathcal{M}/\mathcal{M}_t))]$ can be interpreted as a time-varying "slope of the Keynesian cross."

What are the aggregate consequences of introducing a borrowing constraint, by setting a debt limit tighter than the natural debt limit so that such constraint becomes binding for a nonnegligible fraction of households every period? We address this question by computing the impulse responses to monetary and technology shocks in a calibrated version of HANK-II with $\psi = 2$. The implied borrowing limit is consistent with 30% of households being constrained in the stochastic steady state, consistently with Kaplan et al. (2014). The settings for the remaining parameters are left unchanged. Figure 4 displays the resulting impulse responses, together with those generated by HANK-I.

The first panel of figure 4 shows the response of output to an expansionary monetary policy shock. Perhaps surprisingly, we see that the presence of a binding borrowing constraint does not amplify significantly the response of output, and it dampens it after a certain horizon. The previous finding seems at odds with the fact that in HANK-II, a significant fraction of households behave in a hand-to-mouth fashion, thus generating a large direct multiplier effect captured by coefficient Φ_t—the slope of the Keynesian cross in equation (19). At least two factors account for this result. First, the direct effects of interest rate changes, working through intertemporal substitution by unconstrained households, are now smaller

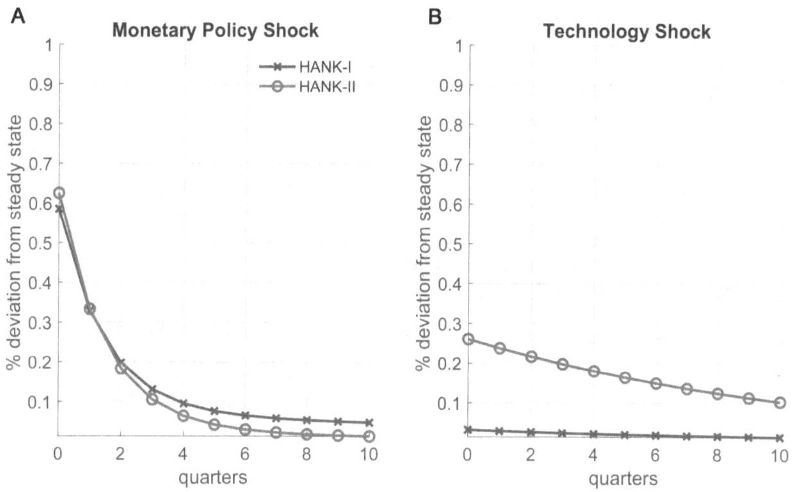

Fig. 4. HANK-I versus HANK-II. The figure shows the response of output to a 1% decrease in the (annualized) real interest rate (panel *A*) and to a 1% positive technology shock (panel *B*) in the heterogeneous agent model with no binding borrowing constraint (line with crosses) and with binding borrowing constraint for 30% of the population (line with circles).

because the latter account only for a fraction $1 - \lambda_t^H$ of all households. Second, because of the tighter borrowing constraint, the distribution of wealth across households in HANK-II is less dispersed than in HANK-I. As a result, the interest rate exposure channel is more muted.

Things are substantially different in response to a technology shock, because in that case, the absence of a monetary policy response neutralizes the interest rate exposure channel as well as the direct effect working through intertemporal substitution by unconstrained households. As a result, the higher multiplier associated with the presence of hand-to-mouth households ends up becoming the key factor, leading to the amplified response to the positive technology shock relative to HANK-I shown on the right panel of figure 4.

To sum up, the introduction of occasionally binding borrowing constraints, with the consequent emergence of hand-to-mouth households, does not necessarily amplify the effects of shocks. Whether this is the case or not depends on the nature of the shock as well as on the strength of potential offsetting effects (including an eventual endogenous response of monetary policy, not modeled here). Next, we look for a tractable framework that can account for all these properties of HANK-II.

A. A Tractable Counterpart to HANK-II

The Standard TANK Model (TANK-I)

The key difference between HANK-I and HANK-II is the presence of a fraction of households that do not satisfy the Euler equation and instead behave in a hand-to-mouth fashion, consuming their current income (net of debt service payments). The "standard" TANK model (Galí et al. 2007; Bilbiie 2008), which assumes ex ante heterogeneity with two types of households (unconstrained and hand to mouth), may naturally be viewed—and has often been portrayed in the literature—as a tractable framework to approximate the equilibrium dynamics of a HANK model with binding borrowing constraints like HANK-II. Standard versions of the TANK model, however, fail to capture some of the mechanisms at work in HANK-II, as we show next.

Consider a standard version of the TANK model, where a constant fraction λ^H of households holds no financial assets and just consumes their current labor income each period, that is, $C_t^H = W_t N_t$. The remaining fraction $1 - \lambda^H$ is unconstrained. Most importantly, households of a given type are identical, both ex ante and ex post; in particular, they experience no idiosyncratic income shocks. Henceforth, we refer to that version of the TANK model as TANK-I (to distinguish it from alternative versions considered below).

Accordingly, in the TANK-I economy, aggregate consumption is given by

$$\begin{aligned} C_t &= \lambda^H W_t N_t + (1 - \lambda^H) C_t^U \\ &= \lambda^H \frac{\mathcal{M}}{\mathcal{M}_t} Y_t + (1 - \lambda^H) C_t^U, \end{aligned} \tag{20}$$

where C_t^U satisfies

$$\hat{c}_t^U = \mathbb{E}_t\{\hat{c}_{t+1}^U\} - \left(\frac{1}{\sigma}\right)\hat{r}_t. \tag{21}$$

A comparison of equations (19) and (20) uncovers several differences between HANK-II and TANK-I. Two of those differences are linked to standard features of TANK models: (1) a constant fraction of hand-to-mouth households and (2) the absence of (first-order effects of) precautionary savings, as reflected in the missing shifter terms in equation (21), due to the absence of idiosyncratic risk. Thus, to the extent that variations in the fraction of hand-to-mouth households and in precautionary savings are significant factors underlying fluctuations in aggregate consumption, TANK models will have little chance to approximate the equilibrium properties and mechanisms in HANK-II.

Other shortcomings, however, are specific to the standard version of the TANK model described above (i.e., TANK-I), and may be amenable to modification. In particular, it is clear that equation (20) fails to capture the interest rate exposure channel revealed by equation (19), because hand-to-mouth households are not indebted in TANK-I. Second, equation (20) points to a negative relation between aggregate consumption and the markup, for a given level of output, due to the negative effect of a higher markups on labor income, a variable tightly connected to aggregate consumption due to the presence of hand-to-mouth households. Thus, the sign of the income distribution channel at work in HANK-II (and captured in eq. [19]) is reversed in TANK-I.

Given the previous differences, it may not be surprising that TANK-I fails to approximate well the aggregate properties of HANK-II. This is illustrated in figure 5*A*, which displays the response of aggregate output to monetary policy and technology shocks in both models. Note that the only new parameter in TANK-I relative to RANK is λ^H, which we set to 0.30, the mean value of λ_t^H in HANK-II.

As figure 5*A* makes clear, the output response to an expansionary monetary policy shock is highly amplified in TANK-I (line with crosses) relative to HANK-II (line with circles), almost trebling the effect on impact. In the case of technology shocks, the difference is even starker because the sign of the output response in TANK-I is reversed relative to HANK-II, due to the fall in labor income. Given the previous discussion and findings, one can hardly view TANK-I as providing a reasonable approximation to HANK-II.

A Modified TANK Model. TANK-II

Next we propose a simple modification of the TANK model that has a better chance to approximate well the aggregate predictions of HANK-II. In our modified model, which we refer to as TANK-II, we make three assumptions that seek to mirror some features of HANK-II, in a way not captured by the standard TANK model. First, we assume that hand-to-mouth households are permanently against the borrowing constraint introduced in HANK-II, that is, $R_t B_t^H = -\psi Y$ for all t. Second, we assume that the productivity of hand-to-mouth households is given by $\Xi^H < 1$, and

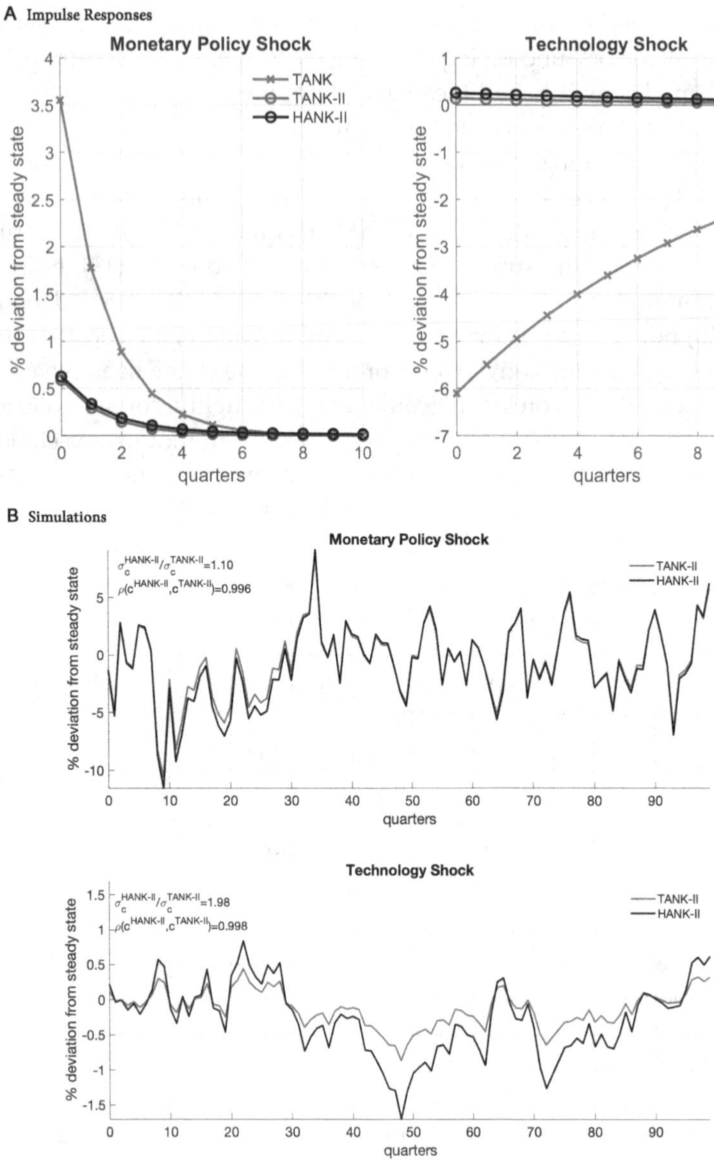

Fig. 5. Simple alternatives to HANK-II. Panel *A* shows the response of output to a 1% decrease in the (annualized) real interest rate (left panel) and to a 1% positive technology shock (right panel) in heterogeneous agent model with binding borrowing constraint for 30% of the population (line with circles) and in the TANK (line with crosses) and TANK-II (line with circles) models. Panel *B* shows a simulated path of consumptions in response to monetary policy and technology shocks.

hence is lower than that of unconstrained households.[18] Finally, we assume that dividends are allocated to all households (including the hand to mouth) according to the same rule assumed in HANK-II, thus implying $D_t^H = \Theta^H D_t$, where $\Theta^H \equiv \vartheta + (1 - \vartheta)\Xi^H > \Xi^H$.

Under the previous assumptions, consumption of hand-to-mouth households in TANK-II is given by

$$C_t^H = \Xi^H W_t N_t + \Theta^H D_t - \psi Y \hat{R}_t,$$

implying the following expression for aggregate consumption:

$$C_t = \lambda^H \left[\Xi^H \frac{\mathcal{M}}{\mathcal{M}_t} + \Theta^H \left(1 - \frac{\mathcal{M}}{\mathcal{M}_t} \right) \right] Y_t - \lambda^H \psi Y \hat{R}_t + (1 - \lambda^H) C_t^U, \quad (22)$$

where C_t^U satisfies equation (21). Note that, in contrast with equation (20), consumption equation (22) captures, at least qualitatively, both the interest rate exposure and income distribution channels at work in HANK-II, as revealed by a comparison with the expression for aggregate consumption in the latter in equation (19), which we reproduce here for convenience:

$$C_t = \lambda_t^H \left[\Xi_t^H \frac{\mathcal{M}}{\mathcal{M}_t} + \Theta_t^H \left(1 - \frac{\mathcal{M}}{\mathcal{M}_t} \right) \right] Y_t - \lambda_t^H \psi Y (\hat{R}_t + \Omega_{t-1}^H - 1) + (1 - \lambda_t^H) C_t^U.$$

Note that TANK-II will be a good approximation to HANK-II if $\lambda_t^H \simeq \lambda^H$, $\Omega_{t-1}^H \simeq 1$, $\Xi_t^H \simeq \Xi^H$, and $v_t^U \simeq v^U$ for all t. Next we turn to a quantitative assessment of the goodness of that approximation.

As in previous sections, we assess the goodness of the approximation by comparing the impulse responses of output in the HANK-II and TANK-II models with monetary and technology shocks. To generate the impulse responses for TANK-II, we set $\lambda^H = 0.30$, $\Xi^H = 0.56$, and $\Theta^H = 0.78$, which match the steady-state values of their (time-varying) counterparts in HANK-II.[19] We also set $\psi = 2$, the value assumed in HANK-II.

As shown in figure 5*A*, and in contrast with the predictions of TANK-I discussed above, the output response to a monetary policy shock in TANK-II matches closely that of HANK-II. For the technology shock, the match is also reasonably good, especially in comparison with TANK-I, which even fails to get the sign right. The reason for the difference is the presence in TANK-II of the interest rate exposure and income distribution channels. As discussed above, those channels play an important role in shaping the aggregate properties of HANK-II but are absent from TANK-I.

Figure 5*B* plots the time series for (log) output generated by TANK-II and HANK-II in response to monetary policy (top panel) and technology shocks (bottom panel). In the case of monetary policy shocks, the gap between the two time series is hardly noticeable, with the ratio of volatilities equal to 1.10 and implied correlations being very close to unity. In the case of technology shocks. the pattern is more different, with a larger ratio of volatilities (1.97), though it is not clear that the latter is much meaningful because the absolute impact of the shock is tiny in the two cases, as figure 5*A* makes clear. The correlation is still very high (0.998), pointing to an insignificant role of changes in the wealth distribution as an additional state variable in HANK-II.

Next, we analyze whether our modified TANK framework is able to capture the impact of a tightening of borrowing constraints predicted by HANK. We illustrate this in figure 6, which reports the impulse responses generated by HANK-II and TANK-II when we tighten the borrowing limit by setting $\psi = 0.8$ so that the fraction of constrained households

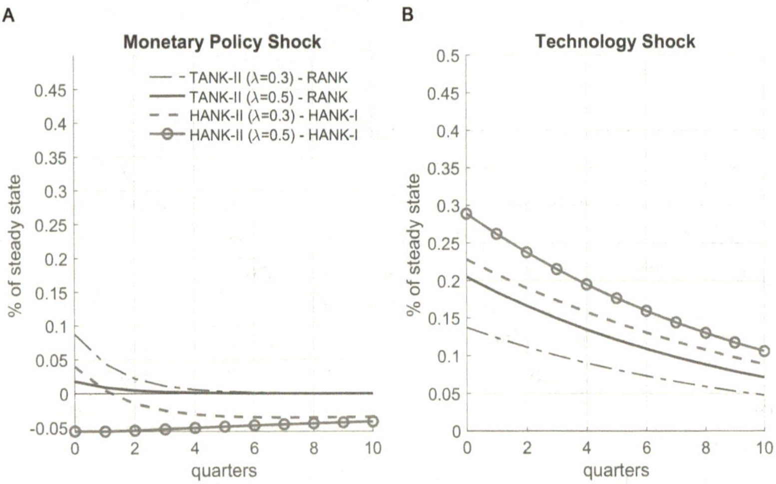

Fig. 6. The role of binding borrowing constraints: HANK-II versus TANK-II. The figure displays the impulse responses in the HANK-II and TANK-II, for the cases where fraction of constrained agents equals 30% (dashed lines) and 50% (solid lines with circles), expressed as a gap relative to their counterparts in the absence borrowing constraints (i.e., HANK-I and RANK, respectively).

in steady state increases from 0.30 to 0.50. The responses are expressed as a gap relative to their counterparts in the absence of borrowing constraints (i.e., HANK-I and RANK, respectively), thus allowing us to isolate the role of the tightening of the budget constraint, independently of initial differences between HANK-I and RANK.

In the case of monetary policy shocks the tightening of the borrowing limit shifts down the impulse response predicted by HANK-II—that is, it dampens the impact of monetary policy. A similar downward shift is observed in the case of TANK-II. With regard to technology shocks, we see that the TANK-II model can also capture well the amplification of the output response predicted by the HANK-II model under a tighter borrowing constraint. We conclude that the TANK-II model can also capture reasonably well the impact of a change in the environment like the tightening of a borrowing constraint.

To further understand the extent to which the TANK-II model provides a good approximation to HANK-II and its underlying mechanisms, we consider the following decomposition of aggregate consumption:

$$C_t = \lambda_t^H C_t^H + (1 - \lambda_t^H) C_t^U.$$

Accordingly, the response of aggregate consumption at different horizons to a shock in period t can be decomposed as follows:

$$\frac{dC_{t+k}}{d\varepsilon_t} = \lambda^H \frac{dC_{t+k}^H}{d\varepsilon_t} + (1 - \lambda^H) \frac{dC_{t+k}^{RA}}{d\varepsilon_t} + \frac{dY_{t+k}}{d\varepsilon_t}, \tag{23}$$

where C_{t+k}^{RA} denotes consumption in the corresponding RANK model.[20] The third term is a residual component resulting from variations in λ_t^H as well as changes in the risk and composition shifters caused by the shock. Note that this residual component is absent in TANK-II, because the latter assumes subsets of unconstrained and hand-to-mouth households that are time invariant in size and composition, and displays no precautionary savings.

Figure 7*A* displays the decomposition of the impulse responses to a monetary policy shock into the components shown in equation (23) for both the HANK-II and TANK-II models. The figure highlights the similarity in that decomposition across the two models, suggesting that the TANK-II model is successful not only in approximating the *aggregate* properties of HANK-II but also in capturing the underlying mechanisms. Figure 7*B* shows the corresponding results for the technology shock. In this case, and given the small output response to the shock,

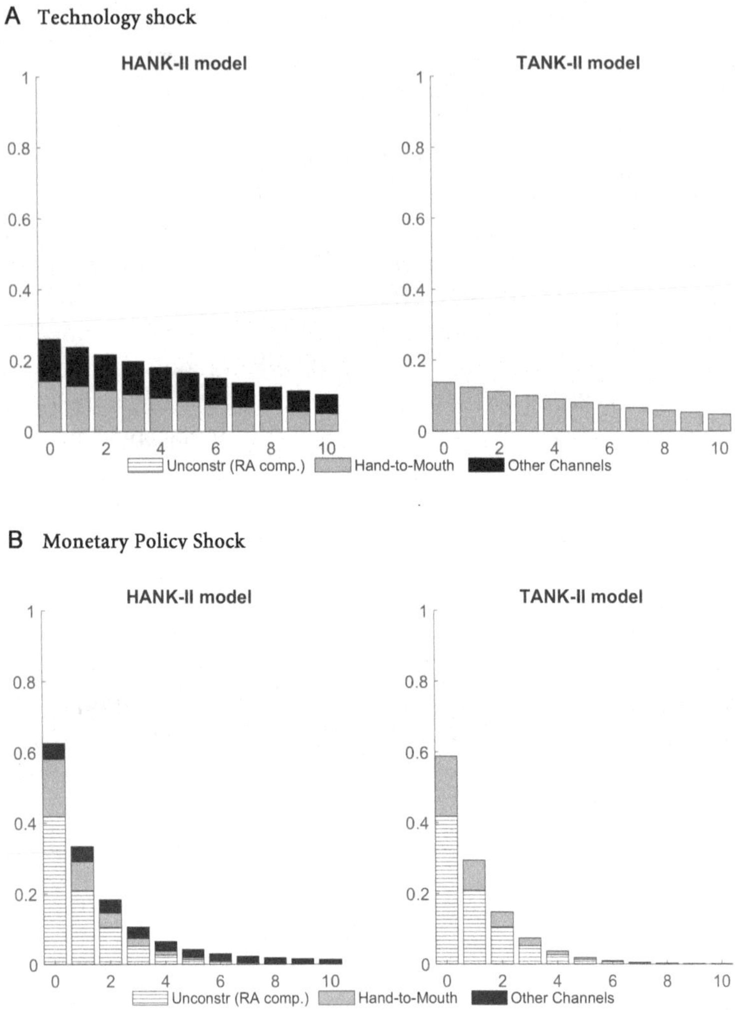

Fig. 7. Decomposition of transmission channels: HANK-II versus TANK-II. The figure shows the decomposition of the impulse responses to monetary policy shocks (panel *A*) and technology shocks (panel *B*) into the three components shown in equation (23) for both the HANK-II (left column) and TANK-II (right column) models.

the residual component (shown as "other" in the figure) is relatively more important, even though still small in absolute terms. That component cannot be captured by the TANK-II model. The latter captures well, however, the size and pattern of the consumption response of hand-to-mouth households.

The Effects of Fiscal Policy

As a complementary exercise, we analyze how heterogeneity may affect the transmission of fiscal shocks. To that end, we modify the models considered above by introducing an exogenous government spending shock (dG_t), which is assumed to be financed through lump-sum taxes—which for simplicity are set to be identical for all households—or by issuing debt (B_t^g), according to the rule $dB_t^g = \rho_b(dB_{t-1}^g + dG_t)$, with $\rho_b \in [0, 1]$.

Similarly to Auclert et al. (2024), we consider two alternative scenarios: (1) a balanced-budget rule (i.e., $\rho_b = 0$) and (2) deficit-financed spending (with $\rho_b = 0.9$). In both cases, we consider the impulse response to a government spending shock equal to 1% of steady-state gross domestic product (GDP) and with persistence $\rho_g = 0.8$, and starting from the same steady state considered above—that is, with $B = G = 0$.

Results are summarized in figure 8. As is well known, and due to Ricardian equivalence, in a RANK economy (black dashed line) the effects of a government spending shock do not depend on whether it is financed with current taxes (left panel) or debt (right panel). Also, under the maintained assumption that the central bank keeps a constant real interest rate, an increase in government spending translate one-to-one into an increase in output—that is, a multiplier equal to one.[21] Things are different in the HANK-II economy, where we find that the effects of

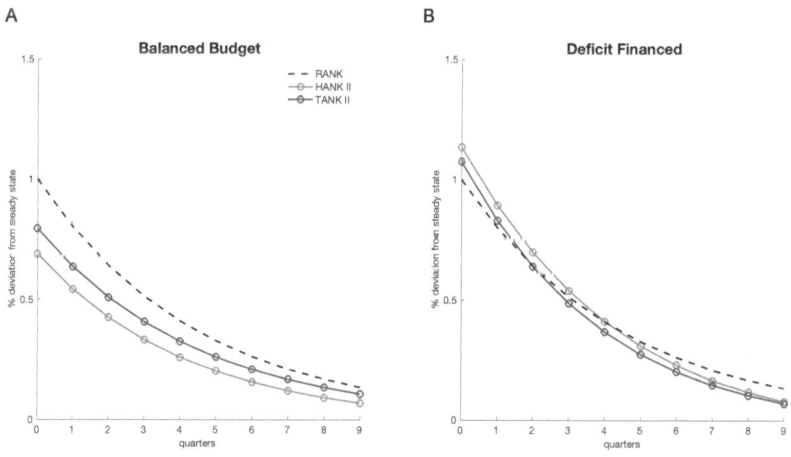

Fig. 8. The effects of government spending shocks: HANK-II versus TANK-II. The figure shows the response of output to a 1% of GDP increase in government spending under a balanced-budget rule (panel *A*) and under deficit financing (panel *B*), in the RANK (dashed line), HANK-II (line with circles), and TANK-II (line with circles) models.

government spending shocks are dampened (relative to RANK) under a balanced-budget rule but amplified (at least on impact) under deficit financing.

Interestingly, the same results are obtained in the TANK-II model, where those patterns can be easily rationalized. Under a balanced-budget rule, the government needs to raise taxes, which, other things equal, leads to a decline in consumption of financially constrained households, and thus to a reduction in aggregate consumption.[22] Such a crowding-out effect implies that the government spending multiplier is lower than one. Conversely, when government spending is deficit-financed, constrained households do not internalize that future taxes will increase, and their consumption increases due to the increase in labor income. Thus, aggregate consumption increases, and the government spending multiplier is larger than one.[23]

Caveats

Two potential aspects of the HANK-II model analyzed above can be criticized on empirical grounds. First, the model assumes an extreme dichotomy with regard to the extent of assets' liquidity: fully liquid bonds, fully illiquid stocks, with profits allocated according to an-hoc rule. In actual economies, most assets can be bought and sold, even though for some assets such transactions may be subject to significant costs. That possibility, assumed away in the HANK models considered above, opens the door for resorting to the sale of less liquid assets for the purposes of consumption smoothing once the borrowing limit is attained. Second, and relatedly, the micro evidence points to the need to distinguish between poor hand-to-mouth and wealthy hand-to-mouth households, based on whether they have or do not have some illiquid (or less liquid) assets that they can deplete once they have attained their borrowing limit (e.g., Kaplan et al. 2014).

Next we analyze a version of the HANK model that seeks to overcome those limitations, and we propose a tractable counterpart to it.

V. A HANK Economy with Binding Borrowing Constraints and Portfolio Choice (HANK-III)

In this section, we take as a starting point the HANK-II model developed above and modify it to allow for endogenous changes in individual equity holdings. That possibility gives an extra margin to equity holders through which they can smooth consumption, even when they have reached their borrowing limit and cannot use bonds for that purpose. Our assumption that such equity changes are subject to a portfolio adjustment cost which limits the extent to which they are effectively used for consumption smoothing purposes. As a result, households whose borrowing constraint is binding will still display high MPCs even when their equity holdings are positive. Following Kaplan et al. (2014), we refer to those households as the "wealthy hand to mouth."

Our model builds on the formalism proposed in Kaplan et al. (2018). In particular, we assume that households are not allowed to hold firms' stocks directly; instead they hold bonds and/or equity issued by financial intermediaries, who in turn invest the proceeds into the available assets (firms' stocks in our case, as we abstract from capital and government debt). We refer to this version of HANK as HANK-III.

Bonds, denoted by $B_t(j)$, can be adjusted at no cost and yield a gross real return R_t. Negative values of $B_t(j)$ can be interpreted as loans from financial intermediaries to household j. As before, we assume a borrowing constraint given by $R_t B_t(j) \geq -\psi Y$. On the other hand, household j's equity position, denoted by $E_t(j)$, yields a stochastic gross return R_{t+1}^e (defined below) and may be adjusted at a cost given by $\chi_t(j)$ given by

$$\chi_t(j) \equiv \frac{\chi_1}{\chi_2} \left| \frac{R_t^e E_{t-1}(j) - E_t(j)}{R_t^e E_{t-1}(j) + \chi_0} \right|^{\chi_2} (R_t^e E_{t-1}(j) + \chi_0),$$

with $\chi_0 \geq 0$, $\chi_1 \geq 0$, and $\chi_2 > 1$. Note that $R_t^e E_{t-1}(j) - E_t(j)$ can be interpreted as net withdrawals from the equity account (net addition to that account, if negative). Note also that a passive strategy consisting of reinvestment of initial balances plus returns is costless.[24] Finally, and most importantly, we assume that individual equity holdings cannot be negative—that is, we impose $E_t(j) \geq 0$ for all t and $j \in [0, 1]$ ("short-sale constraint").

The period budget constraint of household j can thus be written as

$$C_t(j) + B_t(j) \leq R_{t-1} B_{t-1}(j) + \Xi_t(j) W_t N_t + F_t(j), \tag{24}$$

where $F_t(j) \equiv R_t^e E_{t-1}(j) - E_t(j) - \chi_t(j)$ denotes additions to cash on hand linked to equity holdings.

When the short-sale constraint is not binding (i.e., when $E_t(j) > 0$), there is an additional optimality condition that the household must satisfy, given by

$$1 = \beta \mathbb{E}_t \left\{ \left(\frac{C_{t+1}(j)}{C_t(j)} \right)^{-\sigma} \left(\frac{R^e_{t+1} - \frac{\partial \chi_{t+1}(j)}{\partial E_t(j)}}{1 + \frac{\partial \chi_t(j)}{\partial E_t(j)}} \right) \right\}. \tag{25}$$

At each point in time, we can partition households into three groups: the unconstrained, the "wealthy hand to mouth," and the "poor hand to mouth." Unconstrained households satisfy $R_t B_t(j) > -\psi Y$ and $E_t(j) > 0$. For the wealthy hand to mouth, it is also the case that $E_t(j) > 0$, but their borrowing constraint is binding—that is, $R_t B_t(j) = -\psi Y$. Finally, both constraints are binding in the case of the poor hand to mouth—that is, $R_t B_t(j) = -\psi Y$ and $E_t(j) = 0$.

A representative financial intermediary takes bonds and equity from households and invests them into firms' stocks, which are traded at a price Q_t. It faces an intermediation cost ωB_t—which can be viewed as the cost of liquidity transformation—incurred at maturity. The financial intermediary solves the following problem:

$$\max_{S_t, B_t} \mathbb{E}_t \{ \Lambda_{t,t+1} [(Q_{t+1} + D_{t+1}) S_t - (R_t + \omega) B_t] \}$$

$$s.t.\ Q_t S_t = E_t + B_t,$$

where S_t denotes the quantity of firms' stocks, $\Lambda_{t,t+1}$ is the relevant stochastic discount factor, and where Q_t, R_t, $E_t \equiv \int_0^1 E_t(j)dj$ and the distribution of D_{t+1} are taken as given. The solution to the problem above implies the following no-arbitrage condition:

$$\mathbb{E}_t \left\{ \Lambda_{t,t+1} \left[\left(\frac{Q_{t+1} + D_{t+1}}{Q_t} \right) - (R_t + \omega) \right] \right\} = 0.$$

In equilibrium $S_t = 1$, and the ex post return R^e_{t+1} on equity is given by

$$R^e_{t+1} = \frac{Q_{t+1} + D_{t+1} - (R_t + \omega) B_t}{E_t},$$

and, hence,

$$\mathbb{E}_t \{ \Lambda_{t,t+1} [R^e_{t+1} - (R_t + \omega)] \} = 0,$$

implying the steady-state relation

$$R^e = R + \omega.$$

In our quantitative exercise, we set $\omega = 0.002$, which implies an annualized equity premium of 0.8%. Given the steady-state real interest rate, this is consistent with a steady-state return on equity $R^e = 1.0071$ (as in

Kaplan et al. 2018, and Auclert et al. 2024) and a value of total assets equal to 3.20 times annual GDP. For the portfolio adjustment cost function, we set the curvature parameter $\chi_2 = 2$ (i.e., a quadratic function), as well as $\chi_0 = 2.55$ and $\chi_1 = 9.60$ so that the fraction of constrained households (for which $R_t B_t(j) = -\psi Y$) is 30% in steady state, of which 25% hold equity (the wealthy hand to mouth) and 5% hold no equity (the poor hand to mouth). This calibration also implies that the total amount of liquid and illiquid assets equals 0.25 and 2.9 times annual GDP, which are close to the values reported in Kaplan et al. (2018). The remaining parameters are set to the same values shown in table 1.

Figure 9 displays the impulse responses of output to monetary policy and technology shocks generated by HANK-III (solid lines with diamonds), as well as HANK-II (dashed lines). In the case of monetary shocks, we see that the possibility of a portfolio adjustment amplifies significantly (but not dramatically) the response of output. To get some intuition for this result, consider the budget constraint facing hand-to-mouth households, shown in equation (24).

Averaging the budget constraint over poor hand-to-mouth households in period t, we get

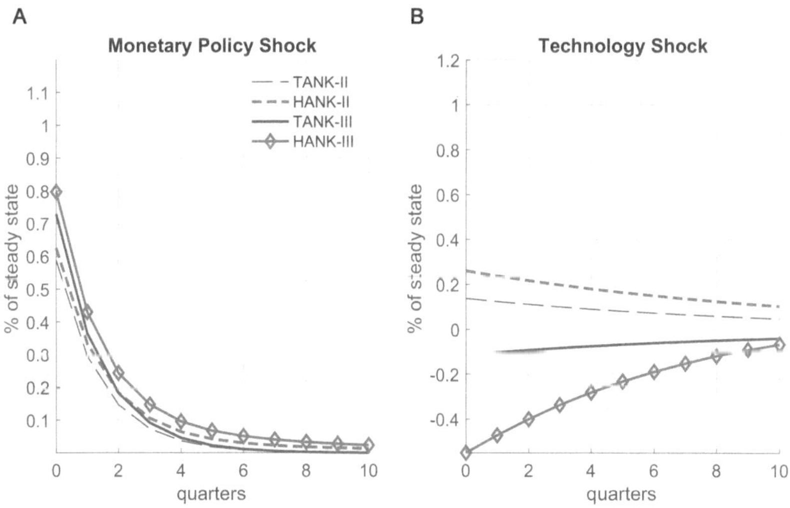

Fig. 9. The role of portfolio adjustment costs: HANK-III versus TANK-III. The figure shows the response of output to a 1% decrease in the (annualized) real interest rate (panel *A*) and to a 1% positive technology shock (panel *B*) in the heterogeneous agent models and two-agent models, for the case without portfolio adjustment costs (HANK-II and TANK-II, dashed lines) and with portfolio adjustment costs (HANK-III and TANK-III, lines with diamonds).

$$C_t^P = \Xi_t^P W_t N_t + F_t^P - \psi Y(\hat{R}_t + \Omega_{t-1}^P - 1),$$

where $F_t^P \equiv R_t^e E_{t-1|t}^P - \chi_t^P$ denotes average withdrawals from the equity account by wealthy hand-to-mouth households and where $E_{t-1|t}^P$ denotes average equity holdings in period $t-1$ among period t poor hand to mouth. Note that $F_t^P \simeq 0$ to the extent that most poor hand-to-mouth households in period t were also in that group in period $t-1$.

Similarly for wealthy hand-to-mouth households

$$C_t^W = \Xi_t^W W_t N_t + F_t^W - \psi Y(\hat{R}_t + \Omega_{t-1}^W - 1),$$

where $F_t^W \equiv R_t^e E_{t-1|t}^W - E_t^W - \chi_t^W$ denotes average net withdrawals from the equity account by wealthy hand-to-mouth households, with obvious notation. Combining both expressions and defining average hand-to-mouth consumption as $C_t^H \equiv (\lambda_t^P C_t^P + \lambda_t^W C_t^W)/(\lambda_t^P + \lambda_t^W)$, we can write:

$$C_t^H = \Xi_t^H W_t N_t + F_t^H - \psi Y(\hat{R}_t + \Omega_{t-1}^H - 1), \tag{26}$$

where $\Xi_t^H \equiv \frac{\lambda_t^P \Xi_t^P + \lambda_t^W \Xi_t^W}{\lambda_t^P + \lambda_t^W}$, $F_t^H \equiv \frac{\lambda_t^P F_t^P + \lambda_t^W F_t^W}{\lambda_t^P + \lambda_t^W}$, and $\Omega_{t-1}^H \equiv \frac{\lambda_t^P \Omega_{t-1}^P + \lambda_t^W \Omega_{t-1}^W}{\lambda_t^P + \lambda_t^W}$.

In the case of HANK-II, we had an identical expression for average hand-to-mouth consumption but with $F_t^H \equiv \Theta_t^H D_t$, which evolves exogenously. By contrast, in HANK-III, F_t^H is an endogenous variable. The difference between the two models lies in the fact that wealthy hand-to-mouth households in HANK-III can smooth fluctuations in their cash on hand by adjusting their equity balance (albeit at a cost). This is not possible in HANK-II because stocks are not tradable, which makes hand-to-mouth households' consumption vary one-for-one with their current income, $\Xi_t^H W_t N_t + \Theta_t^H D_t$, which they take as exogenous. As discussed above, in HANK-II the decline in dividends in response to an expansionary monetary policy shock has a negative effect on the consumption of the hand to mouth through the income distribution channel, which partly offsets the positive impact of the interest rate exposure channel. By contrast, in HANK-III, the decline in dividends does not directly affect their cash on hand unless it is reflected in lower withdrawals from the equity account. As a result, the relative importance of the interest rate exposure channel is enhanced, leading to a stronger response of aggregate consumption and output.

In the case of technology shocks, the difference between HANK-II and HANK-III is more dramatic. As shown in figure 9, aggregate output falls in response to a positive technology shock in HANK-III, which contrasts with the more conventional increase in output predicted by HANK-II. The intuition for that result is as follows: A positive technology shock tends to lower employment and labor income, which by itself should lower consumption of hand-to-mouth households (poor and wealthy). In HANK-II, this is more than compensated by the increase in dividend income, causing a mild expansion. This is not the case in HANK-III, because poor hand-to-mouth households do not benefit at all from the higher dividends, whereas the wealthy hand to mouth cannot freely convert dividends into available cash on hand. Accordingly, the overall cash on hand of hand-to-mouth households declines, and so does their consumption, causing aggregate demand and output to fall.

Note that the previous finding of a fall in output in response to a positive technology shock, which contrasts with existing evidence, should not be held against the empirical merits of HANK-III, because it hinges critically on our (counterfactual) assumption of a constant real rate.[25] In Section VI, we show how the sign of that response switches from negative to positive when we assume a more realistic monetary policy response.

Next, we consider a version of a TANK model which aims at capturing in a stylized way the main features of HANK-III. We refer to this model as TANK-III. As in TANK-II, we assume a constant fraction λ^H of identical hand-to-mouth households, whose consumption is given by

$$C_t^H = \Xi^H W_t N_t + \Theta^H D_t - \psi Y \hat{R}_t, \tag{27}$$

where Ξ^H denotes the productivity of hand-to-mouth households. The difference with TANK-II is that here Θ^H, representing the fraction of aggregate profits accruing to each hand-to-mouth household, is a free parameter, decoupled from Ξ^H.[26]

We can write aggregate consumption as

$$\begin{aligned} C_t &= \lambda^H C_t^H + (1 - \lambda^H) C_t^U \\ &= \lambda^H \Xi^H W_t N_t + \lambda^H \Theta^H D_t - \lambda^H \psi Y \hat{R}_t + (1 - \lambda^H) C_t^U. \end{aligned} \tag{28}$$

We can compare the previous expression with its counterpart in HANK-III:

$$C_t = \lambda_t^H \Xi_t^H W_t N_t + \lambda_t^H F_t^H - \lambda_t^H \psi Y \left[\hat{R}_t + \Omega_{t-1}^H - 1\right] + (1 - \lambda_t^H) C_t^U. \tag{29}$$

As in the analysis of HANK-II and TANK-II, we see that the first, third, and fourth terms on the righthand side of equation (28) will be a good approximation to their counterparts in equation (29) if $\lambda_t^H \simeq \lambda^H$, $\Omega_{t-1}^H \simeq 1$, $\Xi_t^H \simeq \Xi^H$, and $v_t^u \simeq v^u$ for all t. Again, this will be true if variations over time in λ_t^H and Ξ_t^H, as well as the gap between Ω_{t-1}^H and 1, are sufficiently small and if the impact of the shock on aggregate precautionary savings is small.

This leaves us with the second term in equations (28) and (29). In principle, they are not directly comparable because the wealthy hand to mouth in the TANK-III model cannot adjust their equity holdings, in contrast with their counterparts in HANK-III. Our strategy is to calibrate Θ^H to minimize the gap between $\Theta^H D_t$ and F_t^H in response to a unit increase in aggregate dividends D_t, as implied by HANK-III. With that goal in mind we set $\Theta^H = (\partial F_t^H/\partial \varepsilon_t)/(\partial D_t/\partial \varepsilon_t)$, where $\partial F_t^H/\partial \varepsilon_t$ and $\partial D_t/\partial \varepsilon_t$, respectively, denote the impact responses of F_t^H and D_t to a shock ε_t. Because the latter statistic as implied by our calibrated HANK-III model is (slightly) different across the two shocks considered, we take a simple average between the two in our calibration below.

In figure 10, we display the responses of aggregate output to monetary policy and technology shocks in a calibrated version of TANK-III, where we set $\lambda^P = 0.05$, $\lambda^W = 0.25$, $\Xi^P = 0.43$, and $\Xi^W = 0.66$, which correspond to their steady-state counterparts in our calibrated HANK-III model. The previous settings in turn imply an average productivity for hand-to-mouth households of $\Xi^H = 0.62$. Following the procedure discussed above, we set $\Theta^H = 0.58$. The previous calibration implies $\lambda^H\Xi^H - \lambda^H\Theta^H = 0.04 > 0$, a negative relation between the average markup and aggregate hand-to-mouth consumption, given output, in contrast with our calibrated TANK-II model (see previous section). This is a consequence of a relatively lower dividend income share for hand-to-mouth households, which implies a lower income for that group when markups go up. The fact that $\lambda^H\Xi^H \simeq \lambda^H\Theta^H$ in our calibration implies that such an income distribution channel is, however, very weak quantitatively. Furthermore, the fact that $\lambda^H\Xi^H = 0.18$ is relatively small implies that qualitatively similar results can be obtained in a version of the TANK-III model that makes the extreme assumption of $\Theta^H = 0$.

For the sake of comparison, figure 9 also displays the corresponding impulse responses generated by TANK-II. Notably, the TANK-III model is able to capture, at least qualitatively, the difference in the responses originated by the introduction of portfolio choice in its HANK counterpart and, in particular, the amplification of the effects of monetary policy shocks, as well as the reversal of sign in the response to a technology shock.

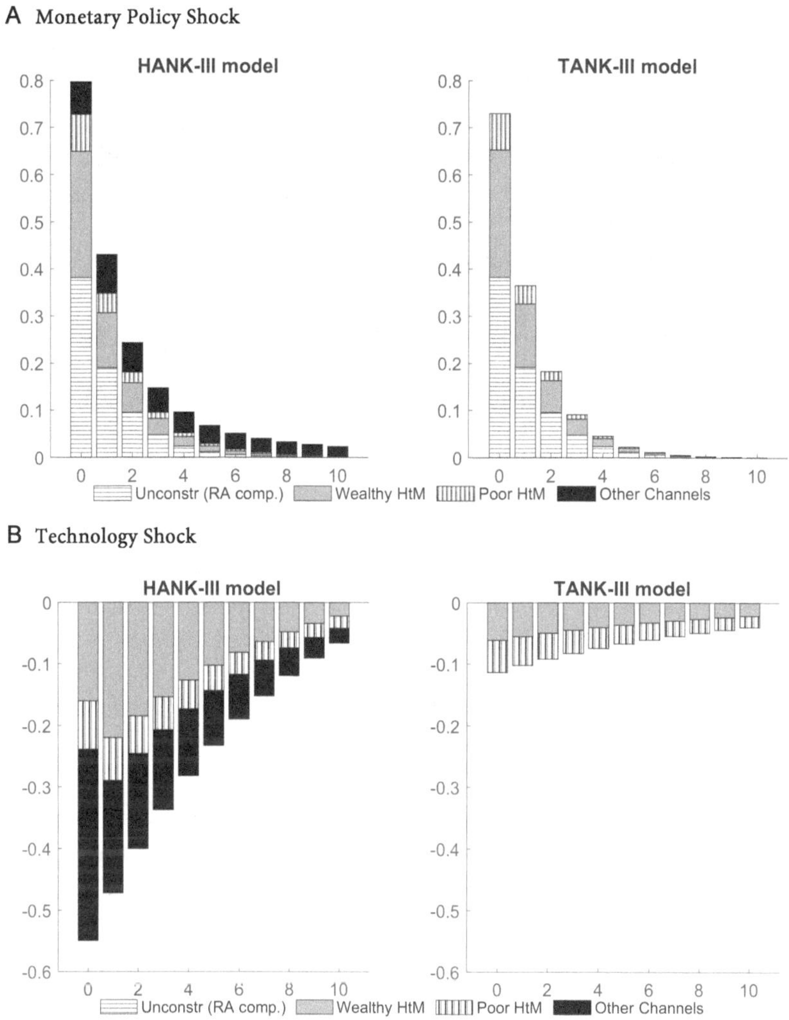

Fig. 10. Decomposition of transmission channels: HANK-III versus TANK-III. The figure shows the decomposition of the impulse responses to a monetary policy shocks (panel *A*) and technology shocks (panel *B*) into the three components shown in equation (23) for both the HANK-III (left column) and TANK-III (right column) models.

Finally, figure 10 displays a decomposition of the response of aggregate consumption to monetary policy and technology shocks in HANK-III and TANK-III into the components associated with the responses of a hypothetical representative household with no precautionary savings, the poor hand to mouth, the wealthy hand to mouth, and (in the case of HANK-III) a residual that combined the effects associated with changes in the risk and composition shifters and the imperfect correlation between dividends and equity withdrawals. In the case of the monetary policy shock, the decomposition is very similar between the two models, suggesting that not only the aggregate effects but also the channels at work are similar. This is less so in the case of technology shocks, in particular given the substantial role of the residual component.

VI. Endogenous Monetary Policy

The analysis in the previous sections has assumed an exogenous real interest rate path. As discussed above, the reason for doing this was to make sure that the economy's aggregate response to those shocks was not affected by the choice of a monetary policy rule, because different assumptions regarding the latter would generally imply different real rate paths, preventing us from insulating the impact of heterogeneity itself. In the present section, we relax that (admittedly unrealistic) assumption by allowing for an endogenous response of monetary policy.

In particular, we consider a simple Taylor-type rule which has the central bank adjust the nominal rate i_t according to

$$i_t = r + \phi_\pi \pi_t + \phi_y y_t + v_t, \tag{30}$$

where v_t is an exogenous monetary policy shifter following the AR(1) process $v_t = \rho_v v_{t-1} + \varepsilon_t^v$.[27]

In addition, and also in the spirit of making the models considered more realistic, we assume bonds are nominal, implying their ex post real return has an unanticipated component, associated with unexpected inflation. The previous two changes imply that equilibrium output is no longer invariant to the evolution of prices, so we need to include the NK Phillips curve (eq. [7]) as part of the set of equations describing the economy's equilibrium.

Figure 11 displays the response of aggregate output in several of the calibrated models considered above to a monetary policy and a technology shock, under the assumption that $\phi_\pi = 1.5$ and $\phi_y = 0.5/4 = 0.125$, as in Taylor (1993). The remaining parameters for each model are calibrated as before. As the figure makes clear, the assumption of an endogenous response reduces even further the gap between the predictions of RANK, TANK, and HANK models regarding the aggregate output response to both monetary policy and technology shocks, thus strengthening the view of a limited role for the presence of idiosyncratic income risk as a factor shaping aggregate fluctuations. Panel *B* displays the simulated path of

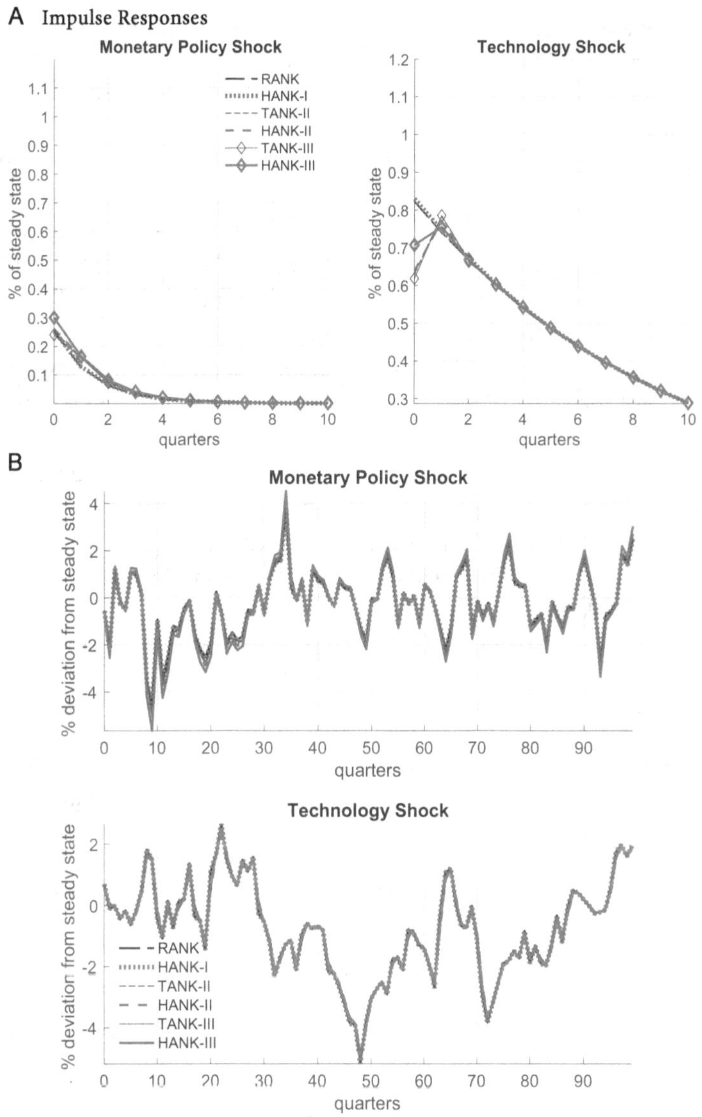

Fig. 11. Heterogeneity, nominal bonds, and endogenous monetary policy. Panel *A* shows the response of output to a 1% shock to the (annualized) nominal interest rate (left panel) and to a 1% positive technology shock (right panel) for the case without portfolio adjustment costs (HANK-II and TANK-II, dashed lines) and with portfolio adjustment costs (HANK-III and TANK-III, lines with diamonds), in the presence of nominal bonds, and assuming the central bank follows a Taylor rule $\hat{i}_t = 1.5\pi_t + 0.5/4y_t$. Panel *B* shows a simulated path of consumptions in response to monetary policy and technology shocks.

log output generated by the different models considered in response to a sequence of monetary policy and technology shocks, respectively. The similarity in the predicted paths is striking, making it hard to distinguish more than a single trajectory.

What is the explanation behind that finding? It follows from two properties of our model. First, as discussed in Section II, the natural level of output, y_t^n, is invariant to the presence of idiosyncratic income risk, being determined by the supply block of the underlying NK framework, which is common across all the models considered. Second, the NK Phillips curve (eq. [7]), which is shared by all the models analyzed above, displays the *divine coincidence* property, namely, stabilization of inflation implies stabilization of the output gap, and vice versa.[28] It follows that a monetary policy rule that tends to stabilize inflation, as it is the case with rule (eq. [30]), will reduce the distance between the equilibrium output path generated by any of the model economies considered above (RANK, TANK, or HANK) and their common natural output path. As a result, the distance between their respective implied equilibrium output paths will also shrink.

The previous reasoning can be taken to the limit and applied to the case of a strict inflation targeting policy. We state its implication in the form a simple proposition.

Proposition *[heterogeneity irrelevance for aggregate output under strict inflation targeting]*: Under a strict inflation targeting policy (i.e., $\pi_t = 0$ for all t), all the HANK, TANK, and RANK models considered above generate an identical equilibrium output path, which corresponds to that of natural output, which is common across models. In that case equilibrium output is invariant to the presence of heterogeneity.

Proof: It follows directly from equation (7).

A caveat is warranted regarding the previous irrelevance result: the fact that equilibrium output is identical across models under strict inflation targeting does not mean that this is also the case for other variables, including the real interest rate and the distribution of consumption.

VII. Caveats and Further Discussion

Our analysis suggests that the role of heterogeneity in shaping economic fluctuations, as stressed in the HANK literature, can be largely understood through simpler frameworks that focus on the distinction between two types of households—unconstrained and hand to mouth—but which abstract from the presence of idiosyncratic risk.

A few considerations are in order regarding the relevance and the limitations of our results.

First, our main result applies to environments where idiosyncratic income risk and the associated precautionary savings motive play a limited role for the transmission of aggregate shocks. This is the case in the HANK models considered above, where the "risk shifter" is largely insensitive to aggregate shocks. In this respect, our quantitative results are consistent with the empirical findings of Berger, Bocola, and Dovis (2023), who use US household survey data on consumption (CEX) to measure the aggregate implications of imperfect risk sharing in a broad class of HANK models, and find that wedges capturing deviations from perfect risk sharing only account for 7% of output fluctuations.

Larger fluctuations in the "risk shifter" would naturally arise in the presence of countercyclical income risk, an aspect that has been ignored in our analysis but that has been shown to be empirically relevant for understanding the cyclical properties of income and wealth distribution (see, e.g., Bayer et al. 2019; Patterson 2023).[29] A separate question is to understand to what extent fluctuations in income risk translate into fluctuations in consumption risk. For instance, Acharya and Dogra (2020) consider a heterogeneous agent model with constant absolute risk aversion (CARA) preferences, where all agents display a low MPC, and thus, where cyclical income risk have quantitatively small effects on the behavior of aggregate consumption. Bilbiie (2024) considers a two-agent model with cyclical idiosyncratic risk, modeled as a time-varying probability that a (rich) unconstrained household could become a (poor) hand-to-mouth household in the future period. In that environment, rich households experience a large drop in consumption when hit by a negative idiosyncratic shock, and the precautionary savings motive plays a more prominent role.

Second, our analysis has focused mainly on the effects of monetary policy and technology shocks while abstracting from other sources of economic fluctuations. In particular, Auclert et al. (2024) study the effects of fiscal shocks through the lens of an intertemporal Keynesian cross logic, where a key role is played by the intertemporal marginal propensities to consume out-of-income shocks (iMPCs) and their interactions with public deficits. Determining whether simple TANK models can account for the empirical evidence on iMPCs remains an open question. For instance, Fagereng, Holm, and Natvik (2021), using rich tax-registry data for Norwegian households, estimate large MPCs out of lottery wins on impact (about 0.5) but which persist for several years. As argued by Auclert et al. (2024), this finding could be rationalized by certain HANK models but is inconsistent with representative agent models—featuring a low MPC at all horizons—and with TANK models—where the MPC falls abruptly after one period. Sahm, Shapiro, and Slemrod (2010), Borusyak, Jaravel, and Spiess (2024), and Orchard, Ramey, and Wieland (2023) estimate the MPCs out of the 2008 rebate using US survey data and find a smaller MPC on impact (below 0.3) that remains positive for at most few months. Similar findings emerge in Boehm, Fize, and Jaravel (2024) using a randomized experiment involving a debit card gift to a subset of bank customers. Some of these findings can be matched by the simple TANK models discussed above, which would then provide a good approximation to study the effects of fiscal shocks.

Third, we have argued that household heterogeneity plays a limited role for aggregate fluctuations when the central bank seeks to stabilize inflation, as is the case when it follows an empirically plausible Taylor rule. This result rationalizes the empirical findings of Bayer, Born, and Luetticke (2024) and Bilbiie, Primiceri, and Tambalotti (2023), who estimate medium-scale heterogeneous agent models and conclude that household heterogeneity does not fundamentally alter our understanding of the causes and consequences of aggregate fluctuations.[30] Also, our results are broadly consistent with the findings in McKay and Wolf (2023), who argue that many of the redistributive channels at work in HANK economies operate in opposite directions and tend to offset each other so that the response of aggregate consumption is not too dissimilar to what would arise in a representative agent model, even though the transmission channels could be different.

Fourth, for the sake of simplicity, we have assumed flexible wages and a constant aggregate wage markup throughout our analysis. Introducing some form of wage stickiness (real or nominal) would affect the relationship between price inflation, the average markup, and output. This would alter the response of profits to shocks and hence how the income distribution channel operates, under an exogenous real rate. Furthermore, under a more general policy rule, the introduction of sticky wages would no longer imply a "divine coincidence" between the stabilization of price inflation and that of the output gap. Accordingly, the proposition in Section VI would no longer hold as stated, though it is likely to hold if the central bank stabilizes "composite inflation."[31] We leave an extension to the case of sticky wages for future research.

Importantly, note that our analysis has deliberately abstracted from heterogeneity having an impact on the economy through supply side channels. An interesting question that we leave for future research is whether HANK economies where heterogeneity affects the supply side of the economy (e.g., due to segmented labor markets and/or the presence of heterogeneous firms) could also be approximated by simpler alternative frameworks.[32] It should be clear, however, that to the extent that the presence of heterogeneity affects the natural level of output, the irrelevance proposition found above will no longer obtain.

Last, our analysis has refrained from normative considerations, such as the implications of heterogeneity for the optimal design of monetary policy. Several studies, using both tractable and rich quantitative models, have shown that stabilizing inflation is no longer optimal in the presence of inequality, as monetary policy may be used to partially offset the redistributional effects of aggregate disturbances (see, e.g., Challe 2020; Bhandari et al. 2021; Acharya, Challe, and Dogra 2023; Dávila and Schaab 2023; Smirnov 2023).

VIII. Concluding Comments

The emergence of HANK models has been viewed as a challenge to the heretofore dominance of the representative household paradigm in the modeling of aggregate fluctuations and their interaction with macro policies.

In the present paper, we have sought to understand the role of idiosyncratic income risk—the key source of heterogeneity in existing HANK models—in shaping aggregate fluctuations by comparing the aggregate properties of three different versions of a HANK model to those of three tractable counterparts that abstract from idiosyncratic risk. In our effort to understand the mechanisms at work in the different HANK models and to design a tractable counterpart to each of them, we have stressed the distinction between unconstrained and hand-to-mouth households, a distinction which is the hallmark of TANK models. For each HANK model considered, we have found a suitably specified and calibrated tractable model that captures reasonably well its implications for aggregate output and the main channels through which aggregate shocks are transmitted. That similarity increases dramatically in the presence of a policy rule that emphasizes inflation stability. Finally, we have shown that heterogeneity becomes irrelevant for the determination of aggregate output in the limiting case of a strict inflation targeting policy.

Appendix

Derivation of the Approximate Individual and Aggregate Euler Equations

Our starting point is the individual Euler equation:

$$C_t(j)^{-\sigma} = \beta R_t \mathbb{E}_t\{C_{t+1}(j)^{-\sigma}\}. \quad \text{(A1)}$$

Substituting a second-order approximation of $C_{t+1}(j)^{-\sigma}$ around $C_t(j)$ into equation (A1) yields

$$C_t(j)^{-\sigma} \simeq \beta R_t \mathbb{E}_t\left\{C_t(j)^{-\sigma} - \sigma C_t(j)^{-\sigma}\left(\frac{\Delta C_{t+1}(j)}{C_t(j)}\right) + \frac{\sigma(\sigma+1)}{2}C_t(j)^{-\sigma}\left(\frac{\Delta C_{t+1}(j)}{C_t(j)}\right)^2\right\}.$$

Rearranging terms,

$$\mathbb{E}_t\left\{\left(\frac{\Delta C_{t+1}(j)}{C_t(j)}\right)\right\} \simeq \frac{1}{\sigma}\left(1 - \frac{1}{\beta R_t}\right) + \frac{\sigma+1}{2}v_t(j),$$

where $v_t(j) \equiv \mathbb{E}_t\{((\Delta C_{t+1}(j))/C_t(j))^2\} \simeq \mathbb{E}_t\{\xi_{t+1}(j)^2\}$, with $\xi_t(j) \equiv c_t(j) - \mathbb{E}_{t-1}\{c_t(j)\}$ being the innovation in individual consumption.

Rearranging terms, we have

$$\mathbb{E}_t\{\Delta C_{t+1}(j)\} \simeq \frac{1}{\sigma}\left(1 - \frac{1}{\beta R_t}\right)C_t(j) + \frac{\sigma+1}{2}C_t(j)v_t(j). \quad \text{(A2)}$$

When all households are unconstrained (as in HANK-I), we can integrate the previous equation over $j \in [0,1]$ and divide the resulting expression by C_t to obtain

$$\mathbb{E}_t\left\{\frac{\Delta C_{t+1}}{C_t}\right\} \simeq \frac{1}{\sigma}\left(1 - \frac{1}{\beta R_t}\right) + \frac{\sigma+1}{2}v_t,$$

where

$$v_t \equiv \int\left(\frac{C_t(j)}{C_t}\right)v_t(j)dj.$$

The previous equation can be approximated around the stochastic steady state to yield equation (9) in the text. Note that in the stochastic steady state

$$\frac{1}{\sigma}\left(1 - \frac{1}{\beta R}\right) + \frac{\sigma+1}{2}v = 0,$$

thus implying $\beta R < 1$. Wealthy households (with high consumption) will have $v_t(j) > v$ and hence will experience a decline in consumption (on average). The opposite will be true for poor households, whose consumption will tend to increase. Consistently with that property, the stochastic steady state is characterized by a well-defined distribution of consumption across households (which also corresponds to the ergodic distribution of individual consumption).

When the individual Euler equation only holds for a subset of households $\mathcal{U}_t$ in period t, we can integrate equation (A2) over that subset and rearrange terms to obtain

$$\mathbb{E}_t\left\{\frac{C^U_{t+1|t} - C^U_t}{C^U_t}\right\} \simeq \frac{1}{\sigma}\left(1 - \frac{1}{\beta R_t}\right) + \frac{\sigma + 1}{2} v^U_t,$$

where $C^U_t = \frac{1}{1-\lambda^H_t}\int_{j\in\mathcal{U}_t} C_t(j)dj$, $C^U_{t+1|t} = \frac{1}{1-\lambda^H_t}\int_{j\in\mathcal{U}_t} C_{t+1}(j)dj$, and $v^U_t \equiv \frac{1}{1-\lambda^H_t}\int_{j\in\mathcal{U}_t} \frac{C_t(j)}{C^U_t} v_t(j)dj$.

Equivalently, we can write:

$$\mathbb{E}_t\left\{\frac{C^U_{t+1} - C^U_t}{C^U_t}\right\} \simeq \frac{1}{\sigma}\left(1 - \frac{1}{\beta R_t}\right) + \frac{\sigma + 1}{2} + h^U_t, \qquad \text{(A3)}$$

where $h^U_t \equiv \mathbb{E}_t\{c^U_{t+1} - c^U_{t+1|t}\}$. Note that h_t emerges as a result of changes in the composition of $\mathcal{U}_t$, which imply that some households that are unconstrained at t become constrained at $t + 1$, and vice versa, so that in general we have $C^U_{t+1} \neq C^U_{t+1|t}$. Approximating equation (A3) around the stochastic steady state yields equation (15) in the text.

Endnotes

Authors email addresses: Debortoli (davide.debortoli@upf.edu), Galí (jgali@crei.cat). This is a heavily revised version of a paper previously circulated under the title "Monetary Policy with Heterogeneous Agents: Insights from TANK Models." We thank Antonio Giribaldi, Kadir Özen, and Danila Smirnov for excellent research assistance. We have benefited from comments by Gianluca Violante, Florin Bilbiie, John Leahy, Valerie Ramey, Johannes Wieland, Matt Rognlie, Paolo Surico, and participants at the CREI Faculty Lunch, NBER SI EFG, NBER Macro Annual, CREI Workshop on Heterogeneity and Economic Fluctuations, and CIGS Conference on Macroeconomic Policy and Theory. Galí acknowledges the financial support from the European Research Council under the European Union's Horizon 2020 research and innovation program (Grant 882332-HEMPEF). Both authors acknowledge financial support from the Agencia Estatal de Investigación (AEI) through the Severo Ochoa Programme for Centres of Excellence in R&D (Barcelona School of Economics CEX2019-000915-S) and grant PID2020-116268GB-I00 (Debortoli) and from the Generalitat de Catalunya through the CERCA Programme. For acknowledgments, sources of research support, and disclosure of the authors' material financial relationships, if any, please see https://www.nber.org/books-and-chapters/nber-macroeconomics-annual-2024-volume-39/heterogeneity-and-aggregate-fluctuations-insights-tank-models.

1. See, e.g., Kaplan et al. (2018) and Auclert et al. (2024) for examples of such models. Our focus in the present paper is on models with household heterogeneity, thus abstracting from firm heterogeneity. The latter is at the core of the literature on Ss pricing and investments policies, firm dynamics, and so forth and may potentially have important implications for aggregate behavior.
2. HANK models may also be used for understanding the distributional impact of shocks or policy interventions. Our focus here is exclusively on its implications for aggregate fluctuations.
3. See, e.g., Galí et al. (2007) and Bilbiie (2008). The idea of partitioning households between hand to mouth and unconstrained can be traced back to Campbell and Mankiw (1989).
4. See, e.g., Auclert et al. (2024) for a recent example.
5. See below for a detailed explanation of each version.
6. See Faia and Shabalina (2024) for recent work in the same spirit, using a larger range of HANK models.
7. Similarly, Bilbiie (2024) uses a TANK model to illustrate the "direct" and "indirect" effects of monetary policy shocks emphasized by Kaplan et al. (2018) in a more general HANK model. Farhi and Werning (2019) use a variety of TANK models to analyze the size of fiscal multipliers in a liquidity trap and in currency unions. Ravn and Sterk (2021) build a tractable heterogeneous agent model with nominal rigidities and labor market frictions, giving rise to endogenous unemployment risk.
8. In our baseline model, we assume a real bond to avoid large reallocations of wealth resulting from unexpected inflation, because the latter is very sensitive to the assumed properties of the Phillips curve.
9. Strictly speaking, the interpretation of $C_t^{\sigma} N_t^{\varphi}$ as an average MRS will be valid in equilibrium only if $\sigma = 1$. The assumed wage equation guarantees that idiosyncratic shocks are not reflected in unrealistic differences in the quantity of labor supplied across households. In addition, it simplifies the analysis by making labor income exogenous to individual decisions. Finally, it is one of the assumptions that guarantee that the supply block of the model corresponds to that in the standard NK model, thus being insulated from the presence of heterogeneity.
10. Under our assumptions, if $\mathcal{M}_w \gg 1$, all households will be willing to supply the amount of labor demanded by firms, as long as shocks are not too large.
11. A similar approach is followed by Woodford (2011) when studying the size of the fiscal multiplier in a NK model.
12. For sufficiently small fluctuations in the previous two variables, the fraction of constrained households in equilibrium can be made arbitrarily close to 0. In our simulations, the fraction of constrained consumer is negligible (below 0.1%) both in steady state and in response to aggregate shocks.
13. See also Boppart, Krusell, and Mitman (2018) for a related perfect-foresight, sequence-based approach.
14. This is the interpretation favored by Kaplan et al. (2018), which assumes $\vartheta = 0$.
15. Note that when $\vartheta = 0$, we have $Y_t(j) = \Xi_t(j)Y_t$; hence, aggregate shocks have no redistributive effects, and that channel is not operative.
16. The absolute difference between the two impulse response functions (IRFs) increases when the autoregressive coefficient is calibrated to a higher value; see the discussion by Rognlie (2025) contained in the present volume. However, the difference in relative terms remains an order of magnitude smaller than the IRF itself.
17. On the other hand, tiny quantitative differences that are highly persistent may end up having significant cumulative effects, often described by means of a cumulative multiplier statistic. That statistic may capture differences that grow very fast in percentage terms with the horizon if the reference response in the denominator gets close to 0.
18. Given our normalization, $\lambda^H \Xi^H + (1 - \lambda^H)\Xi^U = 1$.
19. In his discussion, Wieland (2025, this volume) argues that there is little advantage to using a tractable framework if one has to solve the HANK model to calibrate its parameters. Note, however, that one could instead rely on alternative strategies to calibrate those parameters—e.g., using direct independent evidence on each parameter or matching the empirical impulse responses.

20. Formally, note that

$$\frac{dY_{t+k}}{d\varepsilon_t} = (1-\lambda^H)\left(\frac{dC^U_{t+k}}{d\varepsilon_t} - \frac{dC^{RA}_{t+k}}{d\varepsilon_t}\right) + \frac{d\lambda^H_{t+k}}{d\varepsilon_t}(C^H - C^U)$$

$$= -(1-\lambda^H)\left(\frac{\sigma+1}{2}\sum\nolimits_{l=k}^{\infty}\frac{dv^U_{t+l}}{d\varepsilon_t} + \sum\nolimits_{l=k}^{\infty}\frac{dh^U_{t+l}}{d\varepsilon_t}\right) + \frac{d\lambda^H_{t+k}}{d\varepsilon_t}(C^H - C^U).$$

21. See Woodford (2011).

22. More precisely, because hand-to-mouth households have low productivity, the increase in taxes is larger than the increase in labor income.

23. A similar result was obtained by Galí et al. (2007).

24. The term χ_0 in the denominator is added to avoid infinite adjustment costs when $E_{t-1}(j) = 0$.

25. Galí (1999) and Basu, Fernald, and Kimball (2006) find that employment decreases in response to a positive technology shock, but output does not.

26. Recall that in TANK-II we had

$$\Theta^H \equiv \vartheta + (1-\vartheta)\Xi^H > \Xi^H,$$

where the inequality followed from the fact that Ξ^H was less than 1.

27. Note that the mean of (log) output is normalized to 0 under our calibration. Hence, y_t can be interpreted a deiviations from steady state.

28. See, e.g., Blanchard and Galí (2007) for an early discussion of the divine coincidence.

29. A simple way to incorporate the role of cyclical income risk into our TANK models would be to consider a time-varying difference in the productivity of hand-to-mouth and unconstrained households—e.g., letting $\Xi^H_t - \Xi^U_t$ depend on aggregate output.

30. Similar findings are obtained by Faia and Shabalina (2024).

31. See chapter 6 in Galí (2015).

32. See, e.g., Andreolli, Rickard, and Surico (2024), for an analysis of a TANK economy where a nonhomotheticity in preferences, combined with the interaction of household heterogeneity (à la TANK) and firm heterogeneity (in the composition of their workforce), leads to an amplification of monetary policy shocks.

References

Acharya, Sushant, Edouard Challe, and Keshav Dogra. 2023. "Optimal Monetary Policy According to HANK." *American Economic Review* 113 (7): 1741–82.

Acharya, Sushant, and Keshav Dogra. 2020. "Understanding HANK: Insights from a PRANK." *Econometrica* 88 (3): 1113–58.

Ahn, SeHyoun, Greg Kaplan, Benjamin Moll, Thomas Winberry, and Christian Wolf. 2018. "When Inequality Matters for Macro and Macro Matters for Inequality." *NBER Macroeconomics Annual 2017* 32 (1): 1–75.

Andreolli, Michele, Natalie Rickard, and Paolo Surico. 2024. "Non-Essential Business Cycles." Unpublished manuscript.

Auclert, Adrien. 2019. "Monetary Policy and the Redistribution Channel." *American Economic Review* 109 (6): 2333–67.

Auclert, Adrien, Bence Bardóczy, Matthew Rognlie, and Ludwig Straub. 2021. "Using the Sequence-Space Jacobian to Solve and Estimate Heterogeneous-Agent Models." *Econometrica* 89 (5): 2375–408.

Auclert, Adrien, Matthew Rognlie, and Ludwig Straub. 2024. "The Intertemporal Keynesian Cross." *Journal of Political Economy* 132 (12): 4068–121.

Basu, Susanto, John Fernald, and Miles Kimball. 2006. "Are Technology Improvements Contractionary?" *American Economic Review* 96 (5): 1418–48.

Bayer, Christian, Benjamin Born, and Ralph Luetticke. 2024. "Shocks, Frictions, and Inequality in U.S. Business Cycles." *American Economic Review* 114 (5): 1212–47.

Bayer, Christian, Ralph Luetticke, Lien Pham-Do, and Volker Tjaden. 2019. "Precautionary Savings, Illiquid Assets, and the Aggregate Consequences of Shocks to Household Income Risk." *Econometrica* 87 (1): 255–90.

Berger, David, Luigi Bocola, and Alessandro Dovis. 2023. "Imperfect Risk Sharing and the Business Cycle." *Quarterly Journal of Economics* 138 (3): 1765–815.

Bhandari, Anmol, David Evans, Mikhail Golosov, and Thomas J. Sargent. 2021. "Inequality, Business Cycles, and Monetary-Fiscal Policy." *Econometrica* 89 (6): 2559–99.

Bilbiie, Florin. 2008. "Limited Asset Market Participation, Monetary Policy and (Inverted) Aggregate Demand Logic." *Journal of Economic Theory* 140 (1): 162–96.

———. 2020. "The New Keynesian Cross." *Journal of Monetary Economics* 114:90–108.

———. 2024. "Monetary Policy and Heterogeneity: An Analytical Framework." *Review of Economic Studies*, forthcoming.

Bilbiie, Florin, Giorgio Primiceri, and Andrea Tambalotti. 2023. "Inequality and Business Cycles." http://faculty.wcas.northwestern.edu/gep575/Inequality_BC3-1.pdf.

Blanchard, Olivier, and Jordi Galí. 2007. "Real Wage Rigidities and the New Keynesian Model." *Journal of Money, Credit and Banking* 39:35–65.

Boehm, Johannes, Etienne Fize, and Xavier Jaravel. 2024. "Five Facts about MPCs: Evidence from a Randomized Experiment." Unpublished manuscript.

Boppart, Timo, Per Krusell, and Kurt Mitman. 2018. "Exploiting MIT Shocks in Heterogeneous-Agent Economies: The Impulse Response as a Numerical Derivative." *Journal of Economic Dynamics and Control* 89:68–92.

Borusyak, Kirill, Xavier Jaravel, and Jann Spiess. 2024. "Revisiting Event Study Designs: Robust and Efficient Estimation." *Review of Economic Studies* 91 (6): 3253–85.

Broer, Tobias, Niels-Jakob Harbo Hansen, Per Krusell, and Erik Oberg. 2020. "The New Keynesian Transmission Mechanism: A Heterogeneous-Agent Perspective." *Review of Economic Studies* 87 (1): 77–101.

Campbell, John Y., and N. Gregory Mankiw. 1989. "Consumption, Income, and Interest Rates: Reinterpreting the Time Series Evidence." *NBER Macroeconomics Annual 1989* 4:185–216.

Cantore, Cristiano, and Lukas B. Freund. 2021. "Workers, Capitalists and the Government: Fiscal Policy and Income (Re)Distribution." *Journal of Monetary Economics* 119:58–74.

Carroll, Christopher D. 2006. "The Method of Endogenous Gridpoints for Solving Dynamic Stochastic Optimization Problems." *Economics Letters* 91 (3): 312–20.

Challe, Edouard. 2020. "Uninsured Unemployment Risk and Optimal Monetary Policy in a Zero-Liquidity Economy." *American Economic Journal: Macroeconomics* 12 (2): 241–83.

Dávila, Eduardo, and Andreas Schaab. 2023. "Optimal Monetary Policy with Heterogeneous Agents: Discretion, Commitment, and Timeless Policy." Working Paper no. 30961, NBER, Cambridge, MA.

Debortoli, Davide, and Jordi Galí. 2024. "Idiosyncratic Income Risk and Aggregate Fluctuations." *American Economic Journal: Macroeconomics* 16 (4): 279–310.

Fagereng, Andreas, Martin B. Holm, and Gisle J. Natvik. 2021. "MPC Heterogeneity and Household Balance Sheets." *American Economic Journal: Macroeconomics* 13 (4): 1–54.

Faia, Ester, and Ekaterina Shabalina. 2024. "What Central Bankers Can Learn from Models with Idiosyncratic Risk." Mimeo.
Farhi, Emmanuel, and Iván Werning. 2019. "Monetary Policy, Bounded Rationality, and Incomplete Markets." *American Economic Review* 109 (11): 3887–928.
Galí, Jordi. 1999. "Technology, Employment, and the Business Cycle: Do Technology Shocks Explain Aggregate Fluctuations?" *American Economic Review* 89 (1): 249–71.
———. 2015. *Monetary Policy, Inflation and the Business Cycle*. 2nd ed. Princeton, NJ: Princeton University Press.
Galí, Jordi, J. David López-Salido, and Javier Vallés. 2007. "Understanding the Effects of Government Spending on Consumption." *Journal of the European Economic Association* 5 (1): 227–70.
Gornemann, Nils, Keith Kuester, and Makoto Nakajima. 2016. "Doves for the Rich, Hawks for the Poor? Distributional Consequences of Monetary Policy." https://doi.org/10.17016/IFDP.2016.1167.
Guerrieri, Veronica, and Guido Lorenzoni. 2017. "Credit Crises, Precautionary Savings, and the Liquidity Trap." *Quarterly Journal of Economics* 132 (3): 1427–67.
Kaplan, Greg, Benjamin Moll, and Giovanni L. Violante. 2018. "Monetary Policy According to HANK." *American Economic Review* 108 (3): 697–743.
Kaplan, Greg, Giovanni L. Violante, and Justin Weidner. 2014. "The Wealthy Hand-to-Mouth." *Brookings Papers on Economic Activity* 1:77–153.
Luetticke, Ralph. 2020. "Transmission of Monetary Policy with Heterogeneity in Household Portfolios." *American Economic Journal: Macroeconomics* 13 (2): 1–25.
McKay, Alisdair, Emi Nakamura, and Jón Steinsson. 2016. "The Power of Forward Guidance Revisited." *American Economic Review* 106 (10): 3133–58.
McKay, Alisdair, and Ricardo Reis. 2016. "The Role of Automatic Stabilizers in the U.S. Business Cycle." *Econometrica* 84 (1): 141–94.
McKay, Alisdair, and Christian K. Wolf. 2023. "Monetary Policy and Inequality." *Journal of Economic Perspectives* 37 (1): 121–44.
Orchard, Jacob, Valerie A. Ramey, and Johannes F. Wieland. 2023. "Micro MPCs and Macro Counterfactuals: The Case of the 2008 Rebates." Working Paper no. 31584, NBER, Cambridge, MA.
Patterson, Christina. 2023. "The Matching Multiplier and the Amplification of Recessions." *American Economic Review* 113 (4): 982–1012.
Ravn, Morten, and Vincent Sterk. 2021. "Macroeconomic Fluctuations with HANK & SAM: An Analytical Approach." *Journal of the European Economic Association* 19 (2): 1162–202.
Reiter, Michael. 2009. "Solving Heterogeneous Agent Models by Projection and Perturbation." *Journal of Economic Dynamics and Control* 33:649–65.
Sahm, Claudia R., Matthew D. Shapiro, and Joel Slemrod. 2010. "The Response to the 2008 Tax Rebate: Survey Evidence and Aggregate Implications." *Tax Policy and the Economy* 24 (1): 69–110.
Smirnov, Danila. 2023. "Optimal Monetary Policy in HANK." Unpublished manuscript, Universitat Pompeu Fabra.
Taylor, John B. 1993. "Discretion versus Policy Rules in Practice." *Carnegie-Rochester Conference Series on Public Policy* 39:195–214.
Werning, Iván. 2015. "Incomplete Markets and Aggregate Demand." Working Paper no. 21448, NBER, Cambridge, MA.
Wieland, Johannes. 2025. Comment on "Heterogeneity and Aggregate Fluctuations: Insights from TANK Models." *NBER Macroeconomics Annual* 39:358–65.
Woodford, Michael. 2011. "Simple Analytics of the Government Expenditure Multiplier." *American Economic Journal: Macroeconomics* 3 (1): 1–35.

Comment

Johannes Wieland, *University of California, San Diego and NBER,* United States of America

Heterogeneous agent New Keynesian (HANK) models have become a mainstay in macroeconomics. They are used to elucidate the role of heterogeneity in monetary policy, fiscal policy, and financial frictions.[1] Recent advances in solution methods notwithstanding,[2] these models are more difficult to solve than traditional representative-agent or two-agent New Keynesian models. The additional complexity generally makes it harder to understand the model's workings.

Debortoli and Galí (2025, in this volume) show how to specify two-agent New Keynesian (TANK) models in a way that captures much of the richness of HANK models while preserving their relative simplicity and transparency. The lens of the simpler TANK model elucidates which features of the HANK model are quantitatively important for the transmission of monetary policy and technology shocks. And for both models, the authors show that our choice of the monetary policy rule is crucial for how much heterogeneity matters for aggregate outcomes in equilibrium.

My comments center on (1) how we can specify TANK models to approximate HANK models more generally, (2) whether this is something we should strive for, and (3) the broader role of supply in determining the importance of heterogeneity for aggregate outcomes.

I. Approximating HANK with TANK

A key insight of Debortoli and Galí (2025, in this volume) is that we can successfully approximate a HANK model with a TANK model if the constrained agents in both models are very similar. For example, in their

NBER Macroeconomics Annual, volume 39, 2025.
 https://doi.org/10.1086/735273

HANK-II model,[3] the consumption function of the borrowing-constrained (hand-to-mouth) agent is

$$C_t^H = \Xi^H W_t N_t + \Theta^H D_t + \psi Y - R_{t-1} B_{t-1|t}^H,$$

where C_t^H is the consumption, $W_t N_t$ is the labor income, Ξ^H is the share of labor income going to constrained agents, D_t are the firm dividends, Θ^H is the share ownership by the hand to mouth, ψY is the new borrowing, and $R_{t-1} B_{t-1|t}^H$ is the repayment of old borrowing. We can directly solve for consumption because the borrowing constraint is binding.

To approximate the constrained HANK agent in a TANK model, we assume that its permanent hand-to-mouth agent always sits at the same borrowing constraint, owns the same number of shares, and earns the same share of labor income:

$$C_t^H = \Xi^H W_t N_t + \Theta^H D_t - \psi Y (R_{t-1} - 1),$$

where past debt is equal to the borrowing constraint, $B_{t-1|t}^H = \psi Y$.

The success of this approximation tells us that the transmission mechanism in this HANK model is driven by the relative exposure of constrained and unconstrained agents to labor income, dividend income, and interest rates. Matching the HANK model on these dimensions is crucial for quantitative success. The standard TANK model with hand-to-mouth consumption function $C_t^H = W_t N_t$ does not capture these and therefore fails to approximate the HANK model.

That modified TANK models, in which agent types are fixed, can well approximate HANK models tells us that changes in the number of constrained households in HANK are not important for the transmission of monetary and technology shocks. Similarly, changes in the identity of the constrained households or changes in the expectations of changes in the number or identity of the constrained do not appear to be quantitatively relevant here.

Thus, we may not lose much by focusing only on a few moments of the infinite-dimensional wealth distribution in HANK: the overall fraction constrained and the exposure to different income sources and interest rates. This Krusell and Smith (1998)–type result is consistent with the findings of Ahn et al. (2018) and suggests that one may not need to carry around the entire wealth distribution, which is the source of computational complexity in HANK models.

That we want to mimic the constrained agent in HANK is an important and novel insight; however, implementing this strategy is not straightforward because, generally, it requires solving the HANK model first. The share of labor income going the constrained Ξ^H is endogenous in HANK models. Approximating the two-asset HANK model (HANK-III in the paper) requires additional knowledge of the endogenous dividend distribution rule. But if we need to solve HANK first, how much do we gain by approximating it with TANK?

Finding the right TANK approximation looks even more daunting in models in which one cannot directly solve for consumption of the constrained agent. For instance, in HANK models with durable goods (McKay and Wieland 2021, 2022), one needs to also solve for the allocation of resources between durable and nondurable goods. This is a much more complex problem than the one solved here.

For these reasons, the TANK approximation appears to be most useful in models in which households face a very limited number of choices. But even in more complex environments the TANK approximation may still be useful in elucidating which features of complex HANK model are important in the transmission of shocks.

II. Choosing TANK over HANK?

I next argue that there are instances in which we may want to choose TANK over HANK because TANK matches the data better than HANK. This is not the objective of Debortoli and Galí (2025, in this volume). But I think it is useful to comment on, because a reader of the paper may be forgiven for thinking that HANK is always correct and we simply argue over the quality of the approximation by TANK. There are, of course, many other instances in which HANK is clearly preferred—for instance, by providing microfoundations for high marginal propensity to consume (MPCs)—which I will not cover here, given the context of the paper.

A distinguishing feature of conventionally calibrated HANK models is that they predict significant intertemporal MPCs out of transitory income shocks (Auclert, Rognlie, and Straub 2023). That is, households consume a large fraction of a transitory income shock not just in the period in which it occurs but also in future periods. This is in contrast to standard TANK models, in which those intertemporal MPCs are close to 0.

Table 1 shows a large variation in whether recent empirical studies estimate significant intertemporal MPCs in the data. The Norwegian lottery study by Fagereng, Holm, and Natvik (2021) finds a large intertemporal MPC of 0.15 in the second year following the lottery and further positive

Table 1
Contemporaneous and Intertemporal MPCs in the Data

Study	MPC Contemp.	MPC Intertemp.	Frequency
R. Baker, Farrokhnia, Meyer, Pagel, and Yannelis (2023)	.35	0	Weekly
Boehm, Fize, and Jaravel (2023)	.23	0	Monthly
Borusyak, Jaravel, and Spiess (2024)	.3	0	Monthly
Colarieti, Mei, and Stantcheva (2024)	.17	.12	Quarterly
Fagereng, Holm, and Natvik (2021)	.5	.15	Annual
Golosov, Graber, Mogstad, and Novgorodsky (2024)	.6	0	Annual
Karger and Rajan (2020)	.5	0	Biweekly
Orchard, Ramey, and Wieland (2023b)	.3	0	Quarterly
Parker, Schild, Erhard, and Johnson (2022)	.1	0	Quarterly

Note: Contemporaneous MPCs are computed over the period in which the shock occurs. The period length is one unit of the frequency—for example, 1 week or 1 month. The intertemporal MPC is the measured MPC over the following period.

spending in subsequent years. This is the evidence that HANK models are typically calibrated to match. However, other studies find no evidence of intertemporal MPCs, which suggests that TANK models may be more appropriate in those cases. For instance, in Orchard, Ramey, and Wieland (2023b), we use a TANK model to study the aggregate effects of the 2008 rebate because we and Borusyak, Jaravel, and Spiess (2024) find that intertemporal MPCs are 0 for this fiscal stimulus.

This suggests that the choice between TANK and HANK models is not just about their computational complexity or the quality of the approximation but also about the quality of the fit to the data. In some cases, such as those in which intertemporal MPCs are small, TANK models may better describe the data than HANK models may.

III. Broader Role of Supply

The paper shows clearly that the specification of the monetary policy rule matters a lot for the importance of heterogeneity in aggregate outcomes. In particular, the differences in the output and inflation impulse response functions (IRFs) between representative-agent New Keynesian (RANK), TANK, and HANK models shrink toward zero the more aggressive the central bank becomes at closing the output gap.

This is because in the models considered here, heterogeneity only matters insofar as it affects aggregate demand and, in turn, as aggregate demand affects output. The degree of pass-through from aggregate demand to output is determined by the supply side of the model. The supply side is borrowed from RANK models and specifically set up to be unaffected by heterogeneity. Through a standard New Keynesian Phillips curve, higher aggregate demand raises inflation. The central bank then determines the extent to which it will raise the real interest rate to offset this inflation and the associated shock to aggregate demand.

When monetary policy is relatively accommodating by fixing the real interest rate, then changes in aggregate demand pass-through one-for-one to changes in output. Thus, to the extent that heterogeneity affects aggregate demand, it will also matter equally for aggregate output. However, when monetary policy implements an inflation target, then changes in aggregate demand are offset by changes in the real interest rate. In this case, aggregate output tracks potential output, and heterogeneity is irrelevant.

This is an important insight and suggests that we may want to pay close attention to the specification of monetary policy rules in HANK models. It is very natural to focus on improving the demand block because that is where the heterogeneity is.[4] But far from it being a neutral, the choice monetary rule invokes an implicit stance on how important heterogeneity can be in general equilibrium.

In my view, this conclusion is too narrow because it is based on the premise that "the" real interest rate is the only instrument that determines the pass-through of aggregate demand to output. Of course, standard New Keynesian models work like this. But even slight generalizations of the model can lead to a much broader view of the role of supply.

My view is informed by Orchard et al. (2023b), in which the supply side plays a broader role in determining the pass-through of aggregate demand to output. In this paper, we study the aggregate impact of the 2008 stimulus. Our objective is to reconcile micro and macro data for this episode: We estimate sizable micro MPCs of 0.3, almost all of it on motor vehicles, but the time series for motor vehicle expenditures is flat. We argue that much of this expenditure must have been dampened in general equilibrium to be consistent with plausible counterfactuals—what would have happened absent the stimulus.[5] But movements in the nominal interest rate are too small to account for quantitatively significant dampening in general equilibrium.

Our paper shows that the relative price of motor vehicles spikes up as rebate checks are spent, so the real interest rate for durables is high even when monetary policy is passive, which then crowds out expenditure on this interest-sensitive good. In the model, we capture this fact with an upward-sloping relative supply curve for durables. Our model then predicts that the aggregate effects of the stimulus are modest despite sizable micro MPCs. Thus, supply plays an important role even when monetary policy is relatively passive.

Thus, I believe there is a broader lesson here: that we need to pay attention to the supply side of the model and not only to the monetary rule. This is particularly important in models with interest-rate-sensitive goods. In traditional public finance, the incidence of a tax is determined by the relative elasticities of supply and demand. In the same way, the pass-through of aggregate demand to output is determined by the relative intertemporal elasticities of supply and demand. Estimating and disciplining these elasticities on both the demand and the supply sides is an important agenda for the HANK literature going forward.

IV. Conclusion

Debortoli and Galí (2025, in this volume) have made an important and valuable contribution by showing how to approximate HANK models with TANK models, thereby elucidating which features of HANK models are quantitatively important in the transmission of monetary policy and technology shocks. I expect this paper to become a standard reference in the HANK literature. I also expect TANK models to continue to be part of our toolkit, both on their own merit and by approximating HANK features. Reports of the death of TANK models appear to be greatly exaggerated.

Endnotes

Author email address: Johannes Wieland (jfwieland@ucsd.edu). For acknowledgments, sources of research support, and disclosure of the author's material financial relationships, if any, please see https://www.nber.org/books-and-chapters/nber-macroeconomics-annual-2024-volume-39/comment-heterogeneity-and-aggregate-fluctuations-insights-tank-models-2-wieland.

1. For example, (monetary policy) Werning (2015), McKay, Nakamura, and Steinsson (2016), Kaplan, Moll, and Violante (2018), Auclert, Rognlie, and Straub (2020), McKay and Wieland (2021, 2022); (fiscal policy) Mitman, Auclert, Rognlie, and Straub (2023), Wolf (2021), Angeletos, Lian, and Wolf (2023); and (financial frictions) Guerrieri and Lorenzoni (2017).
2. Reiter (2009), Ahn et al. (2018), Auclert et al. (2021), and Bhandari et al. (2023).
3. Their HANK-II model is a standard, one-asset HANK model.
4. A notable exception is Auclert, Bardóczy, and Rognlie (2023).
5. The use of macro counterfactuals to evaluate the confluence of micro estimates with macro models is described in detail in Orchard, Ramey, and Wieland (2023a).

References

Ahn, SeHyoun, Greg Kaplan, Benjamin Moll, Thomas Winberry, and Christian Wolf. 2018. "When Inequality Matters for Macro and Macro Matters for Inequality." *NBER Macroeconomics Annual 2017* 32 (1): 1–75.

Angeletos, George-Marios, Chen Lian, and Christian K. Wolf. 2023. "Can Deficits Finance Themselves?" Technical report, NBER, Cambridge, MA.

Auclert, Adrien, Bence Bardóczy, and Matthew Rognlie. 2023. "MPCs, MPEs, and Multipliers: A Trilemma for New Keynesian Models." *Review of Economics and Statistics* 105 (3): 700–12.

Auclert, Adrien, Bence Bardóczy, Matthew Rognlie, and Ludwig Straub. 2021. "Using the Sequence-Space Jacobian to Solve and Estimate Heterogeneous-Agent Models." *Econometrica* 89 (5): 2375–408.

Auclert, Adrien, Matthew Rognlie, and Ludwig Straub. 2020. "Micro Jumps, Macro Humps: Monetary Policy and Business Cycles in an Estimated Hank Model." Technical report, NBER, Cambridge, MA.

———. 2023. "The Intertemporal Keynesian Cross." Working Paper no. 25020, NBER, Cambridge, MA.

Baker, Scott R., Robert A. Farrokhnia, Steffen Meyer, Michaela Pagel, and Constantine Yannelis. 2023. "Income, Liquidity, and the Consumption Response to the 2020 Economic Stimulus Payments." *Review of Finance* 27 (6): 2271–304.

Bhandari, Anmol, Thomas Bourany, David Evans, and Mikhail Golosov. 2023. "A Perturbational Approach for Approximating Heterogeneous Agent Models." Technical report, NBER, Cambridge, MA.

Boehm, Johannes, Etienne Fize, and Xavier Jaravel. 2023. "Five Facts about MPCs: Evidence from a Randomized Experiment." Discussion Paper no. 18676, Centre for Economic Policy Research, Paris.

Borusyak, Kirill, Xavier Jaravel, and Jann Spiess. 2024. "Revisiting Event-Study Designs: Robust and Efficient Estimation." *Review of Economic Studies* 91 (6): 3253–85.

Colarieti, Roberto, Pierfrancesco Mei, and Stefanie Stantcheva. 2024. "The How and Why of Household Reactions to Income Shocks." Technical report, NBER, Cambridge, MA.

Debortoli, Davide, and Jordi Galí. 2025. "Heterogeneity and Aggregate Fluctuations: Insights from TANK Models." *NBER Macroeconomics Annual* 39:307–57.

Fagereng, Andreas, Martin B. Holm, and Gisle J. Natvik. 2021. "MPC Heterogeneity and Household Balance Sheets." *American Economic Journal: Macroeconomics* 13 (4): 1–54.

Golosov, Mikhail, Michael Graber, Magne Mogstad, and David Novgorodsky. 2024. "How Americans Respond to Idiosyncratic and Exogenous Changes in Household Wealth and Unearned Income." *Quarterly Journal of Economics* 139 (2): 1321–95.

Guerrieri, Veronica, and Guido Lorenzoni. 2017. "Credit Crises, Precautionary Savings, and the Liquidity Trap." *Quarterly Journal of Economics* 132 (3): 1427–67.

Kaplan, Greg, Benjamin Moll, and Giovanni L. Violante. 2018. "Monetary Policy According to HANK." *American Economic Review* 108 (3): 697–743.

Karger, Ezra, and Aastha Rajan. 2020. "Heterogeneity in the Marginal Propensity to Consume: Evidence from COVID-19 Stimulus Payments." Working Paper no. WP-2020-15, Federal Reserve Bank of Chicago.

Krusell, Per, and Anthony A Smith, Jr. 1998. "Income and Wealth Heterogeneity in the Macroeconomy." *Journal of Political Economy* 106 (5): 867–96.

McKay, Alisdair, Emi Nakamura, and Jón Steinsson. 2016. "The Power of Forward Guidance Revisited." *American Economic Review* 106 (10): 3133–58.
McKay, Alisdair, and Johannes F. Wieland. 2021. "Lumpy Durable Consumption Demand and the Limited Ammunition of Monetary Policy." *Econometrica* 89 (6): 2717–49.
———. 2022. "Forward Guidance and Durable Goods Demand." *American Economic Review: Insights* 4 (1): 106–22.
Orchard, Jacob, Valerie A. Ramey, and Johannes F. Wieland. 2023a. "Micro MPCs and Macro Counterfactuals: The Case of the 2008 Rebates." Technical report, NBER, Cambridge, MA.
———. 2023b. "Using Macro Counterfactuals to Assess Plausibility: An Illustration using the 2001 Rebate MPCs." Technical report, NBER, Cambridge, MA.
Parker, Jonathan A., Jake Schild, Laura Erhard, and David Johnson. 2022. "Household Spending Responses to the Economic Impact Payments of 2020: Evidence from the Consumer Expenditure Survey." Technical report, NBER, Cambridge, MA.
Reiter, Michael. 2009. "Solving Heterogeneous-Agent Models by Projection and Perturbation." *Journal of Economic Dynamics and Control* 33 (3): 649–65.
Werning, Iván. 2015. "Incomplete Markets and Aggregate Demand." Technical report, NBER, Cambridge, MA.
Wolf, Christian K. 2021. "Interest Rate Cuts vs. Stimulus Payments: An Equivalence Result." Technical report, NBER, Cambridge, MA.

Comment

Matthew Rognlie, *Northwestern University and NBER,* United States of America

Following Campbell and Mankiw (1989), the two-agent model, combining hand-to-mouth and permanent-income households, has become a popular alternative to the representative-agent model. Adding a measure of hand-to-mouth agents, who are unable to borrow and lend at the margin, is a simple way to match high marginal propensities to consume (MPCs) in the data. This approach is especially natural when studying fiscal policy (see, e.g., Galí, López-Salido, and Vallés 2007), where MPCs and the associated Keynesian multiplier have long been of interest. TANK (two-agent New Keynesian) models are tractable and well suited for such questions.

More recently, heterogeneous-agent New Keynesian (HANK) models have emerged as another alternative to the representative-agent paradigm. They have been used to revisit the transmission of monetary policy (e.g., Kaplan, Moll, and Violante 2018), fiscal policy (e.g., Auclert, Rognlie, and Straub 2024), and many other core macro topics.

HANK and TANK have important similarities. They both break Ricardian equivalence, can match high MPCs, and have heterogeneous households. But HANK and TANK are also very different: HANK builds on the incomplete-market Bewley-Huggett-Aiyagari tradition, featuring a continuum of heterogeneous households with different incomes and asset positions, whereas TANK's heterogeneity is limited to just two agents. A trade-off emerges between richness and tractability: HANK can speak to the detailed interactions between heterogeneity and macro, but TANK requires less computation and can sometimes be solved analytically.

It is natural to ask, If we opt for TANK rather than HANK, just how much are we giving up? Maybe not that much, Debortoli and Galí argue in

NBER Macroeconomics Annual, volume 39, 2025.
 Published by The University of Chicago Press for the National Bureau of Economic Research. https://doi.org/10.1086/735274

this paper. In particular, if we are interested in the aggregate effects of standard macro shocks—monetary shocks, productivity shocks, and fiscal shocks—then Debortoli and Galí argue that TANK is an effective substitute for HANK. In their words, "a suitably specified and calibrated TANK model (which abstracts from idiosyncratic income risk) can capture reasonably well the aggregate implications of household heterogeneity and the main channels through which it operates."

I think this overreaches—and that, indeed, TANK is a far weaker substitute for HANK than this paper indicates. Although the paper's findings of a close fit between TANK and HANK appear impressive, they are to some extent accidental and specific to the experiments that the paper considers. As I will show, reasonable alternative shocks—such as government spending shocks, financed by debt that is not paid off too quickly—open up a large gap between TANK and HANK.

This is not just a question of quantitative magnitude. It points to a deep, qualitative distinction between TANK and HANK, which is that TANK's departure from the representative-agent paradigm is entirely static—limited to hand-to-mouth agents that spend what they receive within a period—whereas HANK introduces rich, dynamic changes in spending patterns. The difference between TANK and HANK is most apparent when these dynamics are taken into account. I summarize this as the Lesson 1 that I take away from examining this paper.

Lesson 1. The differences between HANK and TANK are clearest when the question of interest has a strong dynamic component.

For instance, both HANK and TANK can be calibrated to have similar MPCs and might behave similarly in response to a government spending shock that is paid for within a few quarters. But they become very different when the debt used to finance spending is more persistent—especially if we look at a cumulative measure of output rather than just the multiplier at date 0. The more dynamic the shock and measurement, the more HANK versus TANK matters.

The paper largely misses this point. It emphasizes short-lived shocks, like a monetary shock with a quarterly persistence of 0.5 or a deficit-financed fiscal shock where the debt is paid back on average within 2.5 years.

Instead, the paper spends much of its time on distributional questions, especially what it calls the interest rate exposure channel (How sensitive is each household's cash-on-hand to changes in interest rates?) and the income distribution channel (How do changes in the aggregate markup affect the distribution of income between households?). There is no doubt these channels are important, but they can easily be made too important with the wrong assumptions. This paper is a case in point: its rule for real wages implies extremely countercyclical profits, such that an extra \$1 in real output leads to an additional \$3 in wage income and −\$2 in dividend income. Needless to say, the paper's HANK and TANK models are extremely sensitive to how this income is distributed. But the premise is absurd: profits are not really so countercyclical, and this fictitious mechanism distracts from other, more economically meaningful ones.

This is a common issue in both HANK and TANK, and I take it as Lesson 2 for the literature.

Lesson 2. In New Keynesian models with heterogeneity, it is easy to make assumptions with extreme and implausible distributional consequences.

This often happens when, like here, papers assume sticky prices with flexible wages. This choice was natural in the early days of HANK and TANK, because the baseline representative-agent New Keynesian model ("RANK") made the same assumption. But one side effect of this assumption is a countercyclical profit margin—*very* countercyclical in most calibrations. This is innocuous enough in RANK models, where the same agent receives all income anyway. But it starts to matter a great deal once there is heterogeneity, and it can easily dominate the analysis.

The same is true for the typical assumption that all debt is short-term, often irrelevant in a RANK model but important once agents have heterogeneous debt positions. The paper's large interest rate exposure channel follows directly from its assumption that when rates change, all debt service is immediately repriced at the new rate.

The paper correctly recognizes these distributional effects as important and engineers a series of TANK models to match them—but again, they are made far too important, especially the income distribution channel, by the paper's assumptions. In my view, the focus on these effects distracts from a more robust comparison of TANK and HANK, as the paper misses not only Lesson 1 but also the following.

Lesson 3. In a simple benchmark where income shares are unaffected by aggregate output, the general equilibrium response of aggregate consumption to real interest rates is identical in RANK, TANK, and HANK.

This important neutrality result is from Werning (2015). In its exact form, it requires that (1) all agents' labor incomes and dividends expand proportionally with output, (2) asset positions held coming into date 0 are claims on future dividends, and (3) the elasticity of intertemporal substitution is 1. Quantitatively, however, it is robust to moderate departures from these assumptions. The result holds despite the fact that partial equilibrium consumption responses to interest rates are very different in RANK, TANK, and HANK—because, in the language of Kaplan et al. (2018), the "indirect" (GE) effects through income exactly offset the varying "direct" (PE) effects of interest rates.

In short, monetary policy is not the first place we should look to find a difference between TANK and HANK—or RANK and HANK, for that matter. There are many reasons, of course, why the Werning (2015) neutrality result might not hold in practice, but it is a very natural starting point and reminds us that very different models, with different implications elsewhere, can have the same aggregate response to interest rates. It is thus unfortunate that this paper chooses monetary shocks as its primary experiment.[1]

Summary and outline of comment. In sum, my critique of this paper is the following: Its assumptions imply a counterfactually volatile income distribution (Lesson 2), which is distracting and requires special attention to handle. This volatility obscures the fact that monetary shocks often have similar aggregate consequences regardless of heterogeneity (Lesson 3), which makes them a bad test of the distinction between TANK and HANK. On top of all this, the paper deals mostly with short-lived shocks, missing the dynamic settings where differences between TANK and HANK are most likely to emerge (Lesson 1).

In the remaining comment, I start in Section I by documenting the profound differences between HANK and TANK, in both the distribution of MPCs and aggregate MPCs, that emerge when we look beyond one period. Then, in Section II, I go through the paper and discuss its main exercises, showing that mild changes in the analysis—a longer-lived shock, or more cumulative measure of output—result in different conclusions. In Section III, I tweak the models to satisfy Werning (2015) neutrality and show that there are vast differences in the response to deficit-financed fiscal shocks, even though RANK = TANK = HANK for monetary policy. Finally, in Section IV, I discuss the path forward and the role of tractable models like TANK versus other approaches to make heterogeneity in macro more accessible.

Throughout my discussion, I use exactly the same models and calibrations as in the paper—all unmodified, aside from my Werning (2015) analysis in Section III. My main goal is to show that even with the same models, a closer look gives us different results.[2]

I. Static TANK, Dynamic HANK: An Overview

TANK models feature stark MPC heterogeneity: agents are either hand-to-mouth consumers, with MPCs of 1, or unconstrained permanent-income consumers, with MPCs very close to 0. HANK models, in principle, are more general: agents can have a range of MPCs between 0 and 1, depending on their distance to the borrowing constraint.

If we look only at the immediate MPC out of a transfer, however, the contrast is not always so clear. Figure 1A compares the distribution of MPCs in Debortoli and Galí's TANK against that in their "HANK-II," where the latter has a standard household side with a binding borrowing constraint. TANK clusters at the extremes: as calibrated, 70% of households are unconstrained with MPCs near 0, and 30% are hand-to-mouth with MPCs of 1. But what about HANK? As targeted by the paper, it features roughly 30% of households with MPCs of 1. Of the remaining 70% of households, around 50% have MPCs below 0.1, and the remaining 20% of households mostly have MPCs in the 0.1–0.4 range. The latter group with intermediate MPCs is special to HANK—impossible to achieve in a TANK model—but one might wonder whether having 20% of the population with mildly elevated MPCs is really such an important distinction.

Figure 1B takes a different approach, looking at the distribution of the expected cumulative MPC over quarters $t = 0, \ldots, 10$ following a transfer. This measure asks, If a household is given \$1 today, what fraction of it do they cumulatively expect to spend, in present value terms, through date 10?[3] Here, TANK has exactly the same distribution as in figure 1A: the hand-to-mouth still have an MPC of 1, whereas the unconstrained have such low MPCs that they spend little, even over many quarters. But the

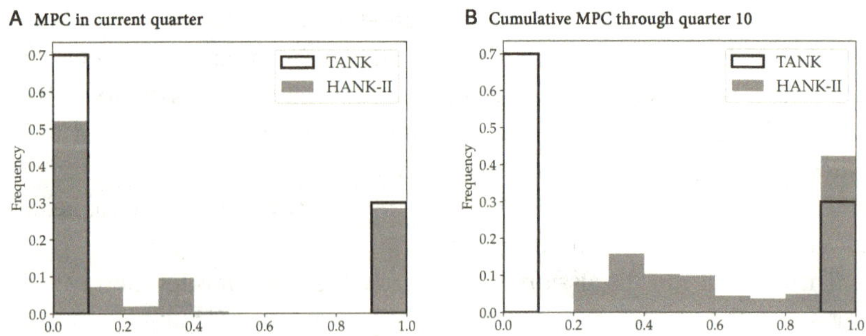

Fig. 1. Histograms of household MPCs, current, and expected cumulative.

HANK distribution has shifted to the right and now looks very different. In this calibration, everyone expects to consume at least 20% of a transfer through date 10. Roughly 45% have expected MPCs between 0.2 and 0.6, and the remaining 55% have expected MPCs above 0.6. The average expected MPC is 0.69, versus 0.34 for TANK.

In short, HANK and TANK might not look so different immediately following a shock—but when we look over a longer horizon, the distinction becomes clear. Here, on impact, they have similar average MPCs; but cumulatively through $t = 10$, HANK has double the average MPC!

What accounts for this difference? In TANK, there are only hand-to-mouth and unconstrained households. The hand-to-mouth have MPCs of 1 immediately when they receive a transfer, but after this, the remaining "excess savings" are all in the hands of the permanent-income households, which hold them forever and consume only the interest income. There is no delayed consumption response of any magnitude—just a static burst when the transfer is received.

In HANK, by contrast, everyone departs to some extent from the permanent-income hypothesis. Households have "buffer-stock" behavior and spend down excess savings. For some households, this spending might not be too impressive in a single quarter, but it adds up over time. On top of all this, households are subject to shocks: over several quarters, some agents who were initially unconstrained will become constrained, and vice versa. It all contributes to much more meaningful dynamics and an obvious difference between figures 1A and 1B.

Intertemporal MPCs. One way to visualize the aggregate distinction between HANK and TANK, as discussed in Auclert et al. (2024), is to look at intertemporal MPCs (iMPCs), which give the aggregate consumption response at each date to income shocks.

In figure 2A, we look at the response to a uniform transfer to all agents at $t = 0$. On impact, the TANK and HANK responses are similar, consistent with figure 1A. But from $t = 1$ onward, HANK consumption remains elevated, summing up to the average cumulative MPCs from figure 1B, whereas TANK consumption falls to almost zero.

Figure 2B shows a similar impulse response but now to a shock that proportionally increases all agents' income at $t = 0$, consistent with Auclert et al. (2024). Here, the impact consumption response is smaller in both models, because high-income agents have low MPCs.[4] But the cumulative difference between HANK and TANK from date 1 onward remains large in absolute terms (at 0.36 vs. 0.04) and is now much larger than the date-0 response. Auclert et al. (2024) show that in general equilibrium,

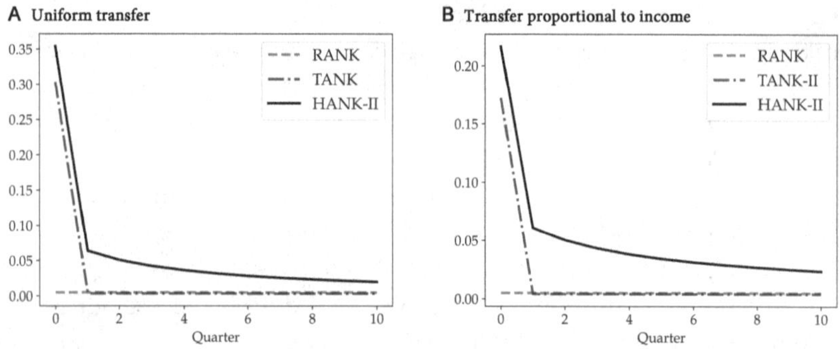

Fig. 2. Aggregate intertemporal MPCs out of uniform and proportional transfers.

these differences imply much larger output multipliers in HANK for deficit-financed spending shocks.

Which is right empirically? We have seen a clear difference between TANK and HANK, summarized by the intertemporal MPCs in figure 2. But which iMPC profile is closer to being correct is an empirical question.

In Auclert et al. (2024), we use administrative Norwegian lottery evidence from Fagereng, Holm, and Natvik (2021) to obtain empirical iMPCs that much more closely resemble HANK. We also use MPC survey data from the Italian Survey of Household Income and Wealth to document that the empirical distribution of MPCs is much less concentrated at the extremes than in TANK, and we leverage this to obtain a lower bound on iMPCs after $t = 0$, which again is a much closer fit for HANK.

But these are just two data sources, and Debortoli and Galí point to several other papers suggesting that the MPC is concentrated within a few months of income receipt, in line with TANK models: Borusyak, Jaravel, and Spiess (2024), Orchard, Ramey, and Wieland (2024), and Boehm, Fize, and Jaravel (2025).[5] This interpretation, however, conflates statistical zeros with economic ones. It is true that these papers find no evidence for a delayed spending response, but they do not rule it out either. They simply do not have the data and statistical power to say anything about plausible intertemporal MPCs. For instance, in Borusyak et al. (2024), the standard errors on the preferred estimates of marginal propensity to spend even just 2 months after the 2008 tax rebate are between 50% and 100% as large as the point estimate for the contemporaneous effect of the rebate—and thus swamp the likely effect.[6] Future months are even noisier.[7] In Orchard et al.'s (2024; table 3) various specifications, the standard errors on the cumulative 6-month MPC range from 0.38 to 1.19. And in Boehm et al. (2025; fig. 2), the confidence interval for the cumulative 9-month MPC out of a 300-euro transfer is from –200 euros to 500 euros! None of these papers has even close to the statistical power that would be necessary to identify the intertemporal MPCs in figure 2, which after the first quarter are between 0.01 and 0.02 (in monthly terms) for HANK.

For now, therefore, the direct evidence on iMPCs (such as Fagereng et al. 2021) seems to favor HANK, but there is still a great deal of uncertainty, and more work is needed. I find it very unlikely, however, that the evidence will ultimately come out in favor of TANK. For one thing, a consistent finding in the literature has been that many households initially use transfers to pay off debt—but as Agarwal, Liu, and Souleles (2007) and Koşar et al. (2024) point out, this leads to a delayed spending response, as these households later run their credit card balances back up. Separately, exploiting a policy change in mortgage amortization rules, Bernstein and Koudijs (2024) have found stark, long-run departures from Ricardian equivalence: in response to forced savings in their mortgages, households cut consumption and leisure nearly one-for-one over a 5-year horizon. This is inconsistent with TANK but possible to explain with HANK. Finally, it is widely believed that "excess savings" contributed to elevated spending in the aftermath of the pandemic. This cannot happen in TANK models—where any excess savings that are not immediately spent are in the hands of permanent-income consumers and held forever—but is possible with more heterogeneity (see Auclert, Rognlie, and Straub 2023).

II. The Paper's Exercises: Chasing HANK with TANK

I now go through the paper's main exercises, which involve a series of HANK models (which the paper calls HANK-I, HANK II, and HANK-III) that are matched by a series of RANK and TANK models (RANK, TANK-I, TANK-II, and TANK-III). Throughout this section, I use the same models and calibrations as the paper.

HANK-I and RANK. In HANK-I, the paper uses the natural borrowing constraint, which households approach but never reach. Here, it turns out that there is plenty of room to self-insure, and average quarterly MPCs are very low (0.014). As a result, the impact effect of the paper's monetary shock, a cut to the real interest rate with a quarterly persistence of 0.5, is similar in HANK-I to a simple RANK model; figure 1A in the paper shows an impact output increase of 0.6% for HANK-I and 0.5% for RANK. The paper concludes that RANK is a decent approximation to HANK-I.

This conclusion, however, turns out to be a bit premature. The reason is that the output response is far more persistent in HANK-I than in RANK, and over time this adds up to a large difference in output. Figure 3A visualizes this by plotting the cumulative (in date-0 present value) output effect, and extending the horizon to 40 quarters. By quarter 40, the difference is enormous and still growing, with HANK-I at 3.5% versus 1% for RANK.

Why such a difference? Figure 3B does a general equilibrium decomposition of the HANK-I output impulse response (Auclert, Rognlie, and Straub 2020) into components originating in the substitution and income effects of interest rates.[8] We see that HANK-I's contribution from substitution almost perfectly agrees with RANK and that the income effects of real interest rates are entirely responsible for the divergence. This may be surprising, because MPCs in the model are low—but because the shock immediately changes the interest rate paid on the entire stock of debt (roughly 300% of annual gross domestic product [GDP]), the implied redistribution here is enormous, and even the tiny gap between the average quarterly MPCs of savers (0.007) and debtors (0.024) is enough to drive a nontrivial and highly persistent effect on demand.

Such a huge distributional effect, of course, seems unlikely—households do not have such a huge stock of debt subject to an immediately adjustable rate. But this all serves as a useful reminder of both Lesson 2 (implausibly large distributional effects are easy to obtain in New Keynesian models) and Lesson 1 (the cumulative effect is much larger than the impact one).

HANK-II, TANK-I, and TANK-II. The paper next modifies the HANK-I model to have a binding borrowing constraint, which it calibrates such that roughly 30% of households are constrained in any given period.

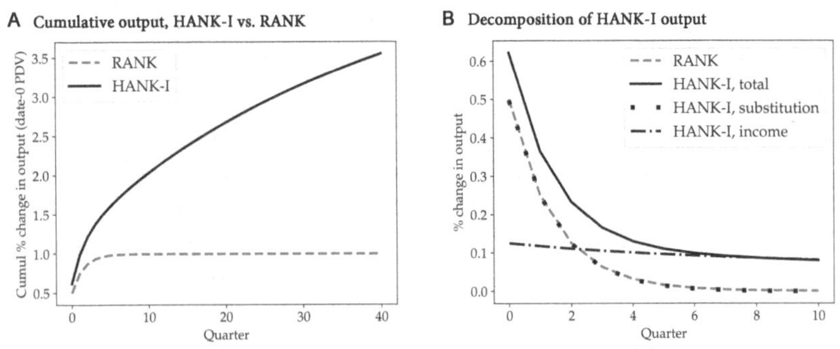

Fig. 3. Output change from 1% (annualized) monetary shock, HANK-I versus RANK models.

This "HANK-II" model is a more conventional HANK model, with higher MPCs that we visualized in figures 1 and 2.

The paper then tries to match HANK-II with a TANK model. It starts with TANK-I—the simplest possible TANK model, which simply makes 30% of households hand-to-mouth and assumes these households receive no dividends. But this results in output that is far too responsive: an impact effect of 3.5% from the monetary shock versus 0.6% in HANK-II. In response, the paper constructs TANK-II, which makes several modifications so that the hand-to-mouth are more similar to the constrained households in HANK-II: It sets the average labor productivity of the hand-to-mouth to a fraction Ξ^H of the average; it gives the hand-to-mouth a share $\Theta^H > \Xi^H$ of dividends; and it also endows the hand-to-mouth with a constant debt burden on which they must pay interest. With these modifications, the paper shows that HANK-II and TANK-II have much more similar responses to its baseline monetary shock.

The analytics of TANK. To understand all this, it is useful to take a brief detour, deriving a formula for output in the paper's TANK models. We start from the equation $C_t^H = \Xi^H W_t N_t + \Theta^H D_t - \psi Y \hat{R}_t$, which says that the hand-to-mouth consume their income minus their required interest rate payments every period. When a monetary shock changes interest rates and output, the first-order change in the hand-to-mouth contribution to consumption is

$$\lambda^H dC_t^H = \lambda^H \underbrace{\left(\Xi^H \frac{dW_t N_t}{dY_t} + \Theta^H \frac{dD_t}{dY_t} \right)}_{\equiv m} dY_t - \lambda^H \psi Y d\hat{R}_t, \tag{1}$$

where we multiply by the λ^H share of hand-to-mouth households, and define m as the marginal share of aggregate income accruing to those households.

To first order, output also equals consumption so that we have $dY_t = \lambda^H dC_t^H + (1 - \lambda^H) dC_t^U$. Substituting in (1) for $\lambda^H dC_t^H$ then gives

$$dY_t = m dY_t - \lambda^H \psi Y d\hat{R}_t + (1 - \lambda^H) dC_t^U,$$

$$dY_t = \frac{1}{1-m} \left(-\lambda^H \psi Y d\hat{R}_t + (1 - \lambda^H) dC_t^U \right), \tag{2}$$

where $1/(1 - m)$ serves as a *multiplier*.

Finally, we observe that the consumption response dC_t^U / C^U of the unconstrained is determined entirely by the forward-looking path of real interest rates and is identical to the output response of a representative-agent economy facing that path, which we denote by dY_t^{RA}/Y. Dividing (2) by steady-state Y and using $\lambda^u \equiv 1 - \lambda^H$, we can rewrite as

$$\frac{dY_t}{Y} = \frac{1}{1-m}\left(-\lambda^H \psi d\hat{R}_t + \frac{\lambda^u C^u}{C}\frac{dY_t^{RA}}{Y}\right). \quad (3)$$

This equation says that the percent change in output, period by period, equals the multiplier $1/(1-m)$ times two impulses to demand: the change in debt service of the hand-to-mouth, and the representative-agent effect of a monetary shock times the unconstrained share of steady-state consumption.

All that remains is to evaluate the coefficients in (3). First, to obtain m, we need dW_tN_t/dY_t and dD_t/dY_t, the marginal shares of aggregate income earned as wage income and dividends. These can be calculated from $W_tN_t = (\mathcal{M}/\mathcal{M}_t)Y_t$ and $D_t = (1-(\mathcal{M}/\mathcal{M}_t))Y_t$. Equation (6) in the paper shows that the elasticity of the inverse markup $1/\mathcal{M}_t$ to Y_t is $\sigma + \varphi$. Evaluating around the steady state where $\mathcal{M} = 1$, at the parameters $\sigma = \varphi = 1$, we get $dW_tN_t/dY_t = 1 + (\sigma + \varphi) = 3$ and $dD_t/dY_t = -(\sigma + \varphi) = -2$. In short, from a marginal \$1 of output, labor earns \$3 and capital earns −\$2.

In the TANK-I model, the $\lambda^H = 0.3$ hand-to-mouth have average labor earnings and no dividends ($\Xi^H = 1$ and $\Theta^H = 0$), so evaluating m in (1), we get $m = \lambda^H \Xi^H (dW_tN_t/dY_t) = 0.3 \cdot 1 \cdot 3 = 0.9$: 90% of a marginal dollar goes to the hand-to-mouth. This leads to a multiplier of $(1/1-m) = 10$. Because the $\lambda^u = 0.7$ hand-to-mouth have no debt in this model ($\psi = 0$) and also $C^u = C$, (3) reduces to $dY_t/Y = (1/1-m)\lambda^u(dY_t^{RA})/Y = 7 \cdot dY_t^{RA}/Y$. Thus, the TANK-I impulse response equals exactly the RANK impulse response, multiplied by 7. This is consistent with the paper's quantitative results (3.5% impact for TANK-I, 0.5% for RANK).

In the TANK-II model, on the other hand, we have $\Xi^H = 0.56$ and $\Theta^H = 0.78$, so that m evaluates to 0.036. This could not be more different from TANK-I: rather than receiving 90% of aggregate income at the margin, the hand-to-mouth get just 3.6%. The multiplier is therefore $(1/1-m) = 1.037$. Combining this with $\psi = 2$ and $\lambda^u C^u/C = 0.83$, (3) evaluates to

$$\frac{dY_t}{Y} = -0.62 \cdot d\hat{R}_t + 0.86 \cdot \frac{dY_t^{RA}}{Y}. \quad (4)$$

Note the conflicting forces in (4): the RANK output response is dampened by a factor of 0.86, but there is also an income effect from the debt owed by the hand-to-mouth, which should amplify the output response.

Quantitative evaluation. Figure 4A shows the impulse responses of RANK, TANK-II, and HANK-II to the paper's baseline monetary shock. Both TANK-II and HANK-II are somewhat more expansionary than RANK (around 0.6%, vs. 0.5%), and they are fairly close to each other—leading the paper to argue that TANK-II is a good approximation for HANK-II.

But (4) suggests that the balance between RANK and TANK-II, at least, depends on dynamics: With a more persistent shock, the forward-looking $0.86 \cdot dY_t^{RA}/Y$ term should dominate, and the dampening factor will make TANK-II respond less than RANK. Figure 4B tests this with a $\rho_v = 0.95$ monetary shock. As expected, we see a reversal: TANK-II now has a smaller output response than RANK.

There is an even more conspicuous reversal for HANK-II: as we move from the less to the more persistent shock, the output response changes from slightly larger than TANK-II to significantly smaller. The reason is that HANK adds a dynamic element to the mechanisms in TANK. In TANK-II, the fact that a tiny marginal share of aggregate income ($m = 0.036$) goes to the hand-to-mouth shows up as static dampening of RANK, with a constant factor of 0.86. But in HANK-II, this mechanism shows up dynamically: if households receive relatively less income when they are constrained, ex ante they perceive this as a risk and consume less, leading to a smaller output boom. This propagates through expectations, causing endogenous discounting of anticipated monetary policy—which is most important for persistent shocks.

We can isolate this effect more cleanly with a forward guidance shock. Figure 5A shows the output response to a 1% (annualized) cut in rates for the single quarter $t = 20$, announced at $t = 0$. The differences between RANK and TANK-II from (4) are very clear: TANK-II output at every date

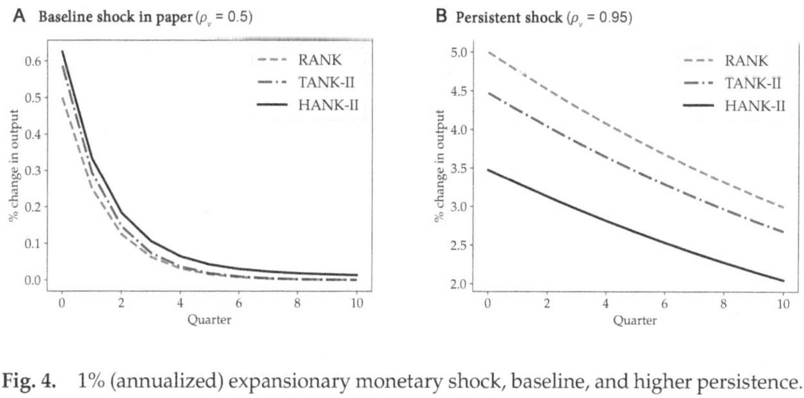

Fig. 4. 1% (annualized) expansionary monetary shock, baseline, and higher persistence.

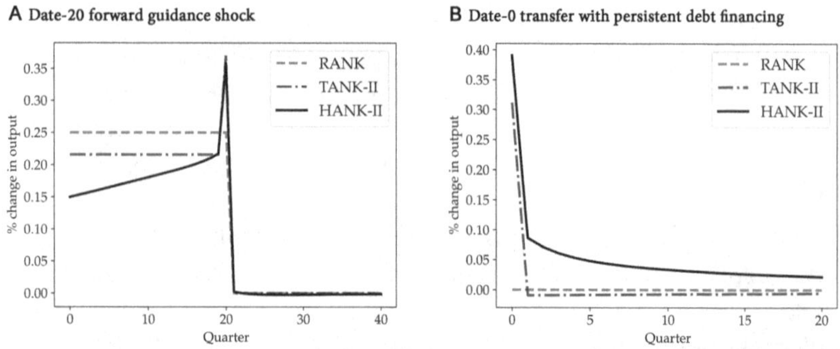

Fig. 5. Experiments that cleanly distinguish TANK and HANK.

other than $t = 20$ equals 0.86 times RANK output, but at $t = 20$, there is also the direct income effect on the hand-to-mouth, which causes a spike in consumption and thus output. HANK-II is similar near $t = 20$ but behaves differently at earlier dates because of the endogenous discounting process just discussed and is substantially weaker than TANK-II at $t = 0$ (0.15% vs. 0.22%).

Here, the ultimate reason for discounting in HANK-II is procyclical inequality, which in turn arises from two questionable features of the model: first, that dividend income is extremely countercyclical (with −\$2 from every marginal \$1 in aggregate income), and second, that poor households earn a higher share of their income from dividends than richer households do. Together, these forces mean that poor households are disproportionately exposed to a countercyclical income stream (dividends) and, therefore, that the gap between rich and poor expands in booms. This procyclical inequality goes hand-in-hand with procyclical risk, which reduces ex ante consumption. As Bilbiie (2020, forthcoming) shows in a tractable version of HANK, procyclical inequality implies discounting in the aggregate Euler equation.[9] Inversely, countercyclical inequality implies amplification.

I take away two points here. First, this is a reminder of Lesson 2: it is easy to have implausible distributional outcomes in New Keynesian models, like the procyclical inequality and risk we see here. But second, once we have interesting general equilibrium feedbacks, those feedbacks are likely to operate intertemporally and will lead to dynamic differences between TANK and HANK (Lesson 1). In the arguably more plausible case of countercyclical risk, for instance, TANK and HANK would still differ in figure 5A—just in the opposite direction.

Fiscal policy. The final version of the paper adds a fiscal policy experiment as well. The two shocks both increase government spending by 1%

of GDP on impact, with a persistence of 0.8. In the balanced-budget shock, the cost of this spending is paid immediately with lump-sum taxation. In the deficit-financed shock, government debt follows the rule $dB_t^g = \rho_b (dB_{t-1}^g + dG_t)$ with $\rho_b = 0.9$, so that government spending is mostly financed by debt at first, which is then paid off with lump-sum taxation over time. The path of real interest rates is held fixed in both cases.

Figure 6A shows the output response to the balanced-budget shock, replicating figure 8 in the paper. The multiplier in RANK is 1, consistent with Woodford (2011). The multipliers in TANK and HANK are lower. This deviation from the balanced-budget benchmark multiplier of 1 in Auclert et al. (2024) is for two reasons: first, the dampening from procyclical inequality discussed above, and second, taxation being lump-sum rather than proportional.

Figure 8 in the paper then shows the output response under deficit financing with $\rho_b = 0.9$. As the paper notes, output is quite similar for both HANK-II and TANK-II, with multipliers now slightly above 1.

Does this mean that HANK-II and TANK-II behave similarly, even for deficit-financed shocks—in apparent contrast to the results in Auclert et al. (2024)? I argue not. The deficit-financed results in the paper look similar only because two forces happen to nearly offset each other: first, the greater dampening in HANK that is visible in the balanced-budget case (fig. 6A), and second, the greater amplification in HANK of deficit-financed spending. This cancellation is highly nongeneric: it depends both on the particular forces that dampen HANK more in the balanced-budget case (countercyclical inequality, lump-sum taxation) and on the persistence ρ_b of debt financing.

I show this in figure 6B by increasing the persistence parameter ρ_b from 0.9 to 0.975. With $\rho_b = 0.9$, debt on average is paid off within 2.5 years;

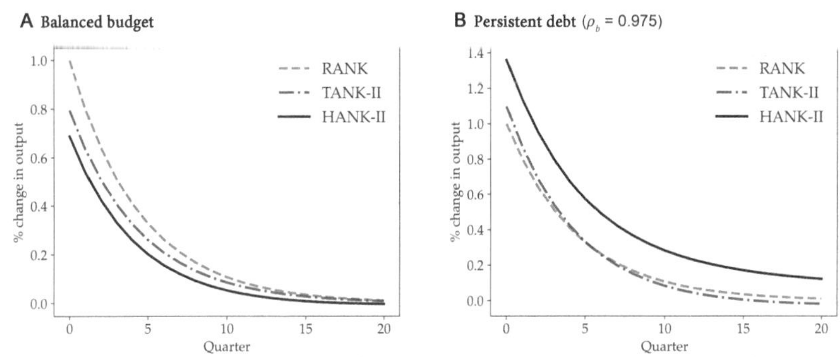

Fig. 6. Output effect of 1% of GDP government spending shock, by financing.

with $\rho_b = 0.975$, this increases to 10 years. Although fiscal rules are difficult to estimate, the higher ρ_b strikes me as more realistic for typical deficit spending—at least in developed countries, policy is rarely so conservative that it pays off extra debt in just a few years.

With this change, the gap between HANK-II and TANK-II becomes noticeably larger, with impact multipliers of 1.36 and 1.10, respectively. But because HANK-II has a more persistent output response, the far more significant gap is in cumulative[10] multipliers, compiled in table 1: 2.44 for HANK-II versus only 0.79 for TANK-II and 1.00 for RANK. Here, there is even a qualitative difference between the two models: cumulatively, HANK-II increases output by far more than RANK, whereas TANK-II increases it by less.

All this reinforces Lesson 1: to best see the difference between HANK and TANK, we need the shock to have more of an intertemporal component (where debt is not paid back within just a few years), and we also need a more cumulative measure of output.

Other exercises: productivity shocks, HANK-III and TANK-III, and the Phillips curve. The paper also has several other exercises, which I briefly cover now.

First, it considers productivity shocks in parallel with monetary shocks. But with an exogenous rule for the real interest rate, productivity shocks only matter in this model through a somewhat obscure channel: because less labor is needed to produce any given amount of output, higher productivity lowers real wages and raises dividends conditional on output. The effect then depends on distributional assumptions: for instance, it is highly contractionary in TANK-I, where constrained agents receive no dividends, but mildly expansionary in TANK-II and HANK-II, where constrained agents receive a higher share of dividends relative to wages. Because it relies on a volatile split between wages and dividends, I do not find this exercise very useful, except as another reminder of Lesson 2.

Table 1
Impact and Cumulative Multipliers by Financing Rule and Model

Financing Rule	Multiplier	RANK	TANK-II	HANK-II
Balanced budget	Impact	1.00	.79	.69
	Cumulative	1.00	.79	.59
Debt ($\rho_b = 0.9$)	Impact	1.00	1.07	1.13
	Cumulative	1.00	.79	.82
Debt ($\rho_b = 0.975$)	Impact	1.00	1.10	1.36
	Cumulative	1.00	.79	2.44

The paper also extends its analysis to the more complex HANK-III, where claims on future dividends are held in an "illiquid" account à la Kaplan et al. (2018) and can be traded subject to an adjustment cost. This reverses the dampening discussed earlier; now there is a very low MPC out of dividends, which are capitalized into illiquid accounts, so that redistribution from dividends to wages is expansionary rather than contractionary. This amplifies the response to monetary shocks.[11] On its own, this is a realistic modification to the model, but in the paper it matters primarily because of the extreme countercyclicality of dividends—which, again, is not very realistic.

Last, the paper moves from an exogenous real interest rate path to a stabilizing Taylor-type rule. It finds that this reduces the gap between all models, for a simple reason: because all models are set up to have the same New Keynesian Phillips curve, which features divine coincidence, an aggressive enough inflation-targeting rule will come arbitrarily close to setting both inflation and the output gap to zero, regardless of model.

This is a useful point that has also been made elsewhere (e.g., McKay and Wolf 2023), but it only goes so far. First, the assumption that all models have the same New Keynesian Phillips curve is made for convenience, not realism; accounting for heterogeneity in Auclert et al. (2024) does change the Phillips curve slightly, and heterogeneity probably has other supply-side effects as well. Second, distributional considerations do matter from a normative perspective, and inflation targeting will generically not be optimal in HANK. Finally, in practice it is very important to understand the demand-side transmission mechanisms of monetary and fiscal policy, even if inflation stabilization is the ultimate goal. Our incomplete understanding of these mechanisms—which vary dramatically across models—remains a major obstacle for effective policy.

III. Comparing Models that Satisfy Neutrality

As discussed, perhaps the most subtle and important mechanism in Debortoli and Galí's paper is distributional: because there are extremely procyclical wages and countercyclical dividends (Lesson 2), different assumptions on who gets the wages and dividends can lead to very different results.

It is natural to ask what would happen with more neutral distributional assumptions—for instance, if wages and dividends both had constant shares of aggregate income.[12] Because the paper assumes that $\sigma = 1$, such a constant-share assumption brings us very close to the setting where

Werning (2015)'s neutrality result holds. The only additional change required is to calibrate the model such that all asset positions coming into date 0 are equity claims on future dividends.

I modify Debortoli and Galí's HANK-II model in the minimal necessary way to achieve this. On the household side, I set the debt limit to zero and instead calibrate the markup $\mathcal{M}$ so that the supply of assets (claims on dividends) is consistent with the same fraction (roughly 30%) of households being constrained in steady state. I assume that the markup $\mathcal{M}$, and therefore the split of output between wage and dividend income, is constant. This requires replacing sticky prices with flexible prices and sticky wages.[13] I impose analogous changes on TANK-II. Figure 7A shows the results for a monetary shock. Consistent with the Werning (2015) result, the output path is exactly the same for RANK, TANK-neutral, and HANK-neutral.[14]

Figure 7B shows the results for the spending shock financed by persistent debt ($\rho_b = 0.975$). Here, the difference between HANK and TANK is large—much larger than in figure 6B. The impact multipliers are 1.77 versus 1.19, whereas the cumulative multipliers are 4.48 versus 1.00.[15] These larger effects in HANK occur because in the neutral case, there is no longer the dampening from procyclical inequality that compressed HANK multipliers in figure 6B.

The moral of figure 7 is that with simple benchmark assumptions, HANK, TANK, and RANK can all have the same response to a monetary shock (Lesson 3)—whereas, at the same time, the implications for other shocks remain very different. This is not to say, of course, that all three models truly have identical implications for monetary policy; in my experience, the Werning (2015) result is fairly robust to reasonable changes in

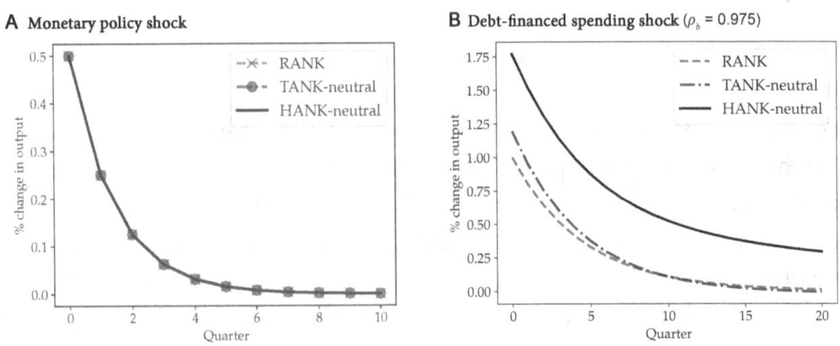

Fig. 7. Monetary and fiscal shocks in Werning-neutral version of models.

income distribution, but the models separate once more complex forces, like endogenous investment that triggers consumption feedback, are in play (Auclert et al. 2020). What is clear is that monetary shocks are a bad first-pass test of the aggregate effects of heterogeneity.

IV. Making HANK Accessible

Although I disagree with the claim that TANK is a close fit for HANK, I share the desire to make models with heterogeneity more accessible. To this end, TANK certainly has a place: it is a simple but limited way to introduce higher MPCs. But there are also many other ways to improve our handle on HANK, and these need not all involve TANK's limitations.

First, there are richer tractable models, which can match intertemporal MPCs and other dynamic features of HANK. Examples include the tractable HANK model in Bilbiie (forthcoming) and the "TABU" mixture of bond-in-utility and hand-to-mouth households in Auclert et al. (2024).[16] As the latter paper points out, the current generation of tractable models is still imperfect, with none of the main contenders matching the low empirical MPC out of capital gains. But progress continues—and a slightly richer mixture of models will likely be able to match this fact as well.

Second, even when working with quantitative HANK models that ultimately require the computer, it is possible to get some analytical traction. Sometimes this involves clean analytical benchmarks, like the balanced-budget multiplier in Auclert et al. (2024) or the neutrality result in Werning (2015). Other times it involves useful representations (e.g., the "Intertemporal Keynesian Cross") or decompositions (e.g., direct vs. indirect effects in Kaplan et al. 2018). These facilitate our understanding of HANK, even without a fully closed-form solution.

Third, one way to make HANK accessible is simply to make computation as fast and easy as possible. To this end, we have made great strides: for instance, all the results in this comment can be obtained in a few seconds on a personal laptop using the sequence-space Jacobian toolkit. Making computation faster and more interactive goes a long way in addressing the traditional weakness of quantitative work, which is the perceived opacity and complexity of a computational solution. Now, if a researcher is curious about what happens if an assumption or parameter is changed, they can edit one or two lines in a Jupyter notebook and get an answer in seconds—faster feedback than we expect from most analytical work!

Rapid progress continues on all three fronts, and I do not expect it to stop in the next decade. TANK will always have its place as a bare-bones way to introduce heterogeneity and non-Ricardian behavior, but as alternatives become increasingly more accessible, I expect it to become less prominent. The future of HANK is bright.

Endnotes

Author email address: Matthew Rognlie (matthew.rognlie@northwestern.edu). For acknowledgments, sources of research support, and disclosure of the author's material financial relationships, if any, please see https://www.nber.org/books-and-chapters/nber-macroeconomics-annual-2024-volume-39/comment-heterogeneity-and-aggregate-fluctuations-insights-tank-models-rognlie.

1. Productivity shocks receive parallel treatment in many places, but given the paper's exogenous-real-rate monetary rule, they only matter because of the effect on distribution, where higher productivity (counterfactually) means much lower wages and higher dividends—making productivity shocks an even less appealing exercise. I discuss these and also fiscal shocks, which were introduced in the final version of the paper, later in this comment.

2. Code that replicates the figures in this comment is available at https://github.com/mrognlie/dg-comment. It uses the sequence-space Jacobian toolkit, available at https://github.com/shade-econ/sequence-jacobian.

3. This is easy to calculate with the help of recursively computed expectation functions (introduced as "expectation vectors" in Auclert et al. 2021).

4. This is true for TANK because here I am using the paper's "TANK-II" calibration, designed to match HANK-II, where the hand-to-mouth households have labor income only $\Xi^H = 0.56$ of average.

5. They also mention Sahm, Shapiro, and Slemrod (2010), a survey that does not measure consumption, in which the vast majority of respondents who retrospectively said that they "spent" their rebates claimed to have done so in the first few months after receipt. To me, this seems like mental accounting: someone is more likely to say that they "spent" a rebate if they spent it right away versus saving it or paying off a credit card and then later using those resources to spend.

6. See table 2, comparing the "Contemporaneous month" and "Second month after" rows of columns 5 and 6.

7. Indeed, Borusyak et al. (2024) point out that their data are unsuited to such questions: "Per Proposition 5, without restrictive assumptions on treatment-effect heterogeneity it is not possible to estimate causal effects beyond 12 weeks."

8. Concretely, we split the real interest rate into a "substitution" interest rate that only enters Euler equations and an "income" interest rate that only enters budget constraints. We then apply the shock to the two rates separately and solve for general equilibrium output in each case. To first order, the resulting two impulse responses sum to the overall impulse response. This is distinct from the partial equilibrium decompositions of consumption popularized by Kaplan et al. (2018) and Auclert (2019), which attribute part of consumption to a labor income effect but do not further decompose that effect into its underlying causes.

9. See also McKay, Nakamura, and Steinsson (2017), who derive a discounted Euler equation under procyclical inequality.

10. As in Auclert et al. (2024), cumulative multipliers here measure the entire output response in date-0 present value.

11. Presumably, it would amplify the response to fiscal shocks too. For productivity shocks, it goes in the other direction: because these shocks lower wages and raise dividends, the lower MPC out of dividends in HANK-III makes them contractionary.

12. The labor share of income is not necessarily acyclical, but its business-cycle pattern is complex, and any cyclicality is far smaller than assumed in this paper—making the neutral case, in my view, a more realistic benchmark.

13. As in Auclert et al. (2024), we can then solve for real outcomes independently of the slope of the Phillips curve.

14. For TANK-neutral, this equivalence is easy to derive from (3): because the marginal income share $1 - m$ of the unconstrained equals the average income share, we have $1 - m = \lambda^U C^U/C$, and with $\lambda^H = 0$ we can cancel to get $dY_t/Y = dY_t^{RA}/Y$.

15. Auclert et al. (2024) prove that with a real rate rule and proportional incidence of income, the cumulative multiplier in TANK is 1.00. The 4.48 cumulative multiplier for HANK here is probably not realistic, because monetary policy would likely lean against such a persistent shock (rather than following the constant-r rule here).

16. Very similar to a bond-in-utility model is a perpetual-youth overlapping generations model, as in Aggarwal et al. (2023) and Angeletos, Lian, and Wolf (2023).

References

Agarwal, Sumit, Chunlin Liu, and Nicholas S. Souleles. 2007. "The Reaction of Consumer Spending and Debt to Tax Rebates—Evidence from Consumer Credit Data." *Journal of Political Economy* 115 (6): 986–1019.

Aggarwal, Rishabh, Adrien Auclert, Matthew Rognlie, and Ludwig Straub. 2023. "Excess Savings and Twin Deficits: The Transmission of Fiscal Stimulus in Open Economies." *NBER Macroeconomics Annual 2022* 37 (1): 325–412.

Angeletos, George-Marios, Chen Lian, and Christian K. Wolf. 2023. "Can Deficits Finance Themselves?" Working paper no. 31185, NBER, Cambridge, MA.

Auclert, Adrien. 2019. "Monetary Policy and the Redistribution Channel." *American Economic Review* 109 (6): 2333–67.

———, Bence Bardóczy, Matthew Rognlie, and Ludwig Straub. 2021. "Using the Sequence-Space Jacobian to Solve and Estimate Heterogeneous-Agent Models." *Econometrica* 89 (5): 2375–2408.

———, Matthew Rognlie, and Ludwig Straub. 2020. "Micro Jumps, Macro Humps: Monetary Policy and Business Cycles in an Estimated HANK Model." Working paper no. 22647, NBER, Cambridge, MA.

———. 2023. "The Trickling Up of Excess Savings." *AEA Papers and Proceedings* 113:70–75.

———. 2024. "The Intertemporal Keynesian Cross." *Journal of Political Economy* 32 (12): 4068–121.

Bernstein, Asaf, and Peter Koudijs. 2024. "The Mortgage Piggy Bank: Building Wealth through Amortization." *Quarterly Journal of Economics* 139 (3): 1767–1825.

Bilbiie, Florin O. 2020. "The New Keynesian Cross." *Journal of Monetary Economics* 114:90–108.

Bilbiie, Florin O. Forthcoming. "Monetary Policy and Heterogeneity: An Analytical Framework." *Review of Economic Studies*.

Boehm, Johannes, Etienne Fize, and Xavier Jaravel. 2025. "Five Facts about MPCs: Evidence from a Randomized Experiment." *American Economic Review* 115 (1): 1–42.

Borusyak, Kirill, Xavier Jaravel, and Jann Spiess. 2024. "Revisiting Event-Study Designs: Robust and Efficient Estimation." *Review of Economic Studies* 91 (6): 3253–85.

Campbell, John Y., and N. Gregory Mankiw. 1989. "Consumption, Income, and Interest Rates: Reinterpreting the Time Series Evidence." *NBER Macroeconomics Annual* 4:185–216.

Fagereng, Andreas, Martin B. Holm, and Gisle J. Natvik. 2021. "MPC Heterogeneity and Household Balance Sheets." *American Economic Journal: Macroeconomics* 13 (4): 1–54.

Galí, Jordi, J. David López-Salido, and Javier Vallés. 2007. "Understanding the Effects of Government Spending on Consumption." *Journal of the European Economic Association* 5 (1): 227–70.

Kaplan, Greg, Benjamin Moll, and Giovanni L. Violante. 2018. "Monetary Policy According to HANK." *American Economic Review* 108 (3): 697–743.

Koşar, Gizem, Davide Melcangi, Laura Pilossoph, and David G. Wiczer. 2024. "Stimulus through Insurance: The Marginal Propensity to Repay Debt." Working Paper no. 2024-14 (September), Federal Reserve Bank of Atlanta. https://www.atlantafed.org/research/publications/wp/2024/09/23/14--stimulus-through-insurance--marginal-propensity-to-repay-debt?item=f42dbbcd-26d6-46b5-acce-73210747f547.

McKay, Alisdair, Emi Nakamura, and Jón Steinsson. 2017. "The Discounted Euler Equation: A Note." *Economica* 84 (336): 820–31.

———, and Christian Wolf. 2023. "Optimal Policy Rules in HANK." Unpublished manuscript, MIT Department of Economics, Cambridge, MA.

Orchard, Jacob, Valerie A. Ramey, and Johannes F. Wieland. 2024. "Micro MPCs and Macro Counterfactuals: The Case of the 2008 Rebates." *Quarterly Journal of Economics* (forthcoming).

Sahm, Claudia R., Matthew D. Shapiro, and Joel Slemrod. 2010. "Household Response to the 2008 Tax Rebate: Survey Evidence and Aggregate Implications." *Tax Policy and the Economy* 24 (1): 69–110.

Werning, Iván. 2015. "Incomplete Markets and Aggregate Demand." Working Paper no. 21448 (August), NBER, Cambridge, MA. https://www.nber.org/papers/w21448.

Woodford, Michael. 2011. "Simple Analytics of the Government Expenditure Multiplier." *American Economic Journal: Macroeconomics* 3 (1): 1–35.

Discussion

Jonathan Parker opened the discussion. He commented that it is crucial to understand whether differences across households' consumption choices are driven by heterogeneity in preferences or by liquidity. The heterogeneous agent New Keynesian (HANK) model can be thought to have both dimensions. However, to an extreme, the two-agent New Keynesian (TANK) model can be interpreted as having only the former kind of heterogeneity because these models feature two types of agents: impatient and patient households. He also pointed out that, according to the consumption literature, heterogeneity in preferences is crucial to understanding consumers' behavior. This could explain why TANK models are a good approximation of the current version of HANK models for many but not all uses.

Deborah Lucas spoke next. She underlined that the model does not include capital for tractability purposes; however, capital seems like an essential force in these models, as it was for the earlier versions of the heterogeneous, consumption-based, asset-pricing models. Indeed, the implied interest rate is sensitive to the ability of agents to smooth consumption across periods by trading capital assets. Given that this mechanism is shut down in the presented paper, the model's predictions could be sensitive to this assumption. For example, she added, the agents' desire to self-insure lowers the interest rate, which should lead to an increase in the stock of capital and, thus, in production.

Afterward, Adrien Auclert, building on Matthew Rognlie's discussion, pointed out that his work with Rognlie and Ludwig Straub showed that

NBER Macroeconomics Annual, volume 39, 2025.
 Published by The University of Chicago Press for the National Bureau of Economic Research. https://doi.org/10.1086/735275

heterogeneity is most relevant for deficit-financed government spending. For this reason, he suggested the authors discuss this point in their paper. He further commented that heterogeneity could also play a role in the supply side of these models, implying a different Phillips curve from what is usually assumed.

Following Adrien Auclert's point, Ricardo Reis also emphasized looking at the effects of deficit-financed government spending in TANK and HANK models. Still within fiscal policy, and whether financed by deficits or not, he noted that targeted transfers, from one group to another, have very different implications in the two models, which could be tested in the data. More generally, fiscal shocks may be better than monetary ones at discriminating which model is the better one to use.

Adam Guren commented next, agreeing with Matthew Rognlie's point that TANK models are suitable for teaching and explaining. He added that TANK models could also be useful when an assumption is needed to cut through complexity for larger and more complicated models, such as multicountry models. In that sense, TANK should be thought of like constant elasticity of substitution (CES) preferences, Calvo price adjustment, or isoelastic money in the utility function—assumptions that allow us to get past a roadblock and consider more complicated models.

Afterward, Jonathon Hazell pointed out that, as Matthew Rognlie discussed, HANK models need sticky wages rather than sticky prices, an established finding in the literature. However, he expressed concern that the microfoundation of sticky wages in HANK models does not seem to have the desired properties arising from the data.

Lawrence D. W. Schmidt next suggested that the normative statements and welfare analysis of HANK and TANK models could be distinct. Furthermore, he added that heterogeneity could matter if a shock itself changes the income dynamics (e.g., income risk) of some but not all agents. Indeed, income risk can be endogenous to monetary policy. He believes TANK models could be suitable for shedding insights into this propagation channel.

Davide Debortoli followed up next. He thanked the discussants and the participants for their comments. Going back to Matthew Rognlie's discussion, he pointed out that, working on this paper, he realized that the results of HANK models are susceptible to the parameter values used. He added that small parameter changes, even those that seem innocuous, could lead to dampening or amplification effects. He believes that TANK models could also help understand why this is the case. Debortoli further noted that the aim of TANK models is to match reality, not HANK models. Indeed, TANK models are suitable for this scope if precautionary saving motives are small, as suggested by the recent paper of Berger, Boccola, and Dovis. This paper shows that precautionary savings motives can, on average, explain a small fraction of business cycle fluctuations. However, precautionary savings could be more relevant in historical examples such as the Great Recession or the COVID-19 crisis. Finally, he concluded by commenting that it is established in the literature that income risk is cyclical and for which agents this cyclical component is more pronounced. However, these patterns are not as well established for consumption. He believes that for heterogeneous models, it is relevant to understand how income risk is translated into consumption risk, which ultimately depends on the ability of agents to insure themselves.

Following his coauthor, Jordi Galí thanked the discussants and participants for their comments. Following up on Johannes Wieland's discussion, he pointed out that he and his coauthors solved HANK models before TANK models in the paper because their aim is to let TANK match HANK. However, if the goal is to match the data, there is no need to solve HANK beforehand. He added that HANK models can be more suitable than TANK models in answering some particular questions. Afterward, he discussed Matthew Rognlie's comments on the equivalence of RANK (representative agent New Keynesian) and TANK: the equivalence shows that the equilibrium representation in the two models is exactly the same, which is an interesting result. However, the coefficients of the two models in such representation are different.

Finally, Valerie Ramey concluded the conference, thanking the authors, the panelists, the discussants, and all the participants for their comments and participation.